Expert One-on-One™
J2EE™ Development without EJB™

Expert One-on-One™
J2EE™ Development without EJB™

Rod Johnson
with Juergen Hoeller

Wiley Publishing, Inc.

Expert One-on-One
J2EE™ Development without EJB™

Published by Wiley Publishing, Inc., Indianapolis, Indiana

Published simultaneously in Canada

For general information on our other products and services please contact our Customer Care Department within the United States at (800) 762-2974, outside the United States at (317) 572-3993 or fax (317) 572-4002.

Trademarks: Wiley, the Wiley Publishing logo, Wrox, the Wrox logo, Programmer to Programmer, Expert One-on-One, and related trade dress are trademarks or registered trademarks of John Wiley & Sons, Inc. and/or its affiliates. J2EE and EJB are trademarks of Sun Microsystems, Inc. All other trademarks are the property of their respective owners. Wiley Publishing, Inc., is not associated with any product or vendor mentioned in this book.

Wiley also publishes its books in a variety of electronic formats. Some content that appears in print may not be available in electronic books.

Library of Congress Cataloging-in-Publication Data

Johnson, Rod, Ph.D.
  Expert one-on-one J2EE development without EJB / Rod Johnson, Juergen Hoeller.
      p. cm.
  Includes bibliographical references and index.
  ISBN 0-7645-5831-5 (paper/website)
  1. Java (Computer program language) 2. Computer software—Development. I. Hoeller, Juergen, 1975– II. Title.
  QA76.73.J38J62 2004
  005.13'3—dc22

                                        2004005516

ISBN: 0-7645-5831-5
Printed in the United States of America
10 9 8 7 6 5 4 3 2 1

About the Authors

Rod Johnson is an enterprise Java architect with extensive experience in the insurance, dot-com, and financial industries. He was the J2EE architect of one of Europe's largest web portals, and he has worked as a consultant on a wide range of projects.

Rod has an arts degree majoring in music and computer science from the University of Sydney. He obtained a Ph.D. in musicology before returning to software development. With a background in C and C++, he has been working with both Java and J2EE since their release. He is actively involved in the Java Community Process as a member of the JSR-154 (Servlet 2.4) and JDO 2.0 Expert Groups. He is the author of the best-selling *Expert One-on-One J2EE Design and Development* (Wrox, 2002) and has contributed to several other books on J2EE since 2000.

Rod is prominent in the open source community as co-founder of the Spring Framework open source project (www.springframework.org), which grew out of code published with *Expert One-on-One J2EE Design and Development*. He speaks frequently at leading industry conferences. He is currently based in London.

Rod can be contacted at expert@interface21.com.

> *I'd like to thank my wife, Kerry, for her continuing love and support. Of those who've given practical help, I'm grateful for contributions from Gary Watson, Andrew Smith, and Jason Carreira for their thorough review of the entire manuscript; Alef Arendsen (reviewing and valuable performance benchmarking); Peter den Haan (thorough review of several chapters); Renaud Pawlak (rigorous review of the AOP material); and Steve Jefferson, Thomas Risberg, and Dmitriy Kopylenko (reviewing).*

> *I'm also grateful to the many developers and architects who have shared their experiences of J2EE development with me, in person and via e-mail.*

> *As always, working with Juergen has been a pleasure.*

Juergen Hoeller is a Senior Systems architect and Consultant at werk3AT, a company that delivers complex web solutions and provides J2EE-based consulting in Austria.

Juergen has a masters degree in Computer Science from the University of Linz, specializing in Java, OO modeling, and software engineering. He has worked on a wide range of projects with numerous J2EE application servers, ranging from enterprise application integration to web-based data visualization. Juergen has particular experience in developing J2EE web applications, O/R mapping, and transaction management.

Juergen is co-lead of the Spring Framework and active in many community forums, including TheServerSide.

> *Most of all, I'd like to thank my spouse, Eva, for her boundless love and support, and for her understanding of my constant lack of time.*

> *Special thanks to my colleagues at werk3AT and in particular to Werner Loibl for respecting all of my activities, and for giving valuable input to Spring and this book.*

> *I'm grateful to Thomas Risberg and Alef Arendsen for their thorough reviews and valuable input, and to all developers who helped sharpen the arguments, both within and outside the Spring team.*

> *It has been a particular pleasure to work with Rod on both Spring and this book.Introduction*

Credits

Vice President and Executive Group Publisher
Richard Swadley

Vice President and Executive Publisher
Bob Ipsen

Vice President and Publisher
Joseph B. Wikert

Executive Editorial Director
Mary Bednarek

Executive Editor
Robert Elliott

Editorial Manager
Kathryn A. Malm

Development Editor
Adaobi Obi Tulton

Technical Editors
Gary Watson
Andrew Smith
Jason Carreira

Production Editors
Felicia Robinson
Eric Newman

Copy Editors
C. M. Jones
Michael Koch

Media Development Specialist
Kit Malone

Text Design & Composition
Wiley Composition Services

Contents

Contents

Contents

Contents

Contents

Contents

Introduction

This is a fairly short book, given its scope, because its subject is less complex than you've been led to believe.

J2EE orthodoxy makes heavy work of many simple problems. Indeed it sometimes seems that the J2EE industry is committed to the belief that there are no simple problems.

Many—probably most—J2EE applications are over-engineered, with unnecessarily complex architectures. Over-engineering can be very costly. J2EE developers tend to assume that increased cost up front will be more than balanced by reductions in future costs. Unfortunately, karma doesn't apply to software engineering, and this is often a fallacy. Greater complexity up front means more code to write and maintain, more potential for bugs, more delay in demonstrating functionality to users: ultimately, greater chance of failure, and at greater cost.

J2EE over-engineering usually involves EJB. As I pointed out in *Expert One-on-One J2EE Design and Development*, EJB is often used inappropriately. This is a real problem, because EJB can introduce more complexity than it conceals. Some services provided by EJB are also overrated. For example, few experienced developers or architects who have worked with entity EJBs to access relational data want to repeat the experience—at least, given the alternatives of JDO, Hibernate, and other transparent persistence technologies.

Critiques of EJB have become commonplace since late 2002. It's easy enough to pick the flaws in an imperfect existing technology, without suggesting alternatives. This book breaks new ground in describing and illustrating better approaches for the majority of J2EE applications that derive no benefit from EJB. This book is no mere theoretical discussion, but a practical guide to designing and implementing high-performance J2EE applications on time and budget. Our suggested architectures are backed up by extensive experience, a realistic sample application, and comprehensive open source solutions that meet typical infrastructure needs.

Despite the significant problems that have emerged with EJB, it continues to be adopted too often largely because of fashion and fear. Fashion because even nontechnical managers have heard of EJB and because many books on J2EE architecture barely mention alternatives to EJB for delivering enterprise services, even where excellent alternatives exist. Fear that the alternatives are worse: for example, that without EJB developers will be left to handle complex issues such as transaction management without the training wheels of the EJB container. This book aims to show that these fears are largely unfounded. Where the potential complexity is real, it shows that there are alternatives that do a better job than EJB at addressing the problems concerned.

> **This book demonstrates a much simpler approach to developing typical J2EE applications than the "classic" J2EE blueprints approach exemplified by the original Java Pet Store. Our approach leads to reduced cost, shorter time to market, greater maintainability, and better performance.**

The architectural approach described in this book is part of a growing movement towards simpler, more rational J2EE architectures. It's suitable for use with agile methodologies. It draws on recently developed technologies such as Aspect Oriented Programming, and borrows where appropriate from alternative platforms to J2EE such as .NET.

I aim to help you build the simplest possible applications that meet your requirements—and hence, also the cheapest, most maintainable and testable.

The merits of EJB have become a surprisingly emotive issue in the J2EE community. There seems to be a stark polarization between those would never use EJB unless compelled and those who believe that the EJB skeptics are lazy, ignorant heretics, with little middle ground.

As you may suspect, I'm not a fan of EJB. However, I have developed many applications with EJB and speak from experience and intimate knowledge of the EJB specification. I'll also strive to justify my position throughout this book. My goal is to help you develop effective applications, not to combat the use of EJB.

After reading this book, you should be able to assess the value proposition of EJB for each application. If, with a strong understanding of EJB and the alternatives, you believe that your requirements are best addressed by EJB, use EJB. The message of this book is not a black-and-white "don't use EJB."

Who This Book Is For

This book is for J2EE architects and developers who have a solid grasp of the technology and want to use it more productively. It's a book about the *why* and *how* of enterprise applications, rather than the *what*. So you won't find API listings here, and you won't find yet another introduction to basic J2EE services such as JNDI and JTA. There are many good books and articles that address these topics.

The material in this book is particularly relevant to those working on web applications. However, most J2EE developers will find something of value. You may well read this book and decide that EJB is the correct choice for your particular application; even in this case, by applying the criteria set out in this book, you'll know exactly why you are using EJB and what value it is providing.

Aims of This Book

This book aims to help you solve practical problems. It aims to demonstrate a simpler and more productive approach to J2EE development than the traditional J2EE approach exemplified in Sun blueprints and based on the use of EJB to manage business logic.

You might end up having a lot more fun, as well.

What This Book Covers

This book covers:

❑   Problems with EJB and received wisdom in J2EE architecture

❑   Key values for successful J2EE projects

❑ Effective architectures for J2EE applications, especially for web applications

❑ Common mistakes in J2EE architecture and implementation

❑ How to find the simplest and most maintainable architecture for your application

❑ Inversion of Control and Aspect-Oriented Programming: two important new technologies that have recently become important to J2EE development.

Chapters 6 through 12 cover replacing EJB services with lighter-weight, more testable alternatives. We emphasize:

❑ Transaction management. This is an essential of enterprise applications, and a popular motivation for using EJB. We'll look at alternative means of transaction management, discussing both declarative and programmatic transaction management.

❑ Data access in J2EE applications: another central problem that—in contrast to transaction management—EJB addresses very badly.

❑ How AOP can be used to solve many common problems in enterprise software development.

We'll also talk about:

❑ Web tier design, and the place of the web tier in a well-designed J2EE application

❑ Testing and test-driven development, and how to test J2EE applications effectively

❑ Performance and scalability

Specific technologies considered include:

❑ Data access with JDBC, Hibernate, and JDO

❑ Web tier technologies such as Struts, WebWork, Spring MVC, and JSP

❑ Using open source products to develop a strong application infrastructure, and minimize the amount of code you'll have to develop, test, and maintain in house. Most problems of J2EE infrastructure have been solved by leading open source products; I'll help you focus on tackling those unique to your applications.

Assumed Knowledge

This is not a primer on EJB or J2EE.

We assume knowledge of core J2EE APIs and services such as JNDI, JTA, and database connection pooling.

We assume sound knowledge of J2SE, including reflection, inner classes, dynamic proxies, JDBC, JAXP, and JNDI.

We assume good working knowledge of OO design.

You won't need detailed knowledge of EJB, as this book is about *alternatives* to EJB, but it will help if you are familiar with EJB. If you want to get up to speed, try Ed Roman's *Mastering Enterprise JavaBeans, Second Edition* (Wiley, 2001).

You will need to understand the basic middleware concepts behind EJB, such as resource pooling, remoting, and transaction management; the basic motivation for adopting n-tier rather than client-server architectures.

You'll need to understand the basic concepts of web interfaces, and the MVC architectural pattern as used in J2EE web applications.

Don't worry if you aren't already familiar with AOP; in Chapter 8 I provide an introduction that enables you to start implementing AOP-enabled applications, and includes a reading list to help you gain deeper knowledge.

Recommended Reading

This book is the sequel to *Expert One-on-One J2EE Design and Development* (Wrox, 2002). You can read this book on its own, but you may want to refer to that book. In particular, it describes in detail many programming practices that are mentioned more briefly here. Chapters 4, 9, and 11–13 are particularly relevant as background to this book.

I also highly recommend Martin Fowler's *Patterns of Enterprise Application Architecture* (Addison-Wesley, 2002): a wise discussion of many problems in enterprise software, with a healthy distance from implementation technologies such as J2EE. Martin Fowler is one of my favorite writers, and he's always worth reading. Fowler's First Law of Distributed Objects ("Don't distribute your objects") is worth the price alone. This book also introduces the term POJO (Plain Old Java Object), coined by Fowler to give plain Java objects buzzword compliance. I'll use it throughout this book.

As I believe that J2EE applications should be OO applications, I highly recommend the classic OO text, *Design Patterns: Elements of Reusable Object-Oriented Software* (Gamma, Helm, Johnson, and Vlissides, Addison-Wesley, 1995). The 23 patterns listed in this book are still the most valuable in J2EE applications—more valuable than technology-centric "J2EE" patterns.

The second edition of *Core J2EE Patterns* (Alur, Crupi, and Malks, 2003) is important reading, partly because it defines a standard naming for J2EE patterns. I'll refer to several patterns from this book, such as Service Locator, Business Delegate, and Front Controller, and it will be helpful if you already understand them. *Core J2EE Patterns* exemplifies more traditional thinking on J2EE architecture (although the second edition is a worthwhile update), but is nonetheless a very useful resource.

I recommend you keep up to date on current J2EE topics. Some of my favorite J2EE websites are:

❑　TheServerSide. The major J2EE portal, this is a great place to keep up to date with developments in J2EE. You'll find discussions on many J2EE issues, and valuable resources such as articles and book chapters and product reviews.

❑　Artima.com (www.artima.com). Java/J2EE-oriented software site, run by Bill Venners.

❑　*Core J2EE Patterns* web site (www.corej2eepatterns.com/index.htm).

❑ Various blogs. Some very important ideas have been explored and discussed amongst Java bloggers. www.javablogs.com is a good starting point for exploring this important information channel. Significant bloggers include Rickard Oberg, Ted Neward, Gavin King, Bob Lee ("Crazy Bob"), and Jon Tirsen.

It's useful to keep up to date on middleware in general, not just J2EE. .NET has a similar overall architecture to J2EE, and the growing patterns literature on .NET is relevant to J2EE. Useful resources include:

❑ MSDN home (http://msdn.microsoft.com/)

❑ "Enterprise Solution Patterns Using Microsoft .NET" website (http://msdn.microsoft.com/architecture/patterns/Esp/default.aspx)

What You Need to Use This Book

To run the sample application and examples, you'll need:

❑ A J2EE web container or/and application server. For examples using a single database, without the need for JTA, we used Tomcat 5.0.16. For examples using JTA, we used WebLogic 8.1 Express. All the code in this book runs unchanged on most other application servers (an incidental benefit of avoiding EJB!), so feel free to deploy the code onto your favorite application server. Please see the release notes with the sample application for information on which application servers it has been tested on.

❑ A relational database and the appropriate JDBC drivers. We used HSQLDB (http://hsqldb.sourceforge.net/) for the examples, but only minor changes should be necessary to use any other transactional database.

❑ The Spring Framework, available from www.springframework.org. This site contains many further resources for developing with Spring. The sample application was written for Spring 1.0 final, but should run unchanged on later versions of Spring.

❑ The Hibernate 2.1 object-relational mapping product, available from www.hibernate.org/.

❑ Jakarta Ant 1.5.3, the standard Java build tool. While you may prefer to build your projects with Maven (a more complex and powerful build tool) you should certainly understand Ant and the importance of script-driven, repeatable project build steps.

❑ Various third-party libraries, including Jakarta Commons Logging and Jakarta Commons Attributes. The necessary jar files are included with the full Spring distribution; see documentation with Spring and the sample application for details.

All this software is open source or free for developer use.

The Sample Application

An innovative feature of this book is that it uses an open source sample application. Authors have limited time; for most of us, writing is a hindrance to earning a living. Thus in many books, the sample application is a poor second to completion of the text. *Expert One-on-One J2EE Design and Development* was no exception in this regard, although it did offer unusually sophisticated infrastructure code.

An open source sample application can be more realistic than would be possible through the authors' effort alone. This has the great advantage of avoiding the simplifications often seen in sample applications. In J2EE applications, the devil is in the detail, and the value of the overall approach is measured by its ability to address problems of real-world complexity, rather than over-simplified examples.

The sample application is an implementation of the familiar Java pet store. The pet store has simple, well-understood requirements, meaning that we don't need to describe the problem domain in detail.

The code base was originally based on Clinton Begin's JPetStore, available from www.ibatis.com: a valuable example in its own right. Our sample application enhances the JPetStore to use the architecture we advocate, introducing greater use of interfaces, use of an Inversion of Control container, and AOP-enabled declarative transaction management. We believe that the result is simpler and more flexible and extensible than the original JPetStore. We also invite you to compare it with the original Sun Java Pet Store to see how much simpler our approach is in comparison to the J2EE blueprints approach, and how it replaces EJB services with lighter-weight alternatives.

The sample application illustrates the following points discussed in the text:

- ❑ A well-defined business interface layer

- ❑ The *Lightweight Container* architecture, discussed in Chapter 3, built on an Inversion of Control container

- ❑ The use of AOP to provide declarative transaction management to POJOs. The underlying transaction-management technology can be switched between JTA, JDBC, or another technology without any change to Java code.

- ❑ Use of an MVC web layer, using either Spring MVC or Struts 1.1. The sample includes both alternative implementations of the web tier, accessing the same business interface layer.

- ❑ Use of the Data Access Object pattern to decouple business logic from database schema and technology for accessing persistent data

- ❑ The use of source-level metadata attributes to simplify the programming model, especially for transaction management

- ❑ Remoting support for multiple protocols, built on the business interface layer.

The sample application is available online at www.wrox.com. Once at the site, simply locate the book's title (either by using the Search box or by using one of the title lists) and click the Download Code link on the book's detail page to obtain all the source code for the book.

> *Because many books have similar titles, you may find it easiest to search by ISBN; the ISBN for this book is 0-7645-5831-5.*

Once you download the code, just decompress it with your favorite compression tool. Alternatively, you can go to the main Wrox code download page at www.wrox.com/dynamic/books/download.aspx to see the code available for this book and for all other Wrox books.

Conventions

To help you get the most from the text and keep track of what's happening, we've used a number of conventions throughout the book.

> **Boxes like this one hold important, not-to-be-forgotten information that is directly relevant to the surrounding text.**

Tips, hints, tricks, and asides to the current discussion are offset and placed in italic like this.

As for styles in the text:

❑   We *highlight in italic* important words when we introduce them.

❑   We show keyboard strokes like this: Ctrl+A.

❑   We show file names, URLs, and code within the text in a monospaced font, like so: `persistence.properties`.

❑   We present code in two different ways:

```
In code examples we highlight new and important code with a gray background.
The gray highlighting is not used for code that's less important in the present
context, or has been shown before.
```

Errata

We make every effort to ensure that there are no errors in the text or in the code. However, no one is perfect, and mistakes do occur. If you find an error in one of our books, such as a spelling mistake or faulty piece of code, we would be very grateful for your feedback. By sending in errata you may save another reader hours of frustration and at the same time you will be helping us provide even higher-quality information.

To find the errata page for this book, go to `www.wrox.com` and locate the title using the Search box or one of the title lists. Then, on the book details page, click the Book Errata link. On this page you can view all errata that has been submitted for this book and posted by Wrox editors. A complete book list including links to each book's errata is also available at `www.wrox.com/misc-pages/booklist.shtml`.

If you don't spot "your" error on the Book Errata page, go to `www.wrox.com/contact/techsupport.shtml` and complete the form there to send us the error you have found. We'll check the information and, if appropriate, post a message to the book's errata page and fix the problem in subsequent editions of the book.

p2p.wrox.com

For author and peer discussion, join the P2P forums at http://p2p.wrox.com. The forums are a web-based system for you to post messages relating to Wrox books and related technologies and interact with other readers and technology users. The forums offer a subscription feature to e-mail you topics of interest of your choosing when new posts are made to the forums. Wrox authors, editors, other industry experts, and your fellow readers participate in these forums.

At http://p2p.wrox.com you will find a number of different forums that will help you not only as you read this book, but also as you develop your own applications. To join the forums, just follow these steps:

1. Go to http://p2p.wrox.com and click the Register link.

2. Read the terms of use and click Agree.

3. Complete the required information to join as well as any optional information you wish to provide and click Submit.

4. You will receive an e-mail with information describing how to verify your account and complete the joining process.

   You can read messages in the forums without joining P2P, but in order to post your own messages, you must join.

Once you join, you can post new messages and respond to messages other users post. You can read messages at any time on the web. If you would like to have new messages from a particular forum e-mailed to you, click the Subscribe to this Forum icon by the forum name in the forum listing.

For more information about how to use the Wrox P2P, be sure to read the P2P FAQs for answers to questions about how the forum software works as well as to many common questions specific to P2P and Wrox books. To read the FAQs, click the FAQ link on any P2P page.

Why "J2EE Without EJB"?

The traditional approach to J2EE architecture has often produced disappointing results: applications that are more complex than their business requirements warrant, show disappointing performance, are hard to test, and cost too much to develop and maintain.

It doesn't need to be so hard. There is a better way for most applications. In this book, we'll describe a simpler, yet powerful architectural approach, building on experience with J2EE and newer technologies such as Inversion of Control and AOP. Replacing EJB with lighter-weight, more flexible, infrastructure typically produces significant benefits. We and many others have used this approach in many production applications, with better results than are usually produced from traditional architectures.

Let's begin with a quick tour of the topics we'll examine in more detail in later chapters.

EJB Under the Spotlight

Like most of my colleagues, I was excited by the promise of EJB when it first appeared. I believed it was the way forward for enterprise middleware. However, I've since revised my opinions, in the light of my experiences and those of many colleagues.

Much has changed since the EJB specification was conceived:

❑   Parts of the specification's design now seem dated. For example, dynamic proxies, introduced in J2SE 1.3, call into question the container code generation envisaged in the EJB specification and the multiple source files needed to implement every EJB.

❑   The traditional link between EJB and RMI remoting is looking dated, because of the emergence of web services and the recognition that EJBs sometimes need only local interfaces. EJB is a heavyweight model for objects that don't need to offer remote access.

❑   This is a special case of the fact that basing typical applications around distributed business objects—the architectural choice EJB implements best—has proved problematic.

❑   Usage of EJB indicates its strengths and weaknesses. Most developers and architects have restricted their use of EJB to stateless session beans and (if asynchronous calls are needed) message-driven beans. The relative simplicity of the services provided by the EJB container to support SLSBs means that the overhead of an EJB container is hard to justify in such applications.

❑   Although EJB has been around for five years, and its use is a given in many J2EE projects, it has become apparent that its complexity means that many developers still don't understand it. For example, many developer candidates I interview can't correctly describe how EJB containers handle exceptions and how this relates to transaction management.

❑   The EJB specification is becoming more and more complex in an attempt to address problems with EJB. It's now so long and complex that few developers or architects will have time to read and understand it. With specifications, as with applications, the need for continual workarounds and constantly growing complexity suggests fundamental problems.

❑   The complexity of EJB means that productivity in EJB applications is relatively poor. A number of tools try to address this, from "Enterprise" IDEs to XDoclet and other code generation tools, but the complexity still lurks under the surface and imposes ongoing costs.

❑   Rigorous unit testing and **test driven development** have become increasingly, and deservedly, popular. It's become clear that applications making heavy use of EJB are hard to test. Developing EJB applications **test first** requires a lot of fancy footwork; essentially, minimization of the dependence of application code on the EJB container.

❑   The emergence of **Aspect Oriented Programming** (AOP) points the way to more powerful—yet potentially simpler—approaches to the middleware problems addressed by EJB. AOP can be viewed in part as a more general application of the central EJB concepts, although of course it's much more than a potential replacement to EJB.

❑   Source level metadata attributes, as used in .NET, suggest a superior alternative in many cases to the verbose XML-based deployment descriptors used since EJB 1.1. EJB 3.0 looks like it's heading down that road as well, but it's a way off and will carry a lot of baggage.

Experience has also shown EJB to incur greater cost and deliver fewer benefits than were initially predicted. Developers have encountered intractable problems that weren't apparent when EJB first appeared. Experience has shown that EJB fails to deliver in several areas:

❑   It doesn't necessarily reduce complexity. It *introduces* a lot of complexity.

❑   The entity bean experiment for persistence has largely failed.

❑   Applications using EJB tend to be less portable between application servers than applications using other J2EE technologies, such as servlets.

❑   Despite the promises that EJB would prove the key to scalability, EJB systems often perform poorly and don't necessarily scale up well. Although statistics are hard to come by, anecdotal evidence suggests that the overhead of excessive use of EJB necessitates re-architecture or causes outright failure in a significant number of projects.

❑   EJB can make simple things hard. For example, the Singleton design pattern (or alternatives) is hard to implement in EJB.

All of these issues suggest that it's wise to analyze exactly what the value proposition is before using EJB. I hope to equip you with the tools to do this effectively and dispassionately.

In Chapter 5, we'll talk more about EJB and its problems. In the meantime, let's look at where J2EE is today, where I feel it's going, and how this book will help you deliver real solutions on time and budget.

What's Left of J2EE?

You may be wondering, "What's left of J2EE without EJB?"

The answer is: a great deal. J2EE is much more than EJB. Many J2EE developers believe otherwise, and will tell you so when they see this book on your desk, but a dispassionate analysis of what EJB does, and what J2EE does overall, shows that EJB is only a part of a much bigger and more important picture.

J2EE is essentially about standardizing a range of enterprise services, such as naming and directory services (JNDI), transaction management offering a standard API potentially spanning disparate transactional resources (JTS and JTA), connection to legacy systems (JCA), resource pooling, and thread management. The true power of J2EE lies in these services, and this standardization has done great service to the industry.

EJB, on the other hand, is merely one way of leveraging those valuable services, through a particular component model.

We can still access JNDI, JTA, JCA, resource pooling, and other core J2EE services without using EJB. We can do this by writing code that uses them directly (not as hair-raising as it may seem) or—better—using proven libraries and frameworks that abstract their use without imposing the complexity of EJB.

Only a few EJB container services are unique to EJB, and there are good alternatives to those. For example:

- ❑ **Entity beans** are the only dedicated data access components in J2EE. However, they're also the most questionable part of J2EE, and there are much better non-J2EE alternatives, such as Hibernate and JDO. In some applications, JDBC is a better option.

- ❑ **Container Managed Transactions (CMT):** EJBs are the only part of J2EE to enjoy declarative transaction management. This is a valuable service, but as we'll see in Chapters 8 and 9 we can also achieve declarative transaction management using AOP. CMT is a relatively thin layer over the underlying J2EE JTA service. It would be hard (and foolhardy to attempt) to replace an application server's global transaction management, but it's not so hard to access it to develop an alternative form of CMT.

- ❑ **Thread pooling for business objects:** We usually don't need this if we're supporting only web clients (or web services clients going through a servlet engine), because a web container provides thread pooling and there's no need to duplicate it in the business object tier. We do need thread pooling to support remote clients over RMI/IIOP, one case in which EJB remains a good, simple technology choice.

❑ (Related) **Thread management for business objects:** the ability to implement EJBs as though they are single-threaded. In my experience this is overrated for stateless service objects (the most useful kinds of EJB). EJB can't eliminate all threading complexity anyway, as problems can remain with objects used by EJB facades. There are good alternatives to EJB thread management, discussed in Chapter 12.

Only in the area of remoting is EJB the only way to implement such functionality in standard J2EE. As we'll see, only in RMI/IIOP remoting is EJB clearly an outstanding remoting technology; there are better alternatives for web services remoting.

There's a strong argument that EJB attempts to address a lot of issues it shouldn't. Take O/R mapping. This is a complex problem to which EJB provides a complex yet under-specified solution (entity beans) that simply ignores some of the central problems, such as mapping objects with an inheritance hierarchy to relational database tables. It would have been better for the designers of the EJB specification to leave this problem to those with much more experience of the issues around object persistence.

> **J2EE is much more than EJB. Using J2EE without EJB, we don't have to reinvent the wheel. We don't need to reimplement J2EE services, just consider alternative ways of tapping into them.**

J2EE at a Crossroads

J2EE is at a fascinating point in its evolution. In many respects it's a great success. It has succeeded in bringing standardization where none existed; it has introduced a welcome openness into enterprise software. It has achieved fantastic industry and developer buy-in.

On the other hand, I feel it has come up short on a number of measures. J2EE applications are usually too expensive to develop. J2EE application projects are at least as prone to failure as pre-J2EE projects. (Which means that the failure rate is unacceptably high; developing software is far too hit-and-miss an affair.) In the areas where J2EE has failed, EJB has usually played a significant part.

J2EE has significant issues with ease of development. As I've said, J2EE applications tend to be unnecessarily complex. This is especially true of J2EE web applications, which, like the Sun Java Pet Store, are often absurdly over-engineered.

J2EE is still a relatively young technology. It's not surprising that it's imperfect. It's time to take stock of where it's worked, and where it hasn't worked so well, so that we can eliminate the negatives and enjoy the positives. Because J2EE contains a lot, this essentially means identifying the subset of J2EE that delivers most value, along with some supplementary infrastructure we need to harness it most effectively.

There is a growing movement in the J2EE community toward simpler solutions and less use of EJB. My previous book, *Expert One-on-One J2EE Design and Development* (2002), was a step in the growth of that movement, but was part of a broader trend. I believe this book represents the next step in defining and popularizing such solutions, but it's important to note that I'm by no means alone. Fellow pioneers include Rickard Oberg and Jon Tirsen (of Nanning Aspects), who have helped to demonstrate the power and simplicity of AOP-based solutions. The revisions in the second edition of *Core J2EE Patterns* suggest that even Sun is not immune; there is a new and welcome emphasis on use of plain Java objects.

Some of the problems with J2EE and EJB relate to its specification-driven origins. History shows that the most successful standards *evolve*, rather than are created by a committee. The danger of a "specification-first" approach is shown by the example of the OMG and CORBA. The OMG was founded to create a distributed object standard. Over 300 vendors signed up; the result was the slow production of complex specifications that never achieved widespread acceptance. As is often the case with committees, usability by developers was barely a consideration; the result was a horribly complex programming model.

J2EE is partly an evolution of existing middleware, because many of the problems it addresses were familiar when it was conceived in the late 1990s. For example, stateless session EJBs are merely an EJB take on a component type of proven value. Service objects with declarative transaction management existed in Microsoft Transaction Server, for example, before the EJB 1.0 specification. It's arguable that where J2EE has tried to innovate, through specifications being developed *before* any real applications using them, it has often failed. *Stateful* session beans, for example, were a new and unproven component type introduced in EJB. Five years on, they remain largely unproven. The tricky issue of state replication remains problematic, and most architects avoid stateful session beans if at all possible.

I suspect that the specification-driven nature of J2EE is going to change in practice, and that this is a good thing. I don't envisage J2EE descending into anarchy, but I do think that developers aren't automatically going to adopt each new feature of the J2EE specifications without considering alternative technologies, especially from the open source community.

This book represents part of that critical process: the recognition that end users of the technology—application developers, project managers responsible for development projects, and those who end up using applications—are the most important stakeholders, and that the reality at the coal face of application development isn't always obvious to those on specification committees.

The Way Forward

This book is not primarily about questioning EJB, but about mapping a path forward. This includes architectural principles, working code, and practical advice you can use in your projects today.

The way forward that this book proposes is to focus on core values—I'll call them *themes*—that help lead to project success, and to examine architectures and implementation choices that express them.

Themes

The central themes of this book are:

❏ Simplicity

❏ Productivity

❏ The fundamental importance of object orientation

❏ The primacy of business requirements

❏ The importance of empirical process

❏ The importance of testability

Let's briefly discuss these.

Simplicity

There *are* simple problems, and architecture and implementation should always be as simple as possible.

As I've already mentioned, J2EE projects are often over-engineered, partly because of an assumption that J2EE applications are necessarily complex. This isn't always true. Areas in which J2EE architects often assume requirements to be more complex than they are include:

❏ **Database distribution.** Many applications use only a single database. This means that they don't need JTA, two-phase commit, or XA transactions. All these high-end features incur cost in performance and complexity.

❏ **Assumption of multiple client types.** An application may have a requirement for a web inter-face. But J2EE architects are also likely to assume that it must also be able to support remote Swing clients. The assumption that all J2EE applications should be able to support multiple client types is deeply ingrained. (Indeed, I only realized that it's actually not that common when a reviewer on one of my previous books pointed it out, prompting me to reflect on real projects I'd been involved with.)

J2EE orthodoxy in both cases is that the user isn't allowed to have such simple requirements. We J2EE architects, in our wisdom, know that the client's business will get complicated enough to justify the com-plexity we're going to make him pay for up front.

There are two problems here. Firstly, including this complexity isn't our choice as architects and devel-opers, as we don't write the checks. Secondly, even if the more complex requirements do ultimately emerge, how do we know it's cheaper to factor them in from day one? It may well be cheaper to wait until these requirements come up. It's quite likely they won't; if they do, we can cross that bridge when we come to it. For example, the eventual remote client choice might be C# or VB.NET on Windows; an EJB-based remoting architecture might not be the best choice to support this. One of the key lessons of XP is that it is often more cost-effective, and more likely to produce a quality implementation, not to try to solve all conceivable problems up front.

> We should minimize complexity up front to what's necessary to support actual (and reasonably foreseeable) requirements. However, it is necessary to design a simple architecture that allows for architectural refactoring to scale up. Refactoring an architecture is not as simple as refactoring code; clearly we don't want to have to scrap much of our code to meet additional requirements.

It's important to have a simple architecture that can scale up. It's not so good to have a complex architec-ture, such as an EJB architecture, that can't scale down to meet simple requirements.

In my experience, the keys to enabling architectural refactoring in J2EE projects are:

❑ To follow good OO design practice and **program to interfaces rather than classes**. This is a fundamental teaching of the classic *Design Patterns* text, and too often neglected.

❑ To conceal technologies such as EJB behind plain Java interfaces.

The architectural approach and frameworks discussed in this book make it easy to practice these principles.

Productivity

Productivity is an immensely important consideration, too often ignored in J2EE.

J2EE has a poor productivity record. J2EE developers typically spend too much of their time wrestling with API and deployment complexity when they should really be concentrating on business logic. The relative proportions are better than in the CORBA days, but still not good enough. Much of this incidental time is associated with EJB.

The approaches advocated in this book are highly productive, partly because they're comparatively simple and dispense with a lot of unnecessary crud.

OO

Surely, since Java is a rather good OO language, object orientation is a given for J2EE applications? While it should be, in fact many J2EE applications are really "EJB" or "J2EE" applications more than OO applications. Many common J2EE practices and patterns sacrifice object orientation too easily.

> **OO design is more important than specific technologies, such as J2EE. We should try to avoid letting our technology choices, such as J2EE, constrain our ability to use true OO design.**

Let's consider two examples of how many J2EE applications sacrifice OO:

❑ **The use of EJBs with remote interfaces to distribute business objects.** Designing an application in terms of distributed business objects with remote interfaces can deliver a fatal blow to OO. Components with remote interfaces must offer interfaces designed to avoid the need for "chatty" calling for performance reasons, and raise the tricky problem of marshaling input and output parameters in terms of **transfer** or **value** objects. There *are* applications that must offer distributed business objects, but most shouldn't and are much better off staying away from this particular minefield. The use of distributed objects is not unique to EJB: EJB wasn't the first distributed object technology and won't be the last. The reason that this problem is linked to EJB is that distributing components is the one thing that EJB makes easy: arguably, too easy.

❑ The assumption that persistent objects should contain no behavior. This has long been an article of faith among J2EE developers. I used to subscribe to it myself—this is one area in which my thinking has changed somewhat since I published *Expert One-on-One J2EE*. In fact, this assumption in a J2EE context owes more to the severe limitations of entity beans as a technology than sound design principles. Objects that expose only getters and setters (for example, to expose

7

persistent data) are not really objects. A true object should encapsulate behavior acting upon its state. The use of entity beans encouraged developers to accept this limitation as the norm, because business logic in entity beans couldn't easily be tested, and was fatally tied to a particular persistence strategy. (For example, if a significant amount of business logic is coded in entity beans, and it becomes apparent that the only way to achieve adequate performance is to perform relational data access using SQL and JDBC, a major refactoring exercise is required.) A better solution is to use a transparent persistence technology, such as JDO or Hibernate, which allows persistent objects to be true objects, with little or no dependence on how they're actually persisted.

> **Whenever you find yourself writing an object that's not really an object—such as an object that contains only methods exposing its data—think hard about why you're doing this, and whether there's a better alternative.**

And there *is* real value in practicing OO. Applied effectively, OO can deliver very high code reuse and elegant design.

In this book we won't forget the value of OO. We'll try to show how J2EE applications can be object oriented.

Primacy of Requirements

It should be obvious, but application architecture should be driven by business requirements, not target technology.

Unfortunately this is not always the case in J2EE. Developers often assume phantom requirements, such as:

❏   Providing support for multiple databases in the one application, already discussed

❏   The ability to port to another application server at zero cost

❏   The ability to port to another database easily

❏   Supporting multiple client types

All of these are *potential* business requirements, but whether they are *actual* requirements should be evaluated for each application. Developers with other technologies, such as .NET, often don't need to worry about such phantom requirements, meaning that sometimes J2EE developers are expending effort only because of their technology choice, not because of client requirements.

It's a great bonus of J2EE that it makes a whole range of things possible that aren't possible with other technologies, but it's also a potential danger when it causes us to forget that all these things have a cost and that we shouldn't incur each cost without good reason.

Empirical Process

My wife is a doctor. In recent years, medical practice has been influenced by the rise of **Evidence-Based Medicine**: a model in which treatment decisions are strongly influenced by the evidence from medical research. Treatment decisions are typically made on the basis of the known outcomes of various choices for the patient's condition.

While the influence of EBM on medical practice may not be wholly positive, this kind of empirical approach definitely has lessons for software development.

The IT industry is strongly driven by fashion and emotion. I seldom pass a day without hearing someone repeat an orthodox opinion they can't justify (such as "EJB applications are inherently more scalable than applications without EJB"), or repeat a religious conviction that's backed up by no real evidence (such as ".NET is not a credible enterprise platform").

Too often this means that people architect enterprise systems based on their own particular bigotry, and without hard evidence backing up the approaches they propose. They just know which way is best.

One of the best comments I've heard about this situation is "Ask the computer" (from fellow author Randy Stafford). We should always "ask the computer" what it thinks of our proposed architecture before we spend too much money and effort on it.

This approach is formalized in iterative methodologies in the form of an **executable architecture** (RUP) or **vertical slice** or **spike solution** (XP). In each case the aim is to minimize risk by building an end-to-end executable as soon as possible. In the case of RUP this aims to tackle the trickiest architectural issues as the best means to mitigate risks; in XP it is driven by key *user stories*. In all cases, it must be relevant to actual requirements. An agile development process can naturally tend toward the creation of a vertical slice, making a distinct activity unnecessary. Once the vertical slice is built, it can be used as the basis for metrics that serve to validate the architectural choices. Important metrics include:

❑ **Performance.** Can non-functional requirements be met? This is the most likely sticking point in J2EE, where many projects that don't do an early vertical slice end up grappling with intractable performance problems at the last minute.

❑ **How hard was it to get here?** Were the development time and costs involved proportionate to the requirements implemented? Is the complexity of the result proportionate to the requirements? Was magic involved or is the process repeatable?

❑ **Maintainability.** How hard is it to add features to the vertical slice? How quickly can a new developer understand the application's architecture and implementation and become productive?

Unfortunately many projects don't do this kind of risk mitigation. Worse still, many proposed J2EE architectures are specification-driven or vendor-driven rather than proven in production, so we shouldn't be too trusting.

> **Don't trust us, or anyone else. Build a vertical slice of your application, and apply metrics based on your critical requirements. "Ask the computer" which architecture meets your requirements.**
>
> **Your requirements just may be unique. However, the architecture described in this book has been used in many successful projects, and proven to deliver very good results.**

Testability

Test first development has become much more popular in the last few years, and usually produces impressive results. Writing effective unit tests for an application isn't just a question of putting in the time and effort; it can be severely constrained by high-level architecture. In this book I'll stress architectures that make it easy to write effective unit tests. This is one of the biggest frustrations with EJB. Due to its heavy dependence on the EJB container, business logic coded in EJB is very hard to test.

Code that is hard to test is usually also hard to re-engineer, reuse in different contexts, and refactor. Testability is an essential characteristic of *agile* projects. The approach to J2EE architecture expounded in this book is ideal for agile projects, and we'll talk about agility throughout.

We'll discuss testability in detail in Chapter 14.

Lightweight Frameworks and Containers

Applications need infrastructure. Rejecting the use of EJB doesn't mean rejecting the need for an infrastructural solution to many of the concerns EJB addresses. We don't want to return to the pre-EJB era of the late 1990s when the first complex Java enterprise applications were developed, each with its own resource pooling, thread management, service lookup, data access layer, and other infrastructure.

This book will look at existing frameworks that provide such alternatives. We believe that such alternative infrastructure is essential to successful J2EE projects. Thus describing the capabilities and use of lightweight frameworks is a central part of this book.

In 2003 there seemed to be a flowering of such "lightweight" frameworks, which provide management of business objects and enterprise services without the heavyweight infrastructure of EJB. This reflects the movement toward simpler, lighter J2EE solutions that I've already mentioned. Many of these frameworks, such as Spring, PicoContainer, and Nanning Aspects, come out of Java's thriving open source community. I'll say more about this in Chapter 5.

There are also commercial products, such as The Mind Electric's GLUE web services product, that provide lighter-weight solutions than EJB in some of the areas that EJB addresses, such as remoting.

The Spring Framework

We couldn't have written this book without working code that illustrates the approaches we advocate, and that has been proved through use in production applications.

The Spring Framework (`www.springframework.org`) is a popular open source product dedicated to providing simple, effective solutions for common problems in J2EE. This project developed in early 2003 from the source code published with *Expert One-on-One J2EE Design and Development*, which was unusual in presenting an integrated and ambitious application framework. Spring has since acquired a thriving developer and user community and become much more full-featured and bulletproof than anything I could have developed alone. (My co-author, Juergen Hoeller, has made an invaluable contribution to making this happen as co-lead of Spring.) The basic framework design predated even *Expert One-on-One J2EE*, being the result of my experience over several commercial projects.

Spring wasn't conceived as an alternative to EJB, but it provides powerful, tested, implementations of features, such as declarative transaction management for plain Java objects, that enable users to dispense with EJB in many projects.

Spring is not the only project in this space. Little of what we say about design is unique to Spring. For example, we advocate the use of AOP to solve some common enterprise problems; there are several other open source AOP frameworks.

The use of a production-quality open source code base is a real differentiator of this book. Most J2EE books come with code examples. Unfortunately the value of the code is often limited, as it represents a simplification of the problems necessary for the pedagogical purpose, which rapidly becomes a problem when trying to apply the code in real applications. Thus illustrating points using a specific, proven framework—even if not all readers will work with that framework—is preferable to presenting unrealistically simple solutions that can be wholly contained in the text.

Spring has excellent support for architectural refactoring. For example, it's possible to add EJBs with local interfaces or AOP to business objects without modifying a line of calling code, so long as we follow the essential discipline of programming to interfaces rather than classes.

Should We Ever Use EJB?

There is a place for EJB. This book describes approaches that offer a simpler, more productive, alternative to EJB for the great majority of J2EE applications. However, we don't claim that this approach is the best solution to all problems.

> In *Expert One-on-One J2EE Design and Development*, I repeatedly invoked the "Pareto Principle." Often referred to as the 80/20 (or 90/10) rule, this states that a small number of causes (10–20%) are responsible for most (80–90%) of the effect. In the architectural context, this emphasizes the value of finding good solutions to common problems, rather than always living with the complexity of solutions to rarer, more complex problems.

EJB stands on the wrong side of the Pareto Principle. It imposes undue complexity on the majority of cases to support the special requirements of the minority. For example, perhaps 10% of applications need distributed business objects; EJB is an infrastructure closely associated with distribution. EJB 2.1 and earlier entity beans are designed to be independent of the data store; the great majority of J2EE applications use relational databases, and gain no benefit from this. (While it offers a portability between data stores that's of more theoretical interest than practical value, it doesn't shine with object databases either. They are best accessed using their own rich APIs, or using a solution such as JDO.)

EJB remains the best choice for applications that genuinely need object distribution, especially if they are implemented wholly in Java or need to use IIOP as the communication protocol. This type of application is rarer than might be imagined.

EJB is also a pretty good solution for applications that are heavily based around messaging, as message driven beans are relatively simple and effective components.

One of the best examples of an application type to which EJB may add real value is financial middleware. Financial applications can involve processing that is so costly in time and computing power that the cost of remote invocation is (atypically) less than the cost of processing. For such applications, object distribution makes sense, and EJB is a good way of implementing it. Financial middleware is also heavily message-oriented, and suited to use of MDBs.

I believe that such applications are part of the 10%.

Of course there may be strong *political*, rather than technical, reasons that dictate the use of EJB. This is outside the scope of this book. In my experience, political battles can be much harder to win than technical battles, and you'll need Machiavelli rather than me as your guide.

> *I believe that EJB is a declining technology, and within three years it will be relegated to legacy status, despite attempts to make it more relevant with EJB 3.0. But this book focuses on what you can do right now to build enterprise applications. So if you have a requirement that's currently best addressed by EJB, I would advise you to use EJB—for now.*

Summary

This chapter has provided a quick tour of the topics we'll discuss in the rest of this book.

Since the inception of J2EE, EJB has been promoted as the core of the J2EE platform. We believe that this is a misconception. EJB has a place, but most applications do better without it. J2EE is much more than EJB; EJB is just one way to tap into J2EE services. Thus, dispensing with EJB does not mean abandoning J2EE.

We believe that lightweight containers, such as the Spring Framework, provide a better way of structuring application code and a better model for leveraging J2EE and other services. We'll look at this architectural approach in detail throughout this book.

We believe that business requirements and basic OO values, not implementation technology, should drive projects and architectures.

In the next chapter, we'll look at the goals identified here in more detail, before moving on to application architecture and specific technologies in the remainder of the book.

2

Goals

In this chapter we'll review some of the themes of this book, examining the values and goals we should keep in mind as we design an application. Architecture and implementation should always be undertaken with clear goals in mind.

In Chapter 1, we identified the following central themes:

- ❑ Simplicity
- ❑ Productivity
- ❑ The importance of object orientation
- ❑ The primacy of business requirements
- ❑ The importance of empirical process
- ❑ The importance of testability

We'll talk about the many benefits of simplicity in Chapter 4. We'll mention testability throughout the book and discuss it in detail in Chapter 14.

Let's discuss the remaining themes in turn. These themes are interrelated, so most can't be discussed in isolation.

We'll focus most heavily on productivity, as it brings up many architectural and other issues, and is often neglected.

Productivity

Productivity should be a central concern in application development. It's only one part of a picture that must include code maintainability, reliability, performance, and scalability, but it's a very important part. Productive teams are cost-effective teams, producing maximum value for their stake-holders.

Many J2EE developers equate calls for enhanced productivity with laziness. This is perhaps partly a manifestation of the "complexity industry" we'll discuss in Chapter 4, and partly the result of instinctive faith in the adage of "no pain, no gain." In reality, it is *not* lazy to want to be able to do things quickly and easily, especially if they're things that need to be done often, such as implementing and deploying a new business object or testing a business method. If such things are hard to do, progress will slow significantly, or developers will take harmful short cuts, such as not bothering to test their code.

The Problem

J2EE projects often experience disappointing productivity. Unfortunately, there's little empirical data available on this important issue. I know of no impartial studies comparing J2EE productivity with that of other technologies, attempting to compare the time taken to develop a J2EE application with the complexity of the requirements it addresses, or comparing the productivity associated with different J2EE architectures. Those productivity studies that have been conducted have been sponsored by vendors such as Macromedia, Microsoft, and Compuware. Although the consultancies who conducted these studies no doubt made every attempt to be impartial, there is clear evidence from the scientific literature that the motivation for a study tends to affect its findings. And none of these studies has been repeated independently: an essential check before drawing too many conclusions.

I would love to see such statistics, which could benefit the industry greatly. In their absence, I'm relying on my own experience across numerous projects, conversations with other consultants and developers who have worked on numerous projects, and the experience of colleagues and many readers who've described their J2EE project experiences.

I believe that far too high a proportion of the time of the average J2EE developer is wasted on incidental tasks. Examples include:

❑ Deploying applications to an application server merely to perform *unit*, rather than integration, testing. Each round trip is lengthy.

❑ Writing verbose EJB deployment descriptors.

❑ Churning out unproductive code as a result of inappropriate architectural choices, such as a layer of verbose transfer objects in applications that don't benefit from object distribution, and business delegates to access EJBs in cases where EJB usage isn't beneficial or codeless client access to EJBs is possible with a suitable application framework.

❑ Writing code to use cumbersome APIs such as JDBC directly.

❑ Writing code to catch and wrap unrecoverable exceptions, including creating new exception classes used as wrappers. In our analysis of some published J2EE applications in Chapter 3, we'll look at the consequences of traditional J2EE error handling in practice.

I don't think productivity problems are inherent to J2EE; I think they are consequences of the way developers tend to use J2EE, and result from orthodox approaches to J2EE architecture, which produce unnecessary complexity.

Fortunately, there are solutions to most productivity problems in J2EE. Anything we can do to remove these hurdles directly reduces project costs and improves our ability to concentrate on what's really important.

> **We should have higher expectations for productivity in J2EE applications.**

The Traditional J2EE Approach to Productivity Issues

What can we do to boost productivity?

The traditional J2EE answer to productivity issues is to either deny that they exist or to argue that they're irrelevant, because tool support can fill the gap. The hoped-for tool support usually amounts to some form of code generation.

Note that, in the following discussion, I'm not referring to Java IDE code generation, such as generating JavaBean getter and setter methods. This is no different from using macros; it merely saves typing and reduces the likelihood of errors. The generated code is hand-maintainable, so there's no round-tripping issue. What I am referring to is code generation that's designed to allow developers to produce code that they wouldn't be able to write manually, because it's too verbose or complex.

There are a number of problems with code generation as the prime solution to J2EE productivity issues, which I believe make this approach dangerous:

❑ **It's easy to generate bad code or code that implements a bad architecture.** Most J2EE code generation tools seem geared toward producing code implementing the "classic" J2EE architecture, with remote EJBs, Data Transfer Objects, and, often, entity beans: the whole enchilada. This isn't an inherent problem in code generation per se, just the reality of the tools available. Specific bad practices we tend to see in generated code (because it makes them so easy to produce) include:

   ❑ **Code duplication:** This is a code smell, which should ideally be avoided by better design, such as abstracting the common code into a framework. A good framework can do this very successfully in J2EE applications, as discussed below. *Don't Repeat Yourself (DRY)* is such an important principle that we should observe it in our application's structure, not just in how we implement it.

   ❑ **Over engineering:** Most J2EE generators and MDA tools are designed to spit out distributed applications. Unfortunately this results in complexity that's unwarranted for the great majority of applications.

❑ **How do we version control generated code?** If generated code is checked into the source control system, regenerating it may cause problems, especially for source control tools that require explicit checkouts. Placing code that isn't intended for manual maintenance in version control is counterintuitive, although, as an essential part of the deployed application, such code must be formally managed.

❑ **How do we round trip generated code?** If any human modification is made, it may need to be merged into a later generated copy. There are some clever solutions to this problem, such as "generational" code generation, where developers can add code to a subclass of a generated class to avoid the need to work with it directly. But still there remains a maintenance issue.

❏ **Projects may become heavily dependent on the code generation tools they use.** While, in theory, code generation should deliver a useful abstraction from the technology (such as the EJB specification version), in practice it often shackles projects to a particular code generation technology, which may prove far less stable and less standard than the J2EE specifications or popular application frameworks. Migrating to a different code generation tool, or even to a later version of the same tool, may be very costly in a large project.

❏ **Maintaining generated code can be problematic.** We may not have had to write the code, but we will need to maintain and support it. There will almost certainly be times when generated code needs to be examined closely because something doesn't behave as expected; at such times the initial productivity gain can disappear. For example, we may encounter complex stack traces and will have to navigate through reams of code to track down bugs. Remember that maintenance accounts for much more of the total cost of a software project than initial development.

❏ **Generated code is not usually configurable at runtime.** Frameworks usually offer superior configurability: often a very important point.

> **Code generation is a useful approach when complexity becomes excessive, but it's usually better to reduce complexity than to resort to code generation to cope with it. Better alternatives include using the simplest possible design, and avoiding code duplication through the use of appropriate frameworks. Code generation is downright dangerous if it is used to mitigate the effects of a flawed architecture.**

When we consider what kind of code is typically generated in J2EE applications, the dangers become clearer. Common uses of code generation include:

❏ **Generating entity beans (or other persistent objects) and related artifacts from database tables.** This results in a one-to-one mapping between relational database tables and supposed domain objects. Unfortunately, such generated entities aren't real objects. They reflect a relational, rather than object-oriented, view of the world, and impose that on all code that uses them. For example, callers must use association (relationship navigation) in place of inheritance. There's no true decoupling between Java application code and relational schema. For example, in a classic J2EE architecture, modifying generated entity bean granularity to improve performance will break all session beans using the entity bean layer.

❏ **Generating DDL from entity beans to create a database schema** if we choose to do things the other way around. This is a recipe for an inefficient database schema and often problems generating reports. The practical limitations of generation tools are apparent in a similar lack of support for inheritance relationships in the object layer; it's difficult to automate this kind of intelligence.

❏ **Generating DAO objects** if we choose yet another alternative approach to data access. Products such as FireStorm (`www.codefutures.com/products/firestorm/`) adopt this approach. The result is usually reams of code that might better be replaced by using a data access framework that simplifies the code in DAOs so that they can easily be hand authored.

❏ **Generating EJB deployment descriptors.** Code generation in this case is essentially a recognition that the EJB specification requires that we express configuration in an unworkably verbose form, split between standard and proprietary deployment descriptors. Code generation solutions require that we supply all necessary information *once*, in a simple form. (In the case of XDoclet, for example, we supply it in Javadoc comments in the source file.)

❑ **Generating XML interchange code.** If we need XML, this might be a real boon. However, we certainly don't want to end up with an XML marshaling infrastructure built into our application unless we require it.

❑ **Generating EJB access code,** such as implementations of the Service Locator and Business Delegate pattern. There are superior, codeless alternatives, using dynamic proxies.

❑ **Generating a whole J2EE stack:** for example, generating a JSP, EJB access layer, EJB, DAO, or entity bean. This is an automatic antipattern generator. There should be decoupling between architectural tiers, and such decoupling requires intelligence and knowledge of the domain. Such press-button tools appeal on paper, but can produce ghastly results in practice.

❑ **Generating boilerplate code in application objects,** such as setting a dirty flag when the state of a persistent object is changed, or security checks before and after methods.

Let's look at each of these reasons in turn, and better alternatives to code generation for each, as shown in the following table.

Motivation for code generation in J2EE applications	Superior alternatives	Notes
Generating persistent classes from an RDBMS schema	Expend the effort to define a more sophisticated, looser, mapping between domain objects and database tables. This will require more effort initially, but the effort will pay off because the resulting domain objects will be much easier to use. Sophisticated persistence mapping solutions such as Hibernate and JDO allow this degree of decoupling. Entity beans don't, but that's a good reason not to use them.

Performance is also likely to be disappointing with the generation of Java code from a relational schema. | Generating Java classes from a relational schema (or the reverse) is an acceptable kickstart for an application, but usually no more than that. Unfortunately it poses a dangerous temptation because of its apparent productivity advantages.

This approach is adequate only if there's limited use of the generated quasi-objects, or if the application is a glorified database entry system.

The only kind of persistent objects that are far too verbose to hand-author are entity beans, and they're the least satisfactory J2EE data access technology.

Generated persistent objects will contain no behavior, and it will be problematic for round-tripping to add behavior. Having "objects" without behavior is profoundly un-OO, as we'll see shortly. |

Table continued on following page

Motivation for code generation in J2EE applications	Superior alternatives	Notes
Generate DDL from persistent classes	As above	As above A database schema derived directly from an object model may prove inefficient and hard to administer. As "data tends to stick where it lands" the unidiomatic database schema may outlive the J2EE application it was generated for, imposing additional cost forever.
Generate DAOs	Use a good data access framework. There shouldn't be vast amounts of boilerplate code in DAOs. Defining methods on DAO interfaces should be the work of developers; method signatures can't meaningfully be autogenerated. *Implementing DAOs shouldn't be too much of a chore either, as we can use a good toolkit such as Hibernate, Spring JDBC, or the iBATIS database layer. Using a JDBC abstraction layer is better than generating JDBC code from a maintainability perspective.* If we see a requirement for boring repetitive code, we should apply an OO solution and abstract it into a framework, rather than generate it and live with the resulting duplication.	Remember the important principle of DRY.
Generate EJB deployment descriptors	Use alternatives to EJB in which configuration data is held in manageable formats. *If you do choose to use EJB, this is one case where code generation is probably a good choice. A simple tool such as XDocLet can greatly simplify configuration and significantly boost productivity.*	This type of code generation is essentially a workaround for problems in the present EJB specification. EJB 3.0 will attempt to address these problems through using source-level attributes to hold much of the configuration presently held in XML deployment descriptors.

Motivation for code generation in J2EE applications	Superior alternatives	Notes
Generate XML-generation code for domain objects	Avoid the use of XML unless it's necessary Consider alternative approaches to XML generation, such as Castor, which don't require verbose Java code.	
Generate EJB access classes	Avoid the use of EJB, and the need for JNDI lookup, if possible. Use a framework such as Spring that provides codeless EJB access via dynamic proxies. Spring completely eliminates the need to write Business Delegates or Service Locators.	Codeless proxy-based EJB access allows a variety of other benefits, such as intercepting calls on EJBs. This can allow bonuses such as caching that is configurable at runtime.
Generation of an entire J2EE stack, from JSPs to entity or other persistent objects	Face it; you need to *design* the application. There's no easy way out.	Usually too good to be true. The result is a close coupling between all application tiers: for example, beans JSPs tied to the database schema. A maintainability nightmare that negates many of the goals of middleware. This approach is valid only for the minority of applications that are essentially thin front ends over an existing database, with minimal business logic and benefiting little from an OO approach in the middle tier. Examples include some Intranet database administration tools. As J2EE components add little value in such cases, database-specific tools may be a better option than a J2EE application.
Generate boilerplate code such as dirty flagging	Use technologies that can externalize such checks. For example, such code may be necessary with TopLink to avoid registering an excessive number of objects with a unit of work, but isn't necessary with JDO.	Again we're dealing with a code smell; we should tackle the reason for the code duplication, rather than learn to live with the symptoms.

Table continued on following page

Motivation for code generation in J2EE applications	Superior alternatives	Notes
	Use AOP to address such cross cutting concerns. This can eliminate boilerplate code through modularizing these concerns into "aspects," while allowing much greater flexibility in deployment.	

Interestingly, Microsoft, which has long led the way in sophisticated tool support, is now working to simplify its underlying enterprise programming model, rather than purely relying on tools to make the model manageable. Consider the task of writing a transactional object today in C# or even Managed C++ versus doing so five years ago in C++ with ATL. The introduction of source level metadata means that there is no longer any need to generate complex code: code that is typically generated by Visual Studio .NET, such as transaction attributes on classes requiring declarative transaction management, is usually easily understandable. As I've noted, EJB 3.0 is also focusing on simplifying the programming model: a clear, if belated, recognition of some of the practical issues posed by the EJB specification.

Although it's become widely accepted in J2EE, relying on code generation to cope with complexity is not consistent with the philosophy of the Java platform itself. Java has always been a simple language, making code easier to understand and author than in predecessors such as C++.

> **There shouldn't be vast amounts of repetitive plumbing code in J2EE applications. Better architectural choices and better frameworks can virtually eliminate such code, meaning that nearly all application code can be hand-authored.**
>
> **I'm not saying that code generation is a bad technology in general—merely that, when properly designed and built on appropriate frameworks, most J2EE applications should not contain enough boilerplate code to justify it and outweigh its negatives.**

The natural path of our industry is toward higher levels of abstraction. Perhaps one day MDA-powered code generation will prove to be an appropriate abstraction. However, I feel that this is 10–15 years away, if it ever happens.

Better Solutions for Higher Productivity

So how *should* we address productivity issues in J2EE applications?

I recommend solutions that reduce complexity, rather than generate complex code. Some of the most valuable techniques I've found for boosting productivity include the following:

❑   Architecture

    ❑   Avoid unnecessary architectural complexity.

    ❑   Avoid unnecessary use of EJB.

    ❑   Use abstraction layers to hide the complexity of core J2EE and J2SE APIs.

    ❑   If possible, use an O/R mapping product to simplify the persistence layer.

    ❑   Use a good application framework.

❑   Focus and methodology

    ❑   Focus! Know what problems you should be solving, and concentrate on them.

    ❑   Use a reference architecture and start from a template application.

    ❑   Use an agile development process.

❑   Use appropriate tools.

Let's discuss these in turn.

Architecture

Architectural choices usually have the biggest impact on productivity throughout the project lifecycle.

Avoid Unnecessary Architectural Complexity

Whenever you encounter complexity, question it. Using the simplest architecture and implementation is a great way of boosting productivity. We'll discuss this further in Chapter 4.

Avoid Unnecessary Use of EJB

Much of the complexity of traditional J2EE applications results from EJB. Remove the EJB and—so long as concerns well addressed by EJB, such as transaction management, are addressed by an adequate alternative solution—applications become a lot simpler. In this book we talk about many techniques to enable us to dispense with EJB. Entity beans are particularly hazardous to productivity, especially when compared with simpler solutions such as Hibernate and JDO.

Use Abstraction Layers to Hide Low-level API Complexity

Many core J2EE APIs, such as JTA, and J2SE APIs critical to J2EE applications, such as JDBC, are not ideal end-user APIs. They do a great job of providing a standard interface to disparate resources, but they aren't very usable by application code. Using them correctly requires a lot of code and substantial developer effort that can better be spent elsewhere.

I've seen many responses to this problem, besides code generation, which we've already discussed:

❑   Ignore the problem.

❑   Use standard ways of avoiding the problem: typically, higher-level J2EE services.

❑   Develop and use an in-house solution.

❑   Use an open source solution.

❑   Use a proprietary solution bundled with an application server.

Ignoring the problem leads to a proliferation of code to do the same thing, such as acquire, use, and release a JDBC connection with the necessary exception handling. Applications become hard to maintain and a fertile breeding ground for bugs. (For example, how many methods may need to be changed if a connection leak becomes apparent?) Different developers do the same thing in different ways, wasting valuable development time and complicating maintenance. Corners will nearly always be cut, either because some developers don't understand the issues in writing robust code using these APIs or because of time constraints.

Sometimes the J2EE specifications offer simpler alternatives to direct API usage. For example, we can use EJB CMT instead of JTA. This is generally a good alternative, although it must be evaluated on its merits against comparable open source solutions. Using entity bean CMP instead of JDBC, however, may be merely exchanging one set of problems for another.

It's possible to develop adequate in-house solutions for many of these problems, but it's unwise. In the early days of J2EE there was no alternative; today the results of in-house infrastructure are usually clearly inferior to those gained by the use of third party solutions. Disadvantages of in-house infrastructure include:

❑   **It's wasted effort.** Typically, the best developers will want to be involved in the development of in-house infrastructure—and they need to be, if it's to succeed. But these developers should be tackling domain problems, not solving problems that other good developers have already solved publicly.

❑   **It's hard.** No matter how capable the developers are, it takes two or three iterations to arrive at a really good infrastructure framework, unless the goals are trivial. In my experience, developers who've already solved these problems once or twice are likely to be aware of good third party solutions, and are least likely to be enthusiastic about tackling them again.

❑   **It's nonstandard.** The result is a proprietary programming model. New developers can't become productive until they're familiar with it, imposing ongoing training requirements. Even if this proprietary programming model is simpler than raw J2EE, it's impossible to hire people who already understand it. This objection doesn't apply to successful open source projects.

❑   **It's seldom documented adequately.** Successful third party products usually come with tutorials and examples that are too expensive to develop in house.

Increasingly, the solution of choice is to look to open source solutions for common problems. The results are typically very good: Open source solutions become widely adopted only if they're reliable and deliver value. In contrast, inferior in-house solutions can survive through being "the way we do things around here," and to avoid embarrassing their designers, who may be politically powerful. The best open source solutions are also far more thoroughly tested than any in-house infrastructure layer. Successful open source projects typically achieve significantly higher unit test coverage than most in-house projects, for example. And successful open source projects are supported by a community. While a few key developers supporting an in-house infrastructure framework going on holiday can adversely affect a project, the size of communities around leading open source projects prevents this danger. Of course, the viability of the open source project is vital. There are a huge number of open source projects without strong communities that are essentially the work of one or two developers, and do *not* offer any likelihood of ongoing support and maintenance.

Another option is to use a simplifying abstraction provided by the application server vendor. BEA is putting particular effort into this, aiming to make much of the work of J2EE developers accessible to developers who might formerly have programmed in "entry-level" languages such as Visual Basic. There's nothing wrong with this from a technical standpoint. It is better (and usually cheaper) than going down an in-house route, so long as you're happy to view your choice of application server as a long-term commitment. However, it's a questionable reason to sacrifice portability between application servers. Also, most application server vendors have a poor record of backward compatibility with their proprietary APIs. They frequently deprecate them in favor of newer, standard APIs, and have few constraints on changing them incompatibly. Open source solutions are more likely to consider their user base as they evolve, as they can't assume a captive market and are thus more likely to produce platform and vendor independent solutions.

> **Do not develop in-house infrastructure to solve standard problems such as resource management or logging. Address only your unique requirements, and perform careful analysis to establish what they are before writing a line of code. Java/J2EE benefits from a rich variety of high-quality open source solutions, which are usually the best choice to address generic requirements.**

O/R Mapping

Because of the *impedance mismatch* between relational and object models, writing code to access a relational database can account for a significant proportion of development effort in J2EE applications. There is often an easier way, with an appropriate mapping tool. Establish whether or not your problem can be solved efficiently by O/R mapping. If it can't, use SQL without guilt to solve it. If it can, use a technology such as Hibernate or JDO that delivers simple yet powerful O/R mapping.

Use a Good Application Framework

Abstraction layers such as those I've mentioned previously are really only part of the function of a good generic *application framework*. Another benefit of a good application framework is that it can bring structure to your whole application—for example, by introducing a good Inversion of Control container such as Spring or PicoContainer. This can significantly improve productivity because you don't need to invent your own solutions to typical problems (as happens with ad hoc use of Singletons, for example) and because it yields a dividend of consistency and understandability. I emphasize a framework-oriented approach throughout this book.

Developers have long realized the importance of using standard frameworks, such as Struts, for the web tier. Even greater value is introduced by the rarer frameworks, such as Spring, that address *all* architectural tiers in a consistent way, providing good solutions to common problems and leaving application developers to focus on their problem domain.

Focus and Methodology

Productivity depends on having a tight focus on those problems that need to be solved, and using streamlined methodologies.

Know What Problems to Solve

Probably the biggest single win in productivity is knowing what *technical* problems to spend effort addressing. These should be the domain problems that your application faces: not generic problems.

Although the J2EE specifications were intended to help developers focus on their problem domain, they didn't quite achieve this goal. However, there is enough accumulated experience in the J2EE community now that it *is* possible, with the right libraries and application framework.

Another common area of misdirected effort is in continually experimenting with new technologies. Don't drag your application to the bleeding edge. Research and experimentation are important, but they are best kept separate from the core development effort in the form of an hour or two per week for research for each developer. Attempt to apply this research in anger only when there's evidence that a new technology delivers clear benefit, given your specific problems.

Use Reference Architectures and Templates

It's also important to cheat. Don't begin from the beginning when starting to develop an application.

I'm not talking about cheating by simple cut and paste; that is a recipe for a bad application. What I'm referring to is starting with a template or skeleton that contains the wiring for your application. Such a template will provide a *reference architecture*: the skeleton that you can flesh out with your own domain logic.

Typically, candidate templates will be provided with one of the central frameworks used in your application. Good starting points include:

- ❑ **Struts resources:** Struts comes with a number of sample applications that provide the necessary WAR structure, Jars, web.xml, and struts-config.xml skeletons.

- ❑ **Spring Framework resources:** Spring provides multiple templates, covering different usage scenarios such as web application with declarative AOP transaction management and web application using Hibernate.

If you have the same requirements in your organization for multiple applications, consider creating your own template based on such a generic starting point and using it each time you begin work on a new application.

> After you've decided on some candidate technologies, such as Spring and Hibernate, begin work using a skeleton application that establishes the overall plumbing. In this case, this would be a simple, generic web application template with the Spring distribution that sets up web.xml, Spring, and Hibernate configuration, giving you placeholders for defining your business objects. A template should include a build script and necessary Jar files.

Don't use something more complex like a complete sample application; that will result in unnecessary complexity extraneous to your application. What you want is plumbing and wiring, not logic: placeholders rather than real behavior.

Of course the key to success in this approach is a good framework. Attempting this kind of approach usually fails when it's based on an *application* rather than on a framework. For example, I've seen some unsuccessful attempts to use the Sun Java Pet Store as a template. The problem is that this is a single application, and that the framework it is built on was not designed for a wider range of scenarios, although it made some effort to abstract generic concepts.

The template approach can also be applied to EJB applications, but it doesn't work so well for them, because even after an EJB application is set up, the cost of adding another EJB is quite high, still involving authoring 3–4 Java classes, adding information to one or two verbose XML deployment descriptors, adding an EJB link in web.xml (for web applications), and writing code or configuration to allow clients to use the EJB.

Using a template-based approach doesn't have the disadvantages of code generation, which I've argued against, because it's merely a way of saving typing. You don't end up with a line of code that you wouldn't otherwise have written by hand, and there's no need for round-tripping. Once the basic infrastructure template is in place, with a good framework you can manually write every line of code thereafter. For example, in a Spring application, adding business objects involves merely:

❑ Implementing two Java classes (interface and implementation). This is no more onerous than plain Java development. Creating this pair of classes is facilitated by any IDE (no J2EE-specific support is required), as is adding JavaBean properties to the implementation class.

❑ Adding a simple XML bean definition to publish the business object.

Use an Agile Development Process

Development process isn't J2EE-specific, so I won't labor this point. In my experience, heavyweight development processes slow down J2EE projects, without adding compensating value. Thus I favor agile methodologies such as XP over heavy-weight methodologies such as RUP (as it is usually practiced). Remember that the goal of a project is maintainable, tested, working code. Other artifacts are essentially optional; beware of approaches in which much of a team's effort goes into producing thick documents or complex models that won't stay in sync with working code. And remember that the more upfront effort before arriving at a working prototype, the greater the risk of inadequate performance or an unworkable architecture.

See the Agile Manifesto (www.agilemanifesto.org/) for a summary of the values of agile software development.

If a project seems so large that only a very bureaucratic methodology seems likely to handle its complexity, try to break it up into smaller sub-projects. This also ensures that team size remains small and manageable.

Use Appropriate Tools

Finally, it's important to use the right tools. A simple, appropriate tool set can greatly boost productivity. Tools should include:

❑ **A good modern IDE, like Eclipse or IntelliJ.** Sophisticated refactoring support, for example, can greatly boost productivity and the quality of application code. I feel that J2EE-specific support, such as the ability to generate WAR deployment units, is less important than is often thought. Java-centric tasks such as refactoring are crucial every day; we don't create a new J2EE deployment unit nearly as often (and a skeleton can provide a good start). A build tool such as Ant can provide good out-of-the-box support for J2EE tasks.

❑ **A unit testing tool and supporting libraries.** JUnit is simple and adequate. It should be possible to run unit tests both within the IDE and from build scripts. Class libraries such as Mock Objects and EasyMock make it easier to write rigorous test cases.

❑ **A standard build tool.** Apache Ant (`http://ant.apache.org/`) is currently the de facto standard for Java development, although Maven (`http://maven.apache.org/`) is a more advanced alternative for teams who are comfortable with its way of working. Having a standard build tool is crucial because it enables application tasks, such as building deployment units, to be scripted. It's important to script every activity that may be repeated in a project. Build scripts make a better place to manage J2EE-specific tasks than IDEs, because they can be version controlled.

❑ **A good XML editor or IDE plugin.** XML is central to J2EE, and many popular frameworks and APIs such as Spring, Struts, JDO, and Hibernate. It's essential to have tools that simplify XML authoring and that understand XML DTDs and schemas. Numerous free and commercial Eclipse plugins offer good XML functionality for Eclipse users. Altova XMLSpy version 5 is an excellent commercial XML editor with full DTD and schema capabilities.

❑ **An effective source control system and good IDE integration.** In my experience, it's counter-productive if a source control system, or usage choice, makes refactoring unduly difficult: for example, by enforcing manual checkouts before modifying code, which obstructs IDE refactoring operations.

Together, such tools enable an agile development process, emphasizing automated testing and refactoring.

J2EE developers are fortunate in that all these requirements can be met by free, open source tools, such as Eclipse, JUnit, Ant, a good Eclipse XML plugin, CVS, and the standard Eclipse JUnit and CVS integration.

A code coverage tool such as Clover is a very worthwhile addition, to help judge the effectiveness and improve the quality of the test suite. Unfortunately I know of no good freeware coverage tools. However, Clover is inexpensive and well worth a small investment.

A profiling tool is also useful to help to analyze application performance. The Eclipse Profiler plugin, discussed in Chapter 15, is free and sufficient for most projects.

OO

I believe that OO is more important than J2EE. The value proposition of OO is clear. Practicing OO isn't easy, but with care we can use OO to:

❑ Elegantly encapsulate domain concepts, hiding implementation details

❑ Express commonality through polymorphism between objects whose implementations differ

❑ Achieve code reuse

❑ Achieve extensibility without needing to modify existing code

Unfortunately, too many J2EE applications fail to enjoy the benefits of OO. Many J2EE patterns are either J2EE-specific versions of true design patterns (which aren't technology-specific), or actively non-OO. One common violation of object orientation in J2EE applications is the existence of what I call *fake objects*: objects in appearance, but which don't exhibit some of the characteristics of objects: identity, state, and behavior.

Let's look at some common fake objects and why to avoid them if possible:

❑ **Transfer objects,** often referred to as Data Transfer Objects (DTOs) or Value Objects. Transfer objects are not true objects because they contain only state, without behavior. Transfer objects are a necessary evil in distributed applications (although there's an argument that this kind of data should really be included in an XML structure rather than Java objects). But if we don't want a distributed architecture, they're redundant and harmful, creating an unwelcome impedance mismatch between business services and callers.

❑ **Entity beans or other persistent objects generated from RDBMS tables.** These reflect a relational, rather than OO, model. They have a harmful effect on code that works with them, which is forced to navigate relationships and cannot benefit from OO concepts such as polymorphism. There's also inadequate decoupling between business logic and persistent data representation.

❑ **Persistent objects in general that contain only getters and setters, without behavior.** Such fake objects force behavior that they should encapsulate to be moved into control classes such as session beans. Not only is encapsulation violated, but the result tends to be verbose code in control classes.

> **Don't tolerate fake objects unless there's no alternative.**

As well as avoiding non-OO idioms, we should practice OO principles where we can. For example, we should program to interfaces, not classes. This frees code from dependence on *how* objects are implemented, as opposed to the contracts they satisfy. I view concrete inheritance as essentially an implementation convenience; an object's concrete inheritance hierarchy is a matter for its implementation, and normally shouldn't be publicly known. Loose coupling through programming to interfaces has an enormous benefit in enabling an alternative implementation of any application object to be dropped in without affecting code using it. It also has many incidental benefits, such as easier testing and the ability to use dynamic proxies.

> **Program to interfaces, not classes. This is a basic OO precept stressed in the classic "Gang of Four" design patterns text. It's hard to overestimate its importance.**

Developers sometimes prefer classes to interfaces because of a belief that programming to interfaces adds complexity. This is a fallacy, so long as we use appropriate frameworks that address the problem of locating the relevant implementation of each interface.

Chapter 4 of Expert One-on-One J2EE Design and Development *includes a lengthy discussion of OO programming practices for J2EE applications. Please refer to that for further discussion of this important topic.*

The Importance of Business Requirements

We should not assume the need to solve problems that don't exist. A particular danger in J2EE projects seems to be assuming business requirements, based on a technical, rather than a business, viewpoint. Just because J2EE makes something possible doesn't mean that the client needs it. Common phantom requirements include:

❑ **Database portability.** This may be a real business requirement, but it's fairly rare. We shouldn't incur unnecessary cost to achieve database portability if there's no realistic likelihood that the application will ever run against a different database. In reality, moving from one *type* of database to another—such as from an RDBMS to an ODBMS—is extremely rare.

❑ **Ability to support remote standalone Java clients,** when this is not initially specified for a web application. If such a requirement ever does come up, it may be for web-services-based remoting, to support clients on different platforms.

❑ **Portability between application servers at zero cost.** It can be surprisingly costly to achieve this, although of course we should not sacrifice portability without good reason.

Such phantom requirements seem partly the result of fashion in the J2EE community, but also result from the natural tendency of architects to focus unduly on *technical* issues during project inception, rather than on domain issues.

Of course when designing an application we should consider the *likely* future requirements. But we shouldn't speculate based on the capabilities of the platform rather than the needs of the business.

The use of agile practices helps to minimize the likelihood of writing unnecessary code. For example, if no code is written without a user story, it's less likely that the technical tail will wag the business dog.

I've previously noted the common project antipattern of excessive effort going into in-house infrastructure development. This is a sure sign of lack of focus on business requirements; this focus can be regained by using existing generic infrastructure.

The Importance of an Empirical Process

I feel that too many assumptions in application development fail to be justified by evidence. Only through gathering evidence can we achieve better and more predictable outcomes.

Empirical process can bring important benefits:

❑ **Within projects:** Validating an application's architecture as early as possible during the development lifecycle. Both RUP and XP methodologies emphasize this through an *executable architecture* or *vertical slice*. It's hard to overemphasize the importance of this to risk management. For example, because some popular J2EE idioms are inherently unperformant, far too many J2EE projects encounter intractable performance problems too late to address them cost-effectively. It's essential to consider business requirements closely when validating an architecture.

❑ **Before project kick-off:** Using data from previous projects to justify choices can bring important benefits. I repeatedly see projects that have been doomed to failure or comparative failure before a line of code has been written, because the overall technology choice or architecture did not fit the problem at hand.

The second of these benefits is much harder to achieve, because organizations are often reluctant to publish the results of projects—especially failed projects. Also, many large users of J2EE, such as financial institutions, are understandably secretive. In some cases, failures are successfully covered up even within an organization. However, this is such a worthwhile goal that I hope it will one day be achieved. (Often it can at least be achieved within an organization. Especially within large organizations, there may have been many previous J2EE projects in other divisions; if information about them can be obtained, it can be very valuable.)

I've recently become increasingly interested in the concept of what I call "Evidence-Based Software Architecture." I would like to reduce the present reliance on opinion and replace it with measurable data. For example, if it were possible to find more than anecdotal and personal evidence of the results of using entity beans versus JDO in practice, architects would be able to make more informed choices than they do at present. Bad technologies would be nipped in the bud before they could adversely affect large numbers of projects; good technologies would be adopted more quickly. Architects would be far less dependent on the power of product marketing.

> **Always develop a vertical slice to validate your application's architecture early in the project. Don't trust our advice or anyone else's without establishing that it's appropriate to your needs.**

Summary

In this chapter we've discussed some of the central themes of this book. We've examined:

❑ Productivity

❑ Object orientation

❑ The primacy of business requirements

❑ The importance of empirical process

Traditional approaches to J2EE projects often fail to deliver in these areas; in this book, we'll outline an approach that does.

In Chapter 3, we'll look at architectural building blocks and candidate architectures in light of these goals.

3

Architectures

In this chapter we'll survey alternative architectures for J2EE applications, focusing on web applications. However, much of the material also relates to other application types.

Architectural Building Blocks

In the light of our goals, let's examine the key architectural building blocks of J2EE applications. Later we'll look at how these building blocks can be put together into an entire application architecture. Three core building blocks are:

- ❏ **Business services layer.** This is central to successful applications.
- ❏ **Presentation layer.** This may be a UI or a remoting facade.
- ❏ **Data access layer.** Objects accessing a persistence store—usually, one or more relational databases.

The Business Services Layer

The key to a sound architecture is a well-defined **service layer**. This is a layer that exposes business logic to clients such as web or other user interfaces or a remoting layer. It will consist of multiple interfaces, each with a well-defined contract.

In the light of our goals, a well-defined service layer should:

- ❏ **Be complete.** It should expose all operations that clients will need. It may need to expose distinct interfaces that support the needs of different clients.
- ❏ **Be simple.** Its complexity should be only that warranted by the complexity of business requirements concerned. Its mechanics shouldn't impose great complexity.

- ❑ **Be defined in terms of interfaces, rather than classes,** following good OO practice.

- ❑ **Be object oriented.** There should be as few constraints as possible on the business objects. For example, they should not be forced to implement special interfaces or extend a particular superclass.

- ❑ **Be independent of presentation technology.**

- ❑ **Be easy to write,** maximizing productivity and reducing costs.

- ❑ **Force no assumptions about the underlying data access technology.** Data access is a lower-level issue. Business objects should not need to deal with data access technologies such as JDBC directly or catch technology-specific exceptions.

- ❑ **Handle transaction management.** Callers of the business service layer should not have to worry about transactions.

- ❑ **Be compatible with horizontal scalability if required.** Nothing in the business services layer should prevent clustering. *However, note that this isn't the same thing as the business services layer itself providing horizontal scalability. It need not be a distribution mechanism.*

- ❑ **Be easy to test and thoroughly tested.** This is crucial, as rigorous testing of business objects is essential to building quality applications.

Stateless or Stateful?

Service objects will usually be stateless. Stateless service layers are highly scalable: They pose no replication issues and there is no need to allocate additional resources for every client. (Remember that one of the key motivations of a middle tier is to share resources between multiple clients.) It is also much easier for stateless service layers to support remote clients, if necessary.

The traditional stateless service objects in J2EE applications are *stateless session beans* (SLSBs). I'll use SLSBs as a starting point for discussion because they illustrate many of the basic concepts of stateless service objects, which predate EJB.

A stateless service layer is one concession of object orientation that I find not too painful. Stateless service objects are semi-objects. Although they cannot expose state to callers, they can hold internal state and they can fully participate in inheritance relationships. If they are local, rather than remote, they can use true objects as parameters and return values.

There are two main potential models for *stateful* service layers in J2EE: *stateful session beans* (SFSBs) and web tier session objects. If we don't use stateful session beans, session data is usually held in Servlet API HttpSession objects. Holding session data in the web tier is usually more scalable than holding it in the EJB tier. (See Chapter 10 of *Expert One-on-One J2EE Design and Development* for detailed discussion of state replication issues.) "Thick" clients such as Swing applications will normally hold their own state.

Because stateless service layers have proven their value in numerous technologies, including both J2EE and Microsoft platforms, we'll focus on them in this book.

> **If possible, design applications to use a stateless service layer. Hold state in the web tier, rather than in the business logic tier, if possible.**

Popular Service Layers

Let's look at some popular technologies for service layers and how they measure up against the above criteria.

Session EJBs

The most familiar type of business service layer is a layer of stateless session beans. These can have either remote or local interfaces.

Stateless Session Beans with Remote Interfaces

Traditionally, session bean services have been accessed via remote interfaces—if not necessarily via RMI. (The application server may optimize to use call-by-reference when remote EJBs and their callers are co-located.)

Such a layer of SLSBs is often called a *Session Facade*. The original intent of this facade was to conceal entity beans behind it; today it will often conceal POJOs: business objects more fine-grained than EJBs, or POJOs persisted with Hibernate, JDO, or the like.

Against our criteria, remote SLSBs score badly on simplicity, object orientation (because of distribution), and productivity. They do well on scalability, although at significant cost in performance overhead. Like all session beans, they provide a good basis for decoupling presentation technology from business logic and business logic from data representation, if used appropriately.

Stateless Session Beans with Local Interfaces

SLSBs with local interfaces are simpler than remote EJBs, and do a lot better on object orientation, as they don't require the use of transfer objects to access them. Otherwise, they are comparable to remote session beans.

Distribution must be handled by an additional remoting facade, as there is no built-in RMI remoting.

Common Issues with EJB Service Layers

All EJB service layers make a distinction between code running in the EJB container and code outside. Even in the case of local EJBs, this is a strong logical, rather than physical, distinction. Although enforcing such a distinction encourages good practice by fostering appropriate decoupling between architectural tiers, it can become a major problem if some business operations cannot be implemented within the EJB container, because of the EJB programming restrictions, defined in section 25.1.2 of the EJB 2.1 specification.

.NET "Serviced Components"

.NET offers "serviced components" as service objects. These are comparable to EJBs in providing declarative enterprise services. However, with no distinct business object container within the overall .NET framework, the distinction between ServicedComponents and their callers is blurred—not necessarily a bad thing if ServicedComponents provide clean interfaces.

.NET serviced components do well with productivity, but not so well on OO, because they are forced to extend the concrete .NET framework `System.EnterpriseServices.ServicedComponent` class.

Overall, the model is fairly similar to EJB, but with less overhead in programming and deployment complexity.

MVC Web Actions

What if there is no distinct service layer, but business logic is implemented in the web tier of a J2EE application in Struts Actions, Spring Controllers, or other web tier classes? This often results from the lack of management for business objects in J2EE applications not using EJB. There are many disadvantages with this approach, such as:

❑ Tying business objects to the servlet API.

❑ Limited reuse of business objects, for this reason. A framework such as XWork, which decouples commands from the Servlet API, can alleviate this concern.

❑ Depending on the web framework, there may be concessions to OO. For example, Struts Actions must extend Struts classes, depriving them of an independent concrete inheritance hierarchy.

❑ Confused responsibilities in the web tier. Each class should have a single, clear responsibility. In this approach, web tier classes have two quite different responsibilities.

❑ Absence of declarative transaction support. (Spring AOP can be applied to Spring web controllers, or Servlet filters can be used for declarative transaction management in any web application, but these are only band-aid solutions for a problem better addressed separately from the Servlet API.)

❑ Business logic is hard to test, as web tier concerns tend to get in the way.

> **Do not put business logic in the web tier, in Struts Actions, or the like. Business logic should be independent of presentation.**

Service Layer Running in a Lightweight Container

In this book we'll recommend a service layer of POJOs, running within a *lightweight container* such as Spring or PicoContainer, which can replace the structure of EJB without most of the complexity.

We'll discuss lightweight containers in Chapter 6. Essentially, a lightweight container will:

❑ Manage the lifecycle of business objects. A key distinction from an EJB container is that a lightweight container can manage POJOs: There is no need to implement special contracts, as with EJB.

❑ Provide a lookup facility, resolving dependencies managed objects may have on collaborators also managed by the lightweight container. Implementing *Inversion of Control* (IoC) is a key responsibility of a lightweight container.

❑ Ideally, provide enterprise services such as declarative transaction management to objects running within it, thus replacing a key value proposition of EJB. This is usually achieved using AOP.

Following good OO practice, callers should work with interfaces, not classes. These interfaces define the contract of the service layer, allowing complete pluggability of different implementing classes. IoC makes interface/implementation separation easy.

Business objects and the presentation tier components that use them run in the same JVM. Horizontal scalability can be achieved by clustering the entire application deployment in additional JVMs.

Service Layers Compared

The following table summarizes how these different service layers perform against the most important of our criteria.

All these approaches successfully deliver independence from presentation and persistence technologies, except for MVC actions, which don't merit further consideration.

Exposing Business Objects to the World

Given a well-defined service layer, servicing clients should be easy.

Limitations of What Can Be Exposed

There are some things that a service layer *should not* or *cannot* expose to the wider world. Let's consider some examples:

- ❑ If the service layer is remote, we can work only with serializable (or, less commonly, remote) parameters and return types. In this case we must also consider efficiency concerns: How long will these objects take to marshal and unmarshal and travel over the wire?

- ❑ With some persistence technologies, we may need to explicitly *disconnect* objects from the persistence store.

Disconnection from a persistence store is a common and important problem.

Persistence technologies fall into two major types. I'm using the terms introduced by Martin Fowler in *Patterns of Enterprise Application Architecture*. In each case a domain object (such as a User object) typically maps to a row in a relational database table.

- ❑ **Active Record:** Data access logic is included in the domain object. This is the approach used in entity beans (with BMP, the application developer writes the data access code; with CMP it's generated by the EJB container) and in many home-grown persistence frameworks.

- ❑ **Data Mapper:** A mapping layer external to the application server, such as TopLink or Hibernate, contains all persistence logic. Domain objects typically don't contain any SQL, although they usually end up making a few concessions to the fact that they must be persisted.

With many persistence technologies, there are challenges in disconnecting persistent objects from the persistence store. For example:

- ❑ Entity beans can't survive outside the current transaction.

- ❑ TopLink uses a shared cache of read-only objects. Hence it's impossible to modify these objects without cloning them, as this will corrupt the shared cache.

Technology	Simplicity	Defined in interfaces?	OO	Productivity	Transaction capable	Horizontal scalability	Testability
Remote EJBs	Complex to implement and use business objects.	Yes	Distribution constrains OO by forcing the use of transfer objects for all interactions.	Poor, because of complexity of distribution and EJB programming model.	Yes	Inherent support for distributing objects. However, this is the correct approach to horizontal scalability only in rare situations.	Poor. It's very hard to test EJBs outside a container. In-container testing is slow and complex.
Local EJB	As complex to implement as remote SLSBs. Slightly less complex to access (no need to catch Remote Exception).	Yes	No significant constraints on OO besides the fact that the EJB component model doesn't fully support Java language inheritance.	Slightly better than for remote EJBs.	Yes	Relies on web container to deliver clustering. Using local EJBs does not constrain horizontal scalability.	Poor. As for remote EJBs.
.NET Serviced Component	Fairly good. It is relatively simple to make an object a "serviced component."	Possible but not enforced.	Serviced Components must extend a framework superclass. No other constraints on OO.	Good, especially given Microsoft tool support. Use of source-level metadata is a productivity boost, compared with XML deployment descriptors.	Yes, but with less fine-grained control than in EJB CMT	Scalability can be achieved through object distribution or clustering whole deployments, as with remote EJBs.	Problematic. Serviced Components, like EJBs, depend on the framework (in this case .NET). Effective unit testing outside that framework is difficult.

No EJB, ad hoc	Varies on implementation. Typically simpler than architectures using EJB.	No standard approach. Can implement using interfaces, but relies on programmer discipline.	Depends on implementation approach. No inherent constraints on OO.	Varies depending on implementation. Productivity is usually better than with EJB architectures.	No. A major weakness in this approach is the need to manage transactions explicitly using JTA or other low-level APIs. If an AOP framework is used to deliver declarative services, this amounts to a lightweight container architecture.	Depends on implementation strategy.	Depends on implementation strategy. Poor if business logic is tied to Servlet API. Poor if heavy use is made of the Singleton pattern, as it usually is in such architectures.
Service layer running in a lightweight container such as Spring	Good, as business objects are POJOs. With an Inversion of Control container they don't usually depend on container APIs.	Use of interfaces is made easy, although not enforced.	No constraints on OO.	High	Yes, using AOP. Spring provides declarative transaction management out of the box, with greater flexibility than EJB or .NET.	Relies on web container to deliver clustering, rather than on object distribution. Does not constrain horizontal scalability.	Good. Easy to test business objects outside an application server. Test first development is a viable option, allowing an agile development process.

Solutions include:

❏ Using a layer of transfer objects to hold disconnected data, even in co-located applications. This is usually best avoided, as it forces us to write fake objects and wastes a key advantage of a co-located architecture.

❏ Using a data access API such as Hibernate or JDO 2.0 that allows for disconnection and reconnection of persistent objects. As with transfer objects, this requires us to materialize all necessary relationships to support the current use case.

❏ Avoiding technologies such as entity beans, which preclude disconnection.

❏ Keeping the persistence "session" open until the work of a co-located client has completed: for example, until a web application has rendered a view. This is a superficially attractive option, as it removes the problem of traversing relationships to the required depth, but it can be dangerous, as persistence-related exceptions can cause unexpected problems in the presentation tier.

Web UI

The most common requirement is to expose business services via a web interface. In this architecture, we have one *enforced* distribution boundary: that between client browser and web server. However, we don't need further distribution barriers, and are usually better off without them. In Chapter 4, we'll talk about the many problems and costs associated with distributed objects.

The Benefits of Co-location

What I call "traditional" or "orthodox" J2EE architectures promote physical separation between web tier and business objects. I believe that this is usually misguided.

> **Co-locate business objects and web container. This is the simplest, most performant, and most object-oriented approach. I believe that the entrenched belief that business objects and web tier should be physically separated is the most harmful and expensive fallacy among J2EE developers.**

There may be a distribution boundary between web server and J2EE web container. For example, Apache may be used as the HTTP server, with a proxy connector sending requests to a J2EE web container behind it. This kind of distribution is not as harmful to design as distributed business objects, because it doesn't impact application code (being invisible to it). Its effect on performance varies. It is usually slower than using the J2EE web container to serve all web content unless there is a high proportion of static to dynamic content. (J2EE web containers are pretty efficient these days.) Beyond the fact that some application servers enforce this distribution, there may be a security argument for it, in that all parts of the J2EE server can be kept behind a further firewall.

The Importance of Logical Separation

So we don't normally want a *physical* separation of business objects from web tier. However, we *do* want a *logical* separation, and rejecting physical separation shouldn't cause us to forget this. The first part of a logical separation is to have a well-defined business services layer. However, we also need to ensure that *accessing* such services is simple and does not produce a dependency in the UI tier on the technology behind the business service interface.

Such a logical separation can be held in a client-side facade for remote EJBs. This is often referred to as the *Business Delegate* pattern, in which client-side code interacts with local objects that hide the complexity of connecting to and using EJBs.

> **A client-side facade of Business Delegates is essential if we use a service layer of remote EJBs. It serves to decouple remoting and service lookup from service access. Ideally, UI tier objects should not need to concern themselves with EJB homes or the EJB API.**

Given a client-side proxy layer, the web tier can focus on its real responsibility: the mechanics of presentation and user interaction.

> **If business objects are running locally in a lightweight container, such a facade is unnecessary, as the presentation tier can use business interfaces directly: a significant architectural simplification.**

Many J2EE web applications contain too much code in the web tier. There are various reasons for this, but I think the most important are that:

❑ Too few books emphasize the importance of a thin web tier. There's a wealth of material emphasizing the importance of a properly designed web tier, separating control logic (in servlets, Struts Actions, etc.) from presentation logic (in JSPs or other templates), but much less on how the web tier should relate to the rest of the application.

❑ Historically, the most popular J2EE frameworks have been MVC web frameworks such as Struts. No framework for organizing business objects has been so widely adopted. This creates a dangerous situation. A basic assumption of the application is a framework that structures the web tier in an orderly way. On the other hand, there's no framework for business objects, or a naïve in-house framework that's less capable or less well understood than the web framework. Thus business objects tend to become an appendage of the web framework. This gives the application the wrong center of gravity.

❑ Putting business logic in the web tier is often perceived as the quickest path to a solution. The previous point helps to understand the cause of this common misconception. However, it *is* a misconception, as working with a more sophisticated architecture will quickly show.

One of the major advantages of the Spring Framework is that it is centered around providing organization for business objects. In both Spring applications and the Spring Framework itself, the web tier is a thin layer on top of this business object framework. This encourages a correct emphasis in coding.

In larger projects, having a well-defined business interface layer makes it easy to develop business and web tier in parallel, once the interfaces have been agreed.

> **A web interface should be thin. It should be built on the service layer and contain only code to interpret user gestures and display the response.**

Supporting Remote Clients

Expose remote interfaces only if you must. However, it should not normally be difficult.

Even if a business services layer doesn't include native support for remoting, adding a remote facade around it should be as straightforward as adding web tier components.

> **If you have a well-defined business service layer, even if it's expressed in terms of local interfaces, you can easily put a remote facade on top of it, just as you can implement a thin web tier on top of it. This is a good practice as it decouples remoting technology from implementation of business logic.**
>
> **Thus, do not build transfer objects into the definition of the service layer, unless this falls out of the design naturally. Transfer objects should normally be defined as part of the remoting facade.**

There are many choices for exposing remote services. The traditional J2EE remoting technology—RMI—is well served by EJB. Hessian's Hessian and Burlap protocols are a lightweight alternative providing a simple programming model, with no need to use EJB.

However, web services remoting is growing in popularity, at the expense of platform-specific protocols such as RMI. There are many good choices for web services remoting. For example, for SOAP services we can use toolkits like Apache Axis or The Mind Electric's GLUE.

We'll discuss remoting choices in Chapter 11.

Data Access Layer, or EIS Tier

Access to persistent data often determines the performance of enterprise applications. Persistent data is usually held in a single relational database, although sometimes there may be multiple transactional data stores or legacy applications.

I prefer the intuitive term *data access layer* when only one or more databases is concerned, although the broader concept of an *Enterprise Information System* (EIS) tier encompasses not just databases, but legacy systems, which are often also transactional.

Technology Choices for Accessing Relational Data

The data access technologies included in J2EE are JDBC (available in J2SE) and entity beans. However, it's easy to use third-party products for data access, and it's often worthwhile.

I feel that entity beans are a poor technology, which produces poor results in practice. This view is now widely accepted in the J2EE community. So where does this leave us for data access?

❏ JDBC is a good technology for SQL-based access to RDBMSs. If we don't want O/R mapping, it's a low-overhead approach. If you do use JDBC, use it indirectly, via a good abstraction layer.

❏ Hibernate is an excellent open source O/R mapping technology.

- ❑ Despite its fairly slow adoption since its release in 2001, JDO is now looking more likely to emerge as a standard Java persistence API.

- ❑ Commercial O/R mapping products. The best of these, such as TopLink, work well, although I prefer Hibernate or JDO.

> **Because most J2EE applications use a relational database, the main persistence options are transparent persistence or SQL-based data access.**

We'll discuss persistence strategies in detail in Chapter 10.

It's possible to mix and match SQL-based and O/R mapping persistence. For example, the "Fast Lane Reader" J2EE pattern is a relational workaround for the problems with entity beans, intended for use when a large number of result objects may be returned. It can be costly to try to use a single persistence technology in all use cases. Although there's a benefit in maintainability from minimizing the number of persistence technologies used, the cost in performance, and complexity of attempting a persistence operation in an inappropriate way can outweigh it.

The *Data Access Object* pattern is the correct choice to allow mixing and matching. It hides the details of persistence operations behind a DAO interface that frees business objects using it from knowledge of the underlying persistence technology.

Accessing Legacy Systems

J2EE 1.3 introduced the *Java Connection Architecture* (JCA) for generic access to backend systems: in particular, non-relational (and, hence, non-JDBC) datastores. It defines generic contracts for resource and transaction management, enabling a JCA resource adapter for any EIS to be plugged into any JCA-compliant J2EE container. The corresponding deployment unit is a *Resource Adapter Archive* (RAR). JCA is an important J2EE service that, like JTA, is provided by an application server, but is independent of EJB.

The services a JCA container offers for connectors are basically the same as for JDBC connections, but in a generic fashion:

- ❑ Connections will be pooled by the container.

- ❑ XA-capable connectors will participate in JTA transactions.

- ❑ On startup, the container will bind the connection factory to a JNDI location.

JCA allows integration of ERP and other backend systems (the original intent of the spec). ERP vendors such as SAP offer JCA connectors for standardized, transactional access to their systems.

> *JCA is also used to integrate some persistence tools and to implement JDBC connection pools in some application servers.*

J2EE Architectures

Let's look at some important J2EE architectures using these building blocks.

We'll primarily focus on web applications, although most of the points are relevant to all types of applications. Essentially the differences between web applications and other applications are confined to the presentation tier. The service layer should be identical.

We'll consider four alternative architectures, two using EJB and two non-EJB:

❑   "Classic" J2EE architecture, using remote EJBs and entity beans.

❑   Local EJB architecture, using local EJBs.

❑   Ad hoc J2EE architecture without EJB.

❑   What I call *Lightweight container architecture*: the architecture advocated in this book for typical applications.

We'll also look at common variations on these architectures.

For each architecture, we'll consider its strengths and weaknesses. Later in this chapter, we'll look at some publicly available examples of these architectures, to see them in practice as well as in theory.

EJB Architectures

EJB has traditionally been regarded as essential to implementing J2EE applications.

> In the J2EE platform, middle-tier business logic is implemented in the middle tier as Enterprise JavaBeans components. . . . The EJB component model is the backbone of the J2EE programming model. (Nicholas Kassem et al, *Designing Enterprise Applications with the Java 2 Platform, Enterprise Edition*, page 9)

Thus we'll begin by considering EJB-based architectures—the orthodox approach to J2EE.

"Classic" J2EE Architecture

This is the architecture that the J2EE platform was supposed to be all about. It reflects the once almost universal view of J2EE as a distributed platform, and the central importance of both session and entity beans.

Let's see how this architecture fits together in a typical application.

Java classes are spread across different JVMs, although it's possible to co-locate them to remove the significant overhead of remote invocation.

The web tier is normally provided by an MVC framework, as in all the architectures discussed here. In a well-designed application there should be a layer of client-side proxies for remote EJBs, to provide a clean decoupling of web and EJB tiers, as noted previously.

All business objects will be stateless session beans with remote interfaces, running inside an EJB container. The EJB container will provide remoting, transaction management, thread management, and (possibly) role-based security.

In a "classic" architecture, all data access will be through entity beans. The use of CMP entity beans with local interfaces is now widely regarded as the best choice if using entity beans, as entity beans with remote interfaces offer little benefit and considerable risk to performance.

The EIS tier will consist of one or more databases and legacy systems. (It's important to remember that a single transactional resource is much the commonest case, in all these architectures.) JTA, accessed via the EJB container, will provide distributed transaction coordination if there are multiple transactional resources.

This architecture is shown in Figure 3-1.

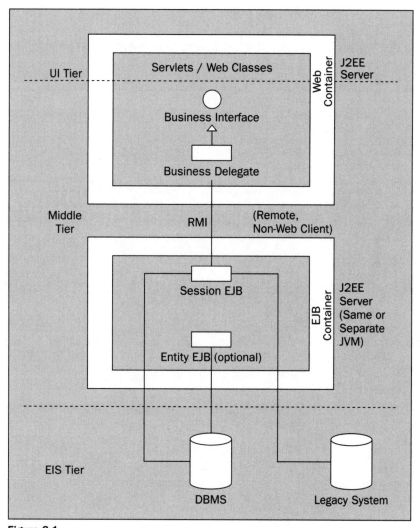

Figure 3-1

Strengths

This architecture has the following advantages:

❏ Remote EJBs provide a well-defined service layer.

❏ EJB services such as declarative transaction management are beneficial.

❏ It can support all J2EE client types by providing a shared middle tier. It's attractive if we need to support Java-based clients such as Swing GUIs. Prior to EJB 2.1 EJBs cannot expose web services without a remote facade in the web tier.

❏ In rare cases, the ability to distribute business objects across multiple servers may lead to high scalability.

❏ Business logic can be updated separately from the web tier if the application is not deployed co-located.

Weaknesses

This architecture has the following weaknesses, which prove problematic in practice:

❏ It has the highest overhead of any architecture we'll consider, in every respect: most important, application performance and development effort. Some of this overhead comes from EJB in general, but much relates to the fact that this is a distributed architecture.

❏ It sacrifices OO to distribution.

❏ It's hard to test, as business logic is usually code in EJB implementation classes, which are heavily dependent on the EJB container.

> **I don't recommend the "Classic" J2EE architecture using remote EJBs. It's seldom the best choice for web applications. Even for other types of J2EE application, it should not be the default choice, as it traditionally has been.**

For those of you who've read *Expert One-on-One J2EE Design and Development*, this is described in Chapter 1 as "Distributed Application with Remote EJBs."

The pointy-haired boss loves this architecture, especially when it's explained in whiteboard sessions, impressive acronyms, and diagrams. When projects using it go over time and budget, as they often do, he's more likely to blame his developers than the architects.

Local EJB Architecture

The architecture we've just discussed isn't the only EJB architecture, and isn't the best EJB architecture in most cases.

The remote EJB architecture can be simplified and optimized by replacing the remote EJBs with local EJBs. This is more than a code refactoring; it is an architectural refactoring, justifying considering it as a different architecture. This change eliminates object distribution, and uses EJB merely to organize business objects and for services such as transaction management. The local EJB architecture is a pretty good architecture, and a big improvement for most web applications.

Let's see how it fits together in a typical application.

All Java classes are co-located in the same JVM.

The web tier is provided by an MVC framework. In the case of local EJBs, we don't need special business delegate interfaces: the EJB "business methods" interfaces can be accessed directly by web tier components without forcing them to work with EJB APIs, so long as we use a framework or helper to hide JNDI lookup and use of the EJB home interface.

Business objects will be stateless session beans with local interfaces, running inside an EJB container. The EJB container will provide transaction management, thread management, and (possibly) role-based security.

Given the goal of simplification, data access is more likely to be through a lightweight O/R mapping product such as Hibernate than through entity beans.

The EIS tier will be the same as in a remote EJB architecture.

This architecture is shown in Figure 3-2.

> **Don't assume that EJB means distribution—a local EJB architecture is a better choice for typical applications than a remote EJB architecture. If you choose to use EJB, consider using local session beans.**

Strengths

This architecture has the following advantages:

- ❑ The many downsides of distribution are gone.

- ❑ The programming model for EJB access is a little simpler. There's no need to handle `RemoteException` on every method.

- ❑ All the strengths of the remote EJB architecture except those related to RMI remoting.

Weaknesses

It also has the following disadvantages:

- ❑ This architecture can't support multiple client types without a remoting facade. However, that can easily be provided for local session beans: for example, in the form of a SOAP servlet that accesses local EJBs in the same way as a web UI. Only where RMI/IIOP remoting is concerned is the use of remote EJBs preferable.

- ❑ Testability problems remain: Business logic is still likely to be implemented in classes that are equally dependent on the EJB container. While accessing EJBs is a little simpler, there is no difference in implementing EJBs.

- ❑ This architecture is still fairly complex. This architecture incurs much of the overhead of EJB without getting that much value from it. Whether the benefits of EJB outweigh the costs depend on how many EJB services are used. None of the services of local EJBs are impossible to provide in lighter-weight containers, as we'll see below.

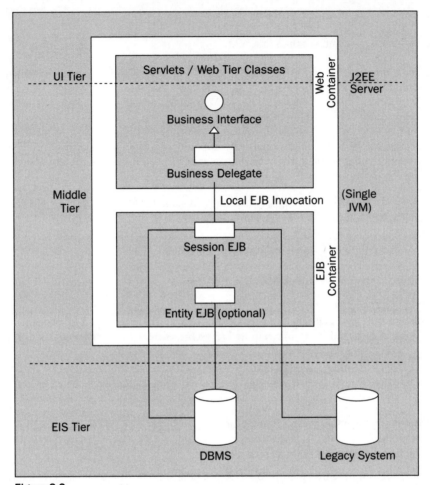

Figure 3-2

> If we use EJB in this limited way, we should question why we need EJB at all. If using local session beans is combined with eliminating the use of entity beans, the difference between this architecture and the "Lightweight Container" architecture without EJB, discussed below, is largely the deployment and programming overhead of EJB.

It is possible for the one EJB to have both remote and local interfaces. This can enable a kind of hybrid architecture. However, I don't advocate this in typical applications.

This architecture is described in Chapter 1 of *Expert One-on-One J2EE Design and Development* as "Web application that accesses local EJBs."

Variations on EJB Architectures

The following common variations are possible on both EJB-based architectures:

❑ Replace entity beans with a transparent persistence solution such as TopLink, Hibernate, or JDO. Session beans use mapped domain objects instead of entity beans. This is nearly always a major improvement, and, in my experience, such architectures are much more likely to succeed. Many projects go down this route, whether with remote or local EJBs.

❑ Replace entity beans with SQL-based data access using JDBC. This is appropriate in cases when O/R mapping doesn't deliver much benefit. This is also a fairly common variation. This is often done in some use cases only, in the "Fast Lane Reader" pattern (or workaround, depending on your point of view).

❑ Refactor business logic out of SLSBs into POJOs behind them. This is also a significant improvement, promoting code reuse by minimizing the dependence of business logic on the EJB container and greatly enhancing testability. I've used this architecture successfully in several applications, and recommend it if you choose to use EJB.

❑ Simplify EJB lookup using a good framework, rather than custom service locators. This simplification works best with local EJBs.

The second edition of *Core J2EE Patterns* (2003) places more emphasis on the use of POJOs behind an EJB facade (whether through transparent persistent or as fine-grained business objects) than the first (2001), reflecting a growing recognition that, even in EJB architectures, it's usually best to use POJOs in preference to EJBs where possible.

Implementation Issues Common to EJB Architectures

Some implementation issues common to all EJB architectures are:

❑ The need for an EJB container: This means a high-end application server, and much more administration complexity than a servlet engine.

❑ The need for Service Locators and/or Business Delegates in the client tier. We'll see code for some of these strategies below.

❑ Problems managing fine-grained objects running within the EJB container, behind the session facade. Even local EJBs are best modeled as relatively coarse-grained objects; we'll need additional infrastructure to manage fine-grained objects behind EJBs. Although EJB deployment descriptors provide a way of declaring "environment variables" in XML and accessing them through JNDI, this is too verbose to be attractive for very fine-grained configuration. EJB provides no lifecycle support for helper POJOs.

❑ Once we start putting business logic in the EJB container, we can't easily stop. If some of our business objects need to do things that are forbidden by the EJB programming restrictions, such as create threads, open network connections, read files, call certain third-party APIs or invoke native code, we have a problem.

Non-EJB Architectures

Let's now consider what happens if we remove the EJB component model. Is it really the "backbone" of J2EE?

Ad hoc J2EE Architecture without EJB

Many—probably most—J2EE applications have been built successfully without EJB. This is particularly true of web applications. While in this book I attempt to describe a consistent and fully featured model for J2EE applications without EJB, practicing J2EE without EJB is not new.

Without EJB, there is less formal structure in "lightweight" J2EE architectures. Such structure as there is is usually defined by the web container. Thus such applications are "ad hoc" in the sense that their structure is largely up to their designers.

In such architectures, all Java objects will run in the same JVM, although it is possible to scale up to a cluster by deploying the web application to multiple servers.

Again, the web tier is usually provided by an MVC framework.

Business objects will be POJOs, running in the web container. Note that this doesn't preclude a *logical* separation of UI tier and business object tier. There is no need for web tier proxies for POJO business objects: web components can work directly with their business interfaces. Typically, the Singleton pattern, or ad hoc factories, are used to enable web tier components to locate business objects. Transaction management will be programmatic, and can be either JTA or resource-specific.

Entity beans are not an option, so data access will be through an O/R mapping solution or JDBC.

The EIS tier will be as in the previous architectures.

This architecture is shown in Figure 3-3.

Strengths

There are many benefits in dispensing with EJB, such as:

❑ Ability to run in a servlet engine. Cheaper licensing, easier administration, and a smaller footprint.

❑ Greater portability between application servers or servlet engine. There are more things that are hard to do in a portable way within an EJB container than within a web container, such as ensuring that certain code runs on startup.

❑ Simpler implementation. For example, accessing POJO business objects is usually much simpler than accessing EJBs: there's no need for JNDI lookups.

❑ No need for verbose deployment descriptors.

❑ Quicker code-deployment cycles. For example, we don't need EJB Jar deployment units; we can simply package code in WARs.

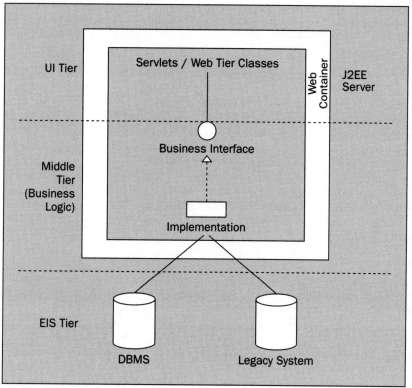

Figure 3-3

Weaknesses

The main negatives are:

❑ Lack of inbuilt support for remoting, although a remoting facade can be added, as with a local EJB architecture.

❑ Lack of a standard environment for and management of business objects.

❑ There may be no clear business service layer. We may end up with an ad hoc arrangement for managing business objects. This may be tacked onto the web tier framework, with Struts plug-ins or the like.

❑ We may end up having to write custom code to solve problems that have already been solved by EJB. For example, declarative transaction management is not available.

❑ There's no standard way of configuring business objects. (However, EJB applications face much the same problem, as EJB provides only clumsy support for parameterizing components.)

❑ Lack of consistency between applications, or even *within* large applications. Each application tends to go down its own path in how it accesses business objects, holds its configuration, and addresses enterprise problems such as transaction management. Each application has its own learning curve.

❑ No guarantee of greater testability than with EJB, although it's at least possible to build highly testable applications.

Whether these weaknesses balance out the strengths depends on the quality of the implementation. It's at least as easy to design bad EJB applications.

The most important potential weakness—the lack of a clear service layer—can be addressed by enforcing standards for consistent use of business interfaces and consistent access to business objects. This typically involves some kind of factory. *Expert One-on-One J2EE Design and Development* describes such standards, calling the resulting architecture "Web Application with Business Component Interfaces." However, an application with such structure will benefit further from a "lightweight" container, as we'll see in the next section.

> **In my experience, with a good architect, a non-EJB web application—even with no overall application framework—is likely to be cheaper to build and maintain and more performant than the equivalent application using EJB.**

The "Lightweight Container" Architecture

Clearly J2EE architectures *can* succeed without EJB. However, we can take some of the successful ideas from EJB to bring a greater level of sophistication to non-EJB architectures.

There's a much better way to address these issues than doing a good implementation of an ad hoc non-EJB architecture. We can enjoy the kind of structure that EJB provides without the disadvantages of EJB.

We call this a *Lightweight Container* architecture. Unlike ad hoc non-EJB architectures, it is similar to EJB architectures in being centered around a layer of managed business service objects. However, this is where the similarity ends. Instead of running inside an EJB container, business objects run inside a *lightweight container*. A lightweight container isn't tied to J2EE, so it can run in a web container, a standalone application, or even an EJB container if necessary. It also isn't tied to the Servlet API, like an MVC web framework, which is a poor choice for managing business objects. Lightweight containers have negligible startup cost and eliminate the deployment step of EJB.

Lightweight containers provide a way to manage and locate business objects. No longer is there any need for JNDI lookups, custom service locators, or Singletons: the lightweight container provides a registry of application objects.

Lightweight containers are both less invasive and more powerful than an EJB container where co-located applications are concerned. We'll say more about their characteristics and benefits in Chapter 6.

Fortunately, a number of lightweight containers are now freely available. Choices include:

❏   Spring Framework (`www.springframework.org`)

❏   PicoContainer (`www.picocontainer.org`)

To provide a complete solution, the lightweight container must provide enterprise services such as transaction management. Typically this will invoke AOP interception: transparently weaving in additional behavior, such as transaction management, before and after the execution of business methods. At the time of writing (early 2004), only Spring provides this in a single integrated distribution. However, it is possible to combine another lightweight container with an AOP framework such as Nanning Aspects to achieve a similar overall result.

The lightweight container architecture is a recent option, made possible by the availability of good open source inversion of control containers.

Let's see how it fits together in a typical application.

All Java classes run in the same JVM.

From the user's perspective, the web tier is provided by an MVC framework. We can use a dedicated web framework such as Struts or WebWork, or—in the case of Spring—a web tier that can itself be managed by the lightweight container and provide close integration with business objects.

Business objects will be POJOs, running inside the lightweight container. They may be "advised" via AOP interception to deliver enterprise services. Unlike EJBs, they don't usually need to depend on container APIs, meaning that they are also usable outside *any* container. Business objects should be accessed exclusively through their interfaces, allowing pluggability of business objects without changing calling code.

Data access will use a lightweight O/R mapping layer providing transparent persistence, or JDBC via a simplifying abstraction layer if O/R mapping adds little value.

The EIS tier will be the same as in other application architectures.

This architecture is shown in Figure 3-4.

> **The "Lightweight Container" architecture is conceptually similar to the "local EJB architecture." However, it tends to work out very differently in practice. This is the architecture that we advocate in this book for typical web applications.**

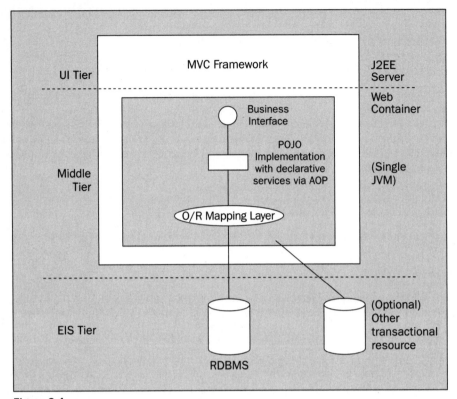

Figure 3-4

Strengths

Following are some of the advantages of using this architecture:

❑ A simple but powerful architecture.

❑ As with local EJBs or an ad hoc non-EJB solution, horizontal scalability can be achieved by clustering web containers. The limitations to scalability, as with EJB, will be session state management, if required, and the underlying database. (However, databases such as Oracle 9i RAC can deliver huge horizontal scalability independent on the J2EE tier.)

❑ Compared to an ad hoc non-EJB architecture, using a lightweight container *reduces* rather than increases complexity. We don't need to write any container-specific code; cumbersome lookup code is eliminated. Yet lightweight containers are easier to learn and configure than an EJB container.

❑ Sophisticated declarative services can be provided by a lightweight container with an AOP capability. For example, Spring's declarative transaction management is more configurable than EJB CMT.

❏ This architecture doesn't require an EJB container. With the Spring Framework, for example, you can enjoy enterprise services such as declarative transaction management even in a basic servlet engine. (Whether you need an application server normally depends on whether you need distributed transactions, and hence, JTA.)

❏ Highly portable between application servers.

❏ *Inversion of Control* allows the lightweight container to "wire up" objects, meaning that the complexity of resource and collaborator lookup is removed from application code, and application objects don't need to depend on container APIs. Objects express their dependencies on collaborators through ordinary Java JavaBean properties or constructor arguments, leaving the IoC container to resolve them at runtime, eliminating any need for tedious-to-implement and hard-to-test lookups in application code. Inversion of Control is discussed in Chapter 6. IoC provides excellent ability to manage fine-grained business objects.

❏ Business objects are easy to unit test outside an application server, and some integration testing may even be possible by running the lightweight container from JUnit tests. This makes it easy to practice test first development.

Weaknesses

Following are some of the disadvantages of using this architecture:

❏ Like a local EJB architecture, this architecture can't support remote clients without an additional remoting facade. However, as with the local EJB architecture, this is easy enough to add, especially if we use web services remoting (which is becoming more and more important). Only in the case of RMI/IIOP remoting are remote EJBs preferable.

❏ There's currently no "standard" for lightweight containers comparable to the EJB specification. However, as application objects are far less dependent on a lightweight container than EJBs are on the EJB API, this isn't a major problem. Because application objects are plain Java objects, with no API dependencies, lock-in to a particular framework is unlikely. There are no special requirements on application code to standardize.

❏ This architecture is currently less familiar to developers than EJB architectures. This is a non-technical issue that can hamper its adoption. However, this is changing rapidly.

> **This architecture has all the advantages of the "ad hoc non-EJB architecture," but eliminates most of the disadvantages.**

Implementation Issues

Following are some of the implementation issues you might encounter:

❏ Declarative enterprise services can be provided by POJOs using AOP, thus taking one of the best features of EJB and applying it without most of the complexity of EJB.

❏ A good lightweight container such as Spring can provide the ability to scale *down* as well as up. For example, Spring can provide declarative transaction management for a single database using JDBC connections, without the use of JTA. Yet the same code can run unchanged in a different Spring configuration taking advantage of JTA if necessary.

❑ A nice variation is ensuring that POJO business objects can be replaced by local EJBs without changes in calling code. Spring provides this ability: all we need to do is create a local EJB with a component interface that extends the business interface, if we wish to use EJB. These last two points make this approach highly flexible, if requirements change. (This results largely from good OO programming practice and the emphasis on interfaces.)

We'll explore lightweight container architectures in detail throughout this book.

J2EE Architectures in Practice

Let's now look at some public examples of these architectures in practice. The detail is the determinant of the success of J2EE architectures, so this is an important exercise.

Implementations of the same basic architecture vary in practice, so not all of these comments apply to all applications built on the architecture in question. However, I've focused on characteristics that I've seen in more than one application, and which I've seen in the real world as well as in sample applications.

"Classic" J2EE Remote EJB Architectures

Let's begin with the "Classic" EJB architecture, using remote session beans and entity beans.

Original Java Pet Store

An early example of this architecture was the original Java Pet Store, described in *Designing Enterprise Applications with the Java 2 Platform, Enterprise Edition*.

This application exposed the J2EE platform to major embarrassment, when its performance and complexity compared badly with that of a .NET implementation in a Microsoft comparison in late 2001. While the Sun application was not intended as a performance benchmark, the massive disparity in performance was alarming, as was the comparison between the lines of code in the Java Pet Store and Microsoft's implementation.

One cause of both problems was the use of BMP entity beans. The n + 1 finder performance problem is sufficiently well known that I won't discuss it here. (See Chapter 8 of *Expert One-on-One J2EE* for details.) However, this was not the only problem.

Some conclusions that can be drawn include:

❑ The orthodox approach to J2EE architecture (which this application partly defined) requires a disproportionate amount of code to solve simple problems.

❑ The use of remote interfaces between web and EJB tier is inappropriate in such a web application. The current Pet Store version 1.3.2 (`http://java.sun.com/blueprints/code/`) reflects a recognition of this, using a local EJB architecture.

❑ BMP entity beans are not a viable choice for persistence. They combine nearly all the disadvantages of JDBC and CMP entity beans without providing any real advantages.

❑ The orthodox approach to J2EE architecture can lead to very poor performance. However, subsequent evolution of the Pet Store has resulted in good performance, as we'll see in a moment, so we shouldn't draw the conclusion that using EJB necessarily leads to bad performance.

Because it dates back so far, the Java Pet Store continues to use its own "web application framework," rather than a standard framework such as Struts. Thus it reflects the many applications written before 2001 that used their own MVC implementations. Like them, it now illustrates the importance of using standard rather than in-house infrastructure where there's a choice. Its take on a command-based web framework is conceptually different from all the popular web frameworks, meaning that the web tier code is little help to developers working with real-world tools. Partly for this reason, I'll look in greater depth at applications that use recognized MVC frameworks, and are more representative of real applications.

OTN J2EE Virtual Shopping Mall

A recent example of this architecture is the Oracle Technology Network "J2EE Virtual Shopping Mall," published in September 2003 (`http://otn.oracle.com/sample_code/tech/java/j2ee/vsm13/docs/Readme.html`). This is an up-to-date version of the Classic J2EE architecture, using local interfaces for CMP entity beans, and a Struts-based web tier. Entity beans have been generated with Oracle 9i JDeveloper. Tables are created from entity beans automatically if necessary when the application first runs. (Most CMP engines offer this feature, but don't recommend it for production use.)

The entity bean layer in the `oracle.otnsamples.vsm.entities` package contains 50 Java classes, amounting to over 3000 lines of code. Deployment descriptors are equally verbose: The `ejb-jar.xml` file is 1900 lines; the Oracle-specific `orion-ejb-jar.xml` almost another 800. This volume of code and configuration is absurd for a simple application that uses only 14 database tables, although it's a typical result of the use of entity beans.

There's a layer of transfer (value) objects in the `oracle.otnsamples.vsm.services.data` package. As with the entities package, there's not a true object in sight here. If there's a genuine need for a distributed application, this is necessary; however, in a local application, many of these 2200 lines of code would be redundant.

The SLSB service layer is responsible for marshaling data obtained from local entities (which can't be exposed to remote clients) into transfer objects. Partly for this reason, but largely because entities are not objects, but merely data holders, it's astonishingly verbose: another 7000 lines of code. As entities don't encapsulate knowledge of their relationships, the session beans must traverse them and iterate over collections of entities themselves.

The entity layer fails completely to decouple the session bean layer from the database schema. Session beans not only depend on the exact table structure, but also the way in which data is stored in those tables. Consider the following line from `OrderManagementBean` (SLSB):

```
if(!Constants.REJECTED.equals(orderItemLocal.getStatus())
```

This represents a serious failure of the `OrderItem` entity. It doesn't even conceal the fact that status—really a boolean—is stored as a String: having an `isRejected()` boolean method on `OrderItem` would be much cleaner.

The `oracle.otnsamples.util` package provides a generic `ServiceLocator` singleton, implementing the *Service Locator* J2EE pattern. This is used in SLSBs to locate entity beans and in Struts actions to locate session beans. The ServiceLocator caches EJB homes in a hash table. The ServiceLocator throws unchecked exceptions (`UtilityException`) in the event of failure to lookup an EJB home. As this would indicate that the caller had provided an incorrect JNDI name, this is a good use of an unchecked exception: Programmers shouldn't be forced to write code to recover from such fatal conditions.

However, the caller is still responsible for calling the `create()` method on the home and catching the checked exceptions that may result, largely negating this benefit. For this reason, session beans and Struts Actions contain a `catch (Exception ex)` block after any EJB invocation, which renders the use of checked exceptions meaningless anywhere in the call stack, as shown in the following code:

```
MallNavigationHome navigationHome =
        (MallNavigationHome)
ServiceLocator.getLocator().getService("MallNavigation");
    MallNavigation navigation = null;

    try {
       navigation = navigationHome.create();


       ...
       navigation.addGuestbookEntry(guestbookEntry);
       ...
    }
catch(ServiceException ex) {
        // code omitted

       return mapping.findForward("failure");

}
catch(Exception ex) {
       ...
       return mapping.findForward("failure");
    } finally {
       // remove SLSB instance
       if(navigation != null) {
         try {
           navigation.remove();
         } catch(Exception ex) {
         }
       }
    }
```

This type of code is a good illustration of the need for a client-side business services proxy when using remote EJBs; if such a layer existed, the Struts actions would be decoupled from the use of EJB and would be much easier to understand and maintain.

Besides service location, the `oracle.otnsamples.util` package provides a simple Mailer class to simplify sending e-mail using JavaMail, support for primary key generation and message lookup.

The web tier is implemented using Struts. Using a popular production quality framework makes this application much more useful as a guide than the Pet Store.

Perhaps partly to justify the use of EJBs with remote interfaces, there's also a Swing client. However, even if this were a real business requirement, it might be more appropriate to add a web services layer to support it (providing a choice of client technology) rather than predicate the entire architecture on the need for it.

Overall this is a fairly good implementation of a remote EJB architecture—better than the average I've seen in industry. However, it illustrates many of the problems associated with implementations of this architecture:

❑   Far too much code in total, and far too high a proportion of "plumbing" code concerning entity beans, transfer objects, and EJB access. This kind of application can't be written cost-effectively without extensive code generation, which has severe drawbacks, as we noted in Chapter 2. Maintaining all this code may be problematic, as there's no support for round-tripping the generated code.

❑   Lack of effective exception handling. Because of the number of checked exceptions that must be caught, code in several layers, such as SLSB service layer and Struts Action layer, effectively gives up and catches `Exception`. This can be dismissed as merely bad programming practice, but it happens too often to ignore as a risk in such architectures.

❑   Failure to decouple business logic from the underlying database. *Note that this is a consequence of the use of entity beans, rather than use of session beans with remote interfaces.*

❑   Failure to decouple the web tier from the use of EJB. Struts actions deal directly with EJB homes.

❑   Unit testing this code outside an application server would be all but impossible. Entity beans are a testing nightmare. Business logic is contained in stateless session beans in the `oracle.otnsamples.vsm.services` package. Testing the web tier would be difficult as it depends on the EJB tier and on the ServiceLocator singleton.

Some of these problems could be solved by using a better overall framework. For example, Spring's `org.springframework.ejb.access` package could be used instead of the very basic OTN `ServiceLocator` implementation to hide the use of EJB from the web tier. However, nothing can make this architecture simple, or the volume of code justifiable.

> **Both these applications contain far too much code for the complexity of the requirements they address. Much of the code is repetitive and mundane, needing to be generated rather than hand-written. It shouldn't be this hard to write a simple shopping application. If this was the best way to implement a typical web application in J2EE, we'd have to draw the conclusion that J2EE is a poor technology for web applications. Fortunately, there is an easier way....**

Local EJB Architectures

Architectures using local session beans are a more recent development: It took some time after the release of EJB 2.0 in mid-2001 before developers realized that local interfaces weren't good only for entity beans.

The Middleware Company mPetStore (February 2003)

The Middleware Company's mPetStore (`www.middleware-company.com/casestudy/`) was built for a performance comparison case study. It is based on original Sun Pet Store, with the following changes to improve performance and reflect community criticism of the original Sun implementation:

❑ Switching from BMP entity beans to CMP 2.0 entity beans. This produced a significant performance improvement.

❑ Switching from remote to local session bean interfaces. This produced no difference in performance, as target application servers were already optimizing to use call-by-reference. However, it's a worthwhile architectural simplification.

❑ Caching of value objects in the web tier.

The Middleware Company did not intend this as an architectural blueprint. However, it's reasonable to consider it as an example of a local EJB architecture, implemented by skilled practitioners.

There is a web tier service proxy layer in the `com.sun.j2ee.blueprints.petstore.control.web` package, with classes such as `CatalogWebImpl`. Unfortunately, this service layer is not expressed in terms of interfaces, making it impossible to vary the implementation without changing existing code, or to test web tier code with stubs rather than real EJBs.

The `com.sun.j2ee.blueprints.shoppingcart.util.EJBUtil` class implements the Service Locator pattern, providing static methods such as `getCatalogHome()` that return EJB homes. There is no exception translation; callers must deal with the checked `javax.naming.NamingException`. Thus callers are shielded only partially from JNDI, and not at all from EJB creation. The `EJBUtil` service locator class is not generic, as there's one lookup method for EJB used. The lack of any exception translation is the direct cause of exceptions being swallowed and thrown away (very dangerously) in the caching layer.

The `com.sun.j2ee.blueprints.petstore.control.web.ModelManager` class serves as a unifying accessor to the service layer, with methods to return all service objects. However, it is dependent on the Servlet API, making testing outside an application server very difficult.

On the positive side, this application proved to have very good performance, partly because of aggressive caching in the web tier. This proves that CMP entity beans can perform well in some cases.

Common Issues with EJB Architectures

One conclusion we can draw from these applications is that the number of checked exceptions that must be caught when working with the EJB API is likely to cause developers effectively to give up on meaningful exception handling when accessing EJB, and write code to catch `Exception`. (This is also borne out by my experience in industry.)

This is an indication of my point regarding overuse of checked exceptions in Chapter 4 of *Expert One-on-One J2EE Design and Development*. Although checked exceptions sound like a guarantee of correctness in theory, in practice the work of dealing with APIs that use them even for unrecoverable conditions, such as the EJB API, can become overwhelming. If all these applications—written as examples of good practice—cannot practice correct exception handling, what likelihood is there that it will happen in the real world?

> **Don't throw away exceptions. Don't create the temptation to throw away exceptions by allowing unrecoverable exceptions to propagate as checked exceptions. Wrap them inside unchecked exceptions, or use frameworks that do so for you.**
>
> *Overuse of checked exceptions makes *any* use of checked exceptions meaningless, negating their value.*

It's also evident that even very capable developers can't develop a really high-quality infrastructure layer for an individual application. In the case of the Sun sample applications, which share some infrastructure code, two or three applications are still not enough to evolve a first-rate infrastructure. In all these applications, infrastructure adds some value over direct use of J2EE APIs such as JNDI, but still fails to effectively decouple web and EJB tier.

Ad hoc Non-EJB Architectures

Let's now look at some applications that don't use EJB. Both the following applications were partially written in response to criticism of the over-engineering of the original Java Pet Store.

Sun Adventure Builder v 1.0 EA 3.1 (July 2003)

The Sun Adventure Builder application (`http://developer.java.sun.com/developer/releases/adventure/`) makes little use of EJB, and also illustrates the exposure of SOAP web services.

The Data Access Objects (DAOs) in this application are a good indication of the productivity pitfalls noted above concerning direct use of low-level J2EE and J2SE APIs. Because each DAO implementation class uses JDBC directly, with no abstraction layer, each contains much cut-and-paste code. For example, the `PointbaseCatalogDAO` class contains seven `try/catch/finally` blocks to ensure that JDBC connections are closed. The amount of JDBC access code dwarfs the amount of code that concerns the SQL issued. (Incidentally, all the `finally` blocks are flawed: If closing the `ResultSet` or `Statement` results in a `SQLException`, the Connection will never be closed. Writing such code correctly is a task that should be centralized in a framework, not spread around application code. As this application shows, even skilled developers can easily err when dealing with such complex but mundane tasks.)

The Adventure Builder's web interface does not use EJB to implement business logic. Instead, there is a well-defined layer of "facade" objects. In this application, these add little value over the DAOs, but they could prove valuable in a more sophisticated application. The facades successfully decouple web tier from middle tier implementation strategy: potentially allowing the use of EJB, for example, without impacting the web tier. The only added value in the facade in the Adventure Builder is the questionable one of wrapping fatal DAO exceptions in another layer of facade-specific exceptions, without adding any useful information. Unfortunately web tier code is written against facade *classes*: There is no interface layer. This lack of a well-defined business *interfaces* is a common pitfall in non-EJB applications which can, however, be easily avoided by applying good OO programming practice.

The Adventure Builder includes a rudimentary effort at parameterization for DAO classes. Static facade methods in the `com.sun.j2ee.blueprints.util.dao.DAOFactory` class look up environment variables specifying the class of each DAO. An interface is used to hide the implementing class from application code using DAOs. This is a step in the right direction, but provides no support for passing configuration information to the DAO, and parameterizes only a small part of the overall application. An IoC container provides a much more powerful and general solution, with no additional complexity.

All exceptions thrown by DAOs are unchecked, although some are caught and re-thrown in the facade layer.

As with the OTN Virtual Shopping Mall, the Adventure Builder uses a generic Service Locator that hides J2EE resource lookup from client code and wraps checked exceptions such as `javax.naming.NamingException` in unchecked exceptions, freeing calling code from catching unrecoverable exceptions. The avoidance of EJB reduces the amount of service location code required overall.

As with the Virtual Shopping Mall, this application would be very hard to unit test effectively—in this case, largely because of the use of Singleton objects and reliance on the JNDI environment for configuration.

iBatis JPetStore v 3.1

Clinton Begin's JPetStore, available from www.ibatis.com/jpetstore/jpetstore.html, demonstrates an alternative approach to the original Sun BluePrints approach. This differs from the Adventure Builder in being built on generic open source infrastructure, making it much more valuable as a real-world example.

The JPetStore uses Struts for the web tier, and a business logic implementation running inside the web container. Data access is SQL-based, although it does not use direct JDBC.

This application uses a well-defined service layer, in the com.ibatis.jpetstore.domain.logic .PetStoreLogic class, which contains the business logic for the whole application. This is a Singleton, thus avoiding the need for factories or Service Locators. Unfortunately, this simplicity is achieved at a price: there is no interface layer—callers use this object directly. The PetStoreLogic class contains less than 400 lines of code, proving the simplicity of the Pet Store's business logic and highlighting the disproportionate amount of code in the EJB version of the same application. Overall, the JPetStore contains less than a quarter of the code in the original EJB Pet Store.

The DAO pattern is used to hide persistence technology details behind technology-agnostic interfaces. The JPetStore illustrates the use of an abstraction layer to avoid direct use of JDBC: in this case the iBatis Database Layer (www.ibatis.com/common/common.html). The result is an impressive reduction in the amount of code required to perform JDBC access, compared with the Adventure Builder's direct use of JDBC. Even though the iBatis database layer moves some of the complexity into XML configuration files, the result is clearly more maintainable and likely to make developers more productive.

The JPetStore illustrates a non-EJB solution for transaction management without the need to resort to direct JDBC: Transaction management is performed programmatically, also via the iBatis Database Layer, as in the following example from the PetStoreLogic class:

```
private void doSimpleInsertOrder(Order order) throws DaoException {
    try {
        storeDaoManager.startTransaction();
        itemDao.updateQuantity(order);
        orderDao.insertOrder(order);

        storeDaoManager.commitTransaction();
    }
    catch (DaoException e) {
        try {
            storeDaoManager.rollbackTransaction();
        }
        catch (Exception e2) {
            /* ignore */
        }
        throw ((DaoException) e.fillInStackTrace());
    }
}
```

The questionable exception handling aside, this code isn't complex and demonstrates that it's feasible to do programmatic transaction management, given an abstraction layer over JDBC. While EJB CMT would simplify transaction management, when the whole application (and not just transactional requirements) is considered, the JPetStore approach is simpler as it removes the incidental complexity of EJB.

The lack of an interface aside, there is a fairly good decoupling between web tier and business logic, via the use of an abstract superclass for all Struts Actions in the application. This provides the PetStoreLogic object to all Actions. (This would be better accomplished using a method, rather than a variable initializer, which doesn't allow this to be changed at test time.) Individual Struts Actions are thus impressively simple, having no need to concern themselves with obtaining business objects.

Data objects in the com.ibatis.jpetstore.domain package contain no behavior: They are merely JavaBeans with getter and setter methods.

The main downsides of this application are that:

❑   Testing is hard because of the use of singletons. It's still impossible to test the business logic without a database.

❑   Web tier code uses classes rather than interfaces when accessing business logic. Thus the web tier is tied to specific implementation code, and it's impossible to plug in different business logic implementations.

❑   Programmatic transaction is required, slightly obscuring business logic. Separate methods are necessary to handle the same business operations in a distributed transaction environment or against a single database.

However, there's little doubt—given the far smaller and simpler code base—that it would require less effort to maintain and enhance this application than the mPetStore or OTN Virtual Shopping Mall.

Overall Notes

The JPetStore shows that using good open source frameworks and libraries it's possible to enjoy alternative solutions to some of the problems solved by EJB, while doing away with the complexity of EJB deployment.

Both these applications show that dispensing with EJB is likely to simplify code and deployment. For example, the amount of code in the JPetStore is reasonable for the complexity of its requirements, unlike that in the original Java Pet Store or Oracle J2EE Virtual Shopping Mall. However, both these applications show the danger that, without the discipline enforced by EJB, there won't be a business *interface* layer.

"Lightweight Container" Architecture: The Sample Application

Our sample application is an evolution of the JPetStore, introducing a lightweight container. In particular, this shows:

❑   The use of a lightweight container to facilitate programming to interfaces, rather than classes. Thus the PetStoreLogic class is abstracted behind an interface.

❏ The use of Spring's IoC capabilities to avoid any need to use the Singleton design pattern. There is no need for Singleton or other lookup; web tier components referencing the business object merely express this dependency via a JavaBean setter method, and Spring performs the necessary wiring at runtime. This increases flexibility, making all application components pluggable, and also significantly improves testability. It's now possible to:

   ❏ Test the web tier against a mock implementation of the PetStoreFacade interface.

   ❏ Test the PetStoreImpl implementation of the business logic interface against mock implementations of the various DAO interfaces.

❏ Not only the web tier now uses a popular open source solution instead of custom coding; using Spring, instead of ad hoc singletons, for middle tier management means that the application's structure is easily understandable to the large Spring user population.

❏ The use of Spring AOP to provide declarative transaction management. This eliminates the programmatic transaction management code shown above, including the questionable exception handling. It eliminates the need for different code to execute in a single-database or distributed transaction environment: this now requires simple reconfiguration of Spring, with no need to change Java code.

❏ Spring's remoting capabilities (integrated with IoC) are used to provide remoting over different protocols with minimal custom coding.

❏ The use of source-level metadata, as in .NET, as an option to drive declarative transaction management.

❏ Two alternative implementations of a thin web tier: one using Spring's MVC framework (integrated with the web application's IoC container), and one using Struts but accessing the same Spring-managed middle tier.

We believe that this is the best architecture we've discussed: the simplest, most testable, object oriented, maintainable, and extensible.

Deciding Whether an Application Needs an Application Server

Aware of these architectural choices, it's possible to make an informed choice as to whether a new application requires a full-blown application server, supporting JTA, JCA along with EJB, as opposed to a web container such as Tomcat.

There are real advantages in avoiding an application server if you don't need one, such as:

❏ Lower license costs, in the case of commercial products. Industry research groups have reported significant overspending on application server licenses for organizations that didn't need their capabilities. (See, for example, www.nwfusion.com/news/2001/0821gartnerapp.html.)

❏ Quicker server startup, saving development time.

❏ Simpler administration and reduced learning curve for developers.

Web applications involving a single database seldom require an application server. Lightweight containers provide a better alternative to an EJB container for managing business objects in most web applications. Distributed transactions—and hence JTA—are not required with a single database.

An application server is indicated:

❑ If you need distributed transactions: for example, if you have multiple databases and transactional legacy systems. It's possible to integrate a third party JTA implementation such as JOTM (http://jotm.objectweb.org/) into a web container, but this may prove more complex than the integrated solution provided by an application server. Products such as WebLogic Express provide a useful half-way house: Much cheaper than full-blown application servers, they lack EJB support, but provide JTA support, which is usually more important.

❑ If you want need remoting, for which EJB is a good choice. However, web services remoting can be supported in a web container using a web services toolkit.

Good web containers provide robust support for web application failover and clustering, so an application server is not necessarily required to ensure scalability and reliability.

With non-EJB architectures, the critical variable in an application server is its transaction management capability, so it's important to ensure this meets your requirements. Application servers vary widely in the sophistication of their transaction capabilities. At the time of writing, some still do not provide a full distributed transaction coordinator.

Of course in many cases, an application server may be available already due to purchase decisions. High-end products such as WebLogic also provide high-quality, efficient, web containers, so there's a return on the investment there.

A good lightweight container, such as Spring, works equally well in all environments. Thus so do applications built using a lightweight container architecture. It's important that an application can take advantage of high-end capabilities such as sophisticated JTA implementations. Thus it's important to note that a lightweight container architecture does not preclude taking full advantage of the services provided by a high-end application server.

Summary

In this chapter we've looked at the key building blocks of J2EE applications, including:

❑ The *business services layer.* This is central to successful applications.

❑ Presentation layer. This may be a UI or a remoting facade.

❑ Data access layer.

We've looked at four J2EE architectures in the light of these issues:

❑ The "Classic" J2EE architecture, using remote EJBs

❑ Local EJB architecture, using local EJBs

❏   "Ad hoc" J2EE architecture without EJB

❏   The *Lightweight Container* architecture, using POJO business objects in a lightweight IoC container that also provides declarative enterprise services using AOP

We've looked at the strengths and weaknesses of each J2EE architecture in theoretical terms, and we've looked at published examples of them in practice.

The *Lightweight Container* architecture differs from most previous attempts to dispense with EJB in that it recognizes the need for a clearly defined service layer. It also involves a container, although a much less cumbersome one than an EJB container, and can provide declarative enterprise services such as transaction management. We advocate using this architecture for typical web applications, and focus on implementing it effectively in the remainder of this book.

In Chapter 4, we'll look at why simplicity is so important.

4

The Simplicity Dividend

So what if many J2EE applications are "over-engineered"? Surely they'll be responsive to future needs, highly maintainable, and highly performant?

Unfortunately, this is not the case. This is one of the costliest myths associated with J2EE. In reality, over-engineered applications are more likely to be bloated, buggy, unmaintainable, and slow. The "over" in over-engineered means "wrongly."

In this chapter, we'll discuss common causes of over-engineering in J2EE application, and its costs. We'll examine the benefits flowing from our goal of simplicity.

The Cost of Complexity

Unnecessary architectural complexity is bad. Complexity costs money and delays deliveries. Complexity provides fertile ground for bugs, and makes it hard to get rid of them. To take just a few issues:

❑ Every line of unnecessary code must be written, tested, and—still more expensively—*maintained* for the lifetime of the application. Writing and maintaining every line of unnecessary code consumes resources that could better be spent on the problem domain.

❑ Complex architectures and code often prove to be inefficient. Too many layers, too much abstraction, too much remote calling: all contribute to poor performance.

❑ Complex code complicates the build process and often creates a dependency on complex tools.

❑ Complex code is hard to understand, making it hard to introduce new developers to the project. Far too much effort goes into understanding and maintaining the complex architecture, and far too little goes into directly addressing business requirements.

> One of the key lessons of XP is to do "the simplest thing that can possibly work." This is particularly relevant to J2EE. Every J2EE developer should repeat this daily, whether or not he or she is comfortable with XP as a methodology. There are great benefits in finding the simplest architecture that can meet business requirements.

I'm continually amazed at the number of J2EE applications I see with over-complex architectures.

In the course of my consulting practice, I regularly perform architectural reviews on projects that are late and over budget. Almost without exception, the main technical cause of the problems is excessive complexity. (Of course, there are also many non-technical reasons why projects fail.) It's difficult to explain to clients that much of the code they've produced is worthless, and that with a better design it could simply be ripped out.

> Question any code that isn't specific to the problem domain.

Causes of Complexity in J2EE Applications

Let's consider some of the reasons that many J2EE applications are unnecessarily complex. These can be divided into *architectural* and *cultural* reasons. Architectural reasons are consequences of applying orthodox J2EE architectures and letting the technology drive the approach to business requirements; cultural reasons are concerned with people, organizations, and software vendors.

Architectural Causes of Complexity

The "Classic" J2EE architecture, discussed in Chapter 3, is highly complex. It is a distributed architecture, centered around EJB, with all the conceptual, implementation, and deployment complexity that entails. Taking this as a blueprint makes many J2EE applications inherently complex, regardless of the specific requirements they need to address.

Use of EJB

Unnecessary complexity often results from unnecessary use of EJB. We've already discussed some of the complexity associated with EJB, and will take a closer look in Chapter 5.

EJB is a complex technology that provides a good solution to certain complex problems, such as implementing a distributed architecture. However, whether the net effect of using EJB is to *reduce* or *increase* complexity depends on how many of those complex problems each application faces in reality. This book sets out to examine how this value proposition stacks up for different kinds of applications.

Object Distribution

Probably the commonest cause of unnecessary complexity in J2EE applications is unnecessary use of distributed objects. In J2EE applications, distributed objects are usually implemented as EJBs with remote interfaces, so distribution goes hand in hand with EJB. Such distribution is especially questionable in web applications, but distribution also tends to be overused in other application types.

Distributed applications are tremendously complex, even if J2EE and EJB can conceal much of the underlying infrastructure required.

Because EJB makes distribution seem a lot easier than it is, it has lulled many J2EE developers into a false sense of security. When you write an application with distributed business objects, *whatever technology you use*, you will encounter some of the toughest challenges in computing. Distributed applications pose difficult error handling problems and are difficult to implement, test, deploy, and maintain. The many problems include:

❑ **Transferring graphs of domain objects between servers.** This requires a layer of messy marshaling code and poses difficult problems. For example, do we use custom marshaling for each use case (writing all the code that requires it), or always traverse all relationships of each domain object when exchanging data? The existence of so many patterns for remote communication demonstrates the complexity of the problems.

❑ **Goodbye OO; hello TO.** Having a layer of transfer objects prevents caller and callee effectively sharing a rich domain model and quickly results in code bloat.

❑ **Deployment issues.** We will need to keep code on different nodes in synch, complicating the rollout of new binaries across a cluster.

❑ **Error handling issues.** All remote calls can face network failures; ability to recover from such failures requires deep understanding of business logic and complex code.

❑ **Testing** becomes far more complicated, because of the need to test failover scenarios and different deployment scenarios.

> **If you care about simplicity, try to avoid writing distributed applications.**

Why Not to Distribute Your Business Objects

If distributed architectures had worthwhile benefits, we would need to accept the complexity that went with them. A distributed architecture, however, is usually a bad idea for many other reasons besides simplicity.

Martin Fowler, in his excellent *Patterns of Enterprise Application Architecture* (Addison-Wesley, 2002), scathingly describes the classic distributed object architecture as "sucking like an inverted hurricane." There are a *lot* of reasons besides simplicity that you don't want to distribute your business objects, so Fowler's condemnation is amply justified. Performance is the most important of these reasons, but it's not the only killer. For example:

❑ **Performance.** Remote method calls are *orders of magnitude* slower than local calls.

❑ **Performance.** If you choose a distributed architecture, you're likely to find performance disappointing, and likely to end up spending a lot of time on performance tuning that simply isn't necessary in applications without object distribution.

❑ **Performance.** Did we mention that remote method calls are slow?

❑ **Loss of OO.** Transfer objects are not true objects. An important point that is often missed is that there isn't really such a thing as a distributed *object*. Distribution places significant constraints on interfaces that should not apply to objects. The pernicious effect on OO is almost as painful in my opinion as the effect on performance.

❑ **Garbage generation.** Transfer objects must continually be created on both client and server, even if many of them contain the same data.

Distribution and Scalability

The main argument in favor of object distribution is the widespread belief that distributed applications are highly scalable. Many J2EE developers believe that the best path to a scalable system is through distributing business objects. In this vision, there might be four web containers and eight EJB containers, with all business objects being invoked remotely by the web tier. The theory is that this can deliver optimal scalability through allowing fine-grained control over processing capacity, with the ability to add web containers or EJB containers hosting business objects as throughput increases.

This is largely a myth. I've never seen it work in practice as well as a co-located solution. I recently raised this issue at a summit with leading enterprise-software experts who had between them worked on dozens of large projects, and none of them had seen it work in practice, either. It *may* work, but there are good theoretical reasons why it won't unless you have unusual requirements. This is one of the areas in which a division between marketing spiel and real-world experience is widest. Jason Carreira summarizes real-world experience succinctly: "The whole Servlet-tier and Business Object tier topography has been pretty well discredited. It doesn't scale to have to make remote calls" (`http://freeroller.net/page/jcarreira/20030726#re_do_you_need_remote`).

The central problem is that the performance penalty for each remote method invocation is so great that any theoretical benefit is overwhelmed by network and marshaling costs.

Furthermore, there's no reason why a distributed architecture should be *more* scalable than a co-located architecture in which each application server hosts all J2EE components—the web tier as well as business objects.

A better path to scalability is usually through clustering whole application deployments, and using hardware or web container load balancing to exercise them. A co-located architecture can scale horizontally very simply, through adding servers that run the whole application. The real limitation of scalability is likely to be the underlying database. The ability to deploy a large number of EJB containers without a web tier doesn't address this.

Clustering entire deployments—including the web interface—is usually easier to administer, also. For example, it may be possible to upgrade the application on one server without directly affecting other servers, as there will be no remote endpoints to consider.

The only situations in which distributed objects may produce excellent scalability are if:

❑ **The cost of processing significantly outweighs the cost of remoting.** As remoting is so amazingly slow, this doesn't happen often. Also, in this case the call may be so slow that it should be made asynchronously through JMS.

❑ **There are no limits to horizontal scaling.** That is, all business objects are stateless, and there are no reasons (such as limited database resources) that more EJB containers cannot be added at will. However, in this case, we could equally well add clustered deployments of the whole application.

❑ **The distributed business objects are stateless.** However, statelessness will *always* benefit scalability, with or without distribution.

Nor are distributed applications necessarily more robust than co-located applications. An incoming web request to a distributed application will still encounter a single point of failure in the web container that accepts it. If the web container fails during a remote business object invocation that succeeds, the request won't complete. Only if the remote server is likely to encounter failures and the web container can retry idempotent invocations will the application be more robust than a co-located application—and in this case, it might be better to attempt to make the business objects more robust than to introduce a distributed architecture to mask their unreliability. (Idempotency is often impossible, in which case dealing with remote failures becomes very difficult, as we have no way of knowing whether or not the failed invocation resulted in an update.)

> **If you believe that distributed objects will provide the greatest scalability for your application, do a vertical slice of your application to verify it through performance and other tests. Don't incur the cost of a distributed architecture without hard evidence that it's worthwhile.**

The true path to scalability is usually through efficiency. The return on horizontal scaling—any form of clustering, with or without distributed objects—will always be limited in practice by the database, state replication, and cache replication in any O/R mapping layer. Wasting CPU cycles waiting for network responses is a dangerous course, as adding servers to make up for the wastage will not produce a linear return.

> **The best basis for a highly scalable application is a highly efficient application. This minimizes the extent of horizontal scalability required, by maximizing throughput per unit hardware. Co-located applications are inherently more efficient than distributed applications.**

Faking It: Phony Distributed Objects

But doesn't J2EE allow us to have our cake and eat it? Can't we avoid the overhead of remote calling, yet have the (debatable) scalability of object distribution should we need it?

Many J2EE architects believe that they can have the best of both worlds, by making applications "distribution ready." This common architecture involves using EJBs with remote interfaces, co-located in the same JVM as callers such as web tier objects. This rests on the fact that an application server will optimize notionally remote calls to local calls. This optimization has always been available, even before local interfaces were added to the EJB specification. Such optimization means that notionally remote calls will be little slower (if at all) than ordinary Java call-by-reference.

Remote EJBs co-located with their clients is one of the commonest EJB deployment options. Often, it's the only way that a notionally distributed architecture can be made to perform acceptably. There are many reasons, however, why it is a poor idea. For example:

❑ **Complexity.** Callers still need to deal with remote exceptions that can never happen. Because remote exceptions are checked in RMI (and hence EJB), this also creates a dependency on remoting in the callers of business objects.

- ❑ **The pernicious effect on OO.** Greater efficiency doesn't reduce the complexity or improve the experience of the basic programming model.

    - ❑ Even though the calls won't actually be remote, the parameters and return types need to be serializable (or remote). All the problems of transfer objects remain.

    - ❑ Because the calls might end up being remote, business interfaces need to be designed to avoid chattiness. This means that business objects do not fall under normal OO design considerations.

- ❑ **Confused semantics.** The application will be deployed in a way that's diametrically opposed to its declared semantics. Code will run with call-by-reference when it's coded to call-by-value. Not only is this illogical; it can produce subtle, hard-to-find bugs if callers by reference modify shared objects returned by the "remote" EJBs.

It's ironic that Java RMI was based on rejection of local-remote transparency, while EJB encourages local-remote transparency in practice by "phony remote interfaces."

> **Do not distribute your business objects unless you need to to meet business requirements. This will provide the single biggest win you can have for simplicity—and performance.**
>
> **If you need to write a distributed application, be upfront about it. Don't pretend you can optimize the cost of remote calling by co-location. If you're relying on this, your architecture is a costly fake.**

Isn't J2EE *about* Distribution?

But isn't J2EE an inherently distributed technology? Am I saying that J2EE is fundamentally misguided, and that the specifications and application server vendors are all wrong?

No. J2EE technologies—especially EJB—offer excellent support for building distributed applications. But there's a lot more to J2EE than distribution, and the fact is that relatively few applications actually need this technology. Just because J2EE *can* make it easier than most other technologies to develop distributed applications doesn't mean that it's usually a good idea.

> **J2EE need not be about distribution. Even today's EJB, with local interfaces, is not necessarily about distribution.**

Focusing on Non Goals: "Phantom Requirements"

This point about the capabilities of the platform is important not just when we consider object distribution. Just because we *can* do something in J2EE doesn't mean that we should.

As I note in Chapter 2, technology-driven "phantom requirements" such as database portability may prove costly. They *may* be business requirements, but most often they're not.

> Just because J2EE makes something possible doesn't mean that we should always choose to do it. Assuming phantom requirements is a common cause of unnecessary complexity in J2EE applications. Base architectural decisions on actual requirements, not on the capabilities of the J2EE platform.

Pattern-sickness

Another cause of unnecessary architectural and implementation complexity that seems particularly common in J2EE is what I call "pattern-sickness." J2EE has a flourishing patterns industry, reflected in countless books, articles, and discussion sites.

Many of these patterns are sound, but many J2EE-specific patterns are workarounds for questionable architectures, and many are irrelevant to most applications. Many architects and developers seem obsessed with how many patterns they can cram into their projects, often with dire results. Patterns are good, but only where they add value.

Again, simplicity is a good guide. Typically, using patterns appropriately will *simplify* an application. Using patterns inappropriately will increase complexity.

The notion of architectural "blueprints," although well intended, has probably proved harmful in this area. Because Sun and others have promoted "blueprints" that combine numerous patterns, the idea of patterns in search of a context is considered normal in J2EE. The notion that a set of "blueprints" and their associated patterns can be applied to almost all J2EE applications is flawed.

Cultural Causes of Complexity: The Complexity Industry

Software architecture is driven by people and organization and industry culture, as well as by technology. Unfortunately, a number of these cultural factors seem to conspire in the case of J2EE to produce unnecessarily complex applications.

Vendor-driven Architecture

Application-server vendors typically promote complex architectures, partly to justify the complexity and cost of their products.

In particular, J2EE application server vendors tend to encourage overuse of distributed objects, and their influence helps to explain why distributed architectures are so undeservedly popular. Several server vendors promote web application architectures that split the web and EJB tiers, and publish examples of this as a best practice. Although the inherent inefficiency of distributed architectures sells a lot of hardware and software licenses, there's no dark conspiracy here. Vendors are proud of having good implementations of complex technologies. The problem is that these technologies are usually inappropriate for the needs of most of the vendors' customers.

I recently learned a great word for this: **markitecture**. Markitecture is extremely dangerous, because it creates trust, especially when backed by the impressive marketing resources of large companies. A markitecture looks great on paper and in diagrams, but doesn't translate at all well into practice.

A surprising number of J2EE developers are seduced by markitecture; it can be difficult even to persuade them to gather evidence to validate fashionable architectures chosen for their application.

> **Trust your own judgment when it's backed up by experimental evidence. Successful application-server vendors are very good at developing low-level infrastructure, but they are seldom authorities on user applications.**

Tools and Complexity

The complexity industry is also fostered by the existence of complex tools, which can be justified only by complex problems. Such tools can act as a band-aid solution to cover unnecessary complexity, and can be an obstacle to necessary simplification.

Many of these tools are graphical; there's nothing like pretty pictures for making complexity look sexy.

I'm not disparaging UML in general. I think it has a valuable role to play in communication. Occasionally I forward engineer code, or work with code and model together. However, I think there are a lot of problems in a UML-centric process, built around complex tools:

- ❑ Rigid use of forward engineering from diagrams prevents the use of an agile process; it's a particular obstacle to practicing TDD and regular refactoring.

- ❑ Rigid use of forward engineering over-emphasizes a particular view of the application, which is often not the most useful. Artifacts other than working code are justified only if they're helpful representations of working code. Heavy emphasis on forward engineering results in a situation in which working code is viewed as justified only if it's a representation of pretty pictures.

- ❑ Overall complexity is likely to be increased, not reduced:
  - ❑ It becomes complex to produce code and round-trip code.
  - ❑ Complex tools are hard to learn and use effectively.

- ❑ Modern Java IDEs provide fantastic support for refactoring. Such refactoring is hard to achieve graphically (although this may change as modeling tools play catch-up with code-based tools in this respect).

- ❑ In reality, models nearly always get out of synch with working code. This is a fact of life; processes that make developers feel guilty about it are not realistic.

Many of these issues are of course the consequences of UML-driven processes, rather than the tools that can be used to support that process.

> **Tool complexity in general is dangerous. There's real value in choosing the simplest tools, as well as the simplest possible architecture.**

A recent project I was involved in used an integrated "enterprise" tool suite, which included a complex, sophisticated version control tool. We and many others on the project couldn't help comparing it with CVS, which we'd used successfully on many projects. This product could do many things that CVS can't. (CVS is far from perfect.) However, on that project, few of those fancy capabilities were used, and none was used to add real value. The net effect was:

❑   **High license costs.** Although the project had a high budget, wasted money can always be spent usefully elsewhere.

❑   **Extraordinary administrative effort,** seeming to amount to one person full time.

❑   **Unreliability.** Obviously, even this level of administration was not enough, or the administrators needed further costly training.

❑   **Steep learning curve** for administrators and developers.

❑   **Excessive complexity in its use.** Partly because the tool could be justified only by complexity, there were a bewildering number of branches in the version control system a year before a single line of code went into production. They looked beautiful in graphical displays of each file, but made no sense in a rational analysis. Incredibly fine-grained control to user access resulted in constant administrative hassle and produced substantial delays when developers could not modify broken code or even check it out locally while debugging.

❑   The tool proved not to be well suited to an agile development process, thus making it difficult to apply a valuable best practice. (In contrast, Eclipse's built-in CVS integration places no obstacles in the way of refactoring.)

Powerful tools such as this can add real value if their full capabilities are needed. But don't adopt them without clear evidence that this value will outweigh the complexity they bring.

> The "simplest thing that can work" should be an important consideration when choosing tools and development processes. Successful open source projects are a good model in many respects. They typically use simple tools that place minimal obstacles in the way of developers. It's usually best to rely on good development practice rather than to trust in tool-enforced processes.

Organizational Delusions

It's natural to want to feel special, and to believe that your organization's requirements are complex or unusual. Few organizations like to admit that many of their requirements are typical.

This can lead to tolerance of excessive complexity and reinvention of the wheel because of failure to acknowledge that lots of applications face similar problems. As an example, I was recently involved in a project that had developed a horrendously complicated common infrastructure layer in-house, ignoring the fact that 80% of the problems it addressed were common to most J2EE applications and had already been solved much better in published frameworks. The result was the waste of millions of dollars in development, and a costly and unnecessary ongoing commitment to maintenance and enhancement.

People

Individual architects and developers often contribute to the complexity industry.

Simplicity Is for Dummies

An important contributing factor is the feeling that Java/J2EE developers are real developers, and that their status is justified by the complexity of the code they write. While developers in Perl and other scripting languages are mere hackers, and Microsoft-technology developers are no better, Java/J2EE developers must do things properly. In this view, doing things properly is inherently harder than doing things in the simplest way. I used to believe this myself. Indeed it's only been in the last two years that I would smile at the statement recently posted on the ServerSide that "it's always easier to do something a dirty way than the correct way." We must be honest in asking ourselves the following questions:

- ❑ If it's the right way to solve the problem, why is it so hard?
- ❑ If it was so hard in the first place, won't it be hard to maintain?
- ❑ If there's such an easy way to solve the problem, why is it so bad?

Career-driven Development

Complex technologies such as EJB are interesting, making them attractive to developers keen to extend their skills out of a sincere desire for intellectual growth. Complex technologies are also sought by recruiters. We were keen to use EJB when it first came out; my enthusiasm very likely encouraged me to use it inappropriately. Curiosity and career enhancement are dangerous drivers for architecture.

> **All good developers are intellectually curious and excited about the technologies they use. Exceptional developers know to subordinate these drives to the real needs of the projects they work on.**

The Hands-off Architect

There's a lot of debate in the industry about the exact meaning of the term "architect"—and whether the concept of an architect (as opposed to a developer) is meaningful and desirable.

I believe that there is an important role for architects but that architects must retain hands-on contact with code. There is a real danger in architects who never work at the coal-face—and hence lack awareness of the myriad of practical issues that dictate the success or failure of projects—defining and dictating architecture in glorious isolation. This is a recipe for failure, and nearly always results in enormous complexity. Unfortunately, the notion that successful career progression involves a complete move away from coding dies hard, and does immense harm.

> **Software architectures can be defined only with detailed knowledge of the issues that implementing them will pose. Architects who spend all their time writing documents and working with models seldom produce realistic architectures.**

Empire Building and Other Political Challenges

There are also less pardonable reasons that individuals and teams implement unnecessarily complex architectures.

Empire building is an unfortunate aspect of the complexity industry. Complexity creates work. In large projects, anything that reduces complexity is sure to affect several empires. Each empire builder will be happily presiding over his or her own area of misdirected effort; expect stiff resistance if you question its foundations. In the project I just mentioned, there was fierce resistance to my criticism of the misguided infrastructure layer, because it justified the existence of a team of eight to ten developers, the prestige of a semi-competent architect, and much of the billing of a large consultancy. Ironically, the fact that this infrastructure project had cost around ten times what it should have cost and delayed the overall project served to protect it from the severe rationalization it required. No one—even if he or she wasn't directly involved—could afford to admit to senior management that so much time and money had been wasted.

Resistance to Simplification

Partly because of the empire-building issue, it can be surprisingly difficult to champion simplicity in many organizations. In the project I mentioned previously, the most complex choice had been made at each architectural decision point—for example, to use distributed business objects rather than local invocation; to use XML-based *internal*, as well as external, communication; and to develop the complex infrastructure framework in-house when superior open source solutions existed. I was unable to create interest in critical examining and debating these choices, all of which I believed were wrong. Needless to say, all this complexity had been described in reams of fine-sounding documentation and UML models. There's nothing like a 100-page document with 20 pages of diagrams to inspire confidence in a misguided, overblown solution. Of course none of this was backed up by working code.

How Much Complexity Is too Much Complexity?

Einstein remarked that things should be "As simple as possible and no simpler." Simplicity may be good, but the difficulty lies is establishing just how much complexity is warranted. As software architecture is more of an art than a science, this is hard. It is in meeting this challenge that architects deliver much of their value.

Simple or Naïve?

How do we decide whether an architecture is simple (good) or naïve (bad)?

> **The answer as to how simple an architecture can be lies in the business requirements rather than in the technological platform. Ideally, its ability to meet business requirements can be tested empirically** *early in the project lifecycle*, **and should not be a matter of faith.**

Remember not to second-guess requirements. Don't try to solve the potential requirements of two years hence right now. Those requirements may never eventuate, or may take a different form. The omniscient architect of today may not even be on the project then, and the solution she envisages today may not meet those requirements. This is an XP teaching that I initially found unappealing. However, I've becoming increasingly convinced, based on real project experience, of its value.

Certainly it's important not to adopt a solution that prevents scaling up or prevents the solution from meeting new requirements. If a simple architecture fails that test, it may in fact be naïve. However, a *good*, simple solution should accommodate future requirements—in fact it's likely to prove easier to change and extend than a more complex architecture.

The *Lightweight Container Architecture* proposed in this book, and implemented using the Spring Framework in our examples, is an example of such a simple architecture that can scale up well, and accommodate additional requirements:

❑ Spring helps to abstract users of business interfaces from the technology dependencies of their implementing classes. This means that:

    ❑ If necessary, it is possible to introduce EJB as an implementation detail rather than as a fundamental architectural change.

    ❑ It is possible to switch to a more sophisticated or performant implementation of any business interface without breaking code that calls it.

❑ Although Spring makes it possible for applications using a single database to use declarative transaction management without JTA when running in a web container such as Tomcat, it's possible to switch to a high-end application server and configure Spring to use JTA for the ability to enlist multiple transactional resources, without changing existing application code.

❑ Spring's ability to manage relationships between business objects of any granularity means that adding application classes as the application becomes more complex is easy.

❑ Spring's AOP capability can be used to introduce cross-cutting code to address security and other concerns that can be problematic for a pure OO programming model.

This architecture has the important advantage of not *imposing* complexity, although it *accommodates* complexity if it becomes necessary.

Proposing a simple solution can take real courage. Proponents of simplicity are likely to be considered naïve. It's a tempting fallacy to believe that greater complexity means greater sophistication.

You'll almost certainly hear comments from some of your colleagues when they see this book on your desk, such as:

❑ *This will be OK for simple projects, but will never scale to the enterprise.* This has the immediate advantage of making the commenter appear smarter than you or I. It's also vague and buzzword compliant (what exactly defines "enterprise" in this context?). In fact, the evidence is that the complex "Classic" J2EE architecture neither performs well nor scales particularly well. EJB is far from a magic bullet for scalability, and there are no inherent limits (beyond those of J2EE and today's technology in general) to the scalability of the Lightweight Container architecture discussed in this book.

❑ *The complexity of classic J2EE architecture merely conceals other complexity. Without distributed objects and EJB, you'll need to reinvent the wheel to solve the same problems in the end anyway.* I used to subscribe to this belief myself. However, the fact is that we usually can safely dispense with distribution, leaving local EJB as the major alternative. As we'll see throughout this book, we should evaluate the value proposition of local EJB on its merits for transaction management, threading, security, and the other services it provides. There is no need for generalizations; we can assess the pros and cons of EJB impartially.

In each case, the answer should be based on evidence. There's no need for it to be subjective. We can progress a little closer to science in this respect.

Just Good Enough?

It's particularly dangerous when unnecessarily complex solutions can be made to work. Total failure before it's too late can actually work out better over the lifetime of a project by forcing a clean-room solution. Remember that most money is spent on software maintenance. The worst case is when a suboptimal, overly complex architecture becomes entrenched and just about manages to meet requirements, at hugely excessive cost and effort. Distinguished computer scientist and inventor of Quicksort, C.H.A.R. Hoare, eloquently described this danger in his 1980 Turing Award Lecture, speaking of the design of the PL/1 programming language:

> At first I hoped that such a technically unsound project would collapse but I soon realized it was doomed to success. Almost anything in software can be implemented, sold, and even used given enough determination. There is nothing a mere scientist can say that will stand against the flood of a hundred million dollars. But there is one quality that cannot be purchased in this way—and that is reliability. The price of reliability is the pursuit of the utmost simplicity. It is a price which the very rich find most hard to pay.

Remember that it's not good enough to be able to make something that just about works, at huge cost. We in the software industry have low expectations, in that we think we've done well if we deliver anything. We shouldn't be proud of this. Consider the expectations of other industries: How many skyscrapers are begun and abandoned when they're three-quarters through (and already over their total budget)? How many city office blocks can never accommodate anything like the number of workers they were intended to?

Hoare's conclusion is similarly illuminating:

> I conclude that there are two ways of constructing a software design: One way is to make it so simple that there are obviously no deficiencies and the other way is to make it so complicated that there are no obvious deficiencies.

> **Don't settle for something that can be made to work. Your goal should be the simplest solution that meets requirements—developed and maintainable at minimum cost.**

The Winds of Change

Fortunately, change is in the air regarding J2EE complexity. I see the following changes amounting to a broad movement:

- ❑   A welcome reluctance to adopt distributed architectures, based on many negative experiences.

- ❑   Greater awareness of the complexity of EJB and a desire to avoid it if possible. Even Sun now acknowledges this, in contrast to its insistence until Java One 2001 that EJB was the best choice for business objects in just about any J2EE application.

❑ The evolution of lightweight infrastructure. This marks an important step beyond mere critiques of EJB. Without a simpler alternative, this was still purely negative; today Spring, PicoContainer, and other solutions provide such simpler solutions.

❑ Widespread rejection of entity beans in favor of simpler, transparent, persistence mechanisms such as JDO and Hibernate.

❑ Greater user of agile methodologies. This has an important influence on J2EE, as it's impossible to practice agile development with the "Classic" J2EE architecture, with its verbose deliverables and need for code generation.

❑ Greater use of open source solutions, which minimize the need for custom infrastructure.

Interestingly, this movement seems to come largely from the grassroots of the J2EE development community, not from Sun or application server vendors, who have traditionally dictated "best practices" in J2EE architecture.

There's still a long way to go, but the bad old days of overblown J2EE architectures and disappointing results are on their way out. And that's a good thing for the future of J2EE—indeed, important to its very survival. This book aims to contribute to this movement by presenting detailed architectural approaches and implementation strategies for building simple, efficient, and maintainable applications.

> **Interestingly, the things that work best about EJB are the simplest things: SLSBs and MDBs. The most complex parts of EJB—entity beans—are pretty much useless.**

Summary

Many J2EE applications are unnecessarily complex. This is costly and wasteful not merely in development but throughout the entire project lifecycle. Complexity is also a major cause of bugs.

There are two main causes of excessive complexity in J2EE applications:

❑ **Architectural causes:** "Classic" J2EE architectures and the EJB technology create a lot of complexity. Very often this complexity is unwarranted by the actual requirements. The use of distributed architectures is probably the greatest cause of unnecessary complexity.

❑ **Cultural causes:** These can be found in the influence of application-server vendors, complex tools, developers' natural desire to work with technology they find interesting, and organizational politics.

Fortunately, there is growing awareness in the J2EE community that many J2EE applications are over-engineered, and that simpler solutions are more appropriate in most cases.

One of the major themes of this book is how to reduce the complexity of J2EE applications. Throughout, we will focus on:

- ❑ How to focus on the problem domain rather than on J2EE technology.

- ❑ Simpler alternatives to EJB that provide enterprise services such as transaction management.

- ❑ How to avoid the need for complex "plumbing" code and custom infrastructure.

> **There is a huge benefit in avoiding unnecessary complexity. Effort that would otherwise have been wasted can go directly into the problem domain.**

The following rules of thumb are helpful in developing the simplest possible J2EE architectures:

- ❑ Don't use a distributed architecture without good reason. Use distributed objects only if they help to meet real business requirements such as the need for remote Java-technology clients.

- ❑ Don't use EJB without good reason.

- ❑ Don't develop complex infrastructure in-house. Use existing solutions, such as open source solutions.

- ❑ Don't speculate on tomorrow's problems today, if doing so incurs additional cost and complexity.

- ❑ *Do* work to understand your business requirements. These, not your technology platform, should dictate the architecture.

- ❑ *Do* seek evidence, in the form of performance and other metrics, before committing to complex architectures. "Ask the computer" before committing to complexity such as that of distributed architectures.

EJB, Five Years On

EJB was once hailed as the core of J2EE. Like most Java architects and developers, I was initially excited by EJB, and believed that it offered the best solution to many enterprise problems.

Unfortunately, the experience of the last five years has taken a lot of the gloss off EJB. I now think of EJB more as a transitional technology that popularized many worthwhile ideas, than as the best choice for most new applications.

In this chapter we'll look at the lessons from EJB, and how I believe that we can enjoy many of its valuable ideas without accepting the significant disadvantages of EJB.

Hype and Experience

EJB was intended to simplify enterprise development. The EJB 1.0 specification promised that:

> Enterprise JavaBeans will make it easy to write applications. Application developers will not have to understand low-level transaction and state management details; multi-threading; resource pooling; and other complex low-level APIs.

Instead of concerning themselves with system-level issues, application developers would be able to concentrate on their domain and on writing business logic.

The EJB specification also promised portability of EJBs and EJB-based applications between application servers:

> Enterprise JavaBeans will follow the "write-once, run anywhere" philosophy of the Java programming language. An enterprise Bean can be developed once, and then deployed on multiple platforms without recompilation or source code modification.

Have these expectations been met?

Before we try to answer this question, let's travel back in time to 1998, and relive the heady early days of EJB and J2EE.

EJB and the J2EE Industry

EJB was enthusiastically embraced by many application server vendors. Today, the market has consolidated and only a few major players remain.

When EJB 1.0 appeared in 1998, we all expected that a host of vendors would compete in implementing the EJB specification, and that sophisticated tools would quickly eliminate niggling problems with EJB, such as all those classes required to implement each EJB, or the fact that a bean implementation class almost—but not quite—implemented the EJB's component interface.

Unfortunately, this didn't prove to be the reality. As the EJB specification grew more and more complex, and the economics of developing an application server became less and less attractive, competition in the application server space diminished.

Tool support is improving, but is still relatively disappointing. Developing EJBs remains relatively hard, and far harder than developing a plain Java class or J2EE web components.

EJB in Practice

It's hardly surprising that there's a gulf between the promise of EJB, as expressed in the specification, and real-world experience. The promise was exactly that: a *promise* of a new era of simplicity in enterprise applications, without practical proof.

While the J2EE specification process has had great benefits for standardization and openness, it has at least one significant flaw. Specifications are developed *before* credible implementations of them. There's a risk that the specifications can be hard to implement efficiently. Even more important, there's no experience as to whether specifications are usable from the developer's viewpoint. Setting a technology in stone before it's been used in real applications is risky.

If viable implementations of specifications take time to appear, best practices take much longer to emerge, as do negative experiences.

In the case of EJB, there seemed to be relatively little open criticism of the specification until 2001–2002, when the floodgates opened and a lot of accumulated frustrations were aired. Only in 2001 had a large number of EJB-based projects run their course, providing data enabling the technology to be assessed.

An Aging Component Model

It's not surprising that EJB is now looking rusty. When EJB first appeared in March 1998, the enterprise software landscape was very different from that of today.

So much has changed since 1998 that it's difficult to remember exactly where the industry was back then. When version 1.0 of the EJB specification appeared, there was no standardization in the enterprise software space. **Microsoft Transaction Server (MTS)** was perhaps the closest thing to an enterprise component framework, but it was proprietary and rested on inelegant Microsoft extensions to C++ and other languages with COM/DCOM bindings.

CORBA was the only open alternative to COM/DCOM. However, CORBA, although powerful, was complex to work with. Bindings to C++ and other languages were daunting, and CORBA was essentially about communication between distributed objects, rather than managing application objects. CORBA ORBs were not true application servers.

In this environment, EJB looked simple and open.

Not only were the background technologies very different from today's: the business environment was benign. The dotcom sector, especially, was awash with money to spend on infrastructure, even if it was of unproven benefit. Although this benign economic climate helped foster the emergence of many valuable technologies, such as J2EE, it also had its downside. Fewer tough questions were asked about new technologies than should have been. EJB was probably the biggest beneficiary of this. A costly technology in terms of application server licensing, performance on given hardware, development time, and training, it would have been unlikely to gain acceptance in leaner times.

Java Language Improvements

The EJB 1.0 specification was released six months *before* the significant API improvements of Java 1.2. Remember Java before the "new" Collections framework, when Swing wasn't part of core Java and lived under `com.sun.java.swing`, and when Javadocs didn't use frames? When class loaders weren't inherently hierarchical?

A lot has changed in the Java world since 1998, but the basic EJB model has not. The addition of local interfaces in EJB 2.0 was essentially an optimization, rather than a fundamental change.

J2SE 1.3 would continue to introduce more significant enhancements, such as **dynamic proxies**, which enable any interface to be implemented by a runtime-generated proxy. Given this capability, the way in which the EJB bean implementation class didn't quite match the component interface looked even clumsier. It also brought into question the idea of a dedicated deployment step: in fact, many EJB container vendors quickly took advantage of this to do away with code generation and compilation as part of the EJB deployment process. Most vendors seem to agree that code generation is no longer necessary to support session beans; only for entity beans is its value still strongly evident.

Dynamic proxies have become steadily more attractive over time, as successive JVMs have improved their performance along with that of reflection in general. The growing popularity and success of dynamic byte code generation using libraries such as CGLIB (`http://cglib.sourceforge.net/`) has provided another high-performance alternative to the traditional EJB Java code generation. (Hibernate uses CGLIB to avoid the need for the code generation associated with entity beans, for example.)

The .NET Challenge

EJB was originally inspired partly by MTS, which in turn was indebted to much older transaction monitor concepts. However, EJB had far wider appeal than MTS.

For most of the history of EJB, Microsoft lacked a credible enterprise framework. COM/DCOM and MTS were unimpressive, and EJB essentially had the field uncontested.

This changed in early 2002, with the release of the ambitious Microsoft .NET enterprise platform. .NET is greatly influenced by J2EE; Microsoft drew on expert knowledge of J2EE. However, .NET has some significant differences from J2EE and—especially—EJB that deserve consideration. (I'm concerned here with architectural differences, rather than the obvious fact that .NET is, in practice, a proprietary system.)

Many Java developers wrongly believe that core EJB services have no counterpart in .NET. In fact, .NET has no direct equivalent of EJBs, yet offers the key services of EJBs.

.NET blurs the distinction between web container and EJB container that is fundamental to "classic" J2EE architectures. Any object in a .NET language can harness enterprise services such as declarative transactions by extending `System.EnterpriseServices.ServicedComponent`; there's no special "container" for business objects distinct from the overall managed environment. Rather than a weakness, I think this is actually a strength. It means that enterprise services can be applied to any object without special deployment steps and without imposing onerous requirements on their implementation. I don't much like the enforced concrete inheritance from `ServicedComponent`, but even this is less painful than implementing an EJB.

The deployment of such "serviced components" is simpler than EJB deployment, because .NET also does away with the many external deployment descriptors in J2EE. For example, rather than place metadata driving declarative transaction management in separate XML deployment descriptors such as `ejb-jar.xml`, such information is usually held in the actual source files, in the form of "metadata attributes." The following example defines a transactional object, whose methods will have access to an implicit transactional context offering methods analogous to the transactional methods on the `EJBContext` interface. Note that the class must extend `ServicedComponent`:

```
[Transaction(TransactionOption.Required)]
public class MyComponent :ServicedComponent, MyInterface {

    public void myMethod(long objectIdentifier)  {
    ...
    }
    ...
}
```

This use of source level metadata is intuitive, because, contrary to the assumptions of the EJB specification, transactional behavior is normally an essential part of business objects. The idea of an "application assembler" role distinct from the "bean developer" role exists only in the minds of the EJB specification committee; I've never seen it observed in a real project, and it's arguably even dangerous, since changing transaction semantics fundamentally changes behavior and can invalidate any unit testing. Source-level metadata also survives refactoring, thus addressing a significant weakness of external XML deployment descriptors.

All this deserves to be taken seriously. Sadly, too few in the J2EE community pay .NET the attention it deserves, as evidenced by the predictable and unenlightening flaming of anyone foolish enough to post .NET-related news of relevance to J2EE on the Serverside.com and other J2EE portals. Fortunately, some important initiatives in the J2EE community show an open-minded approach and willingness to adopt worthwhile features pioneered in .NET. For example:

❑ Java 1.5 will add source-level metadata to Java, along with C#-style "autoboxing" (conversion from primitives to and from objects).

❑ JBoss 4 adopts .NET-style use of source-level metadata to drive enterprise services.

❑ Spring and other AOP frameworks besides JBoss use source-level metadata.

❑ Even EJB 3.0 is likely to adopt source-level metadata for much of the information presently held in XML EJB deployment descriptors.

In comparison with EJB, the .NET ServicedComponent concept simplifies the process of enabling an object to access enterprise services such as declarative transaction management. However, it's possible to do even better, while retaining the portability of J2EE. The ServicedComponent concept is based on concrete inheritance from a framework superclass, which is questionable in languages such as Java and .NET CLR languages that allow concrete inheritance from only a single superclass, since it deprives application classes derived from ServicedComponent of their ability to extend another superclass. The approach I'll describe in this book enables us to apply enterprise services to plain Java objects: still simpler, more elegant, more object oriented, and easier to develop and test.

Web Services

In the era of EJB 1.0 and 1.1, the only significant distributed object technologies, besides Java's own RMI/RMP (then somewhat rudimentary), were CORBA and COM/DCOM. Both were complex and neither had universal industry buy-in. By comparison, EJB offered simplification and consistency, thus serving to introduce object distribution in many systems where it had no place.

Today things are very different. XML-based web services offer a far greater openness than ever before. There is real interoperability, not merely between Microsoft technology- and Java-based solutions, but between Perl, Tuxedo, and a wide range of languages and systems.

There is also a growing appreciation that the use of distributed objects is only appropriate to a minority of applications. Thus the growth area is platform-agnostic remoting for interoperability between systems, rather than Java-only remoting within J2EE applications.

It may seem that EJB has risen to the challenge of web services in EJB 2.1, which adds standard support for web services endpoints. (Of course all leading application servers have long provided proprietary support for exposing EJB services via web services protocols.)

However, there are two major problems with EJB attempting to fold both component model and remoting support into a single standard: addressing component model and remoting together adds complexity; and remoting protocols continue to develop. The assumption evident in the first three versions of the EJB specification that Java RMI, or at least RMI over IIOP, would prove a standard remoting protocol, now looks highly questionable. As more remoting protocols develop, EJB containers can hardly support all of them, yet EJB provides no "pluggable" remoting mechanism.

.NET sidesteps this limitation by providing a common mechanism for components to support remoting (any class derived from `System.MarshalByRefObject` can support remote access), but enabling a number of "channels" to handle the wire protocol, whether binary (DCOM), HTTP (SOAP), or custom.

I prefer an even more modular approach, in which remoting is treated as a service exported by a facade on top of an object model, in much the same way as a web interface is a facade on business objects. I'll discuss this approach in Chapter 11.

The Rise of Agile Methodologies

Finally, thinking on development process and best practices has changed significantly since EJB was conceived in 1998. Probably the most significant event has been the rise of "agile" methodologies such as Extreme Programming (XP).

In particular, **test first development,** or at least rigorous unit testing, has proven its value in many projects. I'll discuss the many benefits of test first development in Chapter 14. The importance of this point for now is that EJB makes effective unit testing very difficult, because EJBs depend heavily on container services. In turn, this means that EJB makes agile development processes hard to apply.

Confusion Regarding the Aims of EJB

Changes in the EJB specification itself have highlighted some tensions at the heart of EJB. Notably:

❑ Is EJB intended as a component model or a remoting model?

❑ *Is* EJB primarily a component model, or are EJBs intended to be objects rather than components?

This confusion is most evident with entity beans. Although they make sense only as components, we usually want to persist *objects*, not components. Hence EJB 2.0 introduced local interfaces to supplement remote interfaces, essentially as an entity bean optimization. However, even with RMI remoting out of the picture, local entity beans remain too heavyweight and invasive a model to be used for fine-grained objects. For example, JNDI lookup is cumbersome for local objects.

Even if most J2EE developers wisely decide to steer clear of entity beans, questions about the exact goals of EJB remain. The EJB 2.1 specification title page describes EJB as a "component architecture for the development and deployment of component-based distributed business applications." The EJB specification remains tied to distribution, although more often than not we don't want to build distributed applications.

> **There's a strong argument that EJB should separate its component and remoting model. This would address the concerns I mentioned earlier about supporting new web services or other remoting protocols.**

And often we don't want components: we want objects. I feel it's unclear exactly what value viewing applications as built of components adds over viewing them as built of objects.

Warning: the following comments reflect my experiences as a practical J2EE architect, and do not claim to theoretical rigor!

Interested to hear the practical experience of others in the field, I recently surveyed a number of my colleagues about what they felt the difference was between a component and an object. The responses were broadly in line with those of texts on component software. The essential characteristics of components were felt to be:

❑ **Granularity.** Components were thought of as coarser grained than objects. Another way of looking at this is that components are at a higher level of abstraction than most objects.

❏ **Encapsulation.** A component may hide details of its dependencies, exposing a contract that's distinct from its internals. This also typically means that components don't expose references to classes behind their facade. (In this view, a local session bean that exposes by-reference objects is not a true component.)

❏ **Deployment.** A component can be deployed independently. EJB reflects this goal by providing partially defined deployment step for EJBs, and the ability to package all their dependencies in a single deployment unit.

❏ **Separation between contract and implementation.** A component is a replaceable unit of software that is defined through its interface(s) and the contracts for those interfaces. It should be possible to switch to another component that honors the same contract.

Interestingly, the only characteristic of a component that appears in the literature on component software that the practitioners *didn't* cite was that components are likely to be sourced from third parties; this is one area in which component theory hasn't been realized in practice.

Components are also often thought of as:

❏ Dependent on a particular environment or context, such as an EJB container

❏ Having no observable state

I feel that all of the most valuable of these features can be realized by *objects* running in a lightweight container (but potentially usable outside any framework). To address each in turn:

❏ **Granularity.** We can define objects of arbitrary granularity. Objects don't need to be fine grained. For example, a facade is naturally coarse grained, yet it's not necessarily a component rather than an object.

❏ **Encapsulation.** If we program to interfaces rather than classes, we are free to conceal the dependencies of our implementing classes.

❏ **Deployment.** If we're writing a web application, we can use WAR deployment to package our objects, along with their dependencies. In any Java application we can use the standard JAR deployment unit, which allows us to express dependencies on other JARs via the manifest class path.

❏ **Separation between contract and implementation.** I feel this is a simple matter of good programming practice, and highly desirable when working with objects. We can achieve separation between interfaces and implementations using lightweight solutions such as Spring or PicoContainer (discussed later in this chapter). Pluggability naturally follows. An object can implement any number of interfaces.

❏ **Dependence on a particular context.** While objects can also have expectations about their environment, there are compelling benefits in minimizing such expectations, such as reuse in different contexts.

❏ **Having no observable state.** This is a matter of the contract; we can easily define a stateless interface. Stateless objects are arguably not true objects, but they are very useful and not necessarily components.

I don't like to view components as distinct from objects, as I feel the benefits of object orientation are greater and better proven than those of component-based software. So I don't like creating a sharp distinction between an object and a component purely based on a technology choice such as EJB. .NET appears to blur this distinction, which I find preferable.

The Component Market That Didn't Eventuate

One disappointment of EJB is its failure to generate a market for third-party components; one of the major hopes it promised. (Remember that the EJB specification envisaged beans provided by various vendors being "assembled" to form applications.)

This component market hasn't eventuated, and it's questionable whether it ever will. The problem is partly the EJB model (with its portability shortcomings and deployment complexity); but, far more important, the fact that enterprise components are too complex and have too many dependencies to be shrink-wrapped. The relatively few supposedly reusable third-party EJB-based "components" I've seen in practice have had extensive dependencies—for example, on an elaborate database schema and proprietary database features. Most have depended on proprietary features of a particular J2EE application server. Such dependencies make a J2EE component market problematic. Successful markets have developed in the past for components such as ActiveX controls and (to a lesser extent) JavaBeans. However, the problems addressed by such components are much simpler than those of enterprise applications.

The New Paradigm on the Block: The Emergence of AOP

Last but not least, a new programming model has emerged that offers to deliver the most valuable capabilities of EJB as part of a far more general solution: **Aspect Oriented Programming (AOP)**. I'll discuss AOP in more detail in Chapter 8. For now, let's look at why a subset of AOP can be regarded as a powerful generalization of EJB.

This subset of AOP primarily concerns **interception**. It provides us with the ability to interpose custom behavior before and/or after method invocations *on any object.* This enables us to address **crosscutting** enterprise concerns that apply to multiple objects, while preserving strong typing. (We don't need to change method signatures to accommodate this.) For example, we can begin a transaction before a method call that we know should be transactional, and commit it or roll it back on return. The use of AOP enables the plumbing related to transaction management to be moved inside a framework. Another good candidate for AOP is custom security checks.

I see AOP as *complementing*, rather than competing with, OOP. OOP works well in general. (As you'll gather after reading this book, I'm something of an OO zealot.) However it is weak in certain areas: for example, if we have to apply the same transactional behavior to multiple objects and methods, we need to cut and paste the same code into each and every method. AOP gives us a better way of modularizing such concerns by packing them into **aspects**. AOP complements OOP by providing a different way of thinking about programming structure by identifying "pointcuts": for method interception, sets of methods to which crosscutting behavior should be applied.

At this point you're hopefully seeing the similarities with EJB. EJB services are essentially about interception. A client invokes a method on an EJB: the EJB container typically uses interception to perform security checks, do thread management, and perform declarative transaction management. This is the same concept as AOP interception. And it's a powerful concept, which delivers the most important benefits of EJB.

One reason that AOP is a more attractive proposition to deliver such services than EJB is that it imposes fewer requirements on the objects to which it adds enterprise services. For example, they don't usually need to depend on a particular API such as the EJB API. They can be POJOs, with a significant gain in ease of development and benefit to application object model.

Another major plus of AOP is that it allows for much greater openness than EJB. For example, we can define custom application aspects if we choose. With EJB, we're limited to those system-level aspects that are required by the EJB specification and implemented by the EJB container.

AOP can be implemented in several ways that are portable between application servers. For example, we can use J2SE dynamic proxies if we're programming against business interfaces, rather than classes—a best practice anyway. Or we can use dynamic byte code generation using CGLIB or the like.

> It's important to note that AOP as I advocate in this book is not experimental. It represents a generalization of some of the most successful features of EJB that have been proven in many applications.

What Do We Really Want from EJB, or Why Stateless Session Beans Are So Popular

Experienced architects tend to use a small subset of EJB. There's consensus that stateless session beans (SLSBs) are the most useful of EJBs, closely followed by message-driven beans, for asynchronous processing. There's an almost equal consensus that stateful session beans are of dubious value. The EJB specification makes it hard for containers to achieve the same robustness with stateful session beans as with HTTP session objects, meaning that HTTP session objects are a better choice in most cases.

Entity beans are probably the weakest part of the EJB specification. Despite drastic changes to the EJB specification, such as the introduction of local interfaces in EJB 2.0, they still offer poor performance in many cases. Worse still, they fail to address most of the important issues in O/R mapping—the practical problem that they're normally used to solve. For example, it's impossible to map an inheritance relationship, such as a `Manager` that extends an `Employee`. Solutions such as JDO, Hibernate, and TopLink successfully address the real problems of O/R mapping, and deliver almost transparent persistence. Unlike entity beans, these products externalize persistence from persistent objects. This allows persistent objects to be true domain objects, with few if any dependencies on the framework used to persist them. Entity beans, by contrast, are hard to test, and cannot survive outside the EJB container. The code generation required in CMP entity beans makes testing outside the container impracticable. Because entity beans are not true domain objects, their use leads to many workarounds, such as avoidance of natural inheritance relationships, and the need to treat persistent objects as dumb data holders. Dumb data holders, which contain no behavior, are not true objects.

> My personal view is that entity beans are simply a bad technology. Their inclusion in the EJB specification has done great harm to the cause of true O/R mapping. Persistence should not be tied to the EJB container, but should be addressed by a specialized solution without the tradeoffs imposed by EJB. This position seems much less controversial in mid 2004 than when I wrote *Expert One-on-One J2EE Design and Development* in 2002.

For a discussion of the pros and cons of stateful session beans and entity beans, see Chapter 8 of *Expert One-on-One J2EE Design and Development*. The arguments around entity beans are sufficiently well known that it's not worth repeating them here.

Why have SLSBs proved so popular? They're simple components (at least by the standards of EJB) and provide a pretty good solution to several common problems in enterprise systems.

The simplest form of SLSBs, *local* SLSBs, has recently (deservedly) surged in popularity, as the problems with distributed architectures become more widely understood.

> The fact that the simplest type of EJB (stateless session beans) are by far the most popular and least maligned suggests that EJB overall is over-complex.

Let's examine the major services provided by SLSBs in turn:

- ❑ Declarative transaction management
- ❑ Remoting
- ❑ Clustering
- ❑ Thread management
- ❑ Instance pooling
- ❑ Resource management
- ❑ Security
- ❑ Management of business objects

Declarative Transaction Management

Probably the most valuable service of SLSBs is **container-managed transactions (CMT)**. Although the J2EE server, rather than its EJB container, is responsible for delivering transaction coordination via JTS/JTA, SLSBs enable us to use **declarative**, rather than programmatic transaction management. That is, we can instruct the EJB container to delimit transactions outside Java code. Of course, if we want to roll back transactions, we'll need to use the EJB API, but in the "happy path" we won't need to write a line of code to manage transactions. And we won't need to work with the complex JTA API.

The value of declarative transaction management had been proven in earlier technologies such as MTS, so it's not surprising that it's been one of the most successful features of EJB.

EJB CMT has proved its worth in a wide range of applications, although it is not ideal for managing complex transaction scenarios. For example, sometimes we require more than one transaction in a single business operation; achieving this through using one EJB entry point to call another EJB method per transaction is usually more complex than delimiting transactions programmatically. There can also be problems with optimistic locking. If we use declarative transactions to drive a persistence technology such as TopLink performing optimistic transactions, optimistic concurrency exceptions will only be apparent after the container tries to commit the transaction, by which time application code has passed control to the EJB container and cannot easily regain it. EJB doesn't provide very good support for more complex scenarios of this kind. EJBs with Bean-Managed Transactions (BMT) need to obtain a JTA `UserTransaction` object from JNDI like any other object running inside an application server, and use the JTA API directly. It is also impossible to mix BMT and CMT in the same EJB, so if only one method requires complex transactional behavior, all other methods must deal with the complexity of BMT and JTA.

However, while CMT is not the solution to all problems, it is a good technology for most scenarios, and deservedly one of the main reasons people use session EJBs.

Yet EJB CMT could be even better. Another limitation with EJB transaction support is that it's tied to global container transactions driven by JTA. While on the surface this seems perfectly appropriate, in fact it's overkill for many applications. Reliance on global JTA transactions introduces a dependency not just on an EJB container, but also on a distributed transaction coordinator provided by the application server. And a distributed transaction coordinator only makes sense if we have multiple transactional resources, such as databases. In reality, many J2EE applications, even quite complex ones, work only with a single database (possibly a database that is itself distributed over a cluster, like Oracle 9i RAC). Thus such applications don't need anything more than local, resource-specific transactions, although they do stand to benefit from declarative transaction management.

Thus there's real value in lighter-weight, less invasive, transaction infrastructure that can scale *down* as well as up. For example, the Spring Framework AOP-based declarative transaction management, discussed in detail in Chapter 8, can switch between JTA for multiple databases or JDBC or other resource-specific transaction management APIs (such as the JDO transaction API) based on configuration, without any change to application code. This means that the most appropriate transaction management strategy can be used, depending on application requirements, and that a high-end application server with JTA support isn't required for single-database applications.

Also, EJB CMT could be more flexible. An EJB container will roll a transaction back automatically only in the event of a business method throwing an unchecked exception. This is treated as a grave problem by the EJB container, which will log the error, destroy the bean instance, and throw `EJBException` to a local client, or `RemoteException` to a remote client. In the event of an "application" exception as defined by the EJB specification (a checked exception other than `RemoteException`), the EJB developer is responsible for specifying rollback via the `setRollbackOnly()` method on the `EJBContext`. This behavior is not normally what we want; it would be good to be able to specify which checked exceptions should cause transaction rollback without needing further intervention, and for such automatic rollback not to be treated as a programming error. Spring's declarative transaction management provides this capability through "rollback rules," with the important benefit of minimizing the need of application developers to call a framework-specific `setRollbackOnly()` method.

Spring's transaction management also provides a good solution when programmatic, rather than declarative transaction management, is appropriate. This tends to be at either end of the complexity scale: in applications with few transactional requirements, in which setting up declarative transaction management is not worth the effort; and for more complex transaction requirements for which declarative transaction management (a good 90/10 solution) isn't appropriate. Spring provides a much simpler approach to programmatic transaction management than JTA, with much more manageable error handling and no need to perform JNDI lookups in application code. It's also possible to mix the equivalents of BMT and CMT in the same object if only one method requires complex transactional behavior. The iBATIS Database Layer also provides a transaction API that's much easier to use than JTA in applications using iBATIS data access.

> **EJB CMT is a good solution for the majority of transaction management requirements. However, it's not always appropriate, and it's not the best possible implementation of declarative transaction management. Although SLSBs provide real value in their declarative transaction management capabilities, they are not the only technology capable of delivering this functionality.**

Remoting

Remoting is another area in which EJB, and especially SLSBs, have proven valuable. Up till EJB 2.0 SLSBs provided only RMI remoting; EJB 2.1 added web services remoting. The EJB container's ability to serve remote requests, as well as manage the lifecycle of EJB instances, is valuable, as anyone who remembers the hell of managing custom RMI servers can confirm.

As I've said, there's an argument that the EJB specification confuses remoting with a component model. But the most important issue is that more often than not *we don't actually want remoting*. This is the one thing that EJB makes easy, and it's a dangerous temptation to adopt an inappropriate and potentially very expensive architecture (expensive in complexity, effort, and performance).

In web applications, it is nearly always a better idea to co-locate web components and business objects in the same JVM. In such applications, using EJB with remote interfaces adds no value and is usually harmful to design.

> **EJB is still usually the best choice for exposing remote interfaces via RMI/IIOP. However, we should be wary of building distributed applications without good reason. The fact that EJB makes this relatively easy is actually a dangerous temptation.**
>
> **If you need to expose web services, EJB is not the only option, and often not the best.**

Clustering

EJB is often hailed as the path to maximum scalability in J2EE applications. One reason for this is the belief that distributed applications are necessarily more scalable than collocated applications. I talked about distribution and scalability in Chapter 4 and explained that this belief is often a misconception. Another belief is that EJB containers have magical clustering capabilities. Commercial EJB containers are usually expensive, so it's reasonable to expect something fancy.

In fact, the clustering functionality of EJB isn't that remarkable. Clustering services for entity beans and stateful session beans are fairly limited.

Entity beans don't tend to perform as well in a cluster as O/R mapping solutions such as good JDO implementations. It's usually necessary to load entity state from the database at the beginning of each transaction in a clustered environment, because of the limitations of the EJB container's data replication capabilities. Dedicated clustered caching technologies such as Tangosol Coherence are much more sophisticated than the replication provided by application server vendors.

Stateful session bean clustering is problematic because the EJB specification doesn't lend itself as easily as the Servlet API to optimizing and minimizing the amount of state replication required between nodes in the cluster. In fact, clustering is generally agreed to be the fatal weakness of stateful session beans.

So the EJB clustering argument boils down to remote stateless session beans. However, clustering *stateless* service objects is in fact a relatively easy problem, because there's no state to replicate.

Remote SLSB clustering isn't rocket science. Many of the things that *are* rocket science to implement in EJB containers, such as effective SFSB state replication or efficient container-managed persistence, are either inadequately implemented or questionable ideas in the first place. (Other pieces of rocket science, like implementing a really good distributed transaction coordinator, are part of the overall application server and J2EE, rather than part of the EJB container and EJB.)

SLSB clustering is in fact fairly straightforward to implement as SLSBs are ... stateless. We can therefore run as many instances of a particular SLSB as we want on any node in a cluster, and client calls can be routed to any one of them at any time. As far as clients are concerned, all instances of each SLSB are identical and interchangeable. All that's required is for an `EJBObject` stub provided by the EJB container to remote clients to offer load balancing, via a round-robin, load-based, or random algorithm.

This kind of behavior can easily be implemented (potentially more efficiently) at the hardware level, with devices such as Cisco Load Balancer.

One additional benefit provided by a good EJB container such as WebLogic is the ability for an `EJBObject` stub to retry an operation transparently if it is marked in a deployment descriptor as being **idempotent:** that is, if it can potentially be called more than once without changing system state. But even this is hardly rocket science. Non-EJB solutions such as the GLUE web services product also provide sophisticated clustering of stateless services, so EJB isn't the only option for building robust and scalable distributed applications.

With local SLSBs, there's no special EJB-specific clustering functionality. Clustering is normally handled by the web container or hardware devices in front of it.

As I discussed in Chapter 3, collocated applications can be clustered very efficiently: Such load balancing by the J2EE web container, a web server or hardware in front of it can produce excellent scalability.

The main game with clustering is usually *not* in the business object tier of a J2EE web application. Clustering services are usually more important in:

❑　　The web tier. It's usually necessary to manage session state here, so a routing solution is required. If there's no session state to keep on the server, a web farm-style approach will normally be most performant.

❑　　The data access layer.

❑　　The database.

The true limitation of horizontal scalability usually concerns data access. If—as with most entity bean implementations—it's necessary for every application server to hit the database on every persistent object access in a clustered environment, performance will be affected, and the load on the database will be increased (limiting scalability). By combining a dedicated persistence solution such as Hibernate or a JDO implementation with a clustered cache we can usually achieve much higher throughput. There usually isn't the need to manage state in the business tier, which means that business layer–specific clustering services are less important.

The database itself must support clustering for maximum scalability, or it will become the limiting factor. High-end products such as Oracle 9i RAC are necessary in this case.

In Chapter 15 I'll discuss clustering and scalability in more detail.

Thread Management

EJB thread management is a more debatable benefit than is often thought. Developers have generally welcomed the fact that EJBs allow them to write their business objects as though they are single-threaded. However, the reality is that EJB's threading support doesn't fully address the problem of concurrent access to objects behind the EJB facade, and that it's a fallacy to think that it is the only good option for addressing concurrency issues. The idea of locking an entire bean instance while any method is executed is fairly naïve, and not always appropriate.

There are good alternatives to EJB thread management for service objects such as SLSBs, including:

❑ *Implementing multi-threaded service objects without read-write instance variables.* This works perfectly well with servlets, Struts Actions and the like. Most stateless services simply don't need complex thread management. Having a single instance of the service object, rather than a pool, also has advantages in many cases. For example, if we need to maintain a cache in a stateless session bean for efficiency reasons, such as a cache of results of expensive calculations, EJB pooling will result in the parallel existence of many caches. A single instance may be preferable.

❑ *Using the **Command** pattern:* It's possible to create a new instance of each service object to handle each request, eliminating concurrency problems within the object. WebWork/XWork successfully applies this approach, and it's also possible in Spring, via "prototype" bean definitions. Modern JVMs cope pretty well with the resulting object creation and destruction, and service objects are typically cheap to instantiate.

❑ *Using a multi-threaded service object that uses plain old Java language synchronization or concurrency class libraries to protect any read-write state during execution of methods that might corrupt it.* Synchronization is simple to implement and may perform perfectly well if access to only a minority of methods needs to be controlled. Of course synchronization can't protect against concurrent execution of the same code in another server in a cluster, but neither can EJB thread management.

I'll discuss alternatives to EJB thread management in detail in Chapter 12.

EJB Instance Pooling

Closely related to thread management is the notion of EJB instance pooling. The most valuable form of EJB instance pooling is the pooling of stateless session beans: the simplest form of EJB pooling, as stateless objects are ideal candidates for pooling.

I feel that the value of SLSB pooling is overrated, although it can be valuable at times. As I've said, modern JVMs are much smarter about generational garbage collection than the Java 1.1 JVMs that existed when the EJB specification was conceived. The absolute need for instance pooling to avoid death by GC is another of the basic EJB assumptions reasonable in 1998, but which now looks questionable.

Server-specific EJB deployment descriptors allow pool size to be configured per SLSB deployment. However, the value of such configuration is debatable. Given the relatively low cost of creating a typical SLSB, having a low pool size can create unnecessary contention. An excessively large thread pool cannot improve throughput. The determining factor is the maximum number of threads the application server will permit to execute concurrently. (Thread pooling is a vital service of an application server, which I'll discuss shortly.) If the SLSB pool size is less than the maximum number of threads able to use particular SLSBs, incoming calls to that EJB will be blocked until an instance becomes available. If the SLSB pool size is greater than the maximum number of threads, there is no gain in throughput. So there's a strong argument that the ideal pool size in all cases is the maximum number of threads that may want to access a particular SLSB.

Another issue with EJB instance pooling is that we end up with multiple copies of the internal state of each SLSB. This can be problematic if we really want a shared cache, for example.

> **EJB instance pooling is primarily motivated by a desire to avoid garbage collection and save memory. Garbage collection is much more efficient in modern JVMs than it was in Java 1.1 JVMs. RAM is also cheap, meaning that both these motivations are now less important than they once were.**

Resource Pooling

The truly valuable form of pooling in J2EE or other three tier applications is *resource pooling*, rather than pooling of business object instances. For example, it is essential to pool database connections to avoid running out of them under load. It is essential for an application server to pool threads of execution to guard against denial of service attacks or simply failing under heavy load.

However, such resource pooling is provided by the overall J2EE application server, rather than EJB, and hence is not tied to the EJB container. Database connection pools are available to any object running inside a J2EE server, such as a Servlet or plain Java class. In web applications, thread pooling is enforced by the web container at the point of entry into the application server; no further thread pooling is required to protect business objects, unless they run out-of-process in a distributed application.

Security

Another declarative service provided by EJB is security management. It's possible to enforce role-based security at method level in EJB deployment descriptors. (EJBs also support programmatic security via the ability to check whether the authenticated user is in a given role, as does the Servlet API.)

This looks good in the J2EE specification, but doesn't work so well in practice. Most of the J2EE applications I've seen with complex security requirements have found J2EE security infrastructure inadequate out of the box. None of them has been able to rely on EJB declarative role-based security: for example, because role-based security is inadequate, or because there is a need for a level of dynamic security credential checking not provided out of the box. This is as much a problem with the J2EE security infrastructure as with EJB, but it still negates what could have been a major positive of EJB.

There is value in declarative security; it's just that EJB can only tie into the standard J2EE security infrastructure, which is still inadequate to meet complex requirements. A good, more flexible, alternative approach is to use AOP to implement declarative custom security. Typically security credentials are held in a `ThreadLocal` object, rather than J2EE security context, and a custom security interceptor is used around business methods that need to be secured.

For web applications with simpler security requirements, it's normally sufficient to check user credentials in the web tier, for example, by using the Servlet API's declarative (`web.xml`-based) or programmatic role-based security. Declarative security can also be enabled in the web tier through the use of Servlet filters around protected content; through interceptors in web frameworks such as WebWork 2 and Spring that support custom interceptor chains for request processing; or through the use of AOP interception around web controllers, in frameworks such as Spring that provide AOP functionality as well as web MVC functionality.

Business Object Management

Finally, an EJB container is a kind of factory. EJB uses JNDI to provide a directory of well-defined service objects (typically SLSBs). The EJB deployment descriptors provide a mapping from service name (JNDI name) to implementing object. This provides a decoupling of the business interface (the EJB's component interface) from the implementing class (the EJB implementation class).

Such decoupling reflects good programming practice. One major positive of EJB is that it *forces* callers to program to interfaces, rather than classes. This has been one of the positive effects of widespread use of EJB on programming practice.

However, EJB isn't the only way of implementing such a separation.

The Java language provides perfectly good decoupling through its first-class support for interfaces. Some supporting infrastructure is needed to enable the choice of the implementing class for each interface to be held outside the Java code, as hard-coding it wastes most of the benefit of programming to interfaces. However, there are many far lighter-weight choices for this infrastructure. In this book I'll use the Spring Framework as an example. It provides a very lightweight way of enabling programming to interfaces, rather than classes, through its generic factories that can return an object instance by name based on configuration rather than Java code. Switching to a new implementation of any of these interfaces is as easy as editing a simple XML file. Other lightweight containers that achieve similar results without the complexity of EJB include PicoContainer (`www.picocontainer.org`).

Both Spring and PicoContainer provide **Inversion of Control** functionality, meaning that the lightweight container, not application code, is responsible for sorting out dependencies on collaborating objects. This can remove a vast amount of the JNDI lookup and other plumbing code that typically exists within EJB implementations, and also greatly facilitate testing. In Chapter 6, I discuss Inversion of Control and the benefits it offers.

Both Spring and PicoContainer, because they are so lightweight, are suitable for managing fine-grained business objects, in contrast to EJB, which is most appropriate for coarse-grained components. The overhead of implementing and deploying an EJB and using JNDI to access it is too great to incur for fine-grained objects, even if it is desirable to enable their implementation to be switched without impacting callers. This means that lightweight solutions such as Spring and PicoContainer are one-stop shops for providing this kind of factory functionality, while EJB is a partial solution that often needs to be supplemented by a lighter-weight solution behind a component facade.

> **EJB provides a heavyweight factory that decouples interfaces from their implementations. However, there are more powerful generic factories—the best of them based on Inversion of Control—that do this much better, with much less overhead and a much simpler programming model.**

EJB Services Summary

Most of the services I've discussed apply to all types of EJB. However, they're not often used except with SLSBs (or MDBs). For example, efficiency considerations preclude the use of remote interfaces with entity beans in almost all cases. Nor does it really make sense for entity beans to manage transactions; experience has shown that entity beans are best made dumb data access objects, without business logic.

EJB helped to prove and popularize a lot of valuable ideas. However, in no area is the EJB implementation perfect, or so complex as to preclude the development of lighter-weight alternatives.

In the light of the experience of the last five years, as well as the lessons of .NET, we're now in a position to take the good things from EJB, and avoid the disadvantages. We can have the positives of SLSBs without all the complexity.

> **In the rest of this book, we'll look at these positive features of EJB and how we can recreate them by simpler means.**

What Don't We Want from EJB?

Unfortunately, EJB takes away as well as gives. In particular, its claim to deliver simplicity is debatable.

EJB is the antithesis of YAGNI. It imposes great complexity out of fear of even greater complexity.

Experience has shown that there are many problems and irritations attached to the use of EJB. These can often be worse than the alternative of not enjoying services such as declarative transaction management. They are considerably worse than alternatives that offer similar services through AOP.

Let's look at some of the more significant EJB irritations.

The Monolithic, Distinct Container Problem

First, using EJB requires an EJB container. This may seem a tautological objection, but there are many real problems here:

❑   It limits our choice of application server. We can't just use a web container such as Tomcat, and (if we use commercial products) licensing costs will be much higher. This isn't purely an issue of cost: if we don't need to use a high-end application server with an EJB container, we will reap a simplicity dividend and stand to make savings in areas such as deployment time, application administration, testing effort and training.

❑   Often we want only a small subset of EJB functionality, such as CMT. Why should we swallow the whole baggage of EJB to address just this one requirement? Using EJB is a bit like being pregnant; it's impossible to use EJB just a little, without greatly increasing complexity overall. If we want only one EJB service, such as declarative transaction management, the math isn't attractive. If we want multiple EJB services, such as distributed objects *and* transaction management *and* business object pooling, EJB is a much better value proposition.

❑   Business objects end up invaded by EJB APIs, unless we make a determined effort to factor business logic into POJOs behind an EJB facade.

❑   We can't use the same business logic outside the EJB.

There's also the problem that the existence of an EJB container, distinct from the application server as a whole, introduces an undesirable division in an application. We want a *logical* division between the web tier and business logic tier but not at the cost of a *physical* one; we don't necessarily want this kind of distinction between different managed environments. This can be a problem, for example, when want to share configuration between web and EJB environments.

Inelegance and the Proliferation of Classes

We need at least three Java source files to implement every session EJB: the home interface; the component interface (local or remote); and the bean implementation class. The bean implementation class can, but shouldn't normally, implement the component interface, making synchronization a common source of errors unless we add a fourth interface, often called a "business methods" interface. (If the bean implementation class implements the component interface it also ends up having to implement either EJBObject or EJBLocalObject. This isn't a good idea because implementing methods that can never be invoked is misleading and gratuitous, and because it makes it possible to return this to remote or local clients in place of the container-generated implementation of the component interface: a subtle and serious programming error.) The business methods interface, if we choose to use it, is a superinterface of the component interface that defines the business methods without dependence on the EJB API.

The necessary Java classes to implement each EJB and their relationships are shown in Figure 5-1.

With local EJBs, using EJB doesn't necessarily impact the business methods interface. This can enable us to view EJB as just one implementation choice for a particular business interface. However, with remote EJBs, all methods on the business interface must throw the checked RMI RemoteException, tying the interface to EJB and its remoting strategy.

That this proliferation of artifacts can be made barely manageable by tools such as IDEs or XDoclet doesn't justify it. However we approach it, it will lead to some loss in productivity versus simply having a Java business interface and a class implementing it.

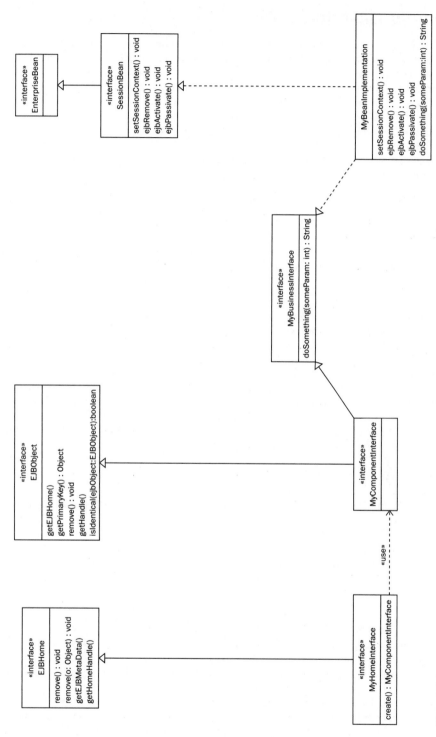

Figure 5-1

Deployment Descriptor Hell

Then there are the EJB deployment descriptors: verbose, almost impossible to hand-author, and not especially intuitive. Because the standard `ejb-jar.xml` deployment descriptor leaves important information (such as specifying the JNDI name of the bean, and configuring instance pooling) to the container vendor, we always need at least one additional, proprietary, deployment descriptor, like `weblogic-ejb-jar.xml`.

With session and message beans, the complexity of the required deployment descriptors is an irritation causing some reduction in productivity and (often) dependence on code generation tools. With entity beans, the complexity in standard and proprietary deployment descriptors makes code generation absolutely essential, and is grossly excessive in contrast to other persistence technologies such as Hibernate and JDO.

Class Loader Hell

Another serious issue with EJB is the class loading complexity it introduces. Even in an integrated J2EE application deployed in a single JVM, the EJB container will not normally use the same class loader as the web container. This means that at least one additional class loader is required.

The more class loaders come into play, the greater the potential problems, and the greater the variations in behavior among application servers. For example, in many application servers, such as WebLogic and Oracle Application Server, the EJB class loader will be the parent of the WAR class loader. Java class loaders are hierarchical, the fundamental rule being that a child class loader must ask its parent to attempt to load a class before it attempts to itself. This can create the following situation: a class loaded by the EJB class loader cannot see classes loaded by the WAR class loader. For example, if `struts.jar` is loaded by the EJB class loader, it will be unable to load application Actions under the WAR's /WEB-INF/classes directory. Yet if any of the many JARs that `struts.jar` depends on is also required in the EJB tier, it must be included in the manifest class path of the relevant EJB jar, as the classes it contains will not be otherwise visible inside the EJB container.

Such problems affect framework developers more severely than application developers, but can have a real impact on developer productivity. Such problems that "shouldn't happen" can write off a surprising amount of team time very quickly. I've seen several projects run into severe problems with J2EE class loading, all of which related to the use of EJB.

J2EE class loading as a whole is rather complex, unintuitive, and insufficiently specified. However, at present it's fair to say that EJB greatly complicates matters where class loading is concerned.

Testing

Because applications built on EJB are so heavily dependent on the EJB container, they are fiendishly difficult to unit test. Typically, applications making heavy use of EJB have no effective unit testing. In-container testing solutions such as Cactus can help to plug this gap, but they're still a complex way of testing, compared to testing plain Java classes with JUnit.

Take a "classic" J2EE architecture. Business logic will be in stateless session "facades," which will do all data access via entity beans with local references. This architecture is particularly difficult to test. Because of their dependence on the container, the SLSBs are difficult to unit test. The entity beans usually can't be unit tested at all, as they'll be abstract classes, with the container responsible for providing concrete subclasses at runtime. Typically architects will minimize the need to unit test entity beans by ensuring that they contain only getter and setter methods, with no behavior, but this is a serious design compromise: true domain objects *should* contain behavior. (As with many of the constraints EJB places on OO, we've become so used to this that it doesn't offend us as much as it should.) We can test such applications *inside* the container, using a testing framework like Cactus. But this means that, even to run a single test case, we need to deploy our application to an EJB container. Test-time deployment and build scripts also become complicated by the need to deploy such a testing framework with the application. With code-test cycles as slow as this, test first development becomes virtually impossible. It also becomes very difficult to achieve comprehensive test coverage. And as we don't control the internals of the container, simulating certain kinds of failure (such as failure to connect to a database) will be difficult, if not impossible.

If using EJB, testability can be improved by treating the session beans (or message beans) as merely a facade to plain Java business objects. This enables us to test the business objects outside the container, unless they depend on EJB APIs or other EJBs. However, managing business objects within the EJB tier can be problematic, because EJB doesn't provide us with any support for managing such fine-grained objects; we'll need to hard-code to classes rather than interfaces, or use additional infrastructure such as an IoC container within the EJB container. If we use entity beans, or need to access other EJBs via JNDI, any testability advantage is lost. In any case, we're now working around EJB rather than working within it.

Now let's consider an alternative architecture: the Lightweight Container architecture described in Chapter 3. We'll abstract our business logic behind ordinary Java interfaces. We can use a transparent persistence solution such as JDO or Hibernate, so that persistent objects are not tied to an EJB container or even a particular persistence framework. We'll use a lightweight framework such as Spring to give us declarative transaction management and to help wire up our business objects, which will be coupled by interfaces, and never dependent on other implementing classes.

With this architecture, we can test all our business logic outside the application server. We can easily use mock objects to replace collaborators in JUnit test cases. In the case of Spring, we can even run integration tests without a container, because we can create a Spring "bean factory" that replaces objects dependent on J2EE services with objects that can run outside a container. For example, we can replace a container-specific `DataSource` with a simple `DataSource` designed to connect to a database outside a container.

Of course it's also essential to run tests against the application deployed in the container, but this is a separate activity from unit testing.

> **The ability to test business objects out of an EJB container (and J2EE server altogether) is essential for practicing test driven development and achieving high unit test coverage.**

With out-of-container testing, we can run unit tests in seconds, rather than endure lengthy deployment to an EJB container even to run individual test cases. Testing will be so easy that it can be welcomed into the development process.

After having worked on easily testable non-EJB applications, it's hard to go back.

Escaping reliance on the container isn't only a testability advantage either: we'll be able to *deploy* our business objects outside an EJB container, too, if we want to.

> **If you're serious about unit testing your code, and especially if you want to practice test first development, you'll find that EJB becomes something you are continually working around, rather than a simplifying model.**

EJB Overdose

Overuse of EJB has severe consequences. Modeling fine-grained business objects as EJB rapidly becomes unworkable because of the complexity of deployment descriptors and EJB lookup, increased deployment time, performance overhead, and reduced testability.

All technologies can be abused, and it's not entirely fair to single out EJB in this respect. However, I've repeatedly seen the "EJB Golden Hammer" antipattern seriously damaging projects, so it's a real concern in practice. Maybe it's the cachet attached to EJB that encourages it; an amazing number of managers I've encountered know the buzzword "EJB" and expect extensive use of EJB on their projects without technical justification. (This is bad management, but that's life.) Even architects are not immune to this; I recently worked on a project where every operation was modeled as a remote EJB invocation. My protestations were in vain; I was viewed as a J2EE Luddite.

The fact that EJB provides no support for managing fine-grained objects behind coarser-grained facades contributes to this problem. Unless we are content to instantiate POJOs behind an EJB facade using the new operator, and abandon any idea of loose coupling and pluggable implementations, we need an additional lightweight container solution in addition to EJB.

In general, I regard one EJB calling other EJBs as an antipattern. An EJB should normally be a component that collaborates with plain Java objects.

> **If you do choose to use EJB, treat EJB as a component model. EJBs should be coarse-grained objects, at the boundaries of your system. If you find that one EJB often invokes another, you probably should rethink.**

Complex Programming Model

EJB imposes a complex programming model. The aim of the EJB specification that EJB should "make it easy to write applications" has not been achieved. Not only do we need to write all those implementing classes, we need to perform JNDI lookups to access each and every EJB. This introduces a dependency on JNDI and the EJB API into code using business objects, and, in traditional approaches to using EJB, involves us hard-coding Service Locator and Business Delegate objects.

Spring improves this situation when using EJBs with its support for codeless Business Delegates—hiding the complexity of JNDI lookup and EJB "creation" inside the framework—but this isn't as good as removing the unnecessary complexity altogether.

Simple Things Can Be Hard

The *raison d'être* of EJB is to make hard things simpler. Unfortunately, EJB negates many of its gains in this area by making simple things surprisingly difficult. Most EJB-based projects I've worked on have encountered problems such as:

- ❑ **Implementing singletons (or the same result by other means) with EJBs.** EJB programming restrictions around read-write static variables make this problematic.

- ❑ **Ensuring that some processing occurs when the EJB container starts up.** It's easy to do this with a Servlet API listener or servlet with "load on startup" specified in web applications, but there's no support for this in the EJB specification. A good IoC container such as Spring allows dependencies to be expressed in configuration, resulting in proper ordering of initialization; EJB fails to address this important requirement of many applications.

- ❑ **Sharing configuration between EJBs and objects running outside the EJB container.** This is a common requirement, but difficult in practice. (JNDI is one way to do it, but it's complex and we end up relying on unspecified behavior as to which tier of our application is fired up by the application server first.)

- ❑ **Restricted access to other Java APIs.** The EJB programming restrictions forbid access to Java APIs required by some business objects. (A recent humorous post on the ServerSide.com portal concerned the number of the EJB programming restrictions violated by `java.lang.String`.)

Once you start putting your business logic in the EJB tier, it's hard to stop. EJBs can't access business objects running outside the container, and business objects outside the container are complicated by the need for EJB lookups.

Is the Goal of Enabling Developers to Ignore the Complexity of Enterprise Applications Even Desirable?

The EJB specification's goal of allowing application developers "not to have to understand low-level transaction and statement management details; multi-threading; resource pooling; and other complex low-level APIs" hasn't been achieved by EJB. Whether it is even a worthy goal is debatable.

We can greatly *reduce* the complexity of working with enterprise concepts: this is the prime focus of this book. However we can't, and shouldn't attempt to, free ourselves from the many design issues they raise. This is the value that enterprise developers currently bring.

In my experience the notion of tiered teams—with a God-like architect, backed by an application server, taking care of all these big picture issues while a team of code monkeys knocks out the code without fully understanding its context, doesn't work well in practice. All too often it results in an inflexible architecture, resulting from the assumption that the architect knows best up front. And I find that there are a lot of very capable J2EE developers out there, with an excellent understanding of middleware concepts.

In a decade or so we may have reached the point where we don't have to worry about transaction management or the other concerns we spend our days pondering today. But we're so far from that point at present that we should be realistic about the fact that current technologies, like EJB, aren't going to take us there.

Loss of Productivity

Put all this together, and EJB can cost a lot of money. EJB scores poorly on productivity, one of our goals from Chapter 2.

In my experience, productivity in projects making heavy use of EJB is far lower than productivity in projects that don't. Although tools such as IDEs or XDoclet can ease the burden of developing and maintaining EJBs, all that complexity is still lurking not far beneath the surface, waiting to cost time and effort.

Portability Problems

Nor does EJB deliver on its goal of portability between multiple application servers "without recompilation or source code modification."

Few non-trivial EJB applications are easily portable between application servers. Issues such as the singleton problem usually dictate some dependence on the target application server, along with a lot of agonizing over accepting them.

Despite its complexity, the EJB specification still doesn't address all the issues that it should. For example:

❑ Entity beans are still under-specified (despite the hundreds of pages devoted to them in the EJB 2.1 specification), and you'll have to resort to proprietary features to use them in realistic applications.

❑ As discussed earlier, class loader behavior varies greatly between application servers. This becomes more of an issue when using EJB and is a real portability hassle.

This is in sharp contrast to the servlet specification. J2EE applications that don't use EJB are typically easy to port between servers.

Can EJB Reinvent Itself?

Aren't these criticisms old and tired? Haven't good workarounds been found? Won't future versions of the EJB specification address these problems?

The fact that many of these criticisms of EJB are not new doesn't make them invalid. There's no smoke without fire, and recurring criticism usually reflects some underlying problem. How many people recently complained to you about servlets? Many other parts of J2EE besides EJB don't generate ongoing criticism, because they self-evidently work and lead to good results and good productivity.

Tool Support

There's a common belief that the irritations of the EJB specification can be negated by improved tool support. Several IDEs provide integrated or plugin support for EJB development; XDoclet-style code generation helps developers to minimize the number of artifacts they need to develop for each EJB.

I remain skeptical. These are workarounds. The complexity is largely unjustifiable; these tools are still relatively feeble in comparison with the amazingly sophisticated tools now available for working with POJOs, such as the IntelliJ and Eclipse IDEs.

As discussed in Chapter 2, I believe that reliance on code generation is potentially dangerous. I prefer to avoid it if I can, and I believe that it *can* be avoided when addressing most problems in developing enterprise applications.

> **It is better to avoid gratuitous complexity than to rely on tools to manage it.**

EJB 3.0

As I began this chapter in June 2003, work had just begun on JSR 220 (EJB 3.0) — several months before the final release of EJB 2.1 (see `http://jcp.org/en/jsr/detail?id=220`). This unusually early start was an indication that Sun had noted the groundswell of concern about the complexity and usability of EJB, and felt a need to mark out its future direction before finalizing J2EE 1.4.

The main motivation for EJB 3.0 is ease of use: "To improve the EJB architecture by reducing its complexity from the EJB developer's point of view." In particular, it aims to use the source-level metadata support in J2SE 1.5 to do away with — or, at least, greatly reduce — the volume of EJB deployment descriptors. As of May 2004, indications are that it will offer a simple Dependency Injection mechanism, also based on annotations, but less powerful than that already proven in production with Spring and other light-weight containers. A new — additional — persistence approach appears to effectively standardize the Hibernate approach to persistence to relational databases. The overall programming model is reminiscent of that offered by Spring (for Dependency Injection) and Hibernate (for persistence). However, as presentations only on work in progress, rather than a specification draft for public review, have been made public, the approach may yet change.

This is encouraging. However, my feeling is that it's too late to reinvent EJB, and it's best to move on. While some of the problems with EJB can be fixed, a simplifying release aiming to win developers' hearts and minds can occur only within the cycle of the overall J2EE specifications. In short:

❑ The timescales are too long. The EJB 3.0 specification is unlikely to be released until mid-2005, and it is unlikely to be widely supported by J2EE servers until well after that. We need to write a lot of enterprise applications between now and then. The timing problems are compounded by the dependency on J2SE 1.5 for annotation support. Upgrading J2SE major version in enterprise-scale applications is a major undertaking, with implications for third-party products such as JDBC drivers, besides the application server itself. Thus it's likely that EJB 3.0 will not be available for use in many projects until 2006.

❑ There's still a danger that the specification-driven approach will not meet the needs of the developer community. As with old-style CMP, such an approach also poses a risk of stifling innovation.

❑ It seems unlikely that a true, general AOP-style approach will be incorporated in EJB 3.0. I firmly believe that this is the way of the future.

The genie is out of the bottle. Frustration with previous versions of EJB has generated powerful ideas and proven solutions, to which EJB 3.0 appears to be playing catch-up. The notion of the monolithic container remains hard to defend in the era of AOP and pluggable persistence and transaction strategies. In particular, the decision to tie persistence to the EJB container (even with the effective deprecation of old CMP entities) is highly debatable. Why should not EJB users choose between best-of-breed solutions such as Hibernate, JDO implementations, or TopLink, which work well inside any EJB container?

The architects of EJB 3.0 will also be constrained by many considerations, including:

❑ **Backward compatibility.** Complete backward compatibility is guaranteed in JSR 220.

❑ **Marketing concerns.** Sun and the application server vendors with a vested interest in the spec cannot afford to acknowledge that EJB got so many things wrong that its future is in doubt.

Most important, some of the negatives of EJB can be removed—bloated deployment descriptors and the proliferation of implementation classes. However, EJB architects need not just correct EJB weaknesses, but they also need to move the technology forward. The unique value propositions of EJB—such as the ability to handle unusual distribution requirements—are not advanced beyond EJB 2.1. These requirements are relatively rare, so the complexity of the programming model entailed to handle them is not usually a major issue. A major release aimed at simplifying the programming model to encourage broader use of EJB is of debatable value, when that simplification is available *today*, over standard J2EE services.

Myths and Fallacies

It's important to refute some common myths about EJB: particularly, that EJB is synonymous with J2EE services; and that to criticize EJB is to attack J2EE as a whole.

J2EE == EJB

We can summarize many of the points made so far in this chapter in two sentences:

> J2EE is more than EJB.
>
> EJB is less than Java.

EJB is *not* synonymous with J2EE services. As I've noted, there is a lot more to J2EE than EJB. Most of the core services, such as transaction management via JTA, resource pooling and thread management are provided by J2EE, rather than EJB. EJB is in fact only one way of tapping into some of these services.

I've discussed alternative solutions to common goals such as declarative transaction management. In the case of persistence, we're better off looking outside J2EE to solutions such as JDO and Hibernate than using entity beans. There were good solutions, such as TopLink, to this particular problem before the EJB specification was released and O/R mapping products have continued to improve.

EJB might be a good way to tap into J2EE services, were it not for the fact that EJB takes away a lot of what we can do with Java. Consider its effect on object orientation. EJBs cannot participate in inheritance at a component interface level, although EJB implementation classes are free to participate in inheritance hierarchy.

> **Rejection of EJB is often thought to be a rejection of J2EE. This is completely incorrect, as EJB is just one part of J2EE.**

Questionable Arguments for Using EJB

The following arguments are often suggested for using EJB. However, they don't withstand scrutiny.

- **Everyone understands EJB.** Really? All 640 pages of the EJB 2.1 specification? This potential benefit is undermined by a number of practical considerations:

  - EJB is complex. While having a standard middleware component model is potentially beneficial, the EJB model is so complex that a deep understanding of it is rare.

  - Apart from the complexity of the EJB model itself, a lot of the understanding required to develop successful applications is actually J2EE understanding and an understanding of the associated enterprise concepts, or middleware understanding. For example, an EJB architect should be able to come to grips with the Microsoft .NET architecture quickly. And anyone who really understands EJB is likely to become more productive with a less complex alternative model.

  - Understanding of EJB provides a good basis for understanding simpler alternatives that keep the best concepts from EJB, such as Container-Managed Transactions.

  - The EJB model is likely to change significantly in EJB 3.0—at least from the point of view of deployment descriptors.

- **You can't possibly want to write asynchronous applications without MDBs.** I'm quite a fan of MDBs: I think they're one of the best parts of the EJB specification. In particular, they're relatively simple. However, as with resource management or transaction management, a lot of the capabilities of MDBs actually come from J2EE, not EJB. For example, JMS message destinations provide thread management without the need for MDBs. I'd be more inclined to use EJB for heavily asynchronous applications than for any other reason. But I'm still far from convinced that messaging warrants accepting all the other problems with EJB.

- **You may build a simpler system without EJB, but it will never scale.** This is untrue except in the rare cases when internal object distribution delivers greatest scalability, and EJB's RMI remoting comes into its own. This is a classic retort of those who lack detailed arguments for exactly why they want to use EJB.

Moving Forward

The remainder of this book will focus on alternatives to EJB that deliver key enterprise services in a simpler, more productive way. In the rest of this chapter I'll focus on moving forward, rather than looking back, beginning by considering when it's appropriate to use EJB today.

Choosing Whether to Use EJB

Should we ever use EJB? How do we decide when EJB is appropriate? Let's consider conventional wisdom, and criteria appropriate today.

Conventional Wisdom

Ed Roman includes a good summary of traditional wisdom in choosing when to use EJB in his excellent, if somewhat dated, *Mastering Enterprise JavaBeans* (Wiley, 2001). This discussion is also available online at www.theserverside.com/resources/article.jsp?l=Is-EJB-Appropriate.

Roman rightly attempts to enumerate the valuable services of EJB, replacing hype with rational argument. The main reasons he gives for using EJB follow. However, the equations have changed since 2001 in nearly every case. I've summarized Roman's points in italics, and included my own discussion in normal font:

❑ *Your system is built faster and more reliably* because without EJB's declarative middleware services such as CMT you'd need to develop your own infrastructure framework. Real-world experience tends to show that systems are not usually built faster because of EJB usage: rather, the reverse. But the crucial development since late 2001 is that you no longer need to develop your own infrastructure to do without EJB's declarative services. For example, the Spring Framework can deliver declarative transaction management without AOP. Before 2003, no credible alternative solutions existed.

❑ *It is easier to hire new employees.* You need to train employees if you use your own framework. This is another powerful argument against developing an in-house infrastructure framework—hardly ever an advisable way to replace EJB. But it's a poor argument against open source solutions such as the three mentioned earlier, which are themselves widely understood. And it's an argument weakened by the complexity of EJB: a good alternative solution may be much simpler and easier to understand.

❑ *You benefit from the best practices the world is building around EJB"* such as EJB design patterns. In practice, the existence of a patterns industry often divorced from reality is a good reason not to use EJB. J2EE applications using EJB are likely to have gratuitous and harmful architectural complexity, such as unnecessary remote method calls. In fact, the popularity of complex and often inelegant "J2EE design patterns" does not guarantee a sensible architecture. Application architecture should be driven by the problem at hand, not popular usage patterns around a technology such as EJB.

❑ *You can support different user interfaces,* such as thick clients and web clients. This is an argument in favor of implementing distributed applications with EJB. However, only for RMI/IIOP remoting is EJB the only reasonable choice for remoting. And the multiple client-type scenario doesn't occur as often in practice as in J2EE texts. If you don't need this complexity, don't incur it.

❑ *You can work with industry-standard tools to rapidly develop your system.* Tool support for EJB development is overrated. No amount of sophisticated tool support can make authoring EJBs as easy as authoring POJOs.

❑ *You can separate your web tier and application server.* Yes, but you rarely want to. If the web container isn't secure that is a major concern in itself. Also, an HTTP server such as Apache can be used to allow a firewall in front of all parts of the J2EE application server, including the web container.

Making a Choice Today

EJB still has a place. It's much less of a place than many J2EE developers think, and I'm convinced that within a few years, EJB will be relegated to legacy status. However, right now, EJB *is* appropriate if:

❑ You are developing a middleware-centric application, with little role for a web interface, and need a distributed (rather than simply *clustered*) architecture. Many large financial applications fit this description. However, distributed architectures are often used inappropriately, impairing performance and increasing complexity without delivering any real gain.

❏ You want a distributed application based on RMI. EJB is one of the simplest technologies you can use to achieve this.

❏ You have a real need for stateful session beans, which cannot be met using HTTP session objects or in thick clients: for example, because you must hold state on behalf of multiple client types. In practice, this is pretty rare.

You do *not* need to use EJB to address the following requirements, which have often been considered indications for EJB usage:

❏ **Transaction requirements.** Transaction coordination is provided by the application server, not the EJB container. EJB CMT is good (especially when used with SLSBs), but it's possible to do better.

❏ **Multi-threading.** It's not that hard to write multi-threaded stateless service objects. In cases where we need pooling, Spring can provide it without EJB.

❏ **Resource pooling.** This is provided by J2EE, not EJB.

You can enjoy these services without using EJB and without the need to roll your own infrastructure code.

You might want to use EJB if you have developers who are very familiar with EJB. However, because of the complexity of EJB, many developers with EJB experience lack in-depth knowledge of EJB, so a little knowledge of EJB can be a dangerous thing.

Of course, your management may force you to use EJB. As this is a book about technical issues, rather than the vagaries of the corporate world, I'll pass on this.

What I hope you'll take away from this book is not the message that EJB is a bad technology, but the basis for making sound decisions as to when (and if) to use EJB. You should be able to run through a checklist that indicates whether or not EJB will deliver value in a particular application. If it does, go ahead and use it!

> Because the design approach advocated in this book emphasizes loose coupling, it can allow you to add EJB into your application without a total rework. Whether or not to use EJB will become more of an implementation choice than a design choice. However, by adopting EJB only if it proves necessary, you'll always have the best design for application at each point along the way.

The Emerging Post-EJB Consensus

Although I've come to my own critical view on EJB independently (based on extensive experience), it's important to point out that I'm not a lone heretic. I'm in good company.

While it was warmly welcomed in the Java community, EJB met a harsher reception outside. For example, in the early days of EJB, former CORBA guru and COM+ expert Roger Sessions attacked stateful session beans as limiting scalability (arguing that stateful middle tier components are a bad idea); and entity beans (on performance and other grounds).

> See **www.objectwatch.com/eddebate.htm** *for a transcript of a debate between Roger Sessions and Ed Roman discussing EJB versus COM+. Although the debate took place in July 1999, many of the points relate to the unchanged basic EJB model.*

Sessions's criticisms were largely ignored in the J2EE community at the time, partly because of his association with Microsoft. But today it's hard to dismiss them so easily.

More important, since 2002, concern about EJB has grown dramatically *within* the J2EE community. Many leaders in the J2EE community are dissatisfied with EJB and many are proposing "post-EJB" solutions. These solutions overlap in some ways.

First, many experts have come to the view that EJB is far from perfect, and is overkill for many applications. These conclusions are based not on theory, but on much real-world experience. (Only now is a post-EJB *theory* beginning to emerge, driven by this practical experience.)

For example, Ted Neward—author of several books on J2EE and .NET—focuses on the deficiencies in the EJB specification and some of the problems that result from it, in an article entitled "The Death of EJB as we know it?" (www.oreillynet.com/pub/wlg/1922?page=last&x-maxdepth=0):

> People are starting to recognize some of the frailty implicit in the EJB specification. In particular, the emphasis on vendor-neutrality within the EJB specification leads to a number of inefficient ways of developing enterprise applications. In order to work around these inefficiencies, developers are forced to adopt "design patterns" that create more work for the average developer, arguably more work than if they'd just abandoned EJB altogether and started from a core architecture of just servlets/JSP and JDBC.

> Developers seek simpler alternatives to EJB for a simple reason: EJB is not only way overkill for most enterprise applications, but it also represents a huge learning curve for the average Java developer.

> EJB is not the sum total of J2EE—in fact, it's probably the one bad apple in the barrel. Servlets, JSP, JMS, RMI, JDBC, all of these are excellent specifications that serve their stated goals quite well. Abandoning EJB doesn't imply you need to abandon them, either—far from it. Instead, embrace them even more fully, and use them to their fullest capabilities.

> In short, next time you're looking into building an enterprise application in Java, maybe spend less time trying to figure out which EJB server to use, and spend a little more time trying to figure out precisely what you need the EJB server for.

James Strachan (http://radio.weblogs.com/0112098/2002/10/30.html) writes that:

> The biggest problem with EJB isn't the technical solution to remoting, to stateful/stateless session beans. It's that it's all so visible and intrusive and damned complicated to use. Also the irony is barely 10% of uses ever even need the EJB solution. Most folks are developing web applications or web services that really don't need EJB at all. This stuff should be hidden and only actually used if stuff really is deployed remotely.

Strachan believes that "Servlets and web services are the future ... I already view EJB as legacy."

Like Neward and other prominent critics of EJB, Strachan cannot be dismissed as naïve or ignorant of the true power of EJB. He's an important contributor to Apache Jakarta, the co-founder of Dom4j, Jaxen, and the Apache Geronimo J2EE server, and a committer on Maven, Apache Commons, and other important Java/J2EE projects. He serves on several Java specification committees and has extensive commercial experience working for software companies and leading financial institutions.

There's also a growing convergence around the idea of lightweight containers and AOP as a replacement for EJB. Carlos E. Perez (`www.manageability.org`), cogently summarizes criticisms of EJB and hopes for a "post-EJB" model (`www.manageability.org/blog/archive/20021030%23blogging_about_post_oo/view`):

> What I see common in all the above endeavors [lightweight containers and AOP-based middleware] is the need to keep the core logic separate from the implementation. Although, this principle seems entirely obvious, EJB in its current incarnation goes completely against it. The conflicting motivations for EJB (Transaction Monitor ideas, compliance with CORBA standards, Business Objects or Beans programming model) have created a Frankenstein. A Technology where a business's core object model is hopelessly lost inside a jungle of design patterns.
>
> Post-EJB is an attempt to separate the core [object] model from the implementation. The core model needs to be preserved at all times. This leads to better traceability and a more agile implementation.

Rickard Oberg (`www.jroller.com/page/rickard`), a distinguished J2EE developer who has implemented several EJB containers, including the innovative interceptor-based JBoss core, now describes EJB as a "dead end." Like many others, he believes that the post-EJB solution rests on AOP and lightweight frameworks.

Jon Tirsen (`www.freeroller.net/page/tirsen`), creator of Nanning Aspects, believes that lighter-weight AOP solutions will supersede EJB, and that the requirements to reach this point are of greater familiarity with and in acceptance of AOP and the emergence of killer aspects for services such as transaction management. (Today, the Spring Framework and some other solutions already provide such aspects.) As with those of the other prominent EJB-skeptics I've quoted, Tirsen's views are based on his experience working with complex EJB-based applications, and alternative architectures.

Bill Burke and Marc Fleury of JBoss promote the use of POJOs with AOP-based declarative enterprise services such as transaction management as an alternative to EJB. JBoss 4 emphasizes the use of AOP to deliver these benefits.

After *Expert One-on-One J2EE Design and Development* was published in late 2002, dozens of readers—many of them experienced architects—have sent their thanks for the critical comments on overuse of EJB, and citing experiences that have led them to share those conclusions.

Prior to 2002, such critical comments about EJB were seldom heard, and there was an absence of credible work toward EJB alternatives. Ed Roman's objections about rejecting EJB meaning developing complex in-house infrastructure were completely valid.

Today, a lot of people are coming together to make a post-EJB world realistic. Not all of them agree in the shape of the post-EJB solution (although there's a consensus on the importance of AOP), but they do agree that an EJB-centric approach has not worked well in practice.

And, at last, there are proven, products that can form the basis of robust J2EE architectures without EJB, including:

- ❏ **The Spring Framework**: a powerful yet lightweight "Inversion of Control" container offering programmatic enterprise services and declarative enterprise services via AOP

- ❏ **Nanning Aspects:** another AOP-based solution, which, like Spring, has been successfully used to replace EJB in numerous applications, with excellent results

- ❏ **JBoss 4:** a J2EE application server that offers enterprise services to POJOs via AOP, without the need to use EJB

- ❏ **PicoContainer:** a lightweight IoC container, which can be integrated with Nanning to provide declarative services through AOP

- ❏ **Hibernate:** a popular O/R mapping solution that provides a much simpler, yet more powerful, persistence solution than entity beans

- ❏ **JDO implementations** such as Kodo JDO: These products offer another good alternative for persistence that doesn't require EJB

- ❏ **HiveMind:** another IoC container which, like Spring and PicoContainer, minimizes the dependence of business objects on their runtime environment

- ❏ **iBatis:** an open source project providing a simple programmatic data access and transaction abstraction

- ❏ **GLUE:** a high-performance, lightweight web services remoting solution

Such products offer a rich menu of choices for dispensing with EJB in typical applications.

In this book, I'll describe a number of "post-EJB" solutions. The examples will use the Spring Framework. However, the architectural concepts apply to many solutions, including those in the list above.

Standards, Innovation, and Open Source

You might be thinking that all this sounds interesting, but that we're advocating moving away from J2EE standards (at least the EJB part of it) toward solutions without the imprimatur of standardization. This issue is worth exploring in detail.

Competition versus Command

The attempt by Sun Microsystems to standardize middleware via J2EE has produced many benefits. No one would want to return to the days of complete fragmentation with multiple proprietary products. Few want monopolistic proprietary vendors controlling the middleware industry. However, there is evidence that standardization through the JCP is not the unalloyed good it was once believed to be:

- ❏ It's arguably not standardization in a true sense; national standards bodies such as British Standards and ISO or independent organizations such as ECMA (www.ecma-international.org/) publish true standards, not hardware and software companies such as Sun. This is more than a trivial point, because Sun and other participants in the Sun-sponsored JCP have vested interests in the technologies they attempt to standardize.

- ❏ Standards work best if they are introduced into a mature area, in which there are successful, mature competing solutions. It's dangerous to try to standardize an approach to an area that still isn't well understood. Practical experience shows that the experimental parts of the EJB specification, such as stateful session beans and entity beans, were not well enough understood when specified to justify standardization. The fact that the JCP amounts to a "standards-first" approach means that:

❏ There's a danger of design by committee, resulting in lack of focus and clear vision. Important specifications may be based not on working products that have produced real value, but on tradeoffs between multiple organizations (usually application server vendors) on the specification committee. An example of this is EJB 2.0, in which local interfaces were a last-minute addition because two of the largest vendors could not agree on other approaches to improve entity bean performance. The necessity for fundamental change in this area at all reflected the fact that entity beans hadn't been proven before they were specified in EJB 1.1.

❏ Bad ideas can be set in stone. Specifications are published before realistic implementations of them, and before real-world experience in applying them. *Reference implementations* do not provide the same value in validating the basic approach, because they are often not robust or performant, and not intended or fit for use in production. This means that poor technologies, such as entity beans and (slightly more contentiously) JSP, can endure far beyond the life span they deserved.

❏ The damage done by premature standardization can last for years. There's no mechanism for killing off unsuccessful specifications or parts of specifications, as backward compatibility is essential to a credible standards effort. The relevant standards provide protection against the market's tendency to cull failing technologies. Backward compatibility and standardization before real-world proof are a dangerous combination.

❏ There are issues with the openness of the JCP, which Sun appears to be trying to address. However, it still does not involve the J2EE community nearly as inclusively as it should.

❏ Standards processes are slow. For example, it will take EJB 3.0 years to catch up with certain worthwhile innovations of .NET, such as source-level metadata, even after these have been successfully delivered in open source products.

❏ The assumption that "standard is always best" means that standard technologies are not always compared on their merits with competing solutions. For example, a proprietary product may do a better job of meeting a specific requirement, but the "standard" alternative is likely to be adopted for political reasons rather than technical merit. For example, I've seen many projects reluctantly switch to proprietary persistence solutions such as TopLink, after wasting significant effort and running into intractable problems with the EJB alternative, which is clearly inferior in a feature-for-feature comparison.

❏ Standards must consider all potential users and uses, meaning that they can be unduly complex for the requirements of the great majority. Commercial or open source products can target particular market segments and provide them with greater value.

❏ Standardization inevitably involves tradeoffs, meaning that it can amount to a lowest common denominator, leaving out essential features.

On the positive side, J2EE standardization has meant that:

❏ J2EE developers are freer from the risk of vendor lock that affects proprietary technologies. However, it is arguable that a good solution that is locked into one vendor is preferable to an inferior, portable solution. There's a tradeoff here: it's important to remember that the primary goal should be a good solution that meets requirements, not a portable solution that may not.

❑ Standardizing core concepts can create a large community, allowing rapid growth of knowledge and experience beyond that possible around a single product.

❑ In some cases, getting together leading organizations involved in the technology can produce a better result than any can alone. However, this doesn't usually happen in practice.

The balance between these issues means that different Java specifications have delivered varying value. The fundamental J2EE infrastructure, such as JTA, has succeeded in shielding developers behind a portable abstraction over difficult low-level code. But some of the higher-level constructs, directly used by application developers, such as EJB, have been less successful.

Today, developers seem to be increasingly wary of the dangers of over-emphasizing standards. For example, Jim Waldo, a Sun Distinguished Engineer, discusses some of the dangers in an article entitled "Why Standards?" (www.artima.com/weblogs/viewpost.jsp?thread=4840):

> Kowtowing to the god of standards is, I believe, doing great damage to our industry, or craft, and our science. It is stifling innovation. It turns technical discussions into political debates. It misunderstands the role that standards have played in the past. Worst of all, it is leading us down absurd technological paths in the quest to follow standards which have never been implemented and aren't the right thing for the problems at hand.

Waldo points up the difference between the formalization of existing *de facto* standards, and what he calls *de jure* standards, in which "a standards effort attempts to invent the standard from the ground up":

> Such a [de jure] standards effort is not descriptive, but rather an attempt to invent by committee. There is no common practice to describe; instead the standards group is trying to tell everyone what they should be doing in the future.

> Those of you who have been part of a *de jure* standard effort know what I mean when I say that they turn all technical questions into political ones. . . . What gets lost in all of this, of course, is whether the technology being blessed by the standard actually helps the customer to solve a real problem. Can the standard be implemented? Will the implementation perform adequately? How much will it cost? All of these sorts of questions are not appropriate in the era of de jure standards.

Author and experienced J2EE architect Stuart Charlton expresses similar views in an article entitled "Proprietary vs. Standard Solutions: Not Always a Clear Choice" (www.theserverside.com/resources/article.jsp?l=Charlton):

> I am continually disappointed by the attitude of some experts towards proprietary solutions vs. standard solutions in the J2EE industry. The general attitude seems to be: "standard approach always better, proprietary approach always bad".

> I find this attitude somewhat foolish and dangerous, for a variety of reasons. The primary reason is that taking a standards-based approach is useful only when the technical domain in question is mature and there is more benefit gained from standardization than from continued innovation. ...

> There is a tradeoff in choosing a proprietary solution over a standard one, and it is my belief that the pro-standards group often oversells the "standards-based" approach, particularly in areas that are technically complex and in need of continuing innovation. No one would question

that standards can be sources of tremendous value, particularly by refocusing R&D efforts on areas in greater need of innovation. But premature standards can cause tremendous strife in delivering quality software (as anyone who has used CMP 1.x can attest to).

Charlton's example of entity beans is particularly compelling. As an example of the danger of stifling innovation and the lowest common denominator, the EJB marketing juggernaut has crushed many promising technologies. For example, Apple WebObjects offered much more sophisticated O/R mapping than EJB 2.0, before EJB 1.0, with its primitive entity bean model, even appeared. Technical merit was not enough for WebObjects to compete with the far less functional—indeed, initially unusable—alternative from Sun.

An interesting example of official standardization ignoring good *de facto* standardization, and adding little value, is the introduction of the Java 1.4 logging API. Apache Log4j is significantly more functional, works brilliantly, and was already widely adopted in the Java community. It had already solved the problem of every application having its own logging infrastructure. Java 1.4 logging served largely to confuse the issue, and the majority of projects seem either to ignore it in favor of Log4j, or to use Jakarta Commons Logging to avoid committing to either solution.

To take another example, the Velocity template engine has had an uphill struggle competing with JSP, which benefits from the Sun imprimatur. Yet Velocity tends to be more performant and more intuitive than JSP. I've seen it lead to productivity and other benefits in several projects. Yet it's still a hard sell, given that JSP is the default choice because of its status as a "standard."

> **Standards have often benefited the industry. But they have sometimes stifled innovation, they have sometimes entrenched poor approaches, and they have caused many developers to suspend disbelief about the merits of the standardized solution. We should always match technologies to actual requirements. It's dangerous to regard the use of a proprietary solution as thought crime, and look only to standard solutions.**

I used to be a passionate supporter of Sun-sanctioned standardization. I have participated and continue to participate in it through the JCP, an experience I am unable to comment on here. But I'm beginning to wonder whether it's the best model for some parts of J2EE, or whether it's better for open source projects (or, potentially, commercial vendors) to take the lead, and for standardization to result from the survival of the fittest.

There are now practical examples of the idea of open source leading the way. Along with Log4j and Velocity, the Hibernate O/R mapping product has achieved remarkable mindshare and proven highly successful in practice. The EJB specification represents the "standards-first" approach; Hibernate represents an "experience-first" approach. In the case of Hibernate, successful commercial products had already developed the power of O/R mapping: Hibernate provided a good, clean-room implementation that has introduced some technical innovations along the way. Significantly, Hibernate benefited little, if at all, from previous standards-based solutions such as CMP or ODMG. Interestingly, the success and user adoption of Hibernate is now having a beneficial effect on JDO 2.0. Hibernate is likely to eventually implement the JDO specification, but some of the experience of its developers and users have helped to strengthen the JDO standard.

Open source solutions partly negate one of the strongest traditional arguments for standardization: the dreaded vendor lock-in. Open source technologies such as Hibernate or Spring do not lock their users into a particular application server or other commercial product. If an open source solution delivers real value right now, in the worst-case scenario, it's possible to maintain the code in-house if necessary. This worst case is unlikely with a wise choice of product. Even if it does occur, it's likely to be significantly less painful than encountering the end of life of a commercial, closed-source product.

Still more important in avoiding lock in, the most recent wave of successful open source products are much less *invasive* than EJB, meaning that application code written to use them has far fewer dependencies on framework APIs. For example, while moving from entity beans to another persistence technology requires major effort because of the heavy dependence of entity beans on the EJB API and the EJB-specific code required in session beans using entity beans, moving from Hibernate to another persistence technology is not so hard. Hibernate can persist POJOs with few, if any, dependencies on Hibernate. Migration isn't such a problem (especially if a DAO layer is used to abstract Hibernate-specific queries), because the same POJO domain objects can often be persisted with JDO or another technology without a rewrite. Similarly, most business objects in Spring applications are simply POJOs, configured by JavaBean setter methods or constructors, with no Spring dependencies. Migration from Spring to another IoC container—or even to no container at all—does not require the business objects to be rewritten. Thus *non-invasiveness*—one of the themes of Chapter 6—has important business, as well as technical, benefits.

Minimizing dependence on the runtime environment is at least as important as standardizing the runtime environment. In the case of POJOs persisted with Hibernate or JDO or POJO business objects used in Spring, the Java *language* is the standard.

> **The JCP remains important. But the JCP hasn't always worked, and where it hasn't produced great results it's important to retain an open mind about innovation outside the specification process. Where a standards-driven approach has failed to deliver shining results—EJB being an example—keep an open mind toward innovative "non-standard" solutions. In the case of open source, they do not incur unacceptable risk of vendor lock in: especially if they are non-invasive.**
>
> **As we've seen, orthodox wisdom on J2EE architecture is out of step with real-world experience. Some of the J2EE specifications are also, to a lesser extent. I feel that we're at an important crossroads in the evolution of the J2EE platform. It clearly needs to evolve and innovate to survive and prosper. Yet the specification of the fundamental enterprise infrastructure such as JTA, JAXP, JDBC and the Java language itself means that there's scope to innovate on how that infrastructure is accessed without destroying the benefits of a consistent, standard approach to the toughest, low-level problems of enterprise software.**

Open Source in Practice

I'm a recent convert to the benefits of open source. I don't wear a beard, I feel comfortable in a suit, and I believe that it's fine to make money by selling software. In short, I'm not Richard Stallman. If I could make as much money as BEA has done out of selling software, I would. My "conversion" to open source is not a matter of ideology. I'm interested in solving real problems, not overturning the software industry.

Well-run open source products such as Hibernate reflect similar pragmatism. They are not ideologically driven, but grow out of their developers' desire for a working solution to practical problems. Over time, great value can be added by responsiveness to the needs of users. It's an experience-driven approach.

The contrast between a specification-driven approach and an innovative, Darwinian, approach is somewhat like the contrast between a command economy (as in the Soviet bloc) and competitive capitalism. Competition may lead to its own problems, but it has proven to generate much faster progress. Like businesses in a market economy, open source products that don't provide real value die. This is not true for J2EE specifications, which are backed by Sun and application server vendors who don't want to rock the boat.

My own involvement in open source has also resulted from practical experience of the benefits it can bring, rather than ideological preference. When I published *Expert One-on-One J2EE Design and Development*, I knew that the code was valuable (I'd used the same concepts with excellent results in several commercial engagements), but didn't have any firm plans about how to move it ahead. In the next few months, I was approached by many readers who believed that it should be open-sourced to move forward.

This resulted in the Spring Framework project in early 2003. I've been very impressed by the experience. The contributors have been of a high quality; a significantly higher quality than most of those I've worked with in commercial engagements. Each is usually the best developer in his or her company. It's been easier to apply test first development than in commercial projects with entrenched bureaucracies: the result has been an impressive ability to respond to users' needs. I find the code base today—incorporating the contributions of many others besides myself—to be significantly more powerful and useful in my day-to-day work than anything I could have created alone. I and others have used it to significantly reduce the costs and increase quality on multiple commercial projects.

In short, Spring and its users have benefited greatly from this open source project. I developed the first version of the code in a commercial environment, and I have no doubt that Spring is of higher quality than it could have been as a closed source product.

> While an open (or at least partially open) specification process is positive, I think one of the biggest advantages of J2EE over .NET is the richness of Java/J2EE open source software.

Avoiding OSS Hell

One practical problem resulting from the flourishing competition in the world of open source J2EE is that finding out what's available and choosing between alternatives can become a time-consuming chore. You may end up building your own complex ecosystem of multiple solutions, each evolving through multiple versions. Although you can benefit greatly from the support of each community, you might find issues that fall down the gaps between different products. (This situation commonly arises with a commercial product stack, as well.)

It's important to adopt a strategy appropriate to your applications and organization to avoid problems.

First, you shouldn't need a vast array of products to meet your requirements. For example, the Spring Framework covers most parts of the infrastructure of typical J2EE applications.

Second, recognize that there is no solution that *won't* leave you dependent on open source solutions, or won't leave you needing to combine commercial solutions. EJB and J2EE as a whole do *not* solve the majority of common problems out of the box. The specifications leave many gaps that will force you to resort to open source or proprietary solutions or do proprietary in-house development even if you base your architecture on standards.

Third, don't think that developing infrastructure in-house is preferable to adopting open source solutions. The support issues are likely to be many times worse, and you also have the cost of all development and maintenance. Only if you have unusual requirements for which no existing solution is a good fit (an increasingly rare situation) is it appropriate to develop complex infrastructure in-house. Typically you can meet your unique requirements by using the extensibility allowed by good generic frameworks.

I recommend the following guidelines to avoid difficulties with integrating open source solutions:

❑ Minimize the number of products and technologies you use, whether they're open source projects or commercial. While every new product may solve a particular problem well, it complicates your overall technology mix for the life of your project. Look for products that add value across your project and use a consistent approach throughout.

❑ Try to combine open source products only if they're a familiar combination. For example, Spring/Hibernate is a common combination, as is Spring or WebWork with Velocity. Don't be a pioneer without good reason.

❑ Unless you absolutely need the latest features, upgrade your framework versions on *your* timetable, not the timetable of each project.

❑ Use well-documented frameworks, ensuring that you don't need deep knowledge of their internals to use them effectively and maintain your applications.

❑ Favor frameworks that minimize the dependencies of your code on the framework. This will avoid lock-in and minimize hassles when upgrading a framework version, as well as simplify testing.

❑ Don't view open source as a no-cost solution, but as a technical choice. (There *are* no no-cost solutions.) Consider purchasing commercial support for open source products critical to your project, especially if that support can ease your integration burden.

Of course you should consider the viability of each open source product you adopt, evaluating the number of developers, size of the user community, quality of documentation, number of open bugs and clear-up rate, and responsiveness in forums and mailing lists.

Summary

EJB provides many valuable services. However, it hasn't lived up to its early promise.

Experience has shown that some of the key goals of the EJB specification have not been met. To return to two cited at the opening of this chapter:

❑ The EJB specification does not "make it easy to write applications." EJB eliminates some complexity, while creating its own set of problems such as slow deployment test cycles.

❑ An Enterprise bean cannot normally be "developed once and then deployed on multiple platforms without recompilation or source code modification." EJB comes up short on portability, compared to other J2EE APIs such as the Servlet API. EJB applications are generally significantly less portable than J2EE applications that don't use EJB.

EJB has clearly failed in some areas:

- ❑ **Persistence.** The entity bean experiment for persistence is a definite failure. While it just about works in EJB 2.0 and 2.1, transparent persistence solutions such as Hibernate and JDO offer much greater productivity and better object orientation. And it is fair to classify entity beans as an "experiment." The idea of persistent distributed components didn't work with CORBA and was unproven when the EJB specification appeared. Local entity beans improve the situation, but still don't match the best alternative solutions.

- ❑ **Productivity.** EJB should have greatly enhanced productivity; in practice it adds many speed humps of its own.

- ❑ **Testability.** EJB applications are much harder to test than they should be because they are so tightly coupled to the EJB container.

EJB has done poorly in some other areas:

- ❑ Stateful session beans don't scale up very well, because of replication issues.

- ❑ Declarative role-based security isn't adequate for many tasks.

EJB has done well in some areas:

- ❑ Stateless session beans perform well and are highly scalable in a clustered environment.

- ❑ CMT declarative transaction management is deservedly popular and delivers real simplification.

- ❑ SLSBs with remote interfaces provide a very good solution for distributed applications built over RMI. However, this is a minority requirement. Experience has shown that we don't want to use a distributed architecture unless we are forced to by requirements. We can still service remote clients if necessary by implementing a remoting facade on top of a good co-located object model.

- ❑ EJB has provided a standard way to separate interface from implementation of business objects. This is valuable; however, there are many ways to achieve this with less effort.

The value of other EJB services varies between applications. For example:

- ❑ SLSB instance pooling is not the essential service it has traditionally been thought to be.

- ❑ The EJB threading model adds more complexity than value for many applications.

There are good alternatives to EJB that solve many of the problems solved by EJB.

There's a growing consensus in the J2EE community that the downsides of EJB outweigh its benefits, and make the search for "post-EJB" solutions an important priority.

2003 saw the emergence of viable "post-EJB" solutions that finally negate many of the previously valid arguments about the necessity of using EJB to access enterprise services. This chapter has surveyed some of these solutions, including:

- ❑ Third-party products such as Hibernate and JDO implementations, which solve persistence much better than the EJB solution

- ❑   Programmatic access to enterprise services using transaction abstraction APIs, which is sometimes simpler than a declarative approach for applications with simple transactional requirements

- ❑   Lightweight frameworks that provide sophisticated management of business-objects without the need for an EJB container

- ❑   AOP as a means of providing declarative enterprise services to POJOs

We've seen that J2EE standardization—at least, the more complex J2EE specifications such as EJB—is not a panacea. Often simpler open source solutions are a better fit for real-world problems. At a time when innovation is flowing in the J2EE community—based on disappointing practical experience with specification-driven solutions, that aren't always proven in actual applications—such solutions are particularly important.

It's important to evaluate alternative solutions, including EJB, on their merits to meet the requirements of each application. The old orthodoxy that EJB is the only alternative to anarchy and reinvention of the wheel is no longer sound.

In the remainder of this book, I'll move beyond EJB to replacing the most valuable EJB services by simpler, yet more flexible, technologies. For example, I'll discuss other ways to manage business objects as well as the use of AOP to deliver declarative transaction management.

6

Lightweight Containers and Inversion of Control

Applications need an infrastructural backbone. We can't responsibly dispense with EJB in medium to large-scale J2EE applications without providing an alternative way of managing business objects. Fortunately, good alternatives exist, and we'll discuss some in this chapter.

Management of business objects will typically involve some form of container. We can try to do without a container, and without an overall application framework, but this is unwise. It typically leads into a morass of an ad hoc mix of Singletons, custom-coded factories, and inconsistent handling of configuration. Some developers might use properties files to hold configuration; others might prefer XML documents or the database. It's likely to be hard to identify a clear service layer in the application, and the overall lack of consistency will prove costly in maintenance.

EJB brings some order in the face of this potential chaos, and if we want to do without EJB, we must provide order and structure in other ways. An EJB container provides a well-defined service layer (normally of SLSBs). It also provides a partial solution for managing business objects. We say "partial" because it leads to complication on the client side, as accessing EJBs is difficult and requires infrastructure itself; because EJB doesn't make it easy to externalize configuration data; and because an EJB container doesn't help to manage fine-grained objects such as DAOs. Even if we use EJB, we can benefit from consistent management of fine-grained objects within the EJB container and on the client side.

There are other types of containers besides EJB containers, and they're arguably better suited to the needs of typical applications. Fortunately, we don't need to write our own container. As usual, we should use pre-existing generic infrastructure, whether open source or commercial.

In this chapter, we'll look at the characteristics of "lightweight" containers, and why I recommend them for use in typical applications. A good lightweight container can bring welcome order and structure to your application, with little of the complexity of EJB.

We'll look at the Dependency Injection flavor of Inversion of Control for configuring managed objects: an approach in which the container takes responsibility for configuring application objects running within it, without the need for lookups in application code. Inversion of Control has important benefits for application code. Popular lightweight containers all offer some form of Inversion of Control.

We'll look at several open source Inversion of Control frameworks: notably, the Spring Framework and PicoContainer.

We'll look at how you can minimize the dependency of your application code on whatever lightweight container you choose, minimizing the risk of being locked in to a particular container. This is a realistic and important goal. As we'll see, Dependency Injection concepts are similar in most frameworks, and only implementation details differ.

We'll also look at how lightweight containers can be integrated with provision of enterprise services. While EJB integrates provision of enterprise services into the core component model, lightweight containers do not. This means that they can offer a simpler and potentially more object-oriented model than EJB, but that enterprise services must be delivered in other ways.

Lightweight Containers

What is a lightweight container, and why do we need one?

What Is a Lightweight Container?

I use *container* to mean a framework in which application code runs. Application objects—most often business objects—run inside the container, and are said to be managed by the container. There are many container architectures and models; EJB is traditionally the most popular in J2EE for managing business objects. A J2EE web container is an example of a specialized container for managing servlets and dependent objects.

Any container should provide a set of services including:

❑ **Lifecycle management:** The container should control the lifecycle of application objects running within it. At a minimum, this must mean that the container can abstract the creation of new objects from code using it. More sophisticated lifecycle management might include callbacks to alert managed objects of their activation in the container or the container's destruction.

❑ **Lookup:** The container should provide a way of obtaining references to managed objects. Lookup functionality abstracts calling code from the knowledge of implementation details, which is hidden inside the container. Lookup is a core service that means that a container is, at its heart, a factory.

❑ **Configuration:** The container should provide a consistent way of configuring objects running within it, to allow parameterization. Simple configuration values should be externalized from Java code, so that they can be changed without recompilation or the need to involve Java developers.

❑ **Dependency resolution:** As well as handling configuration via simple types likes Strings and ints, a container should be able to manage relationships between objects managed by the container.

I use the term "object" for an object running inside a container. However, managed objects are often termed "components": for example, EJBs are generally considered components (as well as objects). We discuss the debatable distinction between objects and components in Chapter5. An object managed by a container has some of the characteristics commonly associated with components: most important, the possibility of replacement with another object fulfilling the same contract. I use the term "object" regardless of granularity. The granularity of managed objects can depend on business requirements and overall architecture, not on any preconceived rules. Thus, managed objects can be coarse grained. The use of the term "object" also suggests that the desirability of running inside a container should not automatically lead to the sacrifice of the values of OO.

There are also some potential value-adds that a container may provide, possibly separately from its core model:

- ❑ **Enterprise services:** Providing transaction management or other declarative services to objects running in the container. These may be declarative.

- ❑ **Thread management:** A container may offer a threading model for access to managed objects.

- ❑ **Object pooling:** A container may provide instance pooling for managed objects.

- ❑ **Clustering:** A container may itself provide clustering support, in which clients can transparently communicate with peer containers, as with EJB clustering. Note that this is often unnecessary when using clustering support at whole application deployment level, in which all application components are deployed on each machine. Container-level clustering is necessary to support a stateful component model such as stateful session beans, but is less important when managed objects are stateless.

- ❑ **Management:** A container may provide management services for objects running within it, such as a management console or possibly management via JMX.

- ❑ **Remoting:** This can be divided into two services. Today there are multiple potential wire protocols, with no clear winner (although SOAP-based web services seem to be growing in popularity).

- ❑ **Exposing remote services:** Providing remote access to objects running in the container. This model is demonstrated by remote EJBs, an excellent remoting technology where RMI/IIOP is concerned.

- ❑ **Consuming remote services:** Providing transparent access to remote objects running outside the container.

- ❑ **Customization and extensibility:** Allowing custom services to be applied to objects running in the container: for example, custom declarative services such as special security checks.

I believe that the following features characterize a lightweight container:

- ❑ A container that can manage application code, but imposes no special dependencies on that code. For example, it should be possible to run legacy code inside a container without modification. We call this non-invasiveness; the infrastructure you use shouldn't impose invasive dependencies on your application code unless absolutely necessary. It should also be possible to run the same application objects both inside or outside a container; they shouldn't be container-specific.

- ❑ A container that is quick to start up.

- ❑ A container that doesn't require any special deployment steps to deploy objects within it.

❑ A container that has such a light footprint and minimal API dependencies that it can be run in a variety of environments, such as web container, standalone client, or even potentially an applet. A lightweight container should be pure Java, not J2EE-only .

❑ A container that sets the bar for adding a managed object so low in terms of deployment effort and performance overhead that it's possible to deploy and manage fine-grained objects, as well as coarse-grained components.

Many of the container services I've defined—especially the optional enterprise services—are reminiscent of the EJB model. Among other things, an EJB container amounts to a factory or registry, with JNDI as the lookup mechanism.

But a lightweight container is very different from EJB in practice. Examining the contrast with EJB is one of the best ways of understanding the characteristics of lightweight containers. An EJB container doesn't meet the criteria we've set out for lightweight containers for the following reasons, discussed in Chapter 5:

❑ Code written to the EJB model doesn't run without the EJB container.

❑ EJB containers are relatively slow to start up.

❑ EJB deployment is fairly onerous, involving multiple Java source files per EJB and possibly a predeployment code-generation and compilation step.

❑ Code is written to run in a single environment.

❑ EJBs are not suited to use as fine-grained objects.

An EJB container doesn't meet all the desirable criteria for a container, either. Specifically:

❑ **Dependency resolution.** An EJB container provides no support for managing relationships between EJBs running within it. It merely guarantees a JNDI context, and EJB code must use it to obtain other EJBs, just like any other code. Even configuration via simple properties is complex, with bean implementation code forced to use JNDI to look up "environment variables" defined in verbose XML deployment descriptors. Environment variables are untyped, requiring type casts in EJB code looking them up.

❑ **Consuming remote services.** An EJB container provides no support for consuming remote services, although it does provide excellent support for exposing remote services over RMI or SOAP.

❑ **Customization and extensibility.** The EJB specification provides no support for customizing services providing to components within the EJB container.

EJB scores well for enterprise services, but not so well as a container model. It's far from ideal. Given the negatives of EJB overall, it's reasonable to consider alternative container models to EJB.

Why Do We Need a Container at All?

In our quest for simplicity, why can't we just get rid of the notion of a container altogether?

There are a number of reasons that containers are important, and that dispensing with one is a step too far:

❑ **Pluggability.** A container allows pluggability of different components. For example, different EJB implementation classes may be used for the same component interface, isolating calling code from the implementation strategy. While Java interfaces provide perfect separation, there has to be some way of looking up what implementation of an interface we want to use. If it's hard-coded in Java code, much of the advantage of using interfaces is lost.

❑ **Consistency.** Without a container infrastructure, service lookup will be haphazard. Different service objects may be located differently, depending on developer preference. Configuration management will be equally haphazard, posing an ongoing maintenance challenge.

❑ **One stop shop.** It's necessary only to find the container to find all its services. There is no need for a dedicated Singleton or factory for every object.

❑ **Delivery of enterprise services.** A consistent approach makes it easier to deliver enterprise services as part of the container model or as an add-on.

> The iBATIS JPetStore, which we discuss in Chapter 3, illustrates typical consequences of doing without a container: in this case, loss of interface-implementation decoupling and hard-coding to a Singleton. In this simple application, the consequences are bearable. In larger applications, such issues become more problematic. My own work on what became the Spring Framework was prompted by repeatedly seeing these kind of problems in project after project, and seeing the value of the infrastructure I gradually developed to add more and more consistency in response to these problems. Without a container, you'll need to write more code, and your applications will be harder to maintain and manage. The greater simplicity of doing without an overall application framework is a dangerous mirage in all but trivial applications.

Lightweight Containers versus EJB

If we can choose between using a lightweight framework and an EJB container, why would we want to choose the lightweight container? Let's look at the pros and cons of lightweight containers versus EJB in typical applications.

Benefits of Lightweight Containers

Let's look at some of the benefits of a lightweight container:

❑ **Escaping the monolithic container.** EJB containers are heavyweight beasts. They're an all-or-nothing approach to an enterprise component model. If we can do without an EJB container to deliver enterprise services to typical web applications, for example, we can often achieve significant architectural simplification. We can also often make do without a high-end application server: not only a potential cost benefit, but also an ongoing benefit in terms of administration complexity. For example, even if we decide to stick with a commercial web container along with an open source lightweight container, we could consider something like WebLogic Express, which is much cheaper and simpler than the EJB-enabled version of WebLogic, yet still offers key J2EE services such as JTA.

❑ **Maximizing code reusability.** As we've noted, code written to the EJB API is only ever going to run in an EJB container. It can be unwise to make assumptions about where code will always run.

❑ **Greater object orientation.** EJBs are often not true objects, in that they are constrained by the characteristics of the EJB component model. For example, they are necessarily fairly coarse grained, even with local EJBs; this poses a restriction on practicing normal OO design. The EJB component model doesn't support inheritance, although EJB implementation classes can participate in inheritance hierarchies. We can often achieve greater object orientation with lightweight containers, which impose fewer constraints on objects.

❑ **Greater productivity.** With a lightweight container, application code can be closer to plain Java. It will have less dependence on heavyweight APIs and will be much easier to write and manipulate in any Java IDE. This will produce a significant productivity gain.

❑ **Better testability.** Testability will also be greatly improved, because of the ability to test objects outside any container: for example, in plain JUnit test cases.

Benefits of EJB

The strength of EJB is integrating enterprise services with the container model. This means that EJB is a single solution for managing business objects and providing managed objects with declarative middleware services. As we've noted, a lightweight container can still be important to complement EJB in areas where it's weak, such as managing fine-grained objects.

Other benefits of EJB are primarily political: for example, the fact that it has great (if slowing) momentum, that it's fairly well understood, and that the EJB market is relatively stable while the lightweight container landscape is still evolving. (However, the EJB 3.0 specification will bring major change.)

> **Think of a continuum of applications ranging from relatively typical web applications accessing a single database to highly transactional middleware-centric applications accessing multiple resources and possibly benefiting from internal distribution via RMI (an architectural choice that should never been taken lightly) and messaging. In general, EJB adds more complexity than value for such web applications, while lightweight containers work extremely well. On the other hand, EJB works pretty well for the latter type of applications. For applications in between, there is not necessarily any right or wrong answer. However, EJB should not be used without consideration of the alternatives and, in particular, the lightweight container option.**

Managing Business Objects

Let's look at some of the implications of managing business objects in lightweight containers rather than in EJB.

Interface-implementation Separation

EJB enforces a separation between interface (component interface or business methods interface) and implementation (bean implementation class). This is a good thing, as programming to interfaces rather than classes is a best practice with many beneficial consequences, such as "pluggability."

Most lightweight containers do not enforce such a separation. However, they do not preclude it, and usage recommendations for most lightweight frameworks encourage it. Plain Java interfaces provide as good a separation as do EJB component interfaces. (While remote EJB interfaces provide physical separation also, the cost of this is prohibitively high in most cases.)

Plain Java interfaces provide excellent decoupling within Java-technology applications. This should be an obvious point, but many architects seem to feel the need to make loose coupling much harder work. Decoupling via remoting is rarely desirable, because it adds so much complexity in many areas, and adds dangerous performance overhead. Decoupling via XML has even higher overheads and even greater complexity.

EJB: Only a Partial Solution

EJB alone isn't enough to manage business objects in any but simple applications. EJB does not deliver all the services we require from a container, because it deals only with coarse-grained objects. Any EJB—even a local EJB—is still a coarse-grained component. Coarse-grained components typically depend on multiple fine-grained components. For example, a typical coarse-grained business object might depend on a DAO and a helper class.

> The DAO pattern is a special case of the Strategy design pattern (GoF), in which a specific implementation "strategy" is refactored into an interface to allow it to be changed independently of the coarser-grained object. The Strategy pattern plays a big part in well-designed OO applications, so there's much value in making it as easy as possible to use.

As best practice suggests the use of POJOs behind an EJB facade to implement business logic, we need a way of managing such fine-grained objects, even if we do use EJB. Developers typically address this limitation of EJB in an ad hoc way, rolling their own infrastructure using Singletons or custom factories. A more consistent approach adds real value here. So a lightweight container can add value even if we use EJB. Spring addresses this through providing convenient superclasses for EJB implementation classes that create a Spring "bean factory" (lightweight container) populated from XML metadata packaged in the EJB Jar file.

> Although the performance penalty in making local EJBs fine-grained is modest, it's not a good idea from the point of view of manageability. Deployment descriptors quickly become enormous; there are three to four Java source files for each fine-grained object; testability is severely compromised; fine-grained objects cannot be used outside the EJB container; and code calling fine-grained objects needs to do JNDI lookups and go through an EJB home interface to obtain references to them.

Another area in which EJB needs to be supplemented from custom infrastructure to achieve best results is on the client side. The JNDI lookup process and indirection through a home interface makes using EJBs cumbersome, even from within the same JVM. A lightweight container can add much value here.

Inversion of Control

We've mentioned the desirability of avoiding application code depending on a container. But how can this be achieved? Only very simple objects work in isolation: Most business objects have dependencies, such as other business objects, data access objects, and resources. Surely, objects need to look up other managed objects and resources, and therefore must depend on a container that can satisfy such look ups?

Satisfying dependencies without introducing a dependency on a container can be achieved in most—if not all—cases by the magic of Inversion of Control and Dependency Injection.

Inversion of Control is an important concept in frameworks generally, and is best understood through the Hollywood Principle: "Don't call us, we'll call you." Throughout this chapter and the rest of the book, I'll use the common abbreviation *IoC*.

Dependency injection is more recently popularized type of IoC, which uses Inversion of Control to eliminate all lookup code, having the container automatically resolve dependencies expressed at language level.

IoC Implementation Strategies

IoC is a broad concept that can be implemented in different ways. There are two main types:

❑ **Dependency Lookup:** The container provides callbacks to components, and a lookup context. This is the EJB and Apache Avalon approach. It leaves the onus on each component to use container APIs to look up resources and collaborators. The Inversion of Control is limited to the container invoking callback methods that application code can use to obtain resources.

❑ **Dependency Injection:** Components do no look up; they provide plain Java methods enabling the container to resolve dependencies. The container is wholly responsible for wiring up components, passing resolved objects in to JavaBean properties or constructors. Use of JavaBean properties is called Setter Injection; use of constructor arguments is called Constructor Injection.

Figure 6-1 illustrates the different kinds of IoC.

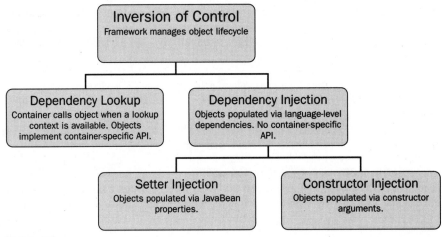

Figure 6-1

Dependency Lookup

EJB and some other J2EE APIs such as the servlet API provide the Dependency Lookup form of IoC. The container manages object lifecycle, while managed objects are responsible for doing their own lookups.

For example, if you are implementing EJBs without any framework beyond EJB, you'll need to use JNDI to look up other EJBs and resources. Consider a Java class designed to be used within the EJB tier. Let's assume that it's created by an EJB's `ejbCreate()` method, and has access to the JNDI environment. For performance and readability, you'll probably want to cache these resources, rather than look them up every time they're needed. So you might end up with a constructor implemented as in this object:

```java
public class MyBusinessObject implements MyBusinessInterface {

        private DataSource ds;

    private MyCollaborator myCollaborator;

    private int myIntValue;

    public MyBusinessObject() throws NamingException {
                    Context ctx = null;
        try {
            ctx = new InitialContext();
            ds = (DataSource) ctx.lookup("java:comp/env/dataSourceName");
                    myCollaborator = (MyCollaborator)
ctx.lookup("java:comp/env/myCollaboratorName");
                    myIntValue = ((Integer)
ctx.lookup("java:comp/env/myIntValueName")).intValue();
        }
        finally {
            try {
                if (ctx != null)
                    ctx.close();
            }
            catch (NamingException ex) {
                logger.warn("InitialContext threw exception on close", ex);
            }
        }
    }

    // Business methods
}
```

In theory, this looks like a good solution. JNDI decouples this object from the implementing `DataSource` and collaborator, and externalizes the value of the myIntValue primitive. We could use a different data source or alter the class implementing the `MyCollaborator` interface without changing Java code, so we have pluggability. The code is portable between application servers, as it uses standard J2EE APIs.

However, the following problems suggest that we can do better:

❑   The class won't run outside an application server environment, as it's dependent on JNDI. JNDI is harder to decouple from an application server than the `DataSource` dependency.

❑   What if we might like to use something other than JNDI to look up resources and collaborators? We'd have to re-factor the JNDI lookup code into a method that could be overridden, or a Strategy interface. There are benefits in externalizing the lookup strategy from the `MyBusinessObject` class altogether.

❑ This class is hard to test. We'll need to provide a dummy JNDI context to do effective unit testing. Implementing your own JNDI stubs is pretty nasty; you could use a pre-existing implementation such as the Spring Framework's `SimpleNamingContextBuilder`, but it's still harder than it should be.

❑ There's too much code. Whatever business logic this class exists to provide, it's a safe bet that it's nothing to do with JNDI. Classes should contain operations at a consistent level of abstraction. The low-level JNDI code in this class represents an intrusion. We could improve things by using a JNDI library to conceal nasty details such as the `try`/`finally` block, but that doesn't remove the basic responsibility for the application code to initiate lookup.

❑ It isn't strongly typed. We need type casts from `Object` in all cases. This is especially annoying with primitive types such as int, in which case we need to use the corresponding object wrapper.

❑ Calling code is complicated by the `NamingException` thrown by the constructor, so complexity cascades outward. As this object's initialization is unlikely to be able to recover from inability to lookup up its environment, such failures should really result in an unchecked exception that doesn't force application programmers to catch it.

We won't be able to use the class easily outside a container, even to test it. If it's implemented as an EJB, we won't be able to use the class outside an EJB container.

This is a business object. It should be responsible for implementing a piece of business logic, not dealing with the mechanics of JNDI.

Thus, while EJB has never been branded *Inversion of Control*, it's comparable to some products that have, such as Apache Avalon (`http://avalon.apache.org/`). Avalon provides a similar approach, with each managed object needing to use a registry such as the Avalon "ServiceManager" passed by the container to a lifecycle callback to look up dependencies. For example, we might resolve a DataSource dependency of an object in the service() method of the Avalon Serviceable interface like this:

```
public void service (ServiceManager sm) throws ServiceException {
    this.dataSource = (DataSource) sm.lookup("dataSource");
}
```

This is slightly preferable to the EJB approach, as it's much simpler to provide a test stub for the Service-Manager interface outside Avalon than to stub the EJB infrastructure, but it suffers from most of the same problems.

There are times when Dependency Lookup is necessary, which we'll discuss in a moment, so any sophisticated IoC container must support it. However, it has some significant disadvantages that mean that it's best avoided if possible.

Dependency Injection

The second IoC strategy—Dependency Injection—is usually preferable: Make the container wholly responsible for dependency lookup, and have the managed object expose JavaBean setter methods or constructor arguments to enable dependencies to be passed into it when the container is initialized. I term this *language-based IoC*, as it does not depend on special container APIs or interfaces.

With Dependency Injection, the IoC container does the plumbing. The container is responsible for looking up the resources, and will provide the necessary resources to the business object. The container can be reconfigured to use a different approach to obtaining the necessary resources without affecting application code.

> **The fundamental principle of Dependency Injection for configuration is that application objects should not be responsible for looking up the resources or collaborators they depend on. Instead, an IoC container should configure the objects, externalizing resource lookup from application code into the container.**

This offers the following advantages:

❑   Lookup is completely removed from application code.

❑   There's no dependence on a container API: We're dealing with Java-language concepts. In fact, it's not even Java-specific; it's a true pattern, which is also growing in popularity in .NET. Thus, it's easy to use application objects outside any container.

❑   No special interfaces are required.

This approach enables us to minimize dependency of application code on the lightweight container: indeed, to eliminate it for most objects.

The same approach can be applied for simple resources such as Strings and ints as for collaborators.

Setter Injection

With Setter Injection, components express dependencies on configuration values and collaborators via JavaBean properties. This builds on the JavaBeans convention. Like Dependency Injection in general, the concept is not Java-specific. Other languages support similar conventions to JavaBeans, such as C# properties.

> *The term Setter Injection (along with Dependency Injection) was coined as a result of discussions among Martin Fowler, me, Paul Hammant, and Aslak Hellesoy in January 2004. However, such use of JavaBean properties is not new. It has long been common in Java GUI development; it is used in the implementation of the Tomcat web container; and I discuss it at length in 2002 in* Expert One-on-One J2EE Design and Development.

Let's look at how our code example would look with Setter Injection:

```
public class MyBusinessObject implements MyBusinessInterface {

    private DataSource ds;

    private MyCollaborator myCollaborator;

    private int myIntValue;
```

```
        public void setDataSource(DataSource ds) {
        this.ds = ds;
    }

    public void setMyCollaborator(MyCollaborator myCollaborator) {
        this.myCollaborator = myCollaborator;
    }

    public void setMyIntValue(int myIntValue) {
        this.myIntValue = myIntValue;
        }

    // Business methods
}
```

The setter methods are invoked immediately after the object is instantiated by the container, before it handles any business methods. Thus, there are no threading issues relating to these properties.

The resource lookup and knowledge of and dependency on JNDI have disappeared. Instead, the dependencies are identified by being expressed in JavaBean properties. JavaBean properties are also used to externalize simple properties such as the int value. This simplifies the code and makes it reusable in a variety of environments. There's a dependence only on the resources and collaborators actually used to achieve the business logic. There's no longer any need for exception handling, as the container can handle configuration-time errors. This addresses all the limitations listed previously.

This is an ordinary Java class, with no dependency on IoC. It can be used in any environment, even without any container.

Constructor Injection

With Constructor Injection, components express dependencies via constructor arguments. This approach to Dependency Injection was invented by the PicoContainer team in mid 2003, and has since been implemented in Spring and other containers besides PicoContainer.

Let's look at how our code example might look with Constructor Injection:

```
public class MyBusinessObject implements MyBusinessInterface {

    private DataSource ds;

    private MyCollaborator myCollaborator;

    private int myIntValue;

    public MyBusinessObject(DataSource ds, MyCollaborator myCollaborator, int
myIntValue) {
                        this.ds = ds;
                        this.myCollaborator = myCollaborator;
                        this.myIntValue = myIntValue;
                }

    // Business methods
}
```

Again, this is a plain Java class: there's nothing specific to IoC or JNDI here.

Choosing between Setter and Constructor Injection

Both Setter and Constructor Injection offer a huge improvement on the traditional need for lookups in application code. Either way, the fundamental Dependency Injection concept is the same. So how do we choose between the two?

Advantages of Setter Injection include:

❑ JavaBean properties are well supported in IDEs.

❑ JavaBean properties are self-documenting.

❑ JavaBean properties are inherited by subclasses without the need for any code.

❑ It's possible to use the standard JavaBeans property-editor machinery for type conversions if necessary.

❑ Many existing JavaBeans can be used within a JavaBean-oriented IoC container without modification. For example, Spring users often use the Jakarta Commons DBCP DataSource. This can be managed via its JavaBean properties in a Spring container.

❑ If there is a corresponding getter for each setter (making the property readable, as well as writable), it is possible to ask the component for its current configuration state. This is particularly useful if we want to persist that state: for example, in an XML form or in a database. With Constructor Injection, there's no way to find the current state.

❑ Setter Injection works well for objects that have default values, meaning that not all properties need to be supplied at runtime.

Disadvantages include:

❑ The order in which setters are called is not expressed in any contract. Thus, we sometimes need to invoke a method after the last setter has been called to initialize the component. Spring provides the `org.springframework.beans.factory.InitializingBean` interface for this; it also provides the ability to invoke an arbitrary init method. However, this contract must be documented to ensure correct use outside a container.

❑ Not all the necessary setters may have been called before use. The object can thus be left partially configured.

Advantages of Constructor Injection include:

❑ Each managed object is guaranteed to be in a consistent state—fully configured—before it can be invoked in any business methods. This is the primary motivation of Constructor Injection. (However, it is possible to achieve the same result with JavaBeans via dependency checking, as Spring can optionally perform.) There's no need for initialization methods.

❑ There may be slightly less code than results from the use of multiple JavaBean methods, although will be no difference in complexity.

Disadvantages include:

❑ Although also a Java-language feature, multi-argument constructors are probably less common in existing code than use of JavaBean properties. Thus, a container that offered only Constructor Injection would be unable to run much valuable legacy code, such as the Commons DBCP connection pool.

❑ Java constructor arguments don't have names visible by introspection. This leaves us dependent on argument index, without a friendly name: a major problem if we have several dependencies of the same type. For example, properties readDataSource and writeDataSource are much more self-documenting in configuration than DataSource with index 0 and DataSource with index 1.

❑ Constructor argument lists are less well supported by IDEs than JavaBean setter methods.

❑ Long constructor argument lists and large constructor bodies can become unwieldy (the downside of concentrating configuration in one method).

❑ Concrete inheritance can become problematic, as constructors are not automatically inherited. Defining constructors that invoke the wrong superclass constructor is a common source of coding errors.

❑ Poor support for optional properties, compared to JavaBeans, which can have default values. In the absence of C++-style default argument lists, optional properties can be given default values only through multiple constructors, with constructors with fewer arguments invoking a constructor with the full argument list providing default values.

❑ Unit testing can be slightly more difficult, as all constructor arguments need to be provided, even those collaborators irrelevant to the particular test case. (Nevertheless, Constructor Injection, like Dependency Injection in general, is very test-friendly, overall.)

❑ When collaborators are passed in on object construction, it becomes impossible to change the reference held in the object. A JavaBeans approach can potentially support dynamic configuration, if a managed object is capable of accepting it; a constructor-based approach can't without changing the identity of the managed object.

I prefer Setter Injection in general. However, a good IoC container should let you, the application developer, choose your preferred flavor of Dependency Injection. You should be able to choose at a per-component level, rather than making an application-wide choice. In contrast to working with older container technologies such as EJB, you should be able to base your choice on Java style concerns, not on container requirements. For example, with or without IoC, I don't like constructors with many arguments.

Setter Injection is preferable when:

❑ An object has more than two or three parameters.

❑ An object has simple type dependencies as well as object dependencies.

❑ An object is likely to participate in a concrete inheritance hierarchy.

❑ An object has more than one dependency of the same type.

❑ An object must provide a means of modifying dependencies at runtime by invoking setters. (This works only if the object is threadsafe.)

Constructor Injection may be preferable for simple objects with only one or two object dependencies, and no simple type dependencies. I often find that in the course of re-factoring I switch objects from using Constructor Injection to Setter Injection.

When Can't We Use Dependency Injection?

While an IoC container can usually resolve all dependencies at configuration time and make collaborators available at runtime via JavaBean properties or constructors, there are some times when this is problematic, and when Dependency Injection can't provide a complete solution. For example:

❑ What if we can't save a simple instance variable for a collaborator or a resource, because we need to work with a different object each time? This might arise because the collaborator isn't thread-safe. The Spring Framework uses AOP to provide a solution where the reference can be an AOP proxy, with creation of a new object with each invocation hidden inside the framework. However, making this behavior explicit may be worth incurring a dependency on the container.

❑ What if the component should be configured differently depending on its context? For example, what if the availability of a SuperFooBar collaborator means that we don't want to fallback on an ordinary FooBar? Conditional configuration logic may require special code in a lifecycle method. This introduces a dependency on the container. It's best to avoid this situation if possible.

❑ What if we need access to container services at runtime? If we want to use the container, rather than merely run within in, that justifies dependence on it.

❑ In some cases it's not attractive to fix all the potential collaborator interfaces up front: for example, if there are lots of them.

Nevertheless, in my experience, most application objects won't need to depend on the container. In our JPetStore sample application, for example, there are no Spring IoC container dependencies or IoC-related imports in Java code.

While it's good to avoid container dependencies if possible, not all container dependencies are as painful as those on an EJB container. For example, a mock implementation of the Spring BeanFactory or Application-Context interface is much easier to set up in a test case than the whole EJB, JNDI, and home interface infrastructure.

IoC Containers

Let's now look at some available IoC containers.

The Spring Framework

The Spring Framework offers sophisticated support for both Setter Dependency Injection and Constructor Dependency Injection.

Just about any Java object can be used in a Spring container. The class must be configurable via JavaBean properties or constructor arguments if it is to benefit from the full power of IoC. (Some classes may require no properties.)

A good IoC citizen will not use its own ad hoc lookup—although of course, it will still work in an IoC environment. Some legacy classes may load their configuration independently, but this dilutes the consistency that IoC aims to provide.

Spring IoC is normally configured using metadata, although it does not mandate any particular metadata representation. It's possible to implement a Spring BeanDefinitionReader that uses a custom representation, and to use it to configure any Spring IoC container. However, users most often use an XML representation, which could be used to configure the JavaBean implementation of MyBusinessObject as follows:

```
<bean id="exampleBusinessObject"
        class="example.MyBusinessObject">
    <property name="dataSource"><ref bean="dataSource"/></property>
    <property name="myCollaborator"><ref bean="myCollaborator"/></property>
    <property name="myIntValue"><value>10</value></property>
</bean>
```

This format should be intuitive. Note how the `<property>` element is used to set JavaBean property values. The `<value>` subelement is used to set String or primitive properties, or any type for which a JavaBeans PropertyEditor is available. The `<ref>` subelement is used to resolve dependencies to other beans in the same or related containers. This enables strong typing in Java code. The preceding XML stanza relies on a bean with id "dataSource" being defined in the same or a related container.

Of course, the Spring XML representation has many features not shown in this simple example:

❑ **Dependency checking:** Spring can check that all JavaBean properties have been populated. Separate checks are possible for object dependencies and simple properties.

❑ **"Autowiring":** Spring can automatically satisfy dependencies expressed in JavaBean properties to objects of the appropriate type in the current factory. Note that this works only if there is one object of the appropriate type.

❑ **Support for collections:** Spring can automatically populate lists, maps, and other core Java collections from an XML representation defined in the Spring beans DTD. Arbitrary nesting of these types is possible, such as a map that contains list values. Collection values can be simple types or references to other objects in the same IoC container.

❑ **Ability to specify an "init" or/and "destroy" method:** This is valuable when using existing objects in a Spring container. If it's not sufficient just to populate their JavaBean properties, but it's necessary to invoke an initialization or shutdown method, the name of that method can be specified in the XML document, meaning that there's no need to subclass the object to implement Spring lifecycle interfaces. Init or destroy methods must take no arguments. Fortunately this is not really a restriction in practice, as classes designed as JavaBeans will normally have all their configuration data available already, and hence won't need more configuration arguments passed into an initialization method.

Spring also defines optional callback methods to enable callback-based Dependency Lookup IoC. At the price of introducing a dependency on the Spring API, managed objects can receive callback methods that enable them to lookup other objects, perform additional initialization, or release resources on container shutdown.

In J2EE applications, a Spring container is normally associated with a J2EE-defined context such as a ServletContext or EJB, meaning that the Singleton pattern (or antipattern) need not be used; it's possible to piggyback on the lifecycle management provided by the J2EE container.

Spring containers are hierarchical. Bean definitions in leaf containers can override those "inherited" from ancestor containers. It's also possible to pull in bean definitions from external documents. This is a powerful way of making applications modular. For example, top-level containers can share common definitions between leaf containers that have their own, private configuration state.

The Spring container infrastructure is not dependent on AOP, but can closely integrate with the Spring AOP framework to deliver declarative enterprise services.

In Chapter 7, we'll look at the Spring container infrastructure in detail.

PicoContainer

Another popular Dependency Injection implementation is PicoContainer (`www.picocontainer.org`): an extremely lightweight container, emphasizing Constructor Injection (which it pioneered).

PicoContainer differs from Spring in that it does not emphasize external configuration such as XML to wire up dependencies. Instead, PicoContainer resolves dependencies based on constructors defined on managed objects. It is also possible for PicoContainer to use Setter Injection, although there is less extensive support than in Spring.

The process of adding an object to a PicoContainer is performed in Java code, and causes PicoContainer to resolve dependencies on other objects running in the same container. Dependencies are identified by type, as in Spring autowiring, which was partly inspired by the PicoContainer approach. Thus, a Pico-Container can manage only one object of each type, unless metadata is provided (in which case the configuration required is similar to Spring configuration).

Rather than a complete application framework such as Spring, PicoContainer is intended more as an IoC container building block for larger frameworks. As metadata is required in many real applications, higher-level layers over PicoContainer, such as NanoContainer (`www.nanocontainer.org`) provide this. The PicoExtras sister project includes an integration with Nanning to complement IoC with AOP. Please refer to the PicoContainer website for up-to-date information on related projects.

Like Spring containers, PicoContainers are hierarchical.

PicoContainer provides simple lifecycle management (start/stop) for managed objects.

Although container configuration is quite different, there need be little (if any) difference between objects written to run in Spring and PicoContainer.

Portability between IoC Containers

The IoC container market is evolving; a number of other lightweight IoC containers are in development. Most focus on Dependency Injection.

You might be worrying at this point about the apparent fragmentation of the IoC market. Are we asking you to replace EJB—a standard, albeit one that doesn't deliver total portability—with one of a host of competing solutions? Is there a risk that you'll pick the wrong solution and end up with a legacy infrastructure?

Fortunately, this is where the non-invasiveness of IoC comes to the fore. It is possible to use the same code with no—or minimal—change in different IoC containers.

> **With Dependency Injection, dependence of application code on container is minimized—indeed, often wholly eliminated. This in turn minimizes the likelihood of lock-in to a particular IoC container.**

Although so far we've focused on the available IoC implementations, portability of components between containers is really about you. You can write your application code for maximum portability. I recommend the following guidelines:

❏ Minimize the dependencies of your code on the container. For example, if you have the choice of doing a lookup or relying on Dependency Injection, use Dependency Injection.

❏ Favor declarative enterprise services over programmatic services if service access introduces a dependency on the container.

If you follow these guidelines, you should be able to migrate components between containers if necessary without significant code changes. (Of course you'll need to migrate configuration, but a good IoC container should minimize the amount of configuration you need, so this shouldn't be too complex.) Still more important, the bulk of your code will be insulated from enhancements to the container. Traditional invasive component models can require major code change on upgrades.

> **Because non-invasiveness is such an important virtue, don't fritter it away by layering your own invasive framework over an IoC container. And—if you must design an in-house framework—ensure that it's as non-invasive as possible. Tight dependencies on any framework are dangerous, even on your own framework. For example, it becomes difficult to enhance the framework without breaking applications built on it; it is difficult to test code with heavy dependencies, as we've noted; and it reduces the potential for code reuse. Fortunately, with appropriate design it's nearly always possible to avoid invasiveness.**

Implications for Coding Style, Testing, and Development Process

Using a lightweight IoC container doesn't impose invasive dependencies on your code, but it does encourage certain coding practices. Fortunately, this largely amounts to fostering good practice.

Coding Style

You won't be forced to adopt any particular coding style. However, you should:

❑ Code to interfaces rather than classes to maximize the benefits of pluggability. Using a lightweight container should reduce the cost of doing this almost to zero. You'll need only the interface and an implementing class, not multiple classes as with EJB.

❑ Ensure that each business object has a clear set of responsibilities, using collaborators to handle distinct responsibilities. If you use a God object, you'll waste the ability to manage fine-grained collaborators.

❑ Favor the Strategy design pattern over concrete inheritance. This is really a special case of "favoring delegation over inheritance," a good practice recommended in the classic "Gang of Four" design patterns text. Again, using a lightweight container can make good practice very easy, as dependencies on strategy classes can be managed by the container.

❑ Avoid writing code to do anything that can be deferred to a container, such as JNDI lookup. This will simplify your code and improve testability.

Chapter 4 of *Expert One-on-One J2EE Design and Development* discusses these and other coding practices for J2EE applications, which help to maximize the benefit of running your code in a lightweight container.

Testability

If you follow the preceding recommendations, you'll miraculously find yourself with code that's easy to unit test. Indeed, you'll be able to practice test-driven development.

Dependencies on collaborators will be expressed through interfaces and will hence be easy to mock. Application code will have minimal dependencies on a container, meaning that simple JUnit test cases will be all you need to exercise it.

Development Process

Because you won't need to deploy code to an application server to test your code, your code-test cycles will be much shorter, increasing productivity. Because your application objects will be ordinary Java classes, rather than EJBs, you'll be able to enjoy the full re-factoring power of modern IDEs.

You may also be able to do some integration testing outside an application server. Because the startup cost of a lightweight container is negligible, you may be able to instantiate one, configuring your application objects, in a JUnit test case. Many Spring users do this successfully.

Applying Enterprise Services

The fundamental approach of EJB is to combine the component model with enterprise services, delivered declaratively to EJBs or available programmatically.

This all-in-one approach has several advantages:

❑ It makes EJB a fairly complete solution for enterprise middleware. I use the qualification "fairly" because the programming restrictions on EJB make some things quite hard to do within the EJB model.

❑ Developers need to learn only EJB to understand how to apply commonly used services. There's no need to integrate with other products besides the EJB container to enjoy declarative transaction management, for example.

❑ All J2EE-compliant application servers must deliver enterprise services to EJBs in the same way.

However, the all-in-one approach has disadvantages which suggest that it is not the ideal way to address enterprise services:

❑ It complicates the component model, and is one reason that EJBs are harder to develop and work with than POJOs. It's also a reason that EJBs aren't really objects. There is real benefit in keeping the object model separate from service provision. The quality of the object model is crucial to an application's success.

❑ It's not extensible. The EJB service menu is fixed. The EJB specification provides no way to enable consistent declarative delivery of custom services.

❑ We can't choose how many of the EJB services we want to use. We incur the same development overhead and ongoing cost if we merely want declarative transaction management when accessing a single database using JDBC as if we are using EJB security and remoting and accessing multiple transactional resources using XA transactions.

❑ Similarly, even when we have modest requirements for enterprise services, we need a full-blown EJB container to deliver them using the EJB model.

❑ If we don't like the way in which EJB delivers a particular service, we can't easily customize it. For example, EJB provides no help in enforcing custom security restrictions, which are often required in real applications.

It's partly to escape the all-on-one model that it's now widely considered a best practice to factor business logic out of EJBs and into POJOs behind an EJB facade.

Thus, there's a strong argument that enterprise services should be externalized from the model provided by a lightweight container. Enterprise services can be delivered in two ways:

❑ Programmatically, via APIs that are provided along with the container, or with additional products.

❑ Declaratively via AOP. We'll discuss this important option in depth in Chapter 8.

In either case, the services will usually be provided by standard J2EE, such as JTA. We're talking about accessing services, rather than reinventing low-level service implementations, which J2EE handles very well.

The advantage of splitting the provision of enterprise services from the core container model is that that model can then be simpler and more object-oriented. The disadvantage is that you may need to combine two or more products—a lightweight container and an enterprise services framework—to achieve a comparable (if arguably superior) result to using EJB.

Thus, it's an advantage if a lightweight container is closely integrated with the provision of enterprise services. The Spring Framework meets this criterion, providing simple access to both programmatic and declarative enterprise services as a closely integrated—but not inherent—part of its lightweight container. This is one of Spring's major strengths, and a key reason for its popularity.

Summary

In this chapter, we've looked at how lightweight containers can be a better alternative to EJB for many applications. The key characteristics of a lightweight container are:

- ❑ Non-invasiveness: imposing minimal special requirements on application objects run within it
- ❑ Quick start up
- ❑ Lack of any special deployment steps
- ❑ Light footprint, enabling it to run in any architectural tier
- ❑ Ability to manage objects of any granularity, including fine-grained objects that cannot be modeled as EJBs

Non-invasiveness is one of the most important benefits of lightweight containers. By minimizing the dependency of application code on the container, we can improve productivity, maximize the opportunity for code reuse, and improve testability.

Non-invasiveness is typically delivered via configuration through Inversion of Control: specifically, the Dependency Injection pattern. An IoC container takes care of plumbing, leaving application developers to concentrate on business logic. This can finally deliver on the initial promise of the J2EE platform, which has been obscured by the complexity of the EJB component model and many J2EE APIs.

> **Lightweight Inversion of Control containers have huge benefits for implementing J2EE applications. I believe that Inversion of Control, along with AOP, provides the basis for next-generation J2EE architectures.**

We've surveyed some popular IoC containers: notably, Spring and PicoContainer. We've seen how it is possible to write application code that can run with minimal change in any IoC container. We've also looked at how to write code to maximize the benefits offered by lightweight IoC containers, and how lightweight container architectures foster good practice such as coding to interfaces rather than classes.

In Chapter 7, we'll look in more detail at the Spring Framework. We'll see how its lightweight container is integrated with abstractions simplifying the use of enterprise APIs, and declarative enterprise services delivered by AOP.

7

Introducing
the Spring Framework

I've already mentioned the Spring Framework: a popular open source application framework that addresses many of the issues outlined in this book. (Indeed, we have contributed to Spring hand-in-hand with our work on this book.) This chapter will introduce the basic ideas of Spring and discuss the central "bean factory" lightweight Inversion-of-Control (IoC) container in detail.

This isn't a "Spring book." "J2EE without EJB" amounts to a *movement*, based on wide-spread experience, rather than a particular book or a popular application framework. Most of our architectural recommendations can be applied using a combination of other frameworks, or through custom coding.

However, Spring makes it particularly easy to implement lightweight, yet extensible, J2EE architectures. It provides an out-of-the-box implementation of the fundamental architectural building blocks we recommend. Spring provides a consistent way of structuring your applications, and provides numerous middle tier features that can make J2EE development significantly easier and more flexible than in traditional approaches.

The following discussion can be considered as a case study in the design of a lightweight container, as well as an introduction to Spring.

History and Motivation

An open source project since February 2003, Spring has a long heritage. The open source project started from the infrastructure code I published with *Expert One-on-One J2EE Design and Development* in late 2002. This code was designed for use in real applications, rather than merely for demonstration purposes. *Expert One-on-One J2EE* also laid out the basic architectural thinking behind Spring, which has provided a strong conceptual basis for ongoing development. The central architectural concepts date back to early 2000, and reflect experience in developing infrastructure for a series of successful commercial projects. Their consistent use across all areas ensures that Spring is particularly well integrated for a relatively ambitious framework.

The basic motivations for Spring are:

❑ **To address areas not well served by other frameworks.** There are numerous good solutions to specific areas of J2EE infrastructure: web frameworks, persistence solutions, remoting tools, and so on. However, integrating these tools into a comprehensive architecture can involve significant effort, and can become a burden. Spring aims to provide an end-to-end solution, integrating specialized frameworks into a coherent overall infrastructure. Spring also addresses some areas that other frameworks don't. For example, few frameworks address generic transaction management, data access object implementation, and gluing all those things together into an application, while still allowing for best-of-breed choice in each area. Hence we term Spring an *application framework*, rather than a web framework, IoC or AOP framework, or even middle tier framework.

❑ **To allow for easy adoption.** A framework should be cleanly layered, allowing the use of individual features without imposing a whole world view on the application. Many Spring features, such as the JDBC abstraction layer or Hibernate integration, can be used in a library style or as part of the Spring end-to-end solution.

❑ **To deliver ease of use.** As we've noted, J2EE out of the box is relatively hard to use to solve many common problems. A good infrastructure framework should make simple tasks simple to achieve, without forcing tradeoffs for future complex requirements (like distributed transactions) on the application developer. It should allow developers to leverage J2EE services such as JTA where appropriate, but to avoid dependence on them in cases when they are unnecessarily complex.

❑ **To make it easier to apply best practices.** Spring aims to reduce the cost of adhering to best practices such as programming to interfaces, rather than classes, almost to zero. However, it leaves the choice of architectural style to the developer.

❑ **Non-invasiveness.** Application objects should have minimal dependence on the framework. If leveraging a specific Spring feature, an object should depend only on that particular feature, whether by implementing a callback interface or using the framework as a class library. IoC and AOP are the key enabling technologies for avoiding framework dependence.

❑ **Consistent configuration.** A good infrastructure framework should keep application configuration flexible and consistent, avoiding the need for custom singletons and factories. A single style should be applicable to all configuration needs, from the middle tier to web controllers.

❑ **Ease of testing.** Testing either whole applications or individual application classes in unit tests should be as easy as possible. Replacing resources or application objects with mock objects should be straightforward.

❑ **To allow for extensibility.** Because Spring is itself based on interfaces, rather than classes, it is easy to extend or customize it. Many Spring components use strategy interfaces, allowing easy customization.

A Layered Application Framework

Chapter 6 introduced the Spring Framework as a **lightweight container**, competing with IoC containers such as **PicoContainer**. While the Spring lightweight container for JavaBeans is a core concept, this is just the foundation for a solution for all middleware layers.

Basic Building Blocks

Spring is a full-featured application framework that can be leveraged at many levels. It consists of multiple sub-frameworks that are fairly independent but still integrate closely into a one-stop shop, if desired. The key areas are:

❑ **Bean factory.** The Spring lightweight IoC container, capable of configuring and wiring up Java-Beans and most plain Java objects, removing the need for custom singletons and ad hoc configuration. Various out-of-the-box implementations include an XML-based bean factory. The lightweight IoC container and its **Dependency Injection** capabilities will be the main focus of this chapter.

❑ **Application context.** A Spring application context extends the bean factory concept by adding support for message sources and resource loading, and providing hooks into existing environments. Various out-of-the-box implementations include standalone application contexts and an XML-based web application context.

❑ **AOP framework.** The Spring AOP framework provides AOP support for method interception on any class managed by a Spring lightweight container. It supports easy proxying of beans in a bean factory, seamlessly weaving in interceptors and other advice at runtime. Chapter 8 discusses the Spring AOP framework in detail. The main use of the Spring AOP framework is to provide declarative enterprise services for POJOs.

❑ **Auto-proxying.** Spring provides a higher level of abstraction over the AOP framework and low-level services, which offers similar ease-of-use to .NET within a J2EE context. In particular, the provision of declarative enterprise services can be driven by source-level metadata.

❑ **Transaction management.** Spring provides a generic transaction management infrastructure, with pluggable **transaction strategies** (such as JTA and JDBC) and various means for demarcating transactions in applications. Chapter 9 discusses its rationale and the power and flexibility that it offers.

❑ **DAO abstraction.** Spring defines a set of generic data access exceptions that can be used for creating generic DAO interfaces that throw meaningful exceptions independent of the underlying persistence mechanism. Chapter 10 illustrates the Spring support for DAOs in more detail, examining JDBC, JDO, and Hibernate as implementation strategies.

❑ **JDBC support.** Spring offers two levels of JDBC abstraction that significantly ease the effort of writing JDBC-based DAOs: the `org.springframework.jdbc.core` package (a template/callback approach) and the `org.springframework.jdbc.object` package (modeling RDBMS operations as reusable objects). Using the Spring JDBC packages can deliver much greater productivity and eliminate the potential for common errors such as leaked connections, compared with direct use of JDBC. The Spring JDBC abstraction integrates with the transaction and DAO abstractions.

❑ **Integration with O/R mapping tools.** Spring provides support classes for O/R Mapping tools like **Hibernate, JDO,** and **iBATIS Database Layer** to simplify resource setup, acquisition, and release, and to integrate with the overall transaction and DAO abstractions. These integration packages allow applications to dispense with custom ThreadLocal sessions and native transaction handling, regardless of the underlying O/R mapping approach they work with.

❑ **Web MVC framework.** Spring provides a clean implementation of web MVC, consistent with the JavaBean configuration approach. The Spring web framework enables web controllers to be configured within an IoC container, eliminating the need to write any custom code to access business layer services. It provides a generic **DispatcherServlet** and out-of-the-box controller classes for command and form handling. Request-to-controller mapping, view resolution, locale resolution and other important services are all pluggable, making the framework highly extensible. The web framework is designed to work not only with JSP, but with any view technology, such as Velocity—without the need for additional bridges. Chapter 13 discusses web tier design and the Spring web MVC framework in detail.

❑ **Remoting support.** Spring provides a thin abstraction layer for accessing remote services without hard-coded lookups, and for exposing Spring-managed application beans as remote services. Out-of-the-box support is included for **RMI**, Caucho's **Hessian** and **Burlap** web service protocols, and WSDL Web Services via **JAX-RPC.** Chapter 11 discusses lightweight remoting.

While Spring addresses areas as diverse as transaction management and web MVC, it uses a consistent approach everywhere. Once you have learned the basic configuration style, you will be able to apply it in many areas. Resources, middle tier objects, and web components are all set up using the same bean configuration mechanism. You can combine your entire configuration in one single bean definition file or split it by application modules or layers; the choice is up to you as the application developer. There is no need for diverse configuration files in a variety of formats, spread out across the application.

Spring on J2EE

Although many parts of Spring can be used in any kind of Java environment, it is **primarily a J2EE application framework**. For example, there are convenience classes for linking JNDI resources into a bean factory, such as JDBC DataSources and EJBs, and integration with JTA for distributed transaction management. In most cases, application objects do not need to work with J2EE APIs directly, improving reusability and meaning that there is no need to write verbose, hard-to-test, JNDI lookups.

Thus Spring allows application code to **seamlessly integrate** into a J2EE environment **without being unnecessarily tied** to it. You can build upon J2EE services where it makes sense for your application, and choose lighter-weight solutions if there are no complex requirements. For example, you need to use JTA as transaction strategy only if you face distributed transaction requirements. For a single database, there are alternative strategies that do not depend on a J2EE container. Switching between those transaction strategies is merely a matter of configuration; Spring's consistent abstraction avoids any need to change application code.

Spring offers **support for accessing EJBs**. This is an important feature (and relevant even in a book on "J2EE without EJB") because the use of dynamic proxies as codeless client-side business delegates means that Spring can make using a local stateless session EJB an *implementation*-level, rather than a fundamental *architectural,* choice. Thus if you want to use EJB, you can within a consistent architecture; however, you do not need to make EJB the cornerstone of your architecture. This Spring feature can make developing EJB applications significantly faster, because there is no need to write custom code in service locators or business delegates. Testing EJB client code is also much easier, because it only depends on the EJB's **Business Methods** interface (which is not EJB-specific), not on JNDI or the EJB API.

Spring also provides **support for implementing EJBs**, in the form of convenience superclasses for EJB implementation classes, which load a Spring lightweight container based on an environment variable specified in the `ejb-jar.xml` deployment descriptor. This is a powerful and convenient way of implementing SLSBs or MDBs that are facades for fine-grained POJOs: a best practice if you do choose to implement an EJB application. Using this Spring feature does not conflict with EJB in any way—it merely simplifies following good practice.

The main aim of Spring is to make J2EE easier to use and promote good programming practice. It does not reinvent the wheel; thus you'll find no logging packages in Spring, no connection pools, no distributed transaction coordinator. All these features are provided by other open source projects—such as **Jakarta Commons Logging** (which Spring uses for all its log output), **Jakarta Commons DBCP** (which can be used as local DataSource), and **ObjectWeb JOTM** (which can be used as transaction manager)—or by your J2EE application server. For the same reason, Spring doesn't provide an O/R mapping layer: There are good solutions for this problem area, such as **Hibernate** and **JDO**.

Spring *does* aim to make **existing technologies easier to use**. For example, although Spring is not in the business of low-level transaction coordination, it does provide an abstraction layer over JTA or any other transaction strategy. Spring is also popular as middle tier infrastructure for Hibernate, because it provides solutions to many common issues like `SessionFactory` setup, ThreadLocal sessions, and exception handling. With the Spring `HibernateTemplate` class, implementation methods of Hibernate DAOs can be reduced to one-liners while properly participating in transactions.

> The Spring Framework does *not* aim to *replace* J2EE middle tier services as a whole. It is an application framework that makes accessing low-level J2EE container services *easier*. Furthermore, it offers lightweight alternatives for certain J2EE services in some scenarios, such as a JDBC-based transaction strategy instead of JTA when just working with a single database. Essentially, Spring enables you to write applications that scale *down* as well as *up*.

Spring for Web Applications

A typical usage of Spring in a J2EE environment is to serve as backbone for the logical middle tier of a J2EE web application. Spring provides a **web application context** concept, a powerful lightweight IoC container that seamlessly adapts to a web environment: It can be accessed from any kind of web tier, whether Struts, WebWork, Tapestry, JSF, Spring web MVC, or a custom solution.

The following code shows a typical example of such a web application context. In a typical Spring web app, an `applicationContext.xml` file will reside in the WEB-INF directory, containing bean definitions according to the "spring-beans" DTD. In such a bean definition XML file, business objects and resources are defined, for example, a "myDataSource" bean, a "myInventoryManager" bean, and a "myProductManager" bean. Spring takes care of their configuration, their wiring up, and their lifecycle.

```
<beans>

  <bean id="myDataSource"
      class="org.springframework.jdbc.datasource.DriverManagerDataSource">
    <property name="driverClassName">
      <value>com.mysql.jdbc.Driver</value>
    </property>
    <property name="url">
      <value>jdbc:mysql:myds</value>
    </property>
  </bean>
```

```
<bean id="myInventoryManager" class="ebusiness.DefaultInventoryManager">
  <property name="dataSource">
    <ref bean="myDataSource"/>
  </property>
</bean>

<bean id="myProductManager" class="ebusiness.DefaultProductManager">
  <property name="inventoryManager">
    <ref bean="myInventoryManager"/>
  </property>
  <property name="retrieveCurrentStock">
    <value>true</value>
  </property>
</bean>

</beans>
```

By default, all such beans have "singleton" scope: one instance per context. The "myInventoryManager" bean will automatically be wired up with the defined DataSource, while "myProductManager" will in turn receive a reference to the "myInventoryManager" bean. Those objects (traditionally called "beans" in Spring terminology) need to expose only the corresponding bean properties or constructor arguments (as you'll see later in this chapter); they do not have to perform any custom lookups.

A root web application context will be loaded by a **ContextLoaderListener** that is defined in web.xml as follows:

```
<web-app>

  <listener>
    <listener-class>
      org.springframework.web.context.ContextLoaderListener
    </listener-class>
  </listener>

  ...
</web-app>
```

After initialization of the web app, the root web application context will be available as a ServletContext attribute to the whole web application, in the usual manner. It can be retrieved from there easily via fetching the corresponding attribute, or via a convenience method in org.springframework.web. context.support.WebApplicationContextUtils. This means that the application context will be available in any web resource with access to the ServletContext, like a Servlet, Filter, JSP, or Struts Action, as follows:

```
WebApplicationContext wac =
    WebApplicationContextUtils.getWebApplicationContext(servletContext);
```

The Spring web MVC framework allows web controllers to be defined as JavaBeans in child application contexts, one per dispatcher servlet. Such controllers can express dependencies on beans in the root application context via simple bean references. Therefore, typical Spring web MVC applications never need to perform a manual lookup of an application context or bean factory, or do any other form of lookup.

Neither do other client objects that are managed by an application context themselves: They can receive collaborating objects as bean references.

Chapter 13 discusses Spring's web support in detail.

The Core Bean Factory

In the previous section, we have seen a typical usage of the Spring IoC container in a web environment: The provided convenience classes allow for seamless integration without having to worry about low-level container details. Nevertheless, it does help to look at the inner workings to understand how Spring manages the container. Therefore, we will now look at the Spring bean container in more detail, starting at the lowest building block: the **bean factory**. Later, we'll continue with resource setup and details on the application context concept.

One of the main incentives for a lightweight container is to dispense with the multitude of custom factories and singletons often found in J2EE applications. The Spring bean factory provides *one* consistent way to set up any number of application objects, whether coarse-grained components or fine-grained business objects. Applying reflection and **Dependency Injection**, the bean factory can host components that do not need to be aware of Spring at all. Hence we call Spring a **non-invasive** application framework.

Fundamental Interfaces

The fundamental lightweight container interface is `org.springframework.beans.factory.Bean Factory`. This is a simple interface, which is easy to implement directly in the unlikely case that none of the implementations provided with Spring suffices. The `BeanFactory` interface offers two `getBean()` methods for looking up bean instances by String name, with the option to check for a required type (and throw an exception if there is a type mismatch).

```
public interface BeanFactory {

    Object getBean(String name) throws BeansException;

    Object getBean(String name, Class requiredType) throws BeansException;

    boolean containsBean(String name);

    boolean isSingleton(String name) throws NoSuchBeanDefinitionException;

    String[] getAliases(String name) throws NoSuchBeanDefinitionException;
}
```

The `isSingleton()` method allows calling code to check whether the specified name represents a *singleton* or *prototype* bean definition. In the case of a singleton bean, all calls to the `getBean()` method will return the same object instance. In the case of a prototype bean, each call to `getBean()` returns an independent object instance, configured identically.

The `getAliases()` method will return alias names defined for the given bean name, if any. This mechanism is used to provide more descriptive alternative names for beans than are permitted in certain bean factory storage representations, such as XML `id` attributes.

The methods in most BeanFactory implementations are aware of a hierarchy that the implementation may be part of. If a bean is not found in the current factory, the parent factory will be asked, up until the root factory. From the point of view of a caller, all factories in such a hierarchy will appear to be merged into one. Bean definitions in ancestor contexts are visible to descendant contexts, but not the reverse.

All exceptions thrown by the BeanFactory interface and sub-interfaces extend org.springframework.beans.BeansException, and are unchecked. This reflects the fact that low-level configuration problems are not usually recoverable: Hence, application developers can *choose* to write code to recover from such failures if they wish to, but should not be forced to write code in the majority of cases where configuration failure is fatal.

Most implementations of the BeanFactory interface do not merely provide a registry of objects by name; they provide rich support for configuring those objects using IoC. For example, they manage dependencies between managed objects, as well as simple properties. In the next section, we'll look at how such configuration can be expressed in a simple and intuitive XML structure.

The sub-interface org.springframework.beans.factory.ListableBeanFactory supports listing beans in a factory. It provides methods to retrieve the number of beans defined, the names of all beans, and the names of beans that are instances of a given type:

```
public interface ListableBeanFactory extends BeanFactory {

    int getBeanDefinitionCount();

    String[] getBeanDefinitionNames();

    String[] getBeanDefinitionNames(Class type);

    boolean containsBeanDefinition(String name);

    Map getBeansOfType(Class type, boolean includePrototypes,
                       boolean includeFactoryBeans) throws BeansException
}
```

The ability to obtain such information about the objects managed by a ListableBeanFactory can be used to implement objects that work with a set of other objects known only at runtime.

In contrast to the BeanFactory interface, the methods in ListableBeanFactory apply to the current factory instance and do *not* take account of a hierarchy that the factory may be part of. The org.springframework.beans.factory.BeanFactoryUtils class provides analogous methods that traverse an entire factory hierarchy.

There are various ways to leverage a Spring bean factory, ranging from simple bean configuration to J2EE resource integration and AOP proxy generation. The bean factory is the central, consistent way of setting up any kind of application objects in Spring, whether DAOs, business objects, or web controllers. Note that application objects seldom need to work with the BeanFactory interface directly, but are usually configured and wired by a factory without the need for any Spring-specific code.

For standalone usage, the Spring distribution provides a tiny spring-core.jar file that can be embedded in any kind of application. Its only third-party dependency beyond J2SE 1.3 (plus JAXP for XML parsing) is the Jakarta Commons Logging API.

> The bean factory is the core of Spring and the foundation for many other services that the framework offers. Nevertheless, the bean factory can easily be used standalone if no other Spring services are required.

Populating Beans via XML

As a simple example, consider an application that needs to load a number of text style definitions to offer them as choice to users. An ad hoc solution could be to define the styles in some custom format in a properties or XML file and parse them into text style object representations. With a Spring bean factory, we can externalize the style configuration data from Java code much more elegantly, through the following steps:

Defining Beans

Let's define an object representation of a text style as a JavaBean:

```java
public class TextStyle {
  private String fontName = "default";
  private int fontSize = 9;
  private boolean bold = false;
  private boolean italic = false;

  public void setFontName(String fontName) {
    this.fontName = fontName;
  }
  public String getFontName() {
    return fontName;
  }
  ...
}
```

The TextStyle class does not have any dependencies on Spring. It simply follows standard JavaBean naming conventions. This allows a Spring bean factory to easily populate it using JavaBean properties.

A set of TextStyle bean instances can be defined in a Spring XML bean definition file as follows:

```xml
<beans>

  <bean id="myStyle" class="style.TextStyle">
    <property name="fontName"><value>Arial</value></property>
    <property name="fontSize"><value>12</value></property>
  </bean>

  <bean id="yourStyle" class="style.TextStyle">
    <property name="fontName"><value>Times</value></property>
    <property name="fontSize"><value>10</value></property>
    <property name="bold"><value>true</value></property>
    <property name="italic"><value>true</value></property>
  </bean>

</beans>
```

The format of this file should be fairly obvious. We provide the name of each bean definition in an "id" attribute, and specify the "class" of the object along with the necessary JavaBean properties. (Of course there are many refinements beyond this basic syntax.)

The bean factory will automatically convert String values to the respective property types, via the standard JavaBeans `java.beans.PropertyEditor` mechanism. So the "fontSize" value will automatically be parsed into an int, and the `"bold"` and `"italic"` values into booleans. The availability of this standard infrastructure is a major advantage of using a JavaBean approach to configuration.

XML is not the only way to specify bean definitions. Bean factories and bean definition readers are decoupled. Bean definition parsing is implemented in readers that can work on any bean factory. (It's even possible to use multiple readers to configure one factory.) The XML format used in the previous example is specified by the "spring-beans" DTD (see `www.springframework.org/dtd/spring-beans.dtd`); the corresponding reader is `org.springframework.beans.factory.xml.XmlBeanDefinitionReader`.

Accessing Beans

Let's look at some code to load a bean factory with the definitions that we've just created. For simplicity's sake, we will use the one-stop shop `org.springframework.beans.factory.xml.XmlBeanFactory` first, showing how to use the more generic approach of reader and factory afterward.

```
Resource resource = new ClassPathResource("styles.xml");
ListableBeanFactory bf = new XmlBeanFactory(resource);

TextStyle myStyle = (TextStyle) bf.getBean("myStyle");
TextStyle yourStyle = (TextStyle) bf.getBean("yourStyle");
Map allStyles = bf.getBeansOfType(TextStyle.class, false, false);
```

The `org.springframework.core.io.Resource` interface used here can be implemented by any resource that provides a `java.io.InputStream`. Spring includes out-of-the-box implementations for all typical scenarios, ranging from class path to ServletContext resources.

Alternatively, you can use a generic `org.springframework.beans.factory.support.Default ListableBeanFactory` with an `org.springframework.beans.factory.xml.XmlBeanDefinition Reader` operating on it. This is essentially what happens underneath the covers of the convenient `XmlBeanFactory`.

```
ListableBeanFactory bf = new DefaultListableBeanFactory();
XmlBeanDefinitionReader reader = new XmlBeanDefinitionReader(bf);
Resource resource = new ClassPathResource("styles.xml");
reader.loadBeanDefinitions(resource);

TextStyle myStyle = (TextStyle) bf.getBean("myStyle");
TextStyle yourStyle = (TextStyle) bf.getBean("yourStyle");
Map allStyles = bf.getBeansOfType(TextStyle.class, false, false);
```

This is the simplest and most flexible usage of a Spring bean factory: The above mechanisms will work in any environment, from an applet to a J2EE web app or an EJB implementation. Obviously, you need to store the reference to the `BeanFactory` somewhere, as singletons in the factory can be costly to create. There is often a natural place for such a factory reference, like an Applet instance variable, EJB instance variable, or ServletContext attribute. Otherwise, you can write a custom bootstrap singleton that holds the reference.

The previous XML file defines singleton beans (meaning singleton scope within the bean factory)—the default and most useful case. If you want to get a new instance on every `getBean` call, using your bean definitions as prototypes, then define your beans as follows:

```
<bean id="myStyle" class="style.TextStyle" singleton="false">
```

This is necessary if the bean factory is used in a multithreaded environment but the bean implementations are not thread-safe, possibly because they hold caller-specific state in instance variables. In many cases, singletons will be fine, however; they avoid object creation and are able to keep shared state. Thus, they are ideal for service objects.

A final example shows how we can use the same classes outside the Spring container, if we prefer this for a specific scenario. Because this class is a JavaBean, there's nothing magic about it: We can construct and use it however we like.

```
TextStyle myStyle = new TextStyle();
myStyle.setFontName("Arial");
myStyle.setFontSize(12);

TextStyle yourStyle = new TextStyle();
yourStyle.setFontName("Times");
yourStyle.setFontSize(10);
yourStyle.setBold(true);
yourStyle.setItalic(true);
```

Using your bean classes with a bean factory is just an option to set them up via IoC. You are free to reuse them in any other context. Perhaps most important, this allows for creating individual instances in unit tests.

> In our experience, externalizing configuration from Java code into an XML or properties format has many benefits, as long as that format isn't overly complex (like EJB deployment descriptors). For example, we can derive maximum benefit from programming to interfaces rather than classes, by plugging in different implementations of particular interfaces without any changes to Java code; we have a central repository of configuration data relating to a particular piece of functionality; and simple configuration changes can be made without Java development skills or the need to recompile Java code.
>
> However, requirements are different during unit testing. If each unit test requires its own XML or other external configuration file, even a relatively simple JUnit test involving a few test methods can require multiple configuration files. This makes tests slow to author and hard to maintain. Thus it is important that application objects can be written so that they can run within a container, or be constructed independently in pure Java. The Spring bean factory delivers this important advantage; we recommend that you keep it in mind if you use a different framework or implement your own framework.

Non-XML Bean Definition Formats

XmlBeanFactory is the most popular and widely used implementation of the BeanFactory interface. Particularly for "application contexts", an extended concept that builds upon the bean factory, XML is the dominant definition format.

Spring provides two other styles of bean definition out of the box: reading a properties file or resource bundle, and programmatic registration. A properties file that defines beans looks as follows:

```
myStyle.class=style.TextStyle
myStyle.fontName=Arial
myStyle.fontSize=12

yourStyle.class=style.TextStyle
yourStyle.fontName=Times
yourStyle.fontSize=10
yourStyle.bold=true
yourStyle.italic=true
```

Again, the format is simple and intuitive. We specify the bean's name to be passed to the getBean method, and JavaBean properties. Again conversion from Strings to primitives or Object types will use the JavaBean PropertyEditor mechanism if necessary. The bean definitions shown in the previous example can be loaded via a org.springframework.beans.factory.support.PropertiesBeanDefinitionReader, assuming that a file styles.properties resides in the root of the class path.

```
ListableBeanFactory bf = new DefaultListableBeanFactory();
PropertiesBeanDefinitionReader reader =
    new PropertiesBeanDefinitionReader(bf);
Resource resource = new ClassPathResource("styles.properties");
reader.loadBeanDefinitions(resource);

TextStyle myStyle = (TextStyle) bf.getBean("myStyle");
TextStyle yourStyle = (TextStyle) bf.getBean("yourStyle");
Map allStyles = bf.getBeansOfType(TextStyle.class, false, false);
```

Alternatively, you can register bean definitions programmatically, without any non-Java metadata. You can use the Spring org.springframework.beans.support.RootBeanDefinition and org.springframework.beans.MutablePropertyValues classes to do this.

```
DefaultListableBeanFactory bf = new DefaultListableBeanFactory();

MutablePropertyValues pvs1 = new MutablePropertyValues();
pvs1.addPropertyValue("fontName", "Arial");
pvs1.addPropertyValue("fontSize", new Integer(12));
RootBeanDefinition bd1 = new RootBeanDefinition(TextStyle.class, pvs1);
bf.registerBeanDefinition("myStyle", bd1);

MutablePropertyValues pvs2 = new MutablePropertyValues();
pvs2.addPropertyValue("fontName", "Times");
pvs2.addPropertyValue("fontSize", new Integer(10));
pvs2.addPropertyValue("bold", Boolean.TRUE);
```

```
    pvs2.addPropertyValue("italic", Boolean.TRUE);
    RootBeanDefinition bd2 = new RootBeanDefinition(TextStyle.class, pvs2);
    bf.registerBeanDefinition("myStyle", bd2);

    TextStyle myStyle = (TextStyle) bf.getBean("myStyle");
    TextStyle yourStyle = (TextStyle) bf.getBean("yourStyle");
    Map allStyles = bf.getBeansOfType(TextStyle.class, false, false);
```

However bean definitions are stored, a `BeanFactory` can be used in a consistent manner in client code. Clients are typically completely shielded from bean factory internals: They solely work with the `BeanFactory` and `ListableBeanFactory` interfaces to look up beans.

Wiring up Application Objects

So far we've populated bean properties with Strings and primitive values. This is already very powerful and convenient for parameterizing application objects. However, the true power of the bean factory approach lies in its ability to **"wire up"** bean instances via bean properties that express object dependencies; that is, to enable the Spring container to **resolve dependencies** on other managed objects.

For example, you could have collaborating objects like the following in an e-business application. A `ProductManager` allows `Products` to be retrieved by ID, loading reference data itself but delegating to an "InventoryManager" to determine the quantity in stock. This is a typical implementation of the **Strategy** design pattern, in which an implementation detail is factored out into a helper interface. (We've already encountered those sample business objects in the web application example earlier in this chapter.)

Defining Beans

First of all, let's assume a simple domain class `Product`, implemented in a JavaBean fashion:

```
public class Product {
    private String productId;
    private String name;
    private int quantityInStock;

    ...
    public void setQuantityInStock(int quantityInStock) {
        this.quantityInStock = quantityInStock;
    }
    public getQuantityInStock() {
        return quantityInStock;
    }
}
```

A `ProductManager` knows how to load `Product` instances by ID:

```
public interface ProductManager {

    public Product getProduct(String productId);
}
```

An `InventoryManager` knows how to retrieve the quantity in stock for a given product ID:

```
public interface InventoryManager {

  public int getQuantityInStock(String productId);
}
```

The default `ProductManager` implementation delegates to an associated `InventoryManager` for filling in the quantity in stock:

```
public class DefaultProductManager implements ProductManager {
  private InventoryManager inventoryManager;
  private boolean retrieveCurrentStock = true;

  public void setInventoryManager(InventoryManager inventoryManager) {
    this.inventoryManager = inventoryManager;
  }

  public void setRetrieveCurrentStock(boolean retrieveCurrentStock) {
    this.retrieveCurrentStock = retrieveCurrentStock;
  }

  public Product getProduct(String productId) {
    Product product = new Product();
    // populate product reference data
    if (this.retrieveCurrentStock) {
      product.setQuantityInStock(
          this.inventoryManager.getQuantityInStock(productId));
    }
    return product;
  }
}
```

The default `InventoryManager` implementation can use an arbitrary way to retrieve the quantity in stock, which we will not worry about here any further:

```
public class DefaultInventoryManager implements InventoryManager {

  public int getQuantityInStock(String productId) {
    . . .
  }
}
```

Again, none of these interfaces and implementation classes need any Spring dependencies. They just follow the standard JavaBean paradigm.

Defining `ProductManager` and `InventoryManager` as interfaces with default implementations allows for a high degree of decoupling and for easy switching to alternative implementations; this is what we call *pluggability*. Note that the interfaces just feature the actual business methods; configuration methods like `setInventoryManager` are details of the implementation classes.

The `Product` domain object is a concrete JavaBean in this example. There is often no need to have fine-grained domain objects implement a domain interface. Creation and persistence logic is normally kept outside domain objects in service classes, especially when using O/R mapping tools. In that case, the domain class itself focuses on implementing domain properties and domain logic that evaluates and manipulates those properties.

How do we wire up these interdependent beans? `ProductManager` is a factory for `Product` domain objects. `ProductManager` and `InventoryManager` should be singleton services, with `ProductManager` needing a reference to an `InventoryManager` to retrieve the current stock. To do this in an ad hoc manner, you would need some custom initialization code that does the wiring up, reading in the implementation class names from a custom configuration file. (The Sun Java Pet Store illustrates this approach, in its parameterization of DAO classes used by SLSBs.) With a Spring bean factory, you can simply define the two as singleton beans:

```
<beans>

  <bean id="myInventoryManager" class="ebusiness.DefaultInventoryManager"/>

  <bean id="myProductManager" class="ebusiness.DefaultProductManager">
    <property name="inventoryManager">
      <ref bean="myInventoryManager"/>
    </property>
    <property name="retrieveCurrentStock">
      <value>true</value>
    </property>
  </bean>

</beans>
```

The bean factory will automatically wire up the `myProductManager` bean with the `myInventory Manager` bean, passing a reference to the latter into the `ProductManager setInventoryManager` method. The type check will happen implicitly; if the `myInventoryManager` bean does not match the argument type of the `setInventoryManager` method, an exception will be thrown on bean creation.

The parameter `retrieveCurrentStock` is optional here. If it isn't specified, the default value of the property in the implementation class will apply.

Accessing Beans

When we use the configured `ProductManager`, we can simply make a single call to the `getBean` method on its owning bean factory. Calling code requires no knowledge of how it's created and how its dependencies are resolved, thus isolating callers from even significant changes in implementation strategy:

```
Resource resource = new ClassPathResource("managers.xml");
ListableBeanFactory bf = new XmlBeanFactory(resource);

ProductManager productManager =
    (ProductManager) bf.getBean("myProductManager");
productManager.getProduct("someId");
```

We have a number of options for locating the `BeanFactory`. In general, we should avoid the use of a singleton that holds the factory itself, for maximum flexibility and testability. In a web application, we could store the owning `BeanFactory` in a `ServletContext` attribute; in an EJB implementation, an EJB instance variable; in a standalone application, we will typically fall back to a custom singleton.

The power of the bean factory is that it allows for easy redefinition of beans. For example, you may want to use a `MockInventoryManager` instead of `DefaultInventoryManager`, or a `MockProductManager` instead of `DefaultProductManager`, for testing purposes: Simply change the class definitions in the respective bean tag and you're done.

Note that no dependencies on custom factory classes are necessary to achieve this kind of flexible wiring up, because the bean factory is able to perform all wiring-up dynamically according to the bean definitions. This is typically not the case with ad hoc custom factories that are often implemented as startup classes with static code-level dependencies for wiring up. Typical code seen in that respect looks as follows:

```
public class DefaultProductManager implements ProductManager {
   private InventoryManager inventoryManager;

   public DefaultProductManager() {
      this.inventoryManager = InventoryManagerFactory.getInventoryManager();
   }

   public Product getProduct(String productId) {
      ...
   }
}
```

Static factory classes like `InventoryManagerFactory` or `ProductManagerFactory`, or a centralized static factory that knows how to create both, can be completely abandoned through the use of a bean factory as seen in the previous snippet.

```
public class InventoryManagerFactory {
   private static InventoryManager inventoryManager;

   public static synchronized getInventoryManager {
      return new DefaultInventoryManager();
      // or some ad-hoc configurability via reading in
      // the class name from a properties file or the like
   }
}
```

As before, we can also configure the objects programmatically if desired, as in the following code fragment:

```
InventoryManager inventoryManager = new DefaultInventoryManager();
ProductManager productManager = new DefaultProductManager();
productManager.setInventoryService(inventoryManager);

productManager.getProduct("someId");
```

In this simple example, pure Java configuration is pretty straightforward. In realistic application scenarios, externalizing configuration is much more attractive. Again, the wiring that the bean factory offers is just an option. You can always reuse your application objects in standalone ways and create them individually in unit tests.

> The ability to express even strongly typed dependencies on collaborating objects via JavaBean properties and have them satisfied by IoC is the key to the power of the Spring lightweight container. If all application objects requiring configuration management are managed via IoC, there is no need for dependence on Spring APIs and no need for bean factory lookups and the necessary type casts.
>
> This benefit can extend to all architectural tiers of a Spring web application, because Spring allows not only business objects, DAOs, and so on, but also web controllers to be configured using IoC. Thus typical Spring web applications can be made up of JavaBeans programmed to depend on collaborator interfaces, offering complete pluggability in external configuration, and with no need for any lookup code whatsoever (JNDI, singleton, custom factory, or Spring-specific code).

Autowire and Dependency Checks

Explicit specification of dependencies is the recommended way to use a bean factory. This is a powerful mechanism as it allows reference to a specific bean instance by name, even if multiple beans of the required type are available. Furthermore, the connections between the various bean instances are immediately obvious from the XML or other representation of the bean factory.

That said, the Spring bean factory also offers a different way of dependency resolution: **autowiring**, partly inspired by PicoContainer. If a bean definition is marked as "autowire," all object dependencies will be resolved via matching beans in the bean factory—if there is a non-ambiguous way to do so. This can be very convenient, because it avoids explicit references to collaborating objects. However, the developer must be aware of the implications of automatic wiring, particularly when defining new beans that implement the same interfaces as existing beans.

For example, if there is exactly one instance of type `InventoryManager` defined in the bean factory, the `DefaultProductManager inventoryManager` property can be wired up with this single instance as it expresses a dependency on a bean of that type. The "autowire" attribute of the `<bean>` element is used here, as shown in the following snippet:

```xml
<beans>

  <bean id="myInventoryManager" class="ebusiness.DefaultInventoryManager"/>

  <bean id="myProductManager" class="ebusiness.DefaultProductManager"
      autowire="byType">
    <property name="retrieveCurrentStock">
      <value>true</value>
    </property>
  </bean>

</beans>
```

Note that there is no explicit reference to `myInventoryManager` in the `myProductManager` definition. Because of its `autowire` attribute, it will automatically receive a reference to the `InventoryManager`, determined by the type of its `inventoryManager` property.

A further autowire option is `byName`, wiring object properties to beans of the same name. So for example, an `inventoryManager` property would automatically be wired to a bean with the name `inventory Manager`. Autowiring by type is the recommended form of autowiring in most cases, as it doesn't require strict name matches, and is less error-prone.

```
<beans>

  <bean id="inventoryManager" class="ebusiness.DefaultInventoryManager"/>

  <bean id="myProductManager" class="ebusiness.DefaultProductManager"
        autowire="byName">
    <property name="retrieveCurrentStock">
      <value>true</value>
    </property>
  </bean>

</beans>
```

Dependency checking automatically ensures that all JavaBean dependencies that a bean expresses have been resolved, which is particularly useful in combination with autowiring.

```
<beans>

  <bean id="myInventoryManager" class="ebusiness.DefaultInventoryManager"/>

  <bean id="myProductManager" class="ebusiness.DefaultProductManager"
        autowire="byType" dependency-check="objects">
    <property name="retrieveCurrentStock">
      <value>true</value>
    </property>
  </bean>

</beans>
```

The `objects` value of the `dependency-check` attribute specifies checking of object references only. The values `simple` and `all` are also supported, checking just *simple* properties (primitives and Strings) or *all* properties (simple and object). A dependency check value of `none` is the default, performing no dependency checks.

Constructor Resolution

Spring supports Constructor Injection as well as Setter Injection, offering resolution of a specific constructor instead of the typical JavaBean no-argument constructor. Constructor Injection is primarily useful for passing in collaborating objects, but it is also capable of applying configuration parameters. Spring support for Constructor Injection is as comprehensive as its support for Setter Injection, with support for type conversions and collections (which I discuss shortly) as well as objects and simple types.

The earlier ProductManager example could look as follows when using Constructor Injection. Instead of two setter methods for `inventoryManager` and `retrieveCurrentStock`, two overloaded constructors are used:

```
public class DefaultProductManager implements ProductManager {
    private InventoryManager inventoryManager;
    private boolean retrieveCurrentStock = true;

    public DefaultProductManager(InventoryManager inventoryManager) {
        this.inventoryManager = inventoryManager;
    }

    public DefaultProductManager(InventoryManager inventoryManager,
                                 boolean retrieveCurrentStock) {
        this.inventoryManager = inventoryManager;
        this.retrieveCurrentStock = retrieveCurrentStock;
    }

    public Product getProduct(String productId) {
        ...
    }
}
```

Setting up this version of `DefaultProductManager` in a Spring bean factory can be achieved via `<constructor-arg>` tags, replacing the former `<property>` tags. For example, if just setting the `InventoryManager`, use the following code:

```
<beans>

    <bean id="myInventoryManager" class="ebusiness.DefaultInventoryManager"/>

    <bean id="myProductManager" class="ebusiness.DefaultProductManager">
        <constructor-arg>
            <ref bean="myInventoryManager"/>
        </constructor-arg>
    </bean>

</beans>
```

The bean factory will match the given constructor arguments by type with the available constructors, in the `DefaultProductManager` case resolving its single-argument constructor. In case of multiple constructors, the "greediest" one that can be satisfied with the given arguments will be chosen.

Unlike bean properties, constructor arguments cannot be accessed by name: a limitation of the Java reflection API. Thus, if you have multiple arguments of the same type—like two `InventoryManager` instances to access or two configuration parameters—you need to specify the corresponding argument index. You can choose to do this even if your arguments can be unambiguously resolved by type, or when you need to convert String values to primitives, like for the two-argument constructor in our example. Note that the index is just *required* for the second argument; the first can easily be resolved by type.

```
<beans>

    <bean id="myInventoryManager" class="ebusiness.DefaultInventoryManager"/>

    <bean id="myProductManager" class="ebusiness.DefaultProductManager">
```

```
        <constructor-arg index="0">
          <ref bean="myInventoryManager"/>
        </constructor-arg>
        <constructor-arg index="1">
          <value>true</value>
        </constructor-arg>
    </bean>

  </beans>
```

The Spring bean factory can also provide autowiring for constructors; this is the PicoContainer default behavior. As constructor argument names aren't available through introspection, this is only possible by type. In our example, the `DefaultProductManager` dependency on an `InventoryManager` can automatically be resolved through matching with the `myInventoryManager` bean definition. The `retrieveCurrentStock` argument still has to be specified, because it represents a simple value.

```
  <beans>

    <bean id="myInventoryManager" class="ebusiness.DefaultInventoryManager"/>

    <bean id="myProductManager" class="ebusiness.DefaultProductManager"
        autowire="constructor">
      <constructor-arg index="1">
        <value>true</value>
      </constructor-arg>
    </bean>

  </beans>
```

Spring allows you to mix Setter Injection and Constructor Injection in the same factory: You can choose at a per-object level. It is even possible to use both constructor arguments and JavaBean properties for the same object.

Lifecycle Callbacks

Beans managed by a Spring bean factory usually do not need any specific callbacks beyond instantiation and property population. This allows most business object implementations to avoid any dependencies on Spring, avoiding lock-in to the framework and allowing maximum potential for reuse in different environments and ease of testing.

Nevertheless, certain objects might want to receive initialization and shutdown callbacks. The bean factory offers two ways to achieve this: implementing callback interfaces or declaratively specifying callback methods.

The two callback interfaces provided by the Spring lightweight container are `org.springframework.beans.factory.InitializingBean` and `org.springframework.beans.factory.DisposableBean`. They provide simple no-argument callback methods after property setting and on bean factory shutdown.

```
public interface InitializingBean {

 void afterPropertiesSet() throws Exception;
}
```

The afterPropertiesSet() method is invoked after all JavaBean properties have been configured, and allows the object to perform any required custom initialization. It is allowed to throw Exception to simplify the programming model. As exceptions thrown from this lifecycle method are considered fatal application configuration failures, there is no value in forcing application developers to catch and rethrow exceptions: Spring will log the exception, regardless of its type. (Note that in general it is poor practice to declare methods to throw Exception, and Spring does not encourage it beyond such callbacks.)

```
public interface DisposableBean {

 void destroy() throws Exception;
}
```

The destroy() method can be used to relinquish any resources the bean has allocated to service requests, in cases where these would not automatically be cleaned up by garbage collection.

Many framework beans implement those callback interfaces. While application objects may choose to do so too, there is an alternative way that does not involve Spring dependencies: declarative specification of callback methods, as shown below.

```
<bean id="myInventoryManager" class="ebusiness.DefaultInventoryManager"
    init-method="initialize" destroy-method="shutdown"/>
```

The DefaultInventoryManager class just has to specify public methods named initialize and destroy without arguments; it does not have to implement any Spring-specific interfaces. This can be leveraged to keep application components independent of Spring even if they require lifecycle callbacks. It is even more useful for hosting third-party components, to avoid the need for writing adapters through specifying their existing lifecycle methods declaratively. Many third-party libraries, such as Jakarta Commons DBCP and util.concurrent, provide JavaBeans that can be used this way in Spring applications, with no requirement for Spring-specific coding.

A further callback is available for beans that want to access their containing bean factory. They can implement the org.springframework.beans.factory.BeanFactoryAware interface to receive a reference on initialization. Such a setBeanFactory method will be invoked before the afterPropertiesSet method of InitializingBean—or a declarative initialization method—if both interfaces are implemented.

```
public interface BeanFactoryAware {

  void setBeanFactory(BeanFactory beanFactory) throws BeansException;
}
```

Again, this is more often used within the Spring framework itself than in application code. But it can be necessary to obtain a reference to the owning BeanFactory at runtime to enumerate other objects in the same BeanFactory (in the case of a ListableBeanFactory), or to repeatedly obtain independent instances of prototype beans. This style of IoC is similar to Avalon.

> If you can, use JavaBean properties or constructor arguments rather than implement
> Spring lifecycle methods. One of the major advantages of Dependency Injection is
> that it enables us to avoid dependencies on a container. The init-method alternative
> allows the invocation of initialization code after all JavaBean properties have been
> set, without creating a dependency on Spring.

Complex Property Values

The Spring bean factory supports not only String values and bean references as property values but also
more complex values, such as arrays, `java.util.List`, `java.util.Set`, `java.util.Map`, or `java.util.Properties`. Array, set, list, and map values can consist of either `String` values or bean references. Map keys and Properties keys and values must be Strings. Map values can even be sets, lists, or
maps themselves. Such complex values are specified using special XML tags when using the XML bean
definition format.

Particularly through allowing the setting of multiple bean references to arrays, the support for complex
property values is a powerful and unique feature of the Spring bean factory. It allows for wiring up virtually any kind of complex dependencies between objects, not just simple one-instance-per-type relationships. The following bean definition illustrates the basic options (omitting set tags and the nesting of tags):

```
<beans>

  <bean id="myBeanWithComplexProperties" class="example.MyComplexBean">
    <property name="myRefArray">
      <list>
        <ref bean="myInventoryManager"/>
        <ref bean="yourInventoryManager"/>
      </list>
    </property>
    <property name="myValueArray">
      <list>
        <value>myArrayValue</value>
        <value>yourArrayValue</value>
      </list>
    </property>
    <property name="myRefList">
      <list>
        <ref bean="myInventoryManager"/>
        <ref bean="yourInventoryManager"/>
      </list>
    </property>
    <property name="myValueList">
      <list>
        <value>myListValue</value>
        <value>yourListValue</value>
      </list>
    </property>
    <property name="myRefMap">
```

```
        <map>
          <entry key="myMapKey">
            <ref bean="myInventoryManager"/>
          </entry>
          <entry key="yourMapKey">
            <ref bean="yourInventoryManager"/>
          </entry>
        </map>
      </property>
      <property name="myValueMap">
        <map>
          <entry key="myMapKey">
            <value>myMapValue</value>
          </entry>
          <entry key="yourMapKey">
            <value>yourMapValue</value>
          </entry>
        </map>
      </property>
      <property name="myProperties">
        <props>
          <prop key="myPropKey">
            myPropValue
          </prop>
          <prop key="yourPropKey">
            yourPropValue
          </prop>
        </props>
      </property>
    </bean>

  </beans>
```

The corresponding class looks like this (setter methods omitted for brevity):

```
public class MyComplexBean {
  private InventoryManager[] myRefArray;
  private String[] myValueArray;
  private List myRefList;
  private List myValueList;
  private Map myRefMap;
  private Map myValueMap;
  private Properties myProperties;

  // corresponding setters of the same types
}
```

Resource Setup

Beyond collaborating application objects, almost all applications work with resources such as **JDBC DataSources** or **Hibernate SessionFactories**. The Spring container treats such a **resource reference** just like a dependency on a collaborating object: The application bean simply needs to expose a JavaBean property of the required type.

We will first review common Java and J2EE ways to access resources, and then show how to define resources in a Spring bean factory and wire them up with application objects. This is IoC applied to a different kind of object: The basic issues, and the bean factory mechanism that we will use to address them, are similar to those in the case of dependencies between collaborating application objects.

Classic Java and J2EE Resource Access

In standalone applications, resources must be created locally within the application. A typical example is the ad hoc setup of JDBC connection infrastructure on startup:

```
// read in driverClassName, url, username, password from custom config file
Class.forName(driverClassName);
MyConnectionPool.initialize(url, username, password);
```

With such custom setup of resources, client code in application objects is tied to custom resource holders that are often implemented as hard-coded singletons. This makes testing such application objects with mock resources hard or even impossible. For example, the DefaultInventoryManager class previously mentioned could look as follows with ad hoc resource access:

```
public class DefaultInventoryManager implements InventoryManager {

    public int getQuantityInStock(String productId) {
        Connection con = MyConnectionPool.getConnection();
        try {
            Statement stmt = con.createStatement();
            // determine nr of items for given product id
            return quantityInStock;
        }
        catch (SQLException ex) {
            // convert to some generic data access exception
        }
        finally {
            MyConnectionPool.returnConnection(con);
        }
    }
}
```

In a J2EE environment, we define such resources via the container and expose them as global *JNDI objects*. The traditional approach is then for client code to access those resources via JNDI, tying application objects to a JNDI infrastructure at runtime. Such code cannot easily be reused or tested outside of a J2EE environment.

```
public class DefaultInventoryManager implements InventoryManager {

    public int getQuantityInStock(String productId) {
        InitialContext ctx = new InitialContext();
        DataSource ds = (DataSource) ctx.lookup("java:comp/env/jdbc/myds");
        Connection con = ds.getConnection();
```

```
      try {
        Statement stmt = con.createStatement();
        // determine nr of items for given product id
        return quantityInStock;
      }
      catch (SQLException ex) {
        // convert to some generic data access exception
      }
      finally {
        con.close();
      }
    }
  }
}
```

The previous example uses raw JNDI and JDBC to illustrate that **DefaultInventoryManager** can be built on plain J2EE APIs. Spring offers more convenient ways of working with those APIs; for example, **JdbcTemplate** allows for writing more concise and cleaner JDBC access code (see Chapter 10). If you are happy to use Spring-specific APIs, we recommend leveraging those convenience features. Typically, the dependence on a particular application framework is far outweighed by the greater convenience, clarity, and reduced likelihood of programming errors.

For another example, consider the ad hoc setup of a local **Hibernate SessionFactory**:

```
Configuration cfg = new Configuration();
cfg.configure();  // loads from default location "/hibernate.cfg.xml"
SessionFactory sf = cfg.buildSessionFactory();
MySessionFactoryHolder.setSessionFactory(sf);
```

Plus the corresponding client code for accessing the SessionFactory:

```
public class HibernateInventoryManager implements InventoryManager {

    public int getQuantityInStock(String productId) {
      SessionFactory sf = MySessionFactoryHolder.getSessionFactory();
      Session session = sf.openSession();
      try {
        // determine nr of items for given product id
        return quantityInStock;
      }
      catch (HibernateException ex) {
        // convert to some generic data access exception
      }
      finally {
        session.close();
      }
    }
  }
```

Or a JNDI lookup in the case of Hibernate being setup as **JCA Connector** in the J2EE container:

```
public class HibernateInventoryManager implements InventoryManager {

  public int getQuantityInStock(String productId) {
```

```
    InitialContext ctx = new InitialContext();
    SessionFactory sf =
        (SessionFactory) ctx.lookup("java:comp/env/jdbc/mysf");
    Session session = sf.openSession();
    try {
      // determine nr of items for given product id
      return quantityInStock;
    }
    catch (HibernateException ex) {
      // convert to some generic data access exception
    }
    finally {
      session.close();
    }
  }
}
```

Either approach ties the client code to the particular resource retrieval strategy. Neither allows for easy reuse of application objects in other environments, or easy testing.

> *Exposing* resources such as JDBC DataSources via JNDI is the recommended approach in J2EE applications, leveraging standard J2EE capabilities. However, locally defined DataSources can be a viable alternative in self-contained scenarios even within a J2EE environment, as you will see in Chapter 10.
>
> *Accessing* such resources in application objects via direct JNDI is not desirable. Spring provides a powerful simplifying abstraction that externalizes resource location from application code.

Resource Definitions in a Bean Container

A major goal of the bean factory concept is to allow for reuse of application objects in any environment, whether within a bean factory or standalone. Hence, Spring also offers means to avoid hard-coded resource lookups for specific environments. The general strategy is to make application objects work with standard resources such as connection factories, received via JavaBean properties.

For example, the DefaultInventoryManager class shown in the previous section might need to access an inventory database. Hence, it could simply expose a property of type javax.sql.DataSource, which is the standard connection factory for JDBC (as of JDBC 2.0), just like a net.sf.hibernate.SessionFactory is for Hibernate. (For a detailed discussion of connection factories and connections, see Chapter 10.)

```
public class DefaultInventoryManager implements InventoryManager {
  private DataSource dataSource;

  public void setDataSource(DataSource dataSource) {
    this.dataSource = dataSource;
  }
```

```
    public int getQuantityInStock(String productId) {
      Connection con = this.dataSource.getConnection();
      try {
        Statement stmt = con.createStatement();
        // determine nr of items for given product id
        return quantityInStock;
      }
      catch (SQLException ex) {
        // convert to some generic data access exception
      }
      finally {
        con.close();
      }
    }
  }
```

This is **IoC applied to resources**: The application object does not look up a resource via a specific mechanism but relies on the connection factory being set from the outside. In a Spring bean factory, the corresponding bean definitions could look as follows:

```xml
<beans>

  <bean id="myDataSource"
      class="org.springframework.jdbc.datasource.DriverManagerDataSource">

    <property name="driverClassName">
      <value>com.mysql.jdbc.Driver</value>
    </property>
    <property name="url">
      <value>jdbc:mysql:myds</value>
    </property>
  </bean>

  <bean id="myInventoryManager" class="ebusiness.DefaultInventoryManager">
    <property name="dataSource">
      <ref bean="myDataSource"/>
    </property>
  </bean>

</beans>
```

The bean factory will automatically wire up the myInventoryManager bean with the myDataSource resource, passing a reference to the latter into the setDataSource method of DefaultInventory Manager. The myInventoryManager is not aware of where the resource came from; it simply does not have to care.

The DriverManagerDataSource class used in the previous example is a simple implementation of the javax.sql.DataSource interface, creating a new JDBC connection on each call to the getConnection() method. It is included in the Spring Framework distribution for convenience, to be used instead of a connection pool DataSource if pooling is not strictly required, as is the case, for example, in test suites.

Switching the previous setup to a locally defined connection pool such as the Jakarta **Commons DBCP** (http://jakarta.apache.org/commons/dbcp) is easy: Drop commons-dbcp.jar and commons-pool .jar into the class path, change the class name of the myDataSource bean to org.apache.commons .dbcp.BasicDataSource, and you're done. The Spring DriverManagerDataSource class uses the same property names as the Jakarta BasicDataSource class to enable easy migration, so there is no need to change the property names.

```
<beans>

  <bean id="myDataSource" class="org.apache.commons.dbcp.BasicDataSource"
      destroy-method="close">
    <property name="driverClassName">
      <value>com.mysql.jdbc.Driver</value>
    </property>
    <property name="url">
      <value>jdbc:mysql:myds</value>
    </property>
  </bean>

  <bean id="myInventoryManager" class="ebusiness.DefaultInventoryManager">
    <property name="dataSource">
      <ref bean="myDataSource"/>
    </property>
  </bean>

</beans>
```

Note that the myDataSource definition specifies a destroy-method: The bean factory will automatically invoke the close() method of BasicDataSource on shutdown. This ensures that the connection pool and its remaining connections are properly closed. Because of the bean factory's support for declarative specification of lifecycle methods, this is possible without the need for an adapter.

Of course, you could also use any other DataSource implementation that follows the JavaBean conventions. For example, **C3P0** (http://sourceforge.net/projects/c3p0) and ObjectWeb **XAPool** (http://xapool.experlog.com) offer such bean-style DataSources too. I'll discuss shortly how Spring allows the use of a J2EE container DataSource located via JNDI through the same mechanism; this is the typical case in J2EE applications.

The DefaultInventoryManager class still does not have any Spring dependencies, and it can still be used without a bean factory easily, for example in a unit test:

```
DataSource ds = new DriverManagerDataSource(...);
DefaultInventoryManager inventoryManager = new DefaultInventoryManager();
inventoryManager.setDataSource(ds);
...
```

> **Wherever possible, move resource lookup code out of your application objects. Your application objects should receive connection factories to work with from the outside, applying the IoC principle in terms of resources. This allows flexible configuration in any environment and—equally important—easy unit testing.**

Factory Beans

A Spring bean factory supports a special concept for creating custom bean instances: *factory beans*, implementing the `org.springframework.beans.factory.FactoryBean` interface. A factory bean introduces a level of indirection, so that a bean defined in the bean factory can act as factory for another object. The object that the factory bean creates will be available for bean references; thus, the factory bean will behave just like the object it produces on `getBean` calls and `<ref>` tags.

The `FactoryBean` interface defines a `getObject()` method that returns the created object, and a flag that indicates whether `getObject()` will return a cached singleton or a new object on each call. Additionally, the `getObjectType()` method can indicate what type of object the `FactoryBean` will create (returning `null` if it is not known in advance).

```
public interface FactoryBean {

  Object getObject() throws Exception;

  Class getObjectType();

  boolean isSingleton();
}
```

This concept is mainly used within Spring itself. While it's easy to implement a custom factory bean, applications will rarely have to implement the `FactoryBean` interface but will normally leverage prebuilt resource factories that ship with Spring, such as:

- ❏ `org.springframework.jndi.JndiObjectFactoryBean`: Generic `FactoryBean` that returns an object obtained by a JNDI lookup. JNDI lookup is performed by Spring, not application code.

- ❏ `org.springframework.orm.hibernate.LocalSessionFactoryBean`: `FactoryBean` to set up a local Hibernate `SessionFactory`.

- ❏ `org.springframework.orm.jdo.LocalPersistenceManagerFactoryBean`: `FactoryBean` to set up a local JDO `PersistenceManagerFactory`.

- ❏ `org.springframework.aop.framework.ProxyFactoryBean`: Generic `FactoryBean` used to obtain AOP proxies.

- ❏ `org.springframework.transaction.interceptor.TransactionProxyFactoryBean`: Convenient `FactoryBean` used to create transactional proxies for objects, allowing for easy declarative transaction management.

- ❏ `org.springframework.ejb.access.LocalStatelessSessionProxyFactoryBean`: `FactoryBean` used as a codeless EJB business delegate. Objects created by the factory bean will implement the EJB's business methods interface, enabling callers to use them without depending on JNDI or EJB APIs.

- ❏ `org.springframework.ejb.access.SimpleRemoteStatelessSessionProxyFactoryBean`: Analogous factory for codeless proxying of remote EJBs.

- ❏ `org.springframework.remoting.rmi.RmiProxyFactoryBean`: `FactoryBean` used to create a proxy for a remote object to be accessed via RMI.

❑ `org.springframework.remoting.jaxrpc.JaxRpcPortProxyFactoryBean`: Similar proxy factory for a WSDL Web Service accessed via JAX-RPC.

❑ `org.springframework.remoting.caucho.HessianProxyFactoryBean`: Similar proxy factory for Caucho's Hession remoting protocol.

❑ `org.springframework.remoting.caucho.BurlapProxyFactoryBean`: Similar proxy factory for Caucho's Burlap remoting protocol.

Two important usages of factory beans will be discussed further in this chapter: JNDI resources and local connection factory definitions. Further usages within the framework include the generation of AOP proxies and access to remote services: Chapters 8 and 11 illustrate those in detail.

Making a JNDI Resource Available

Consider, for example, the `DataSource`-enabled `DefaultInventoryManager` class referenced earlier. We have already seen how it can get wired up with locally defined `DataSource` beans like the Spring `DriverManagerDataSource` or Jakarta `BasicDataSource` classes. What if we want to attach a JNDI-bound container `DataSource` to it? We can do this very simply in a J2EE environment as follows:

```
<beans>

    <bean id="myDataSource"
        class="org.springframework.jndi.JndiObjectFactoryBean">
      <property name="jndiName">
        <value>jdbc/myds</value>
      </property>
    </bean>

    <bean id="myInventoryManager" class="ebusiness.DefaultInventoryManager">
      <property name="dataSource">
        <ref bean="myDataSource"/>
      </property>
    </bean>

</beans>
```

It's as simple as that: just a change of configuration. The `myDataSource` bean has been redefined as `org.springframework.jndi.JndiObjectFactoryBean`, linking in a JNDI object and making it available as a bean in the bean factory. It implements the `FactoryBean` interface to make the bean factory apply special treatment, that is, asking it for an object to register instead of registering the `FactoryBean` itself as object. The lookup will occur once on startup, when the `JndiObjectFactoryBean` caches the located object as singleton.

Note that the JNDI name "jdbc/myds" will get resolved to "java:comp/env/jdbc/myds". The `Jndi ObjectFactoryBean` will append this standard J2EE prefix by default if not already contained in the name. Setting the `JndiObjectFactoryBean` `inContainer` property to `false` will use the given JNDI name without any modification.

When the target of a bean reference, the `FactoryBean` of the previous example will appear as the `Data Source` that it returns. The following code will also work, as the `getBean` call returns a `DataSource` instance, despite `myDataSource` being of type `JndiObjectFactoryBean` in the bean definition:

```
Resource resource = new ClassPathResource("services.xml");
ListableBeanFactory bf = new XmlBeanFactory(resource);
DataSource ds = (DataSource) bf.getBean("myDataSource");
```

> **Spring provides a consistent abstraction over J2EE services such as JNDI, permitting use of alternative resource location strategies: However, Spring does not *compete* with J2EE services in a J2EE environment. A Spring application can use a container DataSource in a J2EE environment like any J2EE application, just as it can use JTA as transaction strategy (see Chapter 9). However, a Spring application can work just as easily with a locally defined DataSource as an alternative.**

Creating a Local Connection Factory

Another popular resource factory bean is `org.springframework.orm.hibernate.LocalSession FactoryBean`. This factory bean creates and exposes a local Hibernate connection factory: It builds a **Hibernate** `SessionFactory` from the given configuration settings, making it available as a bean in the bean factory.

`LocalSessionFactoryBean` offers many setup options: naturally, as JavaBean properties. Hibernate properties can be specified directly as `hibernateProperties`, or read in from a Hibernate XML file at `configLocation` (typically `/hibernate.cfg.xml` in the class path). An important value add is the support for building the `SessionFactory` on an existing `DataSource` bean instead of a Hibernate-managed connection provider. The typical Hibernate configuration in a Spring context uses such an existing `DataSource` bean, and specifies all mappings and properties locally instead of in a separate Hibernate XML file.

```xml
<beans>

  <bean id="myDataSource"
      class="org.springframework.jdbc.datasource.DriverManagerDataSource">
    <property name="driverClassName">
      <value>com.mysql.jdbc.Driver</value>
    </property>
    <property name="url">
      <value>jdbc:mysql:myds</value>
    </property>
  </bean>

  <bean id="mySessionFactory"
      class="org.springframework.orm.hibernate.LocalSessionFactoryBean">
    <property name="dataSource">
      <ref bean="myDataSource"/>
    </property>
    <property name="mappingResources">
      <value>ebusiness/inventory.hbm.xml</value>
    </property>
    <property name="hibernateProperties">
      <props>
        <prop key="hibernate.dialect">
          net.sf.hibernate.dialect.MySQLDialect
```

```
            </prop>
          </props>
        </property>
      </bean>

      <bean id="myInventoryManager" class="ebusiness.HibernateInventoryManager">
        <property name="sessionFactory">
          <ref bean="mySessionFactory"/>
        </property>
      </bean>

    </beans>
```

The corresponding `HibernateInventoryManager` implementation would simply have to expose a property of type `SessionFactory`, with the name `sessionFactory` to match the previous definition.

```
    public class HibernateInventoryManager implements InventoryManager {
      private SessionFactory sessionFactory;

      public void setSessionFactory(SessionFactory sessionFactory) {
        this.sessionFactory = sessionFactory;
      }

      public int getQuantityInStock(String productId) {
        Session session = this.sessionFactory.openSession();
        try {
          // determine nr of items for given product id
          return quantityInStock;
        }
        catch (HibernateException ex) {
          // convert to some generic data access exception
        }
        finally {
          session.close();
        }
      }
    }
```

Like `DefaultInventoryManager`, `HibernateInventoryManager` does not depend on Spring and can easily be reused outside of a bean factory. It is not coupled to any particular `SessionFactory` retrieval strategy; switching to a JNDI-registered `SessionFactory` in case of a JCA Connector is straightforward:

```
    <beans>

      <bean id="mySessionFactory"
          class="org.springframework.jndi.JndiObjectFactoryBean">
        <property name="jndiName">
          <value>jdbc/mysf</value>
        </property>
      </bean>

      <bean id="myInventoryManager" class="ebusiness.HibernateInventoryManager">
        <property name="sessionFactory">
          <ref bean="mySessionFactory"/>
```

```
        </property>
    </bean>

</beans>
```

*Note that the Hibernate access code shown in the previous example is pure Hibernate without leveraging any of the Spring Hibernate access conveniences, to illustrate that such classes do not need to depend on Spring. The Spring **HibernateTemplate** class allows for more convenient data access, providing session handling and exception conversion. See Chapter 10 for a discussion of Spring's Hibernate support.*

Spring provides the same level of support for JDO: `org.springframework.orm.jdo.Local PersistenceManagerFactoryBean` allows for the local setup of a **JDO PersistenceManagerFactory**, while `JndiObjectFactoryBean` can retrieve a JNDI-bound `PersistenceManagerFactory` if the JDO implementation is configured using a JCA connector.

> **Unless you use EJB, there is little reason to keep connection factories of persistence tools in JNDI. Such connection factories are application-specific, thus not suitable for sharing at server level. Nor is there any clustering benefit in using JNDI; locking in a clustered environment typically works via database locks or clustered caches like Coherence, not requiring a connection factory in JNDI either.**
>
> **Both `LocalSessionFactoryBean` for Hibernate and `LocalPersistenceManager FactoryBean` for JDO are much easier to set up and handle than a JCA Connector. Programmatic binding to JNDI is also often a bad idea, because JNDI implementations vary across containers: For example, Tomcat 4.x only provides a read-only JNDI environment.**

The Spring Application Context

Spring builds on the bean factory concept to offer an extended "application context" concept. This provides bean factory capabilities, but adds:

- ❑ **Message source support.** Support for retrieving localized messages via keys in a generic fashion, independent of the underlying source. The default implementation reads in messages from a resource bundle.

- ❑ **Access to file resources.** Loading resources via relative paths without dependence on the actual resource environment, such as the file system or a ServletContext. The "File Resources" section later in this chapter discusses this concept in detail.

- ❑ **Support for application events.** An implementation of the **Observer** design pattern, publishing application events to registered application listeners, decoupling between senders and recipients. Listeners can also receive notifications of context lifecycle events. *Note that the Spring AOP framework is an alternative for setting up notification of application "events."*

The central interface is `org.springframework.context.ApplicationContext`. This extends `org .springframework.beans.factory.ListableBeanFactory`. Thus application code can work with an `ApplicationContext` as though it is a `BeanFactory`. The relation between the involved interfaces is illustrated in Figure 7-1.

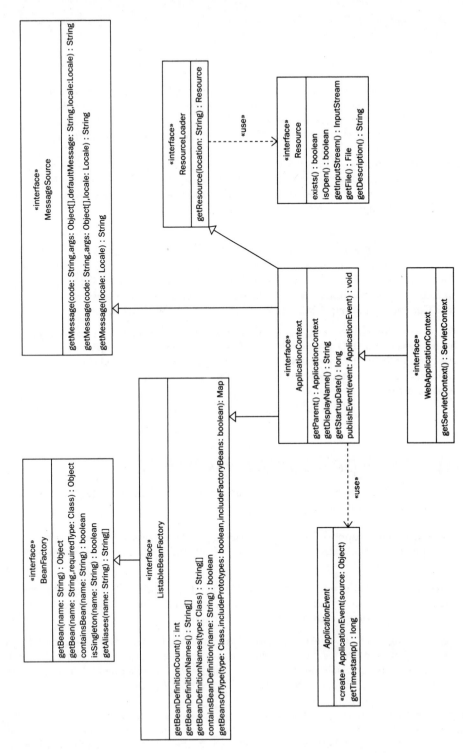

Figure 7-1

Application contexts are intended as **central registries** within an application. They can nest; that is, it is possible to build a tree of application contexts from a root context. Bean resolution will work as with hierarchical bean factories, checking the current context before falling back to the parent context. A typical scenario is a web application with one **root web application context** that hosts the business and data access layers, plus multiple dispatcher servlets with their own child contexts that define mappings and web controllers.

A web-specific sub-interface of `org.springframework.context.ApplicationContext`, `org.springframework.web.context.WebApplicationContext`, adds a method to retrieve the current `javax.servlet.ServletContext`. Most components—if context-aware at all—will rely only on the generic `ApplicationContext` interface, because there is hardly any functionality that the `ServletContext` offers beyond that which the `ApplicationContext` interface already provides in a generic fashion. Thus it's usually best to avoid dependence on a servlet environment; it's better to use the Spring abstraction, which can run in *any* environment.

Out-of-the-box implementations of the `ApplicationContext` interface include:

- ❑ `org.springframework.context.support.FileSystemXmlApplicationContext`
- ❑ `org.springframework.context.support.ClassPathXmlApplicationContext`
- ❑ `org.springframework.web.context.support.XmlWebApplicationContext`

All of them can read in XML bean definition files that conform to the "spring-beans" DTD. For example, with `ClassPathXmlApplicationContext`:

```
ApplicationContext ac =
    new ClassPathXmlApplicationContext("/applicationContext.xml");
MyBean myBean = (MyBean) ac.getBean("myBean");
```

You can also specify multiple file locations to be merged into a single application context instance. Each file must conform to the DTD; they can refer to each other's beans with normal bean references. This is useful for splitting up large middle tier application contexts, for example by module or into a business context and a data access context.

> Generally, it is preferable to work with bean factories if you don't explicitly need application context functionality. Working with the least specific interface is normally a good practice. A bean factory can host all kinds of middle tier functionality like AOP, transaction management, and Hibernate and JDO support. Therefore, it should be powerful enough for most use cases within custom application components.

Lifecycle Callbacks

Since an application context *is* a bean factory, all lifecycle callbacks available in a bean factory are also available in an application context: `InitializingBean`, `DisposableBean`, declarative init and destroy methods, and `BeanFactoryAware`. Note that `BeanFactoryAware` beans will receive a reference to the underlying bean factory of the application context, not to the `ApplicationContext` facade.

Factory-created beans that want to access their containing application context can implement the `org` `.springframework.context.ApplicationContextAware` interface. They will receive a reference to the `ApplicationContext` on initialization, via the `setApplicationContext` callback method. This method will be called immediately after the `setBeanFactory` method of `BeanFactoryAware`, if both interfaces are implemented (which should never be necessary).

```
public interface ApplicationContextAware {

    void setApplicationContext(ApplicationContext context)
        throws BeansException;
}
```

Many components within the Spring framework itself are `ApplicationContextAware`, but it is rarely necessary to implement this callback interface in application beans. There are two main incentives to do so: access to the message source, and access to file resources. However, this can also be achieved via more specific dependencies—for example, the `org.springframework.context.ResourceLoaderAware` interface:

```
public interface ResourceLoaderAware {

    void setResourceLoader(ResourceLoader resourceLoader);
}
```

As an ApplicationContext is required to implement the `org.springframework.core.io.Resource` `Loader` interface, it will typically simply pass itself to the `setResourceLoader` method. The benefit is that the receiving component does not have to be run in an `ApplicationContext`: It can easily be run with a plain `org.springframework.core.io.DefaultResourceLoader`, for example.

We'll discuss specific dependencies for access to the message source and access to file resources, respectively, in the next two sections.

A further important callback interface is `org.springframework.context.web.ServletContextAware`. This can be implemented by objects intended to run in a `WebApplicationContext`, and can be used to save a reference to the `javax.servlet.ServletContext`.

```
public interface ServletContextAware {

    void setServletContext(ServletContext servletContext);
}
```

The `WebApplicationContext` interface itself also provides access to the `ServletContext`, via its `get` `ServletContext()` method. The benefit of using the `ServletContextAware` interface is that the component can be run outside a Spring `WebApplicationContext`, configuring it with a plain `Servlet` `Context` reference.

Message Source

Beyond bean factory functionality, ApplicationContext also extends the `org.springframework` `.context.MessageSource` interface. Messages can be retrieved via a variety of `getMessage` methods, taking message codes, message arguments, and/or default messages.

```
String message = context.getMessage("myCode",
                              new Object[] {"myArg1", "myArg2"},
                              Locale.US);
```

Objects that implement the `org.springframework.context.MessageSourceResolvable` interface can be resolved by direct passing into the corresponding `getMessage` method. An example of such an object is the `org.springframework.validation.FieldError` class from the Spring generic validation support, typically retrieved from a validation errors holder that implements the `org.springframework` `.validation.Errors` interface as follows:

```
Errors errors = ...
FieldError fieldError = errors.getFieldError("myField");
String message = context.getMessage(fieldError, Locale.US);
```

The underlying `MessageSource` is defined as a bean with name `messageSource` in the application context, allowing for arbitrary implementations. (The bean name `messageSource` has a special meaning to an application context.) The default implementation is a `ResourceBundleMessageSource`, wrapping the standard `java.util.ResourceBundle`. The only parameter that it requires is the `basename` of the bundle, for example `messages` for `messages.properties` (`message_en.properties`, `message_de` `.properties`, and so on) file in the root of the class path (according to `java.util.ResourceBundle` rules).

```
<bean id="messageSource"
    class="org.springframework.context.support.ResourceBundleMessageSource">
  <property name="basename">
    <value>messages</value>
  </property>
</bean>
```

As an alternative to the default `ResourceBundleMessageSource` implementation, Spring also includes the `ReloadableResourceBundleMessageSource`, which provides similar services but can be configured to check for modifications of the underlying properties files, in contrast to the permanent caching of `java.util.ResourceBundle`. This is particularly useful in a web application: The properties files can be kept in the WEB-INF directory, allowing for on-the-fly modification when using an expanded WAR file (similar to modifications of JSPs at runtime that trigger automatic recompilation).

Message sources nest like bean factories: If a message cannot be resolved in the current context, the parent source is asked. Thus, child contexts can define their own set of messages, even overriding specific messages of the parent context.

The `MessageSource` can also be accessed directly, simply by specifying a reference to the `messageSource` bean, as follows:

```
<bean id="myApplicationBean" class="mypackage.MyApplicationBean">
  <property name="messageSource">
    <ref bean="messageSource"/>
  </property>
</bean>
```

Thus, an application bean does not have to implement the `ApplicationContextAware` interface to be able to resolve messages. The `messageSource` bean offers the full power of the `MessageSource` directly, including awareness of being nested in a hierarchy. The `ApplicationContext` is simply a facade for the underlying `MessageSource`.

File Resources

An important feature of application contexts is generic access to file resources. The `ApplicationContext` interface extends the `org.springframework.core.io.ResourceLoader` interface: Its `getResource` method returns an implementation of the `org.springframework.core.io.Resource` interface for the given path. Such a resource descriptor allows consistent access to the underlying file resource via `getInputStream()` and `getFile()` methods, regardless of the nature of the resource.

```
Resource logConfig = context.getResource("classpath:log4j.properties");
Properties logProps = new Properties();
logProps.load(logConfig.getInputStream());
```

```
Resource templateDir = context.getResource("file:C:/myapp/templates");
File dirHandle = templateDir.getFile();
```

```
Resource adminFile = context.getResource("WEB-INF/admin.properties");
Properties adminProps = new Properties();
adminProps.load(adminFile.getInputStream());
```

Depending on the given location, an appropriate `Resource` implementation will be returned:

❑   `org.springframework.core.io.ClassPathResource`

❑   `org.springframework.core.io.FileSystemResource`

❑   `org.springframework.web.context.support.ServletContextResource`

All application contexts support standard URLs with protocols like "file:" and "http:", plus the Spring "classpath:" pseudo protocol for accessing class path resources. A plain file path like "WEB-INF/admin.properties" is interpreted in a context-specific fashion:

❑   `ClassPathXmlApplicationContext`: as class path resource

❑   `FileSystemXmlApplicationContext`: as relative path in the file system

❑   `XmlWebApplicationContext`: as ServletContext resource, relative to the WAR root

When leveraging such relative paths, file locations in an application context are not necessarily dependent on a particular runtime environment. For example, a context definition that contains a "WEB-INF/admin.properties" resource path can be loaded either via `XmlWebApplicationContext` or `FileSystemXmlApplicationContext`: Provided that the latter is executed with the root of an expanded WAR as working directory, the same path specification will work in both runtime environments. The exact same bean definition can therefore be run in a non–web application context, for example for testing purposes, as long as the relative file path structure matches.

An application bean that requires access to a file resource can implement the `ApplicationContextAware` interface to receive a reference to the `ApplicationContext` that it runs in, using that reference to invoke `getResource` accordingly. However, this is recommended only if you need the `ApplicationContext` reference for other reasons as well; if not, it's preferable to implement the `ResourceLoaderAware` interface as follows:

```java
public class MyTemplateProcessor implements ResourceLoaderAware {

  private String templateDirLocation;
  private String adminFileLocation;
  private Resource templateDir;
  private Resource adminFile;

  public void setTemplateDir(String templateDir) {
    this.templateDirLocation = templateDir;
  }

  public void setAdminFile(String adminFile) {
    this.adminFileLocation = adminFile;
  }

  public void setResourceLoader(ResourceLoader resourceLoader) {
    this.templateDir = resourceLoader.getResource(this.templateDirLocation);
    this.adminFile = resourceLoader.getResource(this.adminFileLocation);
  }
  ...
}
```

The ResourceLoader reference can be used for loading any number of file resources, using arbitrary naming patterns. For the typical case of single resource locations, a convenient alternative is to expose a bean property of type Resource, expecting to receive a *resource descriptor* instead of looking it up via a String location:

```java
public class MyTemplateProcessor {

  private Resource templateDir;
  private Resource adminFile;

  public void setTemplateDir(Resource templateDir) {
    this.templateDir = templateDir;
  }

  public void setAdminFile(Resource adminFile) {
    this.adminFile = adminFile;
  }
  ...
}
```

The application context can populate such Resource dependencies from location strings, applying the same rules as the ApplicationContext.getResource method:

```xml
<bean id="myTemplateProcessor" class="mypackage.MyTemplateProcessor">
  <property name="templateDir">
    <value>file:C:/myapp/templates</value>
  </property>
  <property name="adminFile">
    <value>WEB-INF/admin.properties</value>
  </property>
</bean>
```

Note that this application bean does not implement `ApplicationContextAware` or `ResourceLoader Aware` but is still able to receive handles to context-specific file resources. This way, the bean can easily be reused in non-`ApplicationContext` environments: All `Resource` implementations in the `org.springframework.core.io` package naturally allow for use in a library style.

```
MyTemplateProcessor myTemplateProcessor = new MyTemplateProcessor();
myTemplateProcessor.setTemplateDir(
    new FileSystemResource("C:/myapp/templates");
myTemplateProcessor.setAdminFile(
    new ClassPathResource("admin.properties");
```

Obviously, this application bean is still dependent on Spring through the use of the `Resource` interface, but this is a less intrusive dependence than an application context.

> The **Resource** concept supported by application contexts is a powerful way to access file resources, supporting all kinds of file locations within a single mechanism. Resource loading via the **ApplicationContext** is also heavily used within the Spring framework itself: for example, to load configuration files from the WEB-INF directory of a web application.
>
> As an alternative, consider loading resources from the class path. This allows your application objects to load their resources in a consistent way without any Spring dependencies. However, the Spring **Resource** support in the **org.springframework. core.io** package also lends itself to programmatic use: It is not dependent on Spring IoC. Hence, we recommend the use of **Resource** bean properties to enable access to any kind of file resource in a generic fashion.

Bean Factory Post-processing

A special capability of an application context is that it allows for *post-processing* of the bean definitions that have been read in by the underlying bean factory. In the commonest case, the beans are defined in an XML file; they can be post-processed to override certain property values or to resolve placeholders in property values. This enables applications to keep certain administration properties in an external file: This way, an administrator doesn't have to understand the application context XML file or the Spring XML format at all.

Such post-processors can simply be defined as beans in the application context that implement the `org.springframework.beans.factory.config.BeanFactoryPostProcessor` interface. They will receive special treatment on context startup, being applied before any other beans and thus being able to change the bean definitions for any other bean.

```
public interface BeanFactoryPostProcessor {

    void postProcessBeanFactory(ConfigurableListableBeanFactory beanFactory)
        throws BeansException;
}
```

An out-of-the-box implementation that comes with the framework is `PropertyOverrideConfigurer`. It reads in a properties file that contains `beanName.propertyName=value` style override values for bean properties. This post-processor can be configured in an application context definition as follows:

```
<beans>

  <bean id="myConfigurer" class="org.springframework.beans.factory.
    config.PropertyOverrideConfigurer">
   <property name="location">
     <value>WEB-INF/admin.properties</value>
   </property>
  </bean>

  <bean id="myInventoryManager" class="ebusiness.DefaultInventoryManager"/>

  <bean id="myProductManager" class="ebusiness.DefaultProductManager">
   <property name="inventoryManager">
     <ref bean="myInventoryManager"/>
   </property>
   <property name="retrieveCurrentStock">
     <value>true</value>
   </property>
  </bean>

</beans>
```

The `admin.properties` file can be taken from any location that the resource mechanism supports, as discussed in the previous section. The file can contain lines like the following that will override the corresponding values in the XML definition file.

```
myProductManager.retrieveCurrentStock=false
```

Another out-of-the-box implementation of `BeanFactoryPostProcessor` is `PropertyPlaceholderConfigurer`. It resolves Ant-style placeholders in a properties file. Note that the actual placeholder syntax is configurable via the `PropertyPlaceholderConfigurer` bean properties.

```
<beans>

  <bean id="myConfigurer" class="org.springframework.beans.factory.
    config.PropertyPlaceholderConfigurer">
   <property name="location">
     <value>WEB-INF/admin.properties</value>
   </property>
  </bean>

  <bean id="myInventoryManager" class="ebusiness.DefaultInventoryManager"/>

  <bean id="myProductManager" class="ebusiness.DefaultProductManager">
   <property name="inventoryManager">
     <ref bean="myInventoryManager"/>
   </property>
   <property name="retrieveCurrentStock">
```

```
            <value>${retrieve_current_stock}</value>
        </property>
    </bean>

</beans>
```

Here, the `admin.properties` file must define values for the *placeholder keys* used in the XML file.

```
retrieve_current_stock=false
```

The latter mechanism *pulls* in values from a properties file while the former *pushes* bean property values from a properties file to the application context. This push approach has the advantage that it can override any bean property value without explicit placeholders in the application context. The pull approach does need explicit placeholders: This makes the replacement more obvious, and allows multiple references to the same placeholder in different bean property values.

You can easily write your own `BeanFactoryPostProcessor` implementation that reads in any custom configuration. However, the out-of-the-box implementations `PropertyOverrideConfigurer` and `PropertyPlaceholderConfigurer` are sufficient for many scenarios, particularly as `Property PlaceholderConfigurer` allows for completely custom keys in the properties file.

A similar mechanism is **post-processing of *bean instances*,** provided via the `org.springframework .beans.factory.config.BeanPostProcessor` interface. A bean post-processor can be used to create AOP proxies automatically, based on pointcuts defined as beans in the current application context. This mechanism is used to create AOP proxies automatically based on source-level metadata attributes, offering a simple programming model similar to the .NET ServicedComponent functionality. This feature is discussed along with the Spring AOP framework in Chapter 8.

> As the **BeanFactoryPostProcessor** mechanism illustrates, Spring gets maximum mileage out of its IoC container: Even framework-specific classes such as bean post-processors, web controllers, and AOP interceptors and pointcuts are defined within the IoC model. This makes Spring configuration highly consistent, and makes Spring easier to learn, because one mechanism is used consistently for application code and framework configuration. And, of course, Spring IoC is a powerful means of configuration for nearly *any* object, framework, or application.

Summary

In this chapter we've surveyed the Spring Framework, focusing on the bean factory concept that serves as the foundation for higher-level services. Through its **lightweight Inversion of Control container**, Spring provides a consistent structure for J2EE applications. This delivers many important benefits:

❑ It **eliminates the need for ad hoc use** of singletons and factories.

❑ It enables us to **write application code against interfaces**, rather than classes, following good OO practice. This has major benefits in terms of pluggability and testability.

❑ It enables us to **manage configuration in a consistent manner** across applications. For example, there is no more need to read the code in a class to find out what magic property keys it relies on.

❑ It builds on the **standard JavaBeans infrastructure.** Application objects are normally implemented as JavaBeans, exposing both simple configuration parameters and dependencies on collaborators via JavaBean properties.

❑ It **improves testability** by eliminating the hard-to-test Singleton pattern, and removing the need for application code to perform resource lookup, which often involves hard-to-stub APIs such as JNDI.

The Spring IoC container—like Spring as a whole—is highly extensible. The **"factory bean"** concept introduces a level of indirection, allowing a factory bean to return objects of a different type, possibly as the result of resource lookup or AOP proxying. **Post-processing** of bean definitions or bean instances can be used to modify the properties of a bean in a bean factory, or to automatically proxy any bean.

Besides its lightweight container, Spring also provides a consistent set of **abstractions for enterprise services** such as transaction management and data access. I haven't focused on these features in this chapter, as they are discussed in other chapters. The final piece of the Spring jigsaw is the **AOP framework**, which enables Spring to provide declarative enterprise services based on its service abstractions.

Together, this combination of a powerful, extensible IoC container and an abstraction for enterprise services, makes Spring a good replacement for local EJB Session Beans in many applications. Its value is particularly obvious in web applications, in which Spring provides a **closely integrated solution** from web tier to EIS tier.

If you want to implement a truly distributed application, EJB remains a good technology to do so: Spring provides support for lightweight remoting protocols but no means for distributed transactional objects. However, Spring can also bring value to EJB applications, by simplifying the implementation of EJBs and client code that accesses EJBs.

Spring is by no means the only way to do J2EE without EJB, or without heavy emphasis on EJB. However, it's important you use *some* generic framework to structure your application. Relying on ad hoc solutions to solve common infrastructure problems is wasteful, and poses ongoing productivity and maintainability issues. Similar programming models can be achieved with other solutions, for example:

❑ IoC containers like **PicoContainer** can provide the foundation for lightweight application development, if enriched with AOP functionality and middle tier services to address enterprise application requirements like transactional execution or seamless remoting. Such building blocks can serve as the foundation for an in-house application framework, gluing together various tools in a custom manner.

❑ Web frameworks like **WebWork** and **Struts** become more flexible with every release. Features like action interceptors or action chains allow for better separation of concerns. If you do not require dedicated middle tier services and do not need to run your business logic outside of a web environment, such a solution might be a good choice. Note that **XWork**, the foundation of **WebWork2**, even provides a framework for web-independent actions.

While all of these are sound solutions, each of them must be combined with a service provision model and an AOP framework in order to achieve the same comprehensive solution as Spring. Spring is also unique in addressing all architectural tiers: None of the other dedicated IoC containers offers a closely integrated web framework. While XWork/WebWork2 is a web-oriented command framework that offers basic IoC, it is typically combined with a more sophisticated container like Spring or Pico.

All things considered, we believe that the Spring solution is the most comprehensive and most consistent approach available today. However, you don't need to adopt Spring to follow our overall architectural advice. IoC in general is a very powerful approach to managing business objects, so we recommend that you use an IoC container like PicoContainer even if you don't choose to use Spring.

8

Declarative Middleware Using AOP Concepts

You must have heard the buzz around AOP in the last year. In this chapter I'll look at why AOP is important to the future of J2EE, and why it can be key to successful use of J2EE without EJB.

EJB owes much of its success to the deserved popularity of declarative middleware services such as container-managed transactions. AOP provides a powerful alternative way of providing such declarative enterprise services without most of the baggage of EJB. AOP service provision can work particularly well in conjunction with a lightweight container infrastructure, and along with source-level metadata attributes. Unlike EJB, AOP can also be used to deliver custom declarative services where appropriate, and to complement OOP for expressing program structure.

As we're primarily interested in a replacement for EJB, the subset of AOP we'll focus on concerns **method interception**. This is not all there is to AOP. However, it's all we need to solve some of the most pressing practical problems in J2EE. It's also a proven paradigm. Such limited use of AOP is not experimental, and won't have unpredictable effects on application structure.

I'll briefly introduce fundamental AOP concepts before moving onto the subset of AOP most important to J2EE, and how you can use it. Please refer to one of the books or articles listed in the "References" section near the end of this chapter for a detailed introduction to AOP.

I'll cover a number of AOP technologies, principally:

❑   **AspectJ:** A language extension to Java that pioneered AOP. AspectJ provides a powerful AOP framework, but no integrated support for enterprise services.

❑   **The Spring Framework:** An application framework including both an AOP framework and a consistent approach to enterprise services.

❑   **JBoss 4:** An open source J2EE application server with an AOP framework designed to allow declarative enterprise services to be applied to POJOs.

Both JBoss and Spring provide aspects addressing common concerns such as transaction management.

AOP 101

AOP stands for **Aspect-Oriented Programming**, a term coined by Gregor Kiczales at PARC in 1996. AOP decomposes systems into **aspects** or **concerns**, rather than objects. This is a different way of thinking about application structure than OOP, which considers objects hierarchically.

Motivation

OOP is a successful and expressive paradigm. Many domain concepts naturally can be expressed as objects, modularizing common code. However, there are areas where OOP doesn't shine.

One measure of the success of OOP is how it serves to avoid code duplication.

> **Code duplication is the ultimate code smell. It's a sign that something is very wrong with implementation or design.**

OOP generally does an excellent job of eliminating code duplication. Concrete inheritance helps us leverage shared behavior; polymorphism enables us to treat objects of different classes consistently when we're interested in their common characteristics. However, there are some cases when we can't use OOP to eliminate code duplication, or where the OO solution is clumsy.

Take the example of custom security checks. Imagine that we want to check whether the user has permission to execute a particular method, and throw an exception if she doesn't. If we address this programmatically, OO can't really help us. We'll end up with code like this:

```java
public class MyBusinessObject implements BusinessObject {
    public void businessMethod1() throws UnauthorizedException {
        doSecurityCheck();
        // Do the work of method1
    }

    public void businessMethod2() throws UnauthorizedException {
        doSecurityCheck();
        // Do the work of method2
    }

    // Other methods requiring a security check omitted

    public void requiresNoSecurityCheck() {
        // Do the work of method
    }

    protected void doSecurityCheck() throws UnauthorizedException {
        // Implement the security check
    }
}
```

Such code duplication is painful to write and maintain. We really want to gather the common code together.

Unfortunately, OO doesn't give us a good way of gathering together and **modularizing** such scattered code. We can *minimize* the amount of code duplication, as in the previous example, which factors the security check into its own method. But we can't eliminate it, and we can't ensure that the necessary boilerplate code is always inserted by the developer. A developer adding a new method requiring a security check to this class could forget to invoke doSecurityCheck(), compromising application security. The reason that OO can't help us here is that in order to identify the points in our execution flow where the security check should be invoked, we need a different way of looking at program structure than the OO hierarchical model provides.

Inheritance doesn't help in this situation, unless we resort to code generation. Each method needing the crosscutting security concern is independent, so it can't inherit from a generic version of that method. The classic implementation of EJB illustrates the code generation approach: the EJB container, or a deployment tool, generates a subclass of MyBusinessObject that overrides each business method, introducing the necessary crosscutting behavior. This eliminates the boilerplate code, but it complicates deployment and requires that objects benefiting from crosscutting must be EJBs. Also, only a fixed list of crosscutting concerns is addressed by EJB. Assuming that the custom security check in the previous example was necessary because J2EE role-based security was inadequate for the security requirements, EJB would not be able to address this requirement.

AOP aims to improve the modularity of programs by modularizing **crosscutting** common concerns in a more general way. Instead of sprinkling code haphazardly around an object model, with the inevitable code duplication, AOP aims to gather code addressing each concern into its own module. The EJB code generation approach illustrates some of the basic concepts of avoiding code duplication by providing a declarative model that can apply to multiple methods. However, a more general AOP solution offers significant advantages over the EJB model, as I'll discuss later in this chapter.

With AOP we would write code addressing the security concern and package it as an **aspect**. We would then tell the AOP implementation how to **weave** the aspect into the program flow at runtime. There are numerous strategies for this, which I'll discuss shortly. We could use code generation and compilation; an AOP language such as AspectJ; dynamic byte code generation; or a J2SE dynamic proxy.

With the AOP Alliance interfaces for method interception, which I'll discuss shortly, we could write the following code to modularize the security concern:

```
import org.aopalliance.intercept.MethodInterceptor;
import org.aopalliance.intercept.MethodInvocation;

public class SecurityInterceptor implements MethodInterceptor {
    public Object invoke(MethodInvocation invocation) throws Throwable {
        // Apply crosscutting code
        doSecurityCheck();

        // Call next interceptor
        return invocation.proceed();
    }
}
```

```
        protected void doSecurityCheck() throws UnauthorizedException {
            // Implementation omitted
        }
    }
```

The code would look similar in the JBoss AOP framework. In this AOP approach, the security concern is addressed by a single call to the doSecurityCheck() logic. Business objects such as MyBusinessObject don't need to concern themselves with security, meaning that the security details are decoupled from business logic and business logic is not obscured by tangential concerns. The interceptor is part of an aspect that can be applied to any method invocation. The AOP framework will provide a mechanism for defining the set of methods (pointcuts) eligible for interception. In this example, the domain problem has been decomposed not only into an object hierarchy, but also into crosscutting concerns. This enables us to refactor so as to remove the initial code duplication.

> **Think of AOP as *complementing*, not competing with, OOP. AOP can supplement OOP where it is weak.**

AOP in J2EE

Why do we need AOP? Doesn't J2EE supplement the Java OO model to address crosscutting enterprise concerns?

Within a J2EE context, we can use EJB to handle some concerns declaratively. With the predefined concerns EJB addresses, such as transaction management, we're in luck; with our own concerns such as custom security checks, we're not.

EJB isn't the only approach for declarative service provision in standard J2EE. We could also choose to use servlet filters to execute before and after HTTP requests in a web application. (The Sun Microsystems Adventure Builder J2EE sample application takes this approach.) This lets us introduce our own arbitrary interception, but it's inappropriately tied to the servlet API. Also, it usually makes sense to deal with declarative middleware issues at business object level, rather than HTTP request level. One HTTP request might result in the invocation of multiple business objects. Sometimes there might be legitimate reasons for each of these to have its own declarative services.

We could also use a framework such as WebWork 2 that provides an interception capability: in this case, via the XWork *interceptor stack* associated with invocations of application-specific action objects. This is a good option if you are already using such a framework. However, again it's less general than a true AOP framework, and is likely to provide less flexibility and potentially lose the benefits of strong typing. You can't put declarative services around any method; only around certain invocations managed by the framework.

Crosscutting can be used to address enterprise concerns such as transaction management, security checks, or acquiring and relinquishing resources such as JDO or Hibernate sessions, as well as application-specific concerns.

> The AOP buzzword may be new, but a *declarative* approach to middleware, involving some form of interception, is familiar from EJB and a number of other technologies. It's common to many technology platforms, including Microsoft MTS and .NET Framework, as well as frameworks such as XWork.

Definitions

Let's begin by defining some of the important concepts in AOP. Much of the terminology was originated by the creators of AspectJ, who pioneered AOP research.

- ❏ **Concern:** A **concern** is a particular issue, concept, or area of interest for an application: typically, a goal the application must meet. The security check shown in the previous section reflects a security concern; transaction management or performance monitoring are other common concerns. A concern may or may not have been captured in a code structure in an OO application.

- ❏ **Crosscutting concern:** A *crosscutting concern* is a concern for which the implementation cuts across many classes, like the security check in the previous example. Crosscuts are often messy in OOP.

- ❏ **Aspect:** An **aspect** is a modularization of a crosscutting concern; the gathering together of code that might otherwise have been scattered.

- ❏ **Join point:** A point during the execution of a program. Examples include:

    - ❏ **Method invocation.** This may include constructor invocation (although not all AOP frameworks support advising object construction).

    - ❏ **Field access.** Read or write access to an instance variable. Not all AOP frameworks advise field access. Those that do distinguish between read and write access.

    - ❏ **Throws.** A particular exception being thrown.

- ❏ **Advice:** Action taken at a particular join point. Many AOP frameworks model an advice as an *interceptor:* an object that receives a callback when the join point is about to be invoked at runtime. Examples of advice include:

    - ❏ Checking security credentials before allowing a join point to execute, as in the earlier security check example.

    - ❏ Beginning a transaction before executing a method join point, and committing it or rolling it back afterward.

- ❏ **Pointcut:** A set of join points, defined to specify when an advice should fire. Pointcuts are often described using regular expressions or another wildcard syntax. Some AOP technologies support composition of pointcuts.

- ❏ **Introduction:** Adding methods or fields to an existing Java class or interface. This can be used to achieve multiple inheritance in Java (see the following bullet item) or to attach a new API to an existing object model. For example, an introduction could cause an object graph to implement the W3C XML Node interface.

- ❑ **Mixin inheritance:** A **mixin** class encapsulates a piece of functionality that is "mixed into" existing classes without the use of conventional inheritance. In an AOP context, mixins are achieved through introductions. Mixins can be used to simulate multiple inheritance in Java.

- ❑ **Weaving:** Assembling aspects into a complete execution flow, or a complete class (in the case of introductions).

A call is said to **proceed** when advice lets execution flow proceed to the operation at the join point, such as a method invocation of field access.

Let's look more closely at the different types of advice:

- ❑ **Before (pre):** Before the join point is invoked.

- ❑ **After (post):** After the join point is invoked. There are three types of **after** advice in AspectJ:

  - ❑ After successful completion of a call, in which no exception was thrown. AspectJ and Spring term this **after returning** advice.

  - ❑ After throwing a particular exception or subclass. AspectJ terms this **after throwing** advice, Spring **throws** advice.

  - ❑ After *any* call to the join point, regardless of whether it threw an exception. AspectJ terms this **after** advice.

- ❑ **Around:** The advice is given control and responsibility for invoking the join point, as well as doing its work. The advice is responsible for causing the call to **proceed**, typically by invoking a special method.

The parameters to different advice types vary: for example, the return value will be available to after advice, but not throws advice.

Around advice can implement all of these advice types, by explicitly causing the join point to proceed. For example, in the case of throws advice, an around advice can catch any exception thrown by the join point's execution and see if it matches the relevant rule. The AspectJ team chose to distinguish between the other forms of advice from a usability perspective. They felt that using the weakest possible advice makes programs clearer. For example, a before or after returning advice can't change any return value from the join point. There is also the risk with around advice that the developer will fail to cause the join point to proceed correctly. Many interception-based frameworks, such as JBoss, offer only around advice. Currently Spring is the only interception-based implementation that supports a full range of advice types.

Pointcuts can further distinguish between **static** and **dynamic** criteria. Static criteria involves conditional advice based on information available at deploy time: for example, intercept the invocations of all getter methods on a particular class. Dynamic criteria involve conditional advice, based on information available only at runtime. For example, a particular method invocation may be included in a pointcut only if its return value is null.

Some other common terminology is AOP technology specific:

❑ **Interceptor:** Many AOP frameworks (such as Spring and JBoss 4, but not AspectJ) use the notion of field and method **interception**. This involves a **chain** of interceptors around a join point such as method interception. Each interceptor in the chain normally invokes the next interceptor in the chain. Interception is really an implementation strategy, rather than an AOP concept.

❑ **AOP proxy:** Object reference that is **advised**—that is, for which AOP advice will execute. As with interception the notion of an AOP proxy doesn't apply to all implementations. In particular, it doesn't apply to AspectJ, in which advice is built into the advised class's byte code. However, the notion of an AOP proxy is fundamental to interception-based AOP frameworks. An AOP proxy may be a J2SE dynamic proxy or may have been generated using byte code manipulation tools.

❑ **Target object:** In frameworks using interception, the object instance at the end of an interceptor chain. Occasionally there will be no target object; in rare cases, the whole of the desired behavior may be achieved by combining interceptors. (For example, an object may be composed of multiple "mixins": see below.) AOP technologies such as AspectJ in which weaving takes place at compile time don't have distinct target objects; in AspectJ, the target object's byte code includes all advice.

To see this terminology in action, let's look at our example again:

```
public class MyBusinessObject implements BusinessObject {
    public void businessMethod1() throws UnauthorizedException {
        doSecurityCheck();
        // Do the work of method1
    }

    public void businessMethod2() throws UnauthorizedException {
        doSecurityCheck();
        // Do the work of method2
    }

    public void requiresNoSecurityCheck() {
        // Do the work of method
    }

    protected void doSecurityCheck() throws UnauthorizedException {
        // Implement the security check
    }
    }
```

We view security management as an **aspect** here. The interceptor we saw in the previous example is an **advice**.

The three public business methods are the relevant **join points** here. As the security check should apply only to selected methods—businessMethod1() and businessMethod2() and other methods omitted from the listing, but not the requiresNoSecurityCheck() method—we would target the security advice with a **pointcut** matching only those methods. When we deploy this business object along with the security interceptor in Spring, Spring will perform weaving at runtime to create an **AOP proxy**: a JDK dynamic proxy invoking the target object after applying the security advice.

Figure 8-1 shows how control flow flows from the AOP proxy through the interceptor chain to the target method and back to the caller.

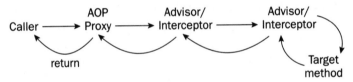

Figure 8-1

History

Many of the ideas associated with AOP are not new—few truly valuable ideas are. For example, **meta-classes**, supported by a number of programming languages, such as Python, offered a way to modify the behavior of classes, helping to eliminate code duplication across multiple methods. Older languages such as CLOS offered before, after, and around constructs. Interception has been used in many technologies and frameworks.

What was genuinely new in the PARC AOP research project was the idea of sophisticated pointcuts, and (compared to most previous interception technologies) of advised classes being oblivious of the advice.

Certain OO design patterns solve some of the problems AOP aims to solve. In particular:

- ❏ The **Decorator** pattern (GoF) allows the addition of custom behavior before and after (*around*, in AOP terminology) a method invocation, in the form of a Decorator class that implements the same interface as the underlying target object and invokes it, as well as executing any custom code. The Decorator is a useful pattern, but requires coding a custom decorator per target class. For example, we would need a transaction decorator for every business object we wanted to make transactional; clearly not a viable option in a large system, and questionably better than programmatic transaction management in the actual business objects. On the positive side, the Decorator pattern preserves strong typing of the target interface, and does help to modularize particular concerns.

- ❏ The **Observer** pattern (GoF) allows multiple objects to receive notification of events concerning an "observable" object. This can sometimes achieve the same results as AOP. However, it doesn't offer around advice, such as executing a method within a transactional context created by an advice; objects need to publish events to support it, meaning that objects aren't oblivious of the necessary plumbing; and there's no way for observers to change the course of execution flow. The Observer pattern is valuable, but it's by no means a substitute for AOP.

- ❏ The **Chain of Responsibility** pattern allows multiple objects in a chain to receive a request until one takes responsibility for handling it. This has some similarities to the common implementation of AOP using a chain of interceptors. However, objects using this approach must be aware of the plumbing, and it's necessary to set up a chain of responsibility for each method requiring one. Like the Decorator, this is not a generic solution for crosscutting concerns.

The **Decorator** and **Chain of Responsibility** allow us to distribute responsibilities amongst objects: that is, for each object to address one aspect. This goes a small part of the way toward AOP. However, in each case the solution to crosscutting problems is less elegant with the OO design pattern than it might be with AOP. In particular, it's impossible to preserve strong typing of advised methods without writing custom code to forward invocations (as in the **Decorator**).

Some existing technologies and frameworks offer interception. For example:

❑ CORBA offered the notion of **interceptors** in remote invocations, as do some web services frameworks, such as Apache Axis.

❑ Servlet filters, introduced in Servlet 2.3, are called before and after processing of web requests.

❑ XWork offers an "interceptor stack."

❑ EJB, which I'll discuss in detail shortly.

The main problem with such solutions is that they tie intercepted code to a particular API or context, such as processing a remote call. Most also sacrifice strong typing.

Thus AOP is an evolution and elegant generalization of previous concepts, rather than a radical new approach. Some of the interception technologies I've described are perfectly adequate for many applications. However, full-blown AOP is not necessarily more complex, yet much more expressive.

Interest in the J2EE community in implementing AOP using pure Java interception frameworks began to grow in late 2002. Rickard Oberg was one of the pioneers of this approach to AOP, and played a major role in popularizing it. Oberg's own AOP framework is part of a proprietary content management system. However, open source frameworks such as Nanning, AspectWerkz, and Spring have been available since early 2003.

EJB as a Subset of AOP

Hopefully the references to *method interception* as a common implementation strategy for AOP frameworks have reminded you of how EJB delivers enterprise services.

An EJB container must *intercept* method invocations to interpose custom behavior. The mechanics of this interception may vary: in some containers it will be implemented using dynamic proxies (discussed later in this chapter), while other containers use the code generation approach envisaged by the creators of the EJB spec, in which the EJB container generates a subclass of the EJB implementation class at deploy time or in a post-compilation step. EJB offers a fixed set of "crosscuts" to address concerns such as:

❑ Transaction management (CMT)

❑ Thread management

❑ Security

Let's look at how EJB addresses some of the key AOP concepts.

An **aspect** in EJB is shipped with the EJB container. For example, a particular server's implementation of CMT is implemented in the internals of the container, building on the overall application server's JTA implementation. A **join point** in EJB is execution of a method on an EJB's component interface. **Pointcuts** are specified in the EJB deployment descriptor. Pointcuts are defined statically, in terms of method names and (optionally) argument lists in the case of method overloading. The EJB server typically **weaves** in aspects either by code generation (generating a subclass of the EJB implementation class at deploy time and compiling it) or by introducing a dynamic proxy or some form of byte code generation.

> **EJB is in part a less general form of AOP interception, used to access a fixed set of J2EE services provided by the application server. This is an important point, because it means that AOP used as I'm advocating here is *not* experimental.**

The EJB interception model is very limited when compared to AOP technologies. For example:

❑ Advice can only apply to EJBs, not arbitrary classes.

❑ The pointcut model is limited. For example, it's not possible to specify particular advice on a particular exception being thrown by a business method. (The EJB container has fixed advice on system exceptions, such as "rollback the current transaction and remove the current EJB instance," but doesn't address application exceptions.)

❑ Pointcuts can't take dynamic information into account. If method doSomething(String name) has a container transaction associated with it, invoking it will *always* result in a transaction. It's not possible to specify non-transactional execution if the name argument is null, for example.

❑ It's impossible to add user-defined actions within standard EJB. (JBoss 3 added this capability, but it was very awkward to use.)

❑ It's impossible to change the implementation of any of the interceptors, beyond the configuration parameters exposed by the application server. For example, we can't decide that we don't want standard J2EE role-based security, but that we do want our own custom declarative security checks. We can't choose not to use JTA if we only need to access a single database.

Thus in comparison with EJB, AOP is much more general. EJB is weak as an interception model, but strong on its support for enterprise services. However, this suggests that, with the availability of suitable enterprise services, AOP may provide a superior replacement for EJB.

The similarities between EJB and AOP are important to emphasize, because it means that *an AOP solution based on method interception is not conceptually very different to an EJB solution.* Thus developers familiar with EJB can quickly understand how AOP can be used to achieve some of the same results.

It's also important to note some conceptual differences between EJB and AOP:

❑ EJB is intended as a component model, whereas AOP advice can apply to any object.

❑ EJBs are *intended* to have explicit knowledge of the runtime infrastructure supporting them: for example, being given a reference to an EJBContext interface. In AOP, objects are meant to be oblivious of the advice applied to them. However, as we've seen, there's a strong argument that business objects should *not* be forced to depend on knowledge of their context in all cases. When it is necessary—for example, to enable programmatic transaction rollback—it can be done in a much less invasive way than with EJB. Using AOP to deliver services non-invasively nicely complements the use of a non-invasive IoC framework.

> **I find it helpful to think of EJB versus AOP solutions in terms of restaurants:**
>
> **EJB provides a set menu—eat whatever the chef prepared, whether you like it or not.**
>
> **AOP offers dining à la carte—eat exactly what you want. You might even be able to order from other restaurants!**

In the remainder of this chapter, we'll look deeper at AOP implementation strategies and AOP frameworks, before focusing on the provision of enterprise services.

AOP Implementation Strategies

This is not a chapter on the mechanics of AOP frameworks, but a quick survey of some of the common implementation strategies for AOP frameworks is helpful even from an end-user perspective. The following are the main strategies used to implement AOP technologies, ordered from least to most powerful. (Note that greater power is not necessarily better, as I'll discuss in the following section):

- ❑ J2SE dynamic proxies
- ❑ Dynamic byte code generation
- ❑ Java code generation
- ❑ Use of a custom class loader
- ❑ Language extensions

Let's consider each of these in turn.

Dynamic Proxies

The most obvious implementation strategy for AOP in Java is to use Java 1.3+ **dynamic proxies**. Dynamic proxies are a powerful language construct that enable us to create an implementation of one or more interfaces on the fly. To implement around advice with a dynamic proxy, the dynamic proxy will invoke the necessary chain of interceptors. The last interceptor in the chain will invoke a target object (if there is one) via reflection.

The main positive with dynamic proxies is that they use a standard Java language feature. There's no need for a third-party library, besides the AOP framework itself, and no risk of strange effects on the behavior of the application server.

The main limitation of dynamic proxies is that it's impossible to proxy classes, rather than interfaces. In general, this constraint is no bad thing: we are primarily concerned with business objects and they should normally be behind interfaces.

Dynamic proxies perform pretty well in Java 1.4 and higher JVMs. However, a dynamic proxy strategy will inevitably incur reflection overhead.

Spring defaults to using dynamic proxies when proxying against interfaces. Nanning currently uses dynamic proxies exclusively.

Dynamic Byte Code Generation

To add the ability to proxy against classes, we need to go beyond the capabilities of dynamic proxies and move to **dynamic byte code generation**. Fortunately, Java's reflection and class-loading capabilities are very open, so this is not complex for libraries to implement.

A popular tool for this kind of byte code generation is CGLIB (Code Generation Library), available at `http://cglib.sourceforge.net/`. CGLIB is used by Spring to proxy classes, rather than interfaces. It achieves method interception by generating dynamic subclasses that override superclass methods and have hooks that invoke interceptor implementations. CGLIB-style byte code enhancement is proven through its use by Hibernate 2.x. Hibernate's success shows that users experience no problem using this approach in an application server environment.

One minor issue is that proxying by subclass cannot proxy `final` methods.

Java Code Generation

As with EJB code generation approaches, we can generate new Java source code that includes code to execute crosscutting code. This approach seems to be declining in popularity because of the availability of dynamic proxies and because dynamic byte code generation is simpler to work with.

Use of a Custom Class Loader

What if we want to advise *all* instances of a particular class? Or if we want to ensure that all instances are advised, however they are created? (That is, to change the behavior of the `new` operator.) In this case, another option is to look to Java's extensible class loading mechanism. By defining a custom class loader, we can apply advice automatically when a class is loaded. Such advice will occur even if the user constructs instances directly using the `new` operator. JBoss and AspectWerkz take this approach, loading information about the advice to weave in at runtime from XML configuration files.

The risks here are that this is taking us farther from standard Java. It may also be problematic in some application servers, as J2EE servers need to control the class-loading hierarchy.

Language Extensions

If we want to elevate aspects to first class status, we need a language that embraces AOP as well as OOP. This can be achieved by extending an existing OO language in the same way as C++ extended C to introduce OO concepts. AspectJ, which I'll discuss in the following section, takes this approach, extending Java.

AOP Implementations

Let's review some of the more important AOP implementations.

AspectJ

The most complete AOP implementation is AspectJ: a language extension to Java that treats AOP concepts as first-class citizens of the language. AspectJ provides its own compiler.

Unlike other AOP frameworks, which use standard Java and move pointcut definition into XML files, AspectJ wholly uses Java/AspectJ code rather than metadata. There are some advantages to this approach: in particular, it's type safe in some cases. However, it also has some disadvantages, as we'll see.

AspectJ has many impressive capabilities. Pointcuts and aspects are first-class language constructs. Aspects can participate in inheritance relationships, for example. AspectJ allows pointcuts to be based on a range of criteria including wildcards (for example, matching all setter methods in a certain package) and "control flow" (such as matching all setter methods invoked under a call initiated by a web controller).

AspectJ can attach advice to any method invocation, field access, object construction, or the throwing of exceptions. Advice will apply regardless of how an object was constructed or obtained, and will work in any class loader. Weaving occurs at compile time, although the AspectJ design aims to avoid committing to any particular weave time. The crosscutting code is compiled into the advised class.

AspectJ has unique capabilities such as the ability to modify the static structure of types in the application. For example, it's possible to introduce members, modify a type hierarchy (with some restrictions), declare compile-time errors and warnings, and "soften" exceptions (allow checked exceptions thrown by certain methods to be treated as unchecked).

Nevertheless, I think there are good reasons why AspectJ is *not* the best choice for the majority of J2EE applications. Let's examine its pros and cons, focusing on our desire to create a superior replacement for EJB.

Pros

AspectJ has many strengths:

- ❏ It's mature.
- ❏ It's well-documented. There are many online resources, and there are also several books on AspectJ.
- ❏ It has growing IDE support, especially in Eclipse, which now offers AspectJ refactorings. (AspectJ is now part of the Eclipse project.)
- ❏ It's very expressive, and supports the full range of AOP constructs.
- ❏ Compile-time weaving can potentially allow optimizations difficult (but not impossible) to achieve with runtime weaving. AspectJ will deliver minimal performance overhead in most cases. The code that AspectJ generates should be as efficient as custom-coding the same crosscutting concerns, with inferior modularization. There is no need to create "invocation" objects, as other AOP frameworks require.

Cons

However, there are significant negatives:

❑ The AspectJ syntax is complex and not especially intuitive. There's a significant learning curve, compared to most other AOP frameworks.

❑ Introducing a new language into an organization is a significant strategic move and probably best avoided, even if it's backward compatible with an existing language. It's possible to use AspectJ in a restricted way, but there's always a danger that this won't happen.

❑ Pointcuts are defined in Java/AspectJ code, along with advice. It's impossible to externalize pointcut configuration in an XML file—for example, enabling a single aspect to be reused in many contexts, each requiring a different pointcut. This is a serious problem for generic, system-level aspects. Such aspects should be applied in configuration, not application code.

❑ There's no concept of per instance advice. Advice will automatically apply to all instances of a class (although it's possible to hold per-instance state in aspects). Sometimes there is a legitimate reason to deploy multiple instances of the same class with different advice.

❑ All advice is built into the resulting class, potentially resulting in memory management issues in large applications.

❑ It's presently impossible to add or remove advice at runtime. Other AOP technologies support this. This is a moot point, as changing the structure of an application at runtime is potentially dangerous. But it may occasionally be useful.

❑ Great power means great responsibility. AspectJ offers a lot of power, and a lot of potential to abuse that power.

> The Pareto Principle has important lessons for using AOP, as in many other areas. To me, most of the value of AOP for J2EE applications at present is method interception, targeted using an expressive pointcut model. Pure Java frameworks can do this perfectly well.

AspectJ is arguably best suited to implementing *application-specific* aspects, closely tied to application code, rather than *generic* aspects such as transaction management aspects. With generic aspects, strong typing as offered by AspectJ is of little value, as an aspect can make no assumptions about the types on which it will operate. In contrast, externalizing pointcut definition from Java into XML code is compelling where generic aspects are concerned. As such generic aspects are the most important in J2EE development (in fact, all the use of AOP that many developers will choose to make), AspectJ is arguably not the ideal tool, and its areas of superiority over other AOP implementations are less significant.

> AspectJ has been used successfully in many applications, and is robust as well as powerful. However, I don't believe that it's the best choice for most J2EE projects needing declarative enterprise services.

AspectWerkz

AspectWerkz (`http://aspectwerkz.codehaus.org/`) is a pure-Java AOP framework, defining point-cuts in XML files.

As this is already a fairly long chapter, there's no room to look at AspectWerkz in detail. However, it has excellent documentation, and a good reputation among its users.

Unlike AspectJ, AspectWerkz supports "per JVM," "per class," "per instance," and "per thread" advice. Like AspectJ, AspectWerkz distinguishes between "pre," "post," and "around" advice. It also offers throws advice. It supports regular expression and control flow advice. However, it also provides the ability to add or remove advice at runtime.

AspectWerkz takes the class loader approach to weaving advice. Weaving is done at runtime, with no need for a special compilation step. There is also a "transformation" option, enabling classes to be "transformed" for use in any application server's class loader. Otherwise, an application server must be started using the AspectWerkz command line tool, customizing class loading.

JBoss 4

JBoss 3 opened up its EJB container by allowing customization of the interception process, and even the addition of application-specific interceptors for EJBs. This was an interesting and powerful capability, but obviously only applied to EJBs. Also, it was complex to configure and hence not widely used.

JBoss 4 takes the next step, making AOP one of the key capabilities of the application server.

Because of the popularity of JBoss, JBoss AOP is an important technology. It will be available to the many projects that use JBoss as their J2EE application server.

The JBoss Group take the view that it is the aspects themselves that are, in Marc Fleury's words, "the crown jewels" of middleware. This reflects a fundamental difference in the goals of JBoss versus other AOP frameworks, apart from Spring. The aim is not to provide an AOP framework as an end in itself, but to help simplify the use of enterprise services provided by the application server. This pragmatic view of AOP has proven controversial. However, I'm inclined to agree. An AOP framework is a means to an end, and JBoss offers a clear and important goal of applying enterprise services to POJOs.

The JBoss framework itself, like AspectWerkz, is based on control of the class loader. The AOP-aware class loader can apply interceptors, implementing a JBoss-specific interface, based on an XML syntax for defining pointcuts. Byte code manipulation is performed by the Javassist library (now part of JBoss).

At the time of writing, it's too early to draw conclusions on the likely quality of the JBoss 4 AOP model or implementation.

Pros

JBoss provides a fairly complete AOP framework. Its strengths include:

- ❑ Support for method, field, and constructor interception and introduction.

- ❑ Because JBoss uses a custom, AOP-aware class loader, object instances are automatically advised, however they are constructed. (That is, instances don't need to be obtained from a special factory.)

This is similar to the ease of use of .NET, in which the .NET runtime can automatically apply enterprise services on object construction.

❑ JBoss AOP integrates with JBoss's metadata attribute support, which can simplify provision of declarative services. (The relationship between AOP frameworks and attributes is discussed later in this chapter.)

❑ A management console providing information about deployed aspects and configuration control.

❑ Integration with the JBoss application server to deliver pre-packaged aspects to address common middleware problems.

Cons

On the negative side:

❑ Using JBoss AOP creates a lock-in to both the JBoss AOP framework and the JBoss application server. This cuts against the portability benefits of J2EE. However, as I've noted before, portability isn't everything. There's also a benefit in JBoss providing both application server and AOP framework, and hence a one-stop shop for common middleware services.

❑ Relatively complex XML configuration format.

❑ At the time of writing, JBoss metadata support uses XDoclet to generate XML interceptor definitions. This means that metadata needs to include specific information about the interceptors to use. (See the discussion about "prescriptive" metadata later in this chapter for details.)

❑ JBoss metadata attribute values are currently limited to Strings and XML fragments. .NET and Spring AOP allow attributes to be objects.

❑ As with other AOP technologies besides AspectJ, there is no strong typing for aspects.

> A major downside of JBoss 4 AOP is that it is non-portable. Although the JBoss AOP framework is available standalone, separate from the JBoss application server, it needs control over the class loader—a potential problem in other application servers. The power of JBoss AOP also results from its tie-in to JBoss internals: remove this, and the value proposition is much reduced.
>
> I recommend using a lightweight, portable AOP framework that does not constrain your choice of application server. However, if you're happy to commit to JBoss 4, and portability is not an issue, the JBoss AOP capabilities are worth a look. And JBoss 4 is less proprietary and more open than .NET.

Implementing interceptors in JBoss is similar to implementing interceptors in AOP Alliance-compliant frameworks. Interceptors must implement the `org.jboss.aop.Interceptor` interface, as demonstrated in the following snippet:

```
public interface Interceptor {
        String getName();
        InvocationResponse invoke(Invocation invocation) throws Throwable;
}
```

Each interceptor in the interceptor chain will normally call the `invokeNext()` method on the `Invocation` to proceed to the next interceptor in the chain.

Spring

Like JBoss, Spring provides aspects out of the box, as well as an AOP framework for exercising them. Like JBoss it reflects the view that the aspects themselves (such as transaction management aspects) are more important for many users and usages than the AOP framework.

Spring AOP integrates AOP support into Spring's lightweight container infrastructure, and combines AOP with Spring's services. While you can use Spring AOP without a Spring bean factory or application context, if you want to enjoy this integration, you can manage your interceptors and pointcuts as IoC components. The powerful "bean post processor" mechanism, described in the last chapter, can also be used to simplify AOP configuration.

Spring's AOP capabilities include:

❑   Full range of advice types. Around, before, after, and throws advice for method invocation, against interfaces or classes.

❑   Support for introductions and mixins. Interceptors can be stateless or stateful, depending on configuration.

❑   Expressive and extensible pointcut model. Regular expression support included. Supports pointcut composition operations.

❑   Control flow pointcuts, such as "all methods invoked from an MVC web controller."

❑   Facility for adding arbitrary advice types without modifying the core framework, by providing an adapter class.

❑   Programmatic or configuration-driven proxying.

Aspects are normally configured in XML files, as JavaBeans. Thus aspects themselves can be configured using the full capabilities of Spring IoC. There is also a metadata-driven option that abstracts above the AOP model, providing standard declarative services without the need for application developers to work directly with the AOP framework. We'll discuss this later in this chapter.

An advice such as an AOP Alliance interceptor or `org.springframework.aop.BeforeAdvice` specifies the behavior at the join point: in this case, around or before. All advices must implement the `org.aopalliance.aop.Advice` tag interface.

An **advisor** is a higher-level Spring concept that includes both advice and a pointcut to target it, providing a complete modularization of an aspect. This also allows pointcuts and advice to be reused independently.

Introductions are made using `IntroductionAdvisors`. Note that, unlike other advisors, introduction advisors do not contain a pointcut. Method-level matching does not make sense for introductions, which can apply only at class level.

Pros

Spring AOP has the following advantages:

❏ The AOP framework is integrated with the Spring IoC container. If you are already structuring your application using Spring, Spring AOP can be added very easily, as required. Consistent with the overall Spring approach, advice, advisors, and pointcuts are JavaBeans, configured in the same lightweight container. Thus familiar Spring concepts are leveraged.

❏ Spring does not offer only AOP, but important enterprise services already modularized. For example, Spring offers a transaction interceptor out of the box.

❏ Spring AOP, like the rest of Spring, is portable between application servers. There's no need to customize class loading.

❏ Spring AOP is integrated with pluggable metadata support, offering .NET-like ease of use without the need to work with AOP concepts directly. I'll discuss this in more detail later in this chapter.

❏ Spring implements the AOP Alliance interception interfaces, offering the ability to avoid vendor lock-in in interceptors.

❏ Negligible learning curve for users familiar with Spring IoC, partly because of the integration of the AOP framework with the IoC container. If there were no AOP buzzword, many users would find the typical application of the Spring declarative middleware services intuitive: especially if they were already familiar with EJB.

Cons

Spring AOP has the following disadvantages:

❏ Field interception is not supported.

❏ It's only possible to use configuration to advise objects obtained from a Spring IoC container, or to use the AOP framework programmatically; it's not possible to advice objects at class loader level so that the new operator returns an advised object. As all business objects in Spring applications are obtained from the IoC container, it's possible to apply advice in a much broader range of cases than is supported by EJB. However, it would be harder to apply advice to all objects to be persisted with Hibernate, for example. Like lack of support for field interception, this partly reflects a conscious decision. Spring is not intended to encourage advising each and every object. (This may pose performance problems, for example.) Spring *is* designed to encourage obtaining business objects from a Spring container, which helps to structure applications. And this way there's never any doubt as to which objects are advised, and what advice applies.

❏ As with most other AOP technologies besides AspectJ, there is no strong typing for interceptor code. However, Spring offers strong typing for implementing introductions and throws advice.

Advice Types and Pointcuts

Let's look at a simple diagnostic interceptor, showing how easy it is to implement interception around advice in Spring. This interceptor logs method invocations to the console:

```
import org.aopalliance.intercept.MethodInterceptor;
import org.aopalliance.intercept.MethodInvocation;
```

```
public class DebugInterceptor implements MethodInterceptor {

    public Object invoke(MethodInvocation invocation) throws Throwable {
        System.out.println("Debug interceptor: invocation=[" + invocation +
"]");
        Object rval = invocation.proceed();
        System.out.println("Debug interceptor: next returned");
        return rval;
    }

}
```

As this is an around advice, it's necessary to invoke the invocation's `proceed()` method to invoke the next interceptor in the chain and, eventually, the target join point. Note that there's no dependence on Spring APIs in this interceptor; it implements the AOP Alliance `MethodInterceptor` interface.

Implementing less powerful advice types is even simpler. For example, a before advice that logs method invocations:

```
public class DebugBeforeAdvice implements
            org.springframework.aop.MethodBeforeAdvice {
    public void before(Method m, Object[] args, Object target) throws Throwable {
        System.out.println("About to invoke method: " + m);
    }
}
```

Note that in this case we don't need to call a method to proceed down the advice chain. Before advice can add custom behavior before a method invocation, but cannot return its own return value. Thus there is less potential for programming errors.

If we're only interested in certain exceptions, **throws advice** is most appropriate. Throws advice is invoked after the return of the join point if the join point threw an exception. Spring offers typed throws advice. This means that the `org.springframework.aop.ThrowsAdvice` interface does not contain any methods: it is a tag interface identifying that the given object implements one or more typed throws advice methods. These should be of the form:

```
afterThrowing([Method], [args], [target], subclassOfThrowable)
```

Only the last argument is required. Thus there can be either one or four arguments, dependent on whether the advice method is interested in the method and arguments.

Spring automatically works out the exceptions that are supported by a throws advice from the method signatures. The following is a simple throws advice that receives RMI `RemoteExceptions`. No type cast is necessary to work with this exception:

```
public class RemoteThrowsAdvice implements ThrowsAdvice {
    public void afterThrowing(RemoteException ex) throws Throwable {
        // Do something with remote exception
    }
}
```

Throws advices can contain multiple throws advice methods, to handle different exception types.

All these advice types can be targeted using a pointcut. If no pointcut is used, the advice will match all method invocations.

The Spring pointcut model enables independent reuse of advice and pointcuts. It's possible to target different advice using the same pointcut, or to target a generic advice using different pointcuts. The org. springframework.aop.Pointcut interface is the central interface, used to target advices to particular classes and methods. The complete interface is shown in the following snippet:

```
public interface Pointcut {
    ClassFilter getClassFilter();
    MethodMatcher getMethodMatcher();
}
```

Splitting the Pointcut interface into two parts allows reuse of class and method matching parts, and fine-grained composition operations, such as performing a "union" with another method matcher.

The ClassFilter interface is used to restrict a pointcut to a given set of target classes. If the matches() method always returns true, all target classes will be matched:

```
public interface ClassFilter {
    boolean matches(Class clazz);
}
```

The MethodMatcher interface is normally more important than the ClassFilter interface. The complete interface is:

```
public interface MethodMatcher {
    boolean matches(Method m, Class targetClass);
    boolean isRuntime();
    boolean matches(Method m, Class targetClass, Object[] args);
}
```

The matches(Method, Class) method is used to test whether this pointcut ever matches a given method on a target class. This evaluation can be performed when an AOP proxy is created, to avoid the need for a test on every method invocation. If the 2-argument matches method returns true for a given method, and the isRuntime() method returns true, the 3-argument matches method will be invoked on every method invocation. This enables a pointcut to look at the arguments passed to the method invocation immediately before the target advice is to execute.

Most MethodMatcher implementations are static, meaning that their isRuntime() method always returns false. In this case, the 3-argument matches method will never be invoked.

Spring supports composition methods on pointcuts, such as union and intersection. Union refers to the methods that either pointcut matches. Intersection refers to the methods that both pointcuts match. Spring also provides convenience classes for implementing pointcuts and advisors. Please refer to the Spring reference documentation and Javadocs for detailed information.

We'll see how the AOP framework integrates with the Spring lightweight IoC container later in this chapter.

Nanning

Nanning Aspects (`http://nanning.codehaus.org`) is the most similar AOP framework to Spring. Nanning is a dedicated AOP framework created by Jon Tirsen in late 2002. Like Spring, Nanning does not offer field interception, and uses dynamic proxies.

Nanning Aspects differs from Spring in that it isn't part of a comprehensive solution offering enterprise services as well as an AOP framework. Its aim is to provide the simplest possible interception implementation. It emphasizes a programmatic style of advising objects, rather than a configuration-driven approach.

Nanning provides only interception around advice.

The AOP Alliance

The AOP Alliance (`www.sourceforge.net/projects/aopalliance`) aims to provide standard interfaces for a subset of AOP functionality. Currently this subset includes interception. This enables interception around advice, like the `MethodInterceptor` implementations shown in the previous example, to be implemented so as to be portable between interception-based AOP frameworks. This offers the ideal of ordering services "from a different restaurant."

As I've noted, it's difficult—indeed, potentially *dangerous*—to standardize an evolving area. Thus the AOP Alliance's goals and achievements to date are modest.

At the time of writing, Spring, Dynaop (`http://dynaop.dev.java.net/`) and JAC (`http://jac.objectweb.org/`) implement the AOP interception interfaces, and Nanning support is under development.

AOP Design Issues

So far we've considered some of the many possibilities of AOP in J2EE applications. We must also consider risks that AOP may introduce, and important decisions about how we use AOP.

Dangers of AOP

Let's begin by looking at the dangers introduced by AOP, real and imaginary.

Should We Intercept Fields?

To my mind, field interception is potentially dangerous. While method interception might change how objects behave, it does not usually change how objects *think they are behaving*. All access to object internals is through the methods provided by the class's original developer, who may, of course, have no knowledge of the aspects used at runtime. In other words, encapsulation is preserved. If we intercept field access, we are breaking encapsulation.

In general, I think that field interception is better avoided. As with field access in OO, AOP field interception can usually be replaced by method-level advice, preserving encapsulation.

> Field interception breaks encapsulation. This use of AOP is beginning to compete with, rather than complement, OOP.
>
> In practice, I've seen relatively few legitimate uses for field interception. Such uses are rare enough that there's a strong case for using specific, rather than generic, solutions when it's necessary. Examples include JDO's byte code enhancement and TopLink's reflection-based field manipulation. Such closely focused solutions are perfectly valid, but there's arguably more danger and benefit in opening up field interception to application developers.

Too Many Aspects?

What if you have so many aspects that it becomes difficult to tell what code will execute on any method invocation?

This is a real danger. However, there are ways to avoid it: primarily, by using discipline and restraint in applying aspects.

I have never experienced this problem, perhaps partly because I'm fairly cautious in my use of aspects. I don't use dozens of aspects in my applications. In fact, as in EJB, it's rare for an object instance to have more than four or five aspects associated with it. Most of the aspects I use are generic middleware aspects such as transaction aspects; I use these in many applications and understand the implications.

This is an issue that concerns me more about AspectJ than other AOP technologies. AspectJ makes it easy to add aspects that can apply to a wide range of objects, yet aren't obvious without examining the entire codebase. (Of course, tool support can solve this problem, and it's arguably an indication that AOP requires a new way of thinking about application structure.)

In the "incremental" use of AOP that I advocate, it's normally easy to work out what's going on. For example, with Spring or JBoss, it's fairly easy to see which aspects are defined for any object instance. In the case of Spring, object instances can only be advised if they come from a Spring factory; in the case of JBoss, aspects are defined in a single XML file.

Used correctly, AOP should *simplify* program structure, making it easier to understand, because it improves modularity, where code would otherwise be scattered. For example, debugging an aspect can involve changing one piece of code, not many classes that address that crosscutting concern individually.

Orthogonality

What about the risk of multiple aspects affecting each other in subtle and unpredictable ways? Isn't there a fatal flaw in the idea of combining the effects of multiple pointcuts?

AspectJ obviates this danger by stressing an **orthogonal join point model**: the various kinds of join points and different kinds of advice should be able to be used in any combination. AspectJ provides limited support for controlling the order of advice execution. If different pieces of advice are independent, they can't interact unpredictably. This orthogonality is an important part of the classic AOP model.

Most other AOP frameworks provide control over the order of advice. This can be used—perhaps abused—to allow advice to depend on the prior execution of other advice. Such dependence can lead to aspects affecting each other's work undesirably, and therefore should not be used without good reason. Ordering issues apply also to other technologies, such as implementations of the Observer pattern, that maintain chains of listeners or interceptors.

Where "prepackaged," generic aspects are used—such as JBoss and Spring transaction aspects—this issue is not so clear-cut. Some generic aspects, like transaction aspects, may have legitimate ordering concerns. For example, we might want all other advice to execute in a transaction context created by a transaction advice. And the behavior of such generic aspects should be well-understood and well-documented. Sometimes, generic aspects will be packaged together: for example, in a generic Spring XML bean definition file that can be imported into an application.

> **If you use application-specific aspects, try not to make them interdependent or dependent on ordering.**

Testing Applications Using AOP

Testing applications using AOP weaving at runtime isn't the problem it might at first appear. In fact, AOP can make application classes easier to test by factoring code with low-level, hard-to-stub, dependencies into aspects.

Take transaction management. If we choose a programmatic approach, we need to provide some transaction infrastructure at test time so that the programmatic transaction management code runs. If we choose a declarative approach using EJB CMT, we need to stub an EJB container. However, imagine that we choose to leave transaction management to an aspect: specifically using the Spring `TransactionInterceptor`. We don't need to write any transaction-specific test code. The transaction will automatically be committed by the AOP interceptor unless an exception that should cause rollback is thrown, or unless the transaction code calls the `setRollbackOnly()` method on the Spring `TransactionStatus` context object. All we need to do is write plain JUnit tests that ensure that the methods return or throw the appropriate exceptions on given input.

As usual, unit testing is about testing in isolation. We write unit tests for application code, assuming that the aspect code has been tested. This is no different from using an EJB container or any application server. In that case, we trust the lower level of abstraction provided by the EJB container: we don't need to write specific tests for WebLogic's transaction management, because BEA has already done that for us. If we write our own aspects, we unit test them as thoroughly as usual. So all we need to concentrate on is how our application code behaves, and the knowledge of how that behavior will affect that of the relevant aspects.

Integration testing of course remains vitally important to ensure that your application code works with the relevant aspects, and that everything is configured appropriately. But this is no different to testing that an EJB container is properly configured, or testing any other kind of middleware application.

> **Although AOP may look like a danger to testability, in fact it usually improves testability by improving modularity. Unit tests can then concentrate on specific responsibilities, without being complicated by aspects that can be modularized using AOP.**

Debugging

The impact of AOP on debugging partly depends on the quality of the AOP framework. For example, does it result in obfuscated stack traces? It also depends on the number of advices applied, as discussed earlier. An excessively large number can be problematic; a small number, largely limited to well-understood and well-documented generic middleware services, does not pose a problem in my experience. Nevertheless, there is a risk that cannot be entirely dismissed. If you are concerned about the ease of debugging an application using AOP, I suggest the use of a vertical slice to verify that you are comfortable with the implications of AOP advice. As I've noted in previous chapters, implementing a vertical slice is a vital part of project inception and has many other benefits.

Again, there's nothing magic with AOP here. As with testability, other ways of delivering the same enterprise services will also complicate stack traces. Take EJB: while it is of course possible to make sense of stack traces in EJB applications running in a J2EE server, there will inevitably be many container classes in a stack trace.

Won't AOP Seriously Affect Performance?

Isn't there a danger that all this interception is going to severely compromise performance?

In the case of AspectJ, the overhead of interception should be little if at all greater than the effect of implementing the crosscutting code manually. However, generic aspects will need to access the join point using reflection, meaning that AspectJ may not have a large speed advantage over other AOP technologies in many cases.

With other AOP technologies, the mechanics of interception may have a significant overhead. Interception will often involve reflection; it will also usually involve the creation of an "invocation" object. It's always going to be much slower than an ordinary method invocation. (However, given the improvements in Java reflection performance and garbage collection, it is not as slow as might be imagined.)

The way I advocate using AOP—to advise business objects that might otherwise be local stateless session EJBs—interception performance is a non-issue. The central point is the granularity at which AOP is applied. If it's applied at a very fine-grained level, the performance issues may be significant. If it's applied only at business object level, the performance overhead is modest and it's not necessary for an AOP framework to be hyper-efficient. Yet we can still enjoy declarative services for POJOs.

To take a practical example: if you add AOP advice to fine-grained persistent objects, hundreds of which are created in every business operation, the overhead of AOP might become problematic. But if you advise business objects that would otherwise have been implemented as local SLSBs, the AOP overhead will be less than the overhead of EJB method interception.

> Benchmarks discussed in Chapter 15 show that the overhead of a Spring AOP invocation is less than that of a local EJB invocation, even in high-end EJB containers, some of which use code generation to avoid any use of reflection. In some popular EJB containers an EJB invocation is much more expensive than a Spring AOP invocation.

AOP Design Recommendations

I recommend incremental or pragmatic use of AOP.

In the first instance, AOP can be applied to business objects: objects that might otherwise be modeled as stateless session beans; or any object managed by an IoC container (including objects such as DAOs). Its most valuable uses are to deliver generic enterprise services relevant at business method granularity, such as declarative transaction management and declarative security checks. Such use of AOP is conceptually proven from EJB, and hence not a radical new paradigm. Its performance in Spring is better than the performance of local stateless session beans for delivering such services.

> **There's a particular synergy between AOP and IoC.**

If you're confident with AOP concepts, you can use AOP to eliminate code duplication that OO can't help to avoid, implementing your own aspects. You can also add new functionality (such as auditing) without modifying existing code—a useful option to avoid the likelihood of breaking existing code. Again, this works best at business object level. Typical candidate concerns include:

- ❑   Tracing and performance monitoring
- ❑   Auditing
- ❑   Notification (such as e-mailing an administrator when a certain exception is thrown)

There are many more possibilities, both generic and application specific. Projects such as Spring will produce an increasing number of generic advisors and advices to draw from; if these implement AOP Alliance interfaces they are not framework specific.

A more adventurous AOP usage option is breaking complex objects into smaller parts and combining those parts through AOP mixins. This can provide the equivalent of multiple inheritance in Java. One advantage here is that the smaller objects may be easier to test, and may be developed by different teams or individuals. More important, some of the individual objects might be generic, providing reuse without using up the single option in Java for concrete inheritance. On the negative side, application structure at runtime can become harder to understand. All AOP frameworks I've discussed support mixins, making this relatively easy to implement. This is a powerful technique that may be worth trying if you feel comfortable with AOP. However, it has much more significant implications for runtime structure, so don't use it lightly.

Mixins are perhaps most useful to mix in a generic concern, rather than as a refactoring of object design. For example, a mixin might keep track of object state to implement a `Modifiable interface` including an `isDirty()` method.

I don't recommend advising very fine-grained objects, such as persistent objects. If you must do this, consider using AspectJ.

J2EE à la carte

Let's move back from theory to practice. How can AOP help you develop J2EE applications?

By now you should be able to see how the picture comes together. An AOP framework enables us to address enterprise services such as transaction management declaratively. If the AOP framework is part of a broader solution that provides a consistent model for service provision, like JBoss or Spring, it's possible to replace the most important EJB services and make them available to POJOs.

Armed with the AOP framework of your choice, instead of accepting the fixed set of services that EJB offers, you can choose just those services your application requires. You can add custom services if you need to. Thus a container is no longer a fixed, monolithic concept, but a runtime infrastructure that can be assembled from existing building blocks. There's no longer a set menu of declarative middleware services; you can create your own selection *à la carte*, to use an analogy I and Marc Fleury of JBoss coined independently.

This changes only how we tap into J2EE services; we can use core application server capabilities such as JTA, under the covers. (However, it is nice to have the choice of user lighter-weight solutions such as JDBC transaction management as offered by Spring, as a configuration choice.)

Spring offers a modular AOP solution, including services, through:

❑ A portable service layer, analogous to JTA, JDBC, and other low-level APIs. This service layer often—but not necessarily—accesses J2EE services provided by the application server.

❑ An AOP service access mechanism analogous to EJB interception. However, this has the advantage in that it doesn't require a monolithic container, is *Java,* rather than J2EE, and can be used for user-defined aspects.

JBoss also provides both services and AOP *à la carte* access, but is non-portable, because it is tied to the application server. Pure AOP frameworks such as AspectWerkz do not provide services, meaning that, on their own, they cannot replace EJB. However, they can be combined with custom code or third-party frameworks to create an alternative to EJB.

> **The ability to decouple declarative services from the EJB container means that many applications can run perfectly well in a web container, rather than requiring a high-end application server. Instead of declarative enterprise services being supplied by the EJB container, declarative enterprise services can be applied by a portable AOP framework.**
>
> **If you need distributed transaction support, a JTA implementation provided by a high-end application server is as essential in an IoC + AOP world as it is to EJB.**

AOP in Practice with Spring

Let's now look at using AOP in the architectural approach we advocate in this book. We'll use Spring AOP and the Spring IoC container for the examples.

We'll focus on applying generic enterprise services such as transaction management, but also look at how you can define and apply your own aspects.

Using the ProxyFactoryBean

The basic way to create an AOP proxy in Spring is to use org.springframework.aop.framework.Proxy FactoryBean. This gives complete control over the pointcuts and advice to apply, and their ordering. There are also simpler options that are preferable if you don't need such control, which I'll discuss later.

We need to perform the following basic steps to advise an object using the Spring ProxyFactoryBean class:

❑ Define the necessary pointcuts, interceptors, or other advice as objects in the application context. Often these can be reused in multiple AOP proxies.

❑ Define a "target object" to be advised.

❑ Create a ProxyFactoryBean that will be referenced in place of the target object. This definition must list the names of all applicable interceptors and advisors, along with the target object, if any.

Let's consider transaction management. We'll first need to define the transaction interceptor as a JavaBean in our Spring application context. Because this interceptor is stateless, it can intercept invocations on any number of target objects. Hence it should be a "singleton" bean definition (the default).

> *"Prototype" definitions must be used for stateful interceptors, for which there is a dedicated instance per advised object. These are usually necessary when performing introductions.*

The transaction interceptor depends on a Spring PlatformTransactionManager strategy, also discussed in Chapter 9, so we'll need that bean definition as well. Note that this is part of setting up the transaction infrastructure, rather than an AOP requirement.

```
<bean id="txManager"
    class="...choice of Spring or custom transaction managers...">
</bean>

<bean id="txInterceptor"
class="org.springframework.transaction.interceptor.TransactionInterceptor">
    <property name="transactionManager"><ref local="txManager"/></property>
</bean>
```

Since these two bean definitions can be used for all transactional AOP proxies, we don't need two additional bean definitions per advised class.

Now we define the business object, along with whatever JavaBean properties it needs. This is our POJO target that will be transactionally advised:

```
<bean id=" businessObjectTarget "
    class="yourcompany.MyBusinessObject">
    <!-- Properties or constructor arguments omitted -->
</bean>
```

To apply transactional behavior to all methods on the target object, we don't need an advisor (including a pointcut as well as the transaction advice): we could simply reference the name of the transaction interceptor bean, as shown in the following example. The following XML stanza illustrates how to define an AOP proxy:

```xml
<bean id="businessObject"
 class="org.springframework.aop.framework.ProxyFactoryBean">

        <property name="target"><ref local="businessObjectTarget"/></property>

<property name="proxyInterfaces">
        <value>yourcompany.BusinessObject</value>
</property>
<property name="interceptorNames">
        <list>
                <value>txInterceptor</value>
        </list>
</property>
</bean>
```

The class of the bean definition is the Spring AOP framework's `ProxyFactoryBean`, although the type of the bean as used in references or returned by the `BeanFactory getBean()` method will depend on the proxy interfaces (which will be detected automatically based on the target, if the `proxyInterfaces` property isn't set). Thus objects referencing or looking up this object can work with its business interface, preserving strong typing. Multiple proxy methods are supported, and it's possible to proxy all interfaces or a class without specifying any proxy interfaces. The "interceptorNames" property of the `ProxyFactoryBean` class takes a list of String. Bean names must be used rather than bean references, as new instances of stateful interceptors might need to be created if the proxy is a "prototype," rather than a singleton bean definition. The names in this list can be interceptors or pointcuts.

The "businessObject" bean in this example can be used like any other bean in the bean factory. For example, other objects can reference it via `<ref>` elements and these references will be set by Spring IoC. It should be referenced instead of "businessObjectTarget", which has no transactional advice. ("Auto-proxying," discussed later in this chapter, makes it impossible to reference the target object directly, without advice. This is usually an advantage.)

Now we have declarative transaction management without EJB!

We can use the same technique for application-specific aspects. Let's look at implementing a custom security aspect, modularized using Spring AOP.

We've seen the implementation of our custom security check earlier. Let's look at it again in more detail:

```java
import org.aopalliance.intercept.MethodInterceptor;
import org.aopalliance.intercept.MethodInvocation;

public class SecurityInterceptor implements MethodInterceptor {

    public Object invoke(MethodInvocation invocation) throws Throwable {
        // Apply crosscutting code

        doSecurityCheck();
```

```
        // Call next interceptor
        return invocation.proceed();
    }

    protected void doSecurityCheck() throws UnauthorizedException {
        // Implementation omitted
    }
}
```

Since we're interested in the AOP framework itself, we won't worry about how the security check is implemented. This interceptor could depend on any number of collaborating objects defined in the same or related application contexts—a powerful feature of the Spring integration of the AOP framework with its IoC container.

The `invoke()` method is defined by the AOP Alliance method interception package. The return value is the return value of the method on the target object. The `MethodInvocation` argument exposes the `java.lang.reflect.Method` being proxied, along with the arguments. It also exposes a `proceed()` method, that returns the value of proceeding down the interceptor chain toward the target. The `Method Invocation` holds the chain of interceptors internally. If the security check passes, this interceptor will pass control to the next interceptor in the chain and, in normal execution, on to the target method invocation. If the security check fails, a runtime exception will be thrown and the `proceed()` method will not be invoked. The caller will receive the security exception thrown by `SecurityInterceptor`.

To add this advice to our earlier `businessObject` bean definition, we will need a definition of the interceptor as a JavaBean, as follows:

```xml
<bean id="securityInterceptor"
    class="yourcompany.SecurityInterceptor">
    <!-- Configuration omitted -->
</bean>
```

Like the transaction interceptor, this interceptor could be reused for all proxied bean definitions, so we wouldn't need a new bean definition per business object benefiting from declarative security.

Now we can add the name of this interceptor bean to the AOP proxy definition like this. The new line is highlighted:

```xml
<bean id="businessObject"
    class="org.springframework.aop.framework.ProxyFactoryBean">

        <property name="target"><ref local="businessObjectTarget"/></property>

    <property name="proxyInterfaces">
        <value>yourcompany.BusinessObject</value>
    </property>
    <property name="interceptorNames">
        <list>
            <value>txInterceptor</value>
            <value>securityInterceptor</value>
        </list>
    </property>
</bean>
```

Note that we have control over the ordering of interceptors and pointcuts. In this case, we've chosen to run the security check inside the transaction context.

If we wanted to advise only specific methods, we use a **pointcut**, rather than an interceptor or other advice directly. In the Spring AOP framework, referencing an advice such as an interceptor directly is the same as a pointcut that matches all method invocations on the target.

It's easy to implement application-specific pointcuts, but Spring also provides useful generic pointcuts, such as:

❑   Pointcuts taking regular expressions specifying class and method names to match

❑   Control flow pointcuts, driven by the call stack

❑   Convenient superclasses simplifying implementation of application-specific pointcuts.

One obvious way to specific static pointcuts is regular expressions. Several AOP frameworks besides Spring make this possible. Spring `org.springframework.aop.support.RegexpMethodPointcut` is a generic regular expression pointcut, using Perl 5 regular expression syntax. Using this class, you can provide a list of pattern Strings, via the patterns JavaBean property. If any of these patterns is a match, the pointcut will evaluate to true. (So the result is effectively the union of these pointcuts.)

Typical usage is shown in the following example:

```
<bean id="gettersAndAbsquatulatePointcut"
    class="org.springframework.aop.support.RegexpMethodPointcut">
    <property name="patterns">
        <list>
            <value>.*get.*</value>
            <value>.*SomeObject.specialMethod</value>
        </list>
    </property>
</bean>
```

This pointcut will match getter methods on any class, and the `specialMethod()` on class `SomeObject` (whatever package it may be in).

An advisor contains both an advice (such as an interceptor or before advice) and a pointcut to target it. It's possible for an advisor to reference an external pointcut, like `RegexpMethodPointcut` in the previous example. Spring also provides convenient implementations if we want to combine pointcut and advisor definition in a single bean definition. For example, a convenience subclass of `RegexpMethodPointcut`, `RegexpMethodPointcutAdvisor`, allows us to reference an interceptor also. This simplifies wiring, as the one bean serves as both pointcut and advisor, as shown in the following example:

```
<bean id="settersAndAbsquatulateAdvisor"
    class="org.springframework.aop.support.RegexpMethodPointcutAdvisor">
    <property name="advice"><ref local="beanNameOfAopAllianceInterceptor"/>
</property>
    <property name="patterns">
        <list>
            <value>.*get.*</value>
            <value>.*absquatulate</value>
        </list>
```

```
        </property>
    </bean>
```

More advanced (but less common) uses of Spring AOP include:

❑ Creating mixins via introduction by using stateful IntroductionAdvisors, defined as prototypes. It is possible to mix stateful and stateless advisors to minimize object creation in creating AOP proxies.

❑ Adding or removing advisors at runtime.

❑ Using "target sources" to allow for dynamic join point policies such as pooling.

Please refer to the AOP chapter of the Spring Reference Manual for a comprehensive discussion of the capabilities of Spring AOP.

> In both examples—declarative transaction management and custom security check— AOP is an implementation detail. Code using the advised objects has no dependency on the use of AOP. We could replace the `ProxyFactoryBean` definitions with proxies to local EJBs or plain Java objects without affecting any Java code or other bean definitions. Of course we'd need to write code to address the concerns addressed by the crosscuts, which could be tedious and proves the value of the AOP approach.

Convenience Factory Beans

The `ProxyFactoryBean` class allows complete control over the ordering of advisors. If we're interested only in a single aspect, we can use a dedicated `FactoryBean` that creates a proxy with the necessary advice, without dealing with AOP concepts.

Normally such `FactoryBeans` are generic, included with Spring, although it's easy to implement a custom factory bean to simplify use of a particular aspect. The most important of these is the `Transaction FactoryBean`; other examples include the `org.springframework.ejb.access.LocalStateless SessionProxyFactoryBean` and `org.springframework.ejb.access.SimpleRemoteStateless SessionProxyFactoryBean` for accessing EJBs without client-side Java code.

The `TransactionProxyFactoryBean` is a subclass of `ProxyConfig`, so basic configuration is shared with `ProxyFactoryBean`.

The following example from the sample application illustrates how the `TransactionProxyFactoryBean` class is used. As with a `ProxyFactoryBean`, there is a target bean definition. Dependencies should be expressed on the proxied factory bean definition ("petStore" here), rather than the target POJO ("petStoreTarget").

The `TransactionProxyFactoryBean` class requires a target, and information about transaction attributes specifying which methods should be transactional and the required propagation and other settings:

```
<bean id="petStoreTarget"
class="org.springframework.samples.jpetstore.domain.logic.PetStoreImpl">
    <property name="accountDao"><ref bean="accountDao"/></property>
```

```
        <!-- Other dependencies omitted -->
    </bean>

    <bean id="petStore"
        class="org.springframework.transaction.interceptor.TransactionProxyFactory
Bean">
        <property name="transactionManager"><ref bean="transactionManager"/></property>
        <property name="target"><ref local="petStoreTarget"/></property>
        <property name="transactionAttributes">
            <props>
                <prop key="insert*">PROPAGATION_REQUIRED</prop>
                <prop key="update*">PROPAGATION_REQUIRED</prop>
                <prop key="*">PROPAGATION_REQUIRED,readOnly</prop>
            </props>
        </property>
    </bean>
```

The `TransactionProxyFactoryBean` class automatically creates a transaction advisor, including a pointcut based on the transaction attributes, so only transactional methods are advised.

Like the `TransactionInterceptor`, the `TransactionProxyFactoryBean` depends on a `Platform TransactionManager` implementation via its `transactionManager` JavaBean property. This allows for pluggable transaction implementation, based on JTA, JDBC, or other strategies.

> **If you're interested only in declarative transaction management, `TransactionProxy FactoryBean` is a good solution, and simpler than using `ProxyFactoryBean`.**

"Autoproxying"

Spring also offers a simpler generic approach, allowing advice to be specified once and applied to many business objects.

Spring ships with several "autoproxy creator" implementations, implemented using the bean post processor mechanism discussed in Chapter 7. Once configured, this mechanism allows the Spring container to transparently proxy any business object.

The most important autoproxy creator is the `DefaultAdvisorAutoProxyCreator`. This will automatically apply eligible advisors in the current context, without the need to include specific bean names in the autoproxy advisor's bean definition.

Using this mechanism involves:

❏ Specifying a `DefaultAdvisorAutoProxyCreator` bean definition
❏ Specifying any number of Advisors in the same or related contexts

The `DefaultAdvisorAutoProxyCreator` bean will automatically evaluate the pointcut contained in each advisor, to see what (if any) advice it should apply to each business object (such as "businessObject1" and "businessObject2" in the example). This means that any number of advices can be applied automatically to each business object. If no pointcut in any of the advisors matches any method in a business object, the object will not be proxied.

This has the advantage of making it impossible for callers or dependencies to obtain an un-advised object. Calling getBean("businessObject1") on the ApplicationContext defined below will return an AOP proxy, not the target business object.

The autoproxy infrastructure is configured as shown in the following example. The DefaultAdvisorAuto ProxyCreator will evaluate whether the advisors defined as "txAdvisor" and "customAdvisor" should apply to each of the business objects. Advisors and the DefaultAdvisorAutoProxyCreator can be given any bean name: the DefaultAdvisorAutoProxyCreator looks for beans of type Advisor, rather than filtering by name.

```
<bean id="autoProxyCreator"
    class="org.springframework.aop.framework.autoproxy.DefaultAdvisorAutoProxy
Creator">
</bean>

<bean id="txAdvisor"
    autowire="constructor"
    class="org.springframework.transaction.interceptor.TransactionAttributeSource
TransactionAroundAdvisor">
</bean>

<bean id="customAdvisor"
    class="com.mycompany.MyAdvisor">
</bean>

<bean id="businessObject1"
    class="com.mycompany.BusinessObject1">
    <!-- Properties omitted -->
</bean>

<bean id="businessObject2"
    class="com.mycompany.BusinessObject2">
</bean>
```

The DefaultAdvisorAutoProxyCreator is particularly useful if you want to apply the same advice consistently to many business objects. Once the infrastructure definitions are in place, you can simply add new business objects without including specific proxy configuration. You can also drop in additional aspects very easily—for example, tracing or performance monitoring aspects—with minimal change to configuration.

Programmatic Usage

It is also possible to create AOP proxies programmatically without using a bean factory or application context, although this is more rarely used. For example:

```
BusinessObject rawBusinessObject = new MyBusinessObject();
TransactionInterceptor ti = new TransactionInterceptor();
// Configure transaction interceptor...
```

```
SecurityInterceptor si = new SecurityInterceptor();
// Configure security interceptor if necessary...

Pointcut myPointcut = // pointcut configuration omitted
Advice myBeforeAdvice = new MyMethodBeforeAdvice();

Advisor myBeforeAdvisor = new DefaultPointcutAdvisor(myPointcut, myBeforeAdvice);

ProxyFactory factory = new ProxyFactory(rawBusinessObject);
factory.addInterceptor(ti);
factory.addInterceptor(si);
factory.addAdvisor(myBeforeAdvisor);

BusinessObject businessObject = (BusinessObject) factory.getProxy();
```

We believe that it's generally best to externalize the wiring of applications from Java code, and AOP is no exception.

Using Source-level Metadata to Provide an Abstraction above AOP

It's not especially difficult to work with the mechanics of AOP frameworks such as AspectWerkz, JBoss, or Spring. However, in many cases, developers don't need full control over the AOP infrastructure, and hence don't need to work directly with AOP concepts.

It's possible to build an abstraction over an AOP framework and service provision that provides an even simpler programming model than Spring autoproxying for typical usage. This involves pulling together some of the concepts I've discussed in this and previous chapters. In addition to AOP, we'll use **source-level metadata**. The ability to attach metadata to classes and methods, in particular, can provide information that enables automatic AOP proxying.

JBoss and Spring adopt this approach. Both are indebted to how the Microsoft .NET platform provides enterprise services to "serviced components," so we'll begin by looking at the .NET model. .NET does demonstrate impressive ease of use, although it's not explicitly based on AOP.

Spring treats attribute-driven advice as a special case of AOP autoproxying. However, the programming model is important enough to consider separately.

.NET Example

I've referred to .NET several times in earlier chapters. For a good introduction to the .NET Serviced Component model, see Chapter 10, ".NET Serviced Components," of COM and .NET Component Services by Juval Löwy (O'Reilly, 2001), available at www.ondotnet.com/pub/a/dotnet/excerpt/com_dotnet_ch10/.

The basic concept is that any class that extends System.EnterpriseServices.ServicedComponent can benefit from COM+ declarative services. As with EJB, services include transaction management and pooling. To tell the .NET runtime what services should be applied, developers add source-level metadata to their classes and methods, as shown in the following C# examples. (Source-level metadata is also available in other .NET languages.)

Transaction management can be specified at class or method level, as shown in the following code:

```
[Transaction]
public class MyComponent : ServicedComponent,IBusinessComponent
{
    [AutoComplete(true)]
    public void MyMethod(...)
    {
        // do work
    }
}
```

As we're interested in how .NET makes enterprise services available, rather than its enterprise services model itself, I won't discuss the meaning of the transaction attributes here. Note that all .NET attributes are *objects*, not string values.

Object pooling can be specified at class level as follows:

```
[ObjectPooling(MinPoolSize = 3,MaxPoolSize = 10,CreationTimeout = 20)]
public class MyPooledComponent :ServicedComponent
{...}
```

However a serviced component is created, it will benefit from the declarative services corresponding to such metadata attributes.

Aside: Conceptual Versus Implementation-level Metadata

Metadata attributes can have different levels of abstraction. Consider the familiar example of transaction management. We could address this with a metadata attribute that described both *whether* a transaction was required and *how* that transaction should occur. The *how* might include the transaction infrastructure to use: JDBC or JTA, for example.

However, if we remove the *how* and restrict the metadata attribute to whether a transaction should be created, we retain greater flexibility. This allows the pointcuts that will apply to methods exposing this attribute to adopt the implementation strategy of their choice, depending on their own configuration.

> **In general it's best to avoid making the information carried in source-level metadata prescriptive. Metadata should be used to identify classes and methods to which services should be applied; it should not usually prescribe exactly how those services should be delivered.**

Of course there is only a benefit in avoiding prescriptive metadata if it's possible to choose between different metadata-aware pointcuts. .NET, with its proprietary model, doesn't provide this choice; Spring, in particular, does.

Programmatic Access to Context Information

As I've noted before, some system-level aspects, such as transaction management, require application code to have a way of obtaining a context object and performing programmatic manipulation. .NET provides the ContextUtil class for this purpose. This provides static methods to "vote" on whether to commit transactions, and obtain other COM+ context information. We also face this issue in attribute-driven J2EE solutions; we'll look at the Spring approach to programmatic transaction rollback later in this chapter.

Spring Example

Both JBoss and Spring provide attribute-driven delivery of enterprise services to POJOs, indebted to .NET's attribute-driven service provision model.

> We'll focus on the Spring approach here, but see the following URL for examples of JBoss AOP in action: www.jboss.org/index.html?module=html&op=userdisplay&id= developers/projects/jboss/aop.

Spring differs from .NET in the following respects:

❑ It's extensible. Attribute-driven advice isn't restricted to a standard set of aspects provided with the application server.

❑ It's portable. It will work in any J2EE application server. It can even work in a web container, with JDBC if other resource-specific transactions are sufficient, and there is no need for JTA.

❑ It can be applied to any POJO managed by a Spring lightweight container. There's no need to extend a particular superclass, such as ServicedComponent, meaning that objects retain full control over their inheritance hierarchy.

On the negative side:

❑ Source-level metadata in Java has no IDE support as yet. When Java 1.5 attributes are available, Spring's pluggable metadata support will allow it to leverage them.

Let's look at an example of declarative transaction management. We need to annotate source files with transaction attributes. Attributes can be applied at class or method level. Class-level attributes are the default for every method, unless a method-level attribute is specified, in which case it overrides them. Attributes defined on superclasses are inherited.

```
/**
 * Real comments here

 * @@ DefaultTransaction ( timeout=-1 )

 */
public class TxClassWithClassAttribute {
```

```
public int inheritClassTxAttribute(int i) {
        return i;
}


/**
  * @@ RuleBasedTransaction ( timeout=-1 )

  * @@ RollbackRule ( "java.lang.Exception" )

  * @@ NoRollbackRule ( "ServletException" )

  */
 public void echoException(Exception ex) throws Exception {
        if (ex != null)
                throw ex;
 }
}
```

The first method inherits the class transaction attribute; the second method defines custom transaction behavior, including "rollback rules"— Spring's unique way of setting up declarative rules for what exceptions (and subclasses) should prompt automatic transaction rollback.

We'll need to run a "metadata compilation" step on this class. Fortunately this is easy. Spring offers pluggable metadata support, and Spring 1.0 integrates out of the box with Jakarta Commons Attributes (http://jakarta.apache.org/commons/sandbox/attributes/). (The previous examples use Commons Attributes attribute definition syntax.) Commons Attributes provides an Ant task that must be invoked before the main javac compile task, which generates additional Java source files based on attribute values. These additional source files must be compiled alongside the original source. Commons Attributes also integrates with Maven. Once the small one-off setup cost is out of the way, the attributes compiler has negligible impact on the compilation process, because it uses incremental compilation.

The bean definition for TxClassWithClassAttribute in the Spring application context is a normal POJO definition:

```
<bean id="txClassWithClassAttribute" singleton="false"
        class="org.springframework.enterpriseservices.TxClassWithClassAttribute">
</bean>
```

The /attributes directory of the JPetStore sample application illustrates the use of attribute-driven auto-proxying. The bean definitions include the following code, in /WEB-INF/declarativeServices.xml. These definitions are generic, and can be used outside the JPetStore sample application (for example, applying to the TxClassWithClassAttribute example). The TransactionAttributeSource TransactionAroundAdvisor defined with the name "transactionAdvisor" is configured to obtain transaction attributes from the Commons Attributes API. Otherwise, the definitions are conceptually the same as the use of DefaultAdvisorAutoProxyCreator shown earlier:

```
<bean id="autoproxy"

class="org.springframework.aop.framework.autoproxy.DefaultAdvisorAutoProxyCreator">
</bean>
```

```
<bean id="transactionAttributeSource"
    class="org.springframework.transaction.interceptor.AttributesTransaction
AttributeSource"
    autowire="constructor">
</bean>

<bean id="transactionInterceptor"
    class="org.springframework.transaction.interceptor.TransactionInterceptor"
    autowire="byType">
</bean>

<bean id="transactionAdvisor"
    class="org.springframework.transaction.interceptor.TransactionAttributeSource
TransactionAroundAdvisor"
    autowire="constructor" >
</bean>

<bean id="attributes"
    class="org.springframework.metadata.commons.CommonsAttributes"
/>
```

With this autoproxying infrastructure in place, application developers can define as many beans as they like with transaction (or other) attributes. Beans without recognized metadata will not be proxied; proxying will be automatic for beans with the relevant attributes.

To use additional, custom metadata attributes we need to perform the following steps:

1. Implement an attribute class. This is normally a simple object, configured via its constructor or JavaBean properties. In some cases it might have no properties, being merely a tag object identifying that certain services should be applied to objects annotated with it.

2. Implement an Advisor whose pointcut understands this attribute.

3. Add a bean definition for the Advisor to the relevant application context.

An instance of each class won't be advised unless it's obtained from the appropriate Spring factory. However, as discussed in Chapter 6, there are many advantages in using an IoC container such as a Spring bean factory or application context, so this is arguably good practice anyway.

This offers a very simple and powerful means of abstracting developers from AOP implementation issues; arguably, combining the ease of use of .NET with the power and portability of J2EE.

> **AOP driven by source-level metadata is not "classic" AOP. Classes are not oblivious of the aspects that may be used to address crosscutting concerns; metadata annotations (but not code to interpret them) are applied to multiple classes. And it often doesn't involve developers working directly with AOP concepts.**
>
> **However, I believe it's very important. Its practical value is demonstrated by the .NET model, which does some things very well. In particular, it provides simple, intuitive, support for common usage cases.**

EJB 3.0

EJB 3.0 will use JSR-175 source-level metadata in EJB implementation classes, reducing the need for verbose XML deployment descriptors and possibly reducing the number of Java source files necessary to implement each EJB. This is more similar to the .NET approach than to the Spring approach described earlier.

Like .NET, it's tied to a particular component model. We can't bring metadata magic to any POJO, only EJBs. (.NET is a little less restrictive in that there's no notion of a distinct EJB container. It's necessary only to write a single class implementing `ServicedComponent`.)

Like .NET, it's tied to a particular model of service provision. EJBs remain tied to JTA, and there's no opening up of the implementation of EJB aspects.

In short, although EJB 3.0 will be a standard, I don't think it's worth the wait. It will probably be somewhat similar in practice to using XDoclet to simplify EJB development—already a popular choice. Technology in this space has already moved on, and EJB 3.0 will probably be playing catch-up.

Implications for Programming Style

Assuming that we accept the value of AOP, is there anything that we need to do in our application code to ensure that we can leverage it effectively?

Fortunately, the answer is "not a lot." Through providing the ability to add crosscutting code to arbitrary classes, AOP helps toward achieving the non-invasive ideal we discussed in Chapter 6. (That is, classes don't need to implement any special interfaces for crosscuts to be applied to them.)

However, there are some relatively minor things that we can consider to make sure that our code can be used most effectively within an AOP framework, and that it is reusable without the use of AOP.

Consistent Naming Conventions

Because many AOP frameworks provide support for expressing pointcuts in terms of regular expressions or another wildcard syntax, adopting a consistent naming convention in application code is helpful. For example, if we know that a method of a name of the form `getXXXX()` can never change an object's state, a caching interceptor can be sure that such methods cannot invalidate a cached version of the object.

Thus adopting a consistent naming convention for methods can be useful. Of course this is good practice anyway. By adopting consistent naming conventions we make code easier to understand, regardless of whether we use AOP.

An alternative to method naming conventions is the use of source-level metadata to annotate classes, as discussed earlier in this chapter. However, in simple cases where consistent method naming is sufficiently expressive, metadata may be unnecessary.

Avoiding Reliance on the AOP Infrastructure

Because of the ideal of non-invasiveness, it's a good idea to avoid making application code depend on execution in a particular AOP framework or on the availability of AOP-delivered services. While such dependence is anathema to pure AOP, the situation can arise in J2EE business objects that will be invoked in a transaction context, for example.

For example, how do we ensure that a transaction will be rolled back? In the case of Spring, there are two ways of rolling back a transaction: throwing an exception for which there's a "rollback rule" (a more flexible declarative equivalent of EJB behavior on encountering an exception); or programmatic rollback by invoking a static method to obtain the Spring `TransactionStatus` object, and call `setRollbackOnly()` on it. In general, a declarative approach is better, because it avoids any dependence on the AOP runtime. Aspects can often be smart enough to allow flexible declarative usage.

However, in some cases, there's no alternative to a `setRollbackOnly` programmatic usage. In this case, there's no way of avoiding a compile-time dependence on Spring. However, this doesn't usually matter; what matters is a *test-time* dependence, and whether it's possible to use the class outside the AOP framework. In such cases, there's a good solution based on an old unit testing trick. A naïve implementation of a business object might look like this:

```
public int myBusinessMethod() {
  try {
          return getMagicValue();
  }
  catch (NastyException ex) {
          // Illustrates a declarative model,
          // which is generally preferable to programmatic model.
          // The transaction aspect will understand that it should roll back
          // on encountering this exception.
          throw new ExceptionCausingRollback("...", ex);
  }
  catch (LessNastyException ex) {
          // Use Spring AOP to roll back transaction
          TransactionInterceptor.currentTransactionStatus().setRollbackOnly();

          // Return distinguished value
          return -1;
  }
}
```

Unfortunately we can't test this class without a Spring transaction context, and we couldn't use it outside any AOP framework, with an alternative transaction infrastructure to Spring's. However, this is easy to correct. We can apply the **Extract Method** refactoring to the highlighted line, creating a protected method like this:

```
protected void setRollbackOnly() {
  TransactionInterceptor.currentTransactionStatus().setRollbackOnly();
}
```

This way we can easily override the new protected method at test time or if we need to use the class in a different environment.

Checked Exceptions and Advice

Checked exceptions are problematic with AOP, where *advice,* rather than application code, is concerned.

There is no problem in having business objects that will be advised throw checked exceptions. So AOP needn't affect the signatures of your business objects. Typically you should choose whether or not to make an application checked based on whether it's likely to be recoverable; potential use of AOP is irrelevant.

However, an aspect can't introduce new checked exceptions of its own. So, in our earlier custom security check example, `UnauthorizedException` would need to be unchecked. Likewise, if we use AOP for transaction management, transaction infrastructure exceptions caught by the transaction interceptor will need to be unchecked. Thus if aspects use APIs using checked exceptions, such as JTA or Hibernate, rather than APIs using unchecked exceptions such as JDO or TopLink, they will need to wrap the checked exceptions in unchecked exceptions. Spring integration with JTA, Hibernate, and other transaction and persistence APIs already does this, so you don't have to.

Callers can catch any unchecked exceptions thrown by aspects (interceptors) as if they were thrown by the target object. Whether or not it's appropriate for callers to make assumptions about runtime exceptions thrown by particular aspects depends on the particular scenario. There may be cases, for example, where a POJO is used in a transactional environment and a caller may be able to recover from a failure in the underlying transaction infrastructure. (However, this scenario is unlikely.)

References

This chapter does not attempt to provide a comprehensive introduction to AOP, but focuses on how to use AOP today in practical J2EE development. For more information, please consult the following resources. However, you won't need to be become an AOP guru to understand the rest of this book.

Books

There are already several books about AspectJ—one of its major advantages. These also provide a useful introduction to AOP technology in general. My favorite is *AspectJ in Action: Practical Aspect-Oriented Programming,* by Ramnivas Laddad (Manning, 2003).

Papers

`www.parc.com/research/csl/projects/aspectj/downloads/ECOOP1997-AOP.pdf`: "Aspect-Oriented Programming" by Gregor Kiczales et al. Proceedings of the European Conference on Object-Oriented Programming (ECOOP), 1997. The original paper on AOP.

Articles and Online Resources

There is a growing body of AOP material on the web. The following are some good starting points:

❑ `www.parc.com/research/csl/projects/aspectj/default.html`: PARC page on AspectJ. Contains links to many useful articles on AspectJ.

❏ www.onjava.com/pub/a/onjava/2003/05/28/aop_jboss.html: "Aspect-Oriented Programming and JBoss" by Bill Burke and Adrian Brock. Introduction to the JBoss 4 AOP framework, with simple examples.

❏ http://aspectwerkz.codehaus.org/index.html: AspectWerkz home page.

❏ http://aosd.net/: "Aspect-Oriented Software Development (AOSD)" home page. Academically oriented, with links to AOP research projects and tools.

❏ Spring reference manual, available from www.springframework.org.

Summary

AOP is one of the central technologies of post-EJB J2EE. AOP is especially useful for addressing common enterprise concerns in J2EE applications, because it allows the provision of **declarative** (rather than programmatic) enterprise services, which have proven valuable in EJB.

We began with a quick summary of AOP, and saw how it aims to address **crosscutting** concerns: concerns that cut across multiple classes. We surveyed key AOP concepts such as:

❏ **Join point:** Point during application execution where we might want advice to execute. The most important kind of join point is method invocation.

❏ **Advice:** Action to take at a join point to address a crosscutting concern. For example, advice might involve a custom security check or creating and committing or rolling back a transaction.

❏ **Pointcut:** Set of join points identifying where to apply advice. The ability to define pointcuts provides much of the power of AOP. In particular, it enables "advised" application code to be **oblivious** to the aspect code to address crosscutting concerns that will be **weaved** in at runtime.

Don't think of AOP as being a radical new paradigm that will overturn software development. It just might be, but that's almost incidental to what I'm interested in here. The limited usage of AOP that I advocate is *evolutionary*, rather than revolutionary, and better for being so.

> I see two futures for AOP: the short to medium term and the long term. In the short to medium term we'll see AOP used as part of an increasingly popular alternative to EJB. In the long term, AOP may alter the way we think about applications, as we begin identifying crosscutting concerns, as well as objects, in domain models.

I see most of the value of AOP in J2EE applications right now in proxying business objects: for example, to provide enterprise services such as declarative transaction management. I don't believe that advising any and every fine-grained object in an application is wise, at least at present. Proxying business objects is a fraction of the full power of AOP, but it's enough to provide elegant solutions to many common problems while minimizing the risk of introducing a completely new paradigm.

Used in this way—method interception with relatively simple pointcuts (such as apply transaction advice on any method on a business object that has a transaction attribute)—AOP is not radical. In fact it's not very different from a generalization of local stateless session beans. Such declarative delivery of enterprise services has proven valuable not just in EJB, but also in MTS, .NET, and other technologies.

However, the AOP approach has some major advantages over EJB. In particular:

❏   It can support greater flexibility in service delivery. For example:

❏   You might require custom declarative security checks that go beyond J2EE role-based security. With standard EJB you can't do this; with AOP you can.

❏   You might want to make different choices for accessing enterprise services. For example, with EJB, transaction demarcation will use JTA even if you use only a single database; with AOP, you could choose to use a JDBC transaction manager, with less overhead, in this case. The Spring Framework provides such pluggable access to enterprise services, which can enable you to use the simplest set of services you require. (And, as a consequence, run on the simplest possible application server: possibly just a web container.)

❏   An AOP approach can apply enterprise services (and arbitrary declarative services) to POJOs. This is consistent with the **non-invasiveness** of good lightweight frameworks, which we've discussed in previous chapters. It also offers much better testability than does the EJB programming model.

Whether you want to move beyond applying enterprise services to POJOs to defining your own aspects is up to you. It can be very beneficial in many cases. I suggest the following guidelines for deciding whether to implement custom aspects:

❏   You and your team feel comfortable with at least the method interception part of AOP.

❏   Your application encounters crosscutting concerns, meaning that otherwise there is significant code duplication.

> **AOP is another important piece of the lightweight J2EE jigsaw. Along with an IoC container and metadata attributes, AOP can provide a powerful declarative solution to many common problems.**

In this chapter, we've looked at some leading AOP implementations, including:

❏   **AspectJ:** Language extension to Java introducing AOP constructs as peers to classes and interfaces.

❏   **JBoss 4:** A J2EE application server including AOP support. Enables the provision of declarative enterprise services to POJOs. However, service delivery is JBoss-specific.

❏   **Spring:** Portable application framework that includes an AOP framework integrated with its IoC container. Spring provides aspects that deliver transaction management out of the box.

All these technologies are open source. Which of these is most appropriate depends on your needs. In this book I focus mainly on Spring. However, it's not the only good approach to AOP.

An AOP framework alone is not sufficient: while AOP gives us a simple and powerful means of delivering enterprise services declaratively, we need services to deliver. Any AOP framework can be used in conjunction with third-party services. For example, developers commonly write transactional aspects for AspectJ. However, application developers shouldn't really need to deal with such low-level plumbing, using AOP or any other technology. Hence JBoss and Spring emphasize enterprise services aspects as heavily as the AOP framework itself. Both provide packaged aspects addressing common enterprise concerns such as transaction management out of the box. Note that they differ in approach; JBoss exposes its application server's functionality, while Spring builds on its portable abstractions for transaction management and persistence.

Finally we've seen how AOP can be an enabling technology that's hidden beneath the covers of an application. It's possible to enjoy most of the benefits of AOP-based declarative middleware without working directly with AOP concepts. We've seen this in action using a combination of source-level metadata attributes and Spring enterprise services. This allows us simply to write metadata attributes specifying eligibility for transactional and other cross-cutting behavior, and have Spring automatically create AOP proxies if necessary. The result combines the power of J2EE with the ease of use of .NET.

9

Transaction Management

Transactions are central to any enterprise application.

Transaction management in J2EE applications is traditionally associated with EJB. **Container Managed Transactions (CMT)** is the most compelling value proposition of Stateless Session Beans (SLSBs). Many J2EE applications use local SLSBs purely for transaction demarcation, needing no other EJB services.

This chapter will take a fresh look at transaction strategies. We'll see that EJB is just one way of managing transactions in J2EE applications, and that there are simpler alternatives that are more appropriate for many applications.

We'll look at JTA, the core J2EE API that EJB CMT serves to access, and how we can leverage JTA without EJB. We'll also consider whether JTA is always appropriate, and when *local* (resource-specific) transactions are appropriate.

We'll consider transaction management with popular O/R mapping tools such as JDO and Hibernate, and re-examine some common but questionable assumptions of J2EE orthodoxy, such as the belief that applications commonly use more than one transactional resource. We'll try to approach transaction management—often considered a dark art—through the values of simplicity, productivity, and object orientation that we've discussed in previous chapters.

This chapter doesn't define transactions, isolation levels, ACID characteristics, or other basic concepts. Please see, for example, Chapter 5 ("Concurrency") of Martin Fowler's *Patterns of Enterprise Application Architecture* (Addison-Wesley, 2002) for background.

High-level Transaction Management

Let's review the basic problem that high-level transaction management attempts to solve.

Consider the following common scenario. A web-based application has complex business requirements. The implementation uses a *logical* three tier architecture with a web layer, a business-object layer, and a data access layer, all running in the same JVM. In such a layered architecture, transaction management belongs in the business object layer, and is typically demarcated at **business facades.** The data access layer will participate in transactions but should not drive them, enabling separate **data access methods** to be used in the one transaction. How do we **propagate transactions** across multiple data access methods (see Figure 9-1)?

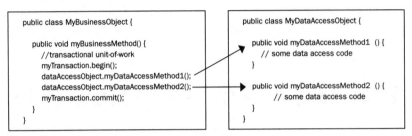

Figure 9-1

A naïve approach might be to fetch a JDBC `Connection` at the beginning of the business object method (`myBusinessMethod` in the preceding example), switch it to manual commit mode, pass it to various data access methods, and trigger a commit or rollback in the business object method before it returns. This has the major drawback of tying both the business objects and the data access objects to the specific transaction strategy and data access strategy (in this case JDBC).

Separating these concerns leads to much cleaner architectures: **Business objects demarcate abstract transactions** without understanding involved resources, and **data access objects fetch transactional resources** without worrying about participation in transactions.

To achieve proper abstract transaction management, we need **coordinating infrastructure**. Existing data access APIs provide only a low-level means of handling specific transactions, like the transactional methods on JDBC's `java.sql.Connection` or Hibernate's `net.sf.hibernate.Session` interface. Transaction infrastructure aims to free the application developer from worrying about such low-level issues, letting the data access objects focus on actual data access code. Such transaction middleware can be built in various ways, but it is typically too expensive to build in-house.

Classic J2EE Transaction Management

The classic J2EE solution is to use **global container transactions**: transactions coordinated by the application server, which can enlist any number of transactional resources such as databases. With global transaction management, if data access objects use transaction-aware resources, the container will coordinate commits or rollbacks as necessary.

The underlying infrastructure for global transaction management is the container's implementation of **JTA (Java Transaction API)**. While global transaction management is often accomplished using EJBs with **CMT (Container-Managed Transactions)**, EJB CMT is in fact only a thin layer—one way of accessing the container's transaction coordinator.

It's also possible to use JTA—J2EE's programmatic transaction demarcation API—directly. In application code, transaction-aware resources and JTA transaction objects must be obtained via JNDI. The setup of transactional resources like JDBC DataSources is not specified by J2EE: It is container-specific, either via server-specific configuration files or a server-specific management console.

Whether initiated via CMT or direct JTA, with global J2EE transactions, the application developer need not concern herself about the number of resources involved in transactions. Neither business objects nor deployment descriptors need to know whether a transaction spans more than one resource and thus classifies as a **distributed transaction**. The container is responsible for handling all cases, hopefully silently optimizing single resource transactions (although such optimization is not *required* by the J2EE specification). Thus, transactions that span a single resource are viewed as a degenerate special case of distributed transactions.

The J2EE Container as Transaction Coordinator

A J2EE application server must provide a **transaction manager** capable of handling distributed transactions. Certain restrictions are allowed, but it is recommended that containers support the full **2-Phase-Commit (2PC)** protocol according to the **X/Open XA** specification. XA defines a low-level contract for transaction managers and resource managers, for enlisting resources in transactions and in particular for 2PC. In contrast to native transactions such as transactions on a JDBC Connection, an XA transaction coordinator will always conduct the processing rather than a resource itself.

In the first phase of committing such a transaction, the coordinator will issue *prepare* calls to all involved resources. In the second phase, it will trigger actual *commits* if no resource objected in the preparation phase. 2-Phase-Commit provides important guarantees of correctness in the event of failure in one transactional resource, although it cannot avoid all errors.

Note that 2-Phase-Commit does not add value for single resources—only for transactions spanning multiple resources. An efficient transaction manager will fall back to simple 1-Phase-Commit if touching only a single resource, although this is merely suggested rather than required by the J2EE specification.

> The range of transaction manager implementations in current J2EE servers runs from basic to highly sophisticated, for example, in terms of recovery capabilities. The transaction manager is still an important differentiator among application servers. However, it's important to note that these differences are merely academic if the transactions do not span multiple resources.

For resources to participate in container transactions, they must be configured appropriately. For JDBC, it's necessary to set up a JNDI DataSource via the 2PC-capable `javax.sql.XADataSource` provided with your JDBC driver. If there is no `XADataSource` available, most application servers will allow a transactional DataSource to be defined even with a non-XA-aware JDBC driver. Such a resource will not be capable of 2PC, but can still participate in container transactions. Thus, it is advisable to upgrade to XA-capable third-party JDBC drivers, at least when actually *needing* to participate in distributed transactions.

J2EE 1.3 introduced a uniform model for transactional resources, beyond specific support for JDBC and JMS. The **Java Connector Architecture (JCA)** provides the means to plug into the container's transaction and resource pooling infrastructure seamlessly—allowing any resource to participate in global, potentially distributed container transactions by using standard interfaces. A JCA connector, such as one for a specific ERP system, can be deployed into any JCA-compliant J2EE container. Currently, JCA is the only completely portable way to plug into J2EE container transactions. Thus, many persistence toolkits including most JDO implementations provide a JCA connector for participating in container transactions, to propagate them to their underlying resource.

Another approach is to use proprietary server features to obtain JTA's internal `javax.transaction.TransactionManager` object (as distinct from `javax.transaction.UserTransaction`), which allows a data access framework to register for **transaction synchronization callbacks**, informing it about global JTA transactions. Unfortunately, the J2EE specifications don't define a standard way of obtaining the TransactionManager object. All servers provide either an API or a well-known JNDI location for obtaining this object. Data access frameworks such as Hibernate and Kodo JDO require server-specific configuration to use this feature.

There is a further solution that dedicated O/R mapping tools like Hibernate can offer: The tools can be configured to perform all data access using a transactional JDBC `DataSource`, so that any JDBC statements that the O/R mapper issues (most important, when flushing changes to the database) will automatically get executed within container transactions. The only issue with this strategy is transactional JVM-level caching: The persistence tool needs proper transaction completion callbacks, provided by container-specific setup of a transaction manager lookup (as described previously). So even for a JDBC-based persistence tool, participating in container transactions requires special configuration.

All these are ways in which persistence products can learn about global transactions at runtime—part of the plumbing that an application developer doesn't want to have to see at runtime.

J2EE *applications* (as opposed to persistence frameworks) typically want to initiate, commit, or roll back transactions, rather than care about synchronization with them. Applications can harness the transaction services of an application server by managing container transactions in two ways:

❑ **Programmatic transaction demarcation** with a JTA UserTransaction object, obtained via JNDI.

❑ **Declarative transaction demarcation** via the component model (that is, EJB CMT). This is a higher-level service built on the underlying JTA infrastructure.

Both approaches are often termed **"managed transactions."** Applications may be said to run in a **"managed environment,"** as they delegate the actual processing to the transaction subsystem of the container.

Everybody Loves CMT

Container-Managed Transactions (CMT) are a well-known and much-loved element of J2EE development. The advantage of CMT is that it keeps transaction demarcation out of the Java code by moving it into the EJB deployment descriptor. Thus, transaction demarcation becomes a cross-cutting aspect that does not need to be hard-coded into application objects. Transactionality is associated with methods on the EJB's component interface, a neat and usually appropriate harnessing of the programming language.

The downsides of EJB CMT are that:

❑ Objects must be EJBs to benefit from declarative transaction management. As we've seen, there's a coding and deployment cost associated with this. Lightweight objects such as POJOs cannot benefit from declarative transaction management.

❑   Declarative transaction management is essentially a Pareto Principle proposition. Eighty percent of the time it works well, but it can make it hard to solve more complex problems.

❑   The only choice under the covers is global-container transaction management. This is overkill if we are accessing only a single transactional resource.

In EJB 1.0 and 1.1, EJBs offered only remote interfaces, meaning that declarative transaction management was an option only if an object was made distributed, or at least pseudo-distributed. Transactionality and distribution should not really be linked, so the complexity of remoteness could be unwelcome and irrelevant. Since the release of EJB 2.0 in 2001, CMT has required less overhead, as it became possible to give EJBs only local interfaces.

It is widely considered a best practice to adopt SLSBs as **business layer facades,** if only for the sake of declarative transactions. Although usage of entity beans seems to be in terminal decline, many developers still tend to agree that CMT via SLSBs provides significant value and justifies the use of EJB, even if just used locally within a web application.

Typical Use: Local Stateless Session Beans

In typical J2EE web applications using EJB for CMT, web controllers access **local SLSB entry points**, delegating the actual processing of business logic to them. Underneath these facades, there might be various persistence mechanisms at work: O/R mapping tools like Hibernate or a JDO implementation, or hand-crafted JDBC code. All of them will participate in container transactions. O/R mapping tools may have to provide JCA connectors, to be able to plug seamlessly into an EJB container, and to receive proper transaction callbacks. This leads to the need to deploy JCA connectors in addition to EJBs, requiring container-specific deployment steps, and a JCA-compliant container in the first place.

So according to J2EE orthodoxy, we need SLSBs and possibly JCA connectors provided by persistence tools to achieve a clean, layered architecture—even for simple J2EE web applications. To make this work for typical J2EE products, the Enterprise Edition of an application server will be required, as both EJB and JCA are needed. On the persistence side of things, for example with JDO, there will also be a need for the Enterprise Edition of a vendor implementation to be able to run in a managed environment. This can lead to high complexity and even higher license costs, even if simply performing transactions on one single database.

All this rests on the assumption that typical J2EE applications need to access more than one transactional resource, incurring the need to delegate transaction coordination to the J2EE container in all cases. While there is a valid argument that true enterprise applications are about integrating multiple, possibly transactional, resources, many J2EE applications do not face this requirement. J2EE web applications typically access a single database, and therefore do not benefit at all from global transaction coordination infrastructure: They suffer from the restrictions and deployment complexity that the latter imposes, for no compelling benefit.

High-end relational databases such as Oracle 9i RAC can deliver huge scalability while providing J2EE applications with a single logical resource. For this and other reasons, many applications simply don't need to concern themselves with transactions spanning multiple resources. Typically, multiple transaction resources are necessary only to coordinate legacy resources. There are many good reasons besides greater complexity in J2EE transaction management that it's unwise to choose to use multiple databases in a new architecture.

That said, if you want to include **JMS (Java Message Service)** processing within your transactions, J2EE's transaction coordination infrastructure is an appropriate choice, even with a single database: Every J2EE 1.3 server is required to include an XA-capable JMS provider, and there are various standalone JMS providers available that can be integrated into J2EE transaction coordination. This is probably the most common scenario where actual distributed transactions are used in J2EE applications.

> **Declarative transaction management has proven its value as a popular feature of EJB. However, as we'll see, EJB isn't the only way to deliver declarative transaction management.**
>
> **Later in this chapter, we will discuss approaches to transaction management that scale *down* as well as up: that provide the same programming model for a single database as for multiple databases accessed via JTA. This enables us to avoid the classic J2EE problem of assuming phantom requirements: We accept only the complexity dictated by our actual business requirements.**

Direct Use of JTA

Container transactions can also be managed programmatically, via a JTA `UserTransaction` that can be fetched from JNDI by a plain Java business object or any other object running inside an application server. This is essentially the approach of EJB *Bean Managed Transactions* (EJB BMT), also. EJB BMT delivers little value over plain use of JTA, and does not justify the use of EJB in itself.

On first sight, JTA's `javax.transaction.UserTransaction` has a simple interface, with only six methods:

```
public interface UserTransaction {

    void begin() throws NotSupportedException, SystemException;

    void commit() throws RollbackException, HeuristicMixedException,
        HeuristicRollbackException, SecurityException, IllegalStateException,
        SystemException;

    int getStatus() throws SystemException;

    void rollback() throws IllegalStateException, SecurityException,
        SystemException;

    void setRollbackOnly() throws IllegalStateException, SystemException;

    void setTransactionTimeout(int timeout) throws SystemException;
}
```

On closer inspection, this simplicity disappears due to the exceptions that may be thrown: a *checked* system exception on each and every method, and a total of three rollback exceptions on commit. Annoyingly, these exceptions do not have a common superclass, so each requires its own catch block. This, in addition to the JNDI lookup required, makes using a `UserTransaction` cumbersome, as it is impossible to avoid extensive "try/catch/rethrow" blocks.

API details aside for now, it is possible to access the transaction services that the container offers with direct JTA. EJB is merely one way of leveraging these services: in this case, via an overarching component model.

However, another problem with direct JTA usage is that it can lead to **transactional code polluting application objects**. Application objects should really be concerned with business logic, not with the incidental, distracting aspect of transaction management. Worse, we can quickly end up with a lot of repetitive demarcation code (including cumbersome "try/catch/rethrow" blocks), for example, in transactional business facades, driving developers toward EJB CMT as a cleaner way of separating the transaction demarcation concern from business logic.

A further limitation is that some **container-specific features** can be addressed only via the EJB deployment descriptor, like custom isolation levels as an important setting for JDBC transactions. Application servers do not offer comparable control at the standard JTA level, one more reason that drives developers into CMT. For example, there is standard JTA support for setting a per-transaction timeout but not for setting isolation levels. (The rationale for ignoring isolation levels in the UserTransaction interface is presumably that not all transactional resources are able to interpret and apply an isolation level. On the other hand, a timeout can be interpreted by the coordinator, not imposing any specific requirements on transactional resources.)

To drive persistence tools with direct JTA, you face similar requirements as with EJB CMT. Transaction callbacks are either provided via workarounds like container-specific transaction manager lookups or via JCA connectors. This again means that you need extra effort and possibly extra license costs, for transactions that span only a single database!

> Direct use of JTA helps to avoid the hassle of EJB deployment but imposes similar requirements in terms of resources. Correct transaction handling with persistence tools can be achieved only with special effort, as with EJB CMT. When needing only local transactions that span one single database—a typical scenario—it is natural to seek a simpler way to achieve high-level transaction management.
>
> JTA also requires application developers to write a lot more Java code for transaction management than EJB CMT. However, as we'll see in a moment, a good abstraction layer provided by a third-party framework can make programmatic transaction management a viable option.

Interlude: Remote Transaction Propagation

So far, we have considered only transactions within a single application server JVM. The rest of the chapter also focuses on this scenario, as it is the commonest. EJB is often used for exactly such transactions via local SLSBs, or SLSBs with remote interfaces that are co-located in the same JVM. Most J2EE applications, especially web applications, do not require any other transaction mechanism.

The EJB component model also supports a different notion of transaction propagation: **propagation across calls to remote servers**. However, such interoperability is not *required* by the J2EE 1.3 specification. The original intention of the EJB 1.x transaction model was to allow for using a **Java Transaction Service**—that is, the Java mapping of the OMG **Object Transaction Service** specification for CORBA—underneath. JTS can propagate transaction contexts across remote calls to other servers. This is a valid goal: A client can call multiple methods of a Stateful Session Bean within the same transaction context, or even demarcate transactions across various Session Beans via a JTA UserTransaction reference of a remote server. An EJB can also call an EJB in a different server with implicit propagation of the transaction context.

Like EJB's remoting in general, its support for remote transaction propagation provides a relatively simple solution to a complex problem. For this and other reasons, remote Stateless Session Beans are a viable choice for distribution at the component level. It is doubtful whether the same programming model provides the easiest solution for local transaction propagation, though. In fact, EJB did not become suitable for purely local components until version 2.0. The heritage of remoting support still shows even for local EJBs: for example, in the central role of JNDI as directory for resources, transactions, and components.

Note that you do not need EJB's remote transaction propagation to execute a single remote method invocation that runs within its *own* transaction, probably the commonest requirement in distributed applications. In such a scenario, a new transaction context will be started when the call arrives at the remote server, and ended when the call returns. This can entirely be handled by the service implementation on the server, and does not have to affect the client or the remoting protocol in the first place. A lightweight remoting solution like RMI-JRMP or Hessian/Burlap (see Chapter 11, "Remoting") can serve perfectly well here.

The main value of remote EJBs lies in the ability to propagate *existing* transaction contexts from one JVM to another, which is often not needed at all. (Keeping transaction contexts open over multiple remote calls, as when making several invocations to a Stateful Session Bean in the same transaction, is inherently dangerous. For example, if there's a network failure, the transaction may be left open, unnecessarily consuming resources and locking out other calls.)

> **Remote transaction propagation is, of course, only an issue for distributed applications. As we emphasize throughout this book, the path of object distribution is usually best avoided, or modeled in a stateless and self-contained fashion, in which case there is no requirement for remote transaction propagation.**
>
> **Significantly simpler solutions can be applied to the problem of local high-level transactions, offering the same power as local EJBs but with easier handling and more flexibility. Such solutions do not diminish the value of remote transactional Session Beans; they just offer compelling alternatives to local SLSBs, the most popular kind of EJB.**

Lightweight Transaction Infrastructure

Within co-located applications, it is normally sufficient to separate the layers *logically* instead of *physically*.

Applications can consist of user interface controllers, business objects, data access objects, or whatever—all modeled as POJOs. Transactional semantics can be achieved very simply on such simple Java objects. Such an application can be deployed as one simple archive: for example, as a WAR for web applications, or as a collection of JAR files for standalone applications. One single deployment descriptor for a web app, one single deployment step—and no requirement for an EJB container.

To be able to achieve such a programming model, we need a sophisticated, lightweight transaction infrastructure, which offers:

❑ **Programmatic transaction demarcation with consistent exception handling.** Exceptions should be unchecked, as transaction infrastructure failures are unlikely to be recoverable, and descended from a common base class, to avoid the need for multiple catch blocks as in JTA.

❑ **Declarative transaction demarcation for POJOs**, not tied to a component model such as EJB. (AOP crosscutting is exactly what we need to implement this.)

❑ Pluggable **transaction strategies**, with associated means for resources to automatically participate in transactions.

❑ JTA for distributed container transactions

❑ A single JDBC `DataSource`

❑ A single JDO `PersistenceManagerFactory`

❑ A single Hibernate `SessionFactory`

The latter transaction strategies should work as simply as possible for the typical case of a single persistence strategy for a single database, while still providing all the power of high-level transaction management. The strategies for JDO and Hibernate should allow for proper transactional caching at the JVM level, without the hassle that comes with container transactions. It should be straightforward to write an appropriate transaction strategy for any other O/R mapping tool, such as TopLink or CocoBase.

Lightweight transaction infrastructure should not depend on J2EE container services like JNDI DataSources or JTA, to allow its use in all kinds of environments, like standalone applications or test suites. A fully managed J2EE environment should be a common scenario, but not an absolute requirement. One should have only to choose JTA and transactional container DataSources (the J2EE equivalent of a hamburger with everything) when actually needing distributed transactions across multiple resources.

Switching between transaction strategies and/or resource definitions should be a matter of configuration. Application code should not need to depend on specific strategies. Business objects should use a generic API with generic exceptions for transaction demarcation. Interfaces of data access objects should not have to contain specific persistence classes or exceptions but just specify generic data access methods with generic exceptions. That way, switching the transaction strategy or the implementation of a data access object does not unnecessarily affect application code.

Transaction Management with the Spring Framework

The Spring Framework provides a ready-made implementation of a lightweight transaction infrastructure that meets the requirements outlined previously. This is a separate subsystem that is not heavily tied to the application context concept or other parts of Spring. Of course, it integrates nicely with an application context in terms of resource and transaction definitions. Declarative transaction demarcation builds upon Spring's AOP framework, so this particular feature demands an AOP-enabled Spring bean factory.

Transaction Definition

For any kind of transaction demarcation, the characteristics of a transaction need to be specified. Spring's `org.springframework.transaction.TransactionDefinition` is an interface that allows for various ways to specify the following properties, for example, programmatically via a `TransactionTemplate` or declaratively via an AOP `TransactionAttribute`. Note that the following concepts are not Spring-specific, or even J2EE-specific. They're common to all transaction managers, and are shared with .NET.

Propagation behavior:

How to deal with the creation of new transactions and propagation of existing transactions. There are six options that correspond to the well-known EJB CMT propagation codes:

"required": execute within a current transaction, create a new transaction if none exists

"supports": execute within a current transaction, execute nontransactionally if none exists

"mandatory": execute within a current transaction, throw an exception if none exists

"requires new": create a new transaction, suspending the current transaction if one exists

"not supported": execute nontransactionally, suspending the current transaction if one exists

"never": execute nontransactionally, throw an exception if a transaction exists

The default is "required," which is typically the most appropriate.

Isolation level:

The database transaction isolation to apply. The options are:

"default": not setting any specific level, typically resulting in the database's default

"read uncommitted" (isolation level defined by JDBC and SQL92)

"read committed" (isolation level defined by JDBC and SQL92)

"repeatable read" (isolation level defined by JDBC and SQL92)

"serializable" (isolation level defined by JDBC and SQL92)

These isolation levels will not be supported by all kinds of resources; but as relational databases are the most important transactional resource, this is still part of the generic transaction definition. (Not all relational databases support all four isolation levels: Oracle doesn't support "read uncommitted," although it offers nonblocking reads, the only merit of "read uncommitted.") Support for management of isolation levels is notably absent in the standard EJB transaction model, due to a different abstraction tradeoff.

Timeout:

The number of seconds after which the transaction should be canceled. The options are *"default"* and any positive number of seconds. Many resources or resource drivers will not support this, but both the JTA API (though not all implementations) and various JDBC drivers do.

> **Read-only:**
>
> A hint whether to optimize for a read-only transaction. A value of *"true"* will just be interpreted by certain resources that can actually perform such optimizations. For example, a Hibernate Session does not try to detect and flush changes in a read-only transaction—a desirable optimization. A JDBC `Connection` will be switched to read-only via `setReadOnly(true)`; this is ignored by most JDBC drivers, though. Some JDBC connection pools use this read-only flag to assign connections from a read-only pool or a read-write pool, respectively.

Transaction definitions will be interpreted by the transaction manager implementation. An application developer does not usually have to be concerned with these inner workings, as this is dealt with by underlying infrastructure classes. As it helps to understand the basic workflow, we will briefly discuss the **central transaction infrastructure interface**, `org.springframework.transaction.Platform TransactionManager`:

```
public interface PlatformTransactionManager {

    TransactionStatus getTransaction(TransactionDefinition definition)
        throws TransactionException;

    void commit(TransactionStatus status) throws TransactionException;

    void rollback(TransactionStatus status) throws TransactionException;
}
```

PlatformTransactionManager abstracts the actual **transaction strategy**, being able to return an `org.springframework.transaction.TransactionStatus` object for a given `TransactionDefinition`, and to trigger a commit or rollback for this status object. An instance of such a transaction manager is typically configured as a bean in a Spring bean factory, to be passed as a bean reference to application objects with transaction demarcation needs.

An important implementation is `org.springframework.transaction.jta.JtaTransaction Manager`, delegating to the JTA subsystem of the J2EE container. For further details and other implementations, see the discussion of transaction management strategies that follows.

A `TransactionStatus` object is a representation of the current (in-flight) transaction. The contained transaction object is just a handle for identifying the transaction on commit or rollback calls. Most application code will not have to use it or even be aware of it, especially when using the AOP `Transaction Interceptor`, which we'll discuss in a moment. The only feature that applications might want to use is to set the current transaction rollback-only, without having to throw an application exception within `TransactionTemplate` or `TransactionInterceptor`. (The `TransactionStatus` object offers the same service as an `EJBContext` object in this respect.)

The UML diagram in Figure 9-2 illustrates the relations between the central classes of Spring's transaction infrastructure.

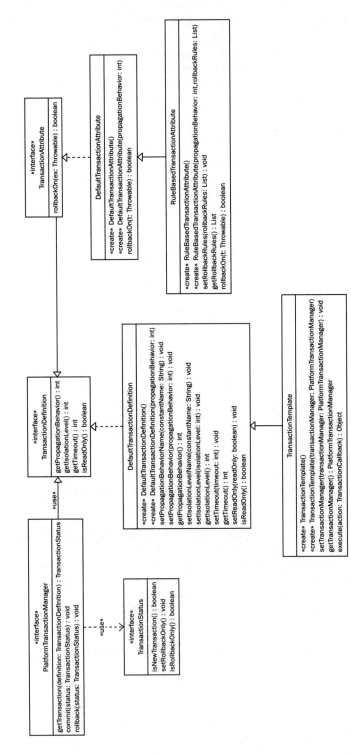

Figure 9-2

All of these classes use a generic hierarchy of transaction exceptions, as defined in the `org.spring framework.transaction` package. In contrast to JTA, these exceptions are unchecked, as transaction failures cannot typically be handled by client code, and properly related through a common hierarchy. Note that unchecked exceptions enable easy use with AOP interceptors. AOP interceptors can't throw checked exceptions, as they are executed in a call stack for which they can't change method signatures by changing the exception contract.

Programmatic Transaction Demarcation

With Spring's transaction API, starting and ending transactions programmatically is easy. Of course, business code still needs to be concerned with transactions, but Spring's transaction exception hierarchy does not enforce any cumbersome "try/catch/rethrow" blocks.

Programmatic demarcation can either happen in the usual style, with a custom `catch` block that triggers a rollback on any exceptions, or via an **Inversion of Control template** class and a callback implementation.

Direct PlatformTransactionManager Usage

Using `PlatformTransactionManager` directly requires manual workflow handling, to trigger a rollback if the transactional code throws any exceptions. The following example defines transaction characteristics and begins a new transaction. Within the try/catch block, any transactional resource access can occur. According to the outcome of the transactional code, either a commit or a rollback will be initiated.

```
TransactionDefinition definition = new DefaultTransactionDefinition();
// set transaction characteristics on definition here
TransactionStatus status = transactionManager.getTransaction(definition);
try {
  // do some resource access
}
catch (MyBusinessException ex) {
  transactionManager.rollback(status);
  throw ex;
}
transactionManager.commit(status);
// return some result object
```

This is the direct equivalent of direct JTA usage via a `UserTransaction` object. As this style of transaction demarcation leads to repetitive code throughout transactional business methods—even if significantly less than direct JTA usage—it is preferable to apply IoC principles and let a template class provide the common workflow, as long as we don't need to throw checked exceptions from within transactional code.

TransactionTemplate

Spring's `org.springframework.transaction.support.TransactionTemplate` class allows for executing transactional code without the need to re-implement transactional workflows. It ensures proper initialization and closing of the transaction, requiring just a callback implementation that performs the actual transactional code.

This callback approach is used consistently throughout Spring to conceal the complexity of dealing with resources that must be closed even in the event of failure: for example, with JDBC and JNDI access. Although the use of a callback interface may initially seem complex, it actually simplifies application code significantly compared to using such resources directly, as there's no need for `finally` blocks and no need to catch low-level exceptions unless a programmer chooses to. Multithreaded Spring utility objects that use this callback approach are called **templates**. Examples include `JdbcTemplate`, `HibernateTemplate`, and `TransactionTemplate`.

The `TransactionTemplate` will trigger a transaction rollback if the callback code throws a runtime exception or if it sets the transaction to rollback-only via the `TransactionStatus` argument to the callback method; otherwise, it will automatically commit the transaction. Application code does not need to implement manual try/catch blocks, and is isolated from the low-level details of the actual transaction strategy.

The following example shows a typical use of a `TransactionTemplate`. The only prerequisite is a reference to the `PlatformTransactionManager`. This will typically come from a bean property, set via Spring's bean factory.

```
TransactionTemplate transactionTemplate = new
TransactionTemplate(transactionManager);
// set transaction characteristics on template here, for this particular
transaction
transactionTemplate.execute(
  new TransactionCallback() {
    public Object doInTransaction(TransactionStatus status) {
      // do some resource access
      // return some result object or throw an unchecked exception
    }
  }
);
```

The resource access code will often be a number of method invocations, enabling the actual business logic to be factored out of the inner class for greater maintainability and testability. If the transactional operation completes without an exception, the return value of the `TransactionCallBack.doInTransaction()` method will be returned by `TransactionTemplate.execute()`.

As `TransactionTemplate` implements the `TransactionDefinition` interface, it carries all transaction characteristics, such as propagation behavior and isolation level. As it extends `org.springframework.transaction.support.DefaultTransactionDefinition`, all of them can be set on the template instance. If not specifically set, the default values are used.

Typically, `TransactionTemplate` will be used in business methods of application objects that need to perform some data access within a transaction. For JavaBeans-style configuration by a Spring bean factory, the `TransactionTemplate` object exposes a `setTransactionManager(PlatformTransactionManager)` method to receive the transaction manager via a bean reference. In addition, it offers a convenience constructor that takes a `PlatformTransactionManager`.

Like all Spring templates, `TransactionTemplate` itself is thread-safe and can thus be kept in an instance variable of the application object: For example, it will often be initialized in a `setTransactionManager` method and used by a business method, if all business methods share the same transaction characteristics.

The following example illustrates a business object that initializes a `TransactionTemplate` when it receives the transaction manager reference, reusing the template instance throughout all of its methods.

```
public class MyBusinessObject {

  private TransactionTemplate transactionTemplate;

  public void setTransactionManager(PlatformTransactionManager transactionManager)
  {
    this.transactionTemplate = new TransactionTemplate(transactionManager);
    // set transaction characteristics on template, for the whole business object
  }

  public void myBusinessMethod() {
    this.transactionTemplate.execute(
      new TransactionCallback() {
        public Object doInTransaction(TransactionStatus status) {
          // do some resource access
          // return some result object or throw an unchecked exception
        }
      }
    );
  }
}
```

The corresponding bean-factory definition looks as follows. The defined instance of `MyBusinessObject` will receive a reference to the `JtaTransactionManager` instance at initialization time.

```
<beans>

  <bean id="myTransactionManager"
      class="org.springframework.transaction.jta.JtaTransactionManager"/>

  <bean id="myBusinessObject" class="mybusiness.MyBusinessObject">
    <property name="transactionManager">
      <ref bean="myTransactionManager"/>
    </property>
  </bean>

</beans>
```

It doesn't matter whether the actual resource access occurs within the same method or in separate data access objects. In any case, the transaction is identified via the current thread. Transaction-aware resource access code will automatically participate in such a transaction as long as it sticks to the required pattern, for example, using transactional container resources in the case of JTA. It does not need to perform any specific checks; it participates automatically.

The `TransactionStatus` object is a convenience for silent rollback-only setting, instead of throwing an exception:

```
transactionTemplate.execute(
  new TransactionCallback() {
    public Object doInTransaction(TransactionStatus status) {
      // do some resource access
      if (someCondition) {
        status.setRollbackOnly();
```

```
        }
        // return some result object
      }
    }
  );
```

Note that the status object does *not* have to be used, and especially not propagated to any data access methods. Lower-level code can use its own `TransactionTemplate` instance and callback implementation to define transaction characteristics, being able to access a current `TransactionStatus` instance even when just participating in an existing transaction.

The programmatic transaction template/callback approach is handy for many usages. However, it has three significant drawbacks:

❑ Transactional application code may only throw unchecked exceptions, to avoid having `throws Exception in TransactionTemplate's execute` method signature and thus the business method signature.

❑ Business-method implementations need to be aware of transaction demarcation, and the containing business objects need to be aware of the `PlatformTransactionManager` interface, although not of any specific implementation.

❑ The use of a callback interface, which is usually implemented as an anonymous inner class, introduces a slight complexity of its own.

Declarative Transaction Demarcation

Programmatic transaction management using the Spring TransactionTemplate is simpler than using JTA out of the box. Code using it is less verbose, less bug-prone, more maintainable, and much easier to test, as it can be tested with a mock `PlatformTransactionManager` rather than with a JTA implementation. And, as with the entire Spring transaction infrastructure, it has the significant benefit that you're not tied to JTA, and hence a high-end application server, unless you need genuinely distributed transactions.

However, there is real value in declarative transaction management in many cases. SLSBs with CMT prove the value proposition, but suffer from negatives such as forcing the use of an EJB container, forcing a dedicated EJB deployment step, and the other productivity and testing implications of EJB.

Ideally, we could enjoy the advantages of declarative transaction management—CMT if you prefer that term—without the downsides of EJB. This would involve making POJOs transactional.

Fortunately, AOP provides us with the ability to have our cake and eat it too. We can "advise" our POJOs to enable a **transaction interceptor** to create transactions for transactional methods, and commit them or roll them back when the methods complete. Of course, we don't want to make every POJO in our application transactional: This strategy is best applied to specific business objects that might otherwise be implemented as local SLSBs. Optionally, we can combine transaction interception with other advice, although transactionality is often the only aspect we care about.

Transaction management is a prime candidate for AOP, as it is a true cross-cutting concern that can otherwise result in code duplication in many methods. The method interception with which EJB CMT is accomplished is essentially a special case of AOP, meaning that using AOP for transaction management is far from experimental, and has been proven through the most successful part of EJB.

There are a number of AOP-based solutions for declarative transaction management, including JBoss 4 AOP. However, Spring's solution is mature, very lightweight, and unique in being portable between application servers and underlying transaction management APIs.

> There is a debate as to whether making plain Java objects transactional is a good thing. The argument goes that EJBs are inherently transaction-aware, while POJOs are not, and that making POJOs transactional is potentially dangerous. After careful consideration, we've concluded that this argument is spurious. EJB's declarative transaction mechanism tends to decouple transaction definitions from source code. Thus, EJBs can be deployed with different transaction attributes in any case.
>
> But the most important counterargument is that an emerging best practice factors business logic out of EJBs into POJOs behind an EJB facade anyway. In this approach, EJBs are used to provide transactional entry points, while actual business logic is in POJOs behind the EJBs. This means that there's very little difference between using local SLSBs for transaction management and advising POJOs serving the same role.

Let's look at how Spring goes about things: There are two declarative ways to create a transactional proxy, either via the **generic AOP ProxyFactoryBean** or the one-stop shop `TransactionProxyFactoryBean`.

AOP ProxyFactoryBean and TransactionInterceptor

With AOP transactions, the business object in the preceding example could look as follows:

```
public class MyBusinessObject {

  public void myBusinessMethod()throws MyCheckedException {
    // do some resource access
    // return some result object or throw MyCheckedException
  }
}
```

In this model, the business object does not to be transaction-aware at all. The business object does not have to receive a `PlatformTransactionManager` reference, and the business method does not have to contain any transaction demarcation code. In contrast to a `TransactionTemplate` callback, any checked exception can be declared in the method signature and thrown whenever necessary.

A Spring application-context definition needs to contain an AOP transaction definition of the following form. The business object is now proxied: Every invocation goes through the transaction interceptor first, continuing with the actual business object, and going through the interceptor again on the way back. The business object implementation itself is defined as "target", which is simply a naming convention to identify its role.

```
<beans>

  <bean id="myTransactionManager"
      class="org.springframework.transaction.jta.JtaTransactionManager"/>

  <bean id="myBusinessObjectTarget" class="mybusiness.MyBusinessObject"/>
```

```
<bean id="myTransactionInterceptor"
    class="org.springframework.transaction.interceptor.TransactionInterceptor">
  <property name="transactionManager">
    <ref bean="myTransactionManager"/>
  </property>
  <property name="transactionAttributeSource">
    <value>
      mybusiness.MyBusinessObject.myBusinessMethod=PROPAGATION_REQUIRED,
        -MyCheckedException
    </value>
  </property>
</bean>
```

```
<bean id="myBusinessObject"
    class="org.springframework.aop.framework.ProxyFactoryBean">
  <property name="interceptorNames">
    <value>myTransactionInterceptor,myBusinessObjectTarget</value>
  </property>
</bean>
```

```
</beans>
```

Note that the target business object now does not receive a transaction manager reference. Both the transaction manager reference and the transaction characteristics are contained in the `TransactionInterceptor` definition, specifying propagation behavior "required" for the business method.

The default exception behavior is to roll back on runtime exceptions as in EJB. This default is partly to simplify the learning curve for developers familiar with EJB transaction management. The preceding definition instructs the `TransactionInterceptor` to also roll back on the custom `MyCheckedException` or subclasses of `MyCheckedException`. Such rollback rules can be defined by strings such as "-ExceptionName ToRollbackOn" or "+ExceptionNameToCommitOn".

Having the ability to specify which checked exceptions should or shouldn't cause automatic rollback has important benefits over the EJB behavior:

❑ There is much less requirement for programmatic rollback via the `setRollbackOnly()` method, if any at all. It's relatively rare to want to rollback without propagating an exception to the client: In this case, it's best to keep all knowledge of transaction management out of the POJO and simply use standard Java exception handling. Thus, Spring's declarative transaction management can enable most POJO business objects to be made transactional without imposing any dependence on Spring or transaction management concepts on them. Typically, they won't even need to import any Spring APIs. This is a remarkable contrast to the highly invasive EJB model.

❑ There's less likelihood of a common error in EJB CMT: forgetting to call `setRollbackOnly()` when throwing a checked exception that won't automatically cause the current transaction to be rolled back. Amazingly, many EJB developers are unaware of the need to do this.

The business object reference that client code will see is the one created by the AOP `ProxyFactoryBean`, wrapping the actual implementation with a transaction-aware proxy that applies the corresponding transaction definitions. It specifies that any call to the object will first go through the transaction interceptor, then to the target object. The `ProxyFactoryBean` definition could also involve other AOP interceptors for the given target object.

The TransactionStatus object for silent rollback-only setting, known from programmatic demarcation, is available here too. It can be obtained from TransactionInterceptor, which manages the status object via ThreadLocals. (This is hidden from application code that doesn't need to work directly with such implementation details.)

```java
public class MyBusinessObject {

  public void myBusinessMethod()throws MyCheckedException {
    // do some resource access
    if (someCondition) {
      TransactionStatus status = TransactionInterceptor.currentTransactionStatus();
      status.setRollbackOnly();
    }
    // return some result object
  }
}
```

AOP ProxyFactoryBean with Interfaces

The preceding ProxyFactoryBean configuration will implicitly use CGLIB to create a runtime subclass of MyBusinessObject as proxy, as there is no proxy interface specified. If one or more "proxyInterfaces" are explicitly specified on ProxyFactoryBean, a plain J2SE 1.3 proxy will be created that implements only the given interfaces. Of course, any interface will do: This should be driven by pure business requirements.

```java
public interface MyBusinessInterface {

  void myBusinessMethod() throws MyCheckedException;
}
```

The business object could thus be implemented as follows:

```java
public class MyBusinessObject implements MyBusinessInterface {

  public void myBusinessMethod() throws MyCheckedException {
    // do some resource access
    // return some result object
  }
}
```

The corresponding bean definition looks like this:

```xml
<bean id="myBusinessObject"
    class="org.springframework.aop.framework.ProxyFactoryBean">
  <property name="proxyInterfaces">
    <value>mybusiness.MyBusinessInterface</value>
  </property>
  <property name="interceptorNames">
    <value>myTransactionInterceptor,myBusinessObjectTarget</value>
  </property>
</bean>
```

> As noted in Chapter 2, programming to interfaces rather than classes is good practice, and AOP is no different. We recommend using proxy interfaces as long as there is no strong need to proxy full target classes.

Simplified Setup: TransactionProxyFactoryBean

For the typical usage of transaction-enabling a certain object, Spring offers an alternative, simplified way of proxy configuration. TransactionProxyFactoryBean allows us to define transaction semantics for a particular target, without having to set up a standard AOP ProxyFactoryBean *and* a Transaction Interceptor. All relevant configuration is contained in a single transaction proxy definition:

```
<beans>

    <bean id="myTransactionManager"
        class="org.springframework.transaction.jta.JtaTransactionManager"/>

    <bean id="myBusinessObjectTarget" class="mybusiness.MyBusinessObject"/>

    <bean id="myBusinessObject"
        class="org.springframework.transaction.interceptor.TransactionProxyFactory
Bean">
        <property name="transactionManager">
        <ref bean="myTransactionManager"/>
        </property>
        <property name="target">
        <ref bean="myBusinessObjectTarget"/>
        </property>
        <property name="transactionAttributes">
            <props>
                <prop key="myBusinessMethod">PROPAGATION_REQUIRED,-MyCheckedException</
prop>
            </props>
        </property>
    </bean>

</beans>
```

The advantages of this simplified configuration style are:

❏ It keeps related things close together: The transaction attributes for the methods of a target are defined in the proxy for the target.

❏ The target can be specified as bean reference, with no need to care about a chain of interceptor names. A bean reference is a simpler concept, familiar from its use throughout Spring.

❏ The proxy interfaces are determined automatically from the target, without the need for explicit specification. A CGLIB proxy can still be enforced via setting the "proxyTargetClass" property to true.

The disadvantage is the loss of configuration power. For full control such as including arbitrary interceptors, proxying specific interfaces, and so on, the standard AOP ProxyFactoryBean should be used. The simplified approach is quite similar to using a local SLSB merely for transaction management: EJB also lacks the ability to add custom behavior.

Source-level Metadata

Spring's transaction-attribute configuration is configurable via the `org.springframework.transaction.interceptor.TransactionAttributeSource` interface, allowing transaction attributes for methods and classes to be sourced from a choice of framework or custom implementations.

An attractive option is the use of source-level metadata: annotations in the source code of business objects. A corresponding `TransactionAttributeSource` implementation uses attribute information at run-time to extract the respective transaction configuration. This allows for the use of source-level metadata without the need for XDoclet-style generation of deployment descriptors. This is comparable to the .NET approach to declarative transaction management.

> **As discussed in Chapter 8 ("AOP"), Spring 1.0 supports source-level metadata via Jakarta's Commons Attributes. The Spring metadata API is pluggable, allowing for other implementations such as Java 1.5 attributes in the future.**
>
> **The use of transaction attributes is an attractive alternative to proxy bean definitions in an application context, keeping transaction attributes in source code itself rather than in the context configuration. The choice of configuration style is largely a matter of taste: Many developers might prefer separated configuration of transactional characteristics via proxy beans, also avoiding additional compilation steps incurred by source-level metadata (pending widespread availability of Java 1.5 attributes).**
>
> **Spring does not restrict you, the application developer, to a specific style of declarative transactions. It offers various out-of-the-box options, even allowing you to implement your own metadata-retrieval strategies, as well as custom proxy factory beans, custom transaction strategies, and so on.**

Transaction Management Strategies

The preceding transaction demarcation mechanisms all delegate the actual transaction execution work to the `PlatformTransactionManager` interface. The rationale is that transaction demarcation code is not tied to any particular transaction strategy. Therefore, switching between transaction manager implementations is just a matter of configuration; no source code changes are required. Replacing the transaction manager bean definition does involve some special requirements for resource setup, however.

The Spring Framework includes various `PlatformTransactionManager` implementations out of the box. As the following explanation shows, there is a strong consistency between these implementations, to allow for easy configuration even when switching between them.

Following the earlier `TransactionTemplate` example, we'll assume a business object that delegates two data access methods with one transactional unit of work. For the sake of simplicity, we use programmatic demarcation here, although declarative demarcation via AOP would allow us to completely remove the transaction handling code from our business object.

It does not matter where those data access methods are defined: We simply assume two methods of a single data access object here.

```java
public class MyBusinessObject {

  private TransactionTemplate transactionTemplate;

  private MyDataAccessObject dataAccessObject;

  public void setTransactionManager(PlatformTransactionManager tm) {
    this.transactionTemplate = new TransactionTemplate(tm);
    // could set transaction characteristics on template here
  }

  public void setDataAccessObject(MyDataAccessObject dao) {
    this.dataAccessObject = dao;
  }

  public void myBusinessMethod() {
    this.transactionTemplate.execute(
      new TransactionCallback() {
        public Object doInTransaction(TransactionStatus status) {
          dataAccessObject.myDataAccessMethod1();
          dataAccessObject.myDataAccessMethod2();
        }
      }
    );
  }
}
```

The wiring of a MyBusinessObject instance with a PlatformTransactionManager and a MyData AccessObject can either happen in a Spring application context or through programmatic setup, invoking the corresponding setters. In the application context case, the bean definitions look as follows:

```xml
<beans>

  <bean id="myBusinessObject" class="mybusiness.MyBusinessObject">
    <property name="transactionManager">
      <ref bean="myTransactionManager"/>
    </property>
    <property name="dataAccessObject">
      <ref bean="myDataAccessObject"/>
    </property>
  </bean>

  <bean id="myTransactionManager" class="...">
    ...
  </bean>

  <bean id="myDataAccessObject" class="mypackage.MyDataAccessObject">
    ...
```

```
        </bean>

    </beans>
```

We will now look at each of Spring's out-of-the-box transaction strategies, and at the requirements for corresponding data access objects.

JtaTransactionManager

If you want to delegate transaction management to your J2EE container, use Spring's JTA transaction strategy: `org.springframework.transaction.jta.JtaTransactionManager` delegates to the JTA subsystem of the J2EE container, providing the ability to manage distributed transactions that span more than one resource. This strategy depends on running in a J2EE application server environment; Spring provides only a means of tapping into the application server's transaction coordination, and does not perform transaction coordination itself.

Transactional resources need to be defined as XA-capable or XA-enabled container resources that are exposed via JNDI (for example, an XA-enabled JDBC DataSource). There are no Spring specifics here: The same requirements regarding resource definitions and resource access apply as with direct JTA and EJB CMT.

Therefore, the `MyDataAccessObject` class in the preceding example can be coded just like any class in a JTA environment. Simply look up the resources you need from JNDI, and work with them as you usually do. The implementation does not have to depend on Spring in any way.

To be able to work with Spring's more specific transaction strategies, the data access implementation must observe a special lookup pattern: for example, the `DataSourceUtils.getConnection` method as shown in the `DataSourceTransactionManager` example that follows. If used with `JtaTransactionManager`, those lookup methods will seamlessly provide standard resource lookups as expected by JTA. But in contrast to standard lookup code, this allows data access code to participate in any JTA environment *and* in any Spring transaction management.

```
    <beans>
      ...

    <bean id="myTransactionManager"
        class="org.springframework.transaction.jta.JtaTransactionManager"/>
    <bean id="myDataAccessObject" class="mypackage.MyDataAccessObject">
      ... // properties expecting references to transactional container resources
    </bean>

    </beans>
```

DataSourceTransactionManager

If you need to perform data access only on a single database via JDBC, use `org.springframework.jdbc.datasource.DataSourceTransactionManager`. It performs transactions on a single `javax.sql.DataSource`, via thread-bound JDBC Connections that it manages internally. This strategy does *not* depend on a J2EE environment: a potentially important benefit, as it can be used without any form of

J2EE container. The DataSource to use can be locally defined: for example, a Jakarta Commons DBCP `BasicDataSource`, or a non-XA container DataSource exposed via JNDI.

To be able to participate in transactions from this strategy, data access code must observe a special Connection lookup pattern, using the `org.springframework.jdbc.datasource.DataSourceUtils` class, shown as follows:

```
public class MyDataAccessObject {

  private void DataSource dataSource;

  public void setDataSource(DataSource ds) {
    this.dataSource = ds;
  }

  public void myDataAccessMethod1 () {
    Connection con = DataSourceUtils.getConnection(this.dataSource);
    try {
      ...
    }
    finally {
      DataSourceUtils.closeConnectionIfNecessary(con, this.dataSource);
    }
  }

  public void myDataAccessMethod2 () {
    // same as above
  }
}
```

This lookup pattern will work with any transaction strategy, such as `JtaTransactionManager`; it is not specific to `DataSourceTransactionManager`. If no thread-bound `Connection` is being managed by Spring, these `DataSourceUtils` methods will behave exactly like `getConnection()` on `javax.sql.DataSource` and `close()` on `java.sql.Connection`, respectively.

> When using Spring's JDBC convenience classes such as JdbcTemplate, this lookup is automatically applied under the hood. These convenience classes also remove the need for custom "try/catch" blocks, managing connection and statement lifecycle, and automatically transforming java.sql.SQLException to Spring's generic DataAccessException hierarchy. See Chapter 10 ("Persistence") for details on Spring's data access support. We recommend using Spring's JdbcTemplate or operation objects as abstraction above JDBC—or an alternative such as an iBATIS SQL Map—as direct use of JDBC is cumbersome and error prone.

The corresponding bean definitions look as follows. Both the `DataSourceTransactionManager` and the `MyDataAccessObject` bean refer to a `myDataSource` bean here, which can be either a local `javax.sql.DataSource` or one fetched from JNDI via Spring's `JndiObjectFactoryBean`. See the discussion of resource definitions in Chapter 7 ("Spring") for details on how to set up such a DataSource.

```
<beans>
  ...

  <bean id="myTransactionManager"
      class="org.springframework.jdbc.datasource.DataSourceTransactionManager">
    <property name="dataSource">
      <ref bean="myDataSource"/>
    </property>
  </bean>

  <bean id="myDataAccessObject" class="mypackage.MyDataAccessObject">
    <property name="dataSource">
      <ref bean="myDataSource"/>
    </property>
  </bean>

</beans>
```

JdoTransactionManager

For transactions on a single JDO datastore, use org.springframework.orm.jdo.JdoTransaction Manager. Like DataSourceTransactionManager, this strategy does not depend on a J2EE environment, and can work with a locally defined javax.jdo.PersistenceManagerFactory.

Data access code must observe an analogous lookup pattern here, using org.springframework.orm .jdo.PersistenceManagerFactoryUtils. As with DataSourceTransactionManager, this lookup pattern will work with any transaction strategy (for example, with JtaTransactionManager). JdoTemplate automatically applies this lookup under the hood.

```
public class MyDataAccessObject {

  private void PersistenceManagerFactory persistenceManagerFactory;

  public void setPersistenceManagerFactory(PersistenceManagerFactory pmf) {
    this.persistenceManagerFactory = pmf;
  }

  public void myDataAccessMethod1 () {
    PersistenceManager pm = PersistenceManagerFactoryUtils.
      getPersistenceManager(this.persistenceManagerFactory);
    try {
      ...
    }
    finally {
      PersistenceManagerFactoryUtils.
        closePersistenceManagerIfNecessary(pm, this.persistenceManagerFactory);
    }
  }

  public void myDataAccessMethod2 () {
    // same as above
  }
}
```

In the corresponding bean definitions, the JdoTransactionManager and the MyDataAccessObject bean refer to a myPersistenceManagerFactory bean here, which needs to be a javax.jdo.Persistence ManagerFactory (local or from JNDI).

```
<beans>
  ...

  <bean id="myTransactionManager"
      class="org.springframework.orm.jdo.JdoTransactionManager">
    <property name="persistenceManagerFactory">
      <ref bean="myPersistenceManagerFactory"/>
    </property>
  </bean>

  <bean id="myDataAccessObject" class="mypackage.MyDataAccessObject">
    <property name="persistenceManagerFactory">
      <ref bean="myPersistenceManagerFactory"/>
    </property>
  </bean>

</beans>
```

HibernateTransactionManager

To perform transactions on a single Hibernate SessionFactory, use org.springframework.orm .hibernate.HibernateTransactionManager. This strategy can work with a locally defined net.sf .hibernate.SessionFactory, independent from a J2EE environment.

The lookup methods for data access code are provided by org.springframework.orm.hibernate .SessionFactoryUtils here. Analogous to JDBC and JDO, it will work with any transaction strategy, and is automatically applied by HibernateTemplate.

```
public class MyDataAccessObject {

  private void SessionFactory sessionFactory;

  public void setSessionFactory(SessionFactory sf) {
    this.sessionFactory = sf;
  }

  public void myDataAccessMethod1 () {

    Session session = SessionFactoryUtils.getSessionFactory(this.sessionFactory);
    try {
      ...
    }
    finally {
      SessionFactoryUtils.closeSessionFactoryIfNecessary(session,
          this.sessionFactory);
    }
  }
}
```

```
    public void myDataAccessMethod2 () {
      // same as above
    }
  }
```

The bean definitions for the `HibernateTransactionManager` and the `MyDataAccessObject` bean refer to a `mySessionFactory` bean here, which needs to be a `net.sf.hibernate.SessionFactory` (local or from JNDI).

```
<beans>
  ...

  <bean id="myTransactionManager"
      class="org.springframework.orm.hibernate.HibernateTransactionManager">
    <property name="sessionFactory">
      <ref bean="mySessionFactory"/>
    </property>
  </bean>

  <bean id="myDataAccessObject" class="mypackage.MyDataAccessObject">
    <property name="sessionFactory">
      <ref bean="mySessionFactory"/>
    </property>
  </bean>

</beans>
```

> **HibernateTransactionManager** can also expose the current transaction for JDBC access code, for a given DataSource that will normally be the one that the Session-Factory was built with. This allows the sharing of transactions between Hibernate access code and plain JDBC access code against the same database, even without JTA. This can be very useful if Hibernate's O/R mapping is not appropriate for some set-based operations that can better be expressed in SQL: no need to switch the transaction strategy to JTA just because of such an additional requirement.

Implications for J2EE Server Choice

With a classic J2EE approach to transaction management, you need to choose a full J2EE server with a JTA transaction subsystem and an EJB container for convenient high-level transaction management. When leveraging Spring's lightweight transaction infrastructure (or possibly that of another lightweight framework), you are able to reconsider that choice, and do the simplest thing that can possibly work. This can help to minimize license costs and runtime complexity.

❑   **Transactions on a single database via JDBC:** For single database applications, the commonest requirement, `DataSourceTransactionManager` is a perfectly viable strategy. As there is no dependency on JTA, such business objects can run in a "simple" J2EE web application server such as Tomcat, or completely outside a J2EE container, as in a standalone desktop application. This enables clean logical layering and transaction management in a very lightweight way, without any EJB deployment hassle or tie-in to a JTA subsystem or EJB container.

❏ **Transactions on a single database via JDO or Hibernate:** If you want to use JDO or Hibernate with proper transactional caching at the JVM level for a single database, `JdoTransaction Manager` or the analogous `HibernateTransactionManager` is an appropriate choice. This allows for the same lightweight style of development as with `DataSourceTransaction Manager`, without tie-in to specific J2EE middle-tier services such as JTA or any need for setting up a JCA connector.

❏ **Transactions that span multiple resources:** If you face distributed transaction requirements (that is, if you need to perform transactions that span more than one database or transactional resource), you need to use the **JtaTransactionManager** transaction strategy. This requires a JTA implementation in your application server, but does not depend on an EJB container. You can choose JTA on a case-by-case basis: Only certain deployments of your applications that actually require distributed transactions need to run in a JTA-enabled container.

Of course, if you need other container services like remote EJBs for exporting a *remote* transactional service, JMS for transactional messaging, or JCA for accessing an ERP, you should choose a full J2EE server.

Even if working with a full J2EE application server, you will still gain a lot of flexibility with lightweight transaction management. Developing with lightweight business objects is significantly simpler in terms of deployment, unit testing, and reuse in other environments.

> A J2EE web container is sufficient for a wide range of typical J2EE web applications, without sacrificing full control over transaction management. Lightweight servers such as Tomcat, Jetty, or Resin are all you need for many typical web applications. Not only are these products free or cheap; they are significantly less complex than full J2EE servers.
>
> Only for distributed transactions do you need to resort to a JTA-enabled server such as JBoss, WebLogic, or WebSphere, for its transaction management capabilities. Note that a low-end version of a commercial server can be a fine choice: For example, WebLogic Express provides JTA support in addition to the core web container—you need the full version of WebLogic Server only if EJB, JMS, or JCA is involved too.

Summary

Contrary to popular belief, the EJB container is not the sole option for effective transaction management in J2EE applications, and not every transaction needs to be capable of spanning multiple resources. The goal of high-level transaction management can be achieved with or without EJB; even with or without JTA. In further contrast to J2EE orthodoxy, it's not always necessary to use global container-managed transactions. All that is necessary is to provide a consistent programming model, regardless of whether transactions span one or more resources.

While it is possible to manage global transactions using the JTA API directly, it's not an attractive option, primarily because of JTA's cumbersome exception handling requirements. However, a good abstraction layer over JTA, such as Spring's `PlatformTransactionManager`, can make programmatic transaction management a good option in many cases. Such an abstraction also means that you're not dependent on JTA in the first place.

It is not necessary to use EJBs (even local EJBs) just for declarative transaction management, as AOP-based solutions can offer the same level of convenience with significantly less effort and more flexibility. AOP can be used to make POJOs transactional, with the potential to make applications simpler and more object-oriented than they might be with use of EJB. In contrast to EJB, the Spring Framework's AOP transaction management even lets you specify which exceptions should cause a rollback.

Compared to local SLSBs, a lightweight transaction infrastructure like that of the Spring Framework offers the same benefits with much simpler means. It applies the same concept and the same API for transaction demarcation to application objects in any environment, be it a J2EE container or a desktop application. Such infrastructure can scale with your requirements *without changes to Java code*. For single database transactions, a simple JDBC-based transaction strategy is perfectly sufficient. If you ever face distributed transaction requirements, you can easily switch to distributed transactions via JTA by a simple change in configuration. But remember, there is a good chance of YAGNI.

The most important benefit of Spring's transaction support is that any POJO can be transaction-enabled without deployment steps or special requirements. If there is an existing service implementation that must be enriched with transactional semantics, it can be defined in a Spring bean factory, with a transactional proxy added for it. There is no need to re-architect the whole application as when migrating to EJB—you just refine the existing configuration. Existing classes need not implement any specific interface or extend any specific base class. As long as you are still accessing only a single database, there is no reason to switch to a more complex J2EE server from a web container such as Tomcat.

> **Transaction management need not be complex. After reading this chapter, you'll see how you can use the simplest possible solution to your transaction management requirements, minimizing overhead and complexity.**

10

Persistence

Nearly every J2EE application needs to access persistent data. Most enterprise applications need to or choose to work with relational databases, which represent an established and well-understood paradigm for keeping persistent data.

> *This is not to disparage object databases, which can provide real benefits to many applications written in object-oriented languages. However, object databases have failed to make significant headway in the market, and are not an option in most projects. This is disappointing from a technical perspective, but unfortunately technical decisions usually need to be made within political constraints.*

Bridging the gap between OO application code and RDBMS concepts can be tricky. Hence data access can account for much of the code in typical J2EE web applications, and much of the complexity and developer effort. Determining an appropriate data access strategy can be difficult, as there are many competing paradigms and solutions. It's crucial to get this decision right, as naïve or otherwise unsatisfactory approaches to data access can doom applications to failure: mired in complexity, performing poorly, or failing to scale.

This chapter focuses on practical ways for accessing relational databases from lightweight J2EE applications. We will discuss basic differences between the major strategies and usage scenarios. We will also address an often neglected issue: the implications of each data access strategy for the overall application architecture.

In this chapter we use terminology for common data access approaches introduced by Martin Fowler in *Patterns of Enterprise Application Architecture* (2002)—further referred to as POEAA. You won't need to consult that book to understand this chapter, although it's recommended reading in any case.

Common Persistence Strategies

Ways of accessing and manipulating relational data vary widely. There is a broad range of data access strategies to choose from, ranging from SQL-based approaches to full-blown O/R mapping.

An Overview of Persistence Patterns

In many applications, it is natural to work directly with the relational model, issuing SQL statements and parsing result sets as necessary. This typically amounts to what Martin Fowler terms a **transaction tcript** (POEAA): business logic organized into procedures for each use case. Direct use of relational operations is well suited for aggregating queries and set-based updates, operations that relational databases perform very efficiently.

Another large group of applications faces different requirements: Relatively simple queries fetch small sets of result rows (often from a single table), which receive selective updates. There is usually little need for set-based updates. These data entities are often mapped to persistent Java objects that make up a **domain model** (POEAA), so that business logic can be implemented to work with these object representations rather than the database tables and fields directly. The general term for such a strategy is **object-relational mapping (O/R mapping)**. It aims to overcome the so-called **impedance mismatch** between object-oriented applications and relational databases.

> The object-relational *impedance mismatch* is a popular term for the gulf between the relational model, which is based on normalized data in tables and having a well-defined mathematical basis, and the world of object-orientation, which is based on concepts such as classes, inheritance, and polymorphism.

A simple form of O/R mapping is an **active record** (POEAA). In this approach, every row of a mapped table is represented by one instance of the corresponding *gateway* class. Such a persistent class features *insert*, *update*, and *delete* methods as explicit persistence operations to be invoked by business controller logic. Additionally, there will typically be a *finder* class per mapped table, with finder methods to retrieve persistent objects in the first place. Business logic is either kept outside the persistent objects in workflow methods or defined on the objects themselves.

In contrast to "active records" that define their own persistence operations within the domain class, a **data mapper** (POEAA), also commonly known as **O/R mapper**, aims to "move data between objects and a database while keeping them independent of each other and the mapper itself." This separates business and persistence aspects into distinct classes: The domain class will focus on data representation and domain logic, while the data mapper will be concerned with the persistence aspects. The term **transparent persistence** is often used to refer to such non-intrusive persistence mechanisms that also provide *unit-of-work* semantics (discussed shortly). It has the important virtue that the difficult problem of data mapping can be addressed largely by a generic framework, rather than application code. Popular products implementing this pattern are Hibernate, TopLink, and various O/R-based JDO implementations.

A data mapper—at least in theory—allows the object model and the database schema to evolve independently. (Of course there are some practical constraints, because of efficiency issues and the capabilities of SQL.) Their sole connection is the data mapping that defines how the various fields of the persistent classes correspond to tables and fields in the data model. The mapping details can either be held in code—for example in **data access objects (DAOs)**—or in metadata such as XML documents. The data mapper will also offer finder functionality for retrieving instances of mapped classes, and means for deleting persistent objects.

A **query object** (POEAA) can complement a finder method: It encapsulates a database query as a reusable command object with domain parameters. Query objects can either be *combined* with DAOs, serving as parameter holders for finder methods, or execute on their own, *replacing* classic finder methods in DAOs. A special kind of query object is a **query-by-example**: An instance of a persistent class is used as a template for retrieving all instances that match the set field values. Another alternative is a **query language** like Hibernate HQL, allowing the specification of queries as (potentially SQL-like) strings rather than programmatic objects.

Sophisticated data mapping products automatically detect changes in retrieved objects and persist them at transaction commit time. This is what we call "full" transparent persistence, not even requiring explicit domain update calls in workflow logic. To achieve this, a **unit of work** (POEAA), such as a Hibernate `Session` object, must maintain a set of objects whose state has been changed by business operations in the current transaction. These objects are said to be *dirty* at commit time. The unit of work can then issue update statements only for data that has actually changed, allowing for highly efficient commits. A Hibernate `Session` also serves as *identity map* (POEAA), "ensuring that each object gets loaded only once by keeping every loaded object in a map."

Popular J2EE Data Access Solutions

Of course, it is possible to work at SQL level with standard Java alone, without additional mapping solutions. The **JDBC** API for SQL-based access to relational databases has been available since Java 1.1, and is still appropriate for many applications. JDBC adds minimal overhead when performing set-based operations, for which SQL is very powerful and intuitive to use. JDBC does not aim to provide an object-oriented view of relational data, nor does it sacrifice any of the power of the target database. JDBC is also handy when we want to use proprietary features of the target database or stored procedures, which may be more difficult to use via an O/R mapping layer.

Unfortunately, JDBC is a low-level API that is relatively cumbersome to use correctly: It requires verbose and error-prone use of try/catch/finally blocks for correct resource and exception handling. However, numerous commercial and open source tools address this difficulty by offering abstraction layers over JDBC: for example the **Spring Framework JDBC support** and the **iBATIS Database Layer** (www.ibatis.com).

Custom O/R mapping mechanisms are often implemented as home-grown data access objects on top of JDBC, serving as data mappers for domain classes. Such in-house solutions are usually not very sophisticated: full transparent persistence via units of work and identity maps is often too hard and too expensive to build. Therefore, business workflow logic will normally need to explicitly invoke update methods on DAOs. Such update implementations will often not perform any dirty detection, but issue their SQL statements every time. Repeated reads may also re-fetch the data from the database instead of using a transactional in-memory cache. The query API is often a primitive form of Query-by-Example or uses SQL clauses.

Such custom solutions are typically thin wrappers above JDBC rather than full-blown O/R mappers. Even if that low level of abstraction is appropriate, there is no need to build it in-house: **iBATIS SQL Maps** provide a good solution that works at the "mapped statement" level with SQL as query language. If you need full transparent persistence—which goes far beyond mapped statements, as outlined earlier—rolling your own solution is hardly ever defensible.

> **If you want O/R mapping, do not implement your own O/R mapping solution. We are amazed at the number of organizations who continue to waste resources doing so. This is a very expensive wheel to reinvent. There is a lot of sophistication to a good solution, even if some basic O/R mapping support can be coded in a couple of days. Fortunately, several very good and surprisingly flexible O/R mapping products are available. The best products are easy to learn and use.**

Sophisticated Java O/R mapping solutions like **Hibernate** (`www.hibernate.org`) and O/R-based **JDO (Java Data Objects)** compliant products are data mappers that offer full transparent persistence including support for units of work. Typically, the mapping information is kept in metadata; certain tools like TopLink also generate Java classes that perform the mapping. An important differentiator between such O/R mapping solutions is how metadata is managed: For example, Hibernate offers a simple, human-editable XML format—with XDoclet support for those who want to keep such metadata in Java source code—while most commercial tools require the use of a graphical mapping tool to generate metadata. Whether it is preferable to edit such metadata in an XML editor or in a graphical mapping tool is to a large degree a matter of taste: In any case, it can be considered an advantage if the metadata format *allows* for human editing, even if typically generated by a tool.

Entity beans are basically a component framework for *active records*, each entity bean being mapped to a single row in a database table. Entity bean instances themselves have load and store operations defined on them; home interfaces serve as finders. With **Bean-Managed Persistence (BMP)**, the application developer must implement the actual persistence operations, typically on top of JDBC. This does not usually add worthwhile benefit to a DAO-based solution, which may be much simpler. **Container-Managed Persistence (CMP)** tries to offer active records with external data mapping. However, this is far from *transparent* persistence, as objects to be persisted depend on the EJB container. Non-intrusive, lightweight persistence, as delivered by solutions like Hibernate and JDO, is more appropriate for typical requirements.

The **Data Access Object** J2EE pattern is very popular, because it often allows for clean separation between the implementation of business and persistence logic. DAOs were originally popularized as implementation helpers for BMP entity beans, making the latter just simple wrappers over lightweight DAOs. However, the DAO pattern has proved valuable in many usage scenarios. It is also common to have session beans or plain Java business objects act as a service layer that delegates to DAOs for persistence operations.

DAOs are typically built on JDBC, although one of the key benefits of the DAO pattern is that it enables persistence operations to be gathered into DAO *interfaces*, which can be implemented with whatever persistence technology is available. With the rise of lightweight solutions for transparent persistence, the value of DAOs is no longer so clear: It can be argued that working with a Hibernate Session or a JDO `PersistenceManager` directly is abstraction enough. We will discuss the Data Access Object pattern more in-depth later in the chapter.

> It is often helpful to differentiate between *business logic* and *persistence logic*. Business logic concerns an application's core workflow, and business rules. Persistence logic concerns access to and manipulation of persistent data. "Logic" may be required to link multiple updates, preserve data integrity, and otherwise conceal the low-level details of the persistence store from business objects.

Choosing a Persistence Strategy

For any project, the persistence strategy should be determined from the outset. Often, requirements are dictated by legacy databases or the need to share a database with other systems, limiting available options. The implementation of a data access layer is a major investment of time and know-how: Appropriate technology will ease the task but cannot make it trivial. Completely abstracting persistence—for example, so that it is totally independent of an RDBMS—is often not worthwhile. Few projects will migrate to a different persistence strategy at a moment's notice. However, reworking a data access layer for a new major release is not uncommon.

A change in data access is always significant, even if within the same persistence strategy. It is a fallacy to believe in drop-in replacements, whether concerning JDBC drivers or JDO implementations. It may be true that not many lines of application code might have to change, but those few have to be identified. The need to rename certain database fields when targeting a different database product or to rewrite mapping metadata for a different JDO implementation are obvious issues. Small but important semantic details may cause the biggest headaches: for example, locking behavior or transaction isolation. Thorough testing is a must in any case.

When to Choose O/R Mapping

O/R mapping is highly fashionable in the J2EE community. (It is less popular in the .NET world, although it is gaining prominence.) O/R mapping can have many benefits, but it is important to remember that *not every application fits the O/R mapping paradigm*. Central issues are heavy use of set access and aggregate functions, and batch updates of many rows. If an application is mainly concerned with either of those and does not allow for a significant amount of caching in an object mapping layer, set-based relational access via JDBC (preferably using a simplifying abstraction layer) is probably the best choice. Because all O/R mapping frameworks have a learning curve and setup cost, applications with very simple data access requirements are also often best to stick with JDBC-based solutions.

Indicators that O/R mapping *is* appropriate are:

❑ A typical *load/edit/store workflow* for domain objects, for example: load a product record, edit it, and update it in the database.

❑ Objects may be possibly *queried for in large sets* but are *updated and deleted individually*.

❑ A significant number of objects lend themselves to being *cached aggressively* (a "read-mostly" scenario, common in web applications).

❑ There is a sufficiently *natural mapping* between domain objects and database tables and fields.

❑ There are *no unusual requirements in terms of custom SQL optimizations*. Good O/R mapping solutions can issue efficient SQL in many cases, as with Hibernate's "dialect" support, but some SQL optimizations can only be done via a wholly relational paradigm.

A major benefit of O/R mapping lies in avoiding the need to write repetitive JDBC code in applications to handle instances of domain objects. For a typical load/edit/store workflow, working with JDBC requires you to implement four statements: *insert*, *select*, *update*, and *delete*. Thus, a renamed field in the database leads to four changes in data access code—in the worst case of building SQL statements without intermediate mapping. If you find yourself writing such statements again and again, do yourself a favor and seriously consider a mapping tool. Even a low-level O/R mapper like iBATIS SQL Maps can ease your task tremendously here.

A further benefit is **transparent persistence**: Sophisticated O/R mapping tools allow you to load any number of objects and automatically persist changes to them at transaction commit. As we've noted, only actual changes will be committed—there is no need for dirty checking in application code. Note that the way in which the various tools achieve this benefit differs: JDO uses **compile-time byte code modification** to make its StateManager aware of field changes, while Hibernate and TopLink use snapshot comparisons. Hibernate uses **runtime byte code generation**, while TopLink (as of version 9.0.4) uses a purely reflection-based architecture. (The use of reflection alone in TopLink means that it's usually necessary to explicitly "register" objects being updated with the unit of work to ensure automatic updates of dirty objects at commit time. This limitation arguably makes TopLink persistence less transparent than Hibernate or JDO.)

> As O/R mapping products have important differences, it often makes sense to consider a specific O/R mapping tool even when deciding on O/R mapping in general versus plain JDBC. A sophisticated O/R mapping tool like Hibernate or TopLink might allow optimizations that a generic query language like JDOQL does not support.
>
> Even within JDO implementations, the potential for optimization differs: Consider leveraging vendor-specific JDO extensions, as you can always encapsulate them in specific DAO implementations, and the loss of standardization is worthwhile if it produces significant simplification or performance benefits.

For an in-depth discussion of data access strategies, particularly regarding O/R mapping, working at the JDBC level, and applying the DAO pattern, see Chapters 7 to 9 of *Expert One-on-One J2EE Design and Development*.

Caching of Persistent Data

The single biggest booster of data access performance in typical applications is aggressive **caching**. Particularly if persistent data is just read and written by one single process—for example, in case of a web content management system—caching is highly advisable: No other process will modify the data, so there is no potential staleness involved as long as the application itself properly notifies the cache of changes to persistent objects.

Of course, caching is not appropriate for data that is frequently updated by various processes, as the database then needs to be hit on each request to avoid the danger of stale results. For read-mostly objects, particularly reference data like user profiles or product categories, caching may still be a good fit. The benefit of keeping data in memory, close to the application, may outweigh the potential staleness. Of course in some applications, *any* risk of staleness may be unacceptable. Tolerance of staleness depends on the nature of the data.

Fine-tuning cache settings is non-trivial. Cache timeouts can typically be set per cached class, for example one hour for product descriptions but one minute for user profiles. The settings need to be balanced for the particular application and user expectations; many caches provide sensible defaults that are at least appropriate for development and demo environments.

Custom caching is often built into particular applications. This is seldom advisable, as many good generic caching products are available, like the Hibernate-affiliated **EHCache** (http://ehcache.sourceforge.net), OpenSymphony **OSCache** (www.opensymphony.com/oscache) and **SwarmCache** (http://swarmcache.sourceforge.net) on the open source side, and **Tangosol Coherence** (www.tangosol.com) on the commercial side.

Many, if not all O/R mapping tools come pre-integrated with caching solutions, notifying them of any changes to mapped objects. Sophisticated tools like Hibernate and Kodo JDO (www.solarmetric.com) offer a cache provider API for plugging in third-party products. Hibernate comes with its sister product EHCache out of the box, and both Hibernate and Kodo offer integration with Tangosol Coherence.

Persistence tools with caching support often provide APIs allowing programmatic **eviction** of selected objects from the cache. This is particularly important when O/R mapping and set-based JDBC access are combined within the same application—a common scenario. Eviction can help to avoid unnecessary staleness of mapped objects after an update through a direct JDBC statement or a stored procedure. Of course, a change applied by a different process—without the application being aware of it—will result in stale cache state in any case. In our experience, a J2EE application having the database to itself is more the exception than the rule.

> **If you need caching, do not implement your own caching solution. This is another very expensive wheel to reinvent. If you choose an O/R mapping tool, learn how to use its integrated caching mechanism. If your caching requirements are highly sophisticated, consider integrating your O/R mapping solution with a specialized caching product.**

A special scenario arises with clustered servers in that a distributed cache is needed for proper cache coherence: If the application itself changes persistent objects on one server, all other instances of the cache need to be notified. Distributed caching is a very tricky issue; often it is advisable to turn off caching for data that is not allowed to be stale in a cluster, delegating the burden of data coherence to the database.

Many caching solutions, like EHCache, are not primarily intended for distributed caching. Check the documentation for your caching product carefully, and do your own tests before adopting a solution for such a scenario. There is a new open source project called *SwarmCache* (mentioned earlier) that addresses distributed caching. This is the domain of Tangosol Coherence—a highly optimized commercial solution.

Many developers incorrectly assume that entity beans provide the best solution for distributed caching. In fact, even the best entity bean implementations, such as the WebLogic implementation, offer less sophisticated distributed caching out of the box than a combination of an O/R mapper such as Hibernate or Kodo and a distributed cache such as Coherence.

Transparent Persistence and Behavior in Domain Objects

When working with O/R mapping, persistent objects are often designed as dumb data holders for persistent state, offering only getters and setters for each field. As we've noted in previous chapters, such dumb data holders are not true objects, having only state and no behavior. Use of dumb data holders probably results from J2EE developers being accustomed to working with primitive persistence mechanisms. If one needs to explicitly save an object whose state has changed, it is preferable to make explicit changes in workflow operations. Implicit changes by business methods in domain objects might not get saved by accident, if the workflow implementation is not aware of those changes.

The entity bean model has also contributed to this view of data objects (or, rather, non-objects). With entity beans, the reasons for keeping business logic out of entities are different but lead to the same result. Entity beans are very hard to test outside a container, therefore business logic is moved out to business objects, which can be unit tested. This is a good example of a "pattern" in the J2EE world that is actually a workaround for a J2EE deficiency: in this case, the failure of entity beans to deliver anything like transparent persistence. Unfortunately, such patterns often endure even after switching to transparent persistence solutions, when the original reasoning is no longer relevant.

With full transparent persistence, there is no reason to avoid implicit changes: They are automatically saved at transaction commit anyway. Domain objects containing business logic do not conflict with a sophisticated external data mapper that offers a unit of work. Such business logic can be unit-tested outside an application server or in the absence of the data mapper, because the domain objects have minimal dependence on the data mapping implementation. Therefore, there is no reason to avoid a rich domain model, that is, true objects with both state and *behavior*. Workflow methods at the business facade level are still responsible for transaction demarcation, for retrieving persistent objects in the first place, and for operations that span multiple objects, but no longer for domain logic that really belongs to the domain model.

What logic to put into domain classes versus what to put into workflow controllers should be decided case by case. Operations that are reusable across multiple use cases should normally be part of domain classes. Single use cases that are hardly reusable are candidates for controller methods; so are operations that span multiple domain objects.

> **With full transparent persistence, use normal OO design criteria to decide where to put business logic in business service objects or your domain model. Often putting logic inside persistent domain objects can improve encapsulation: for example, avoiding the common scenario encountered with entity bean usage, in which session beans iterate over entity bean relationships that could be better concealed inside a domain model.**

A Brief History of Java Persistence Technologies

Sun Microsystems introduced JDBC in 1996 as a standardized low-level abstraction layer for RDBMS resource handling and data access in release 1.1 of the Java platform. Many developers soon realized that working directly with the JDBC API is rather cumbersome: Therefore, various higher-level solutions emerged on top of it within the next few years, both in-house and, increasingly, open source.

The Slow Rise of Java O/R Mapping Solutions

O/R mapping has had a long and somewhat checkered history in server-side Java. However, there is now a richer choice of solutions than ever before, including several mature, established products.

1997–1998: TopLink, CocoBase, ODMG

O/R mapping was not invented for Java or J2EE. The problem of the O/R impedance mismatch applies when accessing relational data from any object-oriented language, and pioneering solutions included the NeXT **Enterprise Objects Framework** (EOF) in the mid 1990s. EOF was originally written in Objective C, and became a part of the **WebObjects** application server, eventually acquired by Apple (www.apple .com/webobjects). EOF had many sophisticated features: However, its port to Java in 2000 sacrificed some of its elegance, and WebObjects was run over in the market by the EJB juggernaut, despite the fact that entity beans failed to provide comparable power as a data access technology.

One of the leading Java O/R mapping solutions, **TopLink**, was initially written in Smalltalk. The Object People released the first Java version of TopLink (thereafter focusing on the growing Java market) in 1997, soon followed by Thought Inc with their **CocoBase** (www.cocobase.com) product. These products were the only major O/R mapping tools for some time, and were unaffordable for many projects because of high license costs. Concern about product complexity also probably reduced the potential adoption rate of O/R mapping products.

In 1997, the **Object Data Management Group (ODMG**; www.odmg.org) published release 2.0 of its standard API for object persistence, defining bindings for Java and other languages. Release 3.0 followed in early 2000, but neither gained significant acceptance. The OMDG was mainly concerned with access to object databases, although it also addressed O/R mapping. To date, there is no complete implementation of the ODMG API for Java O/R mapping. The OMDG layer of Apache **ObjectRelationalBridge (OJB**; http://db.apache.org/ojb) probably comes closest.

Because of fragmentation in the market and the high cost of commercial O/R mapping products, the late 1990s also saw a host of in-house projects developing O/R mapping frameworks of varying sophistication. However, such products generally proved expensive to develop and maintain, and—at least technically— a poor alternative to dedicated O/R mapping products.

1999–2001: Entity Beans, JDO

With the dawn of J2EE, came a new contender for persistence: **entity beans**. They became a mandatory part of J2EE with the EJB 1.1 specification at the end of 1999, gaining wider adoption with the introduction of local interfaces in EJB 2.0 in 2001. Entity beans were heavily promoted by application server vendor marketing, and by their prominent status in the Sun J2EE Blueprints and the Pet Store sample application. However, the popularity of entity beans waned in 2002–03 as their limitations became evident in many projects.

Entity beans arguably set back the cause of true O/R mapping, rather than advancing it. They encouraged thinking of persistent domain objects as dumb data holders; they were the opposite of transparent persistence. And they were cumbersome to implement and work with.

2001 also saw the quiet introduction of the **JDO (Java Data Objects) 1.0** specification, defining a specific way of persisting plain Java objects to any kind of data store. The JDO industry gained momentum in 2002, with the emergence of numerous commercial JDO implementations for both object databases and relational databases. However, JDO has grown in popularity only gradually: perhaps partly due to its generic focus without special regard to O/R mapping; perhaps partly because of (arguably misguided) resistance to the post-compilation byte code "enhancement" step associated with JDO 1.0. A third reason—the existence of the entity bean "standard" solution—is becoming less of an issue. See the discussion of JDO as data access strategy later in this chapter for details.

2002–2003: TopLink, Hibernate, iBATIS Database Layer

After its acquisition by the short-lived WebGain in the late 1990s, **TopLink** underwent another change of ownership in mid 2002, when Oracle acquired it and integrated TopLink into its Oracle 9i product suite (www.oracle.com/appserver). TopLink also introduced a JDO-like API, although it is not compliant with the JDO 1.0 specification and does not provide a standard API in place of the proprietary TopLink API. TopLink representatives now serve on the JDO 2.0 Expert Group, so it is possible (although by no means certain) that TopLink will provide a true JDO interface in the future.

A newcomer that gained momentum in 2002 was Gavin King's **Hibernate**, a dedicated open source O/R mapping tool with a clear focus on being a thin wrapper over JDBC to provide as much flexibility as possible while still providing full transparent persistence. In contrast to JDOQL, the Hibernate query language (HQL) supports key relational concepts like joins, aggregate functions, and fetching certain fields in batch. Hence HQL offers much of the power of SQL without having to specify database table or field names. As of early 2004, Hibernate, approaching 30,000 downloads per release, is probably the most popular O/R mapping tool in the Java industry; an impressive achievement in such a short amount of time.

Another newcomer released in late 2002 was Clinton Begin's **iBATIS Database Layer**, providing SQL Maps as a simple form of O/R mapping. It grew out of Begin's **JPetStore**, an alternative implementation of the infamous Pet Store that Sun introduced in the J2EE Blueprints. Instead of aiming for transparent persistence with units of work, iBATIS SQL Maps target the "mapped statement" level, using SQL as query language.

2004: JDO Evolves; Hibernate Flourishes

The **JDO 2.0** Expert Group formed in late 2003, aiming, among other enhancements, for dedicated support for O/R mapping in *JDO/R*. Gavin King from Hibernate joined the expert group, making it likely that Hibernate will implement the forthcoming JDO/R 2.0 specification as an alternative to its native API. Furthermore, JBoss Group hired Gavin and adopted Hibernate as the backbone for its JBoss 4.0 CMP engine. Since early 2004, JBoss Group is the major driving force behind EJB 3.0's Hibernate-style entity beans, with Gavin also being part of the EJB 3.0 expert group.

Of course, Hibernate is not the only O/R mapping tool on the market beyond JDO implementations. There are other open source projects like Apache **ObjectRelationalBridge (OJB)** which aims to build various standard APIs like ODMG and JDO upon a common persistence broker. TopLink and CocoBase remain options for projects with large enough budgets. Non-JDO commercial products—particularly in the lower price segment—are increasingly coming under pressure from both the Hibernate and JDO fronts. The landscape of O/R mapping tools is still in motion.

The Failure of Entity Beans

The entity bean model has come under severe criticism, even in its EJB 2.0 and 2.1 revisions. See, for example, Chapter 8 of *Expert One-on-One J2EE Design and Development*. Hence, we will merely recap some of the most important issues here.

- ❑ Entity beans are **tightly coupled to the heavyweight EJB component model** and thus to a full J2EE container. They are not well suited for fine-grained domain objects in a reusable business layer. Even if using session beans as middle tier facades, lightweight persistence of POJOs is preferable to entity beans in most scenarios. Typical applications require fine-grained persistent *objects*; the desirability of persistent *components* is still unclear.

- ❑ The **effort of developing and deploying an entity bean is excessive** without code generation tools. Even sophisticated code generation tools cannot hide the complexity of the model. The requirement to specify a home and business interface for any persistent object and the excessive amount of deployment descriptor entries is inappropriate for the typical need of mapping domain objects to a database.

- ❑ BMP entity beans are particularly onerous to implement and pose intractable performance problems such as the well-known **n+1 finder problem.** Using BMP adds significant complexity compared to using the underlying persistence technology (such as JDBC) directly, but delivers little value.

- ❑ To avoid having to work at JDBC level, **Container-Managed Persistence (CMP)** must be used. The configuration and O/R mapping declaration, and also the actual capabilities, of CMP are **highly dependent on the J2EE server product.** This tie-in makes migrating to a different J2EE server a major undertaking.

- ❑ EJB QL (the CMP query language) is limited, forcing developers to **write custom SQL or rely on proprietary extensions** offered by application server vendors.

- ❑ Entity bean **performance is often poor** because of the overhead of component handling and method interception, especially when dealing with large result sets. Performance is more likely to be acceptable for heavily cached objects. EJB patterns like **Fast Lane Reader** and **Value Object** smell like workarounds for such entity bean deficiencies and cannot be considered true design patterns.

> Entity beans in EJB 2.1 finally begin to approach a workable solution for practical O/R mapping. However, the fact that they can work adequately in some applications does not make them credible competitors for simpler, yet more powerful, persistence technologies. Since entity beans are not an appropriate solution for lightweight persistence of fine-grained domain objects, this chapter focuses on popular alternative persistence strategies like JDO and Hibernate.

Data Access Technologies in Practice

The consensus of the last few years is that a fine-grained domain model should be modeled not as heavyweight EJB components but as simple Java objects—**POJOs**. There are a wealth of technologies and tools for persisting POJOs: Hibernate, JDO, and iBATIS SQL Maps are the most popular, and all produce good results in practice, when used appropriately.

Despite the diversity of technologies, there are a number of common issues that application developers will face, whichever product they choose.

Resource Handling

All persistence technologies involve some handling of resources. The basic principle is similar between JDBC, JDO, and Hibernate. There are typically two types of objects involved:

❑ *A connection factory*: This factory represents a specific data store that it can create connections for. A connection factory is typically a thread-safe instance that can be obtained via JNDI or a factory provided by the O/R mapping solution. For JDBC, this is a `DataSource`; for JDO, a `PersistenceManagerFactory`; for Hibernate, a `SessionFactory`.

❑ *A connection*: This represents a communication session with a specific data store. Typically connections are *not* thread-safe, and are thus freshly created by a connection factory for each conversation. For JDBC, this is a `Connection`; for JDO, a `PersistenceManager`; for Hibernate, a `Session`; for TopLink, a `Session` or `UnitOfWork` (depending on usage).

Connection factories often allow for pooling of connections to avoid the repeated overhead of creating new connections. A pooling JDBC `DataSource` will return either a new or a pooled connection. This is transparent to the application; the received connection will always be ready to use. A JDO `PersistenceManager` or Hibernate `Session` will not be pooled in case of a locally defined factory; the factory will return pooled connections only if managed by a JCA connector.

O/R mapping factories like a JDO `PersistenceManagerFactory` or a Hibernate `SessionFactory` are different from a JDBC `DataSource` in that they typically contain shared caches and mapping information with explicit knowledge about application classes. Therefore, they are not well suited for container-managed JCA connectors that do not run within the application's class loader. A JDBC `DataSource` does not involve any application-specific classes; hence it can be managed by the container and shared between multiple applications.

Connections or sessions of O/R mappers are special too in that they cache loaded objects for their client and keep track of modified objects, to be able to automatically persist changes on transaction commit. For accessing relational data, they typically hold onto a JDBC `Connection`; whether this `Connection` is pooled in a shared JDBC `DataSource` or internally within the O/R mapper depends on the configuration of the tool.

Whichever persistence technology you choose, several issues related to resource handling arise:

❑ Where to **define connection factories:** in the J2EE container or locally within the application?

❑ Where to **initialize connection factories:** on application startup, in case of local definitions?

❑ How to **look up connection factories** in application code, whether they are defined in the J2EE container or locally?

❑ How to **reuse connections** across multiple method invocations within the same thread; for example, in processing a web request?

❑ What is the **relationship between transaction and connection:** does the transaction drive the connection or vice versa?

❑ How to guarantee **proper closing of connections** and similar resources in case of exceptions, without the risk of swallowing the original exception?

Common ad hoc solutions to each of these problems are:

❑ Define a JDBC `DataSource` in the J2EE container, using the container's standard functionality. A JDO `PersistenceManagerFactory` or a Hibernate `SessionFactory` may be defined locally within the application or also defined in the J2EE container, using a JCA connector.

❑ Initialize a JDO `PersistenceManagerFactory` or a Hibernate `SessionFactory` in a `Servlet ContextListener`, or one of the proprietary startup classes of a specific J2EE container product.

❑ Use JNDI to look up connection factories that are defined in the J2EE container. Locally defined factories are often looked up via JNDI too, getting bound there in a custom startup class.

❑ Use a `ServletFilter` to look up the connection factory, bind a connection to a `ThreadLocal`, and unbind it at the end of request processing. Application code will then need to fetch the connection from the `ThreadLocal`.

❑ Use the connection to drive native transactions, either in data access methods themselves or in a `ServletFilter`. Alternatively, use the J2EE container's JTA to drive the transactions, and configure your connection factories to return JTA-aware connections.

❑ Write boilerplate `try/catch/finally` blocks for each and every piece of data access code, ensuring that resources are relinquished even in the event of unexpected exceptions.

> While these ad hoc solutions can work, they are often not ideal or particularly elegant. Many of them are *tied* to a J2EE container or a Servlet environment. This is undesirable: When business objects and data access objects are intricately tied to being executed in a specific environment, they cannot easily be reused in other environments or easily tested in test suites. Nevertheless, there must be the option to leverage container resources when they are available. Later in this chapter, we'll see how the Spring Framework addresses these issues.

JDBC

JDBC is still the most common Java/J2EE technology for accessing relational databases. Since its inception in JDK 1.1, it has seen two major revisions:

❑ **JDBC 2.0 and the JDBC Standard Extensions (J2SE 1.2):** This release introduced numerous new features, like scrollable `ResultSets`. An important new feature was the `javax.sql.DataSource` interface, a factory for JDBC `Connection` instances, as an alternative to the `java.sql.Driver` approach. Its main benefit was that it allowed connection pools to share a common interface. The `DataSource` interface has been adopted as the standard way of retrieving JDBC Connections in a J2EE environment. However, it's important to remember that `DataSources` can be used outside a J2EE environment—a point sometimes forgotten.

❑   **JDBC 3.0 (J2SE 1.4):** This consolidation release integrated the JDBC Standard Extensions (`javax.sql`) into the J2SE core, removing the need to include `jdbc2_0-stdext.jar` in the class path of J2EE development projects. It also introduced new features such as *savepoints* (unfortunately not available via the J2EE JTA transaction abstraction), and clarified `ResultSet` holdability and prepared statement caching. (Prepared statement caching was already implemented by a number of J2EE application servers.)

One thing that has *not* changed in the evolution of JDBC is the cumbersome process of using the JDBC API. Using the JDBC API directly requires half a page of code for performing a simple update statement with correct resource and exception handling, as we will see in the next section.

> JDBC is an established and powerful API for working with relational databases at the SQL level. Its main deficiency, the bloated and repetitive infrastructure code necessary for working with it directly, is addressed in different ways by a number of helper libraries. We will look at iBATIS SQL Maps and the Spring Framework template support for JDBC access later on, which both significantly reduce the amount of data access code.

Example Code

An example of an update statement with plain JDBC, assuming a `DataSource` of type `javax.sql.DataSource` has previously been located via JNDI (or otherwise obtained):

```
Connection con = dataSource.getConnection();
Statement stmt = null;
try {
  stmt = con.createStatement();
  stmt.executeUpdate("UPDATE products SET pr_price = 1100 WHERE pr_price = 1000");
}
finally {
  if (stmt != null) {
    try {
      stmt.close();
    }
    catch (SQLException ex) {
      logger.warn("Could not close JDBC Statement", ex);
    }
  }
  try {
    con.close();
  }
  catch (SQLException ex) {
    logger.warn("Could not close JDBC Connection", ex);
  }
}
```

Any `SQLException` thrown during the update, rather than close operations, will be propagated to calling code; handling it in the code fragment would require still more code.

The same example with a prepared statement looks as follows:

```
Connection con = dataSource.getConnection();
PreparedStatement ps = null;
try {
  ps = con.prepareStatement("UPDATE products SET pr_price = ? WHERE pr_price = ?");
  ps.setInt(1, 1000);
  ps.setInt(2, 1100);
  ps.executeUpdate();
}
finally {
  if (ps != null) {
    try {
      ps.close();
    }
    catch (SQLException ex) {
      logger.warn("Could not close JDBC Statement", ex);
    }
  }
  try {
    con.close();
  }
  catch (SQLException ex) {
    logger.warn("Could not close JDBC Connection", ex);
  }
}
```

Note that this code assumes either no transactional execution at all or global transaction management via JTA, because it does not perform any native JDBC transaction handling. Furthermore, it does not reuse connections in any specific way; it would need to be rewritten in order to detect and use a ThreadLocal Connection.

Later in this chapter, we will discuss the Spring Framework support for JDBC: Beyond offering simplified means for coding JDBC access, it also offers integration into its resource and transaction infrastructure, for participating in transactions and reusing a Connection within the scope of a transaction.

iBATIS SQL Maps

A popular tool that works at the SQL level but abstracts the use of JDBC completely is **iBATIS SQL Maps**, part of Clinton Begin's **iBATIS Database Layer** (www.ibatis.com; Apache-style license).

The idea is simple: statements are defined in an XML file, specifying a SQL string with parameter placeholders (optionally specifying SQL types and other details for the parameters). On execution, the placeholders are resolved to given parameter values, either from a **parameter map**, a JavaBean with **bean properties**, or a **simple parameter object**. In case of a SQL query, the definition maps result columns to a result object, supporting the same kinds of values as for parameters.

Beyond plain statement mapping, SQL Maps provide support for **caching query results**, with pluggable cache strategies. Various out-of-the-box implementations are provided, including a default memory cache and a strategy for OpenSymphony **OSCache.** Cache models are applied per mapped query statement; it's possible to specify insert/update/delete statements that should cause flushing of the particular cache (for example to flush the `loadProducts` cache if an `updateProduct` statement is executed). There is no support for evicting specific object instances from the cache; if a single `Product` is updated, all `Product` instances will be evicted.

Note that SQL Maps do *not* provide transparent persistence: that is, they do not perform any kind of change detection for retrieved objects. SQL Maps strictly focus on mapping of input parameters and result values for SQL statements. When using JavaBeans as values, a low-level kind of O/R mapping is provided: Separate statement definitions for insert, select, update, and delete operations are able to reuse the same parameter and result mappings—for example, for the same domain object. Nested objects must be dealt with explicitly; there is *no* implicit cascading of update or delete operations.

Compared to high-level transparent persistence, mapping at the SQL level has the following advantages:

❑ **Retaining the full power of SQL,** allowing full control over all details of the issued statements.

❑ **Set-based updates and deletes** can be applied for efficient manipulation of multiple rows.

❑ **Aggregate functions** like `avg`, `sum`, `max` and `count` can be used without any restrictions.

❑ **Mapping a domain object to fields across multiple tables** is straightforward, allowing for any kind of granularity.

However, an application's data access code is still responsible for:

❑ **Explicitly updating modified objects,** keeping track of potential modifications, and managing relationships between objects.

❑ **Converting application-level values** to database-compatible values, for example in case of booleans or dates.

Full-blown transparent persistence tools like JDO and Hibernate offer a more convenient level of working with persistent objects, typically also allowing for sophisticated type mappings—but imposing restrictions in terms of the relation between domain model and data model.

> iBATIS SQL Maps are a compelling way to perform set-based access to relational databases via declarative statement definitions. The mapping options range from simple values to JavaBeans, allowing SQL Maps to map aggregate values as well as domain objects.
>
> In contrast to full-blown transparent persistence tools like Hibernate, SQL Maps do not implement units of work or identity maps, resulting in a significantly less complex tool: They represent a simple means to work at the SQL level via convenient "mapped statements"—a viable choice for simple needs but also for full control over database access.

Example Code

The earlier update example looks as follows when coded with an iBATIS SQL Map, assuming a `sqlMap` reference of type `com.ibatis.db.sqlmap.SqlMap`. A `SqlMap` is basically a connection factory similar to a JDBC DataSource, but it is not necessary to create connections manually. If the `SqlMap` is fully configured for a specific underlying DataSource, you can simply call the executeUpdate method with a given parameter map.

```
Map param = new HashMap(2);
param.put("oldPrice", new Integer(1000));
param.put("newPrice", new Integer(1100));
sqlMap.executeUpdate("updateProductPrices", param);
```

Underneath, a new JDBC Connection and a PreparedStatement will be created, issuing the mapped SQL statement with the given parameters. Data access code does not have to worry about all the resource handling that direct JDBC usage involves. Corresponding to the example, the SqlMap configuration needs to define a mapped statement for the updateProductPrices key:

```
<mapped-statement name="updateProductPrices">
  UPDATE products SET pr_price = #newPrice# WHERE pr_price = #oldPrice#
</mapped-statement>
```

The #newPrice# and #oldPrice# placeholders will be resolved to the corresponding keys in the parameter map, in our example to 1100 and 1000, respectively. Instead of a parameter map, you can also use JavaBean objects—resolving the placeholders to bean property getters—or simple parameter objects like an Integer, using a #value# placeholder. Therefore, an existing domain object can be used as input parameter as long as it conforms to the JavaBean patterns. For more sophisticated mapping of values, the inline placeholders used above can be moved to a "parameter-map" definition, additionally specifying SQL types, etc.

As an alternative to configuring a SqlMap for a specific underlying JDBC DataSource, you can also use the com.ibatis.db.sqlmap.MappedStatement API and specify a JDBC Connection to work on. You simply have to retrieve the MappedStatement for the given key and invoke its executeUpdate method, passing in the Connection to use.

```
Map param = new HashMap(2);
param.put("oldPrice", new Integer(1000));
param.put("newPrice", new Integer(1100));
Connection con = dataSource.getConnection();
try {
  MappedStatement stmt = sqlMap.getMappedStatement("updateProductPrices");
  stmt.executeUpdate(con, param);
}
finally {
  try {
    con.close();
  }
  catch (SQLException ex) {
    logger.warn("Could not close JDBC Connection", ex);
  }
}
```

Effectively, the MappedStatement API is a very thin wrapper above standard JDBC: The corresponding SqlMap just contains the mapping definitions, while the entire JDBC resource handling is done outside the mapping tool. This usage style allows for easy integration into existing infrastructure; the Spring Framework support for iBATIS SQL Maps leverages this for easy integration into the overall resource and transaction management, as we will demonstrate later in this chapter.

Performing SQL queries is similarly simple: Data access code invokes a query method on a `SqlMap` or `MappedStatement` with a statement key and an input parameter, expecting a list of result objects or a single result object. The statement definition maps the input parameter values as shown in the previous example, but additionally specifies inline result keys (or refers to a "result-map" definition) that map `ResultSet` columns to a result object. As with input parameters, the result object can be a map, a JavaBean, or a simple object like an Integer. We will show a simple query example later in this chapter, when discussing Spring support for iBATIS SQL Maps.

See the excellent article "iBATIS Database Layer Developer's Guide" (available at `www.ibatis.com`) for API and configuration details.

JDO

JDO 1.0, released in March 2002, is concerned with generic object persistence. It defines an API for access to persistent objects, wherever stored, and a specific implementation strategy for state management coupled with a strict lifecycle for persistent objects. As it aims to be agnostic of the underlying data store, the JDO query language **JDOQL** does not support relational concepts like joins or aggregate functions (although JDO 2.0 will introduce an O/R mapping specification that should formalize such extensions). JDOQL is a pure object query language in the tradition of ODMG **OQL**, using a Java query API and Java-based criteria strings. The fact that JDOQL is based on Java makes it easy for Java developers to learn.

JDO 1.0 implementations provide transparent persistence of plain Java objects by **enhancing** their byte code to make them implement the `javax.jdo.PersistenceCapable` interface. The byte code enhancer needs to be run as part of the application's build process. Alternatively, it is possible to implement the `PersistenceCapable` contract directly in domain classes, but this is not recommended by any major JDO vendor.

The central JDO connection interface is `javax.jdo.PersistenceManager`, allowing access to persistent objects. An enhanced class informs the JDO `StateManager` of any changes to its instance fields within an active transaction. At transaction commit, the `PersistenceManager` will flush changes to the data store: in the case of a relational database, issuing the appropriate SQL insert, update, and delete statements.

The JDO specification requires that a `PersistenceManager` caches the instances that it retrieves for its lifetime, which is usually a single transaction. A **second-level cache** at the `PersistenceManager Factory` level is recommended but not required: Major JDO implementations like Kodo provide such a cache in advanced product editions, incurring higher license costs. Caching is applied in a fine-granular fashion at the individual object level, with the option to also cache entire query results. Modifications performed via JDO will automatically update and evict affected objects and query results from the cache.

> **The Expert Group for JDO 2.0 formed in late 2003. JDO 2.0 will contain dedicated support for O/R mapping in the form of the JDO/R sub-specification: among other things, a standard format for mapping definitions. The currently required implementation strategy, based on byte code enhancement, is likely to be downgraded to one implementation option, to allow tools with different strategies like Hibernate and TopLink to comply with the JDO specification.**

Example Code

The update example from the JDBC section would look as follows with JDO. With an O/R mapping tool like JDO, a batch update such as raising prices from 1000 to 1100 needs to retrieve the respective product objects first and then update each of them with the higher price. Such a JDO batch update is of course much less efficient than a set update with a single SQL statement—a problem with any O/R mapping solution when operations are naturally set-based, and not unique to JDO.

The code fragment assumes a reference `pmf` of type `javax.jdo.PersistenceManagerFactory`, whether looked up via JNDI or fetched from some application-specific registry. Furthermore, we assume that the code runs within an active transaction, for example demarcated via JTA (otherwise, objects loaded via JDO would not be modifiable).

```
PersistenceManager pm = pmf.getPersistenceManager();
try {
  Query query = pm.newQuery(Product.class, "price == pPrice");
  query.declareParameters("String pPrice");
  query.compile();
  Collection products = (Collection) query.execute(new Integer(1000));
  for (Iterator it = products.iterator(); it.hasNext();) {
    Product product = (Product) it.next();
    product.setPrice(1100);
  }
}
finally {
  try {
    pm.close();
  }
  catch (JDOException ex) {
    logger.warn("Could not close JDO PersistenceManager", ex);
  }
}
```

Note how a JDO Query object is configured with the type of the returned object, (optional) parameters, and a **JDOQL** string. JDO 2.0 will add support for **named queries**, making it easier to manage queries across an application.

Obviously, the example uses an object representation of the `product` table in the database: the `Product` class. The mapping information is not contained in Java code but in JDO metadata (not shown here). Much of the metadata contents are specific to the JDO product. All *insert*, *select*, *update*, and *delete* operations on `Products` reuse the same mapping definition for the `Product` class.

JDO works exclusively with **instance fields**, which may be private, rather than with getters and setters (JavaBean properties). Getters and setters should be written only if used in application code, and are not required (or recognized) by JDO. Other tools like Hibernate and TopLink allow the use of either instance fields or JavaBean properties. One advantage of JDO using instance fields exclusively is that it discourages the view of a persistent object as an unencapsulated data holder: The public methods of a domain object can focus on the application's needs, providing accessors and business methods for concrete use cases.

For example, the `Product` class might look as follows if all its properties but the price are read-only from the application's perspective. JDO itself directly writes the values into the instance fields instead of going through setter methods:

```
public class Product {
    private int id;
    private String name;
    private double price;

    public int getId() {
        return id;
    }

    public String getName() {
        return name;
    }

    public double getPrice() {
        return price;
    }

    public void setPrice(double price) {
        this.price = price;
    }
}
```

The previous `PersistenceManager` code assumes global transaction management via JTA, as it does not perform any native JDO transaction handling. JDO provides a simple transaction API, which can be used for local transaction management similar to native JDBC transactions; as with JDBC, using it in data access code will not allow the code to participate in higher-level transactions. The code fragment also does not attempt to reuse `PersistenceManagers` across entire transactions; it would have to be rewritten in order to use a ThreadLocal `PersistenceManager`.

As with JDBC, the Spring Framework provides template support for JDO access, offering the same advantages as with JDBC; see the section "Data Access with the Spring Framework" later in this chapter.

State Management

Because of JDO's strict state management, an explicit `makeTransient` call is required to turn JDO-managed instances into objects that behave just like plain Java objects. Without such a call, instance fields are not readable outside an active JDO transaction. With the call, the instances cannot be modified and automatically flushed within the current transaction. This has to be decided explicitly with JDO—a common error for first-time JDO developers.

Making an instance transient can cause some further headaches. It's necessary to make all persistent objects that contain references to the given one transient as well, to avoid their turning to persistent again through JDO's *persistence by reachability* at transaction commit. For a whole object graph, this effectively means making every node transient, by manually traversing the graph and calling `makeTransient` for each node. JDO 1.0 offers no way of making a whole object tree transient in a single operation.

Disassociation must be explicit with JDO 1.0, but the greater problem is its effect on **reassociation**: this is not possible at all in standard JDO 1.0, because JDO instances lose their persistent identity on disassociation. To perform reassociation, an application must copy all field values from the given disassociated instance to a freshly loaded transactional instance, effectively treating the given instance as value object—and requiring explicit accessors for copying the field values. This is cumbersome for the typical case in web applications or remote services. JDO 1.0 also cannot offer optimistic transaction mechanisms like versioning or timestamping for such logical transactions that span multiple requests, because of the reassociation limitation.

The JDO 2.0 expert group plans to introduce a standard means for reassociation of transient instances: a significant enhancement that will make JDO far more appealing for use in typical web applications. Sophisticated JDO implementations like SolarMetric Kodo already offer early support for reassociation as a proprietary extension. It is likely that the `PersistenceManager makeTransient()` method will be deprecated then, as it will no longer be the appropriate way to detach object instances.

> **JDO 1.0 is not ideally suited for web applications and remote services, primarily because of the inability to reassociate persistent objects with a new transaction. Hibernate has a significant advantage on standard JDO 1.0 in this respect.**
>
> **As we've noted before, do not avoid proprietary enhancements to standards such as JDO if they offer real value. Kodo users can benefit greatly from reassociation support right now; it would be misguided to expend the development effort required to achieve a similar result in standard JDO 1.0, or to rule out use of JDO when the need for such a proprietary feature will only be a temporary measure.**

Identity Management

A further special issue is identity management. JDO 1.0 provides several modes of identity management, the most important being *application identity* and *datastore identity*.

A JDO object with **application identity** includes the primary key fields in the persistent object; the actual key values can be generated through database sequences or auto-increment fields. A JDO ID class mirrors the primary key fields in a separate class, even in the common case of one single primary key field. For example, a `ProductId` object that contains a field with the integer value 1 identifies the persistent instance of class `Product` with the primary key 1. Note that in Hibernate, an ID is relative to a persistent class: The class `Product` and an `Integer` object with the value 1 identify the `Product` instance with the primary key 1. With Hibernate, there is no need for an *individual identity class* for each and every persistent class.

With JDO **datastore identity** (advocated by most JDO vendors) it is not necessary to use programmatic ID values at all: In this case, the JDO implementation will transparently keep track of the object ID, which is *not* held in the persistent object. A String representation of the ID can be determined, but only with an active `PersistenceManager`. Unfortunately, referring to objects via their IDs is often a necessity. For example, in web applications, form objects that need to be reassociated with a new transaction need to be aware of their identity, and web views often need to build URLs with the IDs of objects that they are displaying. Application identity is the only standard JDO way to address such needs.

Hibernate

Hibernate (`www.hibernate.org`; licensed under the LGPL) aims to be a thin wrapper over JDBC while offering the full power of transparent persistence, adding O/R semantics but not trying to abstract away the underlying relational database.

Its proprietary query language **HQL** offers important relational concepts such as joins and aggregate functions. In general, HQL is closer to SQL than to other object query languages, with the important difference from SQL that queries are expressed in terms of domain object properties rather than database column values, thus decoupling from the database schema. In many respects, HQL allows developers to leverage SQL's power at the domain object level. It is also relatively easy to learn for developers already familiar with SQL, as any professional J2EE developer must be.

The Hibernate central connection interface is `net.sf.hibernate.Session`, allowing it to retrieve persistent objects, reassociate existing objects, and so on. Hibernate ID handling is extremely simple: Any primitive or `Object` type can be used for lookup, in contrast to JDO's one-identity-class-per-persistent-class approach.

Like TopLink, Hibernate performs change detection via snapshot comparisons. With its optimized reflection usage via CGLIB—creating runtime proxies for persistent objects through dynamic byte code generation—the performance overhead of such comparisons is not as high as might be thought. It is magnitudes higher than JDO's on-demand change detection, but still hardly noticeable in typical scenarios. The advantage of the Hibernate model is that it does not need to modify persistent objects to observe their state.

Hibernate 2.1 supports **pluggable cache strategies**, providing out-of-the-box implementations for EHCache, OSCache, SwarmCache, and Jboss' TreeCache. Like sophisticated JDO implementations, Hibernate applies fine-granular caching of individual objects and optionally query results. Modifications performed via a Hibernate `Session` will automatically update and evict affected objects and query results in the cache.

> Arguably the J2EE community's favorite persistence tool in 2003, Hibernate focuses on doing one thing well: O/R mapping with full transparent persistence. The decision to concentrate on accessing relational databases means that it tackles a narrower—yet extremely important—range of problems than the JDO specification. With its 2.1 release, Hibernate offers a feature set that is closer to established enterprise products like TopLink than to other open source efforts.

Example Code

Like JDO and any transparent persistence tool, our update example needs to retrieve the `Product` instances first to change their prices. The code fragment below assumes the availability of a reference to a `sessionFactory` of type `net.sf.hibernate.SessionFactory`, either looked up via JNDI or fetched from some application-specific registry.

```
Session session = sessionFactory.getSession();
try {
  List products = session.find("FROM example.Product WHERE price = ?",
      new Integer(1000), Hibernate.INTEGER);
  for (Iterator it = products.iterator(); it.hasNext();) {
    Product product = (Product) it.next();
    product.setPrice(1100);
  }
  session.flush();
```

```
    }
    finally {
      try {
        session.close();
      }
      catch (HibernateException ex) {
        logger.warn("Could not close Hibernate Session", ex);
      }
    }
```

The same `Product` class as with JDO can be used, but without the need for compile-time enhancement. Hibernate 2.1 is able to work with either **getter/setter methods** or **instance fields**: We assume to work at the instance field level here, to mimic JDO. Note that when using bean properties, getters and setters that are relevant only for Hibernate persistence can be made protected or even private, to allow for proper application-driven visibility.

Similar to JDOQL, **HQL queries** are written against Java objects and properties. HQL is a textual query language analogous to SQL, however, rather than a Java query API like JDOQL. It aims to provide the same language model as SQL but for mapped objects and object fields instead of database tables and database fields. Hibernate 2.1 also offers **Criteria Queries**, a new Java query API, as an alternative to HQL.

The same restrictions regarding transactions apply as with the JDBC and JDO examples, because there is no native Hibernate transaction handling in the code just shown. Nor does it reuse `Session` instances: `ThreadLocal` **Sessions** are particularly popular with Hibernate to access the same `Session` instance within a transaction (`www.hibernate.org/42.html`). Obviously, the code would have to be adapted to use `ThreadLocal Session` management.

The Spring Framework provides sophisticated template support for Hibernate access, offering the same advantages as with JDBC and JDO plus numerous Hibernate-specific convenience methods. Spring and Hibernate are a popular combination: Hibernate offers a very powerful but still lightweight persistence mechanism, making for a particularly comprehensive middle tier foundation when combined with Spring's lightweight resource and transaction management.

State Management

Hibernate is well suited for web applications and remote services in that it allows persistent objects to be **disassociated** from a `Session` and easily **reassociated** later. This addresses the common case where persistent objects are sent to the client layer for potential modification, being temporarily decoupled from a transaction, and come back when the user submits. Effectively, persistent objects can serve as transfer objects without extra coding such as field-wise copying between objects.

A special benefit of being able to directly reassociate a persistent object is that this mechanism allows for **optimistic locking via versioning or timestamping,** spanning multiple `Session` instances across multiple requests. If the persistent object knows its version or timestamp in the form of a property, Hibernate can compare the marker of a reassociated object with that of the corresponding record in the database, throwing an optimistic locking failure exception if they do not match. This is currently not possible with JDO, which supports optimistic locking only *within the same `PersistenceManager` instance.*

Hibernate's relaxed state management has its roots in the use of **snapshot comparisons**: In contrast to JDO, the persistent classes themselves do not need to be enhanced to be aware of field modification. Instead, a snapshot is taken at load time: When flushing, the snapshot is compared to the current contents of the persistent object, issuing SQL statements for actual changes. Furthermore, Hibernate's own collection implementations carry around snapshots of their contained objects: Therefore even **reassociated object trees** can be checked for actual modifications (but *not* the root reassociated object *itself*), issuing only a minimal set of update statements.

Outside a transaction, persistent objects are literally POJOs: They do *not* have to be made transient explicitly, as they are not aware of being persistent—not even in modified byte code, like with JDO. Snapshots are completely external to the persistent objects themselves, in contrast to the field-intercepting PersistenceCapable code that delegates to the JDO StateManager. So in addition to avoiding the need for a compile-time enhancement step, Hibernate's lenient state management allows for particularly intuitive handling of persistent objects, without having to care about transactional or transient state.

Lazy Loading

A particularly popular Hibernate feature is lazy loading. As with JDO, both collections and object references can be lazily loaded; in the case of the latter, Hibernate generates runtime proxies via CGLIB. This is as non-intrusive as possible, especially compared to the TopLink **value holder** mechanism, which requires a special TopLink class to be used in the domain model to allow for lazy loading of object references. (TopLink offers the option of **proxy interaction** when the relationship is expressed against an interface instead of a class. This uses dynamic proxies at runtime to avoid the loss of transparent persistence and impaired testability resulting from dependence on the TopLink ValueHolder class.) Like TopLink and typical JDO implementations, Hibernate uses its own collection implementations to transparently deliver indirection for collection references.

Lazy loading can cause severe headaches within a layered architecture, however, where Hibernate access is solely performed by DAOs. Lazy loading proxies will only be able to perform their work with an *active* Hibernate session in the background. Typically, a Session is closed at the end of a transaction; therefore, lazy loading will not work afterward. If an application returns a domain object with lazy loading references to a client layer outside a transaction, all the data needs to have been materialized during the transaction. See the section "DAO Design Issues" later in this chapter for details.

In the case of web applications, lazy loading can be addressed through the **Open Session in View** pattern (www.hibernate.org/43.html): The Hibernate Session will be opened during data access initiated by a web controller, but kept open during view rendering rather than closed at the end of the actual data access operation. This allows for accessing lazy-loaded references in views, but has the severe disadvantage of potentially doing data access during view rendering—outside transactional scopes, and without the chance to handle data access errors properly. In case of multiple transactions within a single request, a single Session instance must be used for all of them, potentially introducing side effects that do not occur with isolated transactions.

Figure 10-1 shows the processing of such a web request, performing two separate transactions during controller execution. With classic resource handling, each transaction would have its own Session; with the Open Session in View pattern, a single Hibernate Session will be used for *both* transactions and kept open during view rendering. Thus, lazy-loading references in model objects will be resolved only if actually touched by the view; the controller does not need to pre-initialize such references.

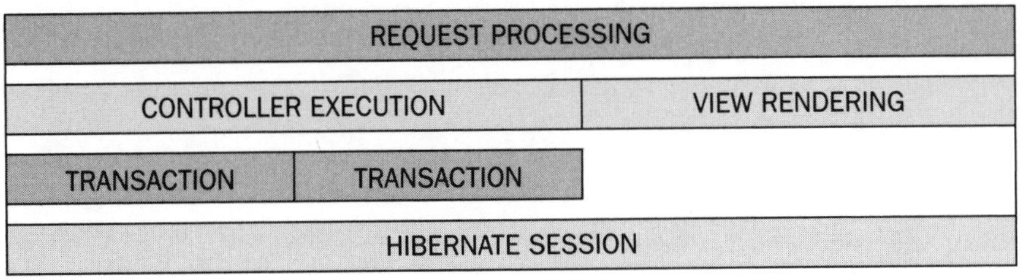

Figure 10-1

A common problem that affects `Session` lifespan is reassociating persistent objects with a new `Session`. Hibernate requires that objects to be reassociated must not have been loaded by the `Session` before, not even as associated objects of other persistent objects. Thus, save or update calls for objects to be reassociated should be performed as early as possible in a data access operation: While this is straightforward within isolated transactions, this cannot be guaranteed when reusing a `Session` across multiple transactions, as when using the Open Session in View pattern. A possible solution in such a scenario is to use the Hibernate 2.1 `saveOrUpdateCopy` method, which copies the field values to the existing instance if already loaded.

The Data Access Object Pattern

One of the most important J2EE patterns is **Data Access Object (DAO)**, a special incarnation of the GoF **Strategy** pattern. The DAO pattern exists to separate persistence code from business logic: that is, to distinguish between business workflows and rules on the one hand and specific persistence issues on the other. The DAO pattern involves a **DAO interface** that conceals the details of data access within particular implementations.

Business Objects and Data Access Objects

Business objects should not be concerned about the details of data retrieval and storage, but should focus on business logic. Data access objects must implement a specific persistence strategy (for example, one based on JDBC), but expose a generic DAO interface for business objects to use. This allows for loose coupling and easy reimplementation of DAO interfaces, for example to be able to leverage specific Oracle features in an Oracle version of a DAO, without having to adapt the business objects.

Data access objects need to **participate in transactions** but should not usually drive them, as their operations are typically fine-grained. Transaction demarcation is the responsibility of the calling business objects, often happening at the level of business facades. (Of course transaction management may be deferred to declarative middleware solutions such as EJB CMT or AOP-based transaction management.) Each business object may invoke multiple DAO methods or even multiple DAOs in a single transaction. (For more details on high-level transaction management and its implications, see Chapter 9.)

Consider the following scenario: A web-based application has a logical three-tier architecture with a *web layer*, a *business layer*, and a *data access layer*. Let's assume that an `OrderManager` business object must store a new order and update the inventory database accordingly. Of course, such a business object would normally contain more sophisticated business logic than shown in this simple example:

```
public class OrderManager {

  private OrderDao orderDao;

  public void setOrderDao(OrderDao orderDao) {
    this.orderDao = orderDao;
  }

  public void placeOrder(Order order) {
    // set business flags of order
    // calculate final prices
    orderDao.storeOrder(order);
    orderDao.updateInventory(order);
  }
}
```

OrderManager performs the business process of placing an order in its placeOrder method: for example, setting any flags of the order according to business rules and calculating the final prices. For actual persistence, it delegates to an implementation of the OrderDao interface that offers storeOrder and updateInventory methods for the two operations that are necessary here:

```
public interface OrderDao {

  void storeOrder(Order order);

  void updateInventory(Order order);
}
```

OrderManager does not care whether the OrderDao implementation uses JDBC, Hibernate, or any other persistence technology to implement its operations. A JDBC-based implementation of the DAO could look as follows:

```
public class JdbcOrderDao implements OrderDao {

  private DataSource dataSource;

  public void setDataSource(DataSource dataSource) {
    this.dataSource = dataSource;
  }

  public void storeOrder(Order order) {
    // perform some JDBC operations on a Connection from dataSource
  }

  public void updateInventory(Order order) {
    // perform some JDBC operations on a Connection from dataSource
  }
}
```

Factoring out a DAO is *not* always appropriate. If an application's business logic consists of data access operations and not much else, it can make sense to include the data access code in the business operations themselves. Such a choice is also appropriate if the business code is heavily intermingled with data access operations: for example, when delegating to stored procedures for efficiency or reuse of business logic with other applications. Since business objects can be pluggable too through implementation of business interfaces, this still allows for specialized implementations (for example for Oracle) but now at the business object instead of the data access object level.

> Don't be too worried about identifying *business* and *persistence* aspects of your code up-front, especially when reworking existing applications. If you cannot draw a clear line, start with a business object that contains the data access operations. You can always refactor the latter into a DAO if you need pluggability because of new requirements, or to achieve greater clarity in your code.

DAOs and Transparent Persistence

The DAO pattern was originally targeted at JDBC as persistence strategy, allowing for alternative implementations that leverage specific non-portable database features, and potentially stub (or, more recently, mock) implementations for testing purposes. Typical DAO interfaces assume a fairly primitive, fine-grained persistence mechanism, with a requirement for explicit store calls for changed objects. There is no strict distinction between **first-class** and **second-class** objects: that is, primary domain objects and dependent objects that are bound to the lifecycle of their parent.

As we've seen, leading transparent persistence solutions such as Hibernate and JDO offer a more sophisticated programming model: They **automatically detect changes** to retrieved objects via a unit of work (see the earlier discussion of persistence patterns). Persistence operations often just deal with first-class domain objects; dependent objects are implicitly addressed via cascading updates and deletes (*"persistence by reachability"*). With such sophisticated mapping solutions, there is no need for explicit save or delete calls on dependent objects, as this can automatically and efficiently be handled by the transparent persistence tool.

It is arguable that working with a JDO `PersistenceManager` or a Hibernate `Session` directly is abstraction enough, and that there is no need for a DAO layer on top. After all, the O/R mapping tool already offers a query language, automatic change detection, and generic delete operations. Working with an O/R mapping tool directly in business objects is also normally significantly more convenient than working directly with JDBC. But there are still valid reasons to use DAOs as thin wrappers on top of an O/R mapping layer:

❑ Encapsulating O/R mapping resource access behind DAO interfaces allows for **easy mock implementations** for testing purposes. For example, mocking a JDO `PersistenceManager` is far more effort than mocking specific DAO operations on domain objects. This is a compelling reason for using a DAO layer if you intend to practice test-driven development (which we recommend).

❑ DAOs offer a **clear, strongly typed persistence API** for a domain: It is immediately obvious which persistent objects are retrieved, created, or deleted. The generic API of an O/R mapping tool allows it to apply any persistence operation to any object, which makes it hard to find out actually available operations for a specific domain.

❑ DAOs allow **finder methods with domain arguments**, removing the need to maintain object query language strings in business objects. Especially regarding vendor extensions to JDOQL, and the need to rewrite even object-level queries for specific underlying databases (for example depending on the availability of sub-selects), it is preferable to encapsulate queries to allow for alternative implementations. **Query objects** can remedy this too, being an alternative to finder methods.

For simple use cases with hardly any business logic, using an O/R mapping tool directly in business objects is a viable choice. There is no need for DAOs then; for testing, you can mock the business objects themselves.

> **The DAO pattern can still offer real benefits when combined with transparent persistence. Such DAO interfaces will look different from classic JDBC-oriented DAOs, however: They will address only *first-class* domain objects (relying on persistence by reachability), and not offer the traditional update methods for persisting changes explicitly. There will still be the need for save methods for persisting new instances, and update methods for reassociating persistent instances with a new transaction, as discussed in the following section.**

Types of Data Access Objects

Unless we settle for a lowest common denominator approach, or are prepared to live with methods that will normally be redundant, DAO interfaces are usually tied to a specific persistence strategy. Even if there are no code dependencies, there will be conceptual ones. As indicated earlier, **DAOs for transparent persistence** look quite different to **JDBC-based DAOs.** The most obvious differences are the granularity of operations—with respect to second-class (dependent) persistent objects—and the lack of conventional update methods.

Of course, one could try to design **portable DAO interfaces** that allow for any kind of implementation, whether JDBC or transparent persistence via Hibernate or JDO. The drawback is that the JDBC option requires fine-grained update methods that need to be invoked for any changed object. Business objects would have to invoke these consistently (making them responsible for keeping track of dirty objects), even if the primary candidate for DAO implementation was a transparent persistence product. This begs the question: Why use a transparent persistence tool, but expend the effort writing business objects capable of working with a *primitive* persistence strategy underneath as an alternative?

It is almost impossible to regard all those limitations and subtle issues *a priori*. This would mean implementing at least a transparent persistence version and a JDBC version of all DAOs to validate the DAO interface design. This is likely to be a waste of time, as applications tend to stick to either transparent persistence or JDBC as strategy (or use both at well-defined places); 100% portability at the DAO layer is normally a non-goal. If there needs to be a complete revision in terms of data access, it is normally acceptable to refine the implementation of the calling business objects too. The XP mantra YAGNI (You Aren't Gonna Need It) springs to mind.

A much more important goal is to allow for leveraging **vendor extensions** and **testability**. The overall strategy (JDBC or sophisticated O/R mapping) should be determined first; then DAO interfaces should be designed for that particular strategy. It might make sense to address multiple, similar persistence strategies like Hibernate and JDO; their programming models are close enough. Adding TopLink to the mix of implementation options should also be possible without too much extra effort, although TopLink's need for explicit registration of objects to be modified might complicate things.

It is significantly easier to target multiple implementation options for read-only operations, that is, operations that return read-only objects or aggregate values. A **read-only DAO** interface can be implemented to be portable between JDBC, iBATIS SQL Maps, JDO, Hibernate, TopLink or just about any alternative persistence technology (such as SQLJ) without much effort. Note that the actual target strategies can be decided on a per-DAO level. For example, the order subsystem might require transparent persistence, but the product catalog and other read-only reference data can allow for JDBC-based implementations too, in case there is ever a need to use set-based operations to boost performance or simplify querying.

All things considered, each DAO should be designed with one of the following categories in mind:

- ❏ **Classic JDBC-based DAO:** with fine-grained explicit update operations (also allowing for data mappers like iBATIS SQL Maps).

- ❏ **DAO for a specific transparent persistence tool:** for example targeted at Hibernate or JDO, respecting the particular lifecycle implications of the tool.

- ❏ **General transparent persistence DAO:** aiming to cover multiple tools, using a variety of access methods with specific semantics.

- ❏ **Portable read-only DAO:** to be implemented on JDBC or a transparent persistence tool, always returning disassociated objects.

- ❏ **Portable read-write DAO:** to be implemented on JDBC or a transparent persistence tool, requiring explicit update operations even when working with a transparent persistence implementation (hardly ever worth the effort).

DAO Design Issues

As should be clear by now, designing DAO interfaces is not as simple and straightforward as it seems at first. It is often advisable to choose targeted implementation strategies from the outset, because there are subtle and not-so-subtle issues that have to be respected in the interface design. DAOs still make sense in case of a single persistence strategy, to be able to adapt the implementation to specific databases, and to plug in mock implementations for testing purposes.

Granularity of Data Access Operations

For flexible reuse of any operation, it is tempting to create very fine-grained methods like `loadOrder`, `loadLineItems`, `storeOrder`, or `storeLineTimes`. To enable efficient implementations of data access operations, it is often preferable to have **coarse-grained** methods in the DAO interface. We recommend as much data access granularity as your business objects allow: Make the DAO interfaces more fine-grained only if you actually need to.

For example, JDBC-based `loadOrder` and `loadLineItems` implementations might simply select from the appropriate tables and turn the required rows into object representations. The `loadLineItems` implementation could populate the `lineItems` property of the given `Order` object with a corresponding collection of `LineItem` objects.

```
public class JdbcOrderDao {

    public Order loadOrder(int orderId) {
        // load order data via SQL
        // build Order object
        return order;
    }

    public void loadLineItems(Order order) {
        // load line item data for given order via SQL
        // build LineItem objects
        order.setLineItems(lineItems);
    }
}
```

A Hibernate-based implementation of loadOrder could fetch an Order and associated LineItems more efficiently in one JDBC statement via an outer join, if appropriate. This can only be allowed through one single loadOrder method with a loadLineItems flag that determines whether to load the LineItems too when loading the Order itself.

```
public class HibernateOrderDao {

    public Order loadOrder(int ordered, boolean loadLineItems) {
        // load and return Order via HQL,
        // indicating whether to fetch the "lineItems" collection too
    }
}
```

Typically, DAO interfaces contain *load*, *store*, and *delete* methods for specific domain objects. Of course, there might be only load operations for domain objects that are never modified by the application. Separate *save* and *update* operations are not necessary if the DAO can determine the status of the domain object: for example, if there is a clear distinction between *saved* and *unsaved* objects. An ID property that contains null or -1 for unsaved objects would be enough to achieve this. A store method can then evaluate the ID value to perform the appropriate operation, without the need to bloat the DAO interface with separate save and update methods.

Transparent Persistence and Object State

DAOs for transparent persistence need update methods only for **reassociating** domain objects with a *new* transaction: for example, when coming back from the user interface layer or coming in via a remote call. If the application does not require reassociation of domain objects at all, transparent persistence DAOs do not need any update methods. If needed, update methods for reassociation can be added, but without the *requirement* for business code to invoke them for changes *within the same transaction*.

Load and find methods are a special case when using transparent persistence, too. JDO's lifecycle model explicitly differentiates between **transactional** and **transient** instances of persistent objects. The former allows for transparent change detection, the latter for use outside a transaction. An instance needs to be explicitly made transient if required. TopLink on the other hand needs explicit cloning of instances that could potentially get modified in a transaction; DAO finder methods need to properly register the persistent instances before returning them. (Cloning is required with TopLink because it uses a shared read-only cache, and otherwise updates would corrupt global state.)

Hibernate does *not* require explicit disassociation from or association with a transaction, as its persistent objects do not have lifecycle ties to the current transaction. A session will always work with its own copies of persistent objects, even when coming from a cache. Hibernate simply throws away snapshots at the end of a transaction, without any implications on the viability of the persistent objects. A DAO interface that aims to cover both JDO and TopLink strict state management and the lenient Hibernate approach needs to offer **distinct finder methods** for the various states of returned objects. For example:

```
public interface OrderDao {

  Order loadOrderAsDisassociated(int orderId);

  Order loadOrderAsTransactional(int orderId);
}
```

The `loadOrderAsDisassociated` method will typically be used to pass the `Order` into a different layer, outside the current transaction, while `loadOrderAsTransactional` is supposed to be called within an enclosing transaction, for automatically persisting changes to the returned `Order` object within the current transaction. As outlined above, a JDO-based implementation needs to make the returned object transient for the former method but keep it transactional for the latter. A Hibernate-based implementation can simply ignore the state hints, delegating to the same order loading code for both methods.

As an example of typical consequences of *not* regarding the detailed semantics of different persistence strategies, let's assume that you initially develop a Hibernate-based implementation of your `OrderDao`. The `loadOrder` method loads an `Order`, either to be passed into a different layer or to be modified within the current transaction, persisting the changes on transaction commit.

```
public interface OrderDao {

  Order loadOrder(int orderId);
}
```

You rely on transparent persistence and do not require store calls after changes, effectively disallowing JDBC-based implementations. Furthermore, you rely on being able to return a transactional instance (with transparent change detection) to a different layer outside a transaction, without explicit disassociation—effectively disallowing JDO-based implementations. As this example shows, it is very easy to design non-portable DAOs by accident.

Transaction Scopes and Lazy Loading

Data access operations should be gathered into transactions, demarcated by business objects. A transaction should never span user think time to avoid unnecessary resource locks, therefore business operations are nearly always the appropriate scope. In the case of web applications or remote services, transactions should be finished within single requests and not span multiple requests. Transactions typically do not affect DAO design: DAOs should normally perform their persistence operations without special regard to transactional execution. There are areas where the design and implementation of DAOs have to consider transaction semantics, though.

A persistent object instance can be either fully or just partly loaded, triggering **lazy loads** on navigation to certain fields and collections. The latter will work transparently within the same transaction that the instance was loaded in. A load method of a DAO should thus state which parts of the returned object have been loaded eagerly, and which other parts will be loaded lazily if touched within the same transaction.

If a business operation returns a persistent object to a web controller or a remote client, *outside* a transaction as the operation has already ended, it should clarify the actually loaded parts, because lazy loading will not work in that case.

Inability to lazily load outside a transaction has special implications for **web views**. As the transaction has typically ended with the business operation, neither the web controller's preparing nor the web view's rendering can rely on lazy loading of model objects. The controller must explicitly prepare the model into the necessary state to back the view, via business operations that it invokes. An alternative would be to keep a connection active during view rendering: for example, implementing the **Open Session in View** pattern with Hibernate. However, it is generally preferable to keep resource access within the controller, to ensure shorter resource allocation (minimize contention for the database), and to avoid the possibility of resource exceptions during view rendering.

If a whole load, edit, and store workflow must execute within one logical long-lived transaction, **optimistic locking** mechanisms *must* be used, because a resource transaction should not span multiple requests. The persistent object can contain a version number or a timestamp marker that indicates the time it has been loaded at. When storing the object in a different transaction, the DAO implementation can compare the **version** or **timestamp** with the currently persistent one, or even compare all initially read fields with the current database state. In case of intermediate changes by a second party, an optimistic locking exception can be thrown to make the user interface reload the object and notify the user. Note that only few persistence tools, such as Hibernate, support such an optimistic transaction mechanism for *disassociated* persistent objects.

DAO Infrastructure Issues

To reap full benefit from the pluggability of DAOs, three further infrastructure issues have to be addressed. They are related to the resource-handling issues discussed earlier; there is a need for a common solution for both kinds of issues.

❑ **Wiring up:** How does a business object *obtain* an appropriate instance of a DAO? Where is the DAO *configured*? The same questions can be applied to the business objects themselves too, from the view of clients like a user interface layer. This leads into the domain of service registries and IoC containers.

❑ **Participating in transactions:** How are DAO implementations *enlisted* in any transaction demarcated by a business object, potentially regarding diverse transaction strategies? What *requirements* are there on resources used within DAOs?

❑ **Exception handling:** To achieve *decoupling* from the specific persistence technology, DAO methods must throw *generic* data access exceptions that are not specific to any strategy such as JDBC or JDO. Of course, we could simply wrap all exceptions in a common data access exception, whether checked or unchecked. Many developers choose to define their own custom exceptions for each DAO, which are used to wrap the root cause. However, this is a lot of arguably unnecessary work. A preferable approach to either of these is to have a fine-grained, generic data access exception hierarchy, to be able to catch specific kinds of exceptions that one wants to address, like optimistic locking failures.

Unfortunately, these issues are not addressed by most frameworks and tools. Data access libraries like JDBC, JDO, and Hibernate address resource access and *native* transaction demarcation, but they do not address such integration within applications and arguably should not try to. This is the domain of middle tier and application frameworks that provide the glue between various libraries and components.

Although O/R mapping is becoming increasingly productized, such DAO infrastructure is still often built in-house, to meet specific transaction and persistence strategies. Very few generic frameworks address these needs. Two that do are **iBATIS DAO**, the DAO framework included in iBATIS Database Layer, and the **Spring Framework**. iBATIS concentrates on DAOs for its SQL Map mechanism, and JDBC and JTA transaction strategies. Spring offers generic DAO support that complements the transaction infrastructure discussed in the previous chapter, with out-of-the-box integrations for JDBC, JDO, Hibernate, and iBATIS SQL Maps.

> **Consider not only a persistence tool but also appropriate infrastructure for data access objects. Such infrastructure does not need to be built in-house. There are comprehensive solutions—like iBATIS DAO and the Spring Framework—that provide transaction management and other glue between business objects and data access objects.**

Data Access with the Spring Framework

The Spring Framework offers support for all of the infrastructure issues we've identified:

❑   The Spring bean factory and application context containers enable **easy wiring up of any kind of application object**. This is a convenient and consistent way of setting up not only business objects and data access objects but also connection factories. Regarding the latter, there are means for definition, initialization, and passing references to application classes, with prebuilt options for JNDI lookups and local singleton factories.

❑   There is a **clean model for transactions** and their relationship to connections, and especially for the reuse of connections within transactions. Basically, transactions and connection handles have the same lifespan; data access objects can participate in any kind of transaction simply by following certain lookup rules for each kind of resource. See the discussion of transaction strategies in Chapter 9 for details.

❑   Spring offers a **generic DataAccessException hierarchy** in its `org.springframework.dao` package, with prebuilt transformation of respective native exceptions in its JDBC, JDO, and Hibernate support. Those exceptions are unchecked, because client code has no chance to specifically react to most of them. One can always catch specific exceptions if one actually wants to handle them.

❑   There is **consistent template support** for proper connection closing and exception handling. This is provided out-of-the-box for JDBC, iBATIS SQL Maps, JDO, and Hibernate. These template classes make data access code in DAO implementations less repetitive and more robust; it also reduces the amount of application code required.

Generic Data Access Exceptions

The UML diagram in Figure 10-2 illustrates the Spring hierarchy of data access exceptions, defined in the `org.springframework.dao` package. Specific subclasses are contained in other packages, like `org.springframework.jdbc` and `org.springframework.orm`; the diagram shows only the most important classes.

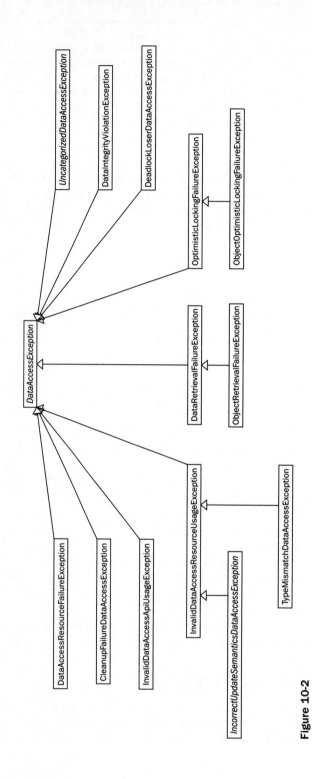

Figure 10-2

As noted earlier, all of the Spring data access exceptions are unchecked, as data access errors are typically fatal. Note that client code can choose to handle certain subclasses like `OptimisticLockingFailure Exception`—provided that those particular exceptions are actually thrown by the underlying data access implementation.

The main value of a generic data access exception hierarchy is decoupling business objects and data access interfaces from specific data access strategies. Client objects can catch certain `DataAccessException` subclasses without having to worry about the underlying data access strategy. For example, JDBC and Hibernate access code will both throw `DataIntegrityViolationException` or `OptimisticLocking FailureException` exceptions if the respective failure is encountered. Of course, data access code may throw specific subclasses of those exceptions; in any case, client code can catch the generic base exceptions.

Data access code may throw appropriate exceptions itself when encountering specific failures. However, it is preferable to delegate this burden to **prebuilt converters** as far as possible: the Spring data access template classes apply such conversion automatically. The exception conversion logic can also be invoked on its own, via provided helper classes. JDBC `SQLException` instances carry vendor-specific error codes: Spring provides a special vendor code translation mechanism to convert them to corresponding `Data AccessException` instances; this can also be customized.

For details on the `DataAccessException` hierarchy, in particular the JDBC-specific subclasses and the provided `SQLException` translators, see Chapter 9 of *Expert One-on-One J2EE Design and Development*.

Business Objects and Data Access Objects Revisited

Let's now look at the benefit that this Spring infrastructure could bring to our earlier example. The `Order Manager` example could look as follows if the objects are defined in a Spring application context. Note how a Spring XML bean definition can be used to wire up the business object and the DAO it depends on, meaning that Java application code need have no knowledge of the DAO implementation in use:

```xml
<beans>

  <bean id="myDataSource" class="org.springframework.jndi.JndiObjectFactoryBean">
    <property name="jndiName">
      <value>jdbc/myds</value>
    </property>
  </bean>

  <bean id="myOrderDao" class="example.JdbcOrderDao">
    <property name="dataSource">
      <ref bean="myDataSource"/>
    </property>
  </bean>

  <bean id="myOrderManager" class="example.OrderManager">
    <property name="orderDao">
      <ref bean="myOrderDao"/>
    </property>
  </bean>

</beans>
```

A Spring-based `OrderDao` interface and the `JdbcOrderDao` implementation would declare that it might throw `DataAccessException`, although this is not strictly necessary as the `DataAccessException` hierarchy is unchecked:

```
public class JdbcOrderDao implements OrderDao {

  private DataSource dataSource;

  public void setDataSource(DataSource dataSource) {
    this.dataSource = dataSource;
  }

  public void storeOrder(Order order) throws DataAccessException {
    // perform some JDBC operations on a Connection from dataSource,
    // preferably via Spring's JdbcTemplate (see below)
  }

  public void updateInventory(Order order) throws DataAccessException {
    // perform some JDBC operations on a Connection from dataSource,
    // preferably via Spring's JdbcTemplate (see below)
  }
}
```

The `OrderManager` class would look just like the non-Spring one you've already seen, but preferably declaring that it may propagate `DataAccessException`:

```
public class OrderManager {

  private OrderDao orderDao;

  public void setOrderDao(OrderDao orderDao) {
    this.orderDao = orderDao;
  }

  public void placeOrder(Order order) throws DataAccessException {
    // set business flags of order
    // calculate final prices
    orderDao.storeOrder(order);
    orderDao.updateInventory(order);
  }
}
```

None of the application objects need perform any custom lookup of collaborating objects. For example, the `OrderManager` instance receives an `OrderDao` implementation as JavaBean reference, via its exposed `setOrderDao(OrderDao)` method. The same principle applies to the `JdbcOrderDao` instance: It does not perform a JNDI lookup itself but receives a JNDI-bound `DataSource` via its `setDataSource(DataSource)` method, needing to have no knowledge of how the `DataSource` is obtained.

Besides offering means for wiring up DAOs, the Spring Framework makes implementing them easier by offering template classes that handle resource acquisition and release, effectively reducing simple data access operations to one-liners. These templates automatically participate in transactions, and convert resource-specific exceptions to the generic Spring `DataAccessException` hierarchy.

Transactional Objects

Making the `OrderManager` instance transactional is straightforward, and does not require any code changes. For example, the following code demonstrates how to leverage Spring's support for declarative transaction demarcation via AOP, introduced in Chapter 9:

```xml
<beans>

  <bean id="myDataSource" class="org.springframework.jndi.JndiObjectFactoryBean">
    <property name="jndiName">
      <value>jdbc/myds</value>
    </property>
  </bean>

  <bean id="myTransactionManager"
      class="org.springframework.transaction.jta.JtaTransactionManager"/>

  <bean id="myOrderDao" class="example.JdbcOrderDao">
    <property name="dataSource">
      <ref bean="myDataSource"/>
    </property>
  </bean>

  <bean id="myOrderManagerTarget" class="example.OrderManager">
    <property name="orderDao">
      <ref bean="myOrderDao"/>
    </property>
  </bean>

  <bean id="myOrderManager"
      class="org.springframework.transaction.interceptor.TransactionProxyFactoryBean">
    <property name="transactionManager">
      <ref bean="myTransactionManager"/>
    </property>
    <property name="target">
      <ref bean="myOrderManagerTarget"/>
    </property>
    <property name="transactionAttributes">
      <props>
        <prop key="placeOrder">PROPAGATION_REQUIRED</prop>
      </props>
    </property>
  </bean>

</beans>
```

The `myDataSource` and `myOrderDao` beans are the same that we had before; the `OrderManager` bean is renamed to `myOrderManagerTarget` here to reflect that it is the target behind a transactional proxy now. That proxy is defined using the `TransactionProxyFactoryBean`, with the `OrderManager` bean as "target", specifying the transaction attribute `PROPAGATION_REQUIRED` for the `OrderManager` `placeOrder` method. The actual transaction management is delegated to the `myTransactionManager` bean: in our example, the Spring `JtaTransactionManager` implementation. (`DataSource` `TransactionManager` would be a viable choice for JDBC-based DAOs too, as long as we needed to access only a single database.)

Spring allows DAOs to participate automatically in transactions from a connection factory–specific transaction manager like DataSourceTransactionManager, JdoTransactionManager, or HibernateTransactionManager. Application code will always receive the same connection within a transaction, without the need for JTA or custom ThreadLocals. The templates handle this automatically; DataSourceUtils, PersistenceManagerFactoryUtils, and SessionFactoryUtils offer respective utility methods for connection retrieval, to allow any kind of data access code to participate transparently in such transactions.

Outside transactions, data access code will simply execute *non-transactionally* using individual connections. This is often not desirable: Even *read-only* operations should arguably be executed in transactions for proper transaction isolation, particularly if they consist of multiple SQL statements. Otherwise, the query statements would return inconsistent state if some transaction (that affects the data to be read in) committed right in the middle of the operation.

See Chapter 9 for a further discussion of transaction management strategies.

JDBC

The Spring Framework offers a convenient means for JDBC access at two different levels: a **template class** and **operation objects.** Either of these two approaches is simpler and much less cumbersome than plain JDBC. It can significantly improve productivity and eliminate many common errors.

Note that the Spring JDBC framework does not attempt any O/R mapping: It is merely a more usable API making a thin layer over JDBC. It is appropriate when SQL-based RDBMS access is appropriate. For simple O/R mapping at the SQL level, with declarative mappings between bean properties and database fields, consider **iBATIS SQL Maps**, which I'll discuss next in the context of Spring.

Note that this part of Spring can be reused as library, as you will see below: It does not depend on being used within a Spring application context. The Spring distribution offers fine-grained JAR files for specific scenarios like usage as a data access library, to avoid the need to include the full spring.jar file in all cases.

JDBC Access via a Template

The JdbcTemplate class and its associated helpers in the org.springframework.jdbc.core package apply a template style to JDBC handling. A JdbcTemplate instance is configured with a javax.sql.DataSource, and offers various query and update methods to perform data access. A simple update statement using a JdbcTemplate can look as follows:

```
JdbcTemplate jdbcTemplate = new JdbcTemplate(dataSource);
jdbcTemplate.update("UPDATE products SET pr_price = 1100 WHERE pr_price = 1000");
```

When a query returns a ResultSet that needs to be evaluated, the query method takes a callback implementation:

```
final List products = new ArrayList();
JdbcTemplate jdbcTemplate = new JdbcTemplate(dataSource);
jdbcTemplate.query(
    "SELECT pr_id, pr_name, pr_price FROM product WHERE pr_price > 1000",
```

```
      new RowCallbackHandler() {
        public void processRow(ResultSet rs) throws SQLException {
          Product product = new Product();
          product.setId(rs.getInt("pr_id"));
          product.setName(rs.getString("pr_name"));
          product.setPrice(rs.getFloat("pr_price"));
          products.add(product);
        }
      }
  );
```

Both methods exist in an overloaded version for the use of `PreparedStatement`. The previous `update` example would look as follows:

```
JdbcTemplate jdbcTemplate = new JdbcTemplate(dataSource);
jdbcTemplate.update(
    "UPDATE product SET pr_price = ? WHERE pr_price = ?",
    new PreparedStatementSetter() {
      public void setValues(PreparedStatement ps) throws SQLException {
        ps.setInt(1, 1000);
        ps.setInt(2, 1100);
      }
    }
);
```

The query example would look like this when using `PreparedStatement`:

```
final List products = new ArrayList();
JdbcTemplate jdbcTemplate = new JdbcTemplate(dataSource);
jdbcTemplate.query(
    "SELECT pr_id, pr_name, pr_price FROM product WHERE pr_price > ?",
    new PreparedStatementSetter() {
      public void setValues(PreparedStatement ps) throws SQLException {
        ps.setInt(1, 1000);
      }
    },
    new RowCallbackHandler() {
      public void processRow(ResultSet rs) throws SQLException {
        Product product = new Product();
        product.setId(rs.getInt("pr_id"));
        product.setName(rs.getString("pr_name"));
        product.setPrice(rs.getFloat("pr_price"));
        products.add(product);
      }
    }
);
```

Compare the update examples to the plain JDBC code in the "Data Access Technologies in Practice" section earlier in this chapter. This style of JDBC programming offers the same power, but with implicit proper resource and exception handling. Callback implementations might seem awkward at first but are actually quite straightforward to implement as anonymous inner classes, especially with an IDE that offers intelligent code completion. The benefits outweigh the requirement for callback implementations, especially as connection leakage due to buggy application code is no longer possible.

The generic Spring `DataAccessExceptions` thrown by `JdbcTemplate` are of particular benefit with JDBC. The JDBC API throws the same `SQLException` class on any kind of error, such as failure to access the database, SQL syntax error, or transaction timeout, the only differentiator is the vendor-specific error code. (Even a meaningful code is not guaranteed for all vendors.) Spring automatically converts well-known vendor codes into the appropriate subclasses of `org.springframework.dao.DataAccess Exception`, such as `org.springframework.dao.DataAccessResourceFailureException` or `org.springframework.dao.DataIntegrityViolationException`. Thus using the Spring JDBC abstraction not only simplifies JDBC code and makes it more readable, it makes JDBC code significantly more portable, by eliminating the need to write vendor-specific catch blocks.

The `JdbcTemplate` autodetects the target database from JDBC metadata, loading the appropriate mappings from vendor code to `DataAccessException` subclass at initialization time. The exception translation strategy is configurable; plugging in custom implementations is straightforward.

`JdbcTemplate` instances, like all Spring template classes, are thread-safe and reusable. Therefore, a `JdbcTemplate` instance variable can be configured on DAO initialization and accessed in each DAO method, without concern for concurrency. Spring provides a convenient prebuilt support class `org.springframework.jdbc.core.support.JdbcDaoSupport` that allows to access the template via `getJdbcTemplate()` in DAO method implementations.

"RDBMS Operation" Objects

The Spring Framework also offers a higher level of JDBC abstraction: reusable "RDBMS operation" objects, representing queries, updates, or stored procedures. The `RdbmsOperation` class hierarchy can be found in the `org.springframework.jdbc.object` package: subclasses include `SqlUpdate`, `MappingSqlQuery`, and `StoredProcedure`. Like `JdbcTemplate` instances, such objects can be created once and held as instance variables of DAO implementations, as they are also reusable and thread-safe.

Using this approach, the update example could be written as follows:

```
SqlUpdate priceUpdate =
    new SqlUpdate(dataSource,
        "UPDATE product SET pr_price = ? WHERE pr_price = ?");
priceUpdate.setTypes(new Types[] {Types.INTEGER, Types.INTEGER});
priceUpdate.compile();
priceUpdate.update(1000, 1100);
```

This example uses an overloaded convenience version of the `update` method, taking two `int` arguments. The general version takes an `Object` array, which will be applied as prepared statement parameters in the order in which they are provided.

The query example would be written as a subclass of `SqlQuery` as follows:

```
SqlQuery productQuery =
    new MappingSqlQuery(dataSource,
        "SELECT pr_id, pr_name, pr_price FROM product WHERE pr_price > ?") {
    protected Object mapRow(ResultSet rs, int rowNum) throws SQLException {
        Product product = new Product();
        product.setId(rs.getInt("pr_id"));
        product.setName(rs.getString("pr_name"));
        product.setPrice(rs.getFloat("pr_price"));
        return product;
    }
```

```
    };
productQuery.setTypes(new Types[] {Types.INTEGER});
productQuery.compile();
List products = productQuery.execute(1000);
```

Note how the `mapRow()` method is overloaded to convert each row of the `ResultSet` into a Java object. The `MappingSqlQuery` superclass is responsible for iterating through the `ResultSet` and building the collection of mapped objects.

Spring also offers an operation class for accessing **stored procedures**. This models a stored procedure as a thread-safe RDBMS operation object with a single stateless method, hiding database-specific syntax and the name of the stored procedure. A stored procedure object can even implement a single-method interface, completely removing the dependency of code using it on the use of a stored procedure.

Because of their higher level of abstraction from JDBC, and concealed use of prepared statements, Spring RDBMS operation objects are often an appropriate alternative to direct `JdbcTemplate` usage. The choice is up to you as the application developer.

iBATIS SQL Maps

Spring also provides convenient means for writing iBATIS SQL Map code, analogous to the support for plain JDBC. These classes reuse the same transaction and exception translation support as `JdbcTemplate`, working with the iBATIS `MappedStatement` API underneath for seamless participation in Spring resource and transaction management.

SQL Map Access via a Template

The `org.springframework.orm.ibatis.SqlMapTemplate` is the equivalent of `JdbcTemplate` for iBATIS SQL Maps: It provides a generic `execute` method for arbitrary operations on an iBATIS `MappedStatement`, and additionally offers convenience methods similar to those found in the iBATIS `SqlMap` class.

The update example looks as follows with `SqlMapTemplate`:

```
SqlMapTemplate sqlMapTemplate = new SqlMapTemplate(dataSource, sqlMap);
Map param = new HashMap(2);
param.put("oldPrice", new Integer(1000));
param.put("newPrice", new Integer(1100));
sqlMapTemplate.executeUpdate("updateProductPrices", param);
```

The same mapped statement definition as in the generic iBATIS SQL Maps section earlier in this chapter can be used:

```
<mapped-statement name="updateProductPrices">
  UPDATE products SET pr_price = #newPrice# WHERE pr_price = #oldPrice#
</mapped-statement>
```

The query example could refer to a mapped query statement with the associated result mapping to `Product` objects:

```
SqlMapTemplate sqlMapTemplate = new SqlMapTemplate(dataSource, sqlMap);
List products = sqlMapTemplate.executeQueryForList("findProductsByPrice",
                                           new Integer(1000));
```

The corresponding mapped statement definition could look as follows, inlining the result keys via "as" clauses instead of referring to a separate `result-map` definition. The "as" names must correspond to bean properties in the `Product` class. The `#value#` placeholder corresponds to the single input parameter of type `Integer`.

```
<mapped-statement name="findProductsByPrice" result-class="ebusiness.Product">
  SELECT pr_id AS id, pr_name AS name, pr_price AS price
  FROM product WHERE pr_price > #value#
</mapped-statement>
```

`SqlMapTemplate` automatically participates in transactions, and converts `SQLExceptions` to the generic Spring `DataAccessException` hierarchy via the same exception translation mechanism that `JdbcTemplate` uses. If configured via Spring IoC, it needs references to the JDBC `DataSource` to work on and to the iBATIS `SqlMap` that defines the mapped statements.

`SqlMapTemplate` is thread-safe and reusable. The Spring support class `org.springframework.org`
`.ibatis.support.SqlMapDaoSupport` offers convenient access to a template instance variable via the `getSqlMapTemplate()` method. `SqlMapDaoSupport` is a convenient superclass for iBATIS-based DAOs.

JDO

The Spring Framework offers a convenient way of writing JDO access code. The level of support is slightly different to the one for JDBC, as JDO is a higher-level API: Spring callbacks implement whole JDO use cases rather than single statements.

JDO Access via a Template

An `org.springframework.orm.jdo.JdoTemplate` instance is configured with `javax.jdo`
`.PersistenceManagerFactory`, and offers an execute method with a callback. Spring IoC is normally used to provide the `PersistenceManagerFactory` to the relevant DAO, although this is not necessary: As with JDBC, Spring JDO support can be used in a programmatic fashion too.

Our update example might look as follows with JDO:

```
JdoTemplate jdoTemplate = new JdoTemplate(pmf);
jdoTemplate.execute(
    new JdoCallback() {
      public Object doInJdo(PersistenceManager pm) throws JDOException {
        Query query = pm.newQuery(Product.class, "price == pPrice");
        query.declareParameters("String pPrice");
        query.compile();
        Collection products = (Collection) query.execute(new Integer(1000));
        for (Iterator it = products.iterator(); it.hasNext();) {
          Product product = (Product) it.next();
          product.setPrice(1100);
        }
        return null;
      }
    }
);
```

The query example assumes that the domain objects will be passed into a different layer of the application and are not supposed to be modified within the current transaction. The JDO instances need to be made transient to achieve this.

```
JdoTemplate jdoTemplate = new JdoTemplate(pmf);
Collection products = (Collection) jdoTemplate.execute(
    new JdoCallback() {
        public Object doInJdo(PersistenceManager pm) throws JDOException {
            Query query = pm.newQuery(Product.class, "price > pPrice");
            query.declareParameters("pPrice");
            query.compile();
            Collection result = (Collection) query.execute(new Integer(1000));
            pm.makeTransientAll(result);
            return result;
        }
    }
);
```

In both cases, the `JdoTemplate` class conceals the acquisition and release of a JDO `Persistence Manager` (which we would otherwise need to do in a `try/catch/finally` block in application code), implicit participation in transactions, and conversion of JDO exceptions to the generic Spring `DataAccessException` hierarchy. There are means to achieve each of those benefits individually, but the template is a convenient one-stop shop for typical needs.

Note that `JdoTemplate`, like all Spring templates, is thread-safe and reusable, and can thus be configured on DAO initialization and subsequently accessed in all of the DAO methods. Spring provides a convenient prebuilt support class called `org.springframework.orm.jdo.support.JdoDaoSupport` that allows to access the template via `getJdoTemplate()` in DAO method implementations.

JDO Access with an Interceptor

As an alternative to `JdoTemplate`, Spring also provides a declarative model for acquiring and releasing a JDO `PersistenceManager`, via the `JdoInterceptor`. Instead of implementing a callback with `JdoTemplate` managing resources, an AOP interceptor responsible for resource handling can be applied to a plain data access method.

Data access code simply fetches the current `PersistenceManager` via the `org.springframework.orm.jdo.PersistenceManagerFactoryUtils` class, working on it directly without caring about closing the `PersistenceManager` in a finally block. For exception conversion, it can delegate to a corresponding `PersistenceManagerFactoryUtils` method too. Note that the `getPersistenceManager` call specifies `false` for the `allowCreate` argument, to participate only in an existing thread-bound `PersistenceManager` but throw an exception if none is found.

```
PersistenceManager pm =
    PersistenceManagerFactoryUtils.getPersistenceManager(pmf, false);
try {
    Query query = pm.newQuery(Product.class, "price == pPrice");
    query.declareParameters("String pPrice");
    query.compile();
    Collection products = (Collection) query.execute(new Integer(1000));
    for (Iterator it = products.iterator(); it.hasNext();) {
        Product product = (Product) it.next();
```

```
        product.setPrice(1100);
    }
  }
  catch (JDOException ex) {
    throw PersistenceManagerFactoryUtils.convertJdoAccessException(ex);
  }
```

This data access code *needs* to be proxied via AOP, applying a `JdoInterceptor` that handles the lifecycle of a thread-bound JDO `PersistenceManager`: This interceptor binds a `PersistenceManager` before the data access method is invoked, and properly unbinds it again after the method finishes its work. If already proxying with a `TransactionProxyFactoryBean`, the `JdoInterceptor` can be registered there; otherwise, the generic Spring AOP `ProxyFactoryBean` can be used. See the Spring documentation for details.

The previous code can also be written to work at the plain `PersistenceManager` level without relying on a `JdoInterceptor`, by calling `getPersistenceManager(pmf, true)` and adding a finally block that invokes `PersistenceManagerFactoryUtils.closePersistenceManagerIfNecessary(pm, pmf)`. However, it is typically preferable to use `JdoTemplate` instead in such a scenario, avoiding the `try/catch/finally` block.

Note that `JdoTemplate` code can also be combined with a `JdoInterceptor`, to achieve *eager* prebinding of a `PersistenceManager` (for example, on transaction begin with `JtaTransactionManager`) while still leveraging the `JdoTemplate` callback approach for data access code. This is not necessary, but only an option, as `JdoTemplate` itself will work well with `JtaTransactionManager`, binding a `PersistenceManager` *on-demand* (that is, on first access).

> As you can see, you have a variety of options to code JDO data access with Spring. For typical usages, JdoTemplate is a perfectly viable way for data access that leverages Spring resource and transaction management. Consider `JdoInterceptor` an advanced feature for special needs rather than an effective replacement for `JdoTemplate`.

Hibernate

After seeing the JDBC and JDO templates, you should find the following listing easily understandable. It uses the analogous `HibernateTemplate` class, a convenient way of writing Hibernate access code.

Hibernate Access via a Template

The `HibernateTemplate` class is configured with a `SessionFactory`, and offers an execute method with a callback. As with JDO, objects that need to be updated must be retrieved and individually modified:

```
HibernateTemplate hibernateTemplate = new HibernateTemplate(sessionFactory);
hibernateTemplate.execute(
```

```
          new HibernateCallback() {
            public Object doInHibernate(Session session) throws HibernateException {
              List products = session.find("FROM example.Product WHERE price = ?",
                                        new Integer(1000), Hibernate.INTEGER);
              for (Iterator it = products.iterator(); it.hasNext();) {
                Product product = (Product) it.next();
                product.setPrice(1100);
              }
              return null;
            }
          }
    );
```

The query example would look as follows. Note that there is no need for a distinction between returning transactional or transient instances, in contrast to JDO.

```
    HibernateTemplate hibernateTemplate = new HibernateTemplate(sessionFactory);
    List products = (List) hibernateTemplate.execute(
          new HibernateCallback() {
            public Object doInHibernate(Session session) throws HibernateException {
              return session.find("FROM example.Product WHERE price > ?",
                                new Integer(1000), Hibernate.INTEGER);
            }
          }
    );
```

`HibernateTemplate` abstracts the same issues as `JdoTemplate`: proper `Session` acquisition and release, implicit participation in transactions, and conversion of Hibernate exceptions to the generic Spring `DataAccessException` hierarchy. Again, the template is a convenient one-stop shop for typical needs.

The `HibernateTemplate` class is thread-safe and reusable. The Spring support class `org.spring framework.hibernate.support.HibernateDaoSupport` manages a template as an instance variable, offering the `getHibernateTemplate()` method. As you can see, the Spring DAO infrastructure uses consistent concepts, across all supported technologies.

As a special feature, Spring allows transactional execution in the middle tier in combination with the "Open Session in View" pattern via its `OpenSessionInViewInterceptor` and `OpenSessionIn ViewFilter` classes. Data access code—typically using `HibernateTemplate`—and configuration does not have to change; transactions will simply be executed on the prebound `Session`. As noted in the general Hibernate section earlier in this chapter, this may introduce side-effects on reassociation of persistent objects, as the objects to be reassociated must not have been loaded by the `Session` before. Furthermore, persistent objects will be cached in the `Session` across multiple transactions, which is strictly speaking not consistent with transaction isolation.

HibernateTemplate Convenience Methods

Beyond a plain `execute` method, the Spring `HibernateTemplate` class offers various convenience methods for single-step actions. This is particularly useful for returning disassociated objects to a web controller or remote caller, or reassociating incoming objects with Hibernate. With such a convenience method, the previous query example could look as follows:

```
HibernateTemplate hibernateTemplate = new HibernateTemplate(sessionFactory);
List products = hibernateTemplate.find("FROM example.Product WHERE price > ?",
                                       new Integer(1000));
```

Note that despite being so concise, this code does correct resource handling and will participate in an enclosing transaction. The fact that there is no need for special distinction of returned instance state eases things significantly. The Hibernate type does not have to be specified (although it can be via an overloaded `find` method), as Hibernate can guess the type via the mapping. Such convenience methods also exist for load, save or update, and delete.

If executed within a transaction, for example driven by `HibernateTransactionManager` or `JtaTransactionManager`, the update example can also be written with the find convenience method. The changes in the loaded objects will automatically get flushed on transaction commit.

```
HibernateTemplate hibernateTemplate = new HibernateTemplate(sessionFactory);
List products = hibernateTemplate.find("FROM example.Product WHERE price = ?",
                                       new Integer(1000));
for (Iterator it = products.iterator(); it.hasNext();) {
  Product product = (Product) it.next();
  product.setPrice(1100);
}
```

If load and store have to happen in different transactions, the code could look like this:

```
HibernateTemplate hibernateTemplate = new HibernateTemplate(sessionFactory);
List products = hibernateTemplate.find("FROM example.Product WHERE price = ?",
                                       new Integer(1000));
```

(... going to a remote client or web controller ...)

```
for (Iterator it = products.iterator(); it.hasNext();) {
  Product product = (Product) it.next();
  product.setPrice(1100);
}
```

(... returning from the remote client or web controller ...)

```
HibernateTemplate hibernateTemplate = new HibernateTemplate(sessionFactory);
for (Iterator it = products.iterator(); it.hasNext();) {
  Product product = (Product) it.next();
  hibernateTemplate.update(product);
}
```

Spring also offers a `HibernateInterceptor` analogous to the `JdoInterceptor` class discussed earlier, for delegating resource handling to an AOP interceptor and writing data access code on a plain Hibernate `Session`. However, as with JDO, `HibernateInterceptor` should be considered an advanced feature for special needs, possibly in combination with `HibernateTemplate` for eager pre-binding of a `Session`. The `HibernateTemplate` convenience methods offer full power with surprisingly little data access code, making it a compelling, particularly simple means for data access.

With the `HibernateTemplate` convenience methods, the implementation of DAOs with disassociation and reassociation requirements, as for web applications or remote services, becomes extremely simple. Many fine-grained operations are effectively reduced to one-liners, if the `HibernateTemplate` instance is kept as an instance variable of the DAO.

Hibernate is already well suited for web applications and remoting, but the Spring `HibernateTemplate` class makes using it even easier and allows for seamless integration into a middle tier infrastructure. As we've noted before, Spring and Hibernate integrate particularly closely, and many users combine them with excellent results.

Summary

This chapter has focused on accessing relational databases: the commonest data access requirement in J2EE applications. Data access can account for much of the code in typical J2EE applications, and the data access strategy can help to determine the success or failure of projects.

The first decision in J2EE data access strategy—and often the most important—is between **set-based SQL access** and **O/R mapping with transparent persistence**.

Despite the hype around it in the J2EE community, not all applications benefit from O/R mapping. With a good abstraction library like the Spring Framework or iBATIS Database Layer, JDBC access does not have to be unduly cumbersome: A SQL-based approach can thus be a viable choice for a data access strategy, negating the FUD often spread about the general inappropriateness of SQL and JDBC.

However, O/R mapping is arguably the best approach for many—perhaps most—J2EE applications. (Of course it's possible—and often necessary—to use JDBC for certain operations within applications that use O/R mapping.) In many applications, a good O/R mapping solution can successfully bridge the object-relational impedance mismatch, enabling business objects to work with persistent domain objects, rather than relational concepts, and eliminating the need for Java developers to work with SQL.

O/R mapping should be done via good **generic O/R mapping solutions**. The best products, such as Hibernate, leading JDO implementations, and TopLink are far more sophisticated than anything that can reasonably be developed in-house. As Hibernate (probably the most popular Java O/R mapping product) is open source and free, there is no longer a prohibitive cost barrier to using a good O/R mapping product.

In this chapter, we've examined leading O/R mapping solutions. We've seen how capabilities differ widely between O/R mapping solutions, not only in terms of implementation, but also in API design and lifecycle semantics. For example, JDO offers a standard model for generic object persistence (not just RDBMS access) that entails several restrictions, while Hibernate concentrates on straightforward O/R mapping with as much relational database power as possible. The TopLink use of pure reflection, rather than byte code enhancement or generation, poses issues for detection of dirty objects (persistent objects modified during a transaction).

We've considered the **Data Access Object** pattern in depth, and looked at how to decide when to use a DAO layer. Almost a necessity with JDBC, DAOs offer less (but still usually worthwhile) value with transparent persistence via good O/R mapping solutions. We've seen how difficult it is to write DAOs that are truly independent of underlying data access technologies. With properly designed data access objects, business code can successfully be shielded from persistence technology details. DAOs also make sense for transparent persistence, although their design will be different from classic JDBC-based DAOs. DAO design is far from being as trivial as it seems; this chapter has outlined and discussed various issues. Achieving complete DAO portability between JDBC and O/R mapping technologies is not usually worth the effort, except for read-only operations, for which it is straightforward.

We've discussed common problems in working with persistence technologies, including locating resource factories such as JDO `PersistenceManagerFactory` objects, acquiring and relinquishing resources such as JDO `PersistenceManager` instances, and participating in transactions.

We concluded by looking at **data access support in the Spring Framework**, which offers dedicated support for DAOs, solving many common problems. This support includes infrastructure for wiring up business and data access objects, a generic data access exception hierarchy that helps to decouple DAOs from specific data access technologies, and participation in transactions.

Our sample application, a reworked version of Clinton Begin's **JPetStore**, illustrates the use of Spring and iBATIS SQL Maps in a layered architecture. Refer to Chapter 16 for an in-depth discussion. The Spring distribution comes with several further examples that show how to apply various data access strategies in a Spring context.

11

Remoting

"Remember the First Law of Distributed Computing: Don't Distribute Your Objects."
(Martin Fowler, *Patterns of Enterprise Application Architecture*)

In previous chapters, we have noted that most J2EE applications, especially web applications, do not benefit from a distributed architecture. In most scenarios, it is preferable to co-locate all application components in a single server, to avoid costly remote calls between different layers of the application and the complexity introduced by any remoting infrastructure and a distributed programming model. *Logical* layering is usually far more important than *physical* layering. We have seen that lightweight frameworks can help to achieve such clean separation of concerns.

That said, there are valid reasons for choosing a distributed architecture for some applications. If you encounter specific requirements that actually require **internal distribution** of the application, you need to choose appropriate mechanisms for your particular scenario. For adaptability, applications should be designed so that they allow for introducing **selective distribution** if needed for exporting certain functionality in a future stage of the project. In this chapter, we will discuss important issues to consider in that respect.

A different kind of remoting is needed for **exposing remote services to external clients**: for example, to rich clients or other external processes. It's important to stress that this does *not* require a distributed application on the server. Co-located web applications can easily expose remote services via various web service protocols. As we'll see, there are several good solutions for exposing such stateless remote services, some of them surprisingly easy to integrate into an existing architecture. Others, like EJB and JAX-RPC, fail in delivering an easy way to bolt on remoting to an existing architecture.

Besides the classic J2SE and J2EE remoting mechanisms, numerous alternative solutions are available, many of them open source. We will discuss both the classic approaches and a couple of alternative wire protocols, tools, and patterns, and show how these can be integrated into overall application architecture. The Spring Framework's generic remoting-integration support is a valuable tool for this task; we will use it for reference purposes here.

We will begin by looking at classic J2SE remoting (RMI) and classic J2EE remoting (EJB), before discussing WSDL-based web services (JAX-RPC) and lightweight remoting alternatives (Hessian and Burlap). Both EJB and JAX-RPC are built on the basic RMI model; to understand the heritage, we will briefly recap Java's remoting history.

Classic J2SE Remoting: RMI

The mother of all Java remoting, **RMI** (Remote Method Invocation), was introduced as early as JDK 1.1. Despite its age, RMI is a powerful remoting mechanism. It is built on Java serialization, with pluggable wire protocols: The default protocol is **JRMP** (Java Remote Method Protocol); **RMI-IIOP** was introduced later on for CORBA compatibility. Both of these protocols are required for J2EE-compliant EJB containers.

Let's start with a brief review of the RMI foundation, which is still more relevant than is often assumed.

All RMI services must implement a remote interface that extends the `java.rmi.Remote` tag interface. Each remote method must throw the checked `java.rmi.RemoteException` in addition to any application-specific exceptions, a much-debated fundamental decision that still shows in EJB remote component interfaces. With raw RMI, client-side stubs and server-side skeletons must be generated using **RMIC** (the RMI compiler), to be invoked after standard Java compilation. This is somewhat dated in the age of dynamic proxies, code-generation libraries like CGLIB, and programming techniques like AOP, but after all, the RMI model *does* date back to 1996.

An RMI service interface and implementation can look as follows. Note that `java.rmi.Remote` does not contain any methods, and that `java.rmi.RemoteException` is checked and needs to be declared by all methods in the service *interface*:

```
public interface MyService extends java.rmi.Remote {

    String doSomething(int someParam) throws java.rmi.RemoteException;
}
```

The corresponding methods in the *implementation class* do *not* need to throw `RemoteException`:

```
public class MyServiceImpl implements MyService {

    String doSomething(int someParam) {
        return "did something: " + someParam;
    }
}
```

The debate about the `Remote` interface and whether `RemoteException` should be checked is as old as RMI itself. We believe that *forcing* services and clients to be **remoting-aware** does not add much value, as most clients will not be able to deal with communication failure other than rethrowing the exception. The remoting concern can be completely transparent to service invokers if they simply work with a plain business interface, with communication failure leading to unchecked exceptions that an invoker can choose to handle but is not forced to. We will show ways to use such plain interfaces with RMI later in this chapter.

In general, we believe that unrecoverable exceptions should normally be unchecked. See Chapter 4 of Expert One-on-One J2EE Design and Development for further discussion of this issue. In this case, because it's normally impossible for clients to usefully handle remote exceptions, it's common for them to be propagated up the call stack to be handled by a generic Struts base action or the like, adding no value over the use of unchecked exceptions in the first place.

The RMI wire protocol can be customized or even completely replaced by implementing custom versions of `java.rmi.server.RMIClientSocketFactory` and `java.rmi.server.RMIServerSocket Factory`. However, working at that level is seldom advisable, unless you have extremely unusual remoting requirements and are happy to work at that low level. Experience shows that you may become mired in debugging your wire protocol instead of focusing on your business logic. Freeing developers from that kind of burden was one of the major aims of EJB, and one area in which EJB largely succeeds.

While it is possible to implement per-client **remote sessions** with RMI, it is not trivial and can lead to severe maintenance headaches. It's almost always preferable to keep remote communication **stateless** — a principle that applies to all types of remoting. If you *really* need stateful sessions, consider using EJB Stateful Session Beans or an HttpSession-enabled web service.

> RMI's standard JRMP protocol does not provide support for authorization, encryption, compression, or HTTP tunneling. If you need any of those, avoid implementing your own RMI wire protocol; consider alternatives like HTTP-based remoting tools or remote EJBs (discussed later in this chapter).

Accessing and Exporting RMI Services

Accessing an RMI service is as simple as looking up an RMI URL via `java.rmi.Naming`. Each lookup returns a proxy for the same server-side RMI service instance; there is no notion of component pooling, as with EJB. This can be considered an *advantage* in most cases. As we have noted in previous chapters, instance pooling does not add any value if service implementations are thread-safe anyway but *does* significantly complicate issues like singleton scope for business objects and shared resources.

```
MyService service = (MyService) Naming.lookup("rmi://myhost:1099/myservice");
```

Alternatively, JNDI can be used with a context factory that accesses the RMI registry: This allows for easy switching from JRMP and an RMI registry to IIOP and a CORBA naming service.

In contrast to EJB, exporting RMI services is done programmatically, usually via the class `java.rmi.server.UnicastRemoteObject`. Service implementations can either derive from `UnicastRemoteObject` directly, or be exported via `UnicastRemoteObject`'s static methods. The latter is normally preferable, as it doesn't impose any restrictions on service implementations other than the basic remote interface requirements. To be available for clients, an exported service has to be registered with an RMI registry, either running in the same process or in its own.

```
MyService service = new MyServiceImpl();
Remote exportedService = UnicastRemoteObject.exportObject(service);
Registry registry = LocateRegistry.getRegistry(1099);
registry.bind("myservice", exportedService);
```

An RMI registry must be started at the given port (1099) to make registration work. Such a registry can be started as a separate process, or within the same JVM. There are many issues in setting up an appropriate RMI environment. Refer to the wealth of RMI documentation for details.

Setup within a Spring Context

In a Spring bean factory or application context, a client-side proxy to an RMI service can be defined using an **RmiProxyFactoryBean**. This factory bean will expose a proxy for the located RMI object, analogous to JndiObjectFactoryBean and other Spring-provided FactoryBeans that expose a created or located object rather than the factory instance itself.

```
<bean id="myServiceProxy"
    class="org.springframework.remoting.rmi.RmiProxyFactoryBean">
  <property name="serviceInterface">
    <value>mypackage.MyService</value>
  </property>
  <property name="serviceUrl">
    <value>rmi://myhost:1099/myservice</value>
  </property>
</bean>
```

This service proxy can be passed to a business object that needs to access the RMI service as follows, using Dependency Injection:

```
<bean id="myServiceClient" class="mypackage.MyServiceClient">
  <property name="service">
    <ref bean="myServiceProxy"/>
  </property>
</bean>
```

The MyServiceClient class simply needs to expose a bean property of type "mypackage.MyService". It need have no concern about how the service was located:

```
public class MyServiceClient {

  private MyService service;

  public void setService(MyService service) {
    this.service = service;
  }

  public void myBusinessMethod() {
    try {
      this.service.doSomething(...);
      ...
    }
    catch (RemoteException ex) {
      ...
    }
  }
}
```

In all the examples in this chapter, we'll show the use of JavaBean properties (Setter Dependency Injection) to provide services to clients. If you prefer Constructor Dependency Injection (defining a constructor taking the required service or services as arguments), this is equally well supported in Spring. As usual, the IoC container avoids imposing a particular model on application code.

On the server side, an existing bean in the same Spring IoC context can be exposed with an **RmiServiceExporter** definition, provided that it conforms to RMI's service implementation requirements. The same "myService" bean could also be used locally — for example, by web controllers, or exported under multiple names.

```
<bean id="myService" class="mypackage.MyServiceImpl"/>

<bean id="myServiceExporter"
    class="org.springframework.remoting.rmi.RmiServiceExporter">
  <property name="service">
    <ref bean="myService"/>
  </property>
  <property name="serviceName">
    <value>myservice</value>
  </property>
  <property name="registryPort">
    <value>1099</value>
  </property>
</bean>
```

Business Interfaces for RMI Services

To avoid the need to code clients against RMI interfaces, RMI service implementations can employ a non-RMI **business interface** in addition to the RMI service interface. The methods in the service implementation class do not need to throw `RemoteException`, so implementing an analogous business interface amounts to declaring an additional "implements" clause. Clients can then expose a dependency for the plain business interface.

```
public interface MyService extends java.rmi.Remote {

    String doSomething(int someParam) throws java.rmi.RemoteException;
}
```

In addition to the MyService RMI interface, a plain MyBusinessInterface with corresponding methods is needed:

```
public interface MyBusinessInterface {

    String doSomething(int someParam);
}
```

The implementation class then implements *both* interfaces, which is possible because there is no need to throw the checked `RemoteException` here:

```
public class MyServiceImpl implements MyService, MyBusinessInterface {
```

```
    String doSomething(int someParam) {
      return "did something: " + someParam;
    }
  }
}
```

Spring's `RmiProxyFactoryBean` can delegate invocations on a non-RMI business interface to the corresponding methods of the underlying RMI object, using reflection. It will automatically throw Spring's `org.springframework.remoting.RemoteAccessException` on remote invocation failure, converting the `java.rmi.RemoteException` thrown by the RMI object. As this exception is unchecked, it does not need explicit declaration.

Client objects can be coded against the plain business interface, without needing to handle the checked RMI `RemoteException`. We believe that this is preferable in most cases: Rare clients that can potentially recover from remoting exceptions can *choose* to catch this exception to do so. Client-side configuration will be as follows:

```
<bean id="myServiceProxy"
    class="org.springframework.remoting.rmi.RmiProxyFactoryBean">
  <property name="serviceInterface">
    <value>mypackage.MyBusinessInterface</value>
  </property>
  <property name="serviceUrl">
    <value>rmi://myhost:1099/myservice</value>
  </property>
</bean>
```

The corresponding MyServiceClient class must express a dependency of type "mypackage.MyBusiness Interface", not needing to be aware of RMI at all:

```
public class MyServiceClient {

  private MyBusinessInterface service;

  public void setService(MyBusinessInterface service) {
    this.service = service;
  }

  public void myBusinessMethod() {
    this.service.doSomething(...);
  }
}
```

A further benefit of having the service implement a business interface is that service implementations can be used locally via the business interface: Local clients will have no dependency on remote-aware interfaces, meaning no unnecessary catching of `RemoteException` on local invocations. The business interface can be considered a simplified *client view* of the remote service: The core RMI infrastructure still works with the RMI interface as usual, and the service implementations themselves are still aware of being RMI services.

The downside is the need to synchronize "business" and "remote" interfaces. To allow for invoking methods on the business interface and seamlessly delegate to the remote interface, each business method must have a corresponding method in the remote interface, typically adding only a `"throws RemoteException"` clause. Letting the service class implement both interfaces will check *each* interface against the service implementation, but the developer must still coordinate the *same* set of methods in *both* interfaces.

From the `RmiServiceExporter` point of view, nothing has to change: The RMI object is still exposed via the standard RMI infrastructure, via its RMI interface "mypackage.MyService". Conventional RMI clients can simply lookup the object and access it via its RMI interface. The difference is that local clients and special proxy clients like `RmiProxyFactoryBean` can choose to use the business interface to access the service.

> **Accessing and exporting RMI services is straightforward, and can easily be integrated into existing applications. On the negative side, setting up an RMI environment is cumbersome and can cause headaches regarding network ports. Development with RMI involves running the RMIC compiler for each service object. RMI service interfaces face similar restrictions to those of EJB component interfaces, having to implement a marker interface and to throw RemoteException on each service method. As an alternative, Spring offers a mechanism to use non-RMI business interfaces for standard RMI services.**

RMI Invoker for Transparent Remoting

A different flavor of RMI is built on sending method invocations through an **RMI invoker** via Java reflection. From the RMI point of view, each exported RMI service is of the *invoker type*, with a common remote interface and stub/skeleton pair that just features a single "invoke" method. Each exported business service is wrapped with an RMI invoker service.

With this model, remote-enabled services can implement any Java interface: There is no need to derive the service interface from `java.rmi.Remote`, no need to throw `java.rmi.RemoteException` in interface methods, and no need to implement a separate business interface. The actual remoting is still done through the underlying RMI infrastructure, with all of its power; but conventional RMI clients will not be able to access an RMI interface for the service, as the exported RMI object is a special invoker.

A similar concept has been implemented in various incarnations, for example, in the open source project TRMI (`http://trmi.sourceforge.net`) or AltRMI (`http://incubator.apache.org/projects/altrmi/`). The Spring Framework offers its own variation in the `org.springframework.remoting.rmi` package, via the `RmiProxyFactoryBean` and `RmiServiceExporter` classes used in the preceding RMI configuration examples.

If `RmiProxyFactoryBean` looks up an RMI object that is an RMI invoker, it automatically handles invocations on the service interface accordingly. Correspondingly, `RmiServiceExporter` exposes an RMI invoker if it is told to export a "service" that does not implement `java.rmi.Remote`. This way, *any* business interface can be used as sole service interface, provided that its method arguments are all serializable: that is, primitives or objects that implement the `java.io.Serializable` marker interface.

Following the transparency concept, `java.rmi.RemoteException` does not have to be declared on service interface methods. Spring's unchecked `org.springframework.remoting.RemoteAccessException` will be thrown by the Spring remoting layer on remote invocation failure. This provides the same advantages as the "business interface" pattern with conventional RMI, with the additional benefit that there is **no separate RMI service interface** to maintain.

```
public interface MyService {

    String doSomething(int someParam);
}
```

The service implementation is a plain Java object that implements the business interface, with no RMI dependencies.

```
public class MyServiceImpl implements MyService {

    String doSomething(int someParam) {
        return "did something: " + someParam;
    }
}
```

Consequently, a client class needs to express a dependency of type "mypackage.MyService". As with a business interface for a conventional RMI service, the client will not be aware of RMI at all.

In many cases, it will be possible to take an **existing local service object** and expose it as remote service *as is*, via the RMI infrastructure. On the other hand, not every existing service object will match the functionality to be exposed directly. It is often preferable to write a dedicated **facade** and expose that as a remote service. Of course, the same facade instance can be used locally too, for example, to be accessed by web controllers — it does not have any signs of a (potentially) distributed object.

> **Transparent remoting via an RMI invoker allows any business interface to be used as remote service interface (so long as serializability requirements are met), and for writing service implementations that do not have to be aware of their potential remote exposure at all. Thus, the same business facades can be used for local and remote access: even the same facade instances. Existing POJO services can be exported without being aware of their use for remoting. An RMI invoker suffers from the same potential complexity of setting up an RMI environment as conventional RMI, but it does not involve the RMIC compiler at all — the stub/skeleton pair for the RMI invoker is prebuilt.**

Classic J2EE Remoting: EJB

The classic J2EE solution for distribution needs are **remote Session Beans**. (Remote *Entity Beans* are now widely, and deservedly, considered an architectural mistake. Potentially fine-grained persistent objects are not good candidates for remoting.) In this part of the chapter, we will review the programming and deployment model of remote EJBs, and discuss convenient access to remote EJBs.

The original promise of EJB remoting was to be able to deploy application components to specific servers if needed, for efficient usage of server resources. Components are modeled for distributed usage in the first place, including numerous restrictions that the EJB specification imposes for portable distribution. Co-locating business components is treated as a special case, similar to how single-database transactions are considered a special case of distributed transactions (in classic J2EE style).

EJB maintains J2SE's original RMI service model. Remote service interfaces must derive from the `java.rmi.Remote` marker interface, and each method in the interface must throw the checked `java.rmi.RemoteException`. Thus, services are explicitly written as remote services. Clients need to explicitly handle the checked `RemoteException`, even if they just propagate it, and even if invoking locally — a design decision that dates back to RMI's origins.

So EJB enforces a certain programming model for remote services, just like RMI. The only choice is using a plain **RMI business interface** as a super interface of an SLSB **component interface**: That way, callers are not aware of calling an EJB, but merely of calling an RMI object. They still need to deal with `RemoteException`, but the same business interface could alternatively be implemented by a plain RMI object. We will come back to this discussion later in this chapter, and show that alternative and simpler remoting models are possible.

Remote EJBs were the only middle tier component model available in EJB 1.x. Orthodox J2EE design guidelines still recommend modeling business components as remote EJBs for **potentially distributed** application components. In the orthodox view, local EJBs are appropriate only for **definitely co-located** components. Remember that the original intent of introducing local EJBs was to allow for efficient container-managed relationships (CMRs) between Entity Beans: Local EJB interfaces were a last-minute addition to the EJB 2.0 specification to support the introduction of CMRs.

Recent trends, at TheServerSide and other community forums, indicate a growing preference for local Session Beans even for business facades. In private conversations with the authors, many leading J2EE architects have indicated that they prefer such use of local EJBs in most cases. This use of EJB was also advocated in 2002 in *Expert One-on-One J2EE Design and Development*. Many developers have realized that their applications are very unlikely to *ever* be deployed in a distributed fashion. If such requirements might appear in the future, it is still possible to refactor a system such that it allows for the introduction of remote EJBs *then*. As we've noted, it is dangerous to assume phantom requirements upfront, particularly if they incur a significant level of extra complexity.

> **Do not follow J2EE orthodoxy in making components distributed because of the** *potential* **for future distribution. If an application is not likely to be clustered at the component level but rather just as a whole, there is no reason to model individual business objects as remote EJBs. If you do choose to use remote EJBs, derive your Stateless Session Bean component interfaces from plain RMI business interfaces to decouple your clients from the use of EJB.**

Wire Protocols

EJB containers are permitted to use any wire protocol for their EJB remoting. Application clients typically include a client JAR file for the particular container that they intend to access, implementing the client side of the protocol. The J2EE specification requires support for **IIOP**, for interoperability with

CORBA clients, and for **JRMP**, the default Java RMI protocol. Many servers additionally provide their own, more efficient wire protocols, like WebLogic's **T3** or Resin's *Hessian*. Those proprietary protocols are typically recommended by the respective vendors for remoting within instances of the same J2EE server.

The J2EE specification recommends the use of the **IIOP transaction propagation protocol** for transaction interoperability across heterogeneous J2EE servers. Such **remote transaction propagation** is a distinctive feature of EJB, available with few other remoting technologies. However, J2EE-compliant servers are *not required* to support the IIOP transaction propagation protocols or remote transaction propagation in general, not even for calls between instances of the same J2EE application server. A significant number of current J2EE servers do not provide *any* means for remote transaction propagation.

Most EJB containers optimize intra-VM calls to remote EJBs as local invocations, achieving performance close to invocations of local EJBs at the price of changed method argument semantics: call by reference instead of call by value. If EJBs are designed to not modify their passed-in arguments, this works well. However, the programming model is still based on distributed components, merely optimized for the special case of co-location. Such assumptions incur a significant development overhead that is often not covered by actual business requirements.

Standard EJB is not well suited for communication between external clients and Internet servers, as most EJB wire protocols are targeted at Intranet usage, using arbitrary network ports. Some EJB containers such as JBoss and Resin provide **HTTP invokers for EJBs,** offering a HTTP-based wire protocol to overcome the firewall issues. Nevertheless, web services are the better choice for service invocations across the Internet, with SOAP or any other HTTP-based protocol.

State Management

The most popular type of remote EJB is the **Stateless Session Bean (SLSB),** which is well suited for implementing stateless remote services. Clients cannot assume they are invoking the same EJB instance on repeated invocations: Each invocation is dispatched to an arbitrary instance from the container's SLSB pool. The server does not have to keep any state associated with a particular client: an important advantage for scalability. The client-side stubs can implement seamless failover to other servers, without disrupting client state (if methods are marked as idempotent). High-end EJB containers provide impressive support for such failover. However, not all J2EE servers provide sophisticated failover support.

A distinctive EJB feature is the **Stateful Session Bean** (SFSB). SFSBs are mainly intended for implementing remote sessions: Each client works with its own SFSB instance; the instance can hold server-side state for the particular client. While this is superficially appealing for implementing client sessions, it has major disadvantages in terms of scalability and failover in clusters, similar to the use of sessions in a web user interface but with less container support for clustering. For this reason, most developers try to model their remote services in a stateless fashion to avoid the use of SFSBs completely. (The ubiquitous shopping-cart example is now less often implemented using Stateful Session Beans, as users tend to be attached to the contents of their shopping carts. If they are held in a database, there is less likelihood of angry calls to the helpdesk!)

Stateful Session Beans offer some unusual capabilities, which are indispensable in certain scenarios, but usually better avoided. When using bean-managed programmatic transactions with SFSBs, it is possible to start a transaction during one method invocation and end it in another. The SFSB will keep the transactional state between method invocations. This feature is, however, of questionable value. If a client disconnects without finishing its work, because of careless programming, network failure, or unexpected user action, the transaction will be left unfinished until the container rolls it back after a timeout. It is almost always preferable to model transactional-use cases so that they correspond to a single method invocation, finishing its transaction before it returns. In general, it is important to keep transactions as short as possible, because they may lock valuable transactional resources, interfering with the work of other clients. Thus optimistic, rather than pessimistic, transactions are normally preferred for "long-lived," user-controlled transactions.

A further questionable feature is the ability to access a server's `javax.transaction.User Transaction` handle directly from a client, to demarcate transactions that span multiple remote EJB invocations, using either SLSBs or SFSBs. This feature is not required by the J2EE specification, but is available in high-end servers such as WebLogic. It suffers from the same important drawback as the SFSB transactional state keeping: If a client disconnects unexpectedly, the transaction will be left open until cleanup after a timeout.

In the case of physically separated web and EJB servers, it is generally advisable to keep state only in the web container to avoid inefficient double management of server-side state. Currently, most web containers implement `HttpSession` failover, but only a few EJB containers implement robust SFSB failover. And if using an SFSB, it is necessary to keep the handle to it in an `HttpSession` anyway, to allow the client to access it in successive requests. Such container limitations are one more reason to not keep client-specific state in the EJB tier.

> **Developers tend to avoid Stateful Session Beans for a good reason: to avoid server-side state wherever possible. Try to model your remote services in a stateless fashion. This is almost always possible through appropriate mapping of use cases to stateless service methods. Most important, do not let a remote client demarcate transactions unless you absolutely need to. In case of a web tier that accesses an EJB tier, do not keep state in both the HttpSession and SFSBs if you can avoid it.**

Accessing Remote EJBs

To access remote EJBs, application clients must connect to the server's **JNDI** environment, and look up the home interface of the desired EJB. An invocation of the appropriate `create` method on the home interface will then return a remote proxy for an actual EJB instance. In the case of a Stateless Session Bean, each invocation of a proxy method will fetch an instance from the server's SLSB pool, invoke the corresponding method on it, and return the instance to the pool.

Lookup code might be as follows:

```
InitialContext initialContext = new InitialContext();
MyBeanHome cartHome = (MyBeanHome) PortableRemoteObject.narrow(
    initialContext.lookup("myBean"), MyBeanHome.class);
MyBean myBean = myBeanHome.create();
myBean.doSomething();
```

The only line that actually performs an operation on the EJB is the last one, which we've highlighted. The preceding lines deal with the plumbing of getting a reference to the bean: accessing the JNDI environment, looking up the home interface, "creating" the SLSB instance. Repeating this code in every client object that needs to access an EJB is cumbersome. A static utility method that reduces the lines of code for an actual lookup helps but still requires explicit lookups that the client business objects are aware of and tied to. Application code containing such JNDI and EJB lookup is typically difficult to unit test outside the application server.

For the preceding example, let's assume that JNDI has been configured to connect to the remote server's JNDI environment via settings in a jndi.properties file. Alternatively, those settings could also be specified for each InitialContext, through an overloaded constructor.

```
java.naming.factory.initial=com.sun.jndi.cosnaming.CNCtxFactory
java.naming.provider.url=iiop://myhost:535
```

The standard IIOP context factory for JNDI is included in Sun's Java Runtime Environment. If you access EJBs via proprietary wire protocols like WebLogic's T3, you need to specify a corresponding **context factory** and include it in the class path. In any case, the interfaces of your EJBs and their proxy implementations must be available: The deployment tools of your J2EE container will create a **client JAR file** for your remote EJBs. Depending on the context factory and wire protocol used, security credentials like username and password can be specified as JNDI environment entries.

It's best to avoid the need to write (and test) such JNDI/EJB lookup boilerplate code altogether. The need to do so repeatedly throughout an application can significantly reduce productivity, flexibility, and maintainability.

Setup within a Spring Context

Fortunately, a sophisticated **IoC container** is able to provide convenient means for looking up EJB instances. This can happen at two levels: either just looking up a home object or creating a proxy for an actual SLSB instance. Both can be passed to business objects via declarative references. The objects themselves need only to expose a dependency on either the home interface or the bean interface itself. That way, business objects are not concerned with how such references are retrieved, easing reuse in other environments, and facilitating unit testing.

The Spring Framework provides JNDI and EJB access classes for this purpose.

Exposing an EJB Home Object

We have already seen how to use the generic Spring **JndiObjectFactoryBean** for looking up JNDI resources like DataSources in Chapter 7 ("Spring Framework"). Leveraging the same JndiObjectFactoryBean for setting up a client business object with the **home interface** of a remote EJB can look as follows. This configuration strategy is not EJB-specific: It will work with any resource in a JNDI context, such as a JMS topic or queue.

```
<bean id="myBeanHome" class="org.springframework.jndi.JndiObjectFactoryBean">
  <property name="jndiName">
    <value>mybean</value>
  </property>
</bean>
```

JNDI environment settings could optionally be specified for each JndiObjectFactoryBean. For simplicity's sake, we assume use of the same jndi.properties file as before, indicating how to connect to the remote server.

The exposed object will be your home interface, in the example of type "mypackage.MyBeanHome", available for bean references. This is the only option with an SFSB, as such a home interface can have any number of custom create methods that client code needs to invoke in a custom fashion. Furthermore, the bean instance needs to be removed when the client is done with it, clearing the state held by the server.

The home object can be passed to a business object that needs to access the EJB:

```
<bean id="myServiceClient" class="mypackage.MyServiceClient">
  <property name="service">
    <ref bean="myBeanHome"/>
  </property>
</bean>
```

The corresponding client object needs to expose a bean property of type "myexample.MyBeanHome". In its business method, it can create an SFSB through calling a custom `create` method.

```
public class MyServiceClient {

  private MyBeanHome service;

  public void setService(MyBeanHome service) {
    this.service = service;
  }

  public void myBusinessMethod() {
    try {
      this.service.create(...);
    }
    catch (CreateException ex) {
      ...
    }
    catch (RemoteException ex) {
      ...
    }
  }
}
```

Exposing an SLSB with a Business Interface

In case of an SLSB—the most important case—expressing a dependency on the component itself (rather than on the home interface) is much preferable. Removing the indirection of working with the home interface reduces the amount of plumbing code we need to write in application code, and significantly eases testing. The dependency type is normally an **RMI business methods interface** that is a super-interface of the SLSB **component interface**. In this common J2EE pattern, the methods in the business interface need to throw RMI's `RemoteException`, to be able to derive the EJB remote component interface from it.

```
public interface MyRmiBusinessInterface extends java.rmi.Remote {

  String doSomething(int someParam) throws java.rmi.RemoteException;
}
```

Using such a business interface, the client object is effectively decoupled from the use of an EJB; it is aware only of working with an RMI object, implementing the business interface. Furthermore, the EJB implementation class can implement the business interface directly; it *has* to implement the specified business methods, allowing for proper compiler checks, in contrast to EJB's inelegant "kind-of" implementing the component interface.

```
<bean id="myBean" class="org.springframework.ejb.access.
                         SimpleRemoteStatelessSessionProxyFactoryBean">
  <property name="jndiName">
    <value>mybean</value>
  </property>
  <property name="businessInterface">
    <value>mypackage.MyRmiBusinessInterface</value>
  </property>
</bean>
```

This factory bean will expose a proxy that implements the given business interface, in the example of type "mypackage.MyRmiBusinessInterface", wrapping the "creation" and invocation of the underlying SLSB component. `SimpleRemoteStatelessSessionProxyFactoryBean` will create a new reference to an EJB instance for every call to the EJB by invoking `create` on the home interface. Custom invocation strategies are possible via subclassing the proxy factory bean.

The EJB proxy can be passed to a business object that needs to access the service via the business interface as follows:

```
<bean id="myServiceClient" class="mypackage.MyServiceClient">
  <property name="service">
    <ref bean="myBean"/>
  </property>
</bean>
```

The corresponding client object looks as follows. As we've noted, it is aware of working with an RMI interface, but is not tied to the EJB API or an application server environment.

```
public class MyServiceClient {

  private MyRmiBusinessInterface service;

  public void setService(MyRmiBusinessInterface service) {
    this.service = service;
  }

  public void myBusinessMethod() {
    try {
      this.service.doSomething(...);
      ...
    }
    catch (RemoteException ex) {
      ...
    }
  }
}
```

Non-RMI Business Interfaces

Alternatively, `SimpleRemoteStatelessSessionProxyFactoryBean` can be used with a **non-RMI business interface**, similar to the business interface pattern for RMI services shown previously, to avoid having to code remote SLSB clients against RMI interfaces.

Remember that the business methods in the EJB implementation class do not need to throw `RemoteException`, so an implemented business interface can be non-RMI too. However, such a plain business interface cannot serve as super-interface of the SLSB remote component interface. In this case, the interfaces need to be manually kept in sync. You can even create a corresponding non-RMI business interface for an *existing* EJB, as it is effectively independent from the component interface, and doesn't *have to* be implemented by the EJB implementation class.

Clients can then expose a dependency on the plain business interface. The non-RMI business interface for the preceding example looks as follows:

```
public interface MyNonRmiBusinessInterface {


    String doSomething(int someParam);
}
```

`SimpleRemoteStatelessSessionProxyFactoryBean` can delegate invocations on such a non-RMI interface to the corresponding methods of the underlying EJB component proxy, via reflection. It will automatically throw Spring's generic `org.springframework.remoting.RemoteAccessException` on remote invocation failure, converting `java.rmi.RemoteException` thrown by the EJB component proxy. As `RemoteAccessException` is unchecked, it does not need explicit declaration.

```
<bean id="myBean" class="org.springframework.ejb.access.
                        SimpleRemoteStatelessSessionProxyFactoryBean">
    ...
    <property name="businessInterface">
      <value>mypackage.MyNonRmiBusinessBean</value>
    </property>
</bean>
```

Of course, the underlying EJB infrastructure will still work with the EJB component interface. To make a non-RMI business interface work, the proxy must be able to delegate invocations on the business interface to the underlying EJB component proxy, which of course does *not* implement the plain business interface (only the EJB implementation class does). Thus, methods are matched by signature: The developer must ensure that the business interface is in sync with the EJB component interface. Each method in the business interface must have a corresponding method in the component interface, typically adding only a `"throws RemoteException"` clause.

The client object will work with the plain business interface, not even being aware of a remote service, but still accessing a remote EJB. The proxy that the service client works with implements the specified non-RMI business interface as a simpler *client view*.

```
public class MyServiceClient {

  private MyNonRmiBusinessInterface service;
```

```
public void setService(MyNonRmiBusinessInterface service) {
  this.service = service;
}

public void myBusinessMethod() {
  this.service.doSomething(...);
  ...
}
}
```

> Use a sophisticated IoC container such as Spring to decouple your client business objects from remote EJB lookups—or effectively *any* EJB lookups—as the issue is similar when using local EJBs. In case of a Stateless Session Bean, express a dependency for an RMI business interface that the EJB implements, to decouple your client objects from the use of EJB—for ease of reuse and ease of testing. With a Spring-created proxy, you can even let your client objects work with a non-RMI business interface for your remote EJB.

Deploying Remote EJBs

In contrast to conventional RMI, EJB imposes a specific deployment model and a **dedicated container** to host the remote components, heavyweight Inversion of Control, while RMI allows for exporting services from within any existing environment. Remote EJBs are exposed via the J2EE container's JNDI environment: The public JNDI names to be used are typically configured in a vendor-specific deployment descriptor.

Upon deployment, an EJB can typically be **parameterized** in vendor-specific ways, such as pool settings, access rules, clustering, and failover behavior. All these options come at the price of complex deployment descriptors, both standardized and vendor specific. Compared to RMI's simplicity, EJB offers much greater functionality, but also much greater deployment effort.

Exporting Existing Services

Like other component models, EJB assumes that business services are implemented in a self-contained fashion. All EJBs of an enterprise application on a server run within their own class loader, typically without access to web application classes or other parts of the application. The only way to access **shared resources** is via JNDI, for example, a JDBC DataSource or a JCA ConnectionFactory.

Implementing business facades as EJBs is further complicated by the various EJB programming restrictions, incurred by the instance pooling model and other characteristics of the EJB model. We have already seen that it is hard to access singleton helper objects or a shared cache from within Stateless Session Beans in Chapter 12, "Replacing Other EJB Services."

So if you want to export existing business services implemented as plain Java objects via remote Session Beans, you must keep instances of those business objects within the corresponding EJB instances, even if you use the same business objects as the foundation of co-located web applications. It is *not* possible to access *shared* POJO business objects from both web tier classes and EJB implementations—at least not in a portable fashion.

Consider an existing web application with a logical business layer. Let's assume that you need to export a *single* service for access by an external rich client, in a revision of the application. One could naïvely assume that exposing the functionality of that existing business service as EJB would be straightforward, but unfortunately the EJB programming model turns this into a major challenge. Effectively, you need to take that business object and all its collaborating objects and resources, and keep separate instances of them as helpers within the implementation of a Stateless Session Bean.

While it can be acceptable to have multiple instances of your business objects, it is typically inappropriate to have multiple instances of shared resources that are local to your application. It is even more awkward to have one instance of a shared resource *per SLSB instance* in an instance pool. Good examples are a Hibernate SessionFactory or a JDO PersistenceManagerFactory: Having just one instance is absolutely necessary for efficient resource handling and guaranteed cache consistency. The only clean way to achieve this with EJB is to keep such resources in JNDI, via a corresponding JCA connector; other solutions involve custom singletons with custom wiring.

In our example scenario, you also need to introduce a different deployment unit just because of that single remote service: While your application could previously be deployed as a plain **WAR file** (Web Application aRchive) with local resources, it now must be deployed as an **EAR file** (Enterprise Application aRchive), and potentially depends on a **JCA connector** for your persistence tool. You even need to include separate copies of your shared classes and libraries in the included WAR, the EJB JAR, and possibly the JCA connector for your O/R Mapping tool.

Remember that the actual requirement was merely to export a single existing local POJO service for external clients . . . .

EJB is designed so that it works seamlessly if all business logic is implemented as EJBs: Turning an existing local Stateless Session Bean into a remote EJB is straightforward. But as we have seen in previous chapters, it is in many cases preferable to implement **business logic in plain Java objects**, for reusability outside a J2EE container, for ease of testing, and so on. Unfortunately, EJB is not at all well suited for implementing a remote service layer for such a POJO business layer.

> While accessing remote EJB services from external clients is straightforward, exporting existing business services as remote Session Beans can amount to a major challenge. The EJB deployment model assumes that you implement all your business logic as EJBs in the first place. Implementing EJB-based remote service exporters for shared POJO business objects is unnecessarily hard: so hard that almost any alternative is preferable in such a scenario. We will discuss some of these next.

WSDL-based Web Services: JAX-RPC

The major focus for the development of **J2EE release 1.4** was web services support, based on **WSDL** (the **Web Service Description Language**) and **SOAP** (the **Simple Object Access Protocol**). WSDL is defined by the World Wide Web Consortium (www.w3.org/TR/wsdl); quoting the specification's abstract:

WSDL is an XML format for describing network services as a set of endpoints operating on messages containing either document-oriented or procedure-oriented information. The operations and messages are described abstractly, and then bound to a concrete network protocol and message format to define an endpoint. Related concrete endpoints are combined into abstract endpoints (services). WSDL is extensible to allow description of endpoints and their messages regardless of what message formats or network protocols are used to communicate; however, the only bindings described in this document describe how to use WSDL in conjunction with SOAP 1.1, HTTP GET/POST, and MIME.

Essentially, WSDL is about describing remote services in a platform-independent fashion. It is heavily backed by Microsoft, which uses WSDL with SOAP on HTTP as its standard remoting solution for the .NET platform. Web Services have also been hailed as the silver bullet for **Enterprise Application Integration (EAI)** by analysts and major vendors.

XML plays a central role in the web services world, as it is the foundation of both WSDL and SOAP. Web services adopt a **specific tradeoff**, namely interoperability and extensibility over ease-of-use and performance. The use of XML for SOAP indicates this tradeoff: An extensive XML format as wire protocol is hardly a good choice for efficient remoting *within the same platform* (for example, for Java-to-Java communication).

> While web services via WSDL and SOAP are an important option for integration efforts, they are just another tool in your toolbox. Do not follow the fashion blindly in adopting the view that web services are a one-size-fits-all solution for all remoting needs. For plain Java-to-Java communication, RMI/EJB or Hessian/Burlap (discussed later in this chapter) is a compelling alternative and is easier to use, offering optimized wire protocols.

J2EE incorporates several sub-specifications for web service support, the most important being:

❑ The **JAX-RPC** specification for client access and **servlet endpoints** (http://java.sun.com/xml/jaxrpc/)

❑ The specification of **EJB endpoints** in EJB 2.1 (http://java.sun.com/products/ejb/)

❑ **JSR-109** ("Implementing Enterprise Web Services") for the **deployment model** (http://jcp.org/aboutJava/communityprocess/final/jsr109/)

Beyond support by J2EE servers, there are numerous standalone web service tools available that comply with the JAX-RPC specification: for example, Apache Axis (http://ws.apache.org/axis/) and webMethods GLUE (www.webmethods.com/solutions/wM_Glue/). Such tools are straightforward to integrate into J2EE web applications, even if running on a full-blown J2EE server which offers its own Web Service support. J2EE's standard web service model is by no means the *only* way to integrate web service support into J2EE applications.

A detailed discussion of J2EE's web service support including the deployment model is beyond the scope of this book. WSDL and SOAP are complex specifications (despite the latter's name); using them is also inevitably somewhat complex, particularly with all the options that typical J2EE web service tools offer. On the other hand, .NET's web service support has shown that exposing remote services does not have to be so hard.

Many J2EE servers already had support for exposing web services, via proprietary WSDL/SOAP tools (like BEA's WebLogic) or integrated third-party solutions (like **Apache Axis** in IBM's WebSphere). With the advent of J2EE 1.4, they now need to support both their own (legacy) configuration model plus the JSR-109 deployment model, which does not particularly simplify finding a way through the J2EE Web Service deployment jungle.

In this part of the chapter, we will focus on JAX-RPC looking at both its *service client API* and **service endpoint model**. We will *not* discuss the JSR-109 deployment model and other J2EE 1.4 specifics.

Accessing Web Services

Each WSDL-based web service consists of a **service** that defines one or more **ports**. Each port corresponds to a **service endpoint** on a server; multiple endpoints can be gathered into a single WSDL-defined Web Service. This is notably different from a classic remote service, like a remote EJB, where no such separation exists. Each web service port corresponds to a Java service interface. In that respect, the port level is comparable to classic remote service interfaces.

> *JAX-RPC terminology can be a bit confusing but is unfortunately dictated by WSDL: A service is a collection of ports, as defined in a single WSDL document; a "port" corresponds to a service endpoint, implementing a specific service interface. Commonly, a remote service is the actual entity that you're calling from client code, matching the "port" concept here. We will explicitly use the terms "JAX-RPC service" and "JAX-RPC port" when referring to the JAX-RPC concepts, to avoid ambiguity.*

According to the specification, JAX-RPC can be used with a **J2EE-based Service Client Programming Model**, looking up service definitions via JNDI, or with a **"J2SE-based"** model, creating local service definitions. This is analogous to the setup of resources like JDBC DataSources, which can also be set up either in a JNDI environment or locally, as we have seen in Chapter 7 ("Introducing the Spring Framework"). Of course, nothing prevents a J2EE web application from setting up local resources: The "J2SE-based" model is often preferable even in a J2EE environment, to keep resource configuration local to the web application.

The central interface in JAX-RPC is `javax.xml.rpc.Service`, which corresponds to a web service specified by WSDL. Each such JAX-RPC service is a factory for proxies that implement the corresponding Java service interface for each JAX-RPC port. A service reference can either be fetched from JNDI or created locally via the `javax.xml.rpc.ServiceFactory`. `ServiceFactory` is an abstract class; a static factory method returns the tool-specific implementation. Alternatively, the implementation class can also be instantiated directly.

A J2EE-based lookup amounts to conventional JNDI usage, as follows:

```
InitialContext initialContext = new InitialContext();
Service myService = (Service) initialContext.lookup("myService");
```

In the J2SE-based model, the `ServiceFactory` is instantiated directly:

```
ServiceFactory serviceFactory = ServiceFactory.newInstance();
Service myService = serviceFactory.createService(
    new URL("http://localhost:8080/service/myService.wsdl"),
    new QName("http://localhost:8080/service/myService", "myService"));
```

As this code shows, JAX-RPC requires several parameters to access a service:

- ❑ The URL of the WSDL document (`http://localhost:8080/service/myService.wsdl` in the preceding example)

- ❑ The namespace URI for the WSDL service (`http://localhost:8080/service/myService` in the example)

- ❑ The name of the WSDL service ("myService" in the example)

JAX-RPC offers three ways of accessing a service endpoint:

- ❑ **Static stubs:** Pregenerated tool-specific lookup classes, with hard-coded `getXxxPort()` methods for retrieving service endpoint proxies, such as `getStockServicePort()`.

- ❑ **Dynamic proxies:** Runtime generation of service endpoint interfaces, via generic `getPort()` methods that return a service endpoint proxy for the given name and interface.

- ❑ **Dynamic Invocation Interface (DII):** Invocations of certain methods of an endpoint by name via the `javax.xml.rpc.Call` interface, similar to Java reflection.

The first option is hardly recommendable for anything other than prototyping, as it involves including generated code in an application despite the lack of a need to do so.

We will focus on the second option in the remainder of this section. It is most similar to classic remote services: a convenient way to access a service via a Java interface, in a configurable manner.

The third option offers the greatest degree of decoupling, by dispensing with a Java service interface altogether and sticking to pure invocation via method names and dynamic arguments.

The **service endpoint interface** used for JAX-RPC ports must correspond to the WSDL-defined port, either by manual matching or through generation of the interface from the WSDL definition. A JAX-RPC endpoint interface must conform to the basic RMI rules (that is, extend the `java.rmi.Remote` marker interface, and throw the checked `java.rmi.RemoteException` on each method). Furthermore, the supported method argument types are restricted: See the JAX-RPC specification (`http://java.sun.com/xml/downloads/jaxrpc.html`) for details.

```
public interface MyPort extends java.rmi.Remote {

    String doSomething(int someParam) throws java.rmi.RemoteException;
}
```

Given a JAX-RPC `Service` reference, a dynamic proxy for a specific JAX-RPC port can be acquired via the `getPort` method. Again, the namespace URI for the WSDL service is needed, plus the name of the port ("myPort") that identifies the port definition in the WSDL file. The returned proxy will be generated at runtime: No pre-generation via extra deployment steps is necessary for this access model.

```
MyPort port = (MyPort) myService.getPort(
    new QName("http://localhost:8080/service/myService", "myPort"),
    MyPort.class);
```

Setup within a Spring Context

Client code can either explicitly work with a *JAX-RPC service* or with the *service endpoint interface* of a specific port. The former is appropriate when multiple ports are needed in the same client objects, or for access via the Dynamic Invocation Interface. The latter is preferable when clients want to access a specific endpoint via a Java service interface (the commonest requirement), avoiding confronting them with JAX-RPC concepts.

Exposing a JAX-RPC Service

In a Spring bean factory (or application context), a reference to a JAX-RPC service can either be looked up with a generic **JndiObjectFactoryBean** or created with a **LocalJaxRpcServiceFactoryBean**. Both will expose the corresponding `javax.xml.rpc.Service` reference.

Looking up a JAX-RPC `Service` from JNDI:

```
<bean id="myServiceProxy"
    class="org.springframework.jndi.JndiObjectFactoryBean">
  <property name="jndiName">
    <value>myservice</value>
  </property>
</bean>
```

Locally creating a JAX-RPC `Service`:

```
<bean id="myServiceProxy"
    class="org.springframework.remoting.jaxrpc.LocalJaxRpcServiceFactoryBean">
  <property name="wsdlDocumentUrl">
    <value>http://localhost:8080/service/myService.wsdl</value>
  </property>
  <property name="namespaceUri">
    <value>http://localhost:8080/service/myService</value>
  </property>
  <property name="serviceName">
    <value>myService</value>
  </property>
</bean>
```

Either of those can be passed to a business object that needs to access the JAX-RPC `Service` as follows:

```
<bean id="myServiceClient" class="mypackage.MyServiceClient">
  <property name="service">
    <ref bean="myServiceProxy"/>
  </property>
</bean>
```

The MyServiceClient class simply needs to expose a bean property of type `javax.xml.rpc.Service`, not caring where the `Service` comes from:

```
public class MyServiceClient {

    private javax.xml.rpc.Service service;
```

```
  public void setService(javax.xml.rpc.Service service) {
    this.service = service;
  }

public void myBusinessMethod() {
  try {
    Call myDynamicCall = this.service.createCall(...);
    ...
  }
  catch (RemoteException ex) {
    ...
  }
}
}
```

Exposing a Service Endpoint

When a specific JAX-RPC port is needed, it is preferable to look up a port proxy and expose the corresponding service endpoint interface. In a Spring context, this can be achieved with **JaxRpcPortProxyFactoryBean**. It can either define the underlying JAX-RPC `Service` via its local properties, or use an existing `Service` reference via the "jaxRpcService" property. The exposed proxy will implement the service endpoint interface.

```
<bean id="myPortProxy"
    class="org.springframework.remoting.jaxrpc.JaxRpcPortProxyFactoryBean">
  <property name="wsdlDocumentUrl">
    <value>http://localhost:8080/service/myService.wsdl</value>
  </property>
  <property name="namespaceUri">
    <value>http://localhost:8080/service/myService</value>
  </property>
  <property name="serviceName">
    <value>myService</value>
  </property>
  <property name="portName">
    <value>myPort</value>
  </property>
  <property name="serviceInterface">
    <value>mypackage.MyPort</value>
  </property>
</bean>
```

The port proxy can then be passed to a business object that needs to access the corresponding service endpoint, working with the actual service interface:

```
<bean id="myServiceClient" class="mypackage.MyServiceClient">
  <property name="port">
    <ref bean="myPortProxy"/>
  </property>
</bean>
```

In this case, the MyServiceClient class simply needs to expose a bean property of type "mypackage.MyPort", which is the service endpoint interface. The client object is aware of RMI and needs to deal with RemoteException, but it is *not* aware of JAX-RPC.

```
public class MyServiceClient {

  private MyPort service;

  public void setService(MyPort service) {
    this.service = service;
  }

  public void myBusinessMethod() {
    try {
      this.service.doSomething(...);
      ...
    }
    catch (RemoteException ex) {
      ...
    }
  }
}
```

Business Interfaces for Service Endpoints

Alternatively, a proxy for a JAX-RPC port can be exposed as **non-RMI business interface**, similar to Spring's business interface support for conventional RMI. Clients can then expose a dependency for the plain business interface: JaxRpcPortProxyFactoryBean can delegate invocations on this non-RMI interface to the corresponding methods of the underlying JAX-RPC proxy, using reflection. The RMI service interface is still used with the JAX-RPC runtime infrastructure underneath.

```
<bean id="myPortProxy"
    class="org.springframework.remoting.jaxrpc.JaxRpcPortProxyFactoryBean">
  ...
  <property name="portName">
    <value>myPort</value>
  </property>
  <property name="portInterface">
    <value>mypackage.MyPort</value>
  </property>
  <property name="serviceInterface">
    <value>mypackage.MyBusinessInterface</value>
  </property>
</bean>
```

The exposed proxy will implement the specified business interface "mypackage.MyBusinessInterface", while the JAX-RPC runtime will work with the RMI service interface "mypackage.MyPort". Clients will just use the generic business interface. Like RmiProxyFactoryBean, JaxRpcPortProxyFactoryBean will automatically throw Spring's unchecked org.springframework.remoting.RemoteAccess Exception on remote invocation failure when working with a non-RMI business interface.

```
public interface MyPort extends java.rmi.Remote {


  String doSomething(int someParam) throws java.rmi.RemoteException;
}
```

The methods in the business interface do *not* throw `RemoteException`:

```
public interface MyBusinessInterface {


    String doSomething(int someParam);
}
```

The corresponding MyServiceClient class needs to expose a bean property of type "mypackage .MyBusinessInterface", which is the *business interface* rather than the service endpoint interface. The client object is aware of neither RMI nor of JAX-RPC.

```
public class MyServiceClient {

    private MyBusinessInterface service;

    public void setService(MyBusinessInterface service) {
        this.service = service;
    }

    public void myBusinessMethod() {
        this.service.doSomething(...);
        ...
    }
}
```

These interface options affect only the *client side* of the web service. The service endpoint might be implemented with a non-Java technology; the only relevant contract is the WSDL definition. Of course, if the service is implemented in Java, it can and should implement the JAX-RPC endpoint interface, and also the corresponding business interface if used (analogous to a conventional RMI service, as shown in the first part of this chapter). This way, the service implementation is checked against both interfaces to guarantee consistency and minimize maintenance overhead.

> **Accessing WSDL-defined web services via JAX-RPC is straightforward; the rather complex service reference model is imposed by WSDL itself, rather than the JAX-RPC API. Service endpoint interfaces must implement the RMI marker interface and throw RemoteException on each service method. As an alternative, Spring offers a mechanism to use non-RMI business interfaces for JAX-RPC service endpoints.**
>
> **Method argument types are restricted owing to JAX-RPC and WSDL and SOAP: This is a severe disadvantage compared to conventional RMI that can leverage standard Java serialization. See the JAX-RPC specification for details.**

Servlet and EJB Endpoints

The JAX-RPC specification describes two kinds of service endpoint implementations: a **Servlet endpoint** model, defined by JAX-RPC itself, and an **EJB endpoint** model, defined by the EJB 2.1 specification. Both have in common that a service endpoint class needs to implement the corresponding JAX-RPC service endpoint interface, as used by JAX-RPC Web Service clients. In the Servlet case, a tool-specific dispatcher servlet will manage separate *endpoint classes*, while a Stateless Session Bean with a web service Client View implements the endpoint interface *itself* in the EJB case.

Endpoint classes can optionally implement the `javax.xml.rpc.server.ServiceLifecycle` interface, providing "init" and "destroy" callbacks.

```
public interface ServiceLifecycle {

  void init(Object context) throws ServiceException;

  void destroy();
}
```

The initialization method receives a "context" object: in the Servlet case, an implementation of the `javax.xml.rpc.server.ServletEndpointContext` interface, providing access to the `ServletContext`, the `HttpSession`, and request-related information:

```
public interface ServletEndpointContext {

  MessageContext getMessageContext();

  Principal getUserPrincipal();

  HttpSession getHttpSession();

  ServletContext getServletContext();
}
```

A JAX-RPC Servlet endpoint can maintain a **session**, via the `HttpSession` available from the `ServletEndpointContext`. The session can be used as with a normal servlet, but the endpoint class does not have control over session creation, which is specified by the caller, via the `"javax.xml.rpc.session.maintain"` property.

> **As with any remoting mechanism, it is preferable to keep remote communication stateless: Use a JAX-RPC session only if there is a real need to.**

JSR-109 defines a quite complex **deployment model** for J2EE web services, to be implemented by J2EE 1.4 servers. See JSR-109 or supporting documentation for details, as a discussion of it is outside the scope of this book. The main goal is to allow for portability in the sense that a J2EE application will leverage the web service runtime infrastructure of the particular server that it gets deployed on. This means that web service infrastructure and J2EE server can be chosen only in fixed combination.

A plain JAX-RPC implementation is allowed to use a proprietary and potentially simpler deployment model, as **Apache Axis** does with its JWS and WSDD mechanisms. A different kind of portability is possible here: A specific web service tool like Axis can be embedded into a web application that can be deployed on any J2EE server.

> Standard J2EE web service deployment leverages the J2EE server's web service infrastructure. In contrast, embedding a standalone JAX-RPC implementation in a web application allows the use of a specific web service tool independent of the J2EE server choice (for example, Axis on Resin)—potentially enhancing portability between application servers.

Exporting Existing Services

Service endpoint classes must be self-contained. In the Servlet case, the tool-specific dispatcher servlet will instantiate the endpoint class and manage its lifecycle. In case of an EJB endpoint, the usual rules of EJB apply, including the drawbacks discussed in the EJB remoting section earlier this chapter. JAX-RPC does not provide any means to directly expose an *existing* plain Java business service as a web service: for example, a service that is prewired with POJO business objects that it delegates to. Again, the specification committee seems to have assumed that all dedicated business logic will be implemented in EJBs.

Of course, a Servlet endpoint class could **wrap an existing business service**, keeping an own instance of it as member variable. However, it might be necessary to access a *preconfigured* instance of the business service; and if directly exposing the business service, the endpoint class can be considered unnecessary glue code. Unfortunately, neither the JSR-109 deployment model nor any of the major standalone web service tools address this need for integration with existing POJO architectures.

Besides access to JNDI resources, the **ServletContext reference in the ServletEndpointContext** is the only integration point with existing business objects and resources, in case of a JAX-RPC Servlet endpoint. If integrating with a Spring-managed business tier, the root `WebApplicationContext` can be fetched from the `ServletContext` via Spring's `WebApplicationContextUtils` helper class. This allows for access to any Spring-managed business object, similar to how a Spring middle tier can be accessed from within a Struts or WebWork action.

Spring provides the `org.springframework.remoting.jaxrpc.ServletEndpointSupport` class as convenience base class for such a scenario, offering access to the root web application context via the `getWebApplicationContext()` method. It internally implements `ServiceLifecycle` to get access to the `ServletContext` via the `ServletEndpointContext`.

```
public class MyServiceEndpoint extends ServletEndpointSupport
    implements MyPort, MyBusinessInterface {

  public String doSomething(int someParam) {
    MyBusinessService myBusinessService =
        (MyBean) getWebApplicationContext().getBean("myBusinessService");
    ...
  }
}
```

The endpoint class still needs to be implemented as a gluing wrapper, but at least there is a straightforward way to access preconfigured business services. This is as good as it gets with current tools: Direct exposure via exporters as with conventional RMI is not yet possible.

> Exporting JAX-RPC service endpoints is far from ideal. The EJB endpoint model is suitable only for existing EJB middle tiers. The Servlet endpoint model is lightweight but does not allow for direct integration with existing business services implemented as plain Java objects.
>
> Portable deployment is still a challenge. Either use J2EE 1.4's complex deployment model as specified by JSR-109, or leverage the proprietary but usually simpler mechanism of your web service tool. Ease of use will depend on the chosen tool.
>
> In the next section, we will see how simple exporting services via alternative HTTP-based protocols can be.

Lightweight Remoting: Hessian and Burlap

An RMI environment can be cumbersome to set up, and uses arbitrary network ports that are not firewall-friendly. WSDL/SOAP-based web services are hard to export in a portable fashion, and waste bandwidth because of their verbose protocol. **Lightweight HTTP-based remoting protocols** address both these issues: They can be run on top of any standard Servlet container, and will work across any firewall.

While there has been much talk about HTTP-based **web services**, it has focused on WSDL and SOAP with the primary focus on language independence. We have already seen that J2EE 1.4 incorporates support for WSDL/SOAP-based web services via JAX-RPC. SOAP mania seems to have suppressed work on alternative wire protocols, another example of the darker side of standardization when it suppresses innovation. There is much scope for slim, focused protocols as alternative to SOAP's one-size-fits-all complexity.

Fortunately, there has been some interesting work in this area. Caucho, the company behind the popular J2EE web application server **Resin**, has developed two slim protocols and offers them under an open source license: **Hessian**, a binary protocol (www.caucho.com/hessian/), and **Burlap**, an XML-based one (www.caucho.com/burlap/). Resin Enterprise supports both as EJB wire protocols, but they are usable on their own in any Servlet container. Hessian and Burlap have been available since early 2002, and are now mature.

Neither of these protocols is tied to Java. They use their own means of serialization, with generic support for collections. However, their main target is still Java-to-Java communication, and this is a good thing, as they can be considered *the simplest protocols that might possibly work* for rich Java remoting. They are simpler to set up than RMI, and much slimmer than SOAP, addressing a common need in between.

The sole advantage of Burlap over Hessian is that it is human-readable and XML-parsable. Thus, it is easy to debug via watching the HTTP request/response contents; and writing non-Java parsers for it might be easier for languages that offer XML parsers. For **Java-to-Java communication**, Hessian will be the preferred choice, as it is slimmer and hence more efficient. With proper infrastructure, switching between the two protocols can be as simple as changing configuration on both endpoints.

The protocols themselves do not impose any special requirements on service interfaces, service clients, or service implementations. They offer the same benefits as an RMI invoker in that they allow for exporting an existing local service as remote service, provided that the method arguments are serializable, and that the granularity of the interface is appropriate for the particular remoting needs.

Effectively, the same service interface plus implementation can be used for local usage, an RMI invoker, Hessian, or Burlap. All you need is a plain Java business interface and a plain Java implementation class, without any syntactical restrictions imposed by potential remoting.

```
public interface MyService {


   String doSomething(int someParam);
}
```

The implementation class is a plain old Java object:

```
public class MyServiceImpl implements MyService {

   String doSomething(int someParam) {
      return "did something: " + someParam;
   }
}
```

A particular advantage of HTTP-based services is that they can easily leverage the web server's standard means for authorization, encryption, and compression: requiring HTTP basic authentication for certain resources, using SSL transport, applying GZIP compression to HTTP responses, and so on. Hessian and Burlap support all of these, which makes them compelling choices even for advanced remoting requirements.

> **Hessian and Burlap (the "Caucho twins") are powerful and flexible HTTP-based remoting protocols that do not impose any restrictions on service interfaces or service implementations. In combination with standard web containers, they are appropriate for a wide range of stateless remoting needs, especially Java-to-Java communication. They are particularly well suited for communication with external clients over the Internet, but also lend themselves for selective internal distribution within a server system.**

Accessing and Exporting Hessian and Burlap Services

A Hessian or Burlap service can be accessed via the com.caucho.hessian.client.HessianProxy Factory and com.caucho.burlap.client.BurlapProxyFactory classes, respectively. Those factories will return proxies that implement the given service interface. In case of communication failure, an unchecked HessianRuntimeException or BurlapRuntimeException, respectively, will be thrown, instead of plain RMI's checked RemoteException. Security credentials can be set via the setUser and setPassword methods, if necessary. Client-side access looks as follows:

```
HessianProxyFactory proxyFactory = new HessianProxyFactory();
MyService service = (MyService) proxyFactory.create(MyService.class,
    "http://localhost:8080/myservice");
```

The standard way of exposing Hessian/Burlap services is via corresponding servlets, `com.caucho.hessian.server.HessianServlet` and `BurlapServlet`, mapped in `web.xml`. While service implementations can extend those servlets, it is preferable to implement services independently, and define servlet mappings with given service classes. That way, a service implementation can be combined with either Hessian or Burlap, reused in other environments, and easily tested on its own. An example of Caucho servlet usage is as follows:

```
<servlet>
  <servlet-name>myservice</servlet-name>
  <servlet-class>com.caucho.hessian.server.HessianServlet</servlet-class>
  <load-on-startup>1</load-on-startup>
  <init-param>
    <param-name>service-class</param-name>
    <param-value>myservice.MyServiceImpl</param-value>
  </init-param>
</servlet>

<servlet-mapping>
  <servlet-name>myservice</servlet-name>
  <url-pattern>/myservice</url-pattern>
</servlet-mapping>
```

Services exported via those standard servlets must be **self-contained**: They are assumed to be ready after instantiation. JNDI resources can be accessed from within service implementations, but there are no other means for accessing collaborating objects or resources. We will see in a moment how exporting from within a Spring application context addresses such needs.

Hessian and Burlap do *not* support sessions, but are inherently stateless. In contrast to JAX-RPC, there is not even the option to maintain a session between remote invocations. However, this is not a disadvantage in most scenarios, as stateless remote communication should always be preferred anyway.

Setup within a Spring Context

In a Spring bean factory or application context, a proxy for a Hessian or Burlap service can be defined with a `HessianProxyFactoryBean` or `BurlapProxyFactoryBean`. These factory beans will expose a wrapped version of the looked-up Hessian/Burlap proxy for bean references, throwing Spring's generic `RemoteAccessException` instead of `HessianRuntimeException` or `BurlapRuntimeException` on remote invocation failure, thus decoupling callers completely from the specific remoting protocol.

```
<bean id="myServiceProxy"
    class="org.springframework.remoting.caucho.HessianProxyFactoryBean">
  <property name="serviceInterface">
    <value>mypackage.MyService</value>
  </property>
  <property name="serviceUrl">
    <value>http://localhost:8080/myservice</value>
  </property>
</bean>
```

Security credentials can be optionally set via the "username" and "password" properties.

The rationale is to make all kinds of remote service proxies behave consistently from the point of view of client objects, including error handling and authorization. Switching among a Hessian proxy, a Burlap proxy, and a transparent RMI proxy should merely be a matter of configuration: that is, replacing the proxy bean definition. This is particularly straightforward in case of the Caucho protocols, as they offer the exact same power. The client object will simply expose a dependency of type "mypackage.MyService", without being tied to any specific remoting protocol—in fact, not even being aware of remoting at all

As in other important areas such as data access and transaction management, Spring provides a layer of abstraction that permits pluggable underlying implementations, in a much simpler way than J2EE standard APIs but without ruling out the option of the "standard" J2EE solution.

An existing bean can be exposed with a `HessianServiceExporter` or `BurlapServiceExporter` definition, provided that the bean interface conforms to the basic requirements of remote-capable method signatures. The same "myServiceImpl" bean could be used locally too, or exported under multiple protocols. A major advantage of this way of exporting is that *pre-configured* service beans can be used: They can be wired up with collaborating beans and resources using all of Spring's IoC and AOP functionality.

```
<bean id="myService" class="mypackage.MyServiceImpl"/>
<bean name="/myservice"
    class="org.springframework.remoting.caucho.HessianServiceExporter">
  <property name="service">
    <ref bean="myService"/>
  </property>
</bean>
```

These exporters are implemented as Controllers for Spring's web MVC: for example, mapped in a Spring `DispatcherServlet` via a name that is recognized by `BeanNameUrlHandlerMapping`. (A more sophisticated mapping strategy can be used if necessary, possibly with custom interceptors and so on.) In an application with no web interface or which uses a web framework other than Spring MVC, a DispatcherServlet can be added to handle only such HTTP-based remote service exporters, without interfering with the rest of the web application.

See Chapter 13 ("Web Tier Design") for a discussion of Spring's web MVC, in particular the mapping options available with Spring's DispatcherServlet. Our sample application, as described in Chapter 16, illustrates the integration of Hessian and Burlap into an existing web application.

> **Accessing a Hessian or Burlap service is no harder than accessing any HTTP resource. There is no registry involved as with RMI; the mapping occurs via HTTP request paths. A single path identifies a specific service; no namespaces and definition names are required, unlike with WSDL.**
>
> **Exporting via the standard HessianServlet or BurlapServlet is straightforward but requires self-contained service implementations. A better option, if using Spring, is exporting from within a Spring DispatcherServlet. This allows for fully pre-configured service instances that can leverage all of Spring's configuration power.**

Summary

A variety of powerful remoting solutions are available for the J2EE platform. While most of them make accessing remote services fairly easy, they differ widely in how services are implemented and exported. The all-or-nothing deployment model of EJB is at one end of the spectrum; at the other end, RMI and the Caucho protocols permit seamless integration into existing environments.

While EJB offers some unique capabilities, such as relatively simple propagation of a transaction context (in servers supporting this feature) and the ability to maintain a transaction over several calls to the same remote Stateful Session Bean, it's usually best to design applications so that they don't require such features. Transactions kept open during remote invocations are potentially dangerous.

RMI and particularly Hessian and Burlap are particularly lightweight solutions in that they not only offer slim wire protocols but also straightforward export of existing business services that are implemented as plain Java objects. EJB fails to address such needs, while JAX-RPC involves tool-specific deployment procedures for service endpoints.

WSDL-based web services have been heavily hyped since 2001, and it is easy to see the appeal in the platform-independent remoting they offer. However, they are not a convincing choice for *Java-to-Java* remoting, because of their restrictions in terms of method arguments and their complex deployment. Plain old RMI solutions or modern HTTP-based remoting protocols like Hessian and Burlap are significantly better suited for such scenarios; fashion should not obscure the technical arguments.

EJB remains a good option for RMI-based remoting. However, it's by no means the *only* option.

In terms of service interface and client programming model, all of the official remoting standards—RMI, EJB, JAX-RPC—use the original RMI model: a marker interface and checked `RemoteException` declared on each method on the remote interface. As we have seen, there are various solutions to proxy such services with plain non-RMI business interfaces, using an unchecked exception for remote invocation failure.

The Spring Framework offers integrated support for remoting within a lightweight architecture. This includes a generic unchecked `RemoteAccessException`, and various proxy factories and exporters that provide consistent behavior for client objects, with a simple programming model and minimal dependence on the underlying remoting infrastructure in typical applications. RMI, EJB, JAX-RPC, and Hessian/Burlap are all supported out of the box.

Our sample application **JPetStore** illustrates the use of Spring with Hessian/Burlap, RMI, and JAX-RPC via Apache Axis for remote service exposure. It also provides a sample remote service client. Refer to Chapter 16 for in-depth discussion.

12

Replacing Other EJB Services

So far we've focused primarily on the EJB container model and EJB declarative transaction management. We've seen how IoC and AOP can provide a superior replacement for these in many cases.

As the EJB solution for persistence (entity beans) is inferior to alternatives such as Hibernate and JDO, we would not choose to use EJB for its persistence capabilities.

We've also considered EJB remoting. *If* you want a distributed architecture—and that's a big if— EJB is a pretty good technology for managing your distributed objects. Most of the time, however, co-locating business objects with their callers is a better architectural choice.

There remain other EJB services that we need to consider. Let's look at how we can replace the most important of these in typical applications.

Besides CMT, the EJB services most commonly cited as justifying use of EJB are:

❑ **Thread management.** The EJB model aims to allow developers to code EJBs without concern as to concurrency. We'll examine whether this goal is as important as is often supposed, whether EJB achieves it, and look at alternatives that achieve the same ends.

❑ **SLSB instance pooling.** Related to thread management: the ability of the EJB container to maintain a pool of SLSB instances and to efficiently delegate incoming requests to a pooled instance.

❑ **Declarative role-based security,** built on the standard J2EE security infrastructure.

In this chapter, we'll discuss these important services.

We'll focus on replacing the thread management offered by stateless session beans (SLSBs): by common consent, the most useful kind of EJB.

Thread Management

EJB, like Microsoft's MTS before it, is designed to enable developers to write business objects as though they are single threaded. Thus a SLSB instance can execute only one method at a time. Each instance is dedicated to one caller, and hence to one thread, at all times (unless it is idle). The EJB container maintains a pool of SLSB instances to ensure that this does not lock out other clients.

The "single-threaded" approach of EJB seems to be one of the principal attractions of EJB for application developers. This is hardly surprising, since it has been heavily promoted as a key value proposition of EJB. Many developers fear that without EJB and its threading magic, they will end up wrestling with nightmarish complexity of synchronization, reinventing a wheel that BEA and IBM have already polished.

In fact, the EJB solution is not so magical, and the problem often doesn't exist. When it *does* exist, there are valid alternative solutions.

Threading Myths

There are several questionable assumptions behind the EJB threading model:

❏ That typical stateless service objects are prone to concurrency issues, and hence that a single shared instance is *never* a good option.

❏ That if a stateless service object does face concurrency issues, creating a new instance for each client is *always* too expensive, because of the cost of memory allocation and the consequent garbage collection.

❏ That the EJB component model (rather than other application-server services such as database connection pooling) must protect limited middle tier resources.

❏ That Java's threading model is too complex for J2EE developers to deal with themselves *under any circumstances.*

❏ That it's really as easy to solve concurrency issues, if they do arise, as the EJB specification implies.

❏ That the tradeoffs inherent in the EJB threading model are always worth the debatable benefit of single-threading *for all business objects.*

Note the phrases that I've italicized. These assumptions make sense in some cases, but EJB forces us into a threading model based on them *in all cases*: It's impossible to approach different business objects differently.

Many of these assumptions looked reasonable in 1998, when the EJB specification first appeared. For example, the cost of creating new objects was extremely high in Java 1.1 JVMs. However, huge advances in JVM technology and accumulated practical experience with EJB applications suggest that many of them are shaky today.

Let's examine the assumptions, in this section and when we discuss pooling later in this chapter.

Do Stateless Service Objects Need to Be Single Threaded?

A stateless service object is an odd beast. By definition, it can't hold state on behalf of individual clients. However, it *can* hold internal state. For example, it can maintain a cache of resources to avoided repeated lookups as it services incoming requests.

This means that it's similar to a servlet or an "action" or "controller" in an MVC web framework such as Struts or Spring that uses a single, shared instance to serve concurrent requests. This begs a question: If there's no particular difficulty in writing such web tier classes that can serve multiple concurrent requests, why is the same approach inappropriate for any business object? (Remember that EJB doesn't give us the choice of using a shared instance approach for *any* business object: It's a single thread model or nothing.)

In fact, the servlet specification offers a "single thread model": a model in which a servlet instance can serve only one thread at a time. Servlet engines are free to optimize the single thread model by maintaining an instance pool. Nevertheless this model was widely criticized, and was deprecated in the Servlet 2.4 specification. (I'll say more about that criticism later.) If such a model isn't considered good for servlets, why is it considered *essential* in the EJB world? Servlets and MVC controllers typically avoid any complex concurrency problems because they don't hold read-write state. In the rarer cases that do have some read-write state, developers usually find it easy enough to use Java synchronization to protect against concurrency problems. The "single thread model" was seen to be a largely unnecessary and naïve partial solution.

> The real concurrency issues faced by servlets concern user session state: for example, double form submission or concurrent access from two browser windows. This is a different problem, and one to which EJB has no answer either: Stateful session beans provide no protection against concurrent access, which is considered a programming error and is typically prevented by web tier code.

In my experience, most SLSBs, like servlets, do not face real concurrency issues. Typically, they don't maintain read-write instance variables. As no state can be held on behalf of clients, read-write state isn't usually of much use; behavior is determined by read-only shared state and the method arguments provided by each client. SLSBs *do* work with resources such as JDBC `DataSources`, but those are threadsafe and don't require any protection. A single, shared, threadsafe object can cache a reference to a `DataSource` and invoke it without concern for synchronization.

Consider a "classic" J2EE application: the Oracle J2EE Virtual Shopping Mall, which we discuss in Chapter 3. *None* of its SLSBs has any instance variables, read-write or otherwise. (There are some stateful session beans, but these are a separate type of object.) All the SLSB business objects are completely threadsafe, their behavior determined by their arguments and collaborators, and no purpose is served by limiting them to serving a single thread of execution. However, they all share a singleton `ServiceLocator` object. EJB concurrency support can't help with this object, which uses a `HashTable` rather than a `HashMap`, probably to ensure synchronization. (It makes sense to have a single cache for EJB homes, as home objects are threadsafe and there's no reason to limit a home to use by a single instance in a pool, or even by a single EJB deployment.) Thus EJB concurrency support contributes nothing to this application, which ends up relying on standard Java synchronization. Technically, such use of synchronization violates the EJB specification, but a complete ban on synchronization is just not realistic, as experience implementing EJB applications quickly shows.

> Most stateless service objects don't need to use a single thread model; they simply don't run into complex concurrency issues.
>
> Thus a middleware platform should not rule out implementing a service object as a shared, threadsafe single object, as EJB does. In fact, it is the best threading model for most service objects.

The Cost of Instance Creation

The assumption that the creation of service objects must be avoided at all costs, and hence that pooling is required, is questionable in model JVMs. We'll discuss this in our discussion of pooling below.

Resource Management

As we've seen in previous chapters, the EJB component model doesn't usually need to protect limited middle tier resources such as database connections. In most cases, the application server as a whole, rather than the EJB container, protects such resources, as in the case of container-managed DataSources obtained from JNDI.

Should the Solution Totally Reject the Java Threading Model?

Another objection to the EJB threading model is the fact that Java provides good *language-level* support for writing multi-threaded code. While correct multi-threaded code is often conceptually complex in any language, it's easy to *implement* in Java. Concurrent programming in Java is far from the nightmare of writing multithreaded C/C++ code in Unix or Windows environments, for example. Thus it's questionable why a middleware component model should prevent *any* attempt by developers to use this core Java capability, as EJB does. Once again, as I noted early in this book, "EJB is less than Java." Part of the price of the EJB "standard" is the loss of many worthwhile features of the much more widely understood and elegant language behind it.

EJB seems partly based on the assumption that middleware developers are semi-competent, needing protection even from the scarier parts of the Java language. This is flawed. Firstly, in my experience, trying to make developers' decisions for them upfront is usually a mistake: A developer facing actual requirements is best placed to make many decisions. And most developers are competent: those who aren't are in the wrong line of work and are going to cause problems sooner or later. Secondly, middleware concepts are complex, and it's impossible to hide that complexity completely and dangerous to think that it is achievable. Finally, it's a contradiction to assume that developers are dumb and expect them to understand and use something as complex as EJB, which requires a small phone book to describe it.

I'm not arguing that middleware solutions should be complex; this book is about reducing complexity. I'm warning against the dangers of believing that it's always right to impose a single solution that deprives the developer of control or of the ability to use the language itself where it can solve the same problem.

Does the EJB Threading Model Provide a Complete Concurrency Solution?

Is the EJB threading model sufficient? That depends on the resources that an SLSB uses. While the EJB concurrency model protects the internal state of a stateless service object itself against multiple threads, it does not protect any shared resources that it may use. Service objects often need to work with shared resources. We've seen this with the Virtual Shopping Mall, which, reasonably enough, shares a Service Locator cache between all EJB instances on a server, whether in the same or even different pools.

As critics of the old servlet "single thread model" pointed out, protecting internal state isn't enough. Here's what noted servlet expert Jason Hunter has to say about the servlet single thread model in O'Reilly's *Java Enterprise Best Practices* (2002):

> This interface was intended to make life easier for programmers concerned about thread safety, but the simple fact is that SingleThreadModel does not help. It's an admitted mistake in the Servlet API. It's about as useful as a dud firecracker on the Fourth of July.
>
> Here's how the interface works: Any servlet implementing SingleThreadModel receives a special lifecycle within the server. Instead of allocating one servlet instance to handle multiple requests (with multiple threads operating on the servlet simultaneously) the server allocates a pool of instances (with at most one thread operating on any servlet at a time). From the outside this looks good, but there's actually no benefit.
>
> Imagine a servlet needing access to a unique resource, such as a transactional database connection. [Note that a DataSource is threadsafe, unlike a connection.—RJ] That servlet needs to synchronize against the resource regardless of the servlet's own thread model. There's no difference if there are two threads on the same servlet instance or two threads on different servlet instances; the problem is two threads trying to use the connection, and that's only solved with careful synchronization.
>
> Imagine instead there are multiple copies of the resources available but access to any particular one needs to be synchronized. It's the same situation. The best approach is not to use SingleThreadModel but to manage the resources with a pool that all servlets share. For example, with database connections it's common to have connection pools. You could instead use SingleThreadModel and arrange for each servlet instance to hold its own copy of the resource, but that's a poor use of resources. A server with hundreds of servlets might require thousands of resource instances.

These objections also apply to stateless session-bean pooling, although, strangely, they're seldom expressed with the same vigor.

Thus the EJB model does not completely free developers from concern about threading. This goal, however attractive, is not realistic. The problem doesn't lie with the EJB implementation of pooling, but in the fact that there's no way to provide a 100% solution to thread management without developer understanding and effort.

The Tradeoffs in the EJB Solution

The EJB single thread model isn't free: It has undesirable as well as desirable implications for programming model.

The EJB Threading Model

Let's look at the EJB threading model in a little more detail.

Locking

The EJB threading model is relatively simplistic. A bean instance is locked if there's a thread of execution in it. This means that the entire bean instance is locked if code is executing any method. This is a rather heavy-handed way of protecting against potential corruption from concurrent threads. What if only one instance variable, which may rarely be accessed, requires protection from concurrency? What if most of the methods are threadsafe and hence require no locking at all, as in the Virtual Shopping Mall? EJB offers a coarse-grained solution that allows no control other than the maximum number of beans in the instance pool, which is set at deploy time. There's no runtime control over pool size.

Because EJBs provide efficient pooling, these aren't really concerns from a performance perspective. While some instances are locked on behalf of a particular client, other instances in the pool for that EJB deployment will remain free to serve incoming requests. EJB containers' instance pools seem to be efficient enough that—assuming that pool size is set correctly—contention for an instance isn't likely to be noticeable to clients. However, as we've seen, there are some negatives about maintaining an unpredictable number of instances of each bean.

Thread Pooling

Another important part of the EJB threading model is that an EJB container can maintain a **thread pool** (as opposed to a pool of SLSB *instances*). Thread pooling is important to application-server design, as without it applications are prone to denial-of-service attacks or overloading under heavy legitimate use. Unless the number of threads that can execute in parallel is limited, the JVM can become overloaded, with catastrophic results. However, thread pooling must be provided *on entry to a JVM*. Unless a business object such as a remote EJB is serving as an endpoint to remote requests, there is no value in EJB thread pooling. For example, in a web application in which local EJBs are invoked by co-located web tier objects, there is no need for thread pooling in the EJB container. Threads are managed by the web container, not by the EJB container. We don't need to solve this problem twice.

> **EJB container thread pooling is unnecessary for co-located web applications or web services architectures using tools such as Axis or GLUE in which the endpoints are exposed by the web container. It's necessary only when remote EJBs serve as publicly accessible end points.**

Resource Pooling

Like thread pooling, **resource pooling** is delivered by the application server, and is part of J2EE, rather than the EJB container.

> **It's such an important point that it deserves reiterating: The application server, not the EJB container, must provide pooling for resources such as JDBC DataSources. Such resources are typically threadsafe.**

EJB Instance Pooling

Pooling instances of service objects is essentially an implementation strategy used to provide a single-threaded programming model to developers.

When Is Pooling Required?

Conventional wisdom is that pooling SLSB instances is important because it:

❑ Ensures that individual objects do not need to worry about concurrency issues. As we've seen, we can't solve all concurrency problems so easily in reality.

❑ Minimizes memory usage and hence garbage collection by minimizing the number of new objects that need to be created.

❑ Prevents the need to initialize each new object, which may be more expensive than allocating memory for it and garbage collecting it.

Unless we accept the necessity for a single-threaded programming model, pooling is simply unnecessary.

The second of these arguments is somewhat debatable with modern JVM technology, as we'll discuss below.

The third argument is more compelling, but not conclusive. When service objects depend on shared collaborators, as they typically do, we can create new instances efficiently setting a shared reference.

The Case Against Instance Pooling

There are theoretical and practical arguments against instance pooling as the *only* choice for service objects.

❑ It's not always necessary from a memory management point of view.

❑ Maintaining multiple instances can complicate rather than simplify the programming model.

Let's examine these arguments.

Memory Management

If we need a single thread model, why can't we simply create a new instance of the service object for each request?

The assumption that creating short-lived objects is hugely expensive—central to the concept of EJB instance pooling—is now highly debatable. This assumption is based more on the likely cost of garbage collection than that of the initial memory allocation, which is not a huge overhead. As I've pointed out before, the EJB specification was conceived in the days of Java 1.1. Today's JVMs are very different. One of the most important parts of the difference, where garbage collection (GC) is concerned, is **generational garbage collection.** Generational garbage collection was introduced in the Java HotSpot VM for Solaris, and is now widely implemented.

Why is generational GC so important? Without it, most JVMs need to scan *all* objects during every GC pass. This could be expensive. Generational GC breaks heap space into **generations**, providing separate memory pools for long-lived (**old**) objects and **new** or young objects. Newly created objects are allocated in a special part of the new generation called **eden**; if they prove to have a long life, they are moved to the old generation. This means that until the old generation fills up, it is not necessary to garbage collect it; GC passes can be restricted to a **minor collection** (collection of the new generation, with surviving objects moved to the old generation), with a **major collection** (GC pass over the entire heap) required less often. If you use a JVM with the `-verbosegc` flag, you can see that major collections are far less frequent than minor collections. As a further optimization, modern JVMs use different algorithms to perform different types of collection for maximum efficiency.

This means that garbage collection is much more efficient overall, especially in server-side applications that run over long periods. Creating short-lived objects, which will never progress to the old generation, is not necessarily a major cost from a garbage-collection perspective.

In cases where a single-threaded programming model is required, this makes the EJB instance pooling model (as opposed to creating a new object to service each client) less compelling than it was back in 1998.

Many recent publications on memory management argue that pooling can adversely affect garbage collection and deliver *worse* performance. The following comments are from the article "Improving Java Application Performance and Scalability by Reducing Garbage Collection Times and Sizing Memory" by Nagendra Nagarajayya and J. Steven Mayer published on java.sun.com (`http://wireless.java.sun.com/midp/articles/garbage/`):

> In general, object pooling is not usually a good idea. It is one of those concepts in programming that is too often used without really weighing the costs against the benefits. Object reuse can introduce errors into an application that are very hard to debug. Furthermore, retrieving an object from the pool and putting it back can be more expensive than creating the object in the first place, especially on a multi-processor machine, because such operations must be synchronized.

> Pooling could violate principles of object-oriented design (OOD). It could also turn out to be expensive to maintain, in exchange for benefits that diminish over time, as garbage collectors become more and more efficient and collection costs keep decreasing. The cost of object creation will also decrease as newer technologies go into VMs.

Of course with EJB the maintainability issues with pooling are largely a non-issue, as the pooling implementation is provided by the EJB container vendor, who can be trusted to ensure that it's robust.

Lack of Shared State

You may be wondering why this matters. Sure, a shared instance model may be theoretically more efficient, and there may no longer be any need to be hung up about avoiding garbage collection. But haven't I just said that EJB instance pools perform well? So what's the problem?

The EJB pooling model in fact causes some problems, which mean that it isn't free, at least not from a programming perspective.

The problem is that we actually *want* shared state in many cases. If we can have a single shared instance of a stateless service object, we probably want to do so.

As usual, EJB offers a one-size-fits-all solution. If we don't need protection from concurrent threads of execution, writing SLSBs forces us to accept irritations that we may not want.

EJB poses two problems in this respect:

❑ Each instance of an SLSB will maintain its own shared internal state. Thus it's hard to get a view of *overall* state.

❑ The EJB specification does not define any initialization point for the all instances of a given EJB, rather than each instance. Although it's possible to use a shared singleton, this poses threading problems as there may be a race condition between individual instances.

For example, what if we want to know how many invocations have been made to a particular business method, or how many orders have been amended in the database? With EJB we can't do this kind of thing. While each EJB can maintain its own threadsafe counters, there is no way to know how many pooled EJB instances we have, and no standard way to query all instances to arrive at a combined result.

Similarly, imagine that we want to cache data that's expensive to retrieve. Each instance in the pool will maintain its own "mini-cache," meaning that invocations to a different instance may result in unnecessary re-retrieval.

Of course in a clustered environment, with incoming requests routed by hardware or the web tier to different nodes, we will have one instance of a per-JVM shared object on each node in any case. But a coherent cache on each node is still likely to be better than multiple caches per node.

Alternatives to EJB Threading and Pooling

Single threading is not usually a worthwhile goal for stateless service objects. However, when it is useful, there are valid alternatives to EJB instance pooling. It's nice to be able to choose among these alternatives on a case-by-case basis, rather than be forced into a particular solution at all times, as EJB does. Let's discuss the alternatives.

Threading Models

Let's survey some alternative threading models for business objects.

Shared Multithreaded Object

The most obvious model is to share a single instance between all threads. This single instance must be threadsafe. This has the following advantages:

❑ **Consistent programming model.** Resources available to the single instance are available to all clients. Thus a cache will be in the same state for all clients hitting that node (if running in a cluster).

❑ **Optimal efficiency.** No matter how efficient a pool is, it can't beat a shared instance unless there's a need for synchronization.

Often, there's no need for synchronization. If there is, however, the shared instance model becomes less attractive, because of the need to write potentially complex code to protect against corruption from concurrent access. However, such code need not always be complex.

Concurrency Support in Application Code

Application developers can also handle concurrency themselves in shared objects, rather than adopt a single thread model. Whether this is a good idea depends on the extent of concurrency problems and the complexity of the code required to handle them correctly.

What Do We Need to Worry About?

As we've noted, we *don't* need to worry about many common scenarios, such as:

❑ Read-only instance variables initialized on startup.

❑ Caches where a race condition will lead only to the same object being retrieved twice. As object references are atomic, this can't produce corruption. The implications of the Java Memory Model mean that the reader thread isn't guaranteed to see the most recently written value, but it won't see a corrupted, meaningless reference (Lea §2.2.7.1).

❑ Threadsafe resources such as JDBC DataSources, which can safely be held in instance variables.

As we've noted, this means that in many service objects, we simply don't have a problem.

We *do*, however, need to worry about some relatively common scenarios, such as:

❑ We always need to see the latest value from such a cache.

❑ We need to assign to a non-atomic type (long or double, unless they are declared `volatile`). Such references *can* be read while in an inconsistent state, with dire consequences.

However, many such scenarios can easily be made threadsafe without critical loss of performance.

Synchronization

If we *do* have a problem, such as a read-write instance variable, the most obvious way to protect a single shared instance against corruption is by using Java language synchronization.

Many developers fear synchronization, both for the complexity correct synchronization can add to the programming model, and for fear of its effect on performance. Complexity and correctness are dangers; performance isn't always a real danger.

It's beyond the scope of this book to attempt a deep discussion of writing threadsafe concurrent code. However, let's quickly consider a few issues, and valuable sources of further information.

Brian Goetz has published some excellent articles on Java threading on IBM's DeveloperWorks site, including an article on synchronization ("Synchronization is not the Enemy": `www-106.ibm.com/developerworks/java/library/j-threads1.html`). Goetz concludes, on the basis of his benchmarks and considerable insight into JVM behavior, that many developers fear synchronization excessively. Specifically:

❑ *Uncontended* synchronization has little performance impact (10% to 200%). ("Uncontended" synchronization means hitting a synchronized piece of code without being forced to wait for a lock.)

❑ Hence it is important to minimize *contention* rather than synchronization.

Techniques for minimizing contention include:

❑ **Synchronizing as little work as possible.** Goetz terms this "get in and out." Synchronize only the code with a potential for corruption, not blocks of code including operations that are actually threadsafe.

❏ **Reducing lock granularity.** For example, if you use three distinct HashMaps to hold different caches in a shared business object, you may be able to improve performance significantly without increasing complexity by synchronizing on the relevant map, rather than the whole class (using this as a lock or synchronizing an entire method) in operations using each map. This technique is called **lock splitting.**

Goetz gives excellent examples of these in a follow-up article (www-106.ibm.com/developerworks/java/library/j-threads2.html). Doug Lea's *Concurrent Programming Java: Design Principles and Patterns* (Sun Press, Second Edition, 2000) is a classic book on concurrency that discusses many valuable techniques and the underlying concepts in detail.

My own benchmarks indicate that the most important determinant of synchronization performance is how long the synchronized code takes to execute. If it takes a long time, you'll get a long queue of threads blocked waiting for locks on that code under load. If it's quick, performance will be enormously better.

Let's consider the idea that we've discussed previously: counting the number of database operations performed by a service. (Of course, if we need this information to survive beyond the life of the service object, it would need to go in the database.) A naïve implementation in the shared object might look like this:

```
private DataSource ds;

private int updates;

public synchronized void doUpdate(... args ...) {
    // Do update based on args using a DataSource instance variable
    // Code omitted
    ++updates;
}
```

As ints are atomic, if we don't care about exact accuracy in reading, we could simply avoid any synchronization. The updates instance variable can't be corrupted, but it can be prone to double updates. For the sake of the example, let's assume we need exact accuracy. We can also declare the int volatile. See Lea's book for a thorough discussion of concurrency options.

This code performs horribly under load. Assuming that the database operation will take an average of 40 milliseconds, it can be made 10 to 15 times faster under load by synchronizing only the increment operation. The DataSource is threadsafe; we don't need to synchronize that. If we synchronize only the increment, the likelihood of contention declines dramatically. So we can rewrite the doUpdate() method like this:

```
public void doUpdate(... args ...) {
    // Do update based on args using a DataSource instance variable
    // Code omitted
    synchronized (this) {
        ++updates;
    }
}
```

The performance improvement is dramatic. It now performs almost the same as if there were no synchronization at all, even under heavy load, confirming that *contention*, not synchronization, is the performance issue.

If other operations in this class needed to be synchronized, we could also apply lock splitting here, by having a lock object to protect the updates field, like this:

```
private int updates;
private Object updatesLock = new Object();

public void doUpdate(... args ...) {
  // Do update based on args using a DataSource instance variable
  // Code omitted
  synchronized (updatesLock) {
        ++updates;
  }
}
```

Now, only other operations on the updates instance variable—which would need to be similarly protected—will be blocked by this operation. We can synchronize operations acting on other state on different locks, minimizing contention without significantly increasing complexity.

> **The cost of synchronization depends on whether the synchronization is contended, and how long it takes to execute the synchronized code. Uncontended synchronization has very little overhead; however, we will assume that business objects are normally satisfying concurrent requests.**
>
> **If we synchronize a lengthy operation such as database access, the result will be many times slower than alternatives such as pooling. Creating a fresh instance each time will provide better performance. If we synchronize only quick-to-execute segments—such as incrementing a counter—the overhead will be very small and contention substantially reduced. We won't see much difference versus other concurrency models.**
>
> **If we find ourselves writing complicated synchronization code, and debating the finer points of Lea's tome, and there's no absolute reason that the same object must be shared between threads, a new instance per request, pooling or a ThreadLocal approach (discussed in a moment) are preferable on maintainability grounds and to minimize the likelihood of bugs. In such cases, we can also consider using a concurrency library to provide a higher level of abstraction.**
>
> **If we need to synchronize just one or two fast operations, synchronization is not the end of the world, and a shared object with such synchronization may be the best option.**
>
> **The real danger with synchronization is often complexity and the risk of bugs, not that synchronization, used correctly, is a performance killer.**

Concurrency Libraries

Of course we may want to abstract concurrency support. EJB is not the only way to attempt to defer the question of thread management to specialists, while getting on with writing application code.

We can also use libraries such as Doug Lea's util.concurrent (`http://gee.cs.oswego.edu/dl/classes/EDU/oswego/cs/dl/util/concurrent/intro.html`). This is a valuable open source package that provides production-quality implementations of many of the concepts discussed in *Lea's Concurrent Programming in Java,* including locks, thread pools, and implementations of core Java collection interfaces with different concurrency characteristics. Util.concurrent can significantly simplify many concurrency issues. It is used internally by JBoss, among other products.

Doug Lea is the spec lead for JSR-166 (Concurrency Utilities), which will offer similar features to util.concurrent as part of Java 1.5. See www.jcp.org/en/jsr/detail?id=166 for further information.

These utilities are particularly valuable when we need shared objects, even if we use a pooling model.

A New, Dedicated Object per Client

So synchronization is not always a menace. But if ensuring thread safety looks like getting really complex, a single thread model becomes attractive.

At the other end of the spectrum from a shared object approach, we can create a new service object instance for use by the lifetime of each client. This will provide a programming model somewhere between a stateless session bean and a stateful session bean. A client can make multiple invocations on the object while it holds a reference, being able to rely on the accumulated state over that time. But state will not endure after the reference is lost. (If the client hangs on to the reference, it will be like a stateful session bean, but will scale still worse because of the lack of stateful session bean passivation support.) In some cases, this programming model is just what we want.

At first glance, this seems an irrational approach: creating an object for each client. But because we're dealing with objects that are typically not created that often—perhaps once or a few times to handle a web request, rather than 100 times in a nested loop—the performance penalty isn't normally an issue. And, as we've seen, the garbage-collection implications are not that problematic either. Such objects will never progress to the old generation, and can be cleaned up efficiently. WebWork has always used this model exclusively, creating a "command" to handle each web request, and has performed well in high-volume web sites.

We can just create such objects using new. But that means that we won't enjoy the many benefits of container-configuration management, such as automatically having collaborators and simple properties set, and ensuring pluggability by freeing calling code of knowledge of the actual class to be constructed.

The real challenge is not object creation, but object configuration. Typical business objects have dependencies on other objects; when they are created, those dependencies must be satisfied. Ideally, those dependencies should be satisfied by a container, not by application code.

Spring and WebWork 2 both provide Inversion of Control functionality that can solve this challenge efficiently.

For example, in Spring, we can define any POJO as a "prototype" bean definition in a Spring "bean factory." This means that every time we ask the factory for a reference to an object with this name, Spring will create and configure an independent instance.

Spring offers more options for managing the lifecycles of managed options than EJB offers, which doesn't automatically resolve dependencies. Because it allows application objects to benefit from the Spring IoC container, they can in turn express dependencies on other objects. Depending on whether these other objects are "singletons" or "prototypes," these references will be set to either a shared instance or an

independent instance. This style of resolution can extend throughout an object graph, with no intervention by the developer. (Of course traversing large graphs will make prototypes expensive to create.)

When only one new service object has to be created—in the common case when a service object depends
only on shared resources such as DataSources—benchmarking indicates that creating a Spring prototype performs quite well, and is an acceptable overhead in normal usage.

To use this threading model, we can define a simple POJO like this in a Spring bean definition file:

```
<bean id="myService"
  class="org.springframework.benchmark.invokers.ServiceImpl"
  singleton="false"
>
  <property name="dataSource"><ref local="dataSource"/></property>
</bean>
```

If we omit the optional singleton attribute, or set it to "true" (the commonest usage), a shared instance
will be used. Note that we've expressed a dependency on a shared resource: in this case a DataSource.
As we've noted, such dependencies can also be on other prototypes.

A client could obtain and use a new, configured object as follows. I've included an assertion to illustrate
how state is preserved for the lifetime of the reference:

```
Service myService = (Service) beanFactory.getBean("myService");
myService.setName("rod");
assert "rod".equals(myService.getName());
```

The necessary Spring BeanFactory or ApplicationContext reference would normally be obtained
through the caller implementing the org.springframework.beans.factory.BeanFactoryAware or
org.springframework.context.ApplicationContextAware interface to save it.

This approach offers a simple programming model that is appropriate in many cases where a shared
instance is not.

> One problem is that this approach creates a dependence on the Spring API. With an IoC solution such
> as Spring, we normally want to—and are able to—avoid such a dependence on framework API.
> However, as both BeanFactory and ApplicationContext are interfaces rather than classes, this depen-
> dency at least doesn't compromise testability. Such dependency is also arguably much less painful for a
> client than dependence on the EJB API!

Non-EJB Instance Pooling

EJB containers don't have a monopoly on instance pooling. Several good pooling libraries are available,
including Apache Commons Pool (http://jakarta.apache.org/commons/pool/), so you don't
need to write your own object pool to enjoy non-EJB pooling.

Spring builds on such pooling libraries to provide a pooling abstraction offering the same threading
model as SLSBs. This offers a huge advantage over EJB that, as with the "prototype" approach discussed
previously, any POJO can be pooled, removing another reason to complicate things by making business
objects EJBs. Again, a lightweight framework can deliver services but remain "non-invasive," in comparison with the heavy tread of EJB.

We merely need some additional configuration in the Spring XML bean definition file to pool any business object. We must define a prototype bean as above. The class can be any POJO. The only difference is that it's given a name other than `myService`, the name we want to use in application code. We reserve that for the AOP proxy that client code will use.

```xml
<bean id="myServiceTarget"
 class="org.springframework.benchmark.invokers.ServiceImpl"
 singleton="false"
>
 <property name="dataSource"><ref local="dataSource"/></property>
</bean>
```

Next we need to define a pooling *target source* (more about this shortly). Such a definition will look like the following, which uses Spring's out-of-the-box Commons Pool integration:

```xml
<bean id="poolTargetSource"
    class="org.springframework.aop.target.CommonsPoolTargetSource">
    <property name="targetBeanName"><value>myServiceTarget</value></property>
    <property name="maxSize"><value>80</value></property>
</bean>
```

Note that we must specify the bean name of the target, not a reference. This is because the pooling target source will need to create more instances of the prototype using the owning factory's `getBean()` method, and has to know what name to pass as a parameter.

Now we define the `myService` AOP proxy. We can do this in several ways. We can use the AOP `ProxyFactoryBean` directly, as follows, using the optional `targetSource` property. We could specify interceptor names here as well, if we needed advice as well as custom management of a pool of target objects:

```xml
<bean id="myService"
 class="org.springframework.aop.framework.ProxyFactoryBean"
>
    <property
name="proxyInterfaces"><value>com.mycompany.Service</value></property>
    <property name="targetSource"><ref local="poolTargetSource"/></property>

</bean>
```

Or we can combine configuring pooling with setting a transaction interceptor, as in the following example. The example assumes that a PlatformTransactionManager has been defined with bean name "transactionManager". This is a common way of creating AOP proxies, as it addresses one of the commonest enterprise concerns:

```xml
<bean id="myService"
class="org.springframework.transaction.interceptor.TransactionProxyFactoryBean">
  <property name="transactionManager"><ref local="transactionManager"/></property>
  <property name="target"><ref local="poolTargetSource"/></property>
  <property name="proxyInterfaces"><value>com.mycompany.Service</value></property>
  <property name="transactionAttributes">
        <props>
            <prop key="do*">PROPAGATION_REQUIRED</prop>
```

```
        </props>
      </property>
    </bean>
```

A third option is to use Spring "autoproxying" (discussed in Chapter 9) to simplify using a custom TargetSource. Once the bean definitions required to set up the autoproxy infrastructure are in place, we don't need a ProxyFactoryBean definition for each bean using the custom TargetSource: We can just use normal bean definitions. We can even drive pooling from source-level attributes, as in .NET.

However we create the AOP proxy, clients can call `getBean()` to get a shared reference to the myService object exhibiting pooling behavior. Better still, client code can benefit from IoC and avoid any Spring dependency by expressing a dependency of type Service (for example, a JavaBean property) that can be resolved transparently to either of these myService definitions or to an actual Service implementation. In this case, neither clients nor business objects have any dependency on Spring APIs.

As Spring uses the same approach for other important purposes, it's worth understanding how this works under the covers. A client obtaining any reference from a Spring container can be given an AOP proxy for the appropriate interfaces and/or target class, instead of a reference to a POJO. The behavior of the proxy depends on its target object, which contains the joinpoint, and a chain of "advisors" (often interceptors). The pooling strategy shown previously depends on how the target object is obtained. After all advisors in the chain have been executed, an implementation of the `org.springframework` `.aop.TargetSource` interface is used to obtain the "target object" containing the joinpoint, which is invoked via reflection. The default `TargetSource` implementation holds a reference to a single target instance that is invoked with every invocation. Hence, Spring users seldom need to delve into Spring's TargetSource API, or even be aware of its presence.

Spring can use different `TargetSource` implementations without affecting callers of AOP proxies. A different proxy configuration—transparent to code obtaining the reference from the container—can use a different `TargetSource`. Thus Spring can handle instance pooling at TargetSource level, with a TargetSource maintaining a pool of target objects. Client code need have no knowledge of pooling, although clients can now assume that their objects will never have more than one thread executing them.

Other special TargetSources included with Spring support "threadlocal pooling," discussed below, and "hot swapping" (the ability to replace the object behind a reference without affecting callers who hold a reference). Many of these invokers can be switched without affecting client code. For example, we could switch from pooling to a threadlocal model without changing a line of client code.

In its spirit of openness and pluggability, Spring provides the `org.springframework.aop.target` `.AbstractPoolingTargetSource` superclass for invokers that can maintain a pool of target objects. The default concrete subclass is `CommonsPoolInvokerInterceptor`, in the same package, which uses Commons Pool. It's possible to examine the behavior of the pool at runtime via the `org.springframework.aop` `.target.PoolingConfig` interface implemented by `AbstractPoolingTargetSource`.

As the best EJB containers provide highly efficient instance pooling, we're unlikely to achieve better performance than an efficient EJB container if we do want pooling. However, as we've seen, we can provide a much simpler programming model, and we can enjoy pooling if we need it without resorting to EJB. Benchmarks indicate that the Spring Commons Pool–based approach significantly outperforms the SLSB pooling of a popular open source application server, and performs on a par with SLSB pooling in a leading commercial application server. We'll look at performance comparisons between the Spring implementations of this various threading models and local stateless session beans in Chapter 15.

> EJB isn't the only option for a single threaded model implemented by instance pooling. Spring provides transparent instance pooling purely handled by configuration, which can offer pooling services to any POJO. Best of all, neither service implementations nor client need normally have any dependence on the pooling infrastructure or import a single Spring class or interface.

ThreadLocal "Pooling"

There is normally only one appropriate size for the instance pool of a business object such as a stateless session bean: the maximum number of threads that will need to access it simultaneously. Any more objects in the pool than this, and they can't all be in use simultaneously; any fewer and there's possibly contention.

This suggests a radically different approach to instance pooling. What if we take the view that thread management should drive management of instance objects? This means that we can simply maintain an instance of each object for each thread. This eliminates the need for any synchronization, and reduces the likelihood of synchronization-related errors. The potential risk of different business object instances concurrently referencing shared objects remains, as with conventional pooling.

J2SE 1.2 introduced the `java.lang.ThreadLocal` class, which can be used to implement this strategy. A ThreadLocal variable is normally declared static, and provides an independent copy of the object it contains for each thread that accesses it.

I first considered this approach as an option in Spring some time before discovering others had had similar thoughts. Brian Goetz has published an interesting article on ThreadLocals at www-106.ibm.com/developerworks/java/library/j-threads3.html, and concludes by mentioning it as a simpler and less error-pone alternative to pooling for preventing undesired interactions between threads.

The programming model is similar to that of pooling. Client requests can be served by any thread managed by the application server; the probability that successive requests from the same client will go to the same thread is as low as the probability that successive requests against a pool will hit the same instance. The difference is that a calling object *can* assume that successive requests in the same method—and hence the same thread—will go to the same instance. In rare cases, this difference may be important.

As with pooling, it is *not* usually a good idea for application code to implement its own ThreadLocal "pooling." The EJB solution is better than a roll-your-own alternative. However, there are off-the-shelf solutions. For example, Spring provides a `ThreadLocalTargetSource` that conceals the use of a ThreadLocal. This requires a trivial change from the `CommonsPoolTargetSource`, shown previously. We also need a prototype target-bean definition that the `ThreadLocalTargetSource` can use to create new instances as necessary, and an AOP proxy. The necessary `ThreadLocalTargetSource`, which would replace the pooling target source in the preceding example, would look like this:

```
<bean id="threadlocalTargetSource"
 class="org.springframework.aop.target.ThreadLocalTargetSource">
 <property name="targetBeanName"><value>myServiceTarget</value></property>
</bean>
```

All we need is a change to this single XML stanza. All this is transparent to application code, and hence no changes are required there.

As usual, Spring provides a flexible abstraction from low-level details. Any object obtained from a Spring container can use ThreadLocal pooling; there are no special requirements on client or business object.

> **Spring uses AOP to modularize thread management and remove it from application code. This modularization is achieved without invasiveness, meaning that it doesn't incur the same tradeoffs as EJB thread management.**

As with the pooling invoker interceptor, it's possible to obtain a reference to a `ThreadLocalInvokerInterceptor`, which implements the `ThreadLocalInvokerStats` interface, to monitor its behavior.

The `ThreadLocalTargetSource` intercepts the `org.springframework.beans.factory.DisposableBean` interface so that it can free the objects it has created when the owning bean factory is shut down. This ensures correct behavior on hot redeploy.

The performance of ThreadLocal pooling appears to be similar to that of conventional pooling, although it appears to vary more among operating systems. Conventional pooling is a safer option in most cases, if you need pooling at all.

Instance Pooling Summary

Instance pooling is often unnecessary. Often, the most natural programming model is a shared, threadsafe instance. While this places the onus on the developer to write threadsafe code, the guarantee of a single instance is actually good in certain cases:

If it's essential to be able to code a particular business object as though it's single threaded, the EJB solution is not the only approach. There are several valid alternatives:

❑ Create a new instance for each client. Although this was not a viable option with the garbage-collection technology available at the time of EJB 1.0, generational garbage collection makes it a valid choice today.

❑ Use synchronization or threading libraries to provide fine-grained protection for code that isn't threadsafe. This is harder to implement and potentially error prone, but it performs perfectly well if we need only to protect a small amount of code.

❑ Use non-EJB pooling solutions.

Thus the EJB one-size-fits-all solution is questionable. You can choose from *all* these approaches using Spring. Spring's solution can provide a single-threaded programming model without an EJB container or a high-end application server.

> **Consider the concurrency requirements of each service object, and use an appropriate solution for each object. However, a shared single instance is usually the best approach.**

Declarative Security

What about security, and the EJB model's support for declarative and programmatic security?

The EJB Model

EJBs deliver role-based security.

EJB guarantees two things:

❑   If there is an authenticated user, the user `Principal` is available programmatically to any EJB, via the `javax.ejb.EJBContext.getCallerPrincipal()` method.

❑   The option of declarative security, by specifying which roles have access to which EJB methods.

Flaws in the EJB Model

The EJB model is only as good as the J2EE role-based security model it builds on. As usual with EJB, if we don't like the standard J2EE infrastructure underpinning it, we're out of luck. There's nothing much wrong with the EJB declarative approach (although, as we'll see, we can do even better with AOP), but the standard J2EE role-based security is inadequate for many applications.

The problems include:

❑   Authentication is not well defined in the J2EE specifications. It's not portable across containers.

❑   Simple role-based security, without refinements such as wildcards or role inheritance, is often inadequate.

❑   User data may already be stored in a form that's hard to reconcile with a container's security infrastructure. Some application servers make implementing concepts such as security realms a living hell, regardless of where the data comes from.

The majority of the applications I see don't use the standard J2EE security infrastructure. Some that *do* use it find that it adds little value compared to implementing their own security approach.

These shortcomings are a pity—it would be good if the standard infrastructure made the grade—but unfortunately J2EE security hasn't moved forward greatly since J2EE's inception.

Declarative Security via AOP

Declarative security, like declarative transaction management, is a crosscutting concern that is an ideal candidate for AOP. As with transaction management, a declarative AOP solution ends up looking pretty much like the EJB solution, with the significant benefits that it is more flexible and can be applied to POJOs.

It's easy to implement a custom security interceptor by using an AOP framework such as Spring. The use of an AOP framework also means that we can define pointcuts to allow fine control over security permissions.

EJB declarative security goes down to the level of methods on the component interface. This is good, but not always as much control as we need. For example, we can say that the huddled masses in the user role, as opposed to the vip role, can't call the giveMeComplimentaryChampagneNow() method on the component interface. But what if we want to modularize more sophisticated checks? For example, we may want all users to be able to access the bookTickets(int howMany) method, but only allow VIP users to book more than a certain number of tickets. With EJB, there's no way to consider runtime information such as the arguments to the method, so we'd have to make such a check programmatically inside the method itself. This is not necessarily bad, but it complicates the business operation with code for a security concern that may better be modularized in a security aspect.

With Spring's AOP framework, or other sophisticated AOP frameworks, we can easily describe such a joinpoint with a dynamic method matcher. Thus an AOP approach to declarative security is superior in both flexibility of possible security model, and ability to define exactly where security rules should be applied. We could even define several security rules—rather than one role-based check—and specify which rules should apply to which methods, using separate pointcuts.

An AOP approach to security need not be incompatible with standard J2EE security. For example, a servlet container can authenticate the user, and the user's Principal can be bound to a ThreadLocal for use by AOP advice around any POJO.

> *As we go to press, a sophisticated add-on security framework for Spring, leveraging Spring AOP, is in development. Please visit the Spring web site for more information.*

JMS and Message-driven Beans

The only major area of EJB service provision we haven't covered is messaging. Message-Driven Beans (MDBs) are dedicated to processing JMS or other asynchronous messages.

MDBs offer the most compelling part of the EJB value proposition. They are the simplest type of EJB, unique in that they require only a bean-implementation class, with no component or home interfaces. Thus they are significantly less onerous to develop than other types of EJB, although the difficulties related to the EJB container remain (such as the Singleton issue).

MDBs are a good choice as message consumers. They are not the *only* choice, as the services provided by MDBs can, like other EJB services, be provided in other ways. (Also, it's important to distinguish between the services provided by JMS and by the EJB container to MDBs.) I expect to see "lightweight" message-consumer solutions reaching maturity in 2004, in the same way that lightweight containers in general matured in 2003. But that's beyond the scope of this book. We haven't focused on asynchronous processing, because of space constraints and because synchronous invocation normally plays a much bigger role in typical web applications.

Summary

Not much in EJB is unique or particularly difficult to replace with more flexible solutions. In this chapter, we've looked mainly at threading and pooling, with a brief discussion of security.

We've seen that EJB-style thread management—aimed at enabling developers to write SLSBs as though they're single threaded—is not always the best solution for such stateless service objects.

- ❑ Often, a shared instance, serving all threads, is a better alternative than EJB-style instance pooling.

- ❑ Stateless business objects typically have no read-write state and don't need protection from concurrent threads.

- ❑ There is a potential problem for the programming model in having an unknown number of instances even on a single node. For example, it's impossible to have a coherent resource cache unless we rely on a shared object invoked by all EJB instances—and therefore, subject to the same supposed problems as a shared business object instance.

- ❑ In a co-located web application, there is no need for EJB thread pooling. The web container manages threads. (The situation is different with remote EJBs, which are themselves published endpoints.)

- ❑ Resources commonly used by business objects in J2EE applications, such as JDBC `DataSources`, are themselves threadsafe and don't need EJB style concurrency support.

- ❑ In cases where shared resources *aren't* threadsafe, the EJB concurrency model does nothing to help us: In fact, it can provide a false sense of security, like the now deprecated servlet "single thread model."

- ❑ Instance pooling is no longer a necessity, even if a single thread model is required. Object creation (and the consequent garbage collection) is no longer the problem it was in Java 1.1 VMs, especially where short-lived objects are concerned. Hence, creating a new object to service each client is a valid option, as WebWork demonstrates.

- ❑ In cases where we appear to need a single thread model, our own concurrency code—typically, targeted synchronization—may allow a shared object to perform very well. If we have only to synchronize quick-to-run pieces of code, the performance penalty of synchronization is slight. Synchronization is *not* a good approach if it brings up excessive complexity. Writing *complex* code to handle concurrency issues is not a good idea.

- ❑ In cases where we need a single thread model, there are alternatives. Spring and other "lightweight" solutions provide the following services for *POJOs*, not just special objects such as EJBs:

  - ❑ Creating a new object for each client
  - ❑ Pooling without EJB
  - ❑ Thread-local based "pooling"

EJB offers a one-size-fits-all solution to all the middleware problems it addresses; threading is no different. In fact, we may want to pick and mix the most appropriate solution for each business object, where threading is concerned. For example, the majority of an application's business objects may have no concurrency issues whatsoever. A single shared instance is the best option for those objects. One or two objects may require small pieces of code to be protected from concurrent access. Selective synchronization will work fine. One or two objects—if that—may need a single thread model. Any of the three solutions listed above can be used for this, without imposing a single threading model everywhere.

The one-size-fits-all approach is also the fatal flaw in the EJB declarative security model. The problem is not with EJB, but that it is tied to the underlying, and often inadequate, J2EE security architecture. If we need declarative security, an AOP approach is simpler and more expressive than EJB. And it can cope with far more complex security checks than standard J2EE security can manage.

> **In sum: None of these reasons justifies the use of EJB, or justifies the need to make business-object development contend with the complexity introduced by EJB.**

13

Web Tier Design

Web applications are ubiquitous. (X)HTML-based web interfaces are the preferred front-end choice, not only for public Internet applications, but for many Intranet applications. Although the return of the *thick* (or *rich* or *fat*) client has been predicted for some years, most Java enterprise applications continue to adopt web-based user interfaces, and this is unlikely to change in the near future.

Many J2EE applications are dedicated web applications *by their very nature*. While this is hardly a revelation, classic J2EE architecture guidelines ignore its implications, in that they still proclaim distributed components as the cornerstone of any J2EE application. A typical J2EE web application demands for a clean architecture built on lightweight *logical* layers rather than (potentially) *physically separated* layers.

In previous chapters, we've emphasized the importance of reusable business interface layers. In a well-designed J2EE application, the business interface layer should be completely independent of the kinds of clients that will use it. In business-logic-driven applications, the business layer and underlying resource layers can often be developed and tested *before* the user interface(s), even before the choice of a particular user-interface technology.

Mixing various access technologies within the same application should pose no problem for a well-designed application, as we have already seen in Chapter 11 *(Remoting)* when we exposed business facades as different kinds of remote services. In this chapter, we will see that mixing of and switching between multiple web-controller and web-view technologies need not be hard either—at least, should not involve unnecessary reimplementation of business logic or controller code.

> In contrast to orthodox J2EE design strategies, we don't believe that it is necessary to decide on the eventual need for web and/or rich clients in the earliest stages of a project. In particular, it is almost always overkill to adopt remote SLSBs for business facades just because there *might* be some nonweb access at an unknown time in the future.
>
> Of course it is wise to consider well-known requirements early. But no such decision should incur a high degree of up-front complexity. Otherwise, applications that initially need only a web interface will suffer from an unnecessarily complex (and possibly underperformant) architecture.
>
> However, we do believe that reusability of business logic is an important goal, and will describe proven strategies for achieving it in a web environment.

Note that lightweight business logic components, implemented as POJOs, are actually *reusable* rather than just ubiquitously *accessible*: For example, a rich client might need to run some business logic locally rather than accessing it remotely, for performance reasons—possibly the same business logic that also runs in the middle tier of a corresponding web application. This kind of reusability is completely neglected by traditional J2EE literature.

This chapter will focus on building a *thin web tier* on top of a *reusable business layer*. After a brief discussion of the **MVC (model-view-controller)** concept in the context of a web application, we will discuss popular web frameworks in detail: **Struts**, **WebWork2**, and **Spring**'s own web MVC framework. To demonstrate the benefits of middle tier/web tier separation, we will show how to use all of those as web frameworks on top of a dedicated middle tier with reusable business objects.

We assume working knowledge of MVC in the context of a J2EE web application. While this chapter includes a short introduction to web MVC, its main focus is on the similarities and differences between approaches to MVC, and on integrating the web tier into overall application architecture. For a thorough theoretical discussion of web MVC and view technologies, covering Struts, WebWork and Maverick and JSP, Velocity, and XSLT / XMLC, among others, see Chapters 12 and 13 of *Expert One-on-One J2EE Design and Development*.

Goals and Architectural Issues

HTML interfaces offer many practical advantages, which explain their popularity. Notably:

- ❏ They are much easier to update than thick clients. Controlling JVM versions on clients is a major hassle, as is rolling out updates to thick-client applications. HTML applications use a universal client already installed on every desktop: a web browser. (Of course, client version issues become more problematic the more JavaScript is used.)

- ❏ HTML interfaces allow extensive control over look and feel: an important business benefit. It is easier to brand a web application than, say, a Swing or VB.NET application.

- ❏ They decouple the user from the technology choice of the server: for example, an Intranet application implemented as a .NET thick client may fail to scale to an Internet application if required, because it excludes Linux or Mac users.

❑   They are firewall-friendly; again, minimizing administrative effort.

❑   They impose only modest demands on client environment, an important concern for Internet applications. Elaborate thick clients may require later operating-system versions or more RAM or processing power.

However, HTML interfaces also pose a number of challenges:

❑   The request-response paradigm can complicate interactions that would be simple in a traditional UI.

❑   HTTP is a stateless protocol, complicating state management.

❑   Today's web applications feature complex HTML, often produced by tools such as DreamWeaver, and often client-side JavaScript. Such content isn't easily edited by Java developers.

❑   Because it is theoretically easy to update web applications, businesses expect that application presentation *can* be updated at little cost. Web applications are often subject to changes in look and feel. This requires a clean separation of presentation from business logic.

The days of pure HTML are gone, as the majority of today's web applications target modern browsers. Appropriate use of JavaScript allows for rich user experiences while keeping the main advantage of thin clients: no need for client-side installation and maintenance.

However, we can't ignore thick clients. Rich client technologies like Flash and Java Web Start are growing in popularity, not only as an alternative to but as an *enrichment* of existing HTML-based interfaces. Thus, any modern J2EE web application should be built such that it facilitates the adoption of non-HTML user interfaces in a later stage of the project. Note that this does not incur upfront design for remote sessions or building on a remotable component model; the primary goal is simply to implement business logic in a reusable fashion, as we have seen in previous chapters.

Web Tier Design Goals

Naïve approaches toward J2EE web tier implementation typically result in JSP pages containing *excessive amounts* of Java scriptlets, with a confused mixture of presentation and business logic. The result is an untestable presentation layer, refactoring headaches, and maintenance hell. Many, if not most, J2EE web developers have either implemented such applications themselves, when less experienced, or inherited such code for maintenance and enhancement, cursing the original developers.

This naive JSP-centric programming model owes its origins to ASP and PHP, two popular web programming environments since 1996. In both, **page-centric** scripting is the only option, with no easy options for separating workflow control and view rendering or delegating to business logic components. While both have advanced since, to ASP.NET and PHP4, respectively, and both now offer better options for application architecture, the classic programming model unfortunately remains very influential.

There has been consensus in the J2EE community for several years that the web tier in a layered J2EE application should be better structured than such scripted pages, to offer comparable levels of maintainability, testability, and reusability as middle tier components. *Expert One-on-One J2EE Design and Development* clearly summarizes the central goals for a maintainable and extensible web tier:

❑   A **clean** web tier separates control flow and the invocation of business objects (handled by Java **controller objects**) from presentation (handled by **view components** such as JSP pages).

❑   The web tier should be as *thin* as possible: That is, contain no more Java code than is necessary to initiate business processing from user actions, and display the results. It should **contain only web-specific control logic**, not business logic.

The first goal is typically achieved by applying the MVC approach, dividing the web tier into three kinds of objects:

❑   **Controller** objects that accept user input and invoke business logic to create and update model objects

❑   **Model** objects, providing the data to display, representing the contract between controller and view

❑   **View** objects that display model data, as provided by the controller that invoked it

In classic desktop GUI frameworks like Swing, the model **pushes** updates to registered views. For web applications, a special variant of MVC applies, due to the fact that web applications are bound to a request/response cycle that does not allow for dynamic display updates: A controller exposes a model to the view, the model being specifically prepared for the current request, and the view **pulls** data from its model as necessary during rendering.

The second goal (a *thin* web tier) is often less emphasized than the first, as many web frameworks do not help to separate web control logic from business logic. This is potentially costly, as lack of separation between web control logic and business logic can compromise several architectural tiers and lead to what could be called *web-only applications*: web applications lacking a reusable business layer. In such applications, the web controller does not delegate to appropriate reusable business objects but implements both workflow and business logic itself. While this may be adequate for small applications, it typically leads to code duplication for similar actions, does not allow for easy testing of business logic, and prevents reuse of the same business logic in other environments.

> A *thin* web tier is at least as important as a *clean* web tier. We will particularly focus on the challenge of accessing reusable business logic from a web tier, a topic not (or poorly) addressed by most of today's application frameworks.

Ad hoc MVC via Servlets and JSPs

An ad hoc implementation of web MVC can simply implement web-control logic in servlets that forward to appropriate JSP views at the end of processing, as shown below. The corresponding model objects will be transferred between servlet controller and JSP view via Servlet API request attributes. This is the essence of basic web MVC.

```
public class MyServlet extends HttpServlet {

  protected void doGet(HttpServletRequest request,
      HttpServletResponse response) throws ServletException, IOException {
```

```
        request.setAttribute("message", "Hello world");
        request.setAttribute("headline", "my ad-hoc servlet controller");
        request.getRequestDispatcher("/myview.jsp").forward(request, response);
    }
}
```

The action URLs must be mapped in the standard `web.xml` deployment descriptor; each action corresponds to one servlet. The JSP names can either be hard-coded in the servlet implementation (in the preceding example), or determined by servlet init-params in `web.xml`.

Such a servlet/JSP approach offers significant advantages over a JSP-only approach:

❑ Controller code is implemented in servlets: normal Java classes that can be compiled in the usual way, subclassed, tested, and so on.

❑ Common workflow logic can be implemented in a controller base class that all application controllers derive from.

❑ A controller can choose one of several views to render in a clean way, avoiding the need for a view component to perform forwards to other views.

❑ If controller code, or business logic invoked by it, throws an exception, no view will have been partially rendered, allowing a proper error page to be displayed.

❑ A level of indirection is possible through specifying views as configurable parameters, resolving symbolic names to actual view URLs.

❑ The model attributes represent a clear contract between controller and view, avoiding the need for views to access HTTP request data or session attributes.

❑ View implementations need only to display the model, reducing or eliminating the need for scriptlets.

While this is adequate for simple scenarios, it still has several disadvantages:

❑ `web.xml`, because of its verbose structure, quickly becomes cluttered with servlet definitions and mappings; there is no standard way to factor those out into modules.

❑ Mapping options are limited to standard servlet mechanisms, defined in `web.xml`.

❑ Controller base classes are not always an appropriate way to implement common checks and workflows, as they offer a fixed class hierarchy, but not flexible combination of aspects.

❑ Views can be implemented only as JSPs; switching to a different view technology like Velocity would require changes in controller base classes or even each controller. (Of course, the same approach can be used with a templating technology other than JSP, such as Velocity or WebMacro.)

❑ Such a simple solution does not provide any means for data binding or validation. Each controller must retrieve request parameters and apply them to commands or forms manually.

❑ Command and form handling workflows must be implemented if more than simple request parameter evaluation is needed.

Of course, each of those could be overcome by implementing another ad hoc mechanism. A common pattern is the **Front Controller** (*Core J2EE Patterns*): a single generic servlet that accepts all requests, performs common checks, and *dispatches* to mapped application handlers. A further option for implementing common behavior is a Servlet 2.3 Filter, intercepting before and after controller execution. Data binding can be implemented via bean population libraries such as Jakarta's Commons BeanUtils.

However, addressing all these requirements would effectively mean implementing yet another **request-driven MVC web framework**. Not only are these concepts well understood; there are good generic solutions that address them. It is almost always preferable to adopt an existing framework that matches the application's requirements, instead of implementing a proprietary solution.

There are numerous good **open source web frameworks**, of which Jakarta's **Struts** is the most popular. Learning to work with such a framework usually pays off quickly, typically being just a fraction of the effort of designing and maintaining your own framework. Furthermore, all frameworks provide means for customizing their workflows. Spring's web framework is particularly flexible; it would be hard to think of any requirement on a request-driven MVC web framework that could not be satisfied through the customization hooks it provides.

> **Do not implement your own custom web MVC framework. There are numerous open source solutions available that should match a wide range of requirements. If you have special requirements, consider customizing an existing framework that is flexible enough.**

Later in this chapter, we'll look at popular concepts and their implementation, focusing on request-driven web MVC frameworks: in particular, Struts, WebWork2, and Spring Web MVC.

Integration into Overall Application Architecture

While there is a wealth of diverse frameworks for clean separation of web-tier concerns, many address integration into overall application architecture poorly, if at all. Therefore, they do not provide an out-of-the-box foundation for achieving a *thin* web tier.

In case of simple web-only applications, it's adequate (if still far from ideal) to perform all business logic within web controllers and dispense with a dedicated middle tier. But more complex applications benefit greatly from a layered architecture, and face the following questions:

- ❑ When to initialize business objects and resources?
- ❑ How to configure business objects and resources?
- ❑ Where to keep business object and resource singletons?
- ❑ How to access business objects from web controllers?

> **A well-defined middle tier is vital to success in nontrivial web applications. All popular web MVC solutions work pretty well, if used appropriately, but overall maintainability, testability, and reusability depends more on how business objects are designed and managed.**

In this section, we will review some common integration approaches in J2EE web applications. Later in this chapter, we will discuss some specific integration issues with popular web MVC frameworks.

Hard-wired Singleton Business Objects

Common ad hoc approaches to integrating the web tier into overall application architecture include the use of custom singletons, typically:

❑ Initializing them on application startup via a custom listener or load-on-startup servlet, or lazily on first access with custom synchronization

❑ Configuring them from some central initialization class that reads in the application's settings file, or reading in a custom properties file in each singleton

❑ Keeping the singletons in static fields of their implementation classes, following the usual singleton pattern

❑ Accessing the singletons via direct reference to the singleton getters in the implementation classes

For example, the ad hoc servlet from the preceding example could access a "MyService" singleton, determining the message and headline to provide as model objects:

```
public class MyServlet extends HttpServlet {

  protected void doGet(HttpServletRequest request,

      HttpServletResponse response) throws ServletException, IOException {
    MyService myService = MyService.getInstance();
    request.setAttribute("message", myService.getMessage());
    request.setAttribute("headline", myService.getHeadline());

    request.getRequestDispatcher("/myview.jsp").forward(request, response);
  }
}
```

The usual consequence is that the whole application is hard-wired. While such a solution may allow for some kind of customization within the web application, reuse of business objects in other environments is often impossible due to dependencies on the particular application's initialization and service infrastructure. Furthermore, cleanly coding to interfaces is hard, as knowledge of the implementing classes is necessary for singleton lookup. Often, as in the original iBATIS JPetStore discussed in Chapter 3, there *are no* business interfaces.

> **Don't use custom singletons for your business objects. As we've shown in previous chapters, there are much better, equally lightweight solutions for holding business objects, data access objects, and resource factories: namely, generic IoC containers that can configure and wire up any kind of application objects, completely replacing custom singletons. Given such solutions, the common approach of all kinds of singletons spread throughout an application is obsolete and an anti-pattern.**

Stateless Session Beans

The classic J2EE solution is to model all business components as EJBs—in particular, Stateless Session Beans—and define all resources via **JNDI**, deferring configuration and instance management to the EJB container:

❑   Letting the container initialize business objects on startup

❑   Configuring them via JNDI environment parameters

❑   Keeping them in the container's JNDI environment

❑   Accessing them via JNDI lookups

For example, the ad hoc servlet from above could access a "MyService" SLSB as follows:

```
public class MyServlet extends HttpServlet {

  protected void doGet(HttpServletRequest request,
      HttpServletResponse response) throws ServletException, IOException {
    try {
      InitialContext ic = new InitialContext();
      MyServiceHome myServiceHome = (MyServiceHome) ic.lookup("myService");
      MyService myService = myServiceHome.create();
      request.setAttribute("message", myService.getMessage());
      request.setAttribute("headline", myService.getHeadline());
    }
    catch (Exception ex) {
      throw new ServletException("Could not look up EJB", ex);
    }
    request.getRequestDispatcher("/myview.jsp").forward(request, response);
  }
}
```

In such an environment, singletons are discouraged within the EJB tier, to enable seamless clustering at the component level. As SLSB instances are pooled, their instance variables are unsuitable for holding singletons. Custom singleton classes can nevertheless be implemented, but not eagerly initialized on startup without resorting to container-specific startup classes.

Although leveraging SLSBs for business objects, with JNDI as central component repository, seems a good idea at first glance, it starts to break down when considering typical application scenarios. In co-located web applications, there is no need to define each and every business object as a local EJB. The heavyweight SLSB machinery is not well suited for serving fine-grained business objects to a web tier, due to its development and deployment overhead. Furthermore, wiring up various business SLSBs is a tedious process that involves verbose JNDI lookups in numerous objects. Web-tier access to SLSB facades usually requires a layer of **service locator** or **business delegate** singletons as well: still more inflexible, verbose application code.

A typical compromise is to define business facades as SLSBs, for access from web controllers, but keep helpers like data-access objects as internal POJOs in the SLSBs. On the web tier side, helper objects are manually configured too, often resorting to hard-coded singletons again. While it may be acceptable to have application objects instantiated per SLSB instance, resources like a Hibernate SessionFactory pose a severe problem, as they must not be loaded multiple times within the same JVM. A possible solution is to hold the SessionFactory in JNDI, registered via a **JCA connector** or a container-specific startup class.

Overall, EJB creates at least as many problems and complexity as it takes away, in this scenario.

ServletContext Attributes

A lightweight integration point between web and middle tier is the **ServletContext**, as an alternative to heavier infrastructure like JNDI. Local business objects and resource factories can easily be kept as ServletContext attributes. Resources managed by the J2EE container like JDBC DataSources and physically separated components like EJBs can still be looked up in the JNDI environment.

The preceding ad hoc servlet example could easily access a service via a ServletContext attribute as follows:

```
public class MyServlet extends HttpServlet {

  protected void doGet(HttpServletRequest request,
      HttpServletResponse response) throws ServletException, IOException {
    ServletContext sc = getServletContext();
    MyService myService = (MyService) sc.getAttribute("myService");
    request.setAttribute("message", myService.getMessage());
    request.setAttribute("headline", myService.getHeadline());
    request.getRequestDispatcher("/myview.jsp").forward(request, response);
  }
}
```

Custom listener or load-on-startup servlet needs to initialize such business objects and resources on startup, registering them with the ServletContext before any other web resource attempts to access them. Such custom factories can allow for a high degree of flexibility and loose coupling; however, it is not desirable to have to reinvent them for each web application.

> While ServletContext attributes are an easy way to keep business objects and resources, allowing for loosely coupled middle-tier objects, it's preferable to hold those objects in a lightweight container which in turn is kept as ServletContext attribute. The latter strategy retains all advantages of the ServletContext-based approach but provides a prebuilt generic factory that covers lifecycle and configuration.

IoC-based Middle Tier Backbone

As most web MVC solutions fail to address support for layered applications, a solid and lightweight middle tier foundation is needed that can easily be integrated with any web tier. Spring provides out-of-the-box support for its application context concept in a web environment, which we will consider as reference implementation here. Similar support can be built on other lightweight containers or might already be provided out of the box.

Spring offers generic web application support in the form of the **WebApplicationContext** concept. The interface org.springframework.web.context.WebApplicationContext is an extension of the generic interface `org.springframework.context.ApplicationContext`, adding web-specific features such as handling of the corresponding `javax.servlet.ServletContext`. Such a web application context can provide a logical middle tier for *any* kind of J2EE web application, whether built with an ad hoc web tier or based on a web MVC framework.

As an extension of the application context concept, a `WebApplicationContext` implementation like `org.springframework.web.context.support.XmlWebApplicationContext` can offer all bean factory and application context services to generic beans in a web environment, as `org.springframework.context.support.ClassPathXmlApplicationContext` can for standalone environments.

In a typical Spring-based web application, the root web application context is loaded via the generic listener `org.springframework.web.context.ContextLoaderListener` or the startup servlet `org.springframework.web.context.ContextLoaderServlet`. If not overridden by one or more file paths specified via the context-param "contextConfigLocation", the XML bean definition file will be expected at the location `/WEB-INF/applicationContext.xml`.

```
<web-app>

  <listener>
    <listener-class>
      org.springframework.web.context.ContextLoaderListener
    </listener-class>
  </listener>

  ...
</web-app>
```

*For Servlet containers that invoke ServletContext startup listeners after "load-on-startup" servlets, such as WebLogic 8.1, a **ContextLoaderServlet** is provided that achieves the same as the above listener. Note that the Servlet 2.4 specification clarifies that startup listeners must be invoked before any other web components. Many Servlet 2.3 containers such as Tomcat 4.1 and Resin 2.1 already implement that behavior; hence ContextLoaderListener will work with them.*

To override the location of the root web application context definition, specify a "contextConfigLocation" context-param in `web.xml`. You can also specify multiple file locations, separated by any number of spaces or commas, that will be merged into a single root application context.

```
<web-app>

  <context-param>
    <param-name>contextConfigLocation</param-name>
    <param-value>
      WEB-INF/mainApplicationContext.xml
      WEB-INF/additionalApplicationContext.xml
    </param-value>
  </context-param>

  <listener>
    <listener-class>
```

```
        org.springframework.web.context.ContextLoaderListener
    </listener-class>
  </listener>


  ...
</web-app>
```

The root `WebApplicationContext` instance is exposed as a ServletContext attribute, for access by all kinds of web resources like controllers or plain servlets. Client objects can access the context via the defined attribute name for the root context, as specified in the `WebApplicationContext` interface, or preferably via the helper class `org.springframework.web.context.support.WebApplication ContextUtils`. The only requirement is to have access to the web application's ServletContext.

```
WebApplicationContext ctx =
    WebApplicationContextUtils.getWebApplicationContext(servletContext);
```

Thus, the preceding ad hoc servlet example could access a Spring-managed middle tier object as follows:

```
public class MyServlet extends HttpServlet {

  protected void doGet(HttpServletRequest request,
      HttpServletResponse response) throws ServletException, IOException {
    ServletContext sc = getServletContext();
    WebApplicationContext wac =
        WebApplicationContextUtils.getWebApplicationContext(sc);
    MyService myService = (MyService) wac.getBean("myService");
    request.setAttribute("message", myService.getMessage());
    request.setAttribute("headline", myService.getHeadline());
    request.getRequestDispatcher("/myview.jsp").forward(request, response);
  }
}
```

Of course, such lookup code can be factored out into a common base class. This approach is not restricted to servlets. Any web resource like a `javax.servlet.Filter`, a JSP, or a Struts action can access the ServletContext and thus Spring's root web-application context.

You may be noting that this is Dependency Lookup, and would prefer Dependency Injection. If you use Spring's MVC framework, as well as a Spring middle tier, your web controllers, like all other applications objects, can themselves be configured using MVC, avoiding the need to code any lookup in the web tier (or anywhere else).

Typical objects held in such a root web application context are business objects, data-access objects, resources, and a transaction manager, as shown in the middle tier examples in previous chapters. It is normally not advisable to keep web MVC objects like controllers or resolvers in the root web application context: The natural place for those objects is the corresponding web tier: for example, if using Spring's web MVC framework, the nested application context of a Spring `DispatcherServlet`. The root application context is intended to host the *middle tier* for the web application.

A lightweight middle tier container can be integrated with a web application in a natural way, making its services available to web tier components. A ServletContext attribute is an obvious place to hold such a container reference in a web environment, as it is guaranteed to have singleton semantics throughout the web application.

Spring provides explicit support for web applications in the form of a WebApplicationContext, an extension of its generic ApplicationContext concept. Typical middle tier objects hosted there do not have any web dependencies: A WebApplicationContext implementation simply makes them accessible in a web environment, adapting lifecycle and resource access accordingly.

Request-driven Web MVC Frameworks

The commonest type of web framework implements a **request-driven** workflow. An HTTP request comes in, is examined by a generic **dispatcher servlet**, and is dispatched to a mapped application handler. The handler in turn processes UI-specific control logic, invokes business objects and manipulates session state (if necessary), prepares a model, and forwards to a view. Each UI action corresponds to one handler, usually termed an **action** or **controller** (depending on the framework). The origin of an action is always a whole view page, not a specific widget on a page, in contrast to classic rich client GUIs.

Applications provide controller and view implementations and mapping configuration (typically specified in an XML document). Depending on the framework, the controller is either modeled as a **reusable, thread-safe handler** analogous to a servlet (Struts, Spring) or a single-use **command** instance (WebWork, Maverick). The model can either consist of a framework-specific form object, the command instance itself, or arbitrary Java objects. Every framework allows views to be implemented more or less elegantly with a variety of technologies: most important, JSP and Velocity.

The programming model of a request-driven web MVC framework usually involves six types of objects, although in some frameworks individual objects take on several roles:

❑ **Controller**: A component invoked by the framework to process a HTTP request and determine a view to render.

❑ **Interceptor**: A component invoked by the framework to intercept controller execution, typically being able to inspect the controller, potentially abort request processing, and apply actions before and after controller execution. Not all frameworks offer interceptors. (In particular, Struts does not.)

❑ **Command** or **form**: A JavaBean to populate with request parameters, for potential use as method argument of a middle tier business method. Typically called a **command object** if it is a single-use object (with request scope), and a **form object** if it is intended for forms that are capable of resubmissions (possibly but not necessarily an object with session scope).

❑ **Validator:** A component that validates a command/form object and generates validation errors for evaluation by a view, either globally for the whole object or specifically for a field.

❑ **Validation errors holder:** A component that collects and exposes validation errors for examination by a view; to be examined programmatically or via framework-specific JSP tags.

- ❑ **Model:** One or more named JavaBeans that are exposed to the view by the controller, representing the contract between a controller and a view.

- ❑ **View reference:** A symbolic name, a resource URL, or an actual view object that a controller can return to be rendered by the framework.

Jakarta's **Struts**, OpenSymphony's **WebWork2**, and the **Spring Framework**'s web MVC framework all fall into the request-driven category. We will now discuss a few basic characteristics of these frameworks, focusing on the design of Spring's web MVC framework in greater detail. For each framework, we'll discuss the following in turn, drawing on the shared concepts we've already examined:

- ❑ Basic controller workflow

- ❑ Model and view handling

- ❑ Configuration example

For a more thorough discussion of individual object roles and framework characteristics, see Chapter 12 of Expert One-on-One J2EE Design and Development. That chapter also explains the design decisions behind what went on to become Spring's web MVC framework in detail. While the text refers to the former com.interface21 package names, most of the information still applies to the current org.springframework version.

Struts 1.1

Struts (`http://jakarta.apache.org/struts`) is the oldest open source web MVC framework and has been hosted at Jakarta since its inception in late 2000. Its original author, Sun's Craig McClanahan, has since been the specification lead for **Java Server Faces**, a proposed standard for event-driven web MVC targeting GUI builder vendors (briefly discussed later in this chapter). Struts 1.0 was released in June 2001; the next major revision (1.1) was released only in mid-2003, introducing a few extensibility and flexibility features but retaining the original programming model.

Basic Controller Workflow

The central Struts concept is an **action** that extends the `org.apache.struts.action.Action` base class. (Note that concrete inheritance is required: there is no action *interface*.) An Action is a controller component that is similar to a servlet in that it is a reusable, thread-safe object that is passed `HttpServletRequest` and `HttpServletResponse` objects in its central workflow method, `execute`, which has the following signature:

```
public ActionForward execute(ActionMapping mapping,
                             ActionForm form,
                             HttpServletRequest request,
                             HttpServletResponse response)
        throws Exception;
```

In contrast to a servlet, a Struts action is not intended to write the response or forward to a JSP itself; like all MVC frameworks, Struts introduces a valuable level of indirection here. Instead, an action processes the request, invoking business objects accordingly, and returns an `org.apache.struts.action`
`.ActionForward` object as view reference that represents the resource URL to forward to. Typically, a preconfigured `ActionForward` is retrieved by name via the passed `org.apache.struts.action`
`.ActionMapping`'s `findForward` method.

Struts 1.1 introduced the **DispatchAction** concept for combining multiple action methods within one action class, to avoid proliferation of action classes—a common issue in MVC web applications, especially where simple interactions are concerned. A subclass of `org.apache.struts.action.Dispatch Action` can specify multiple execution methods with the same signature as `execute`. The actual determination of the method to invoke can either happen by declaratively specifying the method name in the action definition, or at runtime by resolving a request parameter value into a method name.

Struts 1.1 does not provide any sort of action interception in the standard framework. An add-on project called SAIF (Struts Action Invocation Framework, `http://struts.sourceforge.net/saif`) aims to implement such functionality; however, it is limited in scope, still in early beta as of the time of writing, and not part of the Struts distribution.

A Struts command or form object is called an **ActionForm** and must be a subclass of `org.apache .struts.action.ActionForm`. An `ActionForm` is configured and associated with an action in the Struts XML configuration file. It will automatically be instantiated and given request or session scope, depending on configuration. The bean properties of the form object are populated with request parameters before the corresponding `Action`'s `execute` method is invoked, allowing actions to work with valid `ActionForm` properties. Type mismatch errors (such as a non-numeric value for an `int` property) lead to fatal exceptions. Hence, all user-entered form properties need to be of type `String`.

A simple action plus form implementation might look as follows, expecting a "myParam" parameter of type `int` and forwarding to a success or input view accordingly. We'll assume that the parameter is determined by an application-generated link rather than by user input; in this case, a fatal exception in case of a type mismatch on binding is acceptable (as it represents an application error).

```
public class MyActionForm extends ActionForm {

    private int myParam = -1;

    public void setMyParam(int myParam) {
        this.myParam = myParam
    }

    public int getMyParam() {
        return myParam;
    }
}
```

MyAction will automatically receive a MyActionForm instance (if configured accordingly in `struts-config.xml`):

```
public class MyAction extends Action {

public ActionForward execute(ActionMapping mapping,
                             ActionForm form,
                             HttpServletRequest request,
                             HttpServletResponse response) {
    MyActionForm myForm = (MyActionForm) form;
    String forward = myForm.getMyParam() != -1 ? "success" : "input";
    return mapping.findForward(forward);
    }
}
```

Effectively, a distinct Struts `ActionForm` object is created for each HTML form. If it represents a domain object, the application must copy the domain properties into the form object on form initialization and back to the domain object on submit. Because of the `ActionForm`'s dependence on the Servlet and Struts APIs, it cannot serve as business-level command or domain object itself. Because of type mismatches being considered fatal, it cannot nest a typical domain object either.

Validation happens at the `ActionForm` level; every form is its own validator. Each `ActionForm` subclass can override the `validate` method, to be invoked after population with request parameters but before the invocation of `execute`:

```
public ActionErrors validate(ActionMapping mapping,
                             HttpServletRequest request);
```

The returned `org.apache.struts.action.ActionErrors` instance serves as a validation errors holder and is exposed as model attribute to the view. Typically, it is evaluated via the Struts tag library, to mark erroneous field values with error messages, or to enumerate all error messages in some message box. Such validation logic is both web- and Struts-dependent and cannot be reused in the middle tier or in other client environments.

As an alternative approach to validation, Struts 1.1 introduced support for **declarative validation** via Jakarta Commons Validator. Such validation rules could in principle be applied to generic domain objects; unfortunately, they are still defined for `ActionForm` beans and thus inherently tied to Struts usage. Furthermore, it is debatable whether declarative validation rules are actually preferable to concise programmatic validation rules. However, the principal of separating validation rules from the validated objects is important.

Model and View Handling

There is no notion of distinct model attributes in Struts. The `ActionForm` object is automatically exposed to the view as request attribute, as is the `ActionErrors` object. Additional model objects like reference data (for example, a list of categories to choose from) need to be nested in the `ActionForm` object or manually added to the HttpServletRequest as request attributes.

Struts always uses the Servlet API `RequestDispatcher` to forward to a view, and request attributes to expose a model, or alternatively an HTTP redirect. This is natural when working with JSPs but requires bridges to other view technologies, like a VelocityServlet that in turn gathers the request attributes and exposes them as a Velocity template model. So, while Struts can work with view technologies other than JSP, its way of doing so is not particularly elegant.

Struts' HTML tag library adopts the approach of replacing normal HTML controls like `<form>` and `<input>` tags, to be able to set form targets and property values automatically. While this simplifies JSP code, it makes the HTML harder to understand and harder to edit with a HTML-aware editor or GUI builder. Struts' default property access syntax is based on Commons BeanUtils. Alternatively, the **JSP Standard Tag Library (JSTL)** and its **JSP Expression Language (EL)** can be used.

As of Struts 1.1, the templating tool **Tiles** is now integrated into Struts. The central concept in Tiles is a layout page that defines the common layout of a set of pages. Actual content pages —"tiles"—get included at certain locations of the template page via the Tiles tag library. Per-tile **component controllers** can prepare a specific model for a tile in the form of a **component context** or a set of request attributes, allowing for fine-grained view components with their own controllers. Concrete pages are defined in a Tiles XML definitions file, merging a layout page with content tiles.

While Tiles is implemented as an extension to Struts, it can still be integrated with other web MVC frameworks as pure view technology, as we'll see in the discussion of the Spring Framework's web MVC support later in this chapter.

Configuration Example

Struts actions are defined in a `struts-config.xml` file, in a web application's WEB-INF directory (which is used to hold configuration files in most web MVC frameworks). The preceding example action plus form would be defined as follows, including corresponding forward definitions:

```
<struts-config>

  <form-beans>
    <form-bean name="myForm" type="example.MyActionForm" />
  </form-beans>

  <action-mappings>
    <action path="/myaction" type="example.MyAction"
            name="myForm" scope="request">
      <forward name="input" path="/myform.jsp"/>
      <forward name="success" path="/mysuccess.jsp"/>
    </action>
  </action-mappings>

</struts-config>
```

The Struts `ActionServlet` is typically mapped in `web.xml` to the URL pattern `*.do`. (This extension is a tradition, rather than a Struts requirement.) The URL `/myaction.do` will then invoke the action defined as `myaction` previously. More flexible mappings are not directly supported and require a custom `RequestProcessor` subclass.

Struts 1.1 allows large configurations to be broken into multiple files via its **module** concept: an essential capability to ensuring manageability in all but small web applications. (Struts 1.0 offered no such capability.) With multiple modules, the web application will still use a single `ActionServlet` but will dispatch to separate, internally managed namespaces. Each module is defined in a distinct configuration file, to be registered with the Struts dispatcher via servlet init-params.

Integration with a Middle Tier

Because Struts doesn't provide a middle-tier solution itself, its use is often combined with hard-wired middle tier singletons, or with Stateless Session Beans looked up via JNDI. While the fact that all Struts Actions can easily access the ServletContext provides for an easy way to access pre-configured singletons, this is rarely seen in typical Struts applications. Such ServletContext attributes could be set up via a Struts PlugIn or via a Servlet 2.3 ServletContextListener. Configuration could be read in from PlugIn parameters or context-params; there are no means for more sophisticated configuration or wiring up.

A typical Struts application using hard-coded middle tier singletons is Clinton Begin's **iBATIS JPetStore**. It uses a common base class for all of its Struts Actions, setting up a singleton of its central business object, `PetStoreLogic`. Note that this `BaseAction` class still uses Struts 1.0's `perform` method:

```
public abstract class BaseAction extends Action {

    protected static final PetStoreLogic petStore = PetStoreLogic.getInstance();

    public ActionForward perform(ActionMapping mapping,
                                 ActionForm form,
                                 HttpServletRequest request,
                                 HttpServletResponse response)
        throws IOException, ServletException {
      ... Implementation works with PetStoreLogic business object
    }
}
```

This implementation has two major disadvantages, already outlined regarding custom singletons:

❑ PetStoreLogic cannot be replaced with an alternative implementation: for example, with a mock object for testing purposes.

❑ PetStoreLogic implements its own initialization procedure in its private constructor, reading in a custom properties file and instantiating the DAOs defined there. The whole graph of application objects is wired internally. Inevitably, the sophistication available is limited. Management of business objects via ad hoc singletons means that there is no way to benefit from the valuable services of a lightweight application framework, such as IoC and AOP.

Imagine an application with a large number of business objects and data access objects plus associated resources that are all hard-wired in the same way. (Note that the iBATIS JPetStore does at least have pluggable DAOs, in contrast to many other Struts applications.) The lack of pluggability would make unit testing of individual components hard, if not impossible. Each business object would perform its own initialization, or possibly access a shared configuration holder singleton. Unfortunately, this architectural model is very common in today's J2EE web applications. Such applications are unnecessarily hard to develop and maintain.

It is much preferable to replace this tight coupling of application objects with a generic factory that does the configuration and wiring up. With a Spring root application context, the preceding BaseAction could be rewritten as follows (still using Struts for presentation):

```
public abstract class BaseAction extends Action {

    protected PetStoreLogic petStore;

    public void setServlet(ActionServlet actionServlet) {
      super.setServlet(actionServlet);
      ServletContext sc = actionServlet.getServletContext();
      WebApplicationContext wac =
          WebApplicationContextUtils.getWebApplicationContext(sc);
      petStore = (PetStoreLogic) wac.getBean("petStoreLogic");
    }

    public ActionForward perform(ActionMapping mapping,
                                 ActionForm form,
                                 HttpServletRequest request,
                                 HttpServletResponse response)
```

379

```
        throws IOException, ServletException {
  ...
  }
}
```

Provided that `PetStoreLogic` is no longer designed as singleton, but as business interface that allows for pluggable implementations, any kind of configuration and wiring up can happen in the application context now. The context definition file `/WEB-INF/applicationContext.xml` could look like this. (Note that we didn't show the middle tier wiring in the previous example—just the web tier.)

```
<beans>
```

```
    <bean id="petStoreLogic"
          class="com.ibatis.jpetstore.domain.logic.DefaultPetStoreLogic">
      <property name="accountDao">
        <ref bean="accountDao"/>
      </property>
      <property name="categoryDao">
        <ref bean="categoryDao"/>
      </property>
      ...
    </bean>
```

```
    <bean id="accountDao"
          class="com.ibatis.jpetstore.persistence.dao.JdbcAccountDao">
      <property name="dataSource">
        <ref bean="dataSource"/>
      </property>
    </bean>


    ...
</beans>
```

A similar approach can easily be implemented for any Struts application that needs to access middle-tier objects. A simple base class like the preceding one can encapsulate the lookup of the Spring root-application context, either storing and exposing the context reference itself or specific beans that have been fetched from the context. A similar pattern can be applied to a solution that is based on a different lightweight container.

An alternative way to integrate with an IoC container would be to wire up the Struts Actions themselves there. In the case of Spring, this would mean defining the Struts Actions as beans in an application context, referencing those actions from a Struts configuration via some custom factory mechanism. This approach involves double definition of each Struts Action, once in `struts-config.xml` and a second time in a Spring application context XML file; alternatively, autowiring could be used.

As Struts Actions aren't reusable generic objects, and thus not ideal candidates for being hosted in an IoC container, a simple solution that accesses components in an IoC container from within Struts Actions is usually sufficient. The separation between the tiers is then straightforward and clear: middle tier objects are hosted in the application context IoC container; web components in the Struts ActionServlet. As suggested by clear layering, the web components know about the middle-tier objects but not vice versa.

Struts Recap

The following table illustrates the relation between the previously mentioned object types in a request-driven web MVC framework and their equivalents in Struts:

MVC object type	Struts equivalent
controller	Action
interceptor	—
command/form	ActionForm
validator	ActionForm or declarative rules
validation errors holder	ActionErrors
model	ActionForm, manual request attributes
view reference	ActionForward

> **Struts 1.1 is the current de-facto standard for web MVC, but it is far from perfect. Its reliance on deriving from concrete framework classes like Action and ActionForm restricts implementation choices and ties web tier objects to the Servlet and Struts APIs. The fact that Struts cannot handle domain objects for forms leads to an unnecessary proliferation of form holder classes. Its view handling is JSP-centric and not well suited for other view technologies.**
>
> **The advantages of Struts are not in its design but in its broad acceptance, abundant documentation, and good tool support. However, we expect that these advantages will be eroded as other web frameworks grow in popularity: notably, WebWork2, Spring web MVC, and Tapestry.**

WebWork2

WebWork2 (http://wiki.opensymphony.com/space/WebWork2) is a complete rewrite of **WebWork** (www.opensymphony.com/webwork), a popular open-source web MVC framework that aims to offer an alternative programming model to Struts. While WebWork was originally developed by Rickard Oberg in early 2002, WebWork2's development is now led by Patrick Lightbody, Jason Carreira, and Mike Cannon-Brookes, under the OpenSymphony banner. WebWork2 final was released in February 2004.

Note that the original WebWork 1.x is still actively maintained by Hani Suleiman and others, also hosted by OpenSymphony. As WebWork2 introduces many incompatible changes in significant areas, upgrading from WebWork 1.x is not straightforward. Thus, it can be expected that WebWork and WebWork2 will co-exist for some time to come.

Basic Controller Workflow

Unlike Struts (and despite its name!) WebWork has always been designed to minimize dependence in application code on the Servlet API, for greater reusability. WebWork2 makes this more explicit.

In contrast to WebWork 1.x, WebWork2 is a thin layer above the generic action invocation framework **XWork** (http://wiki.opensymphony.com/space/XWork), enriching it with web semantics in the form of a dispatcher servlet, optional interfaces that make actions (commands) aware of Http ServletRequest and HttpServletResponse, and a JSP tag library. As far as possible, action implementations do not need to be aware of the Servlet or WebWork APIs, but only of the core XWork API.

Like the original WebWork, XWork is completely command driven. It creates a new command instance for each request, even if the nature of the request necessitates manual parameter extraction, and thus demands a servlet-style programming model. There is no notion of a controller; WebWork is completely command-centric. A command can be aware of the HttpServletRequest and HttpServletResponse if it needs direct access to them, but there will always be a new command instance for each request. (Note that creating a new command object for each request is *not* normally a performance issue.)

XWork provides sophisticated action creation, population, and chaining options. The central goals are to keep actions non–web-aware and reusable for any environment, and to allow for customization of action handling to the highest possible degree. It also offers IoC options, via "awareness" interfaces or explicit references to external components, as we will see later in the discussion of integration into an overall application architecture. XWork's central interface is com.opensymphony.xwork.Action:

```
public interface Action {

    String execute() throws Exception;
}
```

The return value is the "logical result" of the action execution: that is, the name of a view to forward to in the web case. It is typically the value of one of the constants in the Action interface: SUCCESS, INPUT, LOGIN, ERROR, NONE. View names are always symbolic in WebWork; there is no option to specify a view resource directly. Actions can have multiple execution methods, analogous to the signature of execute but with different names—similar to Struts' DispatchAction.

Our simple action implementation could look as follows in WebWork2, expecting a myParam parameter of type int and forwarding to a success or input view accordingly:

```
public class MyAction extends ActionSupport {

    private int myParam = -1;

    public void setMyParam(int myParam) {
        this.myParam = myParam
    }

    public String execute() throws Exception {
        return myParam != -1 ? SUCCESS : INPUT;
    }
}
```

Although an XWork action does not implement any web-specific awareness interfaces, it is still not ideally suited for a business command object serving as an argument for a business method, as it is modeled for a web-style workflow. It could, however, derive from a generic business command class, sharing its bean properties, and pass itself to a corresponding business method in the execute implementation. In the end, XWork actions are still UI workflow actions: Their decoupling from the web is valuable when they contain business logic themselves; the advantage is not so significant when they mainly delegate.

XWork provides sophisticated action interception via the `com.opensymphony.xwork.interceptor` `.Interceptor` interface. Interceptors are a central concept in XWork: Even populating an action instance with request parameters is done via an interceptor, and plugging in custom interceptors is simple. Furthermore, various utility interceptors are provided out of the box. XWork's interception facilities are a major advantage over Struts, which doesn't provide any such functionality in the standard framework.

Form handling in WebWork is built on actions plus corresponding controls from the WebWork tag library. Each form submission represents a new command: There is no concept of a form object to be kept in the session for the duration of the form workflow; an action and its nested objects always have request scope. While this works well for simple forms, it is not so well-suited for manipulating domain objects in a form. For re-identification and optimistic locking purposes, it can be important to work on the original form object on submission: WebWork does not support this form model out of the box.

Validation is available via the base class `com.opensymphony.xwork.ActionSupport`, by overriding the `doValidation` method and invoking `addActionError` and `addFieldError` accordingly. The action object itself serves both as validator and validation error holder in this case. Type mismatch errors will automatically be recorded if the action implements the `com.opensymphony.xwork.Validatable` interface (which the convenient `ActionSupport` base class does). Such automatic handling of type mismatches is an important advantage over Struts, enabling strong typing of action properties, rather than a fallback to String properties.

An alternative approach to validation is the **XWork Validation Framework**, to be activated via an XWork interceptor for specific actions or whole action packages. It allows declarative configuration of distinct validators that implement the `com.opensymphony.xwork.validator.Validator` interface, with the main method being `validate`:

```
void validate(Action action) throws ValidationException;
```

Validation errors are still recorded in the given `Action` instance, but the actual validation logic resides in separate objects that can be applied via configuration. An XWork `Validator` does not directly correspond to a "validator object" as defined previously as an object role for request-driven web MVC: It validates only a single aspect of an action or a field, while a "validator object" validates a whole command or form object. Several XWork `Validator` implementations are provided out of the box, including range and expression validators.

Model and View Handling

The execution of an XWork result, that is, the rendering of a WebWork view, is done by a corresponding preconfigured instance of the interface `com.opensymphony.xwork.Result`. There are out-of-the-box implementations for various view technologies, most notably JSP and Velocity. In contrast to Struts, it is possible to work with view technologies such as Velocity directly, instead of bridging via request attributes to a VelocityServlet. Furthermore, XWork allows for chaining actions simply by returning a result that is mapped to another action instead of to a view.

The action instances themselves serve as a model; there is no notion of separate model attributes. Because of the recording of type mismatch errors for redisplay instead of considering them fatal, it is possible and recommended to have strongly typed properties in the action object, or nest existing domain objects there. The same applies to reference data: Such objects need to be nested in the action object too. However, as user input is *not* kept for redisplay in case of a type mismatch, it is still often necessary to define distinct form properties of type String when working with an existing domain object.

WebWork2 comes with a complete set of tag libraries. Like Struts, it offers tags that replace standard HTML controls, which also arguably suffer from the same drawback of obscuring the HTML content. A central concept for WebWork's view scripting is the **value stack** that its tags use underneath to push values that they want to expose. In contrast to WebWork 1.x, which uses its own expression language, WebWork2 adopts **OGNL** for any kind of property access in its tag library.

> *OGNL (**www.ognl.org**) stands for "Object Graph Navigation Language." OGNL is an expression language for getting and setting the properties of Java objects, and is used by other projects besides WebWork2, such as Tapestry.*

It is possible to use JSTL tags and the JSP 2.0 **Expression Language (EL)** with WebWork2, but only with some effort. A Servlet 2.3 Filter must be used, replacing the HttpServletRequest with a custom implementation that overrides the getAttribute method: As the JSTL expects model objects to be exposed as attributes, getAttribute needs to check the WebWork value stack to see WebWork-exposed values such as Action objects. The simple approach of exposing the model objects as request attributes (as used by Struts and also by our ad hoc example at the beginning of this chapter) does not need such bridges.

WebWork actions can be invoked directly in a view page, for example, in a JSP via the <webwork: action> tag. The value stack concept allows for exposing the action as a nested model object within the page. The associated view of such a nested action, if defined, will be rendered as an *include*. This mechanism allows for powerful combination of page components that have their own controllers, similar to Tiles's **component controller** concept. The main difference from Tiles is that WebWork's nested actions do not provide means to build reusable layout pages.

Configuration Example

WebWork2 actions are defined in the generic xwork.xml file, interpreted by WebWork2's **ServletDispatcher**. Actions can be grouped into **packages**, sharing common definitions for result types, results, and interceptor stacks. WebWork2 provides a default package, webwork-default, which is typically extended by all custom package definitions.

```
<xwork>

  <include file="webwork-default.xml"/>

  <package name="default" extends="webwork-default">

    <action name="myaction" class="example.MyAction">
      <result name="input" type="dispatcher">
        <param name="location">/myform.jsp</param>
      </result>
      <result name="success" type="dispatcher">
        <param name="location">/mysuccess.jsp</param>
      </result>
      <interceptor-ref name="defaultStack"/>
    </action>

  </package>

</xwork>
```

The WebWork ServletDispatcher is typically mapped to the URL pattern `*.action`. The URL `/myaction .action` will then invoke the action defined as `myaction` previously, an implicit mapping. There is no obvious notion of overriding this with explicit URL-to-action mappings, or mappings based on any other criteria than the URL.

WebWork2 supports the separation of large configurations into multiple files via **includes** in `xwork.xml`. Each include will typically define one package and its actions. As with Struts, a web application will still use only a single `ServletDispatcher`, but will dispatch to separate, internally managed package namespaces.

Result values are matched to view implementations, for example, "dispatcher" for JSPs and "velocity" for Velocity templates. The allowed result types and their implementation classes are defined globally for a package of actions, in the default case inherited from `webwork-default`. Results themselves can either be defined for a specific action or shared for a package of actions. The nested parameters within the `<result>` tags are specific to the view implementation. The action instance will automatically be exposed as model to the view.

Integration with a Middle Tier

XWork and hence WebWork2 offers sophisticated means for wiring up commands, but no appropriate built-in means for managing business components and resources. Therefore, hard-coded singletons are typically found in WebWork applications just as in Struts applications. Kris Thompson's ServerSide article "Building with WebWork2" (www.theserverside.com/articles/article.jsp?l=WebWork2) contains an example that represents a good indication for how hard-coded singletons are commonly used with WebWork:

```java
public class RegisterAction extends ActionSupport {

    String username, email, firstname, lastname, password;
    private User tempUser;

    public String getUserName() {
      return username;
    }

    public void setUserName(String username) {
      this.username = username;
    }
    ...

    public String execute() throws Exception {
      if (hasErrors())
    return INPUT;
      else {
    tempUser = WebLogSystem.getUserStore().create(this.username,
                                                  this.password);
        tempUser.setFirstName(this.getFirstName());
        tempUser.setLastName(this.getLastName());
        tempUser.setEmail(this.getEmail());
        tempUser.save();
        return SUCCESS;
      }
```

```
      }

   public void validate() {
      LOG.info("Validating the registration page");
      try {
         if (WebLogSystem.getUserStore().verify(this.username)) {
            this.addFieldError("Username", "Someone already has that name");
         }
      }
      catch (Exception e)
         e.printStackTrace();
      }
   }
}
```

The preceding usage of the WebLogSystem class and its UserStore singleton suffers from the same drawbacks as the PetStoreLogic in the Struts example: It does not allow for pluggability, and requires its own initialization procedure. Especially in a large application, this will lead to severe restrictions in terms of testability and flexibility, and become a maintenance nightmare in terms of setup and configuration code.

Again, it is important to ensure that such collaborating objects are loosely coupled. One option would be to adopt XWork's own way of IoC, which works via enabler interfaces, to be resolved by an implementation of the interface com.opensymphony.xwork.interceptor.component.ComponentManager. A registered com.opensymphony.xwork.interceptor.component.ComponentInterceptor will invoke the ComponentManager for each action. So if the preceding action class implements a custom interface UserStoreAware, the ComponentManager will create an instance of the desired type with a configured scope, possibly as a ServletContext attribute:

```
public interface UserStoreAware {

   void setUserStore(UserStore userStore);
}
```

There are no sophisticated means to configure the UserStore instance or wire it up with collaborating objects, so this is a rather primitive kind of IoC. Furthermore, the need to implement enabler interfaces is invasive, and can be tedious for a large number of dependencies.

Alternatively, XWork's **external reference resolver** mechanism can be leveraged to access components that are defined outside of XWork, for example, in a root Spring web application context. (That mechanism was added precisely to permit access to a Spring application context.) The central interface is com.opensymphony.xwork.config.ExternalReferenceResolver, allowing WebWork to resolve references declared in the action configuration from an external source. Such a reference resolver can be specified at the XWork action package level; it will be invoked for each action by a registered com.open symphony.xwork.interceptor.ExternalReferencesInterceptor.

The associated action implementation would simply expose a bean property named "userStore" of type UserStore (analogous to the Spring style), to be populated by an ExternalReferenceResolver. (See the XWork documentation for details on how to wire action properties with specific external components.) The passed-in instance will be accessed in execute and validate, without any hard-coded singletons involved, and without the need to implement a corresponding enabler interface.

```
public class RegisterAction extends ActionSupport {

   private UserStore userStore;

   public void setUserStore(UserStore userStore) {
      this.userStore = userStore;
   }
   ...

   public String execute() throws Exception {
      if (hasErrors())
   return INPUT;
      else {
   tempUser = this.userStore.create(this.username, this.password );
         tempUser.setFirstName(this.getFirstName());
         tempUser.setLastName(this.getLastName());
         tempUser.setEmail(this.getEmail());
         tempUser.save();
         return SUCCESS;
      }
   }

   public void validate() {
      LOG.info("Validating the registration page");
      try {
         if (this.userStore.verify(this.username)) {
            this.addFieldError("Username", "Someone already has that name");
         }
      }
      catch (Exception e)
         e.printStackTrace();
      }
   }
}
```

Another option for accessing Spring-managed beans from within a WebWork action is to fetch the Spring application context from the ServletContext with Spring's `WebApplicationContextUtils` helper class, as with Struts. In WebWork2, the ServletContext can be retrieved via the static `ServletActionContext.getServletContext` method; in WebWork 1.x, the corresponding method is `ActionContext.getServletContext`. The external reference mechanism is preferable, however, as it avoids dependencies on the Servlet and Spring APIs.

In principle, XWork actions could also be defined in a Spring application context to get wired up there. As with Struts actions, this would involve double definition of actions, in this case in both `xwork.xml` and a Spring application context XML file. We consider it preferable to leverage either of the previous mechanisms instead, for clear separation of middle tier objects (in the Spring application context) and web-workflow actions (in the XWork/WebWork2 configuration).

Recap

The following table illustrates the relation between the previously mentioned object types in a request-driven web MVC framework and their equivalents in XWork, respectively, WebWork2:

MVC object type	XWork/WebWork2 equivalent
controller	Action
interceptor	Interceptor
command/form	Action
validator	Validatable Action, collection of Validators
validation errors holder	Validatable Action
model	Action
view reference	symbolic view name

The XWork/WebWork2 combo is, like the original WebWork, a command-driven framework for web-style workflows. It enforces the command paradigm for any web interaction, which may not always be appropriate, and arguably combines too many roles in the Action object.

A big plus compared with Struts is that XWork/WebWork2 builds on interfaces and is even more configurable than WebWork 1.x, particularly through the use of interceptors. WebWork's value stack concept allows for interesting ways of componentizing a view page via nested action invocations.

All things considered, WebWork2 offers a viable and more elegant alternative to Struts, if you can live with the all-embracing command paradigm.

Web MVC with the Spring Framework

The Spring Framework offers a web framework that builds on the core Spring IoC application context concept, extends it for web environments, and seamlessly integrates with a generic middle-tier application context. Owing to Spring's layered architecture, a Spring middle tier context can easily be integrated with a different web framework too, as we have seen previously.

A fundamental difference between Spring and dedicated web frameworks such as Struts, WebWork, and Tapestry is that Spring treats its MVC framework as part of an overall architectural solution, and it is thus designed to integrate closely and seamlessly with Spring's rich middle tier management functionality, based on IoC and AOP.

Basic Controller Workflow

Spring MVC does not build around a central controller or action interface. Instead, the central point is the **dispatcher** `org.springframework.web.servlet.DispatcherServlet`, a highly customizable component that dispatches web requests to **handlers**, treating the latter as plain `java.lang.Object` instances. Handlers are defined as beans in the dispatcher's own application context: in case of a servlet named "example," by default loaded from `/WEB-INF/example-servlet.xml`. This context definition file uses the same bean-configuration syntax as other parts of Spring.

Mapping requests to handlers is delegated to implementations of the interface `org.springframework.web.servlet.HandlerMapping`, defined as beans in the servlet's application context. Two out-of-the-box implementations are provided, either identifying mapped handlers via their bean names, or explicitly mapping certain URL patterns to handler instances. (Other strategies can be implemented in a custom fashion, for example, based on request parameters.) A returned handler gets invoked via a corresponding **handler adapter** that knows how to deal with the specific type of handler.

Spring does provide a default interface for handlers, namely `org.springframework.web.servlet.mvc.Controller`, with a single method:

```
public interface Controller {

   ModelAndView handleRequest(HttpServletRequest request,
                              HttpServletResponse response)
      throws Exception;
}
```

In many respects, this can be considered *the* central interface for controllers. The corresponding handler adapter does not have to be defined explicitly, and all pre-built controllers that come with Spring implement this interface. Most application developers will not have to concern themselves with the generic handler support, but will work with the `Controller` interface or the controller base classes in the `org.springframework.web.servlet.mvc` package.

Although few users will want to work with them directly, it is worth mentioning the concept of handler adapters as an example of the flexibility of Spring's web MVC framework (like most parts of Spring). In contrast to Struts' or WebWork's dispatching approach, Spring's DispatcherServlet could deal with any handler object if a corresponding handler adapter were implemented. Instead of having to wrap each and every existing handler object with a specific Spring controller, you could write a handler adapter once and then plug in corresponding handler objects, possibly actions from a different web MVC framework. As multiple handler adapters per dispatcher are allowed, you could even mix multiple kinds of handlers within the same dispatcher servlet.

Focusing on the default `Controller` interface again, we see that the `handleRequest` method mirrors the `service` method of a servlet. A Controller can be considered a servlet that is not managed by a direct definition in `web.xml` but by Spring's DispatcherServlet. Like a servlet, it can write a response directly, simply returning `null` to indicate that it does not want to forward to any view but has already completed processing itself:

```
public class MyDoItYourselfController implements Controller {

   ModelAndView handleRequest(HttpServletRequest request,
                              HttpServletResponse response)
      throws IOException {
     response.getWriter().write("Hello world");
     return null;
   }
}
```

Having Spring, rather than the Servlet API, manage the lifecycle of controllers is an important advantage, rather than a reinvention of a wheel, because it means that controllers can benefit from Spring IoC, AOP and other sophisticated middle tier functionality. Spring offers a much better wheel. By contrast, the Servlet API provides only primitive parameter passing and cumbersome JNDI access.

Spring provides web-specific *interception* via the `org.springframework.web.servlet.Handler` `Interceptor` interface, allowing it to pre-handle and post-handle a request, before and after execution of the mapped handler. Such `HandlerInterceptors` are registered with the appropriate `HandlerMapping` bean, to be applied for all handlers mapped there. Spring's standard AOP facilities can be applied to handlers too, allowing for any kind of generic method interception.

Model and View Handling

To leverage DispatcherServlet's MVC support, a `Controller` can return an `org.springframework` `.web.servlet.ModelAndView` object, gathering:

❑ The symbolic name of a view, to be resolved by a **view resolver** (see below), or an instance of the `org.springframework.web.servlet.View` interface (in which case view resolution is unnecessary).

❑ A `java.util.Map` of model attributes, with model object names as keys and model objects as values, to be exposed to the view (in the case of a JSP, as request attributes).

A minimal controller might look as follows. It examines a given parameter `myParam` of type int, not via data binding to a bean property but via a convenience method that tries to find an int parameter with the given name, returning a default value if no value is found. (Of course Spring also provides sophisticated data binding support, which we'll discuss in a moment.)

```
public class MyMinimalController implements Controller {

  ModelAndView handleRequest(HttpServletRequest request,
                             HttpServletResponse response) {
    int myParam = RequestUtils.getIntParameter(request, "myParam", -1);
    String viewName = (myParam != -1) ? "/mysuccess.jsp" : "/myform.jsp";
    return new ModelAndView(viewName);
  }
}
```

The preceding controller does not specify a model to be exposed to the view. A minimal controller that returns two Strings as model attributes could look as follows, using the keys "message" and "headline":

```
public class MyMinimalControllerWithModel implements Controller {

  ModelAndView handleRequest(HttpServletRequest request,
                             HttpServletResponse response) {
    Map model = new HashMap();
    model.put("message", "Hello world");
    model.put("headline", "my first controller");
    return new ModelAndView("/myview.jsp", model);
  }
}
```

The Spring DispatcherServlet will then resolve the view name and render it with the given model. The actual resolution is delegated to an implementation of the interface `org.springframework.web` `.servlet.ViewResolver`, passing in the view name and the current locale for localized resolution:

```
public interface ViewResolver {

   View resolveViewName(String viewName, Locale locale)
      throws ServletException;
}
```

The default implementation is `org.springframework.web.servlet.view.InternalResourceView Resolver`, which will simply interpret the given view name as internal resource URL (to be reached via a Servlet RequestDispatcher), possibly referencing a JSP. This is what the preceding controller implementations assume for simplicity's sake.

Of course, there are more sophisticated out-of-the-box view resolvers available, like `org.springframe work.web.servlet.view.ResourceBundleViewResolver` or `org.springframework.web.servlet.view.XmlViewResolver` that read in view bean definitions and resolve views by their symbolic name. Such definitions can specify any view implementation class and any predefined properties, such as "static" model attributes that should be available to the view in all cases. `ResourceBundleView Resolver` will even automatically detect localized resource bundles that define specific views for certain languages.

The actual view rendering happens in an implementation of the interface `org.springframework.web.servlet.View`, which is designed to write to the HTTP response:

```
public interface View {

   void render(Map model,
         HttpServletRequest request,
         HttpServletResponse response)
      throws ServletException, IOException;
}
```

Out-of-the-box implementations of the `View` interface include:

❑   `org.springframework.web.servlet.view.InternalResourceView`: For JSPs, servlets, and other resources that can be reached by a RequestDispatcher forward, exposing the model as servlet request attributes.

❑   `org.springframework.web.servlet.view.JstlView`: An extension of `InternalResource View` for JSTL-based JSP pages, additionally exposing JSTL-specific locale and resource bundle attributes.

❑   `org.springframework.web.servlet.view.tiles.TilesView/TilesJstlView`: An extension of `InternalResourceView` for Tiles template definitions, with or without JSTL support (requiring `struts.jar` in the class path for the Tiles classes). Spring also provides a convenience base class for Tiles component controllers, for easy access to Spring-managed beans.

❑   `org.springframework.web.servlet.view.velocity.VelocityView`: For Velocity templates, exposing the model Map as a Velocity template model, without any bridges like a VelocityServlet that re-exposes request attributes as template model. The VelocityEngine can be set up via factory classes included with Spring, allowing for flexible Velocity configuration.

❑   Others such as `AbstractPdfView`, `AbstractExcelView`, and `AbstractXsltView`.

A detailed hands-on guide for specific view technologies is outside the scope of this book. For a further discussion of view technology in the context of request-driven web MVC, see the "Appropriate View Technologies" section later in this chapter.

Configuration Example

Each Spring DispatcherServlet has its own namespace and application context. By default, the context definition is read in from a file "*servletName*-servlet.xml": If the servlet is named `example` in `web.xml`, the associated context definition file is expected at `/WEB-INF/example-servlet.xml`. This allows for separation of large configurations into multiple files simply by defining multiple DispatcherServlets with distinct servlet mappings in `web.xml`. Each DispatcherServlet will load its own application context, potentially with completely different mapping strategies and resolvers.

As already outlined, all components in a DispatcherServlet context are defined as ordinary Spring beans, and hence able to leverage all of Spring's configuration facilities. The most important components are obviously the application's controller implementations. Apart from controllers, a dispatcher context will mainly consist of framework beans like handler mappings and view resolvers. It should typically not contain application objects other than controller helpers: Middle tier definitions should go into the root application context. All DispatcherServlet contexts will implicitly be children of the latter and have direct access to its beans.

> **Web controllers in a Spring MVC web application are defined in a web application context and are thus themselves managed by a Spring IoC container. This means that they benefit from seamless access to application business objects.**

We've already seen how to load a Spring root web application context earlier in this chapter. Note that a root application context is not required: For simple scenarios, a DispatcherServlet context without a shared parent is sufficient. In the simplest case, a DispatcherServlet application context can look as follows. Note that we cannot use the "id" attribute for bean definitions that indicate a URL path, because "/" is invalid in XML IDs, but have to rely on "name":

```
<beans>

    <bean name="/doityourself" class="example.MyDoItYourselfController"/>

    <bean name="/minimal" class="example.MyMinimalController"/>

</beans>
```

If we assume that the DispatcherServlet has been mapped to `/example/*` in `web.xml`, the dispatcher will automatically map `/example/doityourself` to the `MyDoItYourselfController` instance and `/example/minimal` to the `MyMinimalController` instance. It will do so via an implicit handler mapping default, namely `org.springframework.web.servlet.mvc.handler.BeanNameUrlHandler Mapping`, which interprets bean names as URL paths.

We can also define explicit mappings between URL paths and handlers via a `SimpleUrlHandler Mapping` definition. The controller beans can then use any symbolic "name" or "id" to identify them.

```
<beans>

    <bean id="myHandlerMapping"
        class="org.springframework.web.servlet.handler.SimpleUrlHandlerMapping">
      <property name="urlMap">
        <map>
          <entry key="/doityourself">
            <ref local="myDoItYourself"/>
          </entry>
          <entry key="/minimal">
            <ref local="myMinimal"/>
          </entry>
      </map>
      </property>
    </bean>

    <bean id="myDoItYourself" class="example.MyDoItYourselfController"/>

    <bean id="myMinimal" class="example.MyMinimalController"/>

</beans>
```

The preceding definitions will interpret returned view names as resource URLs in the web application, for example, /myview.jsp, via the implicit ViewResolver default org.springframework.web .servlet.view.InternalResourceViewResolver. It is normally preferable to configure Internal ResourceViewResolver to add a prefix and a suffix to the given view name: For example, the controller might return myview, and the resolver might automatically add a prefix of /WEB-INF/jsp/ and a suffix of .jsp to arrive at a resource path of /WEB-INF/jsp/myview.jsp. This allows for a simple version of symbolic view names, as follows:

```
<beans>

    <bean id="viewResolver" class="org.springframework.web.servlet.view.
        InternalResourceViewResolver">
      <property name="prefix">
        <value>/WEB-INF/jsp/</value>
      </property>
      <property name="suffix">
        <value>.jsp</value>
      </property>
    </bean>

    <bean name="/minimal" class="example.MyMinimalController"/>

</beans>
```

While InternalResourceViewResolver allows for even more customization, like the actual subclass of org.springframework.web.servlet.view.InternalResourceView to use, it is not intended for mixing different view technologies. A generic view resolver like the preceding XmlViewResolver or ResourceBundleViewResolver allows for the full power of view definitions with any kind of view implementation, at the price of more configuration effort. This is the application developer's choice: As usual, Spring does not prescribe a single way.

For an example of individual view definitions, consider the following usage of
ResourceBundleViewResolver:

```
<beans>

  <bean id="viewResolver" class="org.springframework.web.servlet.view.
     ResourceBundleViewResolver">
   <property name="basename">
     <value>views</value>
   </property>
  </bean>

  <bean name="/minimal" class="example.MyMinimalController"/>

</beans>
```

The resource bundle basename "views" indicates to look for a views.properties file in the root of the
class path, potentially localized via additional views_en.properties or views_de.properties files
(according to the rules of java.util.ResourceBundle). The view definitions contained there follow
Spring's properties bean definition syntax, an alternative to XML bean definitions. This allows for arbitrary view definitions, with the logical view name as bean name.

```
myview.class=org.springframework.web.servlet.view.InternalResourceView
myview.url=/WEB-INF/jsp/myview.jsp

otherview.class=org.springframework.web.servlet.view.velocity.VelocityView
otherview.url=otherview.vm
```

Command Controllers

At this point, you might wonder where commands and forms come in: So far, we've discussed only the
basic MVC architecture with the generic Controller that takes HttpServletRequest and
HttpServletResponse arguments. As you can see, Spring's web MVC does not impose any specific
form handling or command paradigm: A plain controller works at the same level as a servlet, but is managed by an MVC workflow that allows for flexible dispatching and abstracted model and view handling.

More sophisticated controllers with specific workflows are provided in a hierarchy of out-of-the-box
Controller implementations in the org.springframework.web.servlet.mvc package. These are
entirely optional and completely separated from the core DispatcherServlet workflow. Figure 13-1 illustrates the controller class hierarchy.

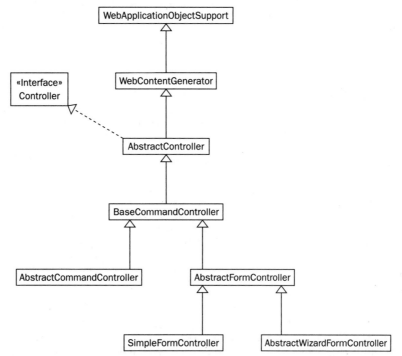

Figure 13-1

The generic base class `org.springframework.web.context.support.WebApplication ObjectSupport` provides access to the current `WebApplicationContext`; `org.springframework .web.servlet.support.WebContentGenerator` encapsulates various settings related to HTTP caching. `AbstractController`, a convenience base class for implementations of the `Controller` interface, applies `WebContentGenerator`'s caching settings to the current HTTP response before delegating to a template method to be implemented by subclasses.

Command-driven controllers can be implemented as subclasses of `org.springframework.web .servlet.mvc.AbstractCommandController`. You simply need to specify a command class, which can be any JavaBean; there is no need to derive a command from a base class or to implement a particular interface. `AbstractCommandController` shares the common base class `BaseCommandController` with Spring's form-controller implementations (discussed in the next section).

Thus the example we've seen for Struts and WebWork could be written as follows using a Spring command controller. First, we need a command class:

```
public class MyCommand {

  private int myParam = -1;

  public void setMyParam(int myParam) {
    this.myParam = myParam
  }
```

```
        public int getMyParam() {
          return myParam;
        }
      }
```

The corresponding controller implementation looks as follows:

```
public class MyCommandController extends AbstractCommandController {

    public MyCommandController() {
      setCommandClass(MyCommand.class);
    }

    protected ModelAndView handle(HttpServletRequest request,
                                  HttpServletResponse response,
                                  Object command,
                                  BindException errors) {
      MyCommand myCmd = (MyCommand) command;
      String viewName = (myCmd.getMyParam() != -1) ? "mysuccess" : "myform";
      return new ModelAndView(viewName, errors.getModel());
    }
}
```

The handle template method is invoked on every request, with a freshly populated instance of the command. All applicable request parameters will have been bound to the command bean properties. Type mismatches will have been recorded in the given "errors" instance, implementing the org.springframework.validation.Errors interface. This validation errors holder can also be thrown as exception if validation errors are considered fatal, as it is passed in as the implementation class org.springframework.validation.BindException.

The handle implementation can perform additional validation of the command before it begins actual processing and returns a view reference. However, it is preferable to let a **Validator** do that work, via setting an instance of org.springframework.validation.Validator to AbstractCommand Controller's "validator" bean property. We'll see how to use a Validator in the form controller example that follows. An additional option is to override AbstractCommandController's onBindAnd Validate method which gets invoked after the validator.

The command object and the validation errors holder will automatically be exposed as model to the view through passing the Map returned by errors.getModel() to the ModelAndView instance. The default attribute key for the command object is "command"; this can be customized by Abstract CommandController's "commandName" property. A command-controller implementation can also decide to return a completely different model or none at all, by returning a corresponding ModelAndView object.

As alternative to AbstractCommandController, org.springframework.web.servlet.mvc. multiaction.MultiActionController allows for multiple handle methods within one controller class, similar to Struts' DispatchAction (except for being much more configurable). The resolution of the handle method name is pluggable via the interface org.springframework.web.servlet.mvc .multiaction.MethodNameResolver. Three out-of-the-box implementations of MethodName Resolver are available: based on the request path, a request parameter, or an explicit mapping between URL patterns and method names.

Each `MultiActionController` handle method can either specify just request and response, or request and response plus command. The command class will be determined via the type of the command argument, automatically creating and populating an instance before the handle method gets invoked.

The preceding command controller example looks as follows with a `MultiActionController`. The configuration has to specify a corresponding `MethodNameResolver`, possibly mapping a certain URL pattern to the `myHandle` method. Binding failures are considered fatal here; there is no way to access the `Errors` object.

```
public class MyMultiActionController extends MultiActionController {

    public ModelAndView myHandle(HttpServletRequest request,
        HttpServletResponse response, MyCommand command) {
      String viewName = (command.getMyParam() != -1) ? "mysuccess" : "myform";
      return new ModelAndView(viewName, "myCommand", command);
    }
}
```

This controller implementation explicitly returns the command instance as model, under the name "myCommand". It uses a convenience constructor of `ModelAndView` here, taking a single model object name and value.

Form Controllers

The `AbstractCommandController` base class shown previously is intended for request-scope commands and does not implement a *form submission* workflow: All requests always go to the `handle` method, regardless of whether there are validation errors. The application controller's `handle` implementation is responsible for applying the correct workflow.

For dedicated form handling, `org.springframework.web.servlet.mvc.SimpleFormController` offers more prebuilt workflow. Besides "commandClass", "commandName", and "validator", it also offers "formView", "successView", and "sessionForm" properties. It can be used in a completely declarative fashion as follows:

```
<beans>

    <bean name="/myform" class=" org.springframework.web.servlet.mvc.
        SimpleFormController">
    <property name="commandClass">
      <value>example.MyCommand</value>
    </property>
    <property name="validator">
      <ref local="myCommandValidator"/>
    </property>
    <property name="formView">
      <value>myform</value>
    </property>
    <property name="successView">
      <value>mysuccess</value>
    </property>
    </bean>
```

```xml
    <bean id="myCommandValidator" class="example.MyCommandValidator"/>

  </beans>
```

The preceding definition reuses the MyCommand class from the command controller example. The result-ing form controller will show the specified form view on a HTTP GET request for /myform, and process a submission on a POST request for /myform. In the latter case, it will first bind request parameters to the command instance, then invoke the validator, and finally return to the **form view** if there were valida-tion errors, or proceed to the **success view** else. It will expose the command object (which serves as form object here) and the validation errors holder to both views.

By default, SimpleFormController will apply a form-handling workflow but still create a new instance of the form object on each request. If it is necessary to use the original form instance for each submission, SimpleFormController's "sessionForm" property needs to be set to "true". This will cause the form object to automatically be put in the HttpSession on first request, and removed from the session after a successful form submission.

The specified Validator needs to validate the form object and register validation errors via the given validation errors holder. The SimpleFormController will then be able to apply its workflow and decide whether to return to the form view or proceed to the success view, depending on whether there are any validation errors. Note that the Errors instance will also contain binding errors that result from type mismatches; such errors will cause a return to the form view too.

```java
    public class MyCommandValidator implements Validator {

      public boolean supports(Class clazz) {
        return MyCommand.class.isAssignableForm(clazz);
      }

      public void validate(Object obj, Errors errors) {
        MyCommand myCommand = (MyCommand) obj;
        if (myCommand.getMyParam() == -1) {
          errors.rejectValue("myParam", "myParamEmpty", "myParam must be set");
        }
      }
    }
```

The Errors instance will automatically store the rejected field values on type mismatch errors; these errors will already be visible to the validator. This allows the use of any existing domain object as form object, because mismatching String values will not result in fatal errors but will be registered in the Errors instance. This is particularly convenient for numbers and java.util.Date values. Rejected val-ues will be kept there too, for convenient redisplay in the form: After all, a user expects to be able to see the rejected value again to be able to correct it before resubmission. Spring's SimpleFormController supports this important functionality without the need for a separate all-String form object.

> With Spring, it's possible to use domain or value objects as form objects if desired, through explicit support for keeping rejected values in case of type mismatches. This helps to minimize the need for object duplication, or for application objects to know about the Servlet API or Spring web API.

In a form view, validation errors can be shown to the user via direct examination of the `Errors` instance or via Spring's **JSP tag library**, in particular the `<spring:bind>` tag. Error codes like "myParamEmpty" in the example will automatically get resolved via the application context's message source, by default a standard Java resource bundle. If the error key cannot be found, the default message will be shown, in the example "myParam must be set". Type mismatch errors will appear via the same mechanism, with the failing field as field name and "typeMismatch" as error code.

Looking at error code resolution in more detail, Spring actually checks for three message keys. Let's consider the example of a "typeMismatch" error on field "myDate" of form "myForm". The error code resolver will first look for "typeMismatch.myForm.myDate", then for "typeMismatch.myDate", and finally for "typeMismatch". This allows for the choice between very specific messages if necessary and general ones for simple cases.

The generic `SimpleFormController` can be subclassed to address more advanced requirements, such as:

- Using a preloaded object as form object, by overriding the `formBackingObject` method, typically in combination with "sessionForm" set to "true"

- Customized form-submission detection (for example, checking for a certain submit request parameter instead of an HTTP POST)

- Registering custom JavaBean property editors in an `initBinder` implementation, for proper display of localized numbers and dates

- Custom `onBindAndValidate` post-processing for additional manual data binding

- A custom submit action, instead of forwarding to a success view (for example, persisting the changes to a domain object)

- Keeping parameter values like for "commandClass" in Java code instead of in metadata, analogous to the command controller example shown earlier

Spring also provides a convenient base class for **wizard-style workflows**: `org.springframework.web.servlet.mvc.AbstractWizardFormController`. It caters for multiple form pages that all work on the same form object, always operating in session form mode. Instead of a simple form view/success view workflow, it allows for changing between form pages and explicit finish and cancel requests. Validation rules are typically implemented per page instead of per form object. See `AbstractWizardFormController`'s Javadocs for details.

Form view implementations that cooperate with Spring's form controllers are straightforward to write. Spring's small but powerful JSP tag library offers convenient access to form fields and validation errors. It is designed to integrate with JSTL, rather than compete with JSTL, which provides excellent solutions to many traditional view scripting needs. Alternatively, Spring offers various convenience classes to access the same model and errors information with Java expressions or in Velocity templates.

Note that Spring does not offer a JSP tag library that wraps HTML controls: It adheres to the design decision not to *generate* HTML code from custom tags, but to use custom tags to *fill dynamic values* into existing HTML templates. This allows for a maximum degree of transparency and control over the HTML code.

Integration with a Middle Tier

A Spring DispatcherServlet's own application context is automatically a child of the root web application context, if the latter exists. This means that all of the beans in the root context can be referenced from the DispatcherServlet context, but not vice versa. For example, let's assume that the root application context consists of the following bean definitions:

```
<beans>

  <bean name="myBusinessObject" class="example.MyBusinessObject"/>

  <bean name="myOtherObject" class="example.MyOtherObject"/>

</beans>
```

A DispatcherServlet application context can then define the following controllers that reference the business objects in the root context. The syntax is the same as for referencing objects in the same context; you obviously need to use the generic `<ref bean="..."/>`, as `<ref local="..."/>` would expect an XML entity with the given ID in the *same XML file*. Controller in this example would be coded to use Setter Dependency Injection:

```
<beans>

  <bean name="/doityourself" class="example.MyDoItYourselfController">
    <property name="businessObject">
      <ref bean="myBusinessObject"/>
    </property>
  </bean>

  <bean name="/minimal" class="example.MyMinimalController">
    <property name="otherObject">
      <ref bean="myOtherObject"/>
    </property>
  </bean>

</beans>
```

> There is no need to handle ApplicationContext references in application code when using Spring's web MVC. Web controllers can be wired up just like any other bean in a Spring application context. Therefore, one consistent IoC approach to configuring objects, via Dependency Injection, is available at all layers.

Recap

The following table illustrates the relation between the previously mentioned object types in a request-driven web MVC framework and their equivalents in Spring's web MVC framework:

MVC object type	Spring web MVC equivalent
controller	Controller, or any handler Object with an adapter
interceptor	HandlerInterceptor, or AOP MethodInterceptor
command/form	Any command or form JavaBean
validator	Validator
validation errors holder	Errors
model	Map of arbitrary model objects in ModelAndView
view reference	View instance or view name in ModelAndView

> **The Spring Framework offers a clean implementation of request-driven web MVC with a very high degree of decoupling and flexibility, built on its generic configuration infrastructure. The dispatching mechanism and the provided base classes for command/form controllers are strictly separated; you can choose appropriate workflows on a per-case basis.**
>
> **The framework respects all six object roles of request-driven web MVC. It supports both the Struts model of controller singletons, with or without session form objects, and request-scoped command objects. Any domain object can serve as form object, as type mismatch errors are registered and the rejected values are kept for redisplay in a separate errors holder.**

Appropriate View Technologies

Request-driven web MVC frameworks offer a clear separation between controller and view: The latter can be any component that is able to render a response for the given model. There are a variety of choices for view implementation, like JSP and Velocity; a good web MVC framework will allow you to switch between them seamlessly, reusing the exact same controllers and model objects. As this is not the main focus of this chapter, please refer to Chapter 13 of *Expert One-on-One J2EE Design and Development* for a more thorough discussion of JSP, Velocity, XSLT, XSL-FO, XMLC, and PDF generation.

As we've seen, all of the popular request-driven web MVC frameworks can directly use **JSP** as a view technology. **Velocity** (`http://jakarta.apache.org/velocity`) is also widely supported, though not always as straightforwardly as JSP. Other template-based view technologies similar to Velocity are available, like **WebMacro** (`www.webmacro.org`) and **FreeMarker** (`http://freemarker.sourceforge.net`). The most important advantage of the templating approach is that it still allows view designers to work with the HTML page concept, interspersed with dynamic snippets for model access and control flow. Syntax is usually simpler and more intuitive than that of JSP.

Alternative approaches are available but less popular. **XSLT** can be used to transform generic XML output into view-specific markup. Although very powerful, it does not share the basic concepts of templating technologies and can hardly be expected to be understood by view designers. XSLT processing also usually carries a large performance overhead, compared to most other view technologies. *XMLC* (`http://xmlc.objectweb.org`) transforms HTML templates into XMLC objects that can be manipulated and rendered via Java code. XMLC was promoted by the Enhydra project (`www.enhydra.org`), but seems to never have reached the mainstream; it is now hosted by ObjectWeb.

A further option is **HTML generation** in Java code, whether by direct `print` statements or using an HTML generation library. This is similar to the original "plain old servlet" approach and the classic CGI approach popularized by Perl. A plain servlet can be used as view for a request-driven web MVC framework, being forwarded to, as with a JSP. With WebWork and Spring, you are free to do a custom implementation of the respective view interface, issuing a set of `print` statements based on the given model. We don't recommend either of these options, however, as any change in HTML code requires a change in a Java class. Furthermore, making Java developers responsible for HTML template content makes it difficult to achieve a division between presentation and content, essential on large projects.

Binary formats like PDF and Microsoft Excel's XLS can also be integrated with request-driven web MVC. Of course, they do not allow for interactive processing like form handling: They are used only for certain views in an application, typically representing reports. In principal, they can be integrated with any web MVC framework, just like HTML generation code. The Spring Framework makes this particularly easy through offering prebuilt base classes for PDF and Excel generation: The Spring *Countries* sample application illustrates this via its PDF and Excel reports.

As outlined previously, integrating a view technology that does not have access to the HttpServletRequest (that is, anything beyond a JSP or a servlet) with Struts requires building a bridge, typically in the form of a rendering servlet. While this has been done for Velocity and XSLT, JSP is still dominant in the Struts world. With the pluggable interfaces of WebWork and Spring, alternative view technologies can be integrated in a more direct and flexible fashion.

Despite being very popular and a part of standard J2EE, JSP is not necessarily an ideal view implementation choice for web MVC. It arguably provides too much power, as it offers means for handling request parameters, forwarding to a different resource, and so on, things that a proper view in an MVC architecture is not supposed to do. With clear coding guidelines and appropriate tag libraries, JSP is still a viable view technology, particularly with the introduction of the **JSTL** and the **JSP Expression Language**, and the general adoption of the EL as an alternative scripting language to Java in JSP 2.0.

There are many view technologies available that suit the request-driven web MVC paradigm. In a good web MVC framework, choosing the view technology per view can be seamless: for example, Velocity for all HTML views but binary PDFs for certain generated reports.

While JSP is by far the most popular choice, template languages like Velocity offer similar strengths with the arguable benefit of less scripting power. If choosing JSP, consider the JSTL and the JSP Expression Language to avoid scattered JSP scriptlets.

Templating languages such as Velocity, although they are interpreted, are often faster than JSP, so there is no compelling performance argument to use JSP (in fact, quite possibly the reverse).

Alternative Approaches to Web MVC

While request-driven web MVC frameworks have proven hugely popular in the last couple of years, the J2EE world keeps seeing a variety of alternative approaches. Two of the most important developments are portlets and event-driven web MVC; in the next sections, we will briefly review them.

Portals and Portlets

Web portals are typically implemented as a single HTML page that consists of multiple completely independent sections, each implemented as controller-view component. In contrast to the classic request-driven MVC approach, there is no workflow controller per UI action that determines the composite view to render. Rather, a **portal container** is in control of the workflow, determining the layout pages where the components get included, and rendering each component wherever placed.

Controller-view components in a portal are called **portlets**. Each portlet is a self-sufficient interactive component rather than a subordinate delegate of a workflow controller. It can receive render requests, typically acting as MVC controller: It examines request parameters, builds a model, and forwards to a view. In such a view, it can submit action requests to itself via a URL that specifically addresses the portlet, performing state changes and other actions. The portal container will then automatically initiate the rendering of the composite view again.

The Java **Portlet specification** (JSR 168; www.jcp.org/en/jsr/detail?id=168) defines a standard API for portlet containers. After a long incubation period, it was finally released in November 2003. All major portal server vendors, such as IBM, BEA, and Oracle, have announced support for it in addition to their existing proprietary portlet APIs.

The Portlet specification defines the notion of a `javax.portlet.Portlet` analogous to a servlet, with a similar API and environment. In contrast to a servlet, a portlet is not a component responsible for processing a complete HTTP request. Instead, it is a callback component that gets notified by the workflow handler of a portal container, reacting to various commands:

- ❑ `doView(RenderRequest, RenderResponse)` is supposed to show the default view of the portlet.

- ❑ `doEdit(RenderRequest, RenderResponse)` is supposed to show the edit view of the portlet, if supported.

- ❑ `doHelp(RenderRequest, RenderResponse)` is supposed to show the help view of the portlet, if supported.

- ❑ `processAction(ActionRequest, ActionResponse)` gets invoked by the container if the portlet has submitted a request to itself, from any view mode.

In a typical JSR 168 portlet, `doView` acts as component controller that prepares a model, possibly accessing middle-tier resources and services, and forwards to a JSP that is specifically designed as portlet view. The latter will issue simple content HTML that can easily participate in the look and feel of a surrounding composite page.

To submit a form to itself, a portlet JSP can define a standard HTML `<form>` tag, specifying the action URL via `<portlet:actionURL>` from the Portlet tag library. The container will then invoke processAction with the submitted parameters, returning to the previous view mode again, that is, invoking doView, doEdit or doHelp. The action implementation can also switch the mode, for example, to the default view after a successful submission from the edit view.

A collection of portlets is deployed as a standard J2EE web-application archive (WAR), with the portlets defined in /WEB-INF/portlet.xml. Such an archive is not intended to be dropped into a normal web container, as it is not supposed to specify any nonportlet web components in web.xml. Rather, it will be deployed to a portal server that will host it in its portlet container. In contrast to servlets or JSPs in a normal web application, portlets will not be available on their own but need to be dropped into a portal page with a portal builder tool for the particular server.

While they share basic request-driven web MVC concepts, there is no strong synergy between portlets and servlet-based web MVC frameworks. The Portlet specification defines its own rudimentary MVC mechanism, specifically adapted to the needs of self-contained portlets. If the portlet container is running in a J2EE server, portlets can access middle tier resources and services via JNDI, just like other web tier components. Unfortunately, it seems to be impossible to share local resources with other components in a web application, as they are hosted in a separate environment: The portlet container is typically a web application itself.

> **Portlets are significantly different from servlets and servlet-based web MVC frameworks in that they do not allow for typical application UI workflows and are not intended for building classic application views. Rather, they represent reusable interactive components for Intranet and Internet portals, with the option of accessing shared resources and services underneath. Portlets should not be considered for building classic workflow-driven web application user interfaces.**

Event-driven Web MVC Frameworks

Besides request-driven frameworks that act as thin MVC wrappers over the servlet request-response workflow, a different kind of framework for web MVC has been gaining interest in the last few years: **event-driven** frameworks that aim to apply well-known patterns from desktop UI programming to the web environment. Apple's **WebObjects** (www.apple.com/webobjects) pioneered this approach, offering a programming model that was later adopted and extended by the **Tapestry** open source framework, briefly discussed later.

Event-driven web MVC frameworks vary widely in terms of their programming model. Their common denominator is that they do *not* focus on form submissions to URLs that are in turn mapped to controllers that handle those requests. Rather, form components are wired to **listeners** that are invoked with **events**. Furthermore, such frameworks typically do not aim for pluggable view technologies that render given model objects, but treat web pages as set of components that keep state and know how to render themselves, potentially with different skins.

Frameworks like **Echo** (www.nextapp.com/products/echo) and **WingS** (http://wings.mercatis.de) offer a programming model close to the well-known desktop GUI framework **Swing**, the latter going as far as imitating Swing classes one by one. The actual HTML code is generated and issued by UI component classes, and is not easily available for customization through web designers. While the similarity to desktop-style UI programming may seem appealing at first sight, this approach has tight limits in terms of customized HTML/JavaScript and flexible interaction. Furthermore, many such user interfaces tend to generate unnecessarily high amounts of session state.

> If maximizing scalability is important, minimizing the amount of session state or avoiding session state altogether is highly beneficial. Thus it's best to avoid unnecessary dependence on session state due to programming model, rather than application requirements.

Other frameworks like **Tapestry** and **Java Server Faces** (JSR 127) combine a templating approach with event handling mechanisms. The HTML layout is defined in templates, as with JSP and Velocity views for request-driven web MVC. Tapestry uses its own templating mechanism while JSF relies on JSP custom tags. The actual MVC workflow and view rendering is managed by a framework servlet that processes events from components on the page.

The latter template-based approaches are not only inspired by Apple's WebObjects but, in some cases, by Microsoft's **ASP.NET** (`www.asp.net`). In many respects, Java Server Faces is intended as the direct equivalent of ASP.NET in the Java world, offering a web programming model that is page-centric and well-suited for tool support, less targeting detail-obsessed web scripters but rather rapid application developers. Of course, in typical Java fashion, JSF is a specification, not a single product: Multiple tool vendors have announced JSF support that is supposed to match Visual Studio .NET's support for ASP.NET.

Neither type of event-driven framework has reached the mainstream yet (with the arguable exception of Tapestry), but there is significant mindshare around the templating approach in the developer community. Tapestry recently gained another boost of momentum through its adoption by Apache's Jakarta project, with the upcoming release 3.0 introducing a general configuration overhaul (at the time of writing, still in beta). Java Server Faces is approaching its final stages, with various early access implementations already available. We will briefly discuss these two solutions in terms of their programming model and differences to request-driven frameworks.

Tapestry

Tapestry (`http://jakarta.apache.org/tapestry`) is an open source web MVC framework developed by Howard Lewis Ship, adopting a completely different approach to request-driven frameworks, inspired by WebObjects. Tapestry has been in development for a few years, and is now mature. In 2003 it joined Apache's Jakarta project, after being hosted on SourceForge for several years.

Tapestry focuses on total separation between Java code and HTML template, dividing each **page** into three artifacts:

- ❑ **An HTML template** containing pure HTML markup, with dynamic parts marked with `jwcid` attributes
- ❑ **A page specification** defining the page implementation class and the components used on the page
- ❑ **A page class** defining the model and the listeners for the page

Each page can consist of any number of **components** that can also be nested. Each component implementation is divided into three similar artifacts:

❑ **An HTML template** containing HTML markup for the component, again with `jwcid` attributes

❑ **A component specification** defining the component implementation class and the nested components used

❑ **A component class** defining the model and the listeners for the component

With Tapestry, HTML templates do not contain scriptlets or custom tags. Rather, certain tags are marked with `jwcid` (Java Web Component ID) attributes, typically `<span jwcid="...">` tags. At runtime, those tags are replaced with HTML code issued by Tapestry components. The original content in the template can either be used by the component, or be replaced by dynamic content if it just serves as illustrating content for the static template.

The main rationale is that such HTML templates can be viewed in any browser or HTML editor, as they contain pure HTML tags, enriched only with non-standard `jwcid` attributes that all browsers and editors will ignore. In contrast to JSPs or Velocity templates, they are not *dynamic* view implementations with markup code, dynamic expressions, and flow logic but just *static* **templates** that need to get **merged with the page specification** to result in an actual dynamic view. Every dynamic element is modeled as such a component that needs to be merged: message placeholders, conditions, loops, forms, buttons, links, and so on.

Tapestry will handle all workflow management, so that the application itself is never confronted with `HttpServletRequest` or `HttpServletResponse` objects. Values submitted by a form are not bound to a command or form object but to properties of the page (or component) instance; controller logic is implemented in listeners defined in page or component classes. A listener can process an action and forward to a different page, just like a controller in a request-driven framework. A Tapestry page thus combines state and event listener, corresponding to model and controller in request-driven web MVC.

Tapestry page instances are pooled: If requested, an instance gets fetched from the pool, populated and used for the request, and returned to the pool in a clean state. Page properties can be marked as persistent if they should keep their state from one rendering of the page to the next for the same user: Then Tapestry will implicitly store the property values in the HttpSession, and populate a Page instance with them when fetching a page from the pool for rendering.

Additionally, the whole Tapestry application needs an **application specification**, defining the available pages. The application specification also determines the **Engine** class to be used: The Engine is the server-side state manager for a Tapestry application, typically stored in the HttpSession. It can hold two kinds of application-specific state objects:

❑ A **Visit** object that contains all state that is associated with the current visit from a user, corresponding to an HttpSession attribute in Servlet API terms

❑ A **Global** object that is shared by all Engine instances in an application, corresponding to a ServletContext attribute

Like pages, Engine instances are pooled, at least as long as there is no session. When an application requests the Visit object for the first time, Tapestry will implicitly create an HttpSession and keep the Engine instance there for the rest of the session. This "lazy initialization" of a session leads to an efficient use of resources, particularly when compared to other event-driven frameworks.

> Tapestry completely abstracts the Servlet API and builds its own page-centric web MVC programming model on top of it. While the strict separation between view logic and template has its merits, you always need to consider both the page specification and the template to understand the behavior of a page. This arguably causes overhead for simple tasks but usually pays off for more complex user interfaces that can reuse components to a high degree.

Tapestry's page class concept is similar to that of ASP.NET, serving the same role of page model with listener methods. However, ASP.NET does not try to abstract HTTP concepts, and offers direct request and response references in page classes, for example to redirect to a different URL. An important difference between Tapestry and ASP.NET is that the latter does not separate HTML template and page specification but rather includes both in a dynamic web page, reducing the number of artifacts and easing rapid application development.

Dynamic view templates that contain markup code interspersed with dynamic snippets like JSPs and Velocity templates include all information that is necessary for understanding the rendering behavior of a page. Combined with controllers in a request-driven web MVC framework, their handling is arguably more natural and straightforward for developers who are familiar with the Servlet API, while Tapestry imposes a completely different world view.

Java Server Faces

At JavaOne 2001, Sun announced a new JSR with the goal to create a JSP-based web MVC framework that is well-suited for GUI builder tools: Java Server Faces (JSF; http://java.sun.com/j2ee/javaserverfaces). After a long phase of relative inactivity, Craig McClanahan (of Struts) took over the JSR in 2002. Java Server Faces was finally released in March 2004, close to three years after its inception.

While also adopting an event-based paradigm, JSF offers a completely different programming model to Tapestry. It focuses on heavy use of **JSP tag libraries** for form building, with references to **validators** and **navigation rules** embedded in the JSP code. Strictly speaking, JSP is not required, but de facto JSF purely concentrates on JSP for the time being. JSF views are invoked via the FacesServlet, normally mapped to /faces/*, typically using the target JSP name directly, like /faces/myView.jsp. Validators, navigation rules, and "managed beans" like form objects can be defined in faces-config.xml.

Actions are implemented as command-style event listeners, to be invoked, for example, on form submission or change of a form field. They return their outcome as String result, typically referencing a navigation rule that leads to a view, and can access their environment via a FacesContext, *very* similar to WebWork. The difference is that those actions are not mapped as handlers for URLs but rather referenced in JSF views as listeners for specific events. Form objects are simple JavaBeans that do not have to extend a common base class: a further non-Struts heritage.

So in contrast to Struts, listeners, validators and form objects do not depend on the Servlet API. But of course, the view implementations are more or less supposed to be JSPs. The main rationale of Servlet API independence is **Portlet compatibility**: As we have learned, the Portlet API defines its own request, response, and context interfaces. The JSF FacesContext lets you access those objects, but only of type java.lang.Object, to be cast to either Servlet or Portlet API interfaces (if necessary).

Components are implemented as custom tags that are skinnable through the use of pluggable **renderers** for markup generation. This is supposed to allow for reuse of the same JSF view for different target formats like HTML and WML, a questionable design goal, as the experience of the last few years has shown that you typically need to adapt view structure for different formats. Pluggable view implementations that access a view-independent model (as seen with request-driven web MVC) are a more appropriate way to address multiple target formats.

The generated markup of forms and other components can only be customized through renderer implementations. In contrast to the classic template approach of JSP, Velocity, and also Tapestry, HTML designers cannot easily fine-tune the markup of components but just the surrounding HTML page. The Spring Framework's web view implementation is most notably different: With Spring, not a single static content character is generated by a custom tag; all presentation is handled in HTML templates.

With respect to separation, JSF is the exact opposite of Tapestry in the event-driven world: As much as possible is kept in the JSF view that is implemented as a JSP, with only event listeners and form objects implemented as Java objects. This facilitates easy rapid application development via JSP-aware **GUI builder tools** like Macromedia's Dreamweaver, but severely hinders suitability for a browser or conventional HTML editor. Furthermore, maintainability and testability also suffer.

A severe limitation of Java Server Faces in its current scope is that it does not include a rich set of GUI components in the specification. It can be expected that tool developers will offer all kinds of out-of-the-box components for JSF, but no doubt in proprietary implementations that tie applications to the particular tool. Many Swing-based applications must include GUI component libraries from JBuilder or other IDEs just because the builder tool offered richer or more convenient components than the GUI framework itself. Do we really want to see a similar effect in the JSF world?

> **Java Server Faces has been hyped as the next big thing in J2EE web development for more than two years and is now taking shape. In its current incarnation, JSF is a JSP-centric affair that is heavily targeted toward GUI builder tools, resulting in code that gathers all sorts of concerns in the web page. There is no notion of view-agnostic controller and model, and no concept of pluggable views. With this programming model, JSF is well-suited for attracting .NET and other RAD developers, but not for becoming the de-facto standard web MVC framework in the Java world.**
>
> **We expect to see a massive vendor marketing push behind JSF. However, we're not convinced that JSF will represent a real advance on existing open source solutions such as Tapestry, WebWork, and Spring web MVC.**

Even if JSF is intended as direct equivalent of ASP.NET, there are significant conceptual differences. JSF does follow ASP.NET in its page-centric approach, which combines dynamic view implementations with validation rules, etc. It does not adopt the "page class" concept, however, preferring per-event action implementations. Tapestry is closer to ASP.NET in that respect. Furthermore, JSF relies on JSP tag libraries, unlike ASP.NET which post-processes certain kinds of innocent-looking HTML tags like `<form>`. The JSP tag library approach is certainly cleaner in terms of control over markup generation.

Craig McClanahan announced a "Struts-JSF integration position" when he took over JSF. This led to the creation of a **Struts-Faces integration library** that attempts to merge the JSF event model with Struts actions. Newer JSF early access releases seem to address everything that Struts does in terms of action and form handling, rendering Struts-JSF integration little use except for migration-path and marketing purposes.

> **Do not try to combine approaches that do not naturally fit. Struts is at its core concerned with request-driven web MVC, while JSF is focused on page-centric RAD with per-event action listeners. Both approaches have merit, but trying to combine them does not add much value except for interim solutions when migrating from one to the other.**

A Word on ASP.NET

While a detailed discussion of ASP.NET or .NET in general is outside the scope of this book, it's useful to review the analogies and differences to the web MVC frameworks above. As noted, both Tapestry and JSF share concepts with ASP.NET: Tapestry on the "page class" side, JSF on the dynamic web page and tool support side. So how does the general level of web user interface support compare between the two platforms, J2EE and .NET?

In typical Microsoft style, Visual Studio .NET is excellent at rapid application development but does not shine when it comes to design and maintenance of complex business objects, for example due to the lack of refactoring support. It will be interesting to see how the Java tool landscape will evolve with the advent of JSF: We might see a split between RAD and "coder's" tools, or attempts at convergence into one-size-fits-all IDEs. In any case, it is likely that Visual Studio will remain ahead in terms of rapid application development convenience for some time to come.

The most important difference between J2EE's and .NET's web support is the number of options in terms of architectural approaches. In .NET, you have ASP.NET, also usable in a plain ASP fashion, to be used for any kind of content, be it markup or binary. In J2EE, you can choose from:

- ❑ ASP-style scripting with plain JSP, for simple markup
- ❑ CGI-style request processing with servlets, mainly for binary content
- ❑ A custom servlet/JSP based MVC solution, for simple workflows
- ❑ A request-driven web MVC framework with JSP, such as Struts: There is a rich choice of open source products here
- ❑ A request-driven web MVC framework with Velocity or other template languages
- ❑ A request-driven web MVC framework with XSLT, XMLC, iText—you name it
- ❑ Swing-style rendering of GUI components with Echo or WingS
- ❑ Page-specification-based GUI building with Tapestry
- ❑ ASP.NET-style GUI building with Java Server Faces

Given all the open source options, along with commercial servlet/JSP containers and JSF implementations, there will be an appropriate option for virtually any scenario and style. This amount of diversity and innovation is hard to overrate. As usual, there are Java/J2EE solutions that meet all requirements; the only downside of the choice on offer is the potential to make a wrong choice.

Summary

Many, if not most, J2EE applications have HTML-based web interfaces. In this chapter we've looked at common approaches to implementing web interfaces in J2EE applications, and how to ensure that J2EE web applications have well-defined middle tiers.

A J2EE web tier should be both **clean** and **thin**. Web MVC frameworks are important tools for achieving clean separation between the various concerns, while proper integration with an underlying middle tier is the key for keeping the web tier as thin as possible. Ensuring that a web layer is thin, concerned only with handling user interaction and presenting content, not with business logic, helps to ensure maximum reusability and testability in business logic: a vital consideration in successful projects.

Struts is currently the most popular web MVC framework, but we have seen that its API and implementation are far from ideal. Of course, there can be compelling reasons for choosing Struts, such as deep in-house expertise in Struts. Alternatives that adhere to a similar request-driven approach include WebWork2 and the Spring Framework's web MVC framework, providing more flexibility, less intrusion into application code, and a higher degree of decoupling between the involved components. As the basic patterns are similar, switching between such request-driven web MVC frameworks does not usually incur a steep learning curve.

We have briefly discussed portlets and event-driven frameworks as alternative approaches to web MVC, illustrating their programming models and target scenarios. While Tapestry is already a mature framework, and JSF promises to be the next big thing pushed by vendors, it remains to be proven that their respective approaches are superior to classic request-driven web MVC for a significant range of real-life applications. Of course, this is also a matter of taste, and of different target audiences: As outlined, JSF mainly targets ASP.NET-style rapid application development.

True web MVC is important; **proper wiring up of web components with the business layer** is even more important. Unfortunately, while the first of these points has been widely recognized in the last few years, the second has been underrated if not completely ignored. However, any web MVC framework allows for more or less elegant integration into overall application architecture, provided that appropriate patterns are applied. We have shown and discussed typical anti-patterns seen in current applications, and outlined how IoC containers (with the Spring Framework serving as reference) can help to achieve cleaner solutions.

14

Unit Testing and Testability

A revolution has occurred in software development over the last few years. From being the poor cousin of development, despised by those with more interesting and important things to do, testing—at least, **unit testing**—has been welcomed into the heart of the development process. At last, rather than seen as a tedious requirement of certain processes (for example, to achieve ISO 9001 compliance), it has been integrated into a highly productive way of working.

I think this is a very important, and very beneficial, change. In this chapter I'll try to explain why I attach so much importance to testability, and why testability considerations should influence how you go about designing and implementing applications.

Late in 2002 I spent several weeks developing a testing strategy for a large J2EE project for a major financial institution. I was working alongside a testing guru, and my remit was to combine my J2EE expertise with his experience formulating testing strategies for large projects to formulate a testing strategy covering the entire project lifecycle. I was asked to recommend changes in development practice where necessary to ensure that the strategy was applied. I was also to ensure the developers came onboard, and mentor them in the coding and testing techniques.

I learned a lot.

- ❑ I discovered that my code was much easier to test than that of most of the developers on the project. My programming style, described in *Expert One-on-One J2EE*, lends itself to effective unit testing. The Spring Framework makes this style easy to practice.

- ❑ I became increasingly convinced of the value of **test driven** (or **test first**) development.

- ❑ I became increasingly convinced that EJB is an enemy of testability.

- ❑ I reached a better understanding of the goals of unit testing.

- ❑ I became more convinced of the value of mock objects in unit testing.

- ❑ I reviewed a number of testing tools.

On the negative side, I was reminded how difficult it is to interest "old school" developers in unit testing or test first development, and how difficult it is to introduce agile practices into a large, bureaucratic organization.

In this chapter, I'll discuss these points in turn. I'll explain how to ensure that your application code is testable and effectively tested, and how to apply test-driven development. I'll survey code coverage tools and other valuable testing tools. I'll cover how to test web applications, and how to test applications built on the Spring framework.

I focus primarily on unit testing: testing classes in isolation. While other forms of testing are important to successful projects, unit testing is especially critical, and should be regarded as a core development activity.

The fundamental Java unit testing tool is **JUnit**. I'll assume familiarity with this basic tool of the trade. If you need to get up to speed with JUnit, I recommend *JUnit in Action* by Vincent Massol and Ted Husted. See the "Resources" section at the end of this chapter for details of this book and other useful resources.

Why Testing Matters

Hopefully it's superfluous, but let's examine the motivations for unit testing:

- ❑ Testing is an essential project activity that helps to ensure a quality deliverable. Unit testing is the best way to pick up many common coding errors. (However, no one activity will find *all* errors, and additional checks such as code reviews remain important.)

- ❑ Writing tests along with application code helps to define the requirements on each class. There's nothing like writing a test to make you think about the requirements of a method. What should it do on null arguments? Should it ever return null? Having to write tests ensures that such scenarios are teased out, their behavior clarified, and notes on usage added to Javadoc.

- ❑ A comprehensive test suite is a powerful and important means of documentation. While other forms of documentation remain important, a test case has the important benefit of being executable. Word documents and other external documentation can become obsolete; a test case can't.

- ❑ A comprehensive test suite gives us effective **regression testing**. As we add new functionality or fix bugs, we can prove that existing functionality still works. This can bring confidence—and great reduction in stress—later in the project lifecycle.

- ❑ The regression testing benefit is so great during the later stages of the project that overall time and effort is likely to be significantly reduced. I have seen a significant reduction in effort and stress levels in the later stages of projects with thorough testing, compared to those without.

- ❑ A comprehensive test suite enables confident **refactoring**. This enables us to ensure that at all times we have the best possible implementation of the required functionality. Without continual refactoring, a code base can rapidly degrade and become unmaintainable. Having a more maintainable code base lessens the likelihood of bugs and reduces maintenance effort.

- ❑ There is evidence from many studies that the earlier a bug is detected, the less it costs to fix. Finding a bug during user acceptance testing will result in many times the cost of finding and fixing the bug at the time of initial development. Hence picking up bugs in unit testing can represent a huge saving.

❑ A comprehensive test suite makes it much easier to fix bugs, because of the regression testing guarantee.

I use the term "comprehensive" test suite to mean a test suite that exercises a sufficient proportion of application code to provide effective regression testing. The proportion of code exercised by unit tests is referred to as the **test coverage**. Test coverage can be measured by tools (discussed later in this chapter); "comprehensive" test coverage will normally be more than 80 percent. It's difficult to find a hard and fast figure; the higher the better.

> **When you become convinced of the value of comprehensive unit testing, you'll find that it begins to influence how you write code, and the frameworks you choose to use.**

While most developers (and managers) agree that an effective, automated test suite is a worthy goal, too many projects don't have one. Of course, in projects with a large legacy code base, it's often not possible to create a comprehensive test suite. In my experience, the main threats to effective unit testing on a *new* project are:

❑ Code that is "too hard" to test

❑ Deadlines resulting in testing being de-prioritized as a non-core activity

❑ Developers who won't write tests

The first problem is technical. We'll examine some common causes of hard-to-test code, and how to avoid them, later in this chapter. EJB, in particular, can make application code built with it hard to test.

We can avoid the second problem by appropriate planning and education. Good project planning should avoid the need to go into regular phases of "just getting it done": this will be harmful in many areas, besides testing. Education can ensure that developers realize that writing tests is not necessarily a waste of time.

The third problem is often harder to tackle. As I've noted before, technical challenges usually pale in comparison with political challenges. A common offender here is the cowboy developer. (He normally is a *he*, so I won't try to avoid gender-specific language.) A cowboy knows that he writes excellent code very fast. He often really does know Java and the APIs he uses well. He knows that his code is so good that he doesn't need to bother with the cumbersome routine of writing tests. I've worked with enough such individuals to shudder when I encounter one. I've never met one who wrote better code than a good developer who was also committed to testing—perhaps a reflection of the fact that desire to write testable code usually means writing *good* code.

Cowboy types can seem like godsends in the short term, but invariably create long-term problems in all but trivial projects. Their code tends to be over-complex—another consequence of their need to continually stroke their egos. The cowboy usually ends up being the only person who understands his code, and will have little interest in communicating knowledge. While this provides him with a satisfying boost to his already overblown ego, it wreaks havoc if he leaves, goes on holiday, or falls sick. The task of writing tests against his code falls to other developers who—in the absence of deep understanding of the code—find this an unfulfilling job that they can't do very effectively. (Spending a large proportion of one's day writing tests for someone else's existing code really *is* boring.)

> **While other forms of testing can usually be validly performed by specialized testers, unit tests should be written by the developer (or pair) that writes each class, along with the code in the class itself. Pair programming is particularly effective here, because two developers are more likely to think of a full range of test scenarios than one.**

Not only cowboy developers feel that testing is boring and unimportant; however, the reasons in other cases are usually less interesting, such as simple ignorance and laziness. This is a political, not a technical issue and must be resolved politically. Tactful mentoring in effective test-driven development may do the trick; if it doesn't, things get messier.

> **As no testing isn't an option, the choice is between repeatable, scripted, structured testing (as with a comprehensive JUnit test suite) or "ad hoc" testing. Ad hoc testing usually involves a chaotic mixture of activities such as running main methods, the odd JUnit test case, sitting in a browser following links and entering form fields, and seeing what happens when the database URL is specified wrongly.**
>
> **Ad hoc testing has a single advantage: zero up-front investment. It also delivers zero ongoing confidence that the software works as expected, and zero documentation of what testing has been run and can be run again and again as the code evolves.**

Goals of Unit Testing

In this chapter I focus primarily on **unit testing**.

Of course, unit testing isn't the only important kind of testing. Component testing and integration testing are also essential. The requirements of each project will determine how these are conducted. For example, must integration tests be performed against a web interface? Must web services be tested? Because this is a book about architecture and development, rather than testing, I'm focusing here on those testing activities that should be an integral part of the development process. This should not be taken to mean that I'm suggesting that other testing activities are not also important.

> *Component and integration testing should also be automated where possible. Often some of the same tools, such as JUnit, can be used as for unit testing. But the goals are different. In my experience, effective unit testing is always essential, and should unfold much the same way in all projects.*

Unit testing is about testing each class in isolation. Tests should be so closely related to the code in the class that it's easy to add tests to exercise a particular piece of code: for example, a catch block invoked in the event of a particular error. As we'll see when we discuss test-driven development, it's probably better to think of the tests driving the code than the reverse.

To test classes in isolation, we need decoupling techniques. If we don't focus each unit test on testing the behavior of a specific object, it becomes hard to get effective test coverage, hard to configure tests, and there's typically a lot of duplication across different tests, when multiple tests indirectly test a particular class.

Testing in isolation has an impact on how we write code. It also has an impact on the testing strategies we use, which I'll discuss later in this chapter.

> **Each test case should test only one class; not indirectly test its collaborators. Unit testing is about knowing what not to test. When we know what not to test, what to test becomes obvious.**

Unit test is normally **glass box** (or "white box") testing. That is, it usually requires knowledge of the internals of the class under test. **Black box** testing is more appropriate in later stages of testing, and requires no knowledge of implementation details.

The term "white box" testing is more commonly used than "glass box" testing, but doesn't really make sense. It's possible to see what's inside a glass box, but a white box is no more transparent than a black box!

Ensuring Testability

Once we accept the importance of comprehensive unit testing, **testability** becomes an important quality of application code. Some developers are still snobbish about allowing testability concerns to influence how they write code; this is misguided, as more testable code is usually better, more understandable and more maintainable code.

Let's look at some dos and don'ts around testability.

Programming Style

We should be prepared to modify programming style to facilitate unit testing. Code that's hard to test is usually hard to maintain and enhance. For example:

- ❑ Code that contains over-long methods that make it impossible to ensure that all code is exercised will also be unreadable and hard to maintain.

- ❑ Code that relies on magic global static state held in singletons cannot be tested in isolation and will be inflexible if the assumptions it was based on ever change. (For example, if there is ever a need for more than one instance of a magic singleton.)

- ❑ Code that is not **pluggable**—where it's impossible to change the implementation of a particular collaborator to a test stub—will make it hard to parameterize and extend an application.

If you don't know how to test something, think seriously about why that is so and how you could slightly modify the implementation to facilitate testing.

> In most cases, the goal of testable application code leads to good application code.

How to Make Your Code Hard to Test

Testability is largely about avoiding untestable idioms. Thus understanding such idioms is important.

Let's look at common causes of untestable code.

EJB and the Potential to Create an Untestable Application

Let's imagine you want to defeat testability. A good way to reach this goal is to begin with heavy use of entity beans, and code all your business logic in EJB implementation classes. (For bonus points, tie your presentation logic inextricably to a web framework such as Struts and to the Servlet API, and you'll struggle to unit test any architectural tier.)

Entity beans are particularly problematic for testability. (I'm talking largely about CMP entity beans, as BMP entity beans have a myriad of productivity and performance problems that rule them out in the great majority of cases. They're also quite hard to test.)

The testability problems with entity beans stem from their dependence on the EJB container at runtime. With CMP, this is taken to an extreme: CMP entities are abstract, making them impossible to instantiate without some form of code generation. Typically, without deploying CMPs, we have no way of even proving that they implement all required EJB lifecycle methods, let alone that they behave as expected.

The classic EJB approach to this problem is to view entity beans as dumb data access objects, and code business logic in session beans. As noted in earlier chapters, this means that a whole layer of our application is not object-oriented. However, it leaves us able to assume that our entities don't need testing, because we can rely on the EJB container to persist them correctly. Unfortunately this approach is not sufficient because all session beans will depend on the hard-to-stub entities, meaning that business logic is also untestable outside an EJB container.

There is growing consensus today that even an EJB architecture should not normally use entity beans. This moves the focus to session beans and message-driven beans: in a "Classic" J2EE architecture, the favored place for all business logic.

Session beans and MDBs are significantly more testable than entity beans, but still significantly less testable than POJOs. The problem is that they also depend on the EJB container at runtime. Replacing such dependencies during unit tests is hard: both JNDI and EJB APIs are complex to simulate.

Can't we get around these problems by testing our EJBs in the application server or simulating an application server? There are three main approaches:

❑   For remote EJBs, we can write RMI clients to test them. On the positive side, this means that we can write relatively normal JUnit test cases, so long as we factor the JNDI and EJB creation code into reusable methods, such as the `setUp()` method. This even allows us to modify tests and add new tests without redeploying application code to the application server. On the negative side, it's no use if we want to test EJBs with local interfaces. As we've seen we don't want a distributed architecture in typical applications, so making a fundamental architectural change from local to remote EJBs is a pretty unpleasant concession to testability, completely different from the code-level changes we *should* happily make for testability.

❑   For remote or local EJBs, use a tool such as Cactus (`http://jakarta.apache.org/cactus/`) that allows us to test EJBs from a test case running in the application server, with local access to the EJB container. The problem with this approach is that running any test case requires a deployment to the application server, greatly increasing the length of deploy-test cycles and practically ruling out test-driven development. Typically we'll need to deploy multiple EJBs to the container to test even a single EJB.

❑   Use a substitute for the EJB container such as the integrated J2EE environment provided with some IDEs, or MockEJB (`www.mockejb.org/`).

Not only do all these approaches make unit testing a lot harder than it should be, most make it very hard to simulate error conditions. What if one EJB needs to access another, and that collaborator isn't available at runtime? How do we test for the required graceful degradation under such circumstances? We can't have a multitude of test deployment scripts that deploy every combination of EJBs. And we can't easily selectively disable services in the EJB container at runtime. We can't really test such scenarios in the container. Thus we have little chance of achieving high test coverage through in-container testing. With a tool like MockEJB we can test outside a full-blown container, and simulate failures, but the overall effort to test each EJB is still high, and even the test-time replacement for the EJB container is necessarily complex.

It's vital to be able to unit test business logic outside the application server. Unit tests are about isolation, so they lose, rather than gain, from being executed in a deployed environment. Not only is unit testing within the container slow and tedious, it makes debugging much harder. Regardless of the available toolset, debugging code running in a container (for example, to help in pinpointing the cause of a failing test) will be slower than debugging a JUnit test within a simple IDE environment.

> **In-container testing is not a viable approach for unit testing. It's too slow, and makes test driven development almost impossible. It also doesn't allow us to simulate error conditions. If you can only unit test your business objects inside an application server environment, redesign your application.**

Cactus-style in-container testing does have a place in some applications. But it's really only appropriate for component-level testing, rather than unit testing.

> **EJB code is inherently hard to test. As it's essential to be able to unit test business logic, this is an important motivation for "J2EE without EJB."**

Thus testability concerns suggest that you don't use EJB unless the value proposition is compelling—such as the need to implement a distributed architecture.

When you do use EJB (local, remote, or MDBs), minimize the number of EJBs. Use plain Java classes behind an EJB facade to implement your business logic. This enables your business logic to be unit tested effectively outside an application server, while still allowing the benefits of EJB such as CMT and remoting at the coarse-grained, facade level. Also, avoid making client-side code that uses EJB business objects dependent on the EJB API using a generic lookup strategy, such as Spring's EJB proxy factories. Otherwise you'll have a problem testing code that uses EJBs as well as code intended to run in an EJB environment.

Spring EJB support and access packages are very helpful in achieving both these goals, if you do choose to use EJB.

The Singleton Antipattern

Another enemy of testability that many take for granted is the Singleton design pattern. As I pointed out in Chapter 4 of *Expert One-on-One J2EE*, the Singleton pattern is greatly overused in J2EE applications.

A singleton is a valid approach in the minority of cases when you really want to enforce the existence of a single instance of a class in the current JVM (or, rather, class loader). But Singletons are often used to provide lookup services that are much better handled by a generic factory such as an Inversion of Control (IoC) container.

> **As commonly used, the Singleton is really an antipattern. The Singleton is a pattern for instance management, not lookup.**

The Singleton pattern is a mortal enemy of testability for many reasons:

❑ Singletons cut against interfaces, by forcing all calling code to have knowledge of a specific class.

❑ It's very hard to replace a Singleton with a test stub.

There are many reasons that you don't want to use Singletons on design grounds. For example:

❑ A Singleton is inflexible. If you ever want to have a pool of such objects, you're stuck. And so are all the callers that have hard-coded dependence on your Singleton. Many libraries and frameworks, such as Velocity and Struts, have found that original assumptions about there being only one of a key resource can end up being wrong and restrictive.

❑ A Singleton can't be configured through any standard mechanism. For example, because if its special construction it can't usually be created and managed by an IoC container.

Consider a typical use of a Singleton in a J2EE application: as a Service Locator for EJB access. This is about service lookup; limiting the number of instances to one is not the issue. Code using such service locators is hard to unit test because it's hard to replace the singleton lookup with a test stub. It's much better to get EJB references from a factory than from a singleton.

In J2EE applications, because the application server provides various well-defined lifecycle structures, such as a `ServletContext`, it's rare to have legitimate reason to use a singleton. For example, an IoC container instance can be associated with a whole web application via the `ServletContext`. In standalone applications, a singleton may be required to bootstrap such a container. In this case, it's much better to use a *single* singleton to bootstrap an IoC container providing many services, than a rash of ad hoc singletons that provide services themselves.

> **If you need any more incentive to avoid using the Singleton pattern, consider its effect on dynamic class loading in a J2EE application server. A library singleton can prevent hot redeploy working correctly, because it can continue to cache out-of-date resources, blocking configuration changes.**

Static Facades

Similar objections apply to facades of static methods. Some developers advocate this approach because it's simple, and because the facades themselves can supposedly be configured (also statically).

Consider the following approach to abstracting a well-known service object:

```
public abstract class MyService {

public static void doSomething() {
      . . .
}

public static void doSomethingElse() {
      . . .
}
}
```

The theory is that this class hides the details of locating the implementation of the `MyService` business logic. The static methods are likely parameterized by a properties or other lookup at load time. The problems are that:

- ❑ There is no service interface.
- ❑ All callers are tied to the `MyService` class. This makes it impossible to plug in a test implementation. (The behavior of the facade may be customizable, but this is less elegant and usually more complex to configure in a test case.)
- ❑ Static methods can't be overridden, so a major capability of OOP has been lost.

Unfortunately, as we'll see below, certain J2SE and J2EE APIs use this approach, so we can't ignore it and have to be prepared to work around it from time to time.

Static methods should be used only for:

❑   Procedural utility methods that don't belong in any class

❑   Working with `ThreadLocal` state

❑   Singleton instance returns (when the Singleton pattern really is appropriate)

> **Static methods can be a valid alternative to coding utility classes in class hierarchies. It's misuse of concrete inheritance to rely on a superclass to deliver utility methods. Often it's best to externalize these into static methods that, ideally, act on an interface rather than a class. This can be a clean design approach, because it provides a way to associate behavior with an interface, rather than a class.**

Standard Library Challenges

Hopefully I've convinced you that Singletons and static magic are generally *A Bad Idea*. However, we have to work with existing code. How should we test applications relying on standard library code that uses the Singleton and other untestable idioms?

Unfortunately, J2SE and J2EE APIs aren't perfect from this perspective, although they are pretty good overall because they do use interfaces fairly extensively.

Certain JDK APIs make testability hard. For example:

❑   JNDI relies on magic static configuration for determining what happens when we create a new `InitialContext`.

❑   JavaMail is truly evil, with a mixture of statics and final classes making stubbing difficult.

❑   JAXP uses a similar approach to JNDI, although as we don't often need to use it directly it has less impact.

Let's look at JavaMail in more detail. To use JavaMail we need to obtain a `javax.mail.Session` object from the static `getInstance()` method defined on that class. The `Session` class's behavior is controlled by a number of properties files. Because `Session` is final and is a class not an interface, it's hard to stub without dependence on the underlying infrastructure. For good measure, the `send` methods on the `Transport` class are static, so we can't override them in a test environment. When unit testing, we really want to verify that our application code attempted to send the correct message to the correct recipients, not that the underlying mail infrastructure is correctly set up and functioning properly.

Thus it's best not to use JavaMail directly, but to work via an abstraction layer that is more testable. This is the motivation behind the Spring `org.springframework.mail` and `org.springframework.javamail` packages, which allow application code to use an interface that can be easily stubbed. As usual, this more testable approach also delivers an architectural bonus: we can use a different mail-sending strategy in environments, such as some standalone clients, in which a JavaMail implementation is not available.

> If you need to rely on a standard library, such as JavaMail, which makes testing prohibitively difficult, use an abstraction layer that is based on interfaces rather than statics. The Spring Framework provides such an abstraction for a number of core J2EE APIs, including JavaMail.
>
> Testing should also be high on your framework or API shopping list. If you have a choice between APIs or frameworks, look for an alternative that makes application code built with it easier to test.

The issues are similar with JNDI. Although it is possible to stub or mock a JNDI environment (the Spring `org.springframework.jndi.SimpleNamingContextBuilder` class implements such an approach), it's best to avoid using the JNDI API directly. Again, this is consistent with architectural best practice. If we obtain a business object from JNDI, we are tied to JNDI as lookup strategy. If we use Dependency Injection, exposing a JavaBean property or constructor argument for the IoC container to set, we move the plumbing work of the necessary lookup into the IoC container, simplifying application code. And we can supply a test object or alternative implementation easily, without any container.

Techniques for Improving Testability

There are a number of techniques we can use to make code easier to test. Some of the most important are:

- ❑ Code to interfaces rather than classes.
- ❑ Use the Strategy design pattern.
- ❑ Consider the Law of Demeter.
- ❑ Minimize dependence on environment-specific APIs.
- ❑ Give each object a manageable and consistent set of responsibilities.
- ❑ Hide implementation details.
- ❑ Refactor into methods to allow overriding at test time.

Let's consider each of these in turn. As we'll see, most of them are consistent with good design practice.

Code to Interfaces Rather than Classes

This is a particularly clear case of testability flowing from good design. The more we code to interfaces, the freer we are to plug in different implementations at runtime or test time. This gives us more architectural flexibility to change implementation details; and makes it easy to provide test stubs that don't need a sophisticated implementation of collaborators' functionality and hence are freed from needing to depend on supporting infrastructure. As an additional consideration, it's easy to use "dynamic" mock objects against interfaces, but not against classes, meaning that coding to classes rules out a particularly valuable unit testing technique. (See discussion of mock objects later in this chapter.)

Use the Strategy Design Pattern

The **Strategy** design pattern (GoF) involves factoring out certain algorithms of functionality into an external interface, enabling the implementation of that functionality to change without changing the rest of the implementation of the class. For example, consider the following code fragment that illustrates how `DefaultMyInterface` delegates part of its work to an implementation of the `MyHelper` interface:

```java
public class DefaultMyInterface implements MyInterface {

    private MyHelper helper;

    public void setMyHelper(MyHelper helper) {
            this.helper = helper;
    }


    public void doWork() {
            // Do some business logic
             int value = helper.calculateSomething(args);
            // Do more work
    }
}
```

This is one of my favorite design patterns, which I use frequently: an excellent pattern from the point of view of testability and architecture. It focuses each class closely around its core responsibilities, breaking up what would otherwise be monolithic classes. It's easy to provide a test stub or mock object for the Strategy interface (`MyHelper` in the previous example). This is particularly beneficial when the strategy involves APIs such as JNDI or JavaMail that might make testing a monolithic object difficult. And it's easy to provide a different strategy implementation to change application behavior. Spring uses the Strategy pattern extensively, which is one of the reasons it is such a flexible and extensible framework.

It's particularly easy to use the Strategy pattern in an IoC container such as Spring or PicoContainer, because the IoC container can do the hard work of managing the dependence on the strategy object. Note that the above example was coded as a JavaBean to allow an IoC container to set the `MyHelper` implementation in `DefaultMyInterface`. A constructor argument could be used for Constructor Dependency Injection.

An alternative to the Strategy pattern is the Template Method pattern (GoF), in which the variant strategy is factored into a concrete subclass of an abstract class. Implemented this way, our example would look like this:

```java
public abstract class AbstractMyInterface implements MyInterface {

    public void doWork() {
            // Do some business logic
             int value = calculateSomething(args);
            // Do more work
    }

    protected abstract int calculateSomething(args);

}


public class DefaultMyInterface extends AbstractMyInterface {
```

```
protected int calculateSomething(args) {
        ...
    }
}
```

This is also relatively easy to test, as we can provide a test subclass that implements `calculate Something()`. However, we can't use mock objects, so we have fewer testing options than with the Strategy pattern approach.

I don't recommend the Template Method pattern in general. Its only real advantage is that it's only necessary to instantiate the correct concrete subclass to get the desired behavior; there's no need to manage a relationship between business object and strategy interface implementation(s). This advantage is irrelevant when running application code in an IoC container. The Strategy pattern is superior to the Template Method design pattern in most cases, because it's more flexible. For example:

❏ We can change the strategy at runtime if we want. Concrete inheritance is defined statically, and inflexible. (As the classic Design Patterns text points out, composition should normally be preferred to inheritance.)

❏ A business object may depend on multiple strategies. With concrete inheritance, the implementation of all of them is linked. With the Strategy pattern we can pick and mix different strategy implementations in any combination.

❏ We can use the same Strategy interface in multiple classes. We may be able to reuse a single instance of an expensive-to-instantiate Strategy implementation in multiple object instances that hold state for other purposes.

❏ We can test using mock objects.

Consider the "Law of Demeter"

The "Law of Demeter" (`http://c2.com/cgi/wiki?LawOfDemeter`) states that objects should "only talk to their immediate friends." That is, an object should invoke methods only on objects available to it (as in the `MyHelper` object in the earlier example), *not* on global objects or on objects resulting from calls on immediate friends.

This should not really be called a "law": it's more a useful guideline, and you should not let it override other OO design considerations—for example in letting it result in the duplication of methods to avoid calling the same methods on objects not directly available.

However, it can be very useful at times, and is worth bearing in mind in your designs. By following the Law of Demeter where possible, you enhance testability by making it much easier to stub or mock helpers. For example, if we merely need to stub the `MyHelper` object in the above example, we can do that easily. But imagine if `DefaultMyInterface` contained the following code, using a `SecondaryHelper` type available to a `MyHelper` implementation:

```
helper.getItsHelper().useMe()
```

Now we'd have to provide a test implementation of the `SecondaryHelper` type as well, significantly complicating testing `DefaultMyInterface`. With a mock object testing strategy the increase of complexity would be significant. Other disadvantages of flouting the Law of Demeter include tight coupling.

Why should one object, such as `DefaultMyInterface`, know about the dependencies of another object (`MyHelper`)? This makes refactoring difficult.

Minimize Dependence on Environment-specific APIs

As I noted earlier regarding JNDI and JavaMail, if your code uses APIs that are tied to a particular runtime environment, it will be hard to test outside that environment, as in plain old JUnit tests. (Unfortunately I don't think POJT is likely to catch on as an acronym, although the concept is nearly as valuable as that of a POJO!) From an architectural perspective, it will also be impossible to reuse outside that environment.

Ensure That Each Object Has a Consistent Set of Responsibilities

"God objects"—big objects with a confusing set of responsibilities and low-level dependencies—are hard to test and maintain. By finding the correct object granularity we can avoid this problem. An IoC container is a big help here, because it enables us to manage graphs of objects at the appropriate granularity, removing lookup issues.

Hide Implementation Details

This is another area in which good OO design practice goes hand in hand with testability. By ensuring appropriate encapsulation within objects you improve your design. But you also ensure that you're free to refactor the internals of those objects without breaking tests that deal with their public interfaces.

Refactor into Methods to Allow Overriding

One interesting case is that of factoring certain code into protected methods. We saw an example of this when discussing AOP, to allow test classes to avoid dependence on the Spring AOP API. We were faced with the need to use a static method that introduced a dependency on Spring. (The Spring API method is static because it works with a `ThreadLocal`.) The necessary code, in a business method, was as follows:

```
TransactionInterceptor.currentTransactionStatus().setRollbackOnly();
```

We refactored this call into a protected method that we can override at test time to ensure that the call was made, rather than to invoke Spring code:

```
protected void setRollbackOnly() {
  TransactionInterceptor.currentTransactionStatus().setRollbackOnly();
}
```

This is essentially a workaround to use when confronted with a hard-to-test API, a `ThreadLocal` or some other environment-specific feature. Unlike all the other techniques we've discussed, it arguably has a minor negative effect on code quality, exposing more of class internals. However, any degradation of code quality is a moot point, as often it does make sense to refactor such operation into a method, meaning that the only issue is the method being `protected` when it would normally be `private`. Of course even protected methods are not visible to callers, who will normally use the appropriate interface.

We can also use this technique to hide Singleton lookup if a Singleton implements an interface.

Inversion of Control

Most of the testability problems with EJB can be avoided, along with the dreaded Singleton, and most of the good practices described above implemented easily, using an IoC container offering Dependency Injection. While EJB predates the Java unit testing revolution, IoC containers such as Spring, PicoContainer, and HiveMind postdate it and one of their motivations is to make it easier to test application code effectively.

> **IoC helps testability enormously by eliminating many needs for singletons, externalizing lookup, facilitating coding to interfaces rather than classes, and potentially making application objects POJOs rather than special objects such as EJBs.**

AOP

AOP also helps testability by providing the ability to factor out concerns such as security and transaction management into aspects, thus simplifying business logic. It's especially important to factor our system-level enterprise concerns from application code, because testing such code often requires a dependence on low-level, hard-to-simulate APIs.

> **Two of the major themes of this book, IoC and AOP, used appropriately, can greatly enhance testability.**

Unit Testing Techniques

Let's now look at some common testing techniques. These are largely concerned with testing in isolation.

Stubs

The most obvious way to test objects in isolation is to use **test stub** objects to replace collaborators at test time. A stub will implement the subset of the collaborator's functionality that is required to support the test case. A stub will not usually aim to be a realistic implementation of the whole of the collaborator's interface. Usually it will require configuration to make it behave appropriately.

It's relatively easy to stub an interface. Often we can provide an abstract implementation that throws UnsupportedOperationException on all methods, and override it at test time to implement those methods that we need to use. Or we can use a more functional generic implementation configured differently in different tests.

Stubbing classes is harder, although we may be able to override methods selectively. Stubbing classes via overriding doesn't work when class construction introduces dependencies on objects that are irrelevant to the test but may be hard to satisfy. Thus programming to interfaces rather than classes makes stubbing, like other unit testing techniques, easier and more effective.

One obvious disadvantage of stubs is the effort required to write them. In some cases, it may be possible to reuse stubs across a project or to use existing third party stubs for common APIs.

Stubbing can also be problematic if we have really complex environment to simulate. For example, stubbing JNDI, or an EJB container, can be difficult. Stubs are usually more valuable the less they depend on realistic implementation considerations and helpers. For example, a stub DAO shouldn't really depend on a database: this makes unit testing in isolation difficult and makes tests hard to configure and slow to run.

Mock Objects

Mock objects are an alternative to test stubs that are particularly valuable in unit testing.

Concepts

Mock objects, or **mocks**, might superficially seem to be similar to stubs. However, there are important differences between the two, and the differences are more important than the similarities.

Mocks are intentionally even less realistic than traditional test stubs. Mocks do not aim to provide anything like a realistic implementation of the interface in question. Unlike stubs, mocks constrain usage, because they are designed to enforce **expectations**. The purpose of a mock is not so much to establish that the code under test behaves appropriately with collaborators behaving in a certain way, but that the code under test invokes the collaborators as expected. That is, mocks are used to create **expectations**. A typical expectation is that a JDBC connection is closed after use, or that a single call is made to a particular method. Stubs don't usually enforce such expectations: for example, a stub will normally let code under test call a stubbed method any number of times, returning the same result each time. See http://c2.com/cgi/wiki?MockObject for a discussion of mocks and link to other resources.

Mocks are typically customized for each test case, providing the minimum functionality required in the relevant scenario. They help to focus unit testing on only the relevant operations, which will be expressed through expectations.

Mocks make it particularly easy to simulate error conditions: for example, what happens when a collaborator throws a particular exception. The ability to easily simulate a range of error conditions is essential to writing robust software, and a key reason that mocks are important to effective unit testing.

Let's look at an example of how a mock object can be used to test code that depends on the Servlet API, outside a servlet engine. The class being tested is a simple servlet that checks for the presence of a request parameter "name." If that parameter is not present, it redirects the user to enterName.jsp. If the parameter is present, it adds the parameter as a request attribute, and redirects to personInfo.jsp. Obviously this is not a particularly realistic or useful servlet, but it serves as a simple yet complete example.

```
public class SimpleServlet extends HttpServlet {
    protected void doGet(HttpServletRequest request,
            HttpServletResponse response) throws ServletException, IOException {
        String name = request.getParameter("name");
        if (name == null) {
            response.sendRedirect("enterName.jsp");
        }
        else {
            request.setAttribute("name", name);
```

```
                response.sendRedirect("personInfo.jsp");
            }
        }
    }
```

The following tests use the Mock Objects Servlet API mocks (available from www.mockobjects.com) to test each case. These include mock `HttpServletRequest` and `HttpServletResponse` objects, which can be used to set up expectations. Remember that the issue is not so much making these objects return expected values, as in the `setupAddParameter()` method in the second test case, because setting up *expectations* that the class being tested behaves appropriately: for example, it invokes the `redirect()` method on the response.

The basic steps in each test case are:

1. Create the necessary mocks.

2. Run a fine-grained test case using the mocks.

3. Conclude by calling the `verify()` method on all mocks. This method is inherited from `com.mockobjects.MockObject`, a convenient superclass for mock objects. Verification checks that all expectations have been satisfied.

The only expectation on our servlet when no name parameter is present is the redirect to `enterName.jsp`:

```
public void testNoNameParameter() throws Exception {
    MockHttpServletRequest mockRequest = new MockHttpServletRequest();
    mockRequest.setupNoParameters();
    MockHttpServletResponse mockResponse = new MockHttpServletResponse();
    mockResponse.setExpectedRedirect("enterName.jsp");
    new SimpleServlet().doGet(mockRequest, mockResponse);
    mockRequest.verify();
    mockResponse.verify();
}
```

In the second case, we use the `addExpectedSetAttribute()` method on `MockHttpServletRequest` to ensure that the value of the name parameter is exposed as a request attribute, as well as the appropriate redirect being sent:

```
public void testValidNameParameter() throws Exception {
    MockHttpServletRequest mockRequest = new MockHttpServletRequest();
    String name = "Rod";
    mockRequest.setupAddParameter("name", name);
    mockRequest.addExpectedSetAttribute("name", name);
    MockHttpServletResponse mockResponse = new MockHttpServletResponse();
    mockResponse.setExpectedRedirect("personInfo.jsp");
    new SimpleServlet().doGet(mockRequest, mockResponse);
    mockRequest.verify();
    mockResponse.verify();
}
```

Using mocks we can easily test this servlet outside a web container. We can simulate any error conditions we want, and our tests run instantly.

427

Dynamic Mock Objects

One objection to mock objects as used above is that, as with stubs, we need to code a mock, with the ability to create expectations, for every interface we need to mock. While a library of mocks is available at www.mockobjects.com for common APIs such as the Servlet API, the volume of code in these mocks suggests that a simpler solution is desirable for mocking application interfaces.

We can extend `com.mockobjects.MockObject` to create application-specific mocks. Extending this class provides handy support for expectations; expectation variables in subclasses will be checked automatically on calls to the inherited `verify()` method. However, there will still be a lot of work in creating mocks.

Fortunately, there is a solution: **dynamic mock objects**. These are created on the fly in test cases to implement interfaces we want to mock. We never need to code an actual implementation of these interfaces. The following code example shows use of the EasyMock dynamic mock object library (www.easymock.org) to create a dynamic mock.

This involves the following steps:

1. Creating the mock instance from a factory provided by the dynamic mock library and casting it to the required type.

2. Creating expectations by **recording** calls to the mock. This involves making the expected method calls on the mock while it is in the *recording* state and, for each call, making a call on the corresponding "mock control" to set the return value. Thus we set both expectations and return values (or exceptions, if we wish to simulate errors).

3. Setting the mock control into "replay" state.

4. Providing the mock as a collaborator to the class under test.

5. Invoking the test case that uses the mock.

6. Verifying the mock to check that the expected calls were made.

Let's look at using this approach to check for expected behavior when a business object using a DAO encounters a data access exception when using it. We need to provide a mock DAO to the business object. The expectations on the mock DAO will be the calls that the business object should make on it if it behaves correctly; we can script the dynamic mock to throw an exception on any method.

```
public void testWithdrawalEncountersDataAccessException() throws Exception {
    DataAccessException expectedException = new DataAccessException("", null) {};

    MockControl mc = MockControl.createControl(BankDao.class);
    BankDao dao = (BankDao) mc.getMock();
    dao.getBalance();
    mc.setThrowable(expectedException);
    // Stop scripting the mock and make it expect calls
    mc.replay();

    BankImpl bank = new BankImpl();
    bank.setDao(dao);
    try {
        bank.withdraw(25.0);
```

```
            fail("DataAccessException should have been thrown");
    }
    catch (DataAccessException ex) {
            // Ok
            assertEquals("Exception was propagated", expectedException, ex);
    }

    // Verify the expected call was made on the mock
    mc.verify();
}
```

After we've obtained our Mock DAO, we invoke the `getBalance()` method on it to *record* the expectation of such a call. The following statement must use the `MockControl` associated with the mock either to set a return value, using the `setReturnValue()` method, or to specify that an exception or other throwable should be thrown, as in the previous example. After recording is complete, we invoke `replay()` on the mock to set it into active state. Finally, we verify as with an ordinary mock.

I found this recording process unintuitive at first. However, dynamic mock objects have become one of the principal unit testing techniques I use.

Dynamic mock objects all but eliminate the need to code dedicated mock objects. In the Spring test suite, the vast majority of tests using mock objects (which account for over half the tests) use EasyMock dynamic mocks.

Libraries such as EasyMock and DynaMock (`www.mockobjects.com`) can dynamically mock only interfaces, not classes: yet another motivation for coding against interfaces.

> *If you have to mock classes, consider using AspectJ to intercept invocations of the class in question. For an interesting article on this see "Testing Flexibly with AspectJ and Mock Objects" by Nicholas Lesiecki (`www-106.ibm.com/developerworks/java/library/j-aspectj2/?open&l=825,t=gr`).*

Deciding When to Use Mock Objects

Mock objects are most useful when you follow good programming practices, such as coding to interfaces and having a manageable set of responsibilities in each class.

Mock objects are not a panacea. Sometimes test stubs are more appropriate.

Mock object problems I've seen in practice in some cases are that:

❑ Constructing mock objects can require a lot of effort where many objects are required to support a test. This problem applies with JDBC, for example: it's necessary to mock connections, statements, and ResultSets. You can end up with a lot of code in tests very quickly. Applying the Law of Demeter in application code can lessen this problem, but you can't solve it so easily with standard APIs. You may be able to refactor the object creation into reusable utility methods, but this can be tricky with mocks.

❑ Mock testing is glass box testing. This can make tests fragile, so they may break on legitimate change in the *implementation* of a method. Mock object expectations are usually valuable, but sometimes we don't want a test to be so tightly coupled to the code we're testing.

Nevertheless, I recommend making mocks a key part of your unit testing strategy. I apply the following guidelines:

❑ Dynamic mock objects are my first approach to mocking most APIs.

❑ If the scripting is problematic, I consider writing a mock class, rather than relying on dynamic mock objects.

❑ For generic objects (rather than application objects used in only a small number of unit tests), it may be best to use traditional test stubs, or perhaps hard-coded mock objects.

❑ The more complex the API that must be simulated, the less effective mocking will be. However, it is also hard to test complex APIs using other methods. In this case, the best solution is to simplify the dependencies of the relevant application objects. We'll look at techniques for this later in this chapter.

Writing Effective Tests

Knowledge of certain testing techniques is also useful when writing tests. It's important to gain the ability to think from a testing perspective when writing unit tests—in particular, to *try* to break the code in question and to think of scenarios that may break it. Thinking of an important, difficult test case is as important as writing the code to satisfy it.

Negative Tests

The key to writing effective test cases is to think of **negative tests**: tests that verify behavior besides the "happy path," in which everything goes well and which is normally obvious. What happens if a DAO throws a data access exception? We need to know how our code will behave in the event of a database failure. What happens if a remote call throws a `RemoteException`? Such scenarios are hard to reproduce in a deployed environment, and hence hard to cover in component and integration testing.

Thinking of all potential negative tests takes a little practice, but it's an important step toward writing robust code.

Equivalence Partitioning

One testing concept that developers should understand is **equivalence partitioning**: determining *classes of inputs* that have similar characteristics. (Note that this use of the word "class" does not relate to the OOP concept of a class.) We can use equivalence partitioning to minimize the number of test cases we need to write, by focusing on one within each equivalence partition.

To illustrate equivalence partitioning, let's consider a `Bank` object's `withdraw` method with the following signature:

```
public void withdraw(float amount) throws InsufficientFundsException;
```

There are the following **equivalence classes** to consider for the `amount` input:

❑ Amount is invalid (negative or zero)

❑ Amount is valid and within the credit limit

❑ Amount is outside the credit limit so the withdrawal should not be authorized

Thinking about equivalence classes is helpful in creating quality tests—and, of course, exactly the way in which most developers go about it intuitively.

Coding Practice

I'm not going to give a JUnit tutorial, but a few quick tips may help you to improve your skills—or confirm that you're on the right track. Later, when covering the Spring Framework's testing strategy, I'll discuss other issues of best practice around JUnit and testing J2EE applications.

Test Cases Should Be Economical Yet Self-documenting

Especially if we practice test-driven development (discussed later in this chapter), it's important that we can write tests quickly. This means that we should minimize the amount of code we need to write in test cases. Yet we must ensure that the test suite is understandably, and, ideally, self-documenting. How do we balance these two goals?

Firstly, we avoid writing code that we don't need in a test case. Consider the following test for a `Bank` object that uses a DAO. I've omitted the code to set up the `Bank` object, which is assumed to be in the helper method `getBank()`.

```
public void testWithdrawal() {
  try {
        Bank bank = getBank();
        bank.setBalance (50.0);
        bank.withdraw(26.0);
        bank.assertTrue(bank.getBalance() == 24.0);
  }
  catch (DataAccessException ex) {
        fail("Failure in bank: " + ex, ex);
  }
  catch (InsufficientFundsException ex) {
        fail("Incorrect throwing of insufficient funds: " + ex, ex);
  }
}
```

There's no need for this test to catch the two exceptions, whether the exceptions are checked or not. The test will fail if it allows an exception to propagate and, especially when coding test first, we don't want to waste time writing unnecessary catch blocks in tests. Thus we can rewrite the method like this:

```
public void testWithdrawal() throws DataAccessException, InsufficientFundsException
{
  Bank bank = getBank();
  bank.setBalance (50.0);
  bank.withdraw(26.0);
  bank.assertTrue(bank.getBalance() == 24.0);
}
```

This is an improvement, making the expected behavior more obvious by removing the extraneous exception handling and avoiding wasted typing, but we can make the test more self-documenting. It's incorrect to use the `assertTrue()` method to assert equality. And we should use the overloaded form of the `assert` method that includes a string that will help explain the problem if something goes wrong. We should also give the test a more meaningful name. We'll need numerous tests for the withdraw method, such as trying to withdraw a negative amount, and ensuring appropriate behavior on a `DataAccess Exception`, and such a generic name is inappropriate:

```
public void testValidWithdrawalSucceedsWithinLimit() throws DataAccessException,
InsufficientFundsException {
  Bank bank = getBank();
  bank.setBalance (50.0);
  bank.withdraw(26.0);
  bank.assertEquals("Balance is correct after withdrawal", 24.0, bank.getBalance());
}
```

What do we do if a method under test *should* throw an exception? We write a `try/catch` block that passes in only the event of the correct exception. We can simply declare other checked exceptions on the test method's signature, so as not to be forced to write irrelevant catch blocks. The result will look like this:

```
public void testWithdrawal() throws DataAccessException {
  Bank bank = getBank();
  try {
          bank.setBalance (50.0);
          bank.withdraw(51.0);
          fail("Bank should have rethrown InsufficientFundsException");
  }
  catch (InsufficientFundsException ex) {
          // Ok
          assertEquals("Correctly calculated amount of unapproved overdraft", 1.0,
  ex.getShortfall());
  }
}
```

Note the all-important `fail()` method. If we omit this, the test will pass even if the required exception isn't thrown: a nasty problem. We also make an assertion about the expected exception.

Documentation in the form of meaningful test case names and assertion messages is usually more important than Javadoc on test cases. When a test fails, the output will show the failed assertion (or an error) and the name of the test in question: not the Javadoc associated with that method. Javadoc and other comments are important to explain non-obvious tests to help in maintaining the test suite, but not so useful to help quickly diagnose failures.

Don't Rely on External Configuration Unless There's No Alternative

Generally it's best for objects to be created in individual test cases or in fixtures. The more configuration files, such as XML files, your tests depend on, the greater the task of managing the test suite over time. (You can quickly end up with *lots* of files.) A file-oriented approach makes sense for certain generic objects that it's desirable to be able to configure outside Java code, but shouldn't be used without good reason.

Refactor the Test Suite as Necessary

Avoid code duplication in your test suite as well as application code: remember that the quality of the test suite is very important. Thus it's important to refactor the test suite as necessary and identify areas in which you can reuse code to speed up writing individual test cases. The use of the `getBank()` method in the previous examples illustrates such reuse.

Avoid Tests with Side-effects

Tests should not change global state. If they *must* change global state, the `tearDown()` method on the relevant test case should restore it. This way we don't need to worry about the ordering of test cases and can let JUnit create a test suite automatically using introspection and reflection. This means less work for us and ensures that JUnit is always able to spot all test methods. If tests use external resources such as databases, the database will need to be returned to a known state between tests; this is one of the major drawbacks with tests depending on a database, and a major reason (besides speed) to avoid them if possible.

Test-driven Development (TDD)

I've already mentioned **test driven development (TDD)**. This is often also referred to as **test first development**. I'm a TDD practitioner myself, and recommend it highly.

Benefits

TDD brings many benefits. For example:

❑ It's the best way of achieving comprehensive test coverage. Retrofitting tests to existing code is a costly exercise in playing catch-up. If your goal is a comprehensive test suite (and it should be), TDD is the quickest and efficient way to achieve it.

❑ It means that application code can be refactored at any point with a secure foundation of regression tests.

❑ It can help you write the simplest possible code. You don't need to write complex code until you have a test that proves it's required.

❑ TDD means that developers have constant feedback about progress, in the form of more and more passing tests demonstrating required functionality. This is very satisfying.

Test first development applies an **iterative**, evidence-based process to coding. Iterative development has many benefits at a *micro* as well as *macro* (project-stage) level.

Test first development avoids the many problems in retrofitting tests. Typically if we want to retrofit tests we encounter the following problems:

❑ Tests are influenced by the code. This means that they're not truly independent. At worst, they can be faked, to write passing tests for code that may not be correct. It is often difficult to derive unit tests from requirements (ensuring independence from existing code), because they're so fine-grained.

❑ It wastes time. Writing tests after the fact is both boring and slow.

❑ Achieving adequate test coverage often requires some refactoring, to eliminate untestable idioms. However, refactoring is dangerous unless there's adequate test coverage: a nasty catch-22.

> Test driven development isn't just about testing. It's an efficient way of structuring coding activities, which has the invaluable benefit of almost guaranteeing a high-quality test suite at all times. Test driven development formalizes working in small steps and getting constant feedback about each small piece of functionality being added.

Arguments against TDD

If TDD is so good, why doesn't everyone practice it? Fortunately, greater awareness of TDD seems to have greatly boosted receptiveness to it. Few developers who have made a serious effort to practice it want to go back to their old ways. However, it's still not universally adopted.

One of the biggest reasons is probably inertia. TDD *is* a different way of working, and does require familiarization.

However, there are also some arguments against TDD in principle that it's worth discussing. Let's look at some of the classic arguments against TDD and why, in my view, they're mistaken.

"TDD Means That There Won't Be an Overall Theme to the Design"

This depends on how you practice TDD. The XP methodology is critical of *big upfront design*, which has caused it (largely wrongly) to be thought of by some as a hacker's charter. However, practicing TDD does not mean that you have to adopt XP as a whole.

In my experience *big upfront design* usually *is* a bad idea. It's impossible to foresee all requirements up front, and misguided to try. However, this doesn't mean that *design* goes out the window.

Personally, I don't write code without having a clear goal. For example, I often design an interface, then code an implementation test first. Of course the testing and coding process may indicate shortcomings in the design, which I will change if necessary, because I accept the fact that the test/coding cycle is iterative.

I only get to the stage of designing an interface on the basis of an overall architectural vision. In tricky cases, I do a lot of sketches and walkthroughs before turning to my IDE. Although my sketches sometimes take the form of UML class diagrams (and far less often, interaction diagrams), I rarely use a modeling tool: I usually use scrap paper. Not only is it cheaper to find a bug during TDD unit testing than retrofitted unit testing or integration testing; it's cheaper to find a problem in a paper or whiteboard walkthrough without writing any code. Note that this only works if the investment in the sketches is small; if the sketches take the form of a fully worked model, they can assume a momentum of their own, creating problems down the track.

This kind of sketching approach seems to work best with one to three people. Writing code to see how it works out often works out better than design by committee, or making a big investment in models before getting down to code. One project I worked on enforced the use of Word documents containing pages of UML models for every "design proposal." These documents were then "discussed" in meetings of 10 to 15 developers. The results were appalling. Because of the high cost of developing each proposal and the excessive number of people involved in the discussion, patently bad designs were seldom revisited. When the time ultimately came to write code, the developers writing the code were blamed for failing to deliver necessary results, when the problems usually related to the initial design, which had not been validated early enough in the form of testable, reviewable, code.

"But TDD Goes out the Window When You Have a Deadline"

Another common argument is that TDD sounds fine in theory, but it's simply unrealistic to apply in the real world, where developers face regular deadlines. Surely TDD will break down under deadline pressure, meaning that a pragmatic approach is to accept that up front and accept that it can't work?

This is emphatically not my experience. TDD, like anything else, needs practice. A developer who has never practiced TDD before *will* find it harder to meet deadlines if forced to adopt TDD, *at first*. But a good developer experienced with TDD can write code as fast as without writing tests, will enjoy the process more, and will deliver a high-quality test suite as well as the functional code.

For deadlines later in the project lifecycle, TDD can produce a huge return. For example, imagine that a sophisticated caching algorithm needs to be introduced to a class to meet a performance requirement. Having comprehensive tests available for the public functionality (virtually guaranteed by TDD) can enable this to be done with the minimum of stress.

"TDD Takes Longer, and the Client Won't Pay for It"

This objection rests on two flawed assumptions: that TDD necessarily takes longer in the development phase, and that the development phase is the most important for costing purposes.

Firstly, TDD does not take longer for experienced practitioners. Secondly, it is widely known that most of the cost of software is associated with *maintenance* throughout the entire lifecycle, rather than initial development. TDD can help to reduce maintenance costs significantly.

"We Want Developers to Generate Code from a Model, Not Hack in Their IDE"

The bad news is that TDD is not compatible with a model-driven approach, in which code is generated from UML modeling tools, after class and interaction diagrams have been completed. The good news is that—in my opinion—this doesn't matter very much because such a rigid emphasis on forward engineering *really* doesn't work in practice, and is incompatible with real-world deadlines.

Modern Java IDEs are far superior to even the best UML modeling tools in generating code. It's impossible to test models: it's easy to test code.

This is not to say that UML isn't a valid way of visualizing code and manipulating it: for example, with one of the excellent UML plugins available for Eclipse. But, in my view, it should be viewed as just one way of looking at code, not privileged as *the* way to produce code. UML is much more valuable in higher-level analysis activities than as part of low-level coding activities.

Organizations with a rigid emphasis on forward engineering from models are not likely to succeed with test first development. Personally, I will always take an effective test suite in preference to a set of models that will inevitably become out of date.

"We Don't Like XP"

TDD is strongly identified with XP in the Java community. Certainly, XP has popularized TDD. But the TDD concept existed before XP, and TDD is just one of the core XP practices. They are not one and the same. It's possible to adopt TDD without adopting XP in general.

Practicing TDD

To practice TDD effectively, you need an up-to-date IDE with refactoring support and integrated support for writing and running JUnit tests. It should be possible to:

❑   Perform sophisticated tool-supported refactoring. IntelliJ and Eclipse both shine in this area. The days when even sophisticated text editors such as vi and emacs were a defensible option are past for Java development.

❑   Run valid tests in a test suite even if some tests do not compile.

❑   Run tests at different granularities within the IDE, from individual test methods to groups of test suites.

My own way of practicing TDD usually involves defining an interface first. Then I use my IDE to generate an implementation, with all generated method stubs throwing `UnsupportedOperationException`. Then, one method at a time, I begin to write tests one at a time, and add code to the implementation to make them pass. Thus I do not write a whole bunch of tests before writing any functional code. On the other hand, I don't usually write test cases that reference non-existing methods (intending to add them later), partly because I want to benefit from my IDE's code helper.

I usually write the simplest implementation code to get my current test suite to pass, thus coding only the necessary complexity up front. I typically begin with negative test cases, such as testing the effect of a null or invalid argument.

Because refactoring is such an important part of TDD, it's important that your tool set doesn't create obstacles to refactoring. Inadequate IDEs are not the only threats. For example, try to avoid source control systems or source control restrictions that make refactoring difficult. Avoid using UML modeling tools in a way that discourages IDE-facilitated, code-driven, test-verified refactoring.

Learning TDD

TDD is a skill in its own right. Being a good Java developer is an enormous help in practicing TDD effectively, but there are new skills to learn, such as:

❑   Knowing what to test

❑   Using JUnit and other tools and libraries effectively

❑   Knowing when to use mock objects and when to use stubs

The best way to learn these skills is by practical experience.

❏ Begin by developing a simple class test first. Chapter 3 of *Expert One-on-One J2EE Design and Development* includes an example of a simple string manipulation test. The Bob Martin article listed in the "Resources" section later in this chapter is a more advanced, and lengthy example to use as a model.

❏ Pairing with experienced practitioners. Check for events in your area. For example, in London, there are several regular events where people get together to "pair" to write code, test first.

❏ Study the test suites for open source projects that are developed test first.

Case Study: The Spring Experience

While your own experience is going to teach you more than anything else, the experience of others can also be helpful. Let's take the Spring Framework open source project as a case study.

I and the other Spring developers apply the following guidelines, which have proven highly successful. I've already discussed some of these issues, but it's useful to see how they all form part of a coherent strategy.

❏ **Accept that the test suite is more important than anything else but the deliverable code itself.** It's powerful documentation, among other things. The test suite must always compile, run, and pass. This means that build scripts must be kept up to date at all times.

❏ **Work in small steps.** Implement one small piece of functionality at a time. This means that you never write a whole bunch of test suites at once, but write one little test then implement one little method. Test first development is *not* about writing all tests in one go before all application code.

❏ **Write code exclusively test first.**

❏ **If you're looking at a piece of code for which tests can be improved, add more tests.**

❏ **Write a unit test that fails because of a reported bug before attempting to fix the bug.** Firstly, this confirms whether or not the issue *is* a bug. If it isn't, a new test case that confirms the current, correct, behavior is a useful addition to the test suite. Secondly, it means that bug fixing also becomes test first. During maintenance, as when writing code in the first place, no code is written except to satisfy a failing test.

❏ **Design code so that it's easy to test, using the techniques discussed earlier.**

❏ **Ensure that even code that depends on J2EE APIs can be unit tested outside an application server.** I can't stress the importance of this too much, because it enables all the following practices to work.

❏ **Ensure that the entire test suite runs in seconds.** There are over 1300 test cases in the Spring 1.0 test suite, which execute in well under a minute, even on a laptop. Thus all developers can regularly run the entire test suite.

❏ **Run the relevant test case continually while working on a piece of code.**

❏ **Run the entire test suite before committing any code to source control.** Not only must all code compile before check in, all tests must pass. The result is that CVS snapshots tend to be so stable that we don't feel we need a nightly build process. Several users have commented on how pleasantly surprised they were to find that code out of CVS worked just fine. *Do not* view a nightly build process at the time when all tests get run. Any "nightly build" is just a bonus, from the unit testing perspective. You, as developer, run the entire test suite many times an hour. If it's too slow or too much trouble to do this, the test suite isn't implemented correctly.

❑ **Use meaningful names for tests that show their purpose,** such as `testTypeMismatchIs Detected()`. Obviously the entire test case relates to a particular class, so you don't have to specify which class the test applies to.

❑ **Minimize the number of configuration files that need to be loaded to run tests.** Sometimes this is necessary, but it's best to define tests in Java code. Any configuration files should have meaningful names, such as `typeMismatch.xml`. The package structure helps define the context for this name (see below).

❑ **Tests should have no side effects.** If they do, use the `setUp()` and `tearDown()` methods in JUnit to put things back into their proper state.

❑ **Don't depend on the ordering of test cases, and don't create test suites programmatically.** If tests are dependent on ordering, test suites become fragile. It's better to rely on JUnit's ability to create a test suite from all eligible `testXXXX()` methods than to create test suites programmatically, because JUnit's use of reflection will then always keep the suite up to date. Otherwise it's easy to forget to add a new test case to the suite.

❑ **Unit tests should not depend on a database or external resources.** This makes tests hard to configure and slow to run. If your test suite takes minutes rather than seconds, you can't practice test first development.

❑ **If a configuration file is used, load it from the class path** and put it in the same directory as the test case, so it's easy for a reader to figure out where configuration comes from. Never load resources from the file system: this is fragile and may not work on different operating systems and directory structures.

❑ **Have Ant scripts that run all tests and run test coverage analysis.** It's vital that your tests are easy to execute. Ideally you should also give developers a choice of IDE, so the build script (Ant or your preferred tool, such as Maven) is a vital central repository of tasks available to all developers and in all environments. I'll discuss coverage tools such as Clover later in this chapter.

❑ **Run individual tests in an IDE.** An IDE's ability to run test suites or test cases individually is very useful during development, as you repeatedly execute a failing test. It may also be useful to run all tests in an IDE, but this is no substitute for a scriptable, repeatable process using Ant or another standard build tool. Forcing experienced developers to use an IDE other than their favorite because of IDE-driven project standardization is misguided.

❑ **Look at test coverage reports regularly.** I estimate that I look closely through the Clover HTML logs once for every day of coding.

❑ **Use mock objects to avoid dependence on external resources.** We use EasyMock for Spring.

❑ **Refactor test code when necessary.** It's important to maintain the quality of test cases, too. Remember that the test suite is a vital part of the code base.

❑ **Refactor application code to eliminate duplication and improve quality.** Refactoring backed by strong test coverage really works. With a comprehensive test suite, you don't have to think "this is really nasty, but sort of works so I don't want to mess with it" ever again about a particular piece of code. For a framework such as Spring with thousands of users, it's an unacceptable risk to have fragile, untouchable pieces of code.

My personal test practices in Spring and other projects include:

- Configuring my IDE to throw `UnsupportedOperationException()` instead of doing nothing or returning `null` in all generated method stubs. I *want* tests to fail until I've implemented the relevant code. This also has the nice result that the exact line where you need to add code will appear in a JUnit stack trace; one click and you're in the right place to add the necessary code.

- For similar reasons, if I need to change the implementation of a particular method—for example, to introduce a faster algorithm—I often begin by modifying the method to throw `Unsupported OperationException`, before making any other changes. This allows me to rerun the test suite and see how many tests are impacted by the breakage of that method. (This technique is especially valuable if you're working on applications with poor test coverage, as it shows that you need to add tests for the *present* behavior before introducing new behavior.)

- Writing each test (each JUnit test method) to test one thing. Methods that perform multiple tests are more fragile, and it's harder to see the cause of the failure of a method that contains multiple tests. Tests with a single responsibility are also superior as documentation.

The Spring experience shows that these techniques work in a project undergoing rapid development of a large and growing code base. Users report that CVS snapshots are very stable. Collective code ownership works well when backed by a comprehensive test suite. As in any open source project, there are some natural, informal constraints on which code developers feel they are entitled to modify, based on status within the project and depth of understanding of the relevant functionality.

> **In my experience, strong test coverage does enable a degree of collective code ownership. However I still think that up-front design has value. There has to be a vision. And while it's legitimate to change design while you write code, it's best to discover mistakes through walkthroughs.**

Open source projects such as Spring are particularly useful case studies of unit testing practice because all their tests, like all their source code, are publicly available. By looking at the test cases along with the relevant source code, you'll see examples of the use of mock objects, how to maximize testability when working with awkward-to-test J2EE and third-party APIs and (from the build scripts) how to measure test coverage.

> **Open source projects with a commitment to comprehensive unit testing provide good examples of unit testing in practice. Besides Spring, just about any project from Codehaus is worth a look.**

From my experience with Spring and discussion with many contributors to leading open source projects, I'm convinced that well-run open source projects use better practices than the majority of in-house development projects. Thus open source projects are a valuable source of guidance as to good practice, and—if you have the time—you will probably sharpen your skills by contributing to a strong open source project. I've learned more from the Spring project than I have in any workplace.

Testing Spring Applications

While Spring and other leading open source frameworks are useful case studies, and provide good examples of test cases, there is a difference between testing frameworks and testing application code.

How should you go about testing *your* applications?

The approach I advocate in this book makes it easy to test business objects—much easier than when using EJB. All unnecessary hurdles to unit testing are removed.

Let's look at testing Spring applications, built using the *Lightweight Container Architecture*. This essentially involves realizing the power of the infrastructure and using it appropriately.

Testing POJOs

Like all Dependency Injection implementations, Spring is designed to encourage developers to implement application objects as POJOs, parameterized via JavaBean properties or constructors, which are used to pass in collaborators and configuration parameters. There is no need to write—or test—lookup code: this function is provided by the container. As lookup code such as JNDI lookups is often harder to test than business logic, this is a major win for testability.

Constructing such objects outside the deployed environment is simple. We create them using new in plain old JUnit test cases (POJTs) and set the necessary properties or constructor arguments. Typically we supply mock objects or stubs for these collaborators. Application code should normally express dependencies on interfaces rather than classes.

Benefiting from Spring Abstractions

One of the key purposes of Spring is to abstract application code from difficult-to-test J2EE APIs. The prime goals are to maximize architectural flexibility—for example, offering the same transaction abstraction in a simple web container without JTA as in a high-end application server—and to provide simple yet powerful abstractions, but there are also huge testability advantages. For example:

❑ You can use Spring's mail abstraction to avoid the testing difficulties around JavaMail. This provides a clean interface, rather than a mix of static methods and final classes.

❑ You can use Spring's transaction abstraction, providing a mock implementation of the `org.springframework.transaction.PlatformTransactionManager` interface to verify that code performing programmatic transaction management behaves appropriately, with no runtime dependence on JTA infrastructure.

❑ You can unit test code intended to access EJBs using the Spring `ProxyFactoryBean` by mocking the Business Methods interface of the EJB. No EJB APIs need to be stubbed or mocked.

❑ You can use Spring's AOP support to modularize solutions to concerns that may use low-level APIs into aspects, removing them and the associated testing challenges from application code.

Although it might seem paradoxical to advocate moving from standard J2EE APIs to the use of a particular framework, it's usually well worthwhile in this case:

❑   Many Spring features, in combination with Dependency Injection, abstract away from *any* API, to plain Java. With the `ProxyFactoryBean`, for example, neither client nor EJB implementation depends on Spring: Spring merely acts as a facilitator, making the EJB Business Methods pattern far more effective. With the `org.springframework.jndi.JndiObjectFactoryBean`, dependency on JNDI *or any other lookup API* can be removed from application code.

❑   Spring APIs are *much* simpler to stub and mock than many J2EE APIs.

❑   Spring abstractions enable you to focus on the relevant concern. Code using JTA, for example, typically depends also on JNDI; the Spring transaction abstraction can be used in isolation from other Spring APIs. This means fewer, simpler objects to stub or mock at test time.

❑   You don't sacrifice the ability to access the full power of the corresponding J2EE APIs, when running in an application server. However, you can potentially reuse your code in different environments.

When You Do Need to Depend on Spring APIs

Spring aims to be non-invasive. Whatever the framework you use, it reduces code reusability and creates lock-in if your code depends on framework APIs. Hence Spring aims to minimize or eliminate the need for application code to depend on its API.

Non-invasiveness is a consistent goal of the Spring design, not merely restricted to Dependency Injection.

For example, AOP complements IoC by providing declarative services to POJOs: there's no need for an object to become more complex or harder to test to benefit from them.

Many other Spring features also reduce the need for programmatic dependence on Spring or J2EE APIs. For example, dependence on a transaction API is inevitable (by definition) to achieve programmatic transaction rollback. However, Spring's provision of *rollback rules* means that you can *declaratively* configure rollback on specific checked application exceptions, greatly reducing the frequency with which you need programmatic rollback, compared to EJB. This enables you to focus on exactly what you want to test. If the contract for a given method is that any exception should cause transaction rollback, you don't need to check transactional behavior, and don't need to set up any transaction infrastructure. You need only to check that exceptions are thrown appropriately.

Even if you *do* need programmatic rollback, it's much easier to test in the case of Spring than with an EJB, for which you'd need to stub its JNDI environment and EJBContext. Your code will call the `org.springframework.transaction.interceptor.TransactionInterceptor`'s static `current TransactionStatus ()` method to find the current `TransactionStatus` (stored in a `ThreadLocal`) to invoke `setRollbackOnly()`. You can easily put this single line of Spring-specific code in a protected method or a strategy interface, allowing you to override the method or use a different strategy at test time. This way you don't have to configure transaction infrastructure at test time, or mock the Spring transaction abstraction (although that's simple enough).

Use the power of Dependency Injection and other Spring capabilities to minimize dependence on Spring and J2EE APIs. Let the Spring IoC container *push* dependencies into your application objects through JavaBean properties or constructor arguments, rather than use pull-style lookup. The jPetStore sample application has *no* dependencies on the Spring IoC container.

Class library–style usage of Spring, as in Spring DAO, is a different issue, and there's no need to minimize it. It's better to leverage the power of a good, well-supported API rather than solve the same problems in in-house code. In my experience, invasive in-house frameworks are a great danger to testability.

There will be rare occasions in complex applications when your code will need to depend on Spring container or AOP APIs.

For example, you might want to implement the `org.springframework.beans.factoryBeanFactory Aware` interface to enable an object to enumerate other objects in the same IoC container. Usually, this is an issue only for framework-style code, not ordinary application objects.

Think about alternatives before using such a mechanism. If there's a non-invasive way to achieve the same thing, use it. Fortunately, because of the way Spring is designed, in contrast to that of some other frameworks (like Struts), dependencies are usually on interfaces, not classes, meaning that they can be mocked easily.

Testing with an Alternate Configuration

With a lightweight IoC container such as a Spring `BeanFactory` or `ApplicationContext` or a Pico-Container, unlike the case of EJB, you have the option of starting the container easily in unit tests. It's simple to write the necessary code, and the startup time is negligible.

This means that, if you want, you can use the container to simplify more complex test cases by wiring application objects together. Consider the following example, testing a JDBC DAO that requires a `DataSource`.

You can configure a simple Spring test `DataSource` as shown in the following code. This DataSource will connect to an HSQL database. The collaborators you will provide for your business objects in such cases will avoid dependence on an application server. If we were to deploy this DAO to an application server, we would obtain a container `DataSource` via JNDI, but of course we don't want to deal with the complexity of supplying JNDI infrastructure at test time.

```
<bean id="dataSource" class="org.springframework.jdbc.datasource.DriverManager
DataSource">
    <property name="driverClassName"><value>org.hsqldb.jdbcDriver</value>
</property>
    <property name="url"><value>jdbc:hsqldb:hsql://localhost:9001</value>
</property>
    <property name="username"><value>sa</value></property>
    <property name="password"><value></value></property>
```

```
</bean>

<bean id="myDao" class="com.mycompany.JdbcMyDao"
    autowire="constructor"
>
```

The DAO would express its dependency on the `DataSource` through a JavaBean property, or via a constructor, as shown in the following example:

```
public class JdbcMyDao implements MyDao {

private DataSource dataSource;

public JdbcMyDao(DataSource dataSource) {
this.dataSource = dataSource;
}

// business methods omitted
```

We can create a Spring `ApplicationContext` by reading the above XML in a test case, as shown in the following code:

```
public class MyDaoTests extends junit.framework.TestCase {

    private ApplicationContext applicationContext;

    private MyDao myDao;

    protected void setUp() {
        applicationContext = new
ClassPathXmlApplicationContext("/com/myCompany/testMyDao.xml");
        dao = (MyDao) ac.getBean("myDao");
    }
```

Each test method would use the DAO saved in the `setUp()` method.

This approach is usually more appropriate for integration testing than unit testing. (The example depends on a database, which, as we've noted, is usually undesirable in *unit* tests.) Using mocks and testing classes purely in isolation is better unit testing practice.

However, it's valuable to have this style of testing as an option. It can also be used to help teams work in parallel. For example, after business interfaces are defined, a web tier team could use simple stub implementations defined in a web application context, enabling them to work in parallel with business object developers. This is a popular approach in companies developing with Spring.

Coverage Analysis and Other Test Tools

While JUnit—a free, simple tool—takes us most of the way toward effective test-driven development, we should consider some other test tools.

Test Generators

Can we automate some of the work of writing test cases? Some tools promise to do just that, based on application code. Jtest (www.parasoft.com) is probably the most popular tool in this space. From the product information sheet: "Jtest analyzes classes, then generates and executes JUnit-format test cases designed to achieve maximum coverage, expose uncaught runtime exceptions, and verify requirements that were expressed using Design by Contract."

I've seen Jtest in practice, in a project where a team who were reluctant to practice TDD saw it as the answer to their prayers, and the end of what they perceived as the hard work of writing test cases.

Auto-generated unit tests sound great, but unfortunately, from what I've seen, they're too good to be true, and little value in practice. They pose the following problems:

❑ Reliance on such tools discourages practicing TDD, meaning that many of its benefits are lost.

❑ They can encourage laziness. Developers *should* be forced to think about null arguments and other negative test scenarios.

❑ Because we *should* think about the content of test cases, there really isn't that much unnecessary grunt work involved in writing test cases. IDEs can do the mundane work of generating JUnit test case stubs perfectly well.

❑ Such tools complicate the build process. The generation step means that it becomes much harder to run all tests; usually too hard to run them all before a commit to the source control system. The result is likely to be more broken code checked in and more developer cycles wasted because of its impact.

❑ It's hard to see what test coverage is meaningful, and what is merely generated based on the tool's best guess as to what should happen. The tool can't guess what outputs should result from a given method call; it *can* guess that if it passes a null argument into a method it shouldn't get a `NullPointerException`. This will show that the method has been exercised (even if all its branches have not), but such coverage means little.

❑ Such tools struggle with understanding object state. For example, what if method calls on an object must be made in a certain order?

If you use the Jtest design by contract syntax in your source files, Jtest has much more to offer and probably will help to raise code quality.

Coverage Tools

Far more useful, in my view, are tools that enable us to see the **code coverage** achieved by unit tests: that is, the application code that was executed by unit tests. A good tool can provide coverage analysis down to individual branches, catch blocks and so on.

This is another important form of evidence that we can integrate into our development process. It can help us improve our test suite, and ensure that it is adequate.

There are several popular code coverage tools. Unfortunately I don't know of any full-featured open source product. However, the commercial Clover product, from www.thecortex.net, is inexpensive, easy to use, and I recommend it.

Figure 14-1 illustrates Clover's Javadoc-style HTML report generation showing coverage for a whole project and individual packages and classes. Green (the left color in the horizontal bars) means exercised code; red no coverage. Follow the links on the Clover home page to see sample reports like the one shown in the figure in color.

Clover reports show test coverage down to individual lines of code. For example, in Figure 14-2, the red bars in the right pane indicate a conditional that always evaluates to false, meaning incomplete code coverage. This might help the developer to write a test in which the advisors collection was empty.

Clover offers integration with the IntelliJ, Eclipse and other IDEs. Clover also provides a Swing coverage browser. Like the HTML reports (which are ideal for publication on an intranet), the Swing UI can be used to view coverage down to individual lines of code.

Clover can easily be integrated with an Ant build process. It needs to instrument source code before compiling it and executing the (un-instrumented) test suite. Scripted appropriately, these steps add little time or complexity to the build process. For example, it's no harder and little slower to run the Spring test suite and generate Clover reports than to run it without Clover.

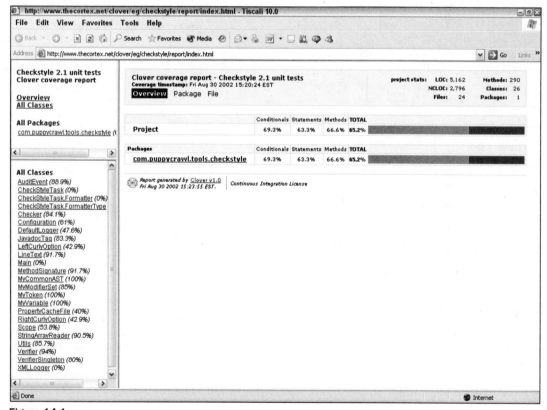

Figure 14-1

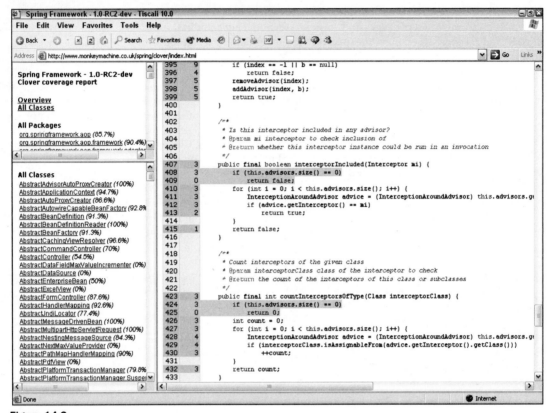

Figure 14-2

Benefits

We can learn a lot from test coverage analysis. It's a valuable form of feedback in improving test cases by identifying code that isn't being exercised. Even with TDD, coverage may not be perfect. While TDD helps us write only the necessary code up front, TDD doesn't necessarily help us eliminate code that is no longer required if the test suite changes. Coverage reports indicate such code, which is typically ripe for removal. (Code that isn't covered should be removed, or further tests written.)

There are no hard and fast rules for coverage. A goal of around 90% is easily achievable for TDD projects, and provides a secure basis for regression testing.

It's important to apply some discrimination in interpreting coverage reports. I've seen obsession with the headline percentage causing wasted work testing JavaBean properties and other code that was too trivial to be particularly important. On the other hand, if higher coverage can be achieved easily, it's usually worthwhile.

Browsing coverage reports is well worth the time it takes. It can help to increase understanding of what is happening at runtime: for example, which code paths are no longer in use.

Dangers

It's important not to let coverage figures become a goal in themselves. Coverage gives us an indication of the quality of the test suite. However, it only gives us *information* about the code we have written; we need to supply the intelligence to make best use of that information. What if we've written the wrong code, or insufficient code? For example, if we lack code to handle an important special case, coverage analysis won't help.

> **Tests should be primarily driven by what the code should *do*, not maximizing coverage.**

Generally, obsession with test coverage is more harmful the more bureaucratic a project is. I've seen projects with coverage targets enforced by management, rather than developer buy-in, in which tests are effectively faked to achieve higher coverage: for example, methods invoked without testing the results of invoking them, just that no runtime exception occurred. Such fake coverage is worse than useless, as it's dangerously misleading.

A few good rules of thumb regarding coverage tools:

- ❑   Code test first; this will guarantee pretty good test coverage.

- ❑   Run coverage reports regularly: once a week or more often. If you can run coverage analysis within your IDE you can run it as you work on individual classes, which is even more useful.

- ❑   If code isn't being used, consider eliminating it.

> **Code coverage tools are an important part of the development toolset, and should be integrated into the build process. Unit test coverage is an important metric, and can be very useful. However, remember that code coverage is an *informative* metric, and should not be viewed as an end in itself.**

Mutation Testing Tools

Another potentially useful type of testing tool is a **mutation testing** tool. Mutation testing tools continually modify application code before rerunning the test suite. For example, they might see whether tests for a class pass if a particular conditional is inverted. Mutation testing tools raise a problem if the tests still pass after such code changes: a strong test suite should fail.

Several academic papers have been published on mutation testing; only recently have practical tools been available implementing the idea.

Mutation testing can be more revealing than coverage analysis because it goes some way toward testing the *quality* of the testing rather than the extent. Mutation testing can find code that is being *executed* by the test suite but not really *tested*. It is a complementary approach to coverage analysis, which is not likely to yield useful results unless test coverage is already high.

The principal problems with mutation testing are that it is so slow, and that mutation testing tools appear still to be immature. The process of continually changing and recompiling code and rerunning the test suite can take much longer than executing tests normally or running coverage analysis.

The most promising Java mutation testing tool appears to be Jester by Ivan Moore (`http://jester.sourceforge.net`). Jester has been favorably reviewed by no less an authority on TDD than Kent Beck. Jester produces simple HTML reports on files where it is able to change code and still find tests pass, which look like Figure 14-3.

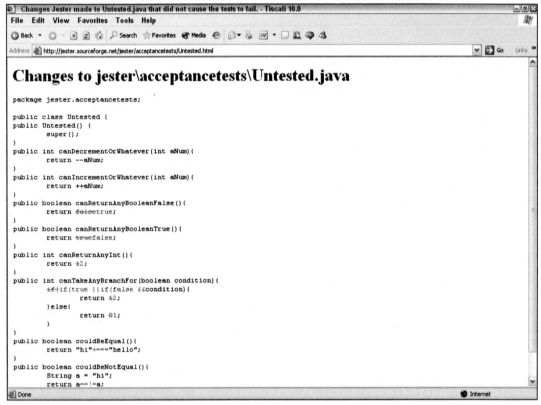

Figure 14-3

I haven't actually used mutation testing tools, so I can't comment from personal experience. However, mutation testing is a very promising area, and on my (lengthy) to do list.

Resources

As I mentioned earlier, you'll learn a lot more by *doing* testing than by reading about it. However, the following resources will help you get started or—even if you're already a testing veteran—improve your skills.

- ❑ www.junit.org. The JUnit portal. A good place to start, with many links to different testing tools and articles.

- ❑ *JUnit in Action* by Vincent Massol and Ted Husted (Manning, 2003). An excellent, highly readable introduction to JUnit, mock objects, and other important testing techniques.

- ❑ www.mockobjects.com. Mock objects home page. See especially www.mockobjects.com/wiki/MocksObjectsPaper for links to articles on mocks.

- ❑ www.ociweb.com/jnb/jnbJun2003.html. "Designing Testability with Mock Objects," by Mario Aquino.

- ❑ www.objectmentor.com/resources/articles/xpepisode.htm. Demonstration of test first development in which Robert C. Martin and Robert S. Koss document the steps in programming a simple game test first. Long but informative.

- ❑ www.thecortex.net/clover/index.html. Clover home page.

As I noted earlier, you'll also find it helpful to study test suites for open source projects with good test coverage, such as the Spring Framework and PicoContainer. These are real-world tests and, as such, more valuable than any examples that can be included in a book.

Summary

Unit testing should be a central part of the development process. There are many benefits in having an effective unit test suite, including a regression testing safety net and the ability to refactor fearlessly to ensure that the code base remains clean over time.

Consider testability when you design and implement applications. Avoid, or at least minimize the use of, the mortal enemies of testability. These include:

- ❑ EJB and anything else that makes code untestable outside a particular runtime environment.

- ❑ The Singleton pattern, or, rather, antipattern.

- ❑ Static locator methods.

- ❑ Classes with too many responsibilities.

- ❑ Programming to classes, rather than interfaces.

In general, there's a synergy between good practice and testable application code. Clean code is usually easy to test; murky, messy code is hard to test as well as hard to understand and maintain.

Fortunately, there's a single way to make these good practices much easier to apply (and bring many other benefits): using an IoC container, as discussed in Chapter 6. This will remove lookup code and other dependencies on hard-to-simulate APIs from application code. You'll be able to implement application code in POJOs, parameterized by JavaBean properties or constructors rather than magic runtime dependencies.

Unit testing is so important that it should be practiced from the commencement of the project, and from the commencement of coding each class. I strongly recommend adopting test-driven development. The chances are that if you've made a serious effort to try test first development, you don't need me to proclaim its many benefits. If you haven't, it's time you tried!

Test-driven development pretty much guarantees adequate test coverage and, therefore, effective regression testing. It also gives continuous feedback about progress.

Test-driven development is a knack that takes a while to develop, but once you feel comfortable with it you won't want to go back. And it saves a lot of time in the end. One of the best ways to acquire skills in unit testing and TDD is to work alongside an experienced TDD practitioner ("pairing" in XP language). Looking at the test suites for well-tested open source projects can also be very helpful in getting started or improving your unit testing skills.

> If you're serious about testing, practice test-driven development. TDD is not only helpful in developing robust code, but it enables fearless refactoring to ensure that the code base is as good as possible at all times.

Understand that unit testing is about testing in isolation. Once you understand this, you'll avoid a lot of duplication in your tests. Write tests that test a single object, rather than all its collaborators indirectly.

Mock objects are a valuable technique for testing classes in isolation. Collaborators can be replaced with mocks at test time, enabling expectations to be created and verified at the end of each test case. Mock objects can be used most effectively when dependencies are expressed on interfaces, rather than classes.

Classes should be testable not only in isolation from each other, but apart from their runtime environment. Unit testing can only effectively be conducted outside the application server. When your unit tests depend on the application server or on the database, you lose your ability to simulate negative conditions such as database failure, and your test suite will take too long to run.

This matters, because it's important to automate your test suite and run it often. Running tests as part of a nightly build process, although a common practice, is far too rare: you should run all tests before you check anything into your source control system.

It's important to continually improve the quality of your test suite, as well as your application code. Remember that an effective test suite is an essential deliverable. Code coverage tools such as Clover can enable you to visualize the percentage of your application code that is covered by unit tests, and even look at individual methods to see which lines of code are exercised by tests. Code coverage should not be an end in itself, but it can be a very useful informative metric.

Performance testing is another important activity. I'll discuss this in Chapter 15.

> Effective testing is another valuable way to base a project on a continual process of evidence gathering, which is one of the themes of this book. It's vital to be able to prove that something works, rather than have faith in unrepeatable, ad hoc testing.

15

Performance and Scalability

Performance and scalability often determine the success or failure of enterprise applications.

A surprisingly large proportion of J2EE applications encounter performance problems: often too late in the project lifecycle for them to be solved cost effectively, leading to the risk of complete failure.

It's not that J2EE is inherently slow. It's that inherently slow architectural patterns are undeservedly popular, and far too many J2EE architects have a blind spot regarding performance. Despite the ample evidence that performance risks should be considered early in the project lifecycle, they believe that performance can safely be addressed after an application is functionally complete, usually through:

- ❑ Code optimization; *or*
- ❑ More, or faster, hardware—often seen as a panacea

Both of these assumptions are wrong. Code optimization often amounts to moving the deckchairs on the *Titanic*. *Architecture*, not implementation, usually determines performance, and optimizing code will seldom radically change performance characteristics. (However, code optimization *is* an excellent way of reducing maintainability and increasing the potential for bugs.) Even if applying more hardware solves a throughput problem—which it often doesn't—it often amounts to a waste of money, when the application requires far greater hardware resources than it should.

The blind spot often extends to a belief that a "pure" architecture is more important than a performant application. This is nonsense: those who pay the bills care whether an application does what they expect far more than whether it follows questionable blueprints.

> **An application that doesn't meet performance and throughput requirements doesn't work.**

In this chapter we'll look at how to avoid performance problems, by considering the performance implications of candidate architectures and verifying those performance characteristics before proceeding to full-blown development. We'll look at:

❑ **The importance of setting clear goals for performance and throughput.**

❑ **Fundamental architectural issues in designing performant J2EE applications, whether or not we use EJB.** Core architecture is usually far more important to performance than implementation detail, which means that understanding and testing the performance implications of an architecture is more valuable than code optimization.

❑ **How the middleware approach I present in this book—built around IoC and AOP—compares with the performance of the EJB alternative.**

❑ **How to tune a J2EE application for optimal performance.**

❑ **The importance of taking an evidence-based approach to performance analysis.** Because performance is so important, it's essential that we base performance decisions on evidence, rather than hunches or prejudices.

We'll largely focus on the performance issues around web applications, but most of the discussion applies to all J2EE applications.

Chapter 15 of Expert One-on-One J2EE Design and Development *discusses performance testing and tuning at length, including a discussion of caching and code optimization techniques. I won't duplicate that discussion here; please refer to it and other references cited below for further information on low-level optimization techniques. In this chapter I'll focus more on the central architectural issues, and the implications for performance of the "J2EE without EJB" vision.*

Definitions

It's important to distinguish between **performance, throughput**, and **scalability**. The definitions I use here are consistent with those of *Expert One-on-One J2EE Design and Development* and (with some minor differences) those of Martin Fowler's *Patterns of Enterprise Application Architecture* (Addison-Wesley, 2002, pp. 7–9).

An application's **performance** is the time it takes to do its work, across a representative range of operations. Performance is typically measured in terms of response times. Performance is often a critical business requirement: for example—"the application must accept a new equities trade and publish a confirmation message in no more than 30 seconds." Performance also has an important effect on user perception, especially for web applications operating in a competitive environment. If users perceive an application to be slow, they will be frustrated and may cease using it.

Response time is the time it takes for an application to process a request—for example, an HTTP request from a user's browser. Normally, we're most interested in average response time, although it's also important to consider consistency of response times, under load. Spikes in response time are often an indication of poor behavior under load, and potential instability.

Latency is the minimum time taken to get a response from the application, regardless of whether the application has to do much work to produce the response. Remote method invocations exhibit high latency: there is a fixed minimum cost, regardless of whether the invoked method does any work.

Throughput is the amount of work that can be performed by an application or component in a given period of time. In the case of web applications, this is often measured in hits per second; for highly transactional applications, the number of transactions completed per second.

Scalability refers to how the application can cope with changed volumes: typically, greater concurrent load, often resulting from a larger user community. By scalability we usually refer to **scaling up** to a larger load. Scalability often amounts to **horizontal scalability**: scaling up to a cluster of servers to increase throughput. We may also try to increase throughput by moving the application on to a more powerful server. Using a more powerful server is far simpler, but of course does not make the application more robust, and can only deliver limited results. Another option is **vertical scaling**, in which we run *multiple servers* on each machine. This might yield good results with application servers such as WebSphere, for which IBM advocate it. See `www-306.ibm.com/software/webservers/appserv/doc/v40/ae/infocenter/was/07010303.html` for a discussion of this technique. The term vertical scaling is also sometimes used, as by Fowler, to refer to the simpler technique of adding more power to a single server, such as more CPUs or RAM.

Performance and scalability are sometimes opposed in practice. For example, an application that is highly performant on a single server may fail to scale up to a clustered deployment: for example, if it maintains a huge amount of session state for each user, which can't be replicated efficiently.

However, it's important to note that applications that perform poorly are not likely to be scalable either. An application that wastes resources on one server will merely have more resources to waste if it is run in a cluster.

We should distinguish between **load** and **stress** testing. Load testing aims to load the system to the limits of its expected capacity. Stress testing aims to load the system *beyond* its expected capacity, to ascertain its behavior. For example, does it simply refuse to accept more connections beyond a certain point, or does it become unstable? Good tools for load and stress testing enable us to measure response time (average and distribution) and latency, as well as throughput.

Setting Clear Goals

It's essential need to have clear goals for performance and scalability. It's essential to know more than it "should run fast" and "be highly scalable." Some of the key questions are:

❑   **What are the throughput and response time goals?** Without clear goals—which should be set by the business, not the application architects—it's impossible to know whether performance is satisfactory, and impossible to know whether we are making the right architectural and implementation decisions from a performance perspective. Far too many projects lack such clear goals.

❑   **Which operations must be fast, and which can be slow?** Not all use cases are equal. Some must be prioritized from a performance perspective.

❑   **What hardware and software (application server, database) must these goals be achieved on?** Without such information, it's impossible to verify success.

❑ **Is making the application faster worthwhile if it costs greater development and maintenance effort?** Slightly higher performance can sometimes be achieved at the cost of maintainability, especially where code optimization is concerned. Hence expending effort achieving further performance increases when we already meet targets can be counterproductive. Only in a small minority of applications—usually infrastructure applications—is it critical to obtain every possible performance improvement.

❑ **What load must the application scale to?** As with response times, it's important to know how many concurrent users (or concurrent transactions) must be supported.

❑ **Is the application intended to run in a clustered environment?** If the application doesn't need to run in a cluster from the outset, is it likely to need to run in a cluster in the future?

Often we can't make *everything* run fast, and must make an informed tradeoff between different use cases. For example, a financial trading system may need to run risk scenarios on current positions as well as provide the ability to recreate historical positions. These requirements may conflict from a performance perspective. For example, the system could store data in a structure allowing efficient temporal access later; or it could prioritize current data, forcing historical positions to be reconstructed through an audit trail. The first option may not be practical if it slows the many accesses to current positions required to support risk calculations. On the other hand, it may be acceptable for construction of historical position data to be slower.

It's important to be realistic about scalability goals. During the dotcom boom, every startup tended to imagine that it was the next Amazon.com. While it's important to avoid an architecture that won't scale, it's unwise to waste effort ensuring scalability to irrelevant levels. And it's important that architects are able to feed back to the business any cost implications of achieving the specified scalability and performance.

Architectural Choices: The Key to Performance and Scalability

Basic architectural choices largely determine the performance characteristics of a J2EE application. It doesn't matter how much we optimize individual method implementations: if the overall architecture dictates unnecessary database access; excessive conversion from Java objects to-and-from XML documents; or excessive remote calls (to take three of the commonest causes of J2EE performance problems), no amount of code-level optimization will do much good.

The most important architectural choices from a performance and scalability perspective are usually:

❑ Whether or not the application is distributed

❑ If the application needs to run in a cluster, the approach to clustering

❑ The approach to accessing persistent data

Let's examine these issues. The first two are closely related.

Object Distribution, Clusters, and Farms

Enterprise applications don't usually run on a single server. One major motivation for **horizontal scaling** (running on more peer servers) is to increase throughput by harnessing more CPU power; another (potentially even more important) is to make the application more robust, by avoiding a single point of failure.

Horizontal scaling is a complex business, so it's important to distinguish between different types of horizontal scaling—notably:

- ❏ **Object distribution**, in which *components* with remote interfaces are the prime unit of distribution. Applications are built out of distributed components.

- ❏ **Deployment clustering**, in which whole application deployments are the prime unit of distribution. When a request is received by one server, it satisfies it through local calls to components in the same process. This is the approach I advocate in general, and which is especially suitable for web applications.

As we'll see, there are different flavors of clustering of each type, depending on what needs to be replicated around the cluster.

Definitions

Object distribution is the classic J2EE approach. Horizontal scaling is achieved by thinking in terms of **components** (remote EJBs) rather than deployments. This model aims to scale by taking web and business objects (remote EJBs in this approach) and distributing them to balance load throughout a cluster. In this model, all business invocations are made using RMI/IIOP or—in some cases—XML or web services invocations.

Deployment clustering involves taking all components and deploying them on each node in a cluster. In a web application, this would involve deploying the whole J2EE stack on each node, from web tier down to database access. In this model, routing decisions are made before a request hits each node, not on individual component invocations. Martin Fowler strongly advocates this approach in *Patterns of Enterprise Application Architecture* (p. 89), citing its advantages for the programming model as well as performance. In this style of clustering, all method invocations are local (call-by-reference) after control has been passed to a particular server.

In either case, EIS tier resources such as databases are normally on separate servers. While this sacrifices some performance, it has benefits in administration. As no enterprise-class database can run in the same process as a J2EE middle tier, there is no way to avoid the cost of interprocess communication in any case.

With either object distribution or deployment clustering, in many cases we need communication between the clustered deployments. For example, replication may be needed between data caches on each node. I'll examine these issues shortly.

There are different styles of cluster, such as a **farm**. In a farm, the whole application runs on multiple servers, but individual servers have no knowledge of each other, and no need to communicate except through the resources they use (such as databases). This means that state replication is not used between servers.

The Trouble with Distributed Objects

The key problem with object distribution is that it achieves scalability by making such a severe sacrifice of performance that much of the scalability serves merely to address inefficiency.

As we noted in Chapter 11, true remote method invocations are slow. (I'm not referring to pseudo-remote invocations of co-located remote EJBs. These are fast because they're not truly remote, and should thus be considered as local method calls.) The overhead of each remote invocation is typically orders of magnitude greater than that of a local invocation, because of the cost of network transfer and serialization and deserialization. Thus while we can have any number of remote business objects (in theory), we may in fact need significantly more hardware to achieve the throughput that we could have achieved on a single server with clustered deployment.

Sometimes RMI is replaced by the use of XML or web services protocols. This is still slower in general, and offers greater complexity. (Remote EJBs make object distribution pretty much as painless as it ever can be.)

The traditional J2EE approach to the high cost of remote invocations is to minimize the number of distributed calls by batching: for example, using transfer objects to communicate a large amount of data in a single request. Fewer remote calls each transporting more data are faster than fine-grained remote calls transporting little data, because the infrastructure overhead in setting up a remote call is usually more significant than the cost of communicating the necessary data. However, removing the distribution boundary altogether, if possible, will perform far better. And using transfer objects can be difficult, because we must know exactly how much data a remote client will need and, hence, how far to traverse a persistent object graph.

While object distribution superficially promises ultimate scalability because it allows heavily hit components to be deployed to more servers, theoretically targeting bottlenecks, in fact deploying the whole application to more servers is usually preferable. This way we don't incur the remote invocation overhead, but still get enough CPU power targeted at the problem components.

In my experience, cases in which distributed objects *do* make sense from a performance perspective are rare. Typically they involve time-consuming, CPU-bound operations, in which the time taken to perform the work significantly outweighs the cost of remote invocations. For example, risk calculations in some financial applications can require so much CPU power that it makes sense to have a large cluster of machines purely devoted to them. In such cases, remote EJBs are a good implementation strategy. But such cases are exceptional. Asynchronous distribution via message queues may be a better alternative to remote method invocation for long-running operations.

Clustering Challenges

However we approach it, there remain major challenges in running a cluster. The major challenges in clustering concern:

❑ **Routing.** How are requests coming into the cluster routed to server within it?

❑ **Replication.** What state or other resources need to be shared across the cluster, and hence replicated? Session state is one of the most important replication challenges; another is ensuring the coherence of a shared data cache across a cluster.

It's not too hard to solve the first problem. In fact, routing may not even need to be solved in software at all. However, replication is a major problem and the biggest limitation in clustering technologies.

We must consider the following limits on horizontal scaling:

❑ **It doesn't produce a linear return.** Running an application on three servers won't usually produce three times the throughput of running the application on one server, unless we're in a farm situation. With object distribution, switching from phony (co-located) remote calls to true remote calls will significantly reduce performance and may increase CPU load so much that it reduces throughput. With clustered deployment the results may be better, but a simple multiplicative effect is unlikely, because of the need for any session replication, and because of the need to access shared resources such as a database. Maintaining a data cache is relatively simple on a single server; maintaining a shared data cache is much more complex, and imposes significantly more runtime overhead.

❑ **There are usually limits to how many servers we can run in a cluster.** There's typically a management overhead. For example, the more servers in the cluster, the greater the overhead of any replication. Although we can limit this by sharing state using the database, this is less performant for smaller clusters. Eventually, unless we have EIS tier resources with infinite scalability, we'll run into their limitations as we grow the middle tier.

> The first essential for a scalable application is an efficient application. Because horizontal scaling seldom produces linear returns, the more throughput that can be achieved per unit hardware, the more scalable the application will be.

An important point often missed is that EJB usually isn't the main game where clustering is concerned. The following table discusses the architectural tiers where applications may face clustering and replication issues:

Architectural Tier	Issue	Where Handled	Issues
Web tier	How are requests routed into web containers?	Hardware routers Plugins for web servers such as Apache	Routing may be based on various algorithms, including round-robin, random, and assessment of load.
		Web container, as with the WebLogic `HttpClusterServlet`.	Routing is a relatively simple problem until state replication is involved, as this places constraints on which servers may handle a request.

Table continued on following page

Architectural Tier	Issue	Where Handled	Issues
	If there is HTTP session state, how is it replicated to allow failover?	Handled by the web container. Strategies include: Broadcast changed data around the cluster Store state in the database Back up state to a single "secondary" server	The different approaches take a different tradeoff between robustness and performance and scalability. For example, backing up data to the database is a robust approach and may allow large cluster sizes (assuming the database can handle the load), but it may have a serious negative effect on performance.
	Is there a cache for frequently displayed data, to avoid repeated trips to the business layer?	Usually handled by a cache in application code in the web tier.	"Classic" distributed J2EE applications often include caches in the web tier, to minimize the number of calls to the remote EJB business objects. This becomes less important if we dispense with remote EJBs, because it means that there's no longer a severe performance penalty for invoking a business object.
Business object layer	Replication of state held by stateful business objects.	EJB container managing stateful session bean instances.	State is usually better managed by the web container in the form of HTTP session objects. Since the web tier will need to hold the handle of the stateful session bean, typically we end up with *two* replication problems, not one, if we hold state in the business layer. With local business objects there's no performance penalty in passing state into them from the web tier, compared with the case of remote session beans, negating a performance argument for using stateful business objects.
	Routing requests to stateless business object instances.	EJB container routing invocations to remote EJBs.	**This is only necessary with a distributed architecture.**

Architectural Tier	Issue	Where Handled	Issues
O/R mapping layer	Maintaining a coherent cache across nodes.	O/R mapping product such as TopLink, Hibernate, or JDO implementation.	Maintaining a transactional-aware distributed cache is a complex problem.
		EJB container if using CMP entity beans.	O/R mapping products often defer the issues of cache coherence to third-party products such as Tangosol Coherence.
			Implementations of CMP entity beans typically offer less sophisticated distributed caches than such solutions. For example, it's usually necessary to invoke `ejbLoad()` before every operation on an entity in a cluster: a huge overhead.
Database	Horizontal scaling; making a database spread across multiple physical servers appear as one logical database.	RDBMS vendor. Oracle 9i RAC is such a product.	Such capability for the database to scale is very important, as otherwise the database may become the limit of the scalability of the entire application.

I've shaded what I consider to be the most important of these replication challenges. In a co-located application that doesn't use entity beans, none of these challenges is addressed by the EJB container. Thus the EJB container doesn't make any contribution, positive or negative, to scalability.

In fact, none of the replication challenges concerns the business object layer at all. The most important replication services are provided by:

❑ **The web container**, replicating any session state

❑ **The O/R mapping layer**, replicating data to ensure a coherent cache in front of the database

❑ **The database itself**, which may be scaled across multiple physical servers

In such an application, using EJBs but not entity beans (consistent with most current views on best practice when using EJB) we might use the web container to manage HTTP session state and use local session beans with JDO for persistence. In this architecture, the crucial replication occurs at two points:

❑ Between the web containers to communicate session state.

❑ Between the second-level (`PersistenceManagerFactory`-level) caches on each node maintained by the JDO implementation. Such replication might involve a specialized third-party caching product. For example, SolarMetric Kodo JDO is often combined with Tangosol Coherence for high-performance transactional caching.

In this architecture, there is no replication, or routing, involved with the local SLSBs. Thus the EJB container has no part in cluster management, and the critical distributed data cache is not handled by the application server, but by the persistence technology.

> *We may be able to help the web container with session state replication by minimizing the amount of data kept in HTTP session objects and using finer-grained session objects instead of a single monolithic object. This allows the server to replicate only the changed objects. Otherwise it may need to serialize the large object each time session state is changed.*

Stateless business objects don't need replication. They need routing services only if servicing remote clients. Otherwise the routing decisions have already taken place before the business objects are invoked.

Data access is usually the key to successful horizontal scaling. The success of clustering will usually be determined by:

❑ How efficiently the O/R mapping layer (if any) can cache data in a distributed environment—something that most entity bean implementations do not do particularly well.

❑ How the database can cope with the overall load. An efficient data cache can help protect the database, but we should remember that databases often themselves include efficient caches, and that high-end databases, such as Oracle 9i RAC, are themselves highly scalable through clustered deployment.

In some applications, there may be little benefit in maintaining a distributed data cache: for example, if data is written as often as read. In this case, direct JDBC access to the database may be appropriate.

> **Often the real replication issues in a clustered J2EE application are not addressed by the EJB container, but by the web container and data access layer. The widely held belief that EJB is necessary to clustering is a fallacy.**

Sacrificing performance in the hope of greater scalability—as by introducing excessive remote calling—is dangerous. Not only can we never recapture the lost performance, but we may need a larger number of servers to achieve the same result, because each of those servers is wasting resources marshaling and unmarshaling data to send over the network. This means that we may run into the problems with the limitations of horizontal scalability.

> **Applications that don't hold server-side state are usually the most scalable. In a web application, for example, if we need to hold only minimal user state, we might be able to hold it in cookies, avoiding any need for HTTP session state replication.**
>
> **Such applications are highly scalable, and also extremely robust. Hardware routing devices can efficiently distribute load between the servers, detecting any failed servers.**

Data Access

How data is accessed will have an important impact on performance. Assuming the use of a relational database, it's important to have:

- An efficient schema, which supports common queries efficiently

- A minimal number of database updates

- Efficient updates, in the fewest possible round trips

- An efficient data cache, if the application's data access is amenable to caching

The ideal for data access—for both maintainability and performance—is to have a natural, efficient, RDBMS schema and a natural, efficient object model. This means that if we use O/R mapping, we need a sophisticated solution that is capable of mapping inheritance relationships, taking advantages of optimizations available in the target database, and accessing stored procedures if required.

For these reasons, entity beans seldom produce as good performance as more sophisticated O/R mapping solutions. (Entity beans are typically used for O/R mapping, despite providing a woefully inadequate solution.) BMP entity beans are usually inherently inefficient, because of the **n + 1 finder problem.** CMP entity beans are better, but are often non-performant because:

- EJB QL is not as expressive a query language as SQL. Some operations that can be done efficiently in SQL or a SQL-like language such as Hibernate HQL, cannot be efficiently performed in EJB QL.

- There is a higher overhead associated with each entity bean instance than with persistent POJOs managed by O/R mapping solutions.

- The entity bean model is inherently transactional, which may not always be appropriate.

- Entity bean implementations are unlikely to provide as efficient distributed caches as the best O/R mapping technologies.

True O/R mapping, as can be done by tools such as Hibernate or good JDO implementations, is often valuable, and often the best route to a good domain model. However, it's important to remember that O/R mapping isn't always appropriate.

Belief that ORM is *always* appropriate reflects a broader distrust of relational databases among J2EE architects. I've repeatedly criticized this, in *Expert One-on-One J2EE Design and Development* and elsewhere, and have never quite fathomed why such distrust runs so deep in the J2EE community. Relational databases do certain things particularly well: in particular, they excel in set-based operations. Also, stored procedures can sometimes minimize the number of round trips to the database, and permit the use of efficient relational operations.

> *Relational databases are not going to go away because the J2EE community doesn't much like them. I'd put my money on RDBMSs to survive J2EE in anything like its present form.*

Of course we don't want to put business logic in the database if we can help it. However, persistence logic is a different matter, and there's a strong argument that it *belongs* in the database. For example, if we can hide knowledge of three database tables by using a stored procedure to update them, we have probably improved design by decoupling our Java code from the structure of the database. We can now change the underlying relational schema if we need to, or migrate to another database, preserving the stored procedure with the same arguments. This approach works so long as there's no business logic in the operations performed by the stored procedure: often the case, for example, if the stored procedure merely generates primary keys and updates several tables to reflect the new data, without performing conditional or other rule-based operations.

In general, if we find that we are forced to retrieve many records via O/R mapping to iterate over them—for example, when working out aggregates—it is better to do that, if possible, in the database. If we need to *display* those records to clients, on the other hand, it makes sense to instantiate Java objects to represent them.

Other Architectural Issues

A number of other architectural issues can also dictate performance characteristics. Three significant issues I've repeatedly seen in practice are usage of XML; presentation tier technologies; and choosing whether to use proprietary features of the application server or other products in the technology stack.

In all these cases, profiling end-to-end operations exercising the entire technology stack can be very useful, indicating exactly how the total time is broken down. I'll discuss profiling later in this chapter.

XML Usage

XML is now almost the *lingua franca* of the Internet. Used to loosely couple systems implemented on different technologies—especially when standardized using web services—XML is a valuable technology. However, using XML for communication *within* a J2EE application is far less desirable, although undeservedly fashionable.

Converting Java objects to and from XML is usually very expensive. XML data binding can reduce the cost, but not eliminate it.

> **Excessive use of XML within applications is a good example of the way in which fashion in J2EE architecture seems directly inimical to performance.**

Presentation Tier Technologies

Presentation tier technologies, and how they're used, can have an important effect on performance. Rendering a JSP page, for example, can be more expensive than direct database access to retrieve the necessary data. Certain idioms, such as excessive use of custom tags, can reduce performance.

Use of XSLT has other merits, but XSLT transforms can be expensive in terms of performance. If they are used throughout the presentation tier, the effect on performance can be significant. XSLT engines vary widely in performance, so making the correct choice is important.

Because presentation tier technology and usage can have such a significant impact on performance, benchmarking the presentation tier in isolation can be useful.

Portability versus Performance

Sometimes a goal of portability can conflict with performance. This is most apparent when certain standards fail to address all requirements. Architects often refuse to use proprietary extensions on grounds of "purity." This can be costly in terms of performance. If your technology platform offers a particularly efficient way of doing something, which is non-standard, it deserves consideration if there are performance constraints on that operation. If possible, follow good OO practice and hide the non-portable code behind a portable interface.

Implementation Choices

By architecture, we refer to the big questions such as: *Do we distribute*? *Do we use O/R mapping*? Once we've made those choices, we still have a number of *implementation* choices, such as:

- ❑ Local EJB vs. POJOs with AOP advice for local business objects?
- ❑ EJB container or IoC container?
- ❑ Hibernate or JDO implementation?

In this section I'll consider some of these choices from the performance perspective, and demonstrate that they don't usually matter as much as the fundamental choices. I'll focus on the performance implications of dispensing with EJB usage.

I'll then consider code optimization, and how we can enjoy quick wins without great effort or many compromises.

The Performance Implications of Dispensing with EJB Service Provision

You may be wondering about the performance and scalability implications of dispensing with EJB and adopting the kind of architecture that we advocate in this book. Proponents of EJB tend to dismiss its other deficiencies—such as its complexity—with the argument that, in return for accepting them, EJB delivers greater scalability and potential throughput than the alternatives.

In this section, I'll survey some evidence to see whether this is true.

I'll consider situations in which we have a service interface that we could choose to implement as either a local stateless session bean, benefiting from EJB enterprise services such as CMT; or a POJO, benefiting from AOP-enabled enterprise services provided by a lightweight container such as Spring. I'll also consider some performance results from true remote EJB invocations, as a comparison.

> *I focus here on performance issues around invoking business objects, for which declarative services are attractive. The cost of delivering declarative services—with EJB or any other technology—is more likely to be an issue with fine-grained objects such as persistent objects returned in a large result set. I'll discuss the performance implications for the whole application stack, as measured through the behavior of the web tier.*

Benchmark Methodology

The following discussion is based on a benchmark of a web application that accesses a relational database.

The web application involved the following operations, intended to simulate the mix of operations in a typical web application accessing a relational database:

❑ Process a request that required repeated invocation of a method on a business object that returned very quickly, simulating the return of cached data. This operation did not require a transaction.

❑ Place an order and update inventory, involving updating two tables. This was performed by a PL/SQL stored procedure.

❑ Query orders by user.

Since these scenarios didn't benefit from caching—and the aim of the benchmark was not to compare caching implementations—data access was performed using JDBC implementations of DAOs accessed from a business object. Random user and item ids were picked from known ranges for order placement and order querying.

The implementation choices tested were:

❑ Remote SLSB deployed remotely, using CMT for transaction management

❑ SLSB deployed locally, using CMT: the recommended EJB architecture for most web applications

❑ Single shared instance of a POJO transactionally advised using Spring AOP: our recommended architecture for most scenarios

❑ A POJO pooled by the Spring AOP infrastructure, also used to provide transactional advice

❑ Shared instance of a POJO implementing programmatic transaction management, without any declarative services

All the POJOs were deployed in the web container of the same application server running the EJBs. The same JSPs were used to generate content in all cases. The underlying transaction infrastructure in each case was the application server's JTA implementation. All the different implementations obtained database connections from the same container `DataSource`. The database was cleaned between runs.

The code in the business object was virtually identical in each case. The EJB extended the POJO implementation to implement the required session bean lifecycle methods. The programmatic implementation was achieved using the Decorator pattern, discussed later in this chapter. The service locator implementation used to obtain EJB references cached the EJBHome object, to minimize the number of JNDI lookups required.

In the case of both EJB and AOP, the only declarative middleware service required was declarative transaction management. In the case of the simulation of the return of cached data, no transaction was required.

Load tests simulated heavy prolonged load, testing for stability as well as throughput. The results shown in the following section were obtained using a popular open source application server. We also benchmarked a high-end commercial product, which produced significantly better results for all benchmarks, but also showed local EJB to underperform the Spring solution—however, by a much smaller margin.

The benchmarks shown below ran under the Sun JDK, version 1.4.2_03. The operating system was RedHat Enterprise Linux 3.0. The application servers were set to use the HotSpot Server JVM, which was optimized for server applications with appropriate settings for garbage collection and heap size. The application server ran on a machine containing two Xeon 2.8 GHz processors, 2 GB of memory and two SCSI hard disks, optimized for performance using RAID 0. For the benchmark involving remote SLSBs, a similar machine served as the front-end, and the two were connected using a Gigabit cross cable to eliminate the influence of network overhead. The database (MySQL 4.0.16) was configured to use appropriate cache and buffer sizes for the volume of data and operations performed by the test. All tests were executed using a clean database and after a server restart and appropriate warm-up time. The tests were conducted using ApacheBench.

We also ran tests on different operating systems, databases (Oracle rather than MySQL), and operating systems (Windows 2000/XP Professional rather than Red Hat). The results were similar to those described earlier. For further discussion of this benchmark, including the source code and detailed results, follow the Performance link on the Spring web site (`www.springframework.org`).

Thanks to Alef Arendsen for gathering most of these performance results, and providing production-quality hardware.

Declarative and Programmatic Middleware Models

Let's first focus on the approach to transaction management, before considering threading model.

Remote SLSB with CMT

When EJBs were truly remote, the overhead of remote invocation had a huge impact on throughput and response time, unless the business operation was itself slow (for example, requiring a database insert).

Local SLSB with CMT

With a local SLSB, performance was much better, and throughput increased dramatically. The cost of invoking an EJB running in-process was clearly modest, in comparison with the work that our business object needed to perform.

AOP Transaction Management

The Spring AOP approach performed significantly better than the local EJB—and, of course, much better than the remote EJB. The Spring AOP framework had a lower overhead for delivering declarative services than even local EJB invocations. The difference was most apparent in invoking methods without declarative services, in which case the Spring AOP implementation appeared to have a fraction of the overhead of the open source EJB container, and slightly less than the commercial EJB container. This was an interesting result, as the commercial EJB container used Java code generation and compilation to avoid any need to use reflection, unlike Spring's AOP, which uses dynamic proxies or CGLIB proxies. Reflection is no longer hugely expensive in Java 1.4 JVMs.

As might have been expected, the difference in overhead between AOP and EJB invocations when the intercepted business method performed an expensive operation such as a database insert was less noticeable. In such cases, the overhead of either the AOP or EJB infrastructure was dwarfed by the time taken *to execute the database operation. However, more efficient interception means more CPU power for IO operations and less time spent in the J2EE server, so it still produced a significant return. It would be possible to run this benchmark in a web container like Tomcat, without JTA, using the Spring JDBC **PlatformTransactionManager** and a third-party connection pool such as Commons DBCP. This approach doesn't work with more than one transactional data source, but it's a useful option, because it allows declarative transaction management in any web container, with no change in programming model. (The Spring AOP approach, unlike the EJB approach, can scale down as well as up). The performance in this case would partly depend on the efficiency of your chosen connection pool, but these results indicate that the Spring interception performance is likely to be better than EJB performance.*

Programmatic Transaction Management

In this case we used a transactional **decorator** subclass. For example, we overrode the `placeOrder()` method on our business facade to begin and commit or rollback a transaction, invoking the superclass's implementation to invoke the necessary business logic. For the operation simulating returning a cached result, there was no need to provide any transaction decoration.

Because, as we've noted, JTA is an awkward API to use, we used the Spring transaction API as a thin layer over the top of JTA. This meant that our code looked like this:

```
public void placeOrder(long userid, Order order) throws NoSuchUserException,
NoSuchItemException, InsufficientStockException   {
  TransactionStatus txStatus = txManager.getTransaction(new
DefaultTransactionDefinition());
  try {
          super.placeOrder(userid, order);
          // Leave txStatus alone
  }
  catch (DataAccessException ex) {
          txStatus.setRollbackOnly();
          throw ex;
  }
  catch (NoSuchUserException ex) {
          txStatus.setRollbackOnly();
          throw ex;
  }
  catch (NoSuchItemException ex) {
          txStatus.setRollbackOnly();
          throw ex;
  }
  catch (InsufficientStockException ex) {
          txStatus.setRollbackOnly();
          throw ex;
  }
  finally {
          // Close transaction
          // May have been marked for rollback
          txManager.commit(txStatus);
  }
}
```

Note that we use the `setRollbackOnly()` method on the Spring `TransactionStatus` object to roll back on the exceptions we've caught.

With the simplifying abstraction API we've used, this code is not *that* complex. If we had a simple application with only one or two transactional methods, this approach might be simpler than setting up the EJB or Spring AOP infrastructure to enable declarative transaction management. However, if we had code like this in multiple methods, we'd get sick of writing it, and we'd have a higher likelihood of making errors.

> **Use of the Decorator pattern in general should suggest an AOP approach.**

This benchmark used the Spring `JtaTransactionManager` implementation under the covers. This is a fairly thin layer on top of JTA. Thus the fundamental transaction infrastructure was identical to that in all the other benchmarks.

> *As with the Spring AOP approach, this Spring programmatic transaction management approach could also use an underlying transaction infrastructure other than JTA—such as JDBC—with no change to application code.*

As we might have expected, the programmatic approach was faster than any declarative approach—however, by only 2% to 10%. These results indicate that there's poor return on the effort involved in implementing such programmatic transaction management. Buying this performance improvement is far too costly in development effort and maintenance hassle.

> **Programmatic transaction management is a more complex programming model, which would require considerable justification. Not only do we need to write more code, meaning more potential for errors; our code becomes harder to test, as we need to provide test stubs or mocks for the transaction infrastructure on which our business logic now depends. If we use the Spring transaction abstraction, this is not too painful, because it decouples us from an underlying, hard-to-configure and hard-to-stub, transaction infrastructure such as JTA. However, it's still not as good as not having written and tested that transaction code at all!**

Threading Models

Let's now look at the threading models I recommended in Chapter 12. How does SLSB instance pooling compare to the following alternatives?

- ❏ Shared, multithreaded object (instead of an SLSB instance pool, a single object that handles all clients)
- ❏ Transparent instance pooling provided for POJOs without using EJB

I'll discuss this in combination with the declarative service provision models considered earlier.

I'll focus on Spring for the non-EJB alternative, as it abstracts the developer away from the lifecycle management of business objects—again, using AoP, as well as the Spring IoC container.

I'll discuss the benchmarks together with transaction management benchmarks later in this chapter.

Shared Multithreaded Object

As I argued in Chapter 12, a single, shared instance is the most appropriate threading model for most stateless service objects.

Normally, no synchronization is required, as such objects don't have read-write state. However, as mentioned previously, if the multithreaded object requires a little synchronization, and the synchronized code runs quickly, performance is not significantly affected.

Because the benchmark aimed to replicate a plausible usage scenario and wasn't designed to include a synchronization requirement, no synchronization was required.

The shared multithreaded object offered better performance than the co-located pooled EJB in all tests, on both open source and commercial application servers.

Spring Instance Pooling

Let's now consider Spring-based instance pooling. This used Spring AOP, with a pooling implementation of the `org.springframework.aop.TargetSource` interface, in this case built on Commons Pool 1.1. The `org.springframework.aop.target.CommonsPoolTargetSource` implementation is shipped as part of Spring. This provides a similar programming model to EJB, with business objects written as though they are single-threaded. In the present case we didn't need to change any code, because we had no threading issues in the business object. We set the pool size to be the same as the SLSB pool size in the EJB test.

In our tests, Spring instance pooling performed worse than a single shared instance *as long as the thread pool was appropriately configured in the web container*. When the web container allowed too many concurrent threads (essentially a misconfiguration), instance pooling around business objects improved performance.

Spring pooling performed significantly better than the EJB instance pool in the open source application server. Spring pooling performed marginally worse than EJB instance pooling in the high-end commercial server, suggesting that that server's pooling implementation is highly efficient, and outperforms Commons Pool 1.1, which was used by the Spring pooling implementation as the actual pooling provider. (It would be interesting to rerun the Spring benchmark with another pooling provider.) Nevertheless, it seems that there's nothing magical about EJB container instance pooling: Spring can achieve the same result for any POJO, and unless the EJB container is highly efficient, Spring pooling performance is likely to be superior.

No changes were required to client code or business implementation code as we switched between shared instance and pooled models, because of the decoupling introduced by the Spring IoC container.

Result Summary and Conclusions

The results of the comparison between the open source application server and the Spring solutions are summarized in the two charts in Figures 15-1 and 15-2. Response time data has been manipulated for ease of graphical representation. The two leftmost results are from true remote and co-located EJBs; the next two the Spring shared instance and pooling approaches; the rightmost, programmatic transaction management, with no use of EJB or Spring declarative services.

Figure 15-1 shows performance when the business operation is almost instant: for example, returning a cached value. This tests the case when we have a non-transactional operation against a facade to which declarative transaction management must be applied for other operations (hence some form of proxying will probably be required for all methods). The cost of remote invocation in this scenario is extremely high. The difference in throughput and response time is around ten times between the remote and slow-est co-located option. Of course, two servers were required to achieve the remote result, so it required twice the hardware of all the other (much more performant) results.

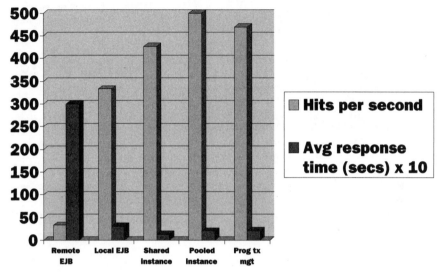

Figure 15-1

This result shows Spring AOP instance pooling achieving the highest result. Rerunning these tests in multiple environments, we found that with optimal web container thread pool size, the shared instance outperformed instance pooling, even under heavy load. However, as we were unable to rerun all tests in the hardware configuration described earlier, we show the initial result.

Figure 15-2 shows performance when the business operation was itself expensive—in this case, querying a database using JDBC (with no caching) and obtaining an average result set of 50 objects. The difference between remote and local invocations is now much less. The relative results for placing an order were very similar. The hardware and software stack was the same as for the previous results.

The true cost of remote invocations in typical applications will fall between these two. Some operations on remote business objects will be quick, meaning that the cost of remote invocation is a huge overhead; for slower operations, the cost of remote invocation is not so problematic. If the machines are connected using a slower network, the cost of remote invocation will be significantly higher. (The connection used in these tests was 1GB.) In all cases, the CPU usage was higher in the case of the remote than local invo-cations, suggesting that although the results for the remote invocations were obtained using two power-ful servers, they consumed more of the capacity of those servers than did the local results, tending to disprove the argument that remote invocation can be used to target CPU power at business operations that might otherwise be bottlenecks. In fact, using remoting means that much CPU power is wasted in marshaling and unmarshaling data to be sent over the wire.

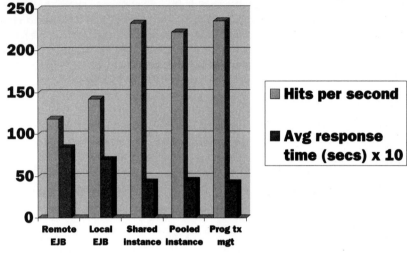

Figure 15-2

In all cases, the Spring solution was clearly superior, in both throughput and response time, to local EJB invocations using the same JTA transaction management.

To summarize:

- ❑ It's wrong to assume that calling EJBs is slow. *Local* EJBs, and remote EJBs co-located with their clients, perform well. Local use of EJB does not have a high overhead in a modern EJB container.

- ❑ Making genuinely remote calls on remote EJBs has a high performance cost—too great to deserve consideration in the majority of web applications.

- ❑ Non-EJB alternatives that achieve the same ends more flexibly are likely to perform better than local EJB. There is no performance case for using local EJBs as opposed to using Spring AOP to deliver the same declarative services; unless you can afford the most high-end application servers, EJB performance is likely to be significantly lower. The Spring AOP approach can provide declarative transaction management with significantly less overhead than local EJB CMT.

- ❑ Programmatic, rather than declarative, transaction management cannot be justified on performance grounds. It delivered an advantage of less than 10% in our tests—not enough to justify the complexity and potential for errors. The overhead of establishing a transaction is more significant than the declarative setup.

- ❑ Instance pooling is likely to perform worse than a shared single instance, so long as the web container's thread pool size is correctly configured.

- ❑ While we advocate a shared, multi-threaded object as the best model for business objects in most cases, if we want a single-threaded model, we don't need to use EJB to achieve it. Spring pooling performed significantly better than the open source application server's SLSB instance pooling in our test, and comparably to the high-end commercial server's.

- ❑ The performance comparison between declarative services via Spring and EJB depends partly on the quality of your application server. While Spring performed better in all benchmarks we ran, its superiority over EJB was much larger when running in a less efficient application server.

> There is no performance case for using local EJBs for declarative transactions *or* to achieve a single thread model: simpler, more flexible, alternative approaches let us apply such behavior to POJOs with comparable or better performance.

Nor is there a stability case for choosing EJB. In our tests, the Spring implementation for all threading models was capable of running equally prolonged load sessions as the EJB test, and used less CPU. Most significantly, it exhibited significantly lower response times and exhibited superior consistency of response times, suggesting that it may prove more stable. (However, it's important to note that both EJB and Spring solutions were stable even under high load.)

Caching and Code Optimization

Let's briefly consider some other implementation issues. These principally concern optimizing code.

Code Optimization and Why to Avoid it

Not only is code optimization often the wrong way to improve performance: it's actively harmful in many cases.

- ❑ It's hard: Code optimization can require a lot of effort
- ❑ It can reduce maintainability and produce bugs
- ❑ It isn't usually necessary

> The eminent computer scientist Donald Knuth remarked that "we should forget about small efficiencies, say about 97% of the time: *premature optimization is the root of all evil*" (my italics). This is wise advice.

Thus we should be parsimonious with optimization, and target it carefully. Optimization—whether architectural or implementation—should normally concern itself with operations that are slow. While this should be an obvious point, it's common to see developers agonizing over the performance of code that is in reality quite fast enough in all realistic scenarios, just because they know that the performance of that particular code could be improved. Obvious candidate slow operations, deserving of consideration for architectural or implementation optimization, include:

- ❑ Excessive database access
- ❑ Remote method invocations

Normally the slowest operations (like these) will be consequences of the overall architecture, rather than poor implementation code.

Of course this isn't to say that we should forget about performance as we write code. Some developers have a flair for finding the slowest way to solve any problem. But, in my experience, the simple, obvious way a capable developers thinks of doing something is usually the best. It's often possible to come up with a faster, less intuitive (and hence less maintainable) solution, but the return doesn't usually justify the complexity.

> **Optimize design, not code.**

Caching

Caching can be an important optimization, on the borderline between architectural and code-level optimization.

Although appropriate use of caching can produce large performance gains, caching can be complex and error-prone, and it's best not to implement any caching without proof that there is a strong reason to do so.

Chapter 15 of *Expert One-on-One J2EE Design and Development* contains a detailed discussion of the pros and cons of caching, including an example of caching and profiling. I won't repeat that here; merely focus on a few basic guidelines for caching.

❑ Caching should only be implemented with clear knowledge of the relevant business requirements. Is it ever acceptable for data to be stale? What would be the implications of a race condition?

❑ Caching is most valuable the more data is read versus written. If there are a significant number of write operations on the cached data, the cache becomes more difficult to implement and the performance benefit is likely to be greatly reduced.

❑ Caching is possible in all architectural tiers. It's often best to avoid duplication of caches, and consider the whole application stack, rather than focus on caching in a particular tier. In order up the architectural stack from the EIS tier, the options are:

    ❑ Database

    ❑ O/R mapping layer

    ❑ Business objects

    ❑ Web tier objects

    ❑ Caching filters and JSP tags

    ❑ Browser and web cache via HTTP header usage

❑ Caching in the data access or business tier is more beneficial if we remove distribution, as in a classic distributed J2EE application a data access cache is too far from the web tier.

❑ Large gains can be made by simple caching scenarios, such as caching read-only data.

❑ If you need to address complex concurrency issues in a cache in application code, consider using a third-party caching product or at least a concurrency library to help with the threading issues.

❑ AOP can be an excellent choice for caching in the business layer.

> **Many J2EE developers (including myself) have an almost instinctive assumption that it's expensive to hit middle tier business objects. This is probably a consequence of experience with distributed EJB applications, in which remote method calls were to be avoided. Question this assumption if using a co-located architecture, especially if you find yourself complicating your design to avoid invoking the middle tier.**

Of course you might still need to limit data access, because it may be *really* slow. However, in this case the best place for a cache may be middle-tier business objects, rather than the web tier.

Let's expand on the last point in the list above, about AOP. One well-known approach to caching is to use the **decorator** design pattern. We implement a caching decorator that implements the same interface as the target class, but which caches some data to minimize the number of invocations of the target. (This can also be thought of as a caching proxy.)

If we use the decorator pattern, we might write an implementation of all the methods that delegate to the original object, with caching around some methods. Or we might subclass the original object, overriding some methods to provide the caching behavior. Neither of these approaches is elegant. With the first approach, we need to write code for all methods, even if we only want to provide behavior for some. There's a lot of boilerplate code here. The subclassing approach avoids that problem, but doesn't allow us to cache around a different implementation of the target object's type, as it's tied to a concrete class.

AOP is an excellent approach to such cross-cutting concerns. We can use a caching *around advice* to separate the caching aspect completely from client code. AOP gives us a powerful way of specifying which methods are targets for caching using pointcuts. We might also consider using metadata attributes to identify cacheable values. (For example, specifying that the result of the getHeadline() method is cacheable for ten minutes.)

Such a generic cache could even offer coherence across a cluster. A different caching implementation could be dropped in without changing application code.

The benefits of such caching would be available to any business object, without any loss of strong typing.

In Spring and other interception-oriented AOP frameworks, this would take the form of a **caching interceptor**.

Potential Code Optimizations

We can minimize the dangers and maximize the return on code optimization through the following techniques:

❑ **Only optimize what we need to.** Target code optimization through benchmarking and profiling (discussed later in this chapter).

❑ **Focus on the low-hanging fruit.** Often we can apply simple optimizations that produce a good return, avoiding trickier optimizations that may not justify the effort or reduced maintainability.

❑ **Work with the safety net of a comprehensive regression test suite.** There are few feelings as satisfying as seeing a comprehensive test suite pass unchanged, and knowing that your code does what it used to do, faster.

There are many optimization techniques, so we won't attempt to enumerate them here. Instead, we'll pick a few simple optimizations that can produce results very easily. See the section "Resources" at the end of this chapter for useful references.

Start with Algorithms

Before worrying about low-level code details, examine the algorithm used by a slow method. Is there any redundancy? Any missed opportunities for caching? Is there are better algorithm for this problem?

Use the Correct Collection Type

In some cases, choosing the correct collection type can have a huge effect on performance. Choosing the correct data structure—for example, a hash table rather than a list, if appropriate—should be second nature. However, different implementations of the same data structure can have very different performance characteristics. For example, if you need to read in a large number of elements, pre-allocating a large `ArrayList` can be dramatically faster than using a `LinkedList`. And random access to an `ArrayList` is much faster than random access to a `LinkedList`.

> *It's easy to see why this is true by looking at the respective implementations in the **java.util** package. Occasionally it's useful to look at the code for the standard libraries.*

Avoid Unnecessary String Operations

String concatenation in Java is slow. Since strings are immutable, a String can't be modified, so string concatenation always results in at least one new object. Often using a `StringBuffer` is more efficient than using a String.

Unnecessary Logging

Consider this statement:

```
for (int i = 0; i < myArray.length; i++) {
  foo.doSomething(myArray[i]);
  logger.debug("Foo object [" + foo + "] processing [" + myArray[i] + "]");
}
```

This innocent-looking logging statement could well end up taking longer than the operation on the array. Why?

Because String operations are slow, and because they are often written without any concern as to efficiency (displaying seldom-used parts of object state that may need to be materialized), `toString()` calls are often slow. Thus the previous unguarded log output is inappropriate in a loop.

So, we could at least put a guard around it like this:

```
for (int i = 0; i < myArray.length; i++) {
  foo.doSomething(myArray[i]);
  if (logger.isDebugEnabled()) {
        logger.debug("Foo object [" + foo + "] processing [" + myArray[i] + "]");
  }
}
```

This is better, because checking whether a particular log level is enabled is a lot quicker than String crunching. But in such situations it's often worth wondering whether the logging is useful at all? Is anyone ever going to enable debug logging to read all that output? Furthermore, the many messages from this loop might end up making other debug logging useless.

If you do a lot of debug logging, even calling methods on the logging infrastructure such as `isDebugEnabled()` can be expensive. (Such method calls are fast, but they still cost something.) In such cases, consider caching the value in a boolean variable.

Contentious Optimizations

The optimizations I've discussed so far are perfectly defensible from a code quality standpoint. However, many code optimizations should only be used in exceptional cases. For example:

❑ **Keep inheritance hierarchies shallow.** Although deep concrete inheritance hierarchies are probably a sign of poor design anyway, we normally *don't* want performance considerations to influence how we practice OO design. However, in extremely performance-critical cases, avoiding the use of inheritance can distinctly improve performance. In exceptional cases, it's worth incurring the cost of cut-and-paste code that could otherwise be refactored into a base class.

❑ **Use direct field access rather than accessor methods.** For example, I was able to use this technique to gain a 20% reduction in the overhead of Spring AOP by allowing AOP proxies to use direct field access instead of method access on the `org.springframework.aop.framework.AdvisedSupport` proxy manager class. This involved changing some variables in `Advised Support` from `private` (my normal default, making for strong encapsulation within a class hierarchy) to `protected`. In this case, such a gain was worthwhile. In general, it is not and more closely coupling the classes involved would be undesirable.

❑ **Use local variables instead of instance variables.** Local variables are allocated on the stack and are therefore faster to access. Copying an instance variable into a local variable can produce performance improvements if the variable is accessed repeatedly.

All these techniques are valuable only if you have an absolute performance imperative. The Spring AOP framework met these criteria because it is part of the fundamental infrastructure for many applications. However, little application code falls into this category, and you should consider such techniques only if you have definitive proof that you need to optimize certain pieces of code aggressively.

> **In general, avoid code optimizations that complicate code or adversely affect maintainability.**

Opportunities to Improve Tests

Sometimes an optimization may occur to you that changes an assumption you or other developers had when writing a test suite. For example, it may be possible to reuse a particular object instead of creating a new object at that point. This may suggest failure scenarios that existing tests haven't covered: for example, in which that object is in an inconsistent state. This suggests that you should write tests that check for that failure scenario *before attempting the optimization*. Even if the optimization doesn't work out, or prove worthy of keeping in the code base, the new tests may help to guard against future bugs.

> **Good developers are constantly on the lookout for opportunities to make tests more rigorous. It's sometimes important to strengthen the test suite before attempting optimization.**

Tuning and Deployment

In general, it's best to explore deployment-tuning options before getting too deep into optimizing application code. Deployment tuning can be less effort and is far less likely to complicate ongoing maintenance. Yet it can sometimes deliver spectacular results, as well as improve application stability.

JVM

Firstly, use the right JVM for your application server and application. I've seen very good results from BEA JRockit, showing it to be around two to four times as fast as the equivalent Sun JRE for long-running server-side applications. However, you should run your own benchmarks, because different JVMs have different strengths and weaknesses, and none is ideal for all applications.

Next, configure the JVM appropriately. Refer to its documentation, and the documentation provided with your application server, to ensure that you configure important settings correctly for it and your application. Such settings include:

❑   Initial and maximum heap size

❑   Garbage collection options

❑   Threading options

See for example, the following resources:

❑   `http://edocs.bea.com/wljrockit/docs81/tuning/`: "Tuning WebLogic JRockit 8.1 JVM"

❑   `http://publib7b.boulder.ibm.com/wasinfo1/en/info/aes/ae/urun_rconfproc_jvm.html`: "Java virtual machine settings: WebSphere Application Server"

Run benchmarks early in the project lifecycle to establish the optimal JVM and the appropriate settings for it.

Application Server

First, choose the right application server for your performance requirements. Application servers are far from equal in performance. Performance on the same hardware can differ widely, meaning that higher server license costs can be outweighed by hardware savings. I've seen a performance variation of up to three or four times between servers in typical web application scenarios.

> *If you must use a less efficient server, a lightweight container solution becomes even more compelling. By replacing an inefficient EJB container with Spring AOP, you can avoid much of the inefficient code in that server, while retaining important features such as JTA implementation and container data sources.*

Next, configure your application server appropriately for your application's characteristics. Application server settings can have an important impact on performance and throughput. These include:

❑   **Database connection pool size.** This can have an enormous impact on throughput. Too small a connection pool size will lead to blocked threads waiting for free connections. Too large a connection pool size can cause problems in a clustered environment, if the database runs out of connection listeners.

❑ **Thread pool size.** Too small a thread pool size will waste CPU capacity; too large a thread pool can degrade performance

❑ **Instance pool sizes, if using SLSBs.** The effect is similar to thread pools. There's no value in setting a pool size larger than that of the thread pool.

❑ **Transaction descriptors, if using SLSBs.** Unless all methods on a business object are transactional, don't apply the same transaction attribute to all methods. Ensure that each method has the appropriate transaction attribute: none if it should not be transactional.

❑ **HTTP session replication options.** Make the correct choice between database-based and in-memory replication for your application, and consider the options offered by your application server carefully.

❑ **JTA settings.** It's important to ensure that if you use a single database, you're not incurring expensive XA transaction overhead.

❑ **Logging settings.** Application servers, as well as applications, produce log output. This can be expensive, so ensure that your server is configured to log only information you might need.

Application server vendors usually provide excellent documentation on the available options.

Framework Configuration

As we've noted, persistence technologies can have a huge impact on performance and scalability. Thus it's particularly important to configure them correctly, especially when caching (and distributed caching) is involved.

If you defer some of the middleware responsibilities to a framework such as Spring, rather than the EJB container, you will need to ensure that you configure it correctly. The *concepts* are likely to be similar to those with EJB, although the means of specifying settings will differ.

For example, if you use the Spring pooling approach discussed earlier, you would apply similar reasoning in setting the pool size for pooled business objects as to determining the pool size for a stateless session bean. Various configuration options in the Spring AOP framework can also have an effect on performance, although the defaults work fine for the great majority of applications. Other important Spring settings include transaction settings for transactional AOP proxying. As with SLSBs, it's important not to cause transactions to be created unnecessarily for methods that do not need to run in a transaction.

As for all settings, it's important to have an easily repeatable benchmark to verify the effect of configuration changes. Ideally the benchmarks should be drawn from prolonged load tests verifying that the application is stable as well as efficient with the new configuration.

Database Configuration

It's critical that your database is correctly configured. Database servers are complex products, and a DBA is important to success. Settings differ between databases, but important settings include:

❑ Threading models

❑ Listener pools

❏ Indexes

❏ Table structure (databases such as Oracle provide many different table structures, appropriate to different usage patterns)

❏ Query optimization options

Database products usually providing profiling tools that can help to indicate potential performance improvements.

An Evidence-based Approach to Performance

Performance *can* and should be addressed in a scientific fashion; unfortunately, it often isn't.

I repeatedly see the following two problems:

❏ Not gathering evidence on performance early enough

❏ Doing work based on performance assumptions without gathering evidence to support them

The first problem can waste effort and valuable time—for example, when an architecture that requires validation is not validated early enough and proves non-performant. In previous chapters, I've discussed the importance of a **vertical slice** or **executable architecture** early in the project lifecycle. This is particularly important to verify performance characteristics. Modern methodologies—even those as different in practice as RUP and XP—stress the importance of such architectural verification. Unfortunately it still happens too rarely in practice.

Not only is it possible that it will simply be too late to address performance problems if they are not identified and avoided early; the whole issue can become politically charged, adding to the technical difficulty in sorting things out, and making successful resolution difficult. (I've seen a number of projects descend into cover-ups, instead of focusing on fixing problems after they eventually emerge.)

> **Do a vertical slice early in the project lifecycle to verify the performance of the candidate architecture, and ensure that it can meet requirements.**

Because of the importance of performance and the costs and dangers associated with optimization, without such a basis in evidence, performance decisions will be ad hoc, with unfortunate results such as wasted effort optimizing slow code that's not causing any problems.

> **Don't make important decisions about performance without real evidence.**

Let's look at how we can gather the necessary evidence to guide our performance work.

Benchmarking

Run benchmarks to ensure that performance targets can be met early in the project lifecycle. I often see architects deferring benchmarking until a project is well advanced, because they don't yet have access to production-quality hardware. This is nonsense: a lot can be learned from performance on a developer's desktop machine. Machines capable of running modern IDEs are capable of very high throughput for server-side applications, given a fast network connection to resources such as databases.

Benchmarks are essentially about risk mitigation. They're most useful when they identify a dangerous bottleneck. It's not hard to estimate that if a P4 desktop can do only 2 transactions per second (TPS), that no amount of hardware will satisfy a requirement of 100 TPS.

> **An application that's worryingly slow on a developer desktop machine will be slow on production hardware.**

Benchmarking must be carefully planned, because there are many variables to control (many of them discussed earlier), such as:

- ❑ JVM version
- ❑ Application server configuration (if running benchmarks in a deployed environment)
- ❑ Logging levels
- ❑ Network configuration
- ❑ Database configuration
- ❑ Load-testing tool

Many tools can be used for benchmarking; however, a discussion of individual tools is beyond the scope of this chapter.

Ideally, many benchmarks can be run outside a container, focusing on application code. However, it's also important that benchmarks can be run against a realistic deployment configuration. Often deployment benchmarks should be run first, with partial-stack benchmarks used to focus on areas that can be improved.

Running in-container benchmarks is particularly easy with applications that have web interfaces, as there are numerous web load-testing tools available, such as:

- ❑ **Microsoft Web Application Stress Tool (WAS)** (`www.microsoft.com/technet/treeview/default.asp?url=/technet/itsolutions/intranet/downloads/webstres.asp`): A dated but easy-to-use free load-testing tool.
- ❑ **Apache JMeter** (`http://jakarta.apache.org/jmeter/`): Pure Java testing tool, which can also be used to load test plain Java classes. Fairly complex to configure.

❏ **The Grinder** (`http://grinder.sourceforge.net/`): Another Java testing tool, which can also be used to load test plain Java classes. Fairly complex to configure.

❏ **ApacheBench** (`http://perl.apache.org/docs/1.0/guide/performance.html#Apache Bench`): The *ab* tool included in any Apache web server distribution. A simple command-line load-testing tool that can push a server to its limits. Does not offer complex scripting options.

It's important that performance tests, like functional tests, are repeatable, and that their methodology is documented. Be sure to avoid common errors. For example:

❏ Don't trust the result of one benchmark. Make sure that it can be repeated.

❏ Be sure that the load test software isn't distorting the results.

❏ Be sure that the load test software isn't competing with the application server running the application for CPU time. For web applications, it's best to run load tests from one or more other machines, to eliminate any such effect.

It can be helpful to benchmark different application tiers in isolation: for example, the presentation tier; business objects (accessing a test database or stub DAOs); and database queries. This can provide a useful way of seeing where benchmarks lie under much heavier load than can be created under profiling.

> The next two sections—on profiling and diagnostics—describe activities that are conditional on worrying benchmark results. If your application meets performance requirements, don't spend much time profiling or optimizing it. Of course it *could* be faster, and it might be intellectually satisfying to *make* it faster. (I love profiling and performance optimization myself. Fortunately, as I spend a lot of time writing infrastructure code, I get to do it more often than the typical application developer.) But there is no purpose to be served by making it faster.
>
> Settle for doing a quick profile run to see if there are any obvious bottlenecks that can be removed, but don't devote too much effort on performance. There are always plenty of other things to do.

Profiling

If we *do* have a problem, how do we track it down?

I strongly recommend using a **profiler**: a tool that can help you analyze exactly which methods are taking too much time.

Why Use a Profiler?

Why do you need to use a profiler if you have performance problems? Isn't it easy enough to work out where the bottlenecks are, just by looking at the code?

Certainly it's possible to predict some common causes of problems. For example:

❑   We known that String operations are slow.

❑   We know that logging statements without a guard such as `isInfoEnabled()` can be slow if they call expensive `toString()` methods or simply concatenate strings.

However, we don't necessarily know whether or not such "slow" code is a problem in our call stack, and we don't know whether or not the gain by addressing them is worthwhile. Techniques such as caching `toString()` values can be error prone and aren't a good idea unless we know that we need them.

There's no substitute for hard evidence. Profiling can indicate *which pieces of slow code matter*. For example, I have a lot of experience in performance profiling, and could probably give a pretty accurate breakdown of the time taken for the various operations in a particular method. But I could not necessarily predict so accurately which of the thousands of methods in an application I need to worry about. Computers are much better at that kind of task than humans. A profiler can do this very easily.

The corollary is that profiling also indicates which pieces of slow code *don't* matter. Developers tend to have a variety of beliefs on performance, which have a varying basis in reality, such as:

❑   Reflection is slow

❑   Object creation is slow

In the absence of firm evidence, I've seen developers eliminate perfectly appropriate uses of reflection, making code more complex and obscure, or implement complex pooling schemes. Yet it's quite likely that these assumptions are wrong. (Reflection is pretty fast in modern JVMs, compared with methods that actually do work. And object creation is seldom an issue any longer.)

Thus it's important to profile application code, both inside and outside the deployed environment.

> **Base profiling on realistic application scenarios. Don't create artificial scenarios that heavily hit slow code, but aren't relevant to real applications.**

I typically do one benchmarking run inside the application server, followed by many profiling sessions outside—within an IDE—when I know which area of application code I want to tune. Often I can guess the broad area within the call stack that's the cause of the problem, and prove that by benchmarking operations that focus on it. If this is not feasible, I profile the application in the application server.

I minimize the number of profile runs I do in an application server. It's possible to run your application server within your IDE, or start up an application server with special JVM configuration to allow remote debugging. However, there are several major disadvantages:

❑   Running JVMs with instrumentation enabled slows things down dramatically. This can mean that application server startup can take minutes, rather than seconds.

❑   It's harder to screen out "noise," such as application server code.

One of the many advantages of freeing as much code as possible from dependence on an EJB container or application server in general is that it's often possible to profile outside the container. For example, by following the architectural guidelines recommended in this book, you can profile most application code in an IDE, without starting up an application server.

The same advantage applies to debugging. It's usually much easier to debug code *outside* than inside an application server. Sometimes, of course, we need to know how the code interacts with the J2EE server. Often, however, we are trying to track down a problem that we have reason to believe is in application code, and, as with unit testing, want to avoid any extraneous concerns.

Remember that profilers may themselves distort performance figures, because of the instrumentation they require. Thus regularly rerun your original benchmark (without profiling) to verify that you see an improvement in it.

You'll almost certainly encounter diminishing returns with profiling. Typically you can deal with the low-hanging fruit quite quickly, removing all your unnecessary string operations and so on. After you've done this, you'll probably find that you're in the swing of things, and getting a real buzz from seeing steady improvements in benchmarks. However, you'll be putting more and more effort into getting smaller performance improvement. You'll also increasingly find yourself tempted to make changes that are potentially damaging to maintainability, to get such minor improvements. Maybe I'm the only programmer subject to such temptations, but I doubt it. With profiling, as with code coverage analysis, it's important not to let what is a very valuable tool when used appropriately tempt you into distorting how you work in general.

Profiling is an invaluable technique for targeting the effort we spend on optimizing code. It can also indicate which part of design should be changed.

Profiling is also an interesting way in looking at the call stack. This can be helpful for gaining understanding of the dynamic behavior of your code, and a useful complement to looking at the static code structure. You may pick up simple coding errors: for example, accidentally invoking a method twice, when you should have used the object reference returned by the first invocation.

For this reason, I tend to use profiling even if I don't think I have a performance problem—although I don't devote much time to it in such cases.

Profiling in Practice

The following notes are based on my own use of profiling tools, on Spring and other projects.

I follow these steps when profiling:

1. Run a realistic, representative benchmark.
2. Run the same benchmark under a profiler, possibly reducing the load or number of operations, to allow for profiler issues with threading and the slowing effect on performance.

3. Change code based on profiling results, rerunning the entire unit test suite after each change.

4. Repeat Steps 2 and 3 regularly, repeating Step 1 less often, to verify that performance is improving without the effect of profiling.

Some important tips:

❑ Ensure that your profile run performs enough operations to avoid distortion from the startup overhead.

❑ Configure your profiler to exclude library classes that might otherwise overwhelm information about your application code.

I normally profile with the Eclipse Profiler plugin (`http://eclipsecolorer.sourceforge.net/index_profiler.html`). This is easy to install (for Eclipse users) and straightforward to use. Any Java application (that is, `main` entry point) can be run under the profiler, with full ability to navigate from profiler output to the relevant source code.

Figures 15-3 and 15-4 illustrate profiling one million invocations of the Spring AOP framework—enough to ensure that the startup cost does not distort the results. I've expanded the thread call tree to show all methods accounting for over 5% of execution time. The thread call tree also indicates the runtime structure.

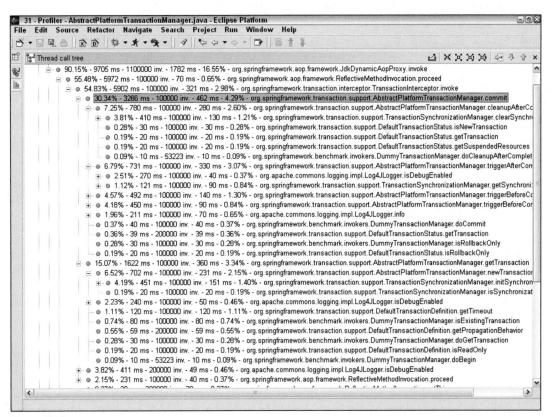

Figure 15-3

Since the profiler runs within the IDE, it's possible to navigate to source code elements directly from the call tree, as well as view graphical representations of "hot" methods.

Another useful view is the "inverted call tree" (shown in Figure 15-4), which shows leaf methods ordered by the amount of execution time they account for. This can be very useful in focusing on which methods it might be worthwhile to optimize.

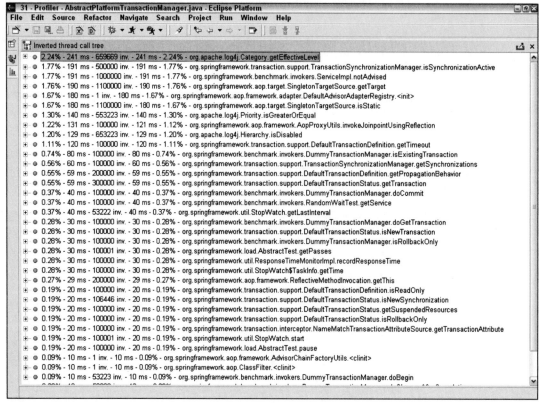

Figure 15-4

I have used Sitraka JProbe in the past, but such commercial products, while excellent, are expensive. I tend to find that Eclipse Profiler is adequate for most requirements: especially as I favor profiling outside the container. However, commercial tools usually offer better support for profiling in an application server, and more sophisticated graph generation.

Diagnostics

In addition to profiling, we can apply some diagnostics, particularly in a deployed environment.

A good profiling tool allows us to see the number of objects of each class being created. It's also possible to obtain such information from the JVM. This can be particularly useful in a deployed environment. If you suspect that the problems are caused by excessive object allocation and garbage collection, refer to your JVM's documentation to see what flags you can apply when you start your JVM to see information about the garbage collection process, such as -verbosegc.

You might also be able to monitor the behavior of your connection pools and inflight transactions in a deployed environment, through application server consoles and other monitoring tools.

Diagnostics are particularly important in production systems, because performance scenarios might differ from load tests. It then becomes important to have some way of analyzing behavior without adversely impacting performance or stability (which rules out profilers).

Resources

For further reading on code optimization and other performance issues, I recommend the following resources:

- ❑ *Java Performance Tuning* by Jack Shirazi (O'Reilly). This book provides an excellent discussion of Java performance issue. Although this book focuses mainly on low-level code optimization techniques, and doesn't cover J2EE in detail, it's well worth reading for any developer interested in writing performant code.

- ❑ Shirazi's web site (www.javaperformancetuning.com). This site has many useful links and more J2EE-related content than *Java Performance Tuning*.

- ❑ *Expert One-on-One J2EE Design and Development*, Chapter 15 ("Performance Testing and Tuning an Application") by yours truly. This book discusses code optimization techniques useful in J2EE applications, along with profiling and load-testing tools and techniques to improve serialization performance if you must use a distributed architecture.

- ❑ *J2EE Performance Testing with BEA WebLogic Server* by Peter Zadrozny, Philip Aston and Ted Osborne (Expert Press, 2002). Although a little dated, this book provides an excellent discussion of many issues, based on actual evidence.

Summary

Fundamental architectural choices largely dictate the performance characteristics of enterprise applications. None is more fundamental than the choice between a distributed and co-located architecture. Our benchmarks have shown that remote EJB invocations are up to ten times slower than local EJB invocations in a comparable, and realistic, web application scenario.

> **If you care about performance, do not adopt a distributed architecture unless business requirements demand it. It is a questionable path to scalability.**

We can avoid the high cost of genuine remote calls by co-locating application components. If necessary, we cluster whole application deployments.

Despite the huge cost of remote invocations, used rationally, there is nothing inherently slow about EJB. Modern EJB containers are efficient, and there is no great overhead in performance attached to invoking a local EJB: as opposed to the undoubted overhead in development, deployment, and testing an EJB. Thus if using EJB we shouldn't be unduly bothered by the supposed performance cost of invoking a local EJB, and we shouldn't discount the use of EJB on the belief that *local* EJB adds performance overhead.

However, there isn't anything magical about EJB from a performance perspective. In this chapter I've shown the results of some benchmarks of typical web application scenarios comparing local EJBs with a Spring AOP architecture that also provides declarative transaction management and—optionally—thread management. Both these alternatives were equivalent in their use of underlying J2EE services, because the Spring deployment was configured to use JTA as the underlying transaction infrastructure.

The Spring approach was *more* performant than the EJB approach in all EJB containers I benchmarked, including a high-end commercial product. The extent of the superiority varied, but it was significant over less efficient EJB containers, such as a popular open source product. In particular, it delivered lower and more consistent response times than the EJB alternatives.

These are important results. Performance is a very important consideration. Given that the lightweight Spring solution I've described is superior to local EJB in virtually every other respect—developer productivity; availability of a sophisticated IoC solution; ease of testing and compatibility with TDD; avoiding unfortunate effects on OOP; more flexible declarative transaction management; availability of a true AOP framework—the fact that the EJB solution fails to better—or even equal—its performance and likely scalability removes one of the only potential arguments in favor of EJB.

> There is no performance or scalability argument for using EJB declarative services (such as CMT) versus an efficient AOP implementation delivering the same services to POJOs, as we've seen in comparing the performance of a local EJB solution with a Spring AOP solution.

Data access strategy has an important impact on performance and scalability. Two of the important decisions here are whether O/R mapping is appropriate; and how to achieve a coherent data cache in a distributed environment. O/R mapping is *not* appropriate in use cases that benefit from set-based relational operations. When O/R mapping is appropriate, we recommend using a specialized O/R mapping product such as Kodo JDO or Hibernate, possibly in conjunction with a dedicated distributing caching product.

> Don't be rigid about the use of O/R mapping. If you do use O/R mapping, use a sophisticated and flexible O/R mapping tool.

Overall, it's important to remember that simplicity usually helps deliver good performance—as well as timely delivery and maintainability. Use of EJB often adds that unnecessary complexity. Prominent J2EE author and consultant Bruce Tate stresses this in an interview on JavaPerformanceTuning.com (`www.javaperformancetuning.com/news/interview036.shtml`). Tate repeatedly notes the performance virtues of simplicity and answers the question "What change have you seen applied in a project that gained the largest performance improvement?" with "We ditched EJB, in favor of a simple POJO solution."

Because performance and scalability has an important impact on the success or failure of an application, it's vital to base performance decisions on evidence. I recommend:

- ❑ Benchmarking a vertical slice early in the project lifecycle
- ❑ Repeating performance tests throughout the development process to check against regression
- ❑ Using a profiling tool to track down any bottlenecks, ensuring that optimization is carefully targeted

I covered some specific code-level optimization techniques that can produce performance gains, but warned against compromising code quality or maintainability in the pursuit of minor performance optimization.

A more significant return than from code optimization is likely to come from choosing the best application server to meet your requirements, and ensuring that the server, the JVM, and other central products to your software stack, such as your database, are correctly configured.

16

The Sample Application

In previous chapters, we have discussed lightweight architectures and technologies for each architectural layer. In this chapter, we will show how to put them together into a typical J2EE web application.

The sample application is an implementation of the familiar J2EE Pet Store requirements. Although the Pet Store is somewhat hackneyed, there is an undeniable advantage in taking a familiar problem as an illustration of the consequences of different architectural and implementation approaches. So we've chosen practicality over originality.

Instead of starting from scratch, we took as our starting point Clinton Begin's **iBATIS JPetStore 3.1**, an open-source alternative to the Sun J2EE BluePrints **Java Pet Store**. Begin's JPetStore was motivated by a desire to illustrate a simpler, more appropriate architecture than that of the original Sun Java Pet Store, which was widely, and deservedly, criticized for poor performance and over-engineering.

We believe that our version of JPetStore represents a significant improvement over the iBATIS JPetStore. Comparing our version with the iBATIS version is straightforward, because we've stayed as close to the original as possible, to show how the architecture we advocate can be introduced in a relatively straightforward refactoring. However, there's no need to refer to the original JPetStore unless you are interested in the comparison. Our JPetStore stands on its own, illustrating a typical Spring web application.

After briefly reviewing the Pet Store requirements, we'll look at the iBATIS JPetStore and identify room for improvement. We'll then look at the Spring JPetStore version in greater detail, seeing how implementing a Lightweight Container architecture with Spring can improve on such an architecture. We'll conclude by discussing deployment issues in such web applications.

Pet Store Requirements

The Pet Store features a product catalog, a shopping cart, account management, order history, and basic personalization options. It is a fairly typical database-driven J2EE web application, without EIS integration or messaging requirements.

Although messaging and EIS functionality are beyond the scope of this chapter, it's important to note that both could be added to our sample application within the overall architecture. Nothing in the architecture or implementation constrains such enhancements. In fact, the use of the Spring lightweight IoC container makes it easier than it would otherwise be to add new functionality.

The business requirements were formalized by The Middleware Company in 2002 and refined in 2003, with the special requirement of supporting both:

❑ A single database to hold all persistent data

❑ Two databases: one for customers' orders and one for product and account data

The first of these scenarios, of course, will produce many times better performance, and is more realistic for such a relatively simple application.

The second scenario requires inventory tracking in the main database holding product and account data, while customers' orders are held in the separate order database. This requires distributed transactions for order placement, if running on two databases.

While the TMC specification (`www.middleware-company.com/casestudy`) does not dictate a specific architecture for Pet Store implementations, it defines two **architectural categories** for J2EE-based submissions:

❑ **J2EE–Servlets–JSP:** Implementation without EJB, using JSP as the view technology.

❑ **J2EE–EJB–CMP2:** Implementation using EJB and Entity Bean CMP for data access.

CMP Entity Beans are the only object-relational mapping approach permitted by the 2003 TMC specification; direct use of JDBC is the only other option permitted for persistence.

Neither the iBATIS JPetStore nor the Spring JPetStore complies fully to either of these categories, as they do not use EJB but do use a persistence framework (the iBATIS Database Layer), which is not allowed in the first category. However, this restriction in the specification is somewhat arbitrary, and these two sample applications are more valuable as examples for using a robust, generic data access layer.

The iBATIS JPetStore 3.1

We briefly discuss the high-level architecture of the iBATIS JPetStore, release 3.1.1, in Chapter 3 ("Architectures"), and look at its use of Struts in Chapter 13 ("Web Tier Design").

JPetStore is a lightweight implementation of the Pet Store specification, relying on logical layering via POJOs. It does not use EJB. Some of its key attributes are:

- ❏ A central business object that web tier classes use to access business logic (the PetStoreLogic class, discussed later).

- ❏ The use of a DAO layer and a JDBC abstraction framework to simplify data access.

- ❏ Support for both a single database and separate main/order databases.

- ❏ Support for exporting a Web Service via Apache Axis.

JPetStore can run in either a web container or a full-blown J2EE application server, as it can either use a local connection pool or a JNDI DataSource, and either local transactions or JTA transactions.

Middle Tier

The `com.ibatis.jpetstore.domain.logic.PetStoreLogic` business object singleton initializes itself from a configuration file in its private constructor, thus enforcing the Singleton pattern:

```
private PetStoreLogic() {
  try {
    Properties props = new Properties();
    props.load(
        Resources.getResourceAsStream("properties/petstore.properties"));

    String resource = null;
    useSimpleConfiguration = Boolean.valueOf(
        props.getProperty("useSimpleConfiguration")).booleanValue();
    if (useSimpleConfiguration) {
      resource = "properties/simple/dao.xml";
      System.out.println("Using SIMPLE configuration. ("+resource+")");
    }
    else {
      resource = "properties/distributed/dao.xml";
      System.out.println("Using DISTRIBUTED configuration. ("+resource+")");
    }

    Reader reader = Resources.getResourceAsReader(resource);
    DaoManager.configure(reader);

    storeDaoManager = DaoManager.getInstance("StoreDaoManager");
    if (useSimpleConfiguration) {
      orderDaoManager = storeDaoManager;
    }
    else {
      orderDaoManager = DaoManager.getInstance("OrderDaoManager");
    }

    accountDao = (AccountDao) storeDaoManager.getDao("Account");
    categoryDao = (CategoryDao) storeDaoManager.getDao("Category");
    productDao = (ProductDao) storeDaoManager.getDao("Product");
    itemDao = (ItemDao) storeDaoManager.getDao("Item");
    sequenceDao = (SequenceDao) storeDaoManager.getDao("Sequence");
    orderDao = (OrderDao) orderDaoManager.getDao("Order");

  } catch (Exception e) {
```

```
      throw new RuntimeException("Could not initialize BaseLogic. Cause: " + e);
    }
  }
```

The `petstore.properties` file is read in and used to configure the `com.ibatis.db.dao.DaoManager` singleton. Depending on the value of the "useSimpleConfiguration" setting, the "orderDaoManager" is set to either the implementation for the main database ("StoreDaoManager") or to that for the order database ("OrderDaoManager"). The DAO instances are obtained via the `DaoManager` and kept in member variables. This is a typical use of the Singleton pattern, combined with ad hoc configuration, in an application that does not use an IoC container or another generic infrastructure backbone.

The `DaoManager` class, acting as a factory for DAO instances and as the transaction manager, is part of the iBATIS Database Layer's generic DAO framework and thus not specific to the JPetStore. The `DaoManager` reads its configuration from a `dao.xml` file, which is somewhat similar to a Spring bean definition XML file, but less general and capable.

As an example of a transactional business method implementation in the `PetStoreLogic` class, let's review the `insertOrder` method. As it needs to execute within either a local or a distributed transaction, depending on whether running on a single or two databases, it delegates to either the `doSimpleInsertOrder` or `doDistributedInsertOrder` method:

```
public void insertOrder(Order order) throws DaoException {
  int orderId = getNextId("ordernum");
  order.setOrderId(orderId);
  if (useSimpleConfiguration) {
    doSimpleInsertOrder(order);
  }
  else {
    doDistributedInsertOrder(order);
  }
}
```

Both `doSimpleInsertOrder` and `doDistributedInsertOrder` perform programmatic transaction management on the corresponding `DaoManager` instances. In the distributed case, both `DaoManagers` will be configured to use JTA, but both cases require explicit transaction demarcation.

```
private void doSimpleInsertOrder(Order order) throws DaoException {
  try {
    storeDaoManager.startTransaction();
    orderDao.insertOrder(order);
    itemDao.updateQuantity(order);
    storeDaoManager.commitTransaction();
  }
  catch (DaoException e) {
    try {
      storeDaoManager.rollbackTransaction();
    }
    catch (Exception e2) {
      /* ignore */
    }
    throw ((DaoException) e.fillInStackTrace());
  }
}
```

In the distributed case, programmatic transaction is required on both data sources:

```
private void doDistributedInsertOrder(Order order) throws DaoException {
  try {
    orderDaoManager.startTransaction();
    storeDaoManager.startTransaction();

    orderDao.insertOrder(order);
    itemDao.updateQuantity(order);

    storeDaoManager.commitTransaction();
    orderDaoManager.commitTransaction();
  }
  catch (DaoException e) {
    try {
      storeDaoManager.rollbackTransaction();
    }
    catch (Exception e2) {
      /* ignore */
    }
    try {
      orderDaoManager.rollbackTransaction();
    }
    catch (Exception e2) {
      /* ignore */
    }
    throw ((DaoException) e.fillInStackTrace());
  }
}
```

PetStoreLogic is not an ideal business object, as it is heavily tied to data access concerns like database separation, and must implement programmatic transaction management for both the single and the multiple database case.

Remoting

As we see in Chapter 13, JPetStore uses a common base class for all its Struts Actions, looking up its Pet StoreLogic business object singleton and providing it as reference to subclasses. The same PetStore Logic singleton is also used from JPetStore's Web Service implementation com.ibatis.jpetstore. service.PetStoreService, illustrating how a remote facade can be layered on top of a business object:

```
public class PetStoreService {

  public Order getOrder(int orderId) throws DaoException {
    return PetStoreLogic.getInstance().getOrder(orderId);
  }
}
```

A PetStoreService instance can be exported as a SOAP Web Service via the included **Axis** deployment descriptor PetStoreService.wsdd. A sample PetStoreClient looks up a remote PetStoreService and invokes the getOrder method via **Axis's Dynamic Invocation Interface**. No service interface is used; the method is invoked dynamically by name.

Thus the iBATIS JPetStore's support for Web Services is not **JAX-RPC**-compliant, despite the use of Axis. A JAX-RPC service implementation, exportable via any JAX-RPC compliant tool, must implement an RMI service interface. The `PetStoreClient` implementation is also heavily dependent on Axis, particularly because of the need to register JavaBean deserializers (an Axis requirement).

Room for Improvement

The iBATIS JPetStore is a valuable example, and a significant improvement on the Sun Pet Store. In particular:

❑ It's much simpler than the Sun Pet Store, which made heavy use of EJB. It is easier to understand and more maintainable.

❑ Rather than the home-grown, semi-generic infrastructure of the Sun Pet Store, it uses robust open source frameworks—Struts and the iBATIS Database Layer—to address generic problems and reduce the amount of application-specific code, as a real application would.

However, there is still room for improvement:

❑ **Business logic is not abstracted behind an interface.** Web tier classes access the `PetStoreLogic` singleton class directly, without a facade interface or pluggable lookup mechanism. Running the web tier on top of a different business layer implementation or testing the web tier classes with mock business objects is impossible.

❑ **The middle tier is hard-wired:** The central business object, `PetStoreLogic`, is a singleton, which reads in a configuration file and in turn looks up the DAOs to use via a `DaoManager` singleton. It is impossible to reuse or test any part of the application without a `DaoManager` or without a database in the first place.

❑ **The business object must perform programmatic transaction management.** The `PetStoreLogic` class does programmatic transaction demarcation via the `DaoManager`, with explicit handling of local transactions on a single database versus distributed transactions on separate main and order databases. This complicates code, obscures business logic, and reduces potential for reuse. Ideally, the same business logic code should run unchanged in different transactional configurations.

❑ **The remoting support is tied to Axis.** The `PetStoreService` implementation does not implement a JAX-RPC-compliant service interface and can thus be exported only with a minority of web service tools. The ad hoc `PetStoreClient` implementation is also tied to Axis.

Spring JPetStore

In our adapted version of JPetStore, we address these issues by introducing a loosely coupled middle tier, using the Spring Framework's IoC container:

❑ Following good OO practice, the PetStoreLogic business object is refactored into a **PetStoreFacade interface** plus **PetStoreImpl implementation**, to be accessed by web tier classes via the interface.

❑ DAO interfaces are refactored to use Spring's technology-agnostic **data access exception hierarchy,** making it possible to switch to a different data access technology without affecting business logic.

- ❑   The business object and its collaborating DAOs **are configured via Spring's IoC capabilities**, removing all infrastructure concerns from their implementations.

- ❑   The PetStoreImpl business object implementation is proxied by a Spring TransactionProxyFactory Bean, using PetStoreFacade as an interface, to deliver **declarative transaction management via AOP**. The actual transaction strategy is determined by the PlatformTransactionManager implementation that the proxy is configured for. Another implementation option illustrates AOP declarative transaction management driven by source-level metadata attributes, as in .NET.

- ❑   The Spring JPetStore offers **generic remoting with pluggable protocols**, supporting JAX-RPC, traditional RMI, and Caucho's Hessian and Burlap. The out-of-the-box configuration uses Axis via JAX-RPC for web service export and access.

> It's important to note that because the Spring lightweight container is non-invasive, application code in the Spring JPetStore has minimal dependence on Spring. The PetStoreImpl business object does not import a single Spring class or implement any special requirements to run within a Spring application context: It is a normal POJO that could easily be used outside the Spring container.
>
> The DAO interfaces depend only on Spring's DataAccessException hierarchy, not on the Spring container. They use these exceptions because of the valuable decoupling from data access technology they provide; this is a matter of choice, not a Spring requirement. Both DAO interfaces and implementations merely use Spring DAO as a class library, and thus would run in any other environment (including an EJB container).
>
> Such non-invasiveness is an important differentiator from an EJB architecture, or an architecture using many older frameworks.

Our JPetStore version uses **iBATIS SQL Maps** for data access, like the original JPetStore, leveraging Spring's iBATIS SQL Maps support classes. This decision was made partly to keep the persistence strategy close to the original, to preserve the same data model and SQL scripts, and to allow easy comparison.

As the iBATIS Database Layer delivers real simplification to the original JPetStore, there was no reason to change this. iBATIS SQL Maps allow easy mapping of fields from multiple database tables into single objects. With the given data model, this is a valid technique for modeling domain objects. Hibernate, for example, does not support such coarse-grained objects as of 2.1, but requires the domain model to be at least as fine-grained as the data model. The original JPetStore domain model would need to change significantly for a Hibernate-based implementation.

Furthermore, JPetStore would not benefit from the kind of transparent persistence that Hibernate and JDO offer: that is, automatic flushing of changes applied within a transaction. All changes to persistent objects happen in web tier forms, spanning multiple HTTP requests. Objects are stored explicitly by web controllers when a form is successfully submitted. This is a further indicator that a JDBC abstraction layer with basic O/R mapping capabilities, such as iBATIS Database Layer or Spring's own JDBC support, is a good fit.

> *Spring JDBC would have been the other obvious candidate for implementing the data access layer. However, making this switch would not deliver any benefit, as the iBATIS Database Layer works well in this application.*

Middle Tier

The Spring JPetStore offers a dedicated, loosely coupled middle tier. In contrast to the original JPetStore, declarative transactions are applied to the central business object via AOP. Transaction management strategies can be configured without any changing application code. Any DataSource implementation can be used via a bean definition in the application context, without Java code changes and with minimal configuration effort.

Configuration Using IoC

In the Spring version, the business object `PetStoreImpl` is set up via a bean definition in the file `/WEB-INF/applicationContext.xml`. It receives references to its collaborating objects via bean references:

```
<bean id="petStoreTarget" class="org.springframework.samples.jpetstore.
    domain.logic.PetStoreImpl">
  <property name="accountDao">
    <ref bean="accountDao"/>
  </property>
  <property name="categoryDao">
    <ref bean="categoryDao"/>
  </property>
  <property name="productDao">
    <ref bean="productDao"/>
  </property>
  <property name="itemDao">
    <ref bean="itemDao"/>
  </property>
  <property name="orderDao">
    <ref bean="orderDao"/>
  </property>
</bean>
```

Note that "autowiring" could be used to simplify configuration even further, making Spring find the collaborators of the required type in the same or related application contexts. However, making the wiring explicit provides better documentation.

The `PetStoreImpl` class simply exposes corresponding bean property setter methods to receive the DAO objects. No lookup code is necessary: merely saving the parameter values in instance variables:

```
public class PetStoreImpl implements PetStoreFacade, OrderService {
  ...

  public void setAccountDao(AccountDao accountDao) {
    this.accountDao = accountDao;
  }

  public void setCategoryDao(CategoryDao categoryDao) {
    this.categoryDao = categoryDao;
  }

  public void setProductDao(ProductDao productDao) {
    this.productDao = productDao;
  }
```

```
public void setItemDao(ItemDao itemDao) {
  this.itemDao = itemDao;
}

public void setOrderDao(OrderDao orderDao) {
  this.orderDao = orderDao;
}

    ...
}
```

Note that we could also use the **Constructor Injection** flavor of IoC, with dependencies expressed via constructor arguments. This is an implementation choice for the application developer: Spring does not impose it, supporting both types of IoC.

There is no longer any need for a Singleton, or for ad hoc configuration files. Other objects needing a reference to the `PetStoreFacade` implementation will receive one from the IoC container, without needing to perform any lookup. This makes the application much easier to test, and improves the potential for reuse in different environments.

Transaction Management: TransactionProxyFactoryBean

Transactional semantics are applied via AOP through a Spring **TransactionProxyFactoryBean**, with the previously defined `PetStoreImpl` instance as target. The TransactionProxyFactoryBean creates an AOP proxy for the target object (in this case a dynamic proxy), adding transactional behavior before and after method invocations on the target. The AOP proxy implements the `PetStoreFacade` interface, appearing as an ordinary object to objects referencing it.

All business methods whose names start with "insert" or "update" will be executed within normal read-write transactions, while all other methods will execute within read-only transactions (potentially leveraging JDBC driver or database optimizations).

```xml
<bean id="petStore" class="org.springframework.transaction.interceptor.
    TransactionProxyFactoryBean">
  <property name="transactionManager">
    <ref bean="transactionManager"/>
  </property>
  <property name="target">
    <ref bean="petStoreTarget"/>
  </property>
  <property name="transactionAttributes">
    <props>
      <prop key="insert*">PROPAGATION_REQUIRED</prop>
      <prop key="update*">PROPAGATION_REQUIRED</prop>
      <prop key="*">PROPAGATION_REQUIRED,readOnly</prop>
    </props>
  </property>
</bean>
```

The `insertOrder` method in `PetStoreImpl` no longer needs to include any transaction management code, simply invoking the corresponding DAO methods. Spring's transaction management will take care of transaction propagation behind the scenes, using the configured transaction manager (whether local or distributed).

```
public void insertOrder(Order order) {
  this.orderDao.insertOrder(order);
  this.itemDao.updateQuantity(order);
}
```

Note how much simpler this is than the original JPetStore's programmatic transaction management. Not only is the business logic much more readable; it's also much easier to test.

Transaction Management: Source-level Attributes

An alternative means of declarative transaction management involves **source-level metadata attributes**, as in .NET. This offers an arguably simpler model, at the (one-off) cost of a slightly more complicated build script. See the /attributes directory of the sample application distribution for the alternative configuration files required for this approach to transaction management.

In this approach, the configuration and programming model involves:

❑   Configuring the Spring application context to perform attribute-driven autoproxying.

❑   Adding source-level metadata to transactional classes and/or methods.

There is no need to use the TransactionProxyFactoryBean in this approach. Business objects are defined using normal bean definitions, specifying the actual class (PetStoreImpl), rather than a factory bean. The autoproxy infrastructure, configured in the /attributes/WEB-INF/declarativeServices. xml file, will cause the Spring AOP framework to search for transaction attributes when the application starts up, and automatically proxy objects with transaction attributes. The autoproxy infrastructure, discussed in Chapter 8 ("Declarative Middleware Using AOP Concepts"), also provides out-of-the-box support for pooling and other common infrastructure requirements, and is extensible to support arbitrary custom attributes, other than transaction attributes. The definitions in the declarativeServices.xml file are generic and can be used in any application.

Transaction attributes are specified as follows on the PetStoreImpl class:

```
/**
 * @org.springframework.transaction.interceptor.DefaultTransactionAttribute()
 */
public class PetStoreImpl implements PetStoreFacade, OrderService {
  ...
}
```

This definition means that all methods will be transactional. Unlike in .NET, but as with EJB, it is also possible to specify transaction attributes at the method level. A unique Spring capability is specifying **rollback rules**, declaratively indicating which exceptions—other than the default, of any throwable other than a checked exception—should cause automatic transaction rollback. (This is, of course, also supported using the TransactionProxyFactoryBean.)

Spring supports pluggable attribute implementations, which will allow support for the attribute syntax due to be introduced in Java 1.5. Presently, Jakarta Commons Attributes (http://jakarta.apache. org/commons/sandbox/attributes) is the recommended attribute implementation.

Commons Attributes integration relies on a precompilation step using a Commons Attributes precompiler to generate additional Java files carrying attribute information, for compilation along with the original Java source. Note that this precompilation step, once in place, doesn't add any noticeable complexity to the build process, and doesn't significantly affect compilation speed.

Attribute-driven autoproxying has significant benefits for applications with many transactional objects, as, once the precompilation step and autoproxy configuration is in place, there is no added effort in defining a new transaction object. In a simple application such as the JPetStore, which has a single business object requiring declarative transaction management, there is no real advantage in avoiding the use of a single TransactionProxyFactoryBean.

Data Access Tier

The preceding business object bean definitions refer to DAOs and a transaction manager. While those could all be defined in the same `applicationContext.xml`, they are defined in distinct `dataAccessContext-local.xml` and `dataAccessContext-jta.xml` files for clearer separation. The data access context to be used is determined by the application context loader: in the web case, via the "contextConfigLocation" context-param in `web.xml`.

Local Transactions

In the local case using a single database, the necessary bean definitions look as follows. All DAOs refer to the same DataSource: in this case, a local **Jakarta Commons DBCP BasicDataSource**, which provides connection pooling without the need for connection pool support in the web container or application server. Transaction management is delegated to the Spring **DataSourceTransactionManager**, which does not require JTA. With this configuration, the application can be deployed in a plain web container like Tomcat or Jetty, yet offer declarative transaction management.

```xml
<bean id="dataSource" class="org.apache.commons.dbcp.BasicDataSource"
    destroy-method="close">
  (...BasicDataSource bean property values for driver name etc...)
</bean>

<bean id="transactionManager" class="org.springframework.jdbc.datasource.
    DataSourceTransactionManager">
  <property name="dataSource">
    <ref local="dataSource"/>
  </property>
</bean>

<bean id="sqlMap" class="org.springframework.orm.ibatis.SqlMapFactoryBean">
  <property name="configLocation">
    <value>classpath:/sql-map-config.xml</value>
  </property>
</bean>

<bean id="itemDao" class="org.springframework.samples.jpetstore.dao.
    ibatis.SqlMapItemDao">
  <property name="dataSource">
    <ref local="dataSource"/>
  </property>
  <property name="sqlMap">
```

```
      <ref local="sqlMap"/>
    </property>
  </bean>

  <bean id="orderDao" class="org.springframework.samples.jpetstore.dao.
      ibatis.SqlMapOrderDao">
    <property name="dataSource">
      <ref local="dataSource"/>
    </property>
    <property name="sqlMap">
      <ref local="sqlMap"/>
    </property>
    <property name="sequenceDao">
      <ref local="sequenceDao"/>
    </property>
  </bean>

  <bean id="sequenceDao" class="org.springframework.samples.jpetstore.dao.
      ibatis.SqlMapSequenceDao">
    <property name="dataSource">
      <ref local="dataSource"/>
    </property>
    <property name="sqlMap">
      <ref local="sqlMap"/>
    </property>
  </bean>
```

Note that the "orderDao" definition refers to the "sequenceDao", which it needs to generate unique IDs for inserted orders. For database-specific ID generation strategies, corresponding subclasses of SqlMap OrderDao or SqlMapSequenceDao can be used. In contrast to Hibernate, iBATIS Database Layer does not provide an abstraction of ID generation strategies.

Distributed Transactions

In the distributed case with two databases, the DAOs refer to two different **JNDI DataSources**, "jdbc/ jpetstore" and "jdbc/jpetstore-order", representing the main database and the order database. Spring's **JtaTransactionManager** is used as transaction strategy, delegating to the J2EE container's JTA subsystem. This configuration must be deployed to a J2EE application server providing JTA. However, JNDI DataSources and JTA are the only services needed, allowing, for example, deployment to WebLogic Express instead of the full WebLogic Server. No Java code changes are required to take advantage of JTA.

```
  <bean id="dataSource" class="org.springframework.jndi.JndiObjectFactoryBean">
    <property name="jndiName"><value>jdbc/jpetstore</value></property>
  </bean>

  <bean id="orderDataSource" class="org.springframework.jndi.
      JndiObjectFactoryBean">
    <property name="jndiName"><value>jdbc/jpetstore-order</value></property>
  </bean>

  <bean id="transactionManager" class="org.springframework.transaction.jta.
      JtaTransactionManager"/>

  <bean id="sqlMap" class="org.springframework.orm.ibatis.SqlMapFactoryBean">
```

```
      <property name="configLocation">
        <value>classpath:/sql-map-config.xml</value>
      </property>
    </bean>

    <bean id="itemDao" class="org.springframework.samples.jpetstore.dao.
        ibatis.SqlMapItemDao">
      <property name="dataSource">
        <ref local="dataSource"/>
      </property>
      <property name="sqlMap">
        <ref local="sqlMap"/>
      </property>
    </bean>

    <bean id="orderDao" class="org.springframework.samples.jpetstore.dao.
        ibatis.SqlMapOrderDao">
      <property name="dataSource">
        <ref local="orderDataSource"/>
      </property>
      <property name="sqlMap">
        <ref local="sqlMap"/>
      </property>
      <property name="sequenceDao">
        <ref local="sequenceDao"/>
      </property>
    </bean>

    <bean id="sequenceDao" class="org.springframework.samples.jpetstore.dao.
        ibatis.SqlMapSequenceDao">
      <property name="dataSource">
        <ref local="orderDataSource"/>
      </property>
      <property name="sqlMap">
        <ref local="sqlMap"/>
      </property>
    </bean>
```

Here, "itemDao" refers to the main database ("dataSource"), while "orderDao" and "sequenceDao" refer to the order database ("orderDataSource"). These are the only changes necessary when switching to the distributed case: Neither the DAO implementations nor the PetStoreImpl business object nor the transactional proxy for the business object needs to be aware of the different deployment scenario.

DAO Implementation

For a DAO implementation example, the insertOrder method of SqlMapOrderDao looks as follows. The SqlMapOrderDao implementation is derived from Spring's org.springframework.orm.ibatis .support.SqlMapDaoSupport convenience class, accessing its prepared org.springframework.orm .ibatis.SqlMapTemplate instance via getSqlMapTemplate() calls.

```
public class SqlMapOrderDao extends SqlMapDaoSupport implements OrderDao {

    private SqlMapSequenceDao sequenceDao;
```

```
public void setSequenceDao(SqlMapSequenceDao sequenceDao) {
  this.sequenceDao = sequenceDao;
}

    ...

public void insertOrder(Order order) throws DataAccessException {
  order.setOrderId(this.sequenceDao.getNextId("ordernum"));
  getSqlMapTemplate().executeUpdate("insertOrder", order);
  getSqlMapTemplate().executeUpdate("insertOrderStatus", order);
  for (int i = 0; i < order.getLineItems().size(); i++) {
    LineItem lineItem = (LineItem) order.getLineItems().get(i);
    lineItem.setOrderId(order.getOrderId());
    getSqlMapTemplate().executeUpdate("insertLineItem", lineItem);
  }
}
}
```

Each DAO method declares `org.springframework.dao.DataAccessException`, the root of Spring's generic DAO exception hierarchy, to be thrown. This way, the `OrderDao` interface decouples business logic using DAOs from low-level exceptions like `java.sql.SQLException`. In contrast to iBATIS Database Layer's own DAO framework used in the original JPetStore implementation, Spring offers a rich hierarchy of non–technology-specific exceptions, with out-of-the-box integration with JDBC, Hibernate, JDO, and iBATIS SQL Maps.

The corresponding iBATIS SQL Maps mapping for the "insertOrder" statement is defined in the class-path resource `org/springframework/samples/jpetstore/dao/ibatis/maps/Order.xml`. The "#xxx#" values correspond to bean properties in the passed-in Order object.

```
<mapped-statement name="insertOrder">
  insert into ORDERS (ORDERID, USERID, ORDERDATE, SHIPADDR1, SHIPADDR2,
  SHIPCITY, SHIPSTATE, SHIPZIP, SHIPCOUNTRY, BILLADDR1, BILLADDR2,
  BILLCITY, BILLSTATE, BILLZIP, BILLCOUNTRY, COURIER, TOTALPRICE,
  BILLTOFIRSTNAME, BILLTOLASTNAME, SHIPTOFIRSTNAME, SHIPTOLASTNAME,
  CREDITCARD, EXPRDATE, CARDTYPE, LOCALE)
  values (#orderId#, #username#, #orderDate#, #shipAddress1#,
  #shipAddress2:VARCHAR#, #shipCity#, #shipState#, #shipZip#,
  #shipCountry#, #billAddress1#, #billAddress2:VARCHAR#, #billCity#,
  #billState#, #billZip#, #billCountry#, #courier#, #totalPrice#,
  #billToFirstName#, #billToLastName#, #shipToFirstName#,
  #shipToLastName#, #creditCard#, #expiryDate#, #cardType#, #locale#)
</mapped-statement>
```

Web Tier

The Spring JPetStore offers two alternative web tier implementations, which both rely on the same middle tier: one based on Struts as in the iBATIS JPetStore and one based on Spring's own MVC web framework. Both use JSTL-based JSPs as views: The original Struts web tier has been ported to Struts 1.1, and uses JSTL exclusively for model access. As a consequence, the Spring web MVC and Struts view implementations are *very* similar, the main difference being the framework-specific form tags.

As in the original JPetStore, all web tier classes, whether from the Struts or from the Spring web tier, access the business logic via the central business object: in this case, the "petStore" bean defined in `applicationContext.xml`, implementing the `PetStoreFacade` interface. The root application context is loaded in the `web.xml` standard deployment descriptor, combining the data access context definition and the business context definition into a single `WebApplicationContext` instance:

```xml
<context-param>
  <param-name>contextConfigLocation</param-name>
  <param-value>
    /WEB-INF/dataAccessContext-local.xml   /WEB-INF/applicationContext.xml
  </param-value>
</context-param>

<listener>
  <listener-class>
    org.springframework.web.context.ContextLoaderListener
  </listener-class>
</listener>
```

The ease with which it is possible to support web tiers using different MVC frameworks illustrates one of the benefits of having a well-defined business interface layer. As we'll see in a moment, supporting different remoting technologies is similarly easy, if we can build on well-defined business interfaces.

Struts 1.1

The Struts actions of the Spring JPetStore use a common **BaseAction** superclass that provides access to the "petStore" business object, retrieving Spring's root `WebApplicationContext` from the ServletContext:

```java
public abstract class BaseAction extends Action {

  private PetStoreFacade petStore;

  public void setServlet(ActionServlet actionServlet) {
    super.setServlet(actionServlet);
    ServletContext servletContext = actionServlet.getServletContext();
    WebApplicationContext wac = WebApplicationContextUtils.
        getRequiredWebApplicationContext(servletContext);
    this.petStore = (PetStoreFacade) wac.getBean("petStore");
  }

  protected PetStoreFacade getPetStore() {
    return petStore;
  }
}
```

Because of the lack of support for an interceptor concept in Struts, the logon check (that is, whether the user is correctly logged in if required for the requested action) is implemented in the action base class **SecureBaseAction**. All actions that require logon are derived from this base class. Thus, the security aspect is hard-wired into action implementations, and code changes would be required if security rules were to change. While it would be possible to use a Servlet Filter to get around this limitation, this is not ideal either, as the filter, which would need to be configured in `web.xml`, would not be integrated with the other MVC layer code.

Simple Controllers

ViewItemAction is a good example for a simple Struts action that prepares a model for a view. It retrieves the Item instance via the `PetStoreFacade` reference from `BaseAction`'s `getPetStore()` method.

```
public class ViewItemAction extends BaseAction {

  public ActionForward execute(ActionMapping mapping, ActionForm form,
      HttpServletRequest request, HttpServletResponse response)
      throws Exception {
    String itemId = request.getParameter("itemId");
    Item item = getPetStore().getItem(itemId);
    request.setAttribute("item", item);
    request.setAttribute("product", item.getProduct());
    return mapping.findForward("success");
  }
}
```

`ViewItemAction` is mapped in `struts-config.xml` via an "action" definition. The symbolic view name "success" gets mapped to the `Item.jsp` page in the forward mapping. The model objects "item" and "product" are passed to the view as request attributes, in typical Struts style.

```
<action path="/shop/viewItem"
    type="org.springframework.samples.jpetstore.web.struts.ViewItemAction"
    name="emptyForm" scope="session"
    validate="true" input="/WEB-INF/jsp/struts/Product.jsp">
  <forward name="success" path="/WEB-INF/jsp/struts/Item.jsp"/>
</action>
```

Form Controllers

As a further example, let's consider the order-creation process. In the Struts web tier, the following components are involved:

❑ **org.springframework.samples.jpetstore.web.struts.OrderActionForm:** the form object derived from Struts' `ActionForm` class, also containing the validation logic for the Order object, and holding reference data (in this case, credit-card types).

❑ **org.springframework.samples.jpetstore.web.struts.NewOrderFormAction:** creates a new Order object from the current shopping cart, and sets up the corresponding view `NewOrderForm.jsp`.

❑ **org.springframework.samples.jpetstore.web.struts.NewOrderAction:** handles the actual order-creation workflow, using the views `NewOrderForm.jsp`, `ShippingForm.jsp`, and `ConfirmOrder.jsp` for input.

An interesting detail is the *lifecycle* of `OrderActionForm`: An instance is created and put into the session by Struts on a new invocation of `NewOrderFormAction`. After persisting the order in `NewOrderAction`'s submission code, it needs to be manually removed with a `session.removeAttribute` call. Struts does not offer the notion of **workflow-scoped form objects**.

The order-form handling in our Struts web layer has been adapted straight from the original iBATIS JPetStore implementation. Interestingly, there are two action classes involved, plus one form object that also serves as validator and validation errors holder. Alternatively, one could also leverage declarative validation rules via Struts 1.1's Commons Validator support to factor out the validation logic.

As an example of a Struts **form view**, let's look at a snippet from NewOrderForm.jsp, illustrating how Struts forms are built with Struts' HTML tag library, wrapping standard HTML tags with form-aware Struts tags. The form-aware tags will automatically issue the corresponding HTML code, including populated form values.

```
<html:form action="/shop/newOrder.do" styleId="workingOrderForm"
    method="post">
...
<TR bgcolor="#FFFF88"><TD>
First name:</TD><TD>
<html:text name="workingOrderForm" property="order.billToFirstName"/>
</TD></TR>
...
```

Spring Web MVC

The Spring web controller implementations are themselves defined as beans in the web application's IoC application context, and can thus receive a reference to the "petStore" bean (or any number of business objects, in more complex applications) via a bean reference. They simply need to expose a JavaBean setter method of type PetStoreFacade (or a constructor argument, depending on one's preferred flavor of IoC). Thus, although it is easy to implement a Struts web tier on top of an application configured using Spring's IoC container, the integration between web tier and business objects is tighter, and no lookup or plumbing code is required, when using a Spring web tier.

Simple Controllers

As an example, the ViewItemController class looks as follows. Like the Struts ViewItemAction, ViewItemController retrieves the Item instance via the PetStoreFacade.

```
public class ViewItemController implements Controller {

  private PetStoreFacade petStore;

  public void setPetStore(PetStoreFacade petStore) {
    this.petStore = petStore;
  }

  public ModelAndView handleRequest(HttpServletRequest request,
      HttpServletResponse response) throws Exception {
    String itemId = request.getParameter("itemId");
    Item item = this.petStore.getItem(itemId);
    Map model = new HashMap();
    model.put("item", item);
    model.put("product", item.getProduct());
    return new ModelAndView("Item", model);
  }
}
```

In contrast to the Struts version, the model objects are passed to the view as a model Map, to be exposed in a way appropriate for the particular view technology. Note that ViewItemController implements Spring's Servlet-style Controller interface instead of being forced to extend a base class: Spring MVC is much more interface-oriented than Struts, which helps to make it more flexible.

ViewItemController is mapped in the context of the corresponding Spring DispatcherServlet, petstore-servlet-xml. The mapping from URL to controller happens via the bean name, leveraging the **BeanNameUrlHandlerMapping** strategy.

```
<bean id="defaultHandlerMapping" class="org.springframework.web.servlet.
    handler.BeanNameUrlHandlerMapping"/>
```

```
<bean id="viewResolver" class="org.springframework.web.servlet.view.
    InternalResourceViewResolver">
  <property name="viewClass">
    <value>org.springframework.web.servlet.view.JstlView</value>
  </property>
  <property name="prefix">
    <value>/WEB-INF/jsp/spring/</value>
  </property>
  <property name="suffix">
    <value>.jsp</value>
  </property>
</bean>
...
```

```
<bean name="/shop/viewItem.do" class="org.springframework.samples.jpetstore.
    web.spring.ViewItemController">
  <property name="petStore">
    <ref bean="petStore"/>
  </property>
</bean>
```

The symbolic view names are resolved by a ViewResolver that is shared by all controllers, in this case an **InternalResourceViewResolver** that prepends a prefix "/WEB-INF/jsp/spring/" and appends a suffix ".jsp" to the view name: Thus, "Item" is resolved to "/WEB-INF/jsp/spring/Item.jsp".

Of course, a more sophisticated view resolution strategy can be used if required (for example, an XmlViewResolver or ResourceBundleViewResolver that allows for arbitrary mappings of view names to view definitions).

Form Controllers

The order-creation process is handled in a different fashion than in the Struts web tier. There are still three components involved, but with significantly different roles:

❑ **org.springframework.samples.jpetstore.web.spring.OrderForm:** A form object that is not derived from a base class, holding an Order plus two flags used by the order-creation workflow. Note that if those two flags weren't necessary, the Order object itself could serve as form object: Any JavaBean can be used as a form object in Spring MVC.

❑ **org.springframework.samples.jpetstore.web.spring.OrderFormController:** A form controller derived from Spring's AbstractWizardFormController, handling the complete order-creation workflow from setting up the order form to persisting the finished order.

❑ **org.springframework.samples.jpetstore.domain.logic.OrderValidator:** Implementation of Spring's `org.springframework.validation.Validator` interface, containing the validation logic for Order objects, used by OrderFormController.

The *lifecycle* of `OrderForm` objects is completely handled by the `org.springframework.web.servlet.mvc.AbstractWizardFormController` base class. It will create a new instance on opening a new form, and automatically remove it after form processing has finished, essentially implementing a **workflow-scoped form object**.

This lifecycle is shown in Figure 16-1.

The gray activities are completely covered by the `AbstractWizardFormController` base class, while only the white activities remain to be implemented in a specific fashion by JPetStore's `OrderForm Controller`. The distinction between generic workflow in a base class and specific behavior via template method implementations in a concrete subclass is unique to Spring's web MVC; neither Struts nor WebWork offers such sophisticated management of form objects in a workflow.

Note that the `OrderValidator` is placed in the business logic package instead of in the web package, as it represents a generic implementation of validation logic for Order objects—not being tied to web environments. So there are three clear object roles involved: the workflow-specific **form object**, the workflow-specific **form controller**, and the generic **validator**.

For a **form view**, the Spring form tags adhere to the principle that custom tags should not issue HTML code but should just be placeholders for dynamic values or control the rendering flow—like the JSTL does too. Therefore, standard HTML form and input tags are used, spiced with JSTL tags that fill in URLs or form values. The "bind" tag exposes a status object for the given form object property, to be used by JSTL EL expressions.

```
<form action="<c:url value="/shop/newOrder.do"/>" method="post">
...
<TR bgcolor="#FFFF88"><TD>
First name:</TD><TD>
<spring:bind path="orderForm.order.billToFirstName">
  <input type="text" name="<c:out value="${status.expression}"/>"
      value="<c:out value="${status.value}"/>"/>
</spring:bind>
</TD></TR>
...
```

Note that JSP 2.0 makes it even easier to use EL expressions, as they can be used outside JSTL "out" tags like ordinary Java expressions, resulting in significantly simplified code, as follows:

```
<spring:bind path="orderForm.order.billToFirstName">
  <input type="text" name="${status.expression}" value="${status.value}"/>
</spring:bind>
```

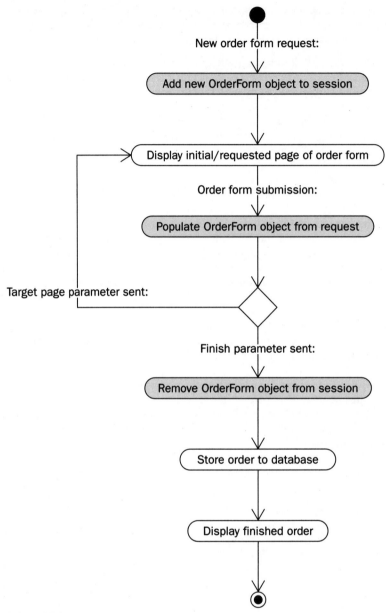

New order form request:

Add new OrderForm object to session

Display initial/requested page of order form

Order form submission:

Populate OrderForm object from request

Target page parameter sent:

Finish parameter sent:

Remove OrderForm object from session

Store order to database

Display finished order

Figure 16-1

SignonInterceptor

In contrast to the Struts web tier, the logon check is not implemented in a controller base class, but in **SignonInterceptor**, implementing Spring's `HandlerInterceptor` interface.

A `HandlerInterceptor` is somewhat similar to a Servlet Filter, but is integrated into Spring's web MVC framework: It can be defined as a bean in a DispatcherServlet context, leveraging Spring's IoC capabilities, and mapped via a Spring HandlerMapping. Note that a `HandlerInterceptor` can intercept request processing but cannot wrap the HttpServletRequest or HttpServletResponse instances used further down the chain. The latter is hardly ever necessary for application-level functionality.

Servlet Filters are typically used for generic, orthogonal content-processing tasks: for example, for transparent GZIP compression. Of course, this is still possible with Spring web MVC, no matter whether `HandlerInterceptors` are used. So while Filters and `HandlerInterceptors` share capabilities, they also complement each other in some respects. Servlet Filters are less closely integrated with other application objects.

In the DispatcherServlet context, a separate HandlerMapping is defined for all secured controllers, applying the `SignonInterceptor`:

```xml
<bean id="secureHandlerMapping" class="org.springframework.web.servlet.
    handler.SimpleUrlHandlerMapping">
  <property name="interceptors">
    <list>
      <ref bean="signonInterceptor"/>
    </list>
  </property>
  <property name="urlMap">
    <map>
      ...
      <entry key="/shop/newOrder.do">
        <ref local="secure_newOrder"/>
      </entry>
  <entry key="/shop/viewOrder.do">
        <ref local="secure_viewOrder"/>
      </entry>
    </map>
  </property>
</bean>

<bean id="signonInterceptor" class="org.springframework.samples.jpetstore.
    web.spring.SignonInterceptor"/>

<bean name="secure_newOrder" class="org.springframework.samples.jpetstore.
    web.spring.OrderFormController">
  <property name="petStore">
    <ref bean="petStore"/>
  </property>
  <property name="validator">
    <ref bean="orderValidator"/>
  </property>
</bean>

<bean name="secure_viewOrder" class="org.springframework.samples.jpetstore.
    web.spring.ViewOrderController">
  <property name="petStore">
    <ref bean="petStore"/>
  </property>
</bean>
```

The `SignonInterceptor` will be invoked for all handlers that are mapped via "secureHandlerMapping". It will simply check for a proper logon, and redirect to the logon page if the check failed.

Remoting

The Spring JPetStore offers multiple remoting options, all exporting the same `OrderService` business object, but over different protocols. Spring's remoting-support classes are used for minimal effort in exporting and accessing those services. See Chapter 11 ("Remoting") for details on the supported remoting strategies.

❑ **Caucho's Hessian:** A slim binary protocol over HTTP.

❑ **Caucho's Burlap:** A slim XML-based protocol over HTTP.

❑ **JAX-RPC via Apache Axis:** SOAP-based web services over HTTP, with Axis-specific extensions.

❑ **RMI invoker:** RMI-based remoting with non-RMI business objects.

All of these tools can export the existing `OrderService` implementation, with only simple configuration required. The only exception is JAX-RPC, which requires a thin JAX-RPC-compliant wrapper to be written for the specific service to export.

The use of RMI is commented out in the default Spring JPetStore distribution to avoid potential conflicts with EJB containers. Custom RMI should be used only in a web container, without an EJB container. Remote EJBs are a good RMI remoting implementation, and are usually the best choice for RMI if available.

Exporting Remote Services

The natural export mechanism for HTTP-based services is a servlet. In case of Hessian and Burlap, Spring provides out-of-the-box `Controller` implementations for exporting services as Spring-integrated alternative to the standard Caucho servlets. (The added value is closer integration with Spring IoC and, hence, any application object configured via IoC.) For RMI, Spring provides an exporter bean that can be used in any application context.

All Spring-integrated exporters use analogous configuration properties: for example, "service" for a reference to the service object to export, and "serviceInterface" to specify the interface to expose. Configuration consistency is important for easy switching between protocols. The goal is to consider the wire protocol a configuration detail, as far as possible, of course. Each wire protocol has its own restrictions in terms of service interface arguments and so on.

Hessian and Burlap

In the case of the Caucho protocols, the Spring JPetStore uses a distinct **DispatcherServlet** that defines the Hessian and Burlap exporters, mapped to the URL pattern "/caucho/*". The DispatcherServlet context definition looks as follows:

```
<beans>

    <bean name="/OrderService-hessian" class="org.springframework.remoting.
        caucho.HessianServiceExporter">
```

```
        <property name="service">
          <ref bean="petStore"/>
        </property>
        <property name="serviceInterface">
          <value>
            org.springframework.samples.jpetstore.domain.logic.OrderService
          </value>
        </property>
      </bean>

      <bean name="/OrderService-burlap" class="org.springframework.remoting.
          caucho.BurlapServiceExporter">
        <property name="service">
          <ref bean="petStore"/>
        </property>
        <property name="serviceInterface">
          <value>
            org.springframework.samples.jpetstore.domain.logic.OrderService
          </value>
        </property>
      </bean>

    </beans>
```

No HandlerMappings or ViewResolver need be defined. The Spring-provided HessianServiceExporter and BurlapServiceExporter instances, both implementing the `org.springframework.web.servlet.mvc.Controller` interface, are defined with the mapped URLs as names, leveraging DispatcherServlet's default BeanNameUrlHandlerMapping.

Both exporters refer to the "petStore" business facade defined in the root application context, to which they have implicit access, as a DispatcherServlet context is automatically a child of the root context. The "serviceInterface" parameter specifies the interface to expose: Only the methods defined there will be accessible by remote clients.

WSDL Web Service via Axis

To export a service via Axis, the **AxisServlet** must be mapped in `web.xml`, in the case of JPetStore to the URL pattern "/axis/*". The Axis deployment descriptor `server-config.wsdd` needs to specify the service endpoint class, in this case the Spring JPetStore's **JaxRpcOrderService** class, implementing the JAX-RPC-compliant **RemoteOrderService** interface:

```
public interface RemoteOrderService extends Remote {

    Order getOrder(int orderId) throws RemoteException;
}
```

The `JaxRpcOrderService` implementation extends Spring's `org.springframework.remoting.jaxrpc.ServletEndpointSupport` class, which provides easy access to the root web application context. Unfortunately, it is not possible to export a Spring-defined bean directly here: A JAX-RPC-compliant service wrapper derived from `ServletEndpointSupport` is as easy as it gets.

```
public class JaxRpcOrderService extends ServletEndpointSupport
    implements RemoteOrderService, OrderService {

  private OrderService orderService;

  protected void onInit() {
    this.orderService =
      (OrderService) getWebApplicationContext().getBean("petStore");
  }

  public Order getOrder(int orderId) {
    return this.orderService.getOrder(orderId);
  }
}
```

Note that `JaxRpcOrderService` implements both `RemoteOrderService` and OrderService, to be able to proxy it not only with the JAX-RPC-compliant `RemoteOrderService` interface but also with the `OrderService` business interface and to guarantee them to be in synch. Later we'll see an example of how to access such a service.

The Axis deployment descriptor also needs to specify appropriate serializers and deserializers for the service: In the JPetStore case, Axis **BeanSerializers** are applied via "beanMapping" entries in `server-config.wsdd`. JavaBeans are not SOAP standard data types; therefore such mappings need to specify how to serialize and deserialize such objects. On the server side, this can be done in the web service deployment descriptor.

Usually, an Axis web service must be deployed via the Axis admin tool. The Spring JPetStore distribution comes with a predeployed web service, defined in the included `server-config.wsdd` file. Therefore, no deployment steps are necessary beyond standard WAR file deployment.

RMI Invoker

As RMI is not HTTP-based, no servlet definition is necessary for exporting an RMI service. Instead, the corresponding exporter can be defined in the root application context (`applicationContext.xml`):

```
<bean id="order-rmi" class="org.springframework.remoting.rmi.
    RmiServiceExporter">
  <property name="service">
    <ref bean="petStore"/>
  </property>
  <property name="serviceInterface">
    <value>
      org.springframework.samples.jpetstore.domain.logic.OrderService
    </value>
  </property>
  <property name="serviceName">
    <value>order</value>
  </property>
  <property name="registryPort">
    <value>1099</value>
  </property>
</bean>
```

As with Hessian and Burlap, the `OrderService` interface implemented by the "petStore" business facade gets exported. Instead of a URL, an RMI service name needs to be specified: in this case, "order". An RMI registry is expected at the specified registry port: If none is running there, a new one will be started automatically.

RmiServiceExporter will automatically export an RMI invoker for the given service, as "petStore" does not implement an RMI interface but only the plain Java `PetStoreFacade` business interface. The exported service will not be accessible via plain RMI, but only via Spring's RmiProxyFactoryBean, which will automatically detect the use of an RMI invoker and adapt to it.

Accessing Remote Services

The Spring JPetStore distribution includes a sample standalone **OrderServiceClient**, which can access the exported services via all protocols. It is a simple class that reads in its own application context from `clientContext.xml`, and invokes all `OrderService` proxies defined there.

As with exporters, Spring provides prebuilt proxy factories for all the protocols it supports, enabling clients to work directly with the service interface, without any lookups in Java code or, equally important, protocol-specific implementation. This results in a lot less code that is a lot more testable than traditional approaches. A client might, for example, merely expose a JavaBean property of the service interface type, leaving a client-side Spring IoC container to supply a remote proxy at runtime. (A test stub or mock object could be provided at test time, significantly improving testability.)

Again, configuration is as consistent as possible: For example, "serviceInterface" is used in every case to specify the service interface for the proxy. With the exception of JAX-RPC, the only other required configuration property is "serviceUrl", determining the HTTP respectively RMI URL that the service is bound to.

Hessian and Burlap

For accessing Hessian and Burlap services, corresponding proxies need to be defined via Spring's remote access support classes. In the Spring JPetStore, they are defined in `clientContext.xml`:

```xml
<bean id="hessianProxy" class="org.springframework.remoting.caucho.
    HessianProxyFactoryBean">
  <property name="serviceInterface">
    <value>
      org.springframework.samples.jpetstore.domain.logic.OrderService
    </value>
  </property>
  <property name="serviceUrl">
    <value>
      http://${serverName}:${httpPort}${contextPath}/caucho/
      OrderService-hessian
    </value>
  </property>
</bean>

<bean id="burlapProxy" class="org.springframework.remoting.caucho.
    BurlapProxyFactoryBean">
```

```
    <property name="serviceInterface">
      <value>
        org.springframework.samples.jpetstore.domain.logic.OrderService
      </value>
    </property>
    <property name="serviceUrl">
      <value>
        http://${serverName}:${httpPort}${contextPath}/caucho/
        OrderService-burlap
      </value>
    </property>
  </bean>
```

The placeholders for connection parameters are read in from a client.properties file via a corresponding **PropertyPlaceholderConfigurer** definition. This separation allows us to keep administration settings in a properties file, avoiding the need to touch the application context definition for customization.

```
serverName=localhost
httpPort=8080
rmiPort=1099
contextPath=/jpetstore
```

The defined beans will expose the located remote service proxies, to be used like as follows, assuming a FileSystemXmlApplicationContext that loads the clientContext.xml file:

```
BeanFactory factory = new FileSystemXmlApplicationContext("clientContext.xml")
OrderService orderService = (OrderService) factory.getBean("hessianProxy");
Order order = orderService.getOrder(1000);
```

As you can see, accessing Hessian and Burlap services is simple and straightforward. The only required parameters for the proxy factories are the service interface to use and the service URL to access.

WSDL Web Service via Axis

Accessing a Web Service via JAX-RPC requires much more effort. Spring's standard **JaxRpcProxyFactoryBean** must be subclassed to register Axis **BeanDeserializers** for the JPetStore domain objects. On the server side, this was done in the Axis deployment descriptor; on the client side, this needs to be done in application code or application configuration.

```
<bean id="jaxRpcProxy" class="org.springframework.samples.jpetstore.
    service.client.AxisPortProxyFactoryBean">
  <property name="serviceInterface">
    <value>
      org.springframework.samples.jpetstore.domain.logic.OrderService
    </value>
  </property>
  <property name="portInterface">
    <value>
      org.springframework.samples.jpetstore.service.RemoteOrderService
    </value>
  </property>
```

```
      <property name="serviceFactoryClass">
        <value>org.apache.axis.client.ServiceFactory</value>
      </property>
      <property name="wsdlDocumentUrl">
        <value>
          http://${serverName}:${httpPort}${contextPath}/axis/OrderService?wsdl
        </value>
      </property>
      <property name="namespaceUri">
        <value>
          http://${serverName}:${httpPort}${contextPath}/axis/OrderService
        </value>
      </property>
      <property name="serviceName">
        <value>JaxRpcOrderServiceService</value>
      </property>
      <property name="portName">
        <value>OrderService</value>
      </property>
    </bean>
```

While the JAX-RPC-compliant `RemoteOrderService` is used as interface for the SOAP port, the exposed service interface is the `OrderService` business interface: JaxRpcProxyFactoryBean will automatically delegate invocations to the underlying port proxy. Of course, the two interfaces need to be in synch: This is why `JaxRpcOrderService` implements both `RemoteOrderService` and `OrderService`.

Note the numerous parameters required for accessing a specific port of a WSDL web service, in contrast to the service URL from Hessian and Burlap. Even if default values are automatically chosen by the Web Service tool used for export, they still need to be specified for web service access.

- ❑ The WSDL document URL
- ❑ The namespace URI of the service
- ❑ The name of the service
- ❑ The name of the port

RMI Invoker

Setting up a remote service proxy for an RMI invoker is as simple as for Hessian and Burlap:

```
    <bean id="rmiProxy" class="org.springframework.remoting.rmi.
      RmiProxyFactoryBean">
      <property name="serviceInterface">
        <value>
          org.springframework.samples.jpetstore.domain.logic.OrderService
        </value>
      </property>
      <property name="serviceUrl">
        <value>rmi://${serverName}:${rmiPort}/order</value>
      </property>
    </bean>
```

Instead of a HTTP service URL like with Hessian and Burlap, RmiProxyFactoryBean expects an RMI URL to access, specifying the server and the RMI registry port. It will automatically detect that the located service is an RMI invoker and adapt accordingly.

Build and Deployment

A typical J2EE web application such as the original iBATIS JPetStore or the Spring JPetStore can be built with a simple Ant script and deployed as a **WAR file**. This is significantly simpler than deploying an **EAR file** that contains both WARs and EJB JARs: In particular, it is normally possible to avoid container-specific deployment descriptors—in contrast to EJB deployment, which always requires such additional descriptors, if only for specifying the target JNDI locations.

Alternatively, a J2EE web application can also be deployed as an **expanded** WAR directory. This is particularly useful in development environments: An IDE can be configured to compile to the `/WEB-INF/classes` directory, with the necessary libraries kept in `/WEB-INF/lib`. This avoids dedicated deployment steps in the first place—simply compile your changes and restart the container. Changes in JSPs will be picked up on the fly, without the need for a restart.

A significant advantage of lightweight containers is that they do not complicate web application deployment, despite all their power and convenience (except when using source-level metadata, which requires an extra precompilation step). Using an expanded WAR directory for development is possible as with any web app: The lightweight container including AOP support, transaction management, and so on is simply embedded there like a conventional class library.

For a direct comparison, a web application that uses Stateless Session Beans for declarative transaction demarcation needs to be redeployed on each change in the EJB layer, even if using only local EJBs. Advanced J2EE containers allow for selective redeployment of EJB JARs, but this needs to be supported by your IDE—and still involves dedicated deployment steps.

> **Web applications that leverage lightweight containers are as simple to deploy as plain web applications and are significantly simpler than EAR files and EJB JARs. Most important, an expanded WAR directory eliminates dedicated deployment steps in development environments.**

WAR Deployment Issues

Despite being significantly simpler than EAR deployment, the usage of WAR files is still not trivial. Subtle and not-so-subtle differences between Servlet containers can cause severe headaches, particularly if encountered on production deployment to a different J2EE server.

Listeners and Startup Servlets

Unfortunately, the Servlet 2.3 specification did not clarify whether ServletContextListeners have to be invoked *before* or *after* load-on-startup servlets like Spring's DispatcherServlet or Struts' ActionServlet. The spec hinted through an example at listeners being invoked *before*, but it did not actually state a requirement. Thus, it is not fully portable to use Spring's **ContextLoaderListener** for loading the root context in Servlet 2.3 containers: For fully portable behavior, **ContextLoaderServlet** must be used, the default in Spring's sample application distributions.

Servlet 2.4 clarifies that ServletContextListeners should be invoked *before* load-on-startup servlets. Many Servlet 2.3 containers already implement this behavior, including:

- ❑ Tomcat 4.x
- ❑ Jetty 4.x
- ❑ Resin 2.1.8+
- ❑ Orion 2.0.2+

Unfortunately, the Servlet 2.3 incarnations of several high-end J2EE servers do not follow the Servlet 2.4 strategy, but invoke ServletContextListeners *after* load-on-startup servlets:

- ❑ BEA WebLogic up to 8.1
- ❑ IBM WebSphere 5.x
- ❑ Oracle OC4J 9.0.3

The major drawback of a load-on-startup ContextLoaderServlet, besides being a servlet that does not actually serve any requests, is that the Servlet container will continue the startup of the web application *even if the servlet initialization fails.* Follow-up servlets like a DispatcherServlet or ActionServlet will then fail because of the missing root application context, obscuring the error log with **follow-up failures**. This does not happen with ContextLoaderListener: If it fails, the web application startup will be aborted in all popular containers (although this behavior is not actually required by the spec).

> For full portability across all Servlet 2.3 containers or to also support Servlet 2.2 containers, prefer load-on-startup servlets over ServletContextListeners. However, if targeting only Servlet 2.4–compliant containers or Servlet 2.3 containers with 2.4-style listener behavior, choose ServletContextListeners, as they provide clearer startup failure behavior.
>
> Of course, in most real applications, unlike our sample application, there is no need to be particularly paranoid about minor portability issues, especially in areas in which the J2EE specifications are becoming more explicit and clearing up any confusion.

Resource References

WAR files can declare JNDI resource dependencies in their web.xml files, in the form of "resource-ref" tags:

```
<resource-ref>
  <res-ref-name>jdbc/jpetstore</res-ref-name>
  <res-type>javax.sql.DataSource</res-type>
  <res-auth>Container</res-auth>
</resource-ref>
```

```
<resource-ref>
  <res-ref-name>jdbc/jpetstore-order</res-ref-name>
  <res-type>javax.sql.DataSource</res-type>
  <res-auth>Container</res-auth>
</resource-ref>
```

While Servlet containers like Tomcat and Resin typically ignore such dependency declarations, lazily discovering missing resources on first access, full-blown J2EE application servers tend to match them against resources in the container on deployment, eagerly reporting failures.

A further difference is that Servlet containers typically allow for matching resource references names *directly* onto JNDI names of actual resources, while full J2EE servers usually require an explicit entry in their container-specific deployment descriptor.

As an alternative to J2EE container resources, JDBC DataSources and O/R mapping factories can also be defined locally within the web application. We have already discussed the advantages and disadvantages of both strategies in Chapter 10 ("Persistence"). Note that if you want distributed transactions across multiple databases, you *must* use JTA and corresponding transactional DataSources: Hence, you *must* use an application server and JNDI resources, unless you combine your web container with a JTA implementation (for example, with a local instance of ObjectWeb's JOTM: http://jotm.objectweb.org).

The Spring JPetStore's default distribution uses a locally defined Commons DBCP BasicDataSource for a single HSQL database, defined in dataAccessContext-local.xml. The alternative configuration for JTA uses two JNDI DataSources, "jdbc/jpetstore" and "jdbc/jpetstore-order", defined in dataAccess Context-jta.xml.

JPetStore's web.xml contains the preceding "resource-ref" declarations, but they are needed only when using JTA. Therefore, they are commented out; otherwise, some J2EE servers will complain on deployment and require you to set up corresponding resources, even if they are not actually needed in your configuration scenario. Unfortunately, you won't discover this early if you develop on a Servlet container like Tomcat or Resin that does not validate resource reference entries.

> Do not embed "resource-ref" entries in your "web.xml" files just for certain configuration scenarios of your application: Some J2EE servers might complain on deployment, forcing you to set up corresponding resources. Preferably, keep such optional resource references commented out.

JSP and JSTL

JSP engines can cause subtle deployment issues. The most common source of problems is the use of **tag libraries**. JSP engines vary slightly in how exactly they translate custom tags into generated servlet code. Unfortunately, this will normally just become obvious when actually rendering a JSP: Precompilation of JSPs still takes too much time to perform on deployment, and even a properly compiled JSP may still result in erroneous behavior at runtime.

Even using the JSTL (JSP Standard Tag Library) has been unnecessarily hard: For example, **Jakarta's reference implementation of the JSTL** had a couple of nasty bugs in its early 1.0 releases. Furthermore, some Servlet 2.3 containers like Resin offer optimized JSTL implementations integrated into their JSP engine. Unfortunately, such implementations are not always fully compatible with the reference implementation.

Deploying tag libraries has become particularly easy with JSP 1.2's automatic scanning of deployed JARs for TLD files. However, it is still not entirely clear how to deploy JSTL-based applications in a portable way. For Servlet containers that do not provide their own JSTL implementation, Jakarta's reference implementation has to be included in the `/WEB-INF/lib` directory. However, Servlet containers with their own JSTL implementations might not be able to deploy such a WAR that includes a JSTL implementation.

Deploying the Jakarta reference implementation in the server's library directory if the server does not provide its own implementation is not an attractive option either, as the TLDs cannot be auto-discovered in the JAR files; only `/WEB-INF/lib` JARs are scanned for TLDs. Fortunately, any decent Servlet container that provides its own JSTL implementation will ignore JSTL JARs included in a WAR, simply overriding the included tag declarations with its own version.

Note that JSTL 1.0 implementations are suitable only for JSP 1.2; for JSP 2.0, JSTL 1.1 must be used. This will only affect applications that actually are Servlet 2.4 / JSP 2.0 applications according to their `web.xml` deployment descriptors. Therefore, it should not cause deployment hassles.

> **If you do not have to rely on absolute out-of-the-box portability of your JSTL-enabled WAR, include Jakarta's JSTL reference implementation in the /WEB-INF/lib directory. If you encounter a server that cannot cope with the included JSTL implementation, remove the corresponding JSTL JAR files on demand. Alternatively, prepare two WAR files: one for Servlet containers that provide their own JSTL implementation, and one that includes the Jakarta JSTL JARs. As we've noted, targeting all servers without any configuration or code changes is not an issue for most real applications anyway.**

Deploying the Spring JPetStore

The Spring JPetStore distribution takes account of all of the previously mentioned issues, for maximum portability:

❑ The Spring ContextLoaderServlet is used for loading the root web application context, rather than the ContextLoaderListener.

❑ Resource references in `web.xml` are commented out, as the local data access context with a local Commons DBCP BasicDataSource is the default.

❑ Jakarta's JSTL reference implementation is included in the `/WEB-INF/lib` directory, because the JPetStore JSPs all require the JSTL.

Hence, deploying JPetStore should be straightforward. We'll assume your server is running on JDK 1.4, which includes an XML parser:

1. If not already set, set the JAVA_HOME environment variable to the path of your JDK installation.

2. Open the directory "samples/jpetstore" of the Spring distribution.

3. Run "ant warfile" respectively "warfile.bat" to generate the WAR file.

4. Copy the generated "jpetstore.war" from the "dist" subdirectory to the WAR deployment directory of your Servlet container (for example, "webapps" in case of Tomcat).

5.   Start the included HSQLDB instance via "server.bat" respectively "server.sh" from the "db/hsqldb" subdirectory.

6.   Start your Servlet container (we'll assume on running port 8080).

7.   Open "http://localhost:8080/jpetstore" in an Internet browser.

8.   If you already have the WAR file, start the database and drop the WAR file into the deployment directory of your Servlet container, without touching server configuration in any way—deployment can hardly be simpler. Note that Servlet containers like Tomcat and Resin are particularly good matches here: Their download sizes are below 10MB, and they can be installed by simply unzipping the distribution.

9.   If you have successfully run the JPetStore WAR and want to try remote service access, use the provided client setup.

10.   Create an order with the JPetStore web UI (the first order number will be 1000).

11.   Open the directory "samples/jpetstore/client" of the Spring distribution.

12.   Adapt the server URL in the "client.properties" file (if not using the default).

13.   Run "ant -buildfile run.xml 1000" or "client.bat 1000" to fetch and show the order with number 1000, using each remoting protocol.

14.   Run "ant -buildfile run.xml 1000 10" or "client.bat 1000 10" to fetch the order 10 times per remoting protocol (testing accumulated response times per protocol).

Summary

In this chapter, we have seen how lightweight technologies can be leveraged to build a database-driven J2EE web application. We have discussed the architecture of the original iBATIS JPetStore, and how Spring's JPetStore version significantly improves on it in a variety of important areas:

❑   Introducing a well-defined business layer abstraction.

❑   Wiring business objects and data access objects via IoC, eliminating ad hoc configuration management and greatly improving testability.

❑   Using declarative transaction management via AOP, simplifying business logic and maximizing reuse between single and multiple database environments.

❑   Offering the option of switching data access technology without changing data access interfaces or affecting business logic.

❑   Supporting generic remoting with pluggable protocols, and a minimum of protocol-specific application code.

Furthermore, we have learned how the Spring JPetStore offers alternative web tier implementations for Struts and Spring's own web MVC framework—built on the same business layer—and discussed some of the similarities and differences between the two web MVC programming models.

Finally, we reviewed various deployment issues and demonstrated how simple it is to deploy the standard JPetStore distribution to any web container.

17

Conclusion

In this book we've attempted to describe architectures, principles, and coding practices that help to produce simple, high-quality, maintainable, performant, and scalable J2EE applications, on time and within budget.

We feel that the main problem with J2EE is the complexity that often surrounds its use. We've attempted to demonstrate simpler approaches to solving common problems in J2EE.

We've argued that EJB often adds to this complexity. While EJB promises to *reduce* complexity in areas such as transaction management and threading, this claim is highly debatable. There are simpler alternatives to solving most problems that EJB addresses.

We've focused on web applications, but the architectural principles we've discussed are by no means limited to web applications.

There are some applications—especially distributed applications—in which EJB still offers much value. Unlike advocates of EJB itself for most of the history of EJB, we don't claim to have the perfect solution for all middleware problems but merely a very good solution for the majority of problems we see in real applications.

Looking Back

The J2EE platform is a remarkable achievement, with immense buy-in from vendors, managers, and developers. However, we can't ignore the fact that, for many applications, J2EE has not been a shining success. Failures are probably commoner than glowing successes. J2EE projects are often poor value for money: Many projects are late; most go over budget. Many applications exhibit poor performance; some fail altogether to satisfy requirements. The hoped-for and hyped reliability and scalability often don't materialize. The complexity of application code is often disproportionate compared with the complexity of the requirements it addresses. Some of these problems are common across software technologies (and sometimes consequences of non-technical issues), but J2EE in practice has certainly failed to rise above the failings of previous technologies, and has added new problems of its own. Such experiences have long been the territory of conversations over the water-cooler or in the pub. In addition to my own experience, and the experience of companies I've been brought in to help as a consultant, I've heard such criticisms in the reports of the many readers—mainly experienced J2EE architects and developers—who have written to me to share their experiences. Some formal studies have also produced shocking findings—see for example a recent survey from Wily Technologies (www.wilytech.com/solutions/chartingJ2EE.html) that prompted the Javalobby headline ".88888—The Fabled "Five Eights" of J2EE Availability."

We point out these unpleasant realities, not to attack J2EE, but as a call to use it better. We see two main causes for these problems, neither reflecting an inherent weakness in J2EE as a technology:

- ❑ **Architectural fashion:** The tendency toward over-engineering and the application of "blueprints" of dubious value in the design of J2EE applications. We feel that this is the main cause of the problems noted previously.

- ❑ **The need for simplifying infrastructure:** Working with J2EE out of the box is difficult, and we need frameworks and libraries to simplify it.

We can do much better by avoiding common architectural and implementation mistakes, by supplementing J2EE with simplifying technologies, and by focusing on application requirements, not on technology.

The key problem with J2EE in practice—following the traditional architectural prescription—is complexity. Coping with complexity has been widely acknowledged as a priority since 2002. The traditional J2EE solutions have been to ignore complexity, or rely on tools to manage it. As those tools have failed to deliver, more and more developers want to reduce the complexity of J2EE rather than apply band-aid solutions. While J2EE is a powerful platform, its complexity means that many J2EE applications are hard to maintain, unreliable, and inefficient. Developers spend too much of their time wrestling with complex APIs and a cumbersome programming model (long development-test cycles) and too little time focusing on the problem domain. EJB was meant to enable developers to concentrate on business logic. However, it hasn't delivered, but has become more a part of the problem than part of the solution.

These challenges cannot be ignored. Without significant change—at least in usage patterns—J2EE won't survive the arrival of a well-funded competing platform such as .NET.

We believe that the problems are more in how J2EE is used than in its basic building blocks. Most of the technological building blocks of J2EE are excellent: JTA; JNDI; JDBC; the Java language itself. No competing platform can boast such a range of standard and proven building blocks for enterprise applications. Many of the J2EE APIs and J2SE APIs that underpin J2EE (such as JDBC) are not best suited as end-user APIs. (As we've seen, if we add an abstraction layer above JDBC or JTA, for example, we can significantly simplify development and lessen the likelihood of errors.) But they provide great value through offering a consistent, integrated model for accessing enterprise services.

Things *are* gradually improving. J2EE application servers are more solid and easier to use than ever before. Java development tools are maturing: IDEs such as IntelliJ and Eclipse now offer outstanding refactoring support, and a degree of understanding of Java code that's a great help to developers. Tools such as JUnit provide a simple and effective support for agile processes. But the traditional approach to J2EE architecture—which produces complex designs—is the key cause of the problem, and must change for things to improve significantly.

It's important to note that this is not purely a technical issue. Over-engineering is endemic to J2EE applications. There seems to be a common belief that J2EE applications cannot—indeed perhaps *should not*—ever be simple. In fact, many J2EE web applications have quite straightforward requirements, such as relatively simple business logic backed by a single relational database. Such applications don't require complexity such as object distribution; they don't even require distributed transaction support via JTA. They require a simple, object-oriented solution: precisely what over-complex implementations don't deliver.

For any application, it's vital to focus on requirements rather than on technology. Whatever technology we use, it should be a means to an end; it should not determine the way in which we address requirements. Because of the complexity of traditional J2EE solutions, and these cultural issues, many J2EE developers focus too much on the technology they use, at the expense of the problem domain. Developers working with many other technologies seem less prone to this distortion of priorities.

J2EE 1.5—including EJB 3.0—will attempt to reduce the complexity of writing J2EE applications, building on Java language improvements: most important, the introduction of source-level metadata attributes in Java 1.5. However, we feel that this is likely to be too little, too late. Although Sun has finally realized some of the issues developers have been facing, the J2EE community has long been aware of these problems, and several innovative frameworks have already solved them. We feel that there are several problems in the attempt to modify the EJB specification to provide a simpler, more productive model:

- ❑ **The EJB specification tries to solve too many problems.** It's hard to find a focus in EJB 2.1. It's a muddled mix of remoting infrastructure, component model, half-baked O/R mapping solution, and provision of declarative enterprise services.

- ❑ **EJB is dated.** Some of its fundamental assumptions date back to Java 1.1, and are no longer relevant.

- ❑ **EJB is not easily amenable to unit testing.** As more and more developers recognize the value of agile processes such as test-driven development, this problem is likely to become more and more pressing.

We believe that EJB is not the way of the future for most J2EE applications. EJB 3.0 will address some of its weaknesses, but it won't provide a true next-generation component model, which is both simpler and more powerful.

We believe there is a simpler way to design most applications. In this book, we've tried to outline an alternative to the traditional, highly complex approach to J2EE architecture and development.

Moving Forward

J2EE is now a mature platform. Its maturity is measured not only in the solidity of application servers and specification versions, but in the large volume of experience that has been built up in the J2EE development community over the last five years.

It is this experience, above all, that we believe points in the direction of simpler, more effective J2EE architectures.

Until 2003, although the problems flowing from the traditional approach to J2EE architecture—heavily emphasizing EJB—were apparent, there was no credible alternative for the majority of enterprise applications. For example, there was no satisfactory alternative to EJB CMT for declarative transaction management. This has now changed, with the emergence of AOP and powerful "lightweight" containers.

Choosing the Best Architecture for Your Application

In the early years of J2EE, EJB was regarded as the core of J2EE, and was actively marketed by Sun as *the* implementation strategy for business objects. Experience has shown this advice to be wrong in many cases. This prompted a widespread backlash against EJB, beginning in 2002. Since then, debate has raged between the pro- and anti-EJB camps in the J2EE community.

Despite our forthright criticism of EJB, we want to take the emotion out of this debate. We advocate evaluating the use of EJB on its merits.

> **As using EJB introduces much complexity, ensure that there's enough of a return on a decision to use EJB. A good return is most likely if you require a distributed architecture—remote EJBs still provide a good infrastructure for distributed applications. Evaluate EJB services, such as the concurrency model, declarative transaction management, along with the alternatives. Base decisions for non-trivial projects on a prototype—don't blindly follow blueprints, our advice, or that of anyone else, without verifying that it's appropriate for your particular requirements.**

Our experience is that the EJB value proposition often doesn't add up. We feel that EJB won't play nearly as big a part in the future, which is why we refer to the "Post EJB Era." EJB won't—and shouldn't—disappear altogether, but we feel that EJB use will be confined to a shrinking problem area, as alternatives prove themselves. In the case of the majority of web applications—which should use co-located, rather than distributed, architectures—"lighter weight" alternatives have already proven themselves in many production applications.

The Lightweight Container Architecture

In Chapter 3, we outlined what we believe is a better architecture for many J2EE applications—especially, for the great majority of J2EE web applications.

We call this the **Lightweight Container Architecture**.

In this architecture, all Java classes run in the same JVM. Business objects are implemented as POJOs, running within an Inversion of Control container. While these objects run within an IoC container in a deployed application, they are not dependent on it. In particular, they can be tested outside an application server using ordinary JUnit test cases. All callers code to business interfaces, rather than to the implementing classes of the business objects, ensuring a high degree of pluggability. Declarative transaction management and other crosscutting enterprise services such as security checks are provided to POJO business objects using AOP. The business logic layer—or, rather, the container infrastructure that supports it—will be responsible for transaction demarcation.

Business objects will normally be stateless, analogous to stateless session beans (the most successful kind of EJB). In most cases, POJO business objects can be multithreaded stateless service objects. In the rarer case where a single-threaded programming model, as provided by EJB, is required, this can be provided using AOP, as we discuss in Chapter 12.

The web tier will be a thin layer over the business logic layer, responsible only for processing user input and displaying the results of business operations. By keeping the web tier as thin as possible, we minimize the amount of application code that is dependent on the Servlet API and whatever MVC web framework we choose, maximizing the potential for code reuse. The web tier should be based on an existing framework such as Struts, WebWork, or Spring MVC (for traditional request-based MVC) or Tapestry or JSF (for an event-driven alternative). The presentation tier will consist of templates—often JSP or Velocity—that are purely concerned with presenting data exposed by MVC controllers, and will never invoke business objects.

Data access will use a lightweight O/R mapping layer, providing transparent persistence. Hibernate and leading JDO implementations are an excellent choice here. When an application requires a full-blown domain model, some business logic may be included in persistent objects. Both persistent objects and business objects are *true* objects in that they can both participate in normal inheritance relationships.

If remote access is required, a remoting facade will be added to expose the business objects to remote clients.

We distinguish this architecture from what we refer to as the **Classic J2EE Architecture**. This is exemplified by the original Sun Java Pet Store and more recent sample applications such as the Oracle Virtual J2EE Shopping Mall. The "classic" J2EE architecture is characterized by modeling business objects as EJBs with remote interfaces, and using entity beans for persistence. The choice of EJBs with remote interfaces is inappropriate unless the architecture should be distributed. As we've seen, this is much less often the case than J2EE developers have been led to believe.

"Classic" J2EE architectures are complex to develop, deploy, and test. Even if they are not deployed with calling code co-located with remote EJBs—as they often are—the distributed semantics dictate a layer of transfer objects, contributing to code bloat and making applications less object oriented.

The use of entity beans has many disadvantages, such as primitive O/R mapping, without support for inheritance in mapped objects; under-expressive query language; and the fact that entity beans are almost impossible to test, making them no place for business logic and thus reducing a "domain model" to a set of structs that are merely dumb data holders.

The Lightweight Container Architecture is now realized by a choice of mature infrastructure such as IoC containers and O/R mapping products—there's no need to create your own framework to support your applications.

Note that in some cases, we don't need the full J2EE stack. For example, if an application needs to access only a single database, there's no need for JTA. There's real benefit in choosing the simplest possible architecture, such as reduced development complexity, simpler administration, and (possibly) reduced license costs, without the need for a high-end application server. With supporting infrastructure such as Spring, a web container is perfectly adequate for the majority of web applications. "Lightweight" solutions can scale down as well as up, without changing application code; EJB can't.

Standards

Doesn't rejecting the EJB component model mean that we reject standardization? Are we advocating returning to the middleware jungle of the mid- to late 1990s?

No. This is an obvious criticism, so it's important to point out that it's unfounded. We are *not* talking about ripping up J2EE as a whole—just about replacing one way of accessing J2EE services.

Imagine J2EE as a building. JNDI, JTA, JDBC and the other fundamental APIs and services are the foundation; application-server implementations of thread and connection pooling the structural members; and EJB the dated flock wallpaper, awkwardly laid out floor plan and inadequate air conditioning. Redecoration may make the building far more pleasant to work in, but it won't threaten its integrity. We don't change the structure of a building often (although in software, we do have the ability to progressively refine it). But interiors become shabby and dated and need replacement every few years.

There are many reasons why what we advocate does *not* represent a rejection of valuable standardization:

❑ **By removing EJB, we give back Java.** For example, by adopting EJB we lose the ability to have component-level inheritance; we lose the ability to use Java language concurrency control where appropriate. Java is a much more worthwhile de facto standard than J2EE. (Note that even Java itself, like all J2EE specifications, is *not* in fact a standard in the true sense of the word.)

❑ **The solution we propose is built on J2EE rather than on EJB.** Thus the most important standards, such as JTA and JNDI, are preserved. As has often been pointed out over the last few years, EJB != J2EE.

❑ **With IoC and AOP we can avoid most dependencies of application code on Spring or any other "lightweight" framework we use to replace EJB services.** Many in the J2EE community are skeptical about such claims, fearing that adopting a "lightweight" container will produce another lock-in to a particular framework and API. However, our experience, and the experience of the Spring, PicoContainer, and other IoC container communities, is that it really is possible to minimize dependence on a framework yet benefit from rich framework functionality. The combination of IoC with AOP is still more powerful, enabling system-level aspects such as transaction management to be completely externalized from application code. While EJB is a highly *invasive* model, with profound effects on the whole of the business object layer, IoC is about minimizing the impact of the container on the programming model—and hence, maximizing scope for plain old Java objects and plain old object orientation. Because of the real decoupling of application code from framework implementation, application code is largely isolated from the evolution of the supporting infrastructure, something that is impossible when application code is forced to implement container-determined APIs.

❑ **Standardization is not an end in itself; unless a "standard" solution is also a *good* solution, the existence of the standard does far more harm than good.** We don't believe that the fact that EJB is a "standard" justifies its many disadvantages for most applications. Standardization is one consideration, but technical merit must always be a decisive consideration. It's dangerous for the J2EE community to ignore worthwhile innovation in the belief that the official process is always best. History shows that the JCP has not delivered in a number of areas; innovative open source (and commercial) products have, in areas such as persistence and AOP.

❑ **The Java standardization process is not a charity or disinterested process.** While Sun and other major players certainly have mainly good intentions, commercial concerns can override technical merit or the interests of users of the technology. There is also the danger of "design by committee": On many specification committees, reconciling the opinions of different participants can result in a compromise that is not the best solution. For example, prior to its resurgence in late 2003, JDO languished without any support from Sun, clearly because it was seen as a competitor to entity beans, a widely adopted (but unloved) existing standard. The fact that JDO was far more promising as a technology was not enough. While there is no dark conspiracy of major vendors, commercial considerations inevitably play a role in JCP deliberations.

❑ **The JCP standardization process is too slow and too concerned with backward compatibility.** For example, the custodians of the EJB specification are unlikely to admit that it contains some mistakes, which should be corrected. The JCP has achieved great things in some areas, but it isn't infallible. Belief in infallibility is always dangerous, and especially so in a field as fast-moving as software. With less invasive frameworks, backward compatibility occurs naturally, without requiring a standards process, because application code isn't intimately tied to the runtime environment.

❑ **Where innovation from the open source communities (or commercial vendors) can produce clear benefit for application developers, "standardization" is a poor argument for using an inferior solution.**

Standards work best where they codify existing successful approaches. The EJB specification is a good example of this. Where it has standardized existing ideas, such as declarative transaction management and stateless service objects such as stateless session beans, it has succeeded. Where it has attempted to standardize unproven concepts such as stateful session beans and fine-grained persistent components (entity beans), it has largely failed.

A good example of the value of innovation *before* standardization is shown by the success of Hibernate. The experimental entity bean model, developed before any experience of using it in practice or any production-quality implementations, often proved inefficient, and complex to use. It failed to address the real problems of developers and, as a result, was widely rejected by those who were supposed to benefit from it. Hibernate, on the other hand, focused on the need of most users for a simple, efficient mapping to relational databases that supported a full range of O/R mappings. While the specification of entity beans largely ignored all experience of previous O/R mapping products such as TopLink, Hibernate built on successful, proven concepts.

The JDO 2.0 specification is now benefiting the innovation of Hibernate and other "proprietary" persistence technologies, creating a standard technology that *will* be relevant to typical applications and is likely to become popular among developers.

> As we note in Chapter 5, J2EE is more than EJB, and EJB is less than Java.

Is Spring the Only Alternative to EJB?

Throughout this book, we've used Spring for most of the examples, and looked in detail at Spring's implementation of the concepts we advocate.

Spring is a particularly good reflection of our architectural principles, and its large and growing user community proves that it delivers real value. Spring grew from code published with *Expert One-on-One J2EE Design and Development* in 2002, and we are joint lead developers. Spring probably owes its success in large part to the fact that it has always been based on a clear architectural vision.

However, we believe that "J2EE without EJB" amounts to a *movement*, rather than a particular framework's user community. It's bigger than any one project. Thus it's important to emphasize that you can take the message of this book and apply it without adopting Spring, if you prefer to use different frameworks. We see the core consensus of this movement as:

❑ **Agreement that EJB is an invasive component model that hasn't delivered in practice.** In this book, we've examined the EJB value proposition at length, and shown that there are now good or better alternatives in most cases for all EJB services except remoting. Spring is an important part of this story, but not the only framework that provides such alternatives.

❑ **A belief in the importance of simplicity:** for example, that web applications should not normally be distributed; that plain Java objects should be preferred to components such as EJBs with dependence on complex infrastructure, even at test time.

❑ **Agreement on the importance of agile practices, especially TDD.** A feeling that EJB stands in the way of effectively practicing agile development.

❑ **Growing agreement that Inversion of Control (IoC) and AOP are a key part of any EJB replacement.**

❑ **Agreement that the entity bean persistence experiment has failed,** and that transparent persistence solutions such as Hibernate or JDO are the way forward. (Even most advocates of EJB would today agree with this point.)

You can develop simpler architectures for some applications by replacing EJB with ad hoc infrastructure and simplifying helper libraries. Clinton Begin's JPetStore application illustrates such an approach, dispensing with the over-complex EJB-based architecture of the original Sun Java Pet Store with a much simpler, Struts-based application using a POJO business object and programmatic transaction management based on Begin's excellent iBATIS DB framework.

However, we don't recommend such approaches. We feel that the notion of a **container** is very important, although the EJB approach to a container leaves much to be desired. We feel that a lightweight IoC container brings valuable structure and consistency to an application, and provides a means of removing complex resource lookup and other configuration from application code. While we believe that Spring provides the most powerful lightweight IoC container available, you can use IoC in several other open source frameworks, such as:

❑ WebWork

❑ PicoContainer

❑ HiveMind

There is also wide choice in AOP frameworks. You can choose from products such as:

❑ Nanning Aspects

❑ AspectWerkz

❑ JBoss 4, if you are happy to commit to the JBoss application server

❑ AspectJ, if you are happy to make a new language part of your development tool set

Many choices for persistence are superior to entity EJBs. You can do true O/R mapping with:

❑ JDO implementations

❑ Hibernate

❑ Mature proprietary products such as TopLink

We advocate Hibernate or JDO for most projects.

You can perform efficient data access in scenarios where O/R mapping is not appropriate using the iBATIS database layer, as well as Spring's JDBC packages.

Thus there are alternatives to Spring that reflect the same architectural goals, with the exception of Spring's transaction abstraction. We know of no framework that provides a comparable ability to isolate application code from the underlying transaction infrastructure.

We feel that Spring provides a superior, more integrated model for most applications than these alternatives. Spring integrates IoC, AOP, and a simple, consistent model for working with different persistence technologies. But they are all good technologies, and each of them is far better for typical web applications than the "classic" J2EE architecture.

> **You don't need to use Spring to enjoy post EJB architectures. However, we believe that it offers a unique value proposition, and thousands of users agree.**

Key Messages

The core of this book can be summarized in four TLAs:

❑ **IoC:** Inversion of Control

❑ **AOP:** Aspect Oriented Programming

❑ **TDD:** Test Driven Development

❑ **OOP:** which should require no spelling out

These all complement each other, helping to develop simpler, better-quality applications, faster than is possible with traditional J2EE architecture. For example:

❑ IoC and AOP together minimize the dependence of application code on the runtime framework. This makes it easy to apply TDD, which is very difficult to apply with traditional use of EJB, and easy to practice OOP.

❑ Using an IoC container reduces to zero the cost of programming to interfaces instead of classes— a crucial best practice in OOP, which also significantly enhances testability.

❑ Practicing TDD enables fearless refactoring, making pursuit of elegant orientation realistic as a code base develops. Thus the ability to practice TDD, which results from reduced dependence on a runtime framework, can make it easier to pursue OOP.

It shouldn't really be necessary to emphasize the importance of object orientation in a book on Java-based middleware. However, we feel that it is, because traditional approaches to J2EE have been anything but object oriented:

❑ They have tolerated and promoted non-objects such as value objects and dumb data holders (as opposed to transparently persisted domain objects).

❑ The limitations of EJB have encouraged developers to forget that business objects should be objects first, and should not be forced into contortions to run in a container.

One area in which EJB *has* had a beneficial effect on practicing OOP is in its enforcement of the use of interfaces for all business objects. We also advocate this, and, as we've noted, using an IoC container makes it far easier.

We'll say more about the first three TLAs under the *Guidelines* section below.

Not many books so far face up to this, but EJB is not compatible with TDD. If you want to practice TDD—and you should!—you will find yourself trying to eliminate EJB usage or, at least, minimize it.

TDD is a form of what we call an **evidence-based** approach to development. We believe that applying evidence throughout the project lifecycle—to architecture as well as coding—is central to reducing risk and achieving the optimal solution. Other important applications of an evidence-based approach to the development process include:

❑ Building a **vertical slice** or **executable architecture** early in the project lifecycle to verify the architecture. This is particularly important from a performance perspective.

❑ Performing regular benchmarks throughout the project lifecycle to verify that performance targets can be met.

❑ Profiling application code to track down any performance issues.

Guidelines

Let's conclude with some guidelines, based on what we've covered in this book. We've categorized these into:

❑ Architecture

❑ Programming style

❑ Inversion of Control

❑ AOP

❑ TDD

Architecture

The guidelines concerning architecture are:

☐ **Don't use a distributed architecture unless business requirements dictate doing so.** Remember Martin Fower's First Law of Distributed Objects: "Don't distribute your objects." J2EE is not an inherently distributed platform, although it was often regarded as such in its early years. Distributed applications are much slower and more complex to write and maintain than co-located applications. In our experience, few web applications benefit from distribution.

☐ **Consider the value proposition before using EJB.** EJB adds complexity. In some cases, it may produce a counterbalancing reduction in complexity—for example, if you want its distribution capability. It's important to asses the cost-benefit equation of using EJB for each application; do not use (or reject!) EJB use without carefully considering the implications of doing so—and without backing that consideration by evidence.

☐ **If you do use EJB, implement your business logic in POJOs behind an EJB facade.** If you use EJB, leverage the services it provides, such as remoting and declarative transaction management, while minimizing the complexity it introduces to your development process. Try to ensure that business logic is not directly implemented in EJBs, but in POJOs used by an EJB facade. This enables you to test much of your business logic outside the EJB container.

☐ **If you use EJB, use local SLSBs unless you need a distributed architecture.** Local stateless session beans provide most of the worthwhile services of EJB, while minimizing the negatives attached to EJB.

☐ **Use declarative transaction management if you have more than a few transactional operations.** Programmatic transaction management may work out simpler than an EJB or even simpler AOP-based declarative transaction management if you have few transaction requirements. However, if you have many transactional methods, programmatic transaction management will lead to code duplication, greater potential for coding errors, and ongoing maintenance hassle. Container-Managed Transactions (CMT) used to be considered the killer application for EJB.

☐ **Consider whether O/R mapping is appropriate for your application.** O/R mapping is appropriate for many but not all applications. Don't feel that you need to use O/R mapping if you're working with a relational database and you need to work with relational concepts.

☐ **If O/R mapping is appropriate, use a transparent persistence solution.** Transparent persistence has many benefits. It enables domain objects to contain business logic shared across multiple use cases. Hence *it allows the domain model to consist of objects, not of dumb data holders.* We consider this a very important benefit. Products such as JDO implementations and Hibernate offer near-transparent persistence, much more flexible O/R mapping and a far preferable programming model than entity beans. Even in EJB applications, steer clear of entity beans. Technologies such as Hibernate and JDO work perfectly well in an EJB container.

☐ **Consider the threading model for each business object.** Most stateless business objects are most simply modeled as a single multi-threaded instance.

☐ **Consider the performance implications of an architecture before committing to it.** Architecture, not implementation, largely determines the performance and scalability of an application. Validate your architecture before going ahead with full-blown development.

Programming Style

Good OO practice is essential to successful projects.

> **We believe that applications should be OO applications before being J2EE applications.**

While discussing object orientation is beyond the scope of this book—and we are confident that our readers are already skilled OO practitioners—it's worth stressing one point in particular: the importance of interfaces to define the relationships between objects.

> *See Chapter 4 of* Expert One-on-One J2EE Design and Development *for a detailed discussion of coding style and OO design practices for J2EE applications. The approach taken in this book follows from that discussion.*

Applications should be built of **pluggable** building blocks. Pluggability has many advantages. To name just a few:

❑   It allows significant changes to be made to an application without major impact on application code. For example, it should be possible to switch from a POJO business object to a local EJB implementation of the same business interface without affecting calling code.

❑   It facilitates testing, enabling us to provide test stubs or mock objects as collaborators along with the objects under test.

❑   It provides scope for code optimization.

❑   It decouples developers and teams, allowing them to work in parallel.

In the EJB model, the unit of pluggability is a component. We feel that plain Java interfaces do a great job of achieving this essential pluggability.

IoC is a powerful tool for ensuring pluggability. However, it's also important to avoid some common antipatterns, such as inappropriate use of the Singleton design pattern. Application code should not normally use Singletons, which are usually incompatible with coding to interfaces rather than to classes.

Inversion of Control (IoC) and Dependency Injection

Pluggability via interfaces is fine in theory, but supporting infrastructure is needed to make it workable. **IoC** containers provide such infrastructure. They are capable of:

❑   Avoiding dependence of application code on container infrastructure.

❑   Avoiding the need to use the Singleton antipattern.

❑   Externalizing configuration, avoiding hard-coded magic values, and providing consistency, in the place of a hodge-podge of different configuration sources and formats.

❑   Running in any environment, from applet to EJB container.

We've focused on the newer wave of IoC containers, such as Spring and PicoContainer, which emerged in 2003. These differ from older IoC containers such as Avalon in that they are designed to minimize—often, wholly *eliminate*—dependence of application code on the container managing application objects. Such IoC containers configure objects using JavaBean properties or constructor arguments: a pattern known as Dependency Injection. In each case, standard Java idioms are used, without any need to make concessions to the runtime IoC environment. This is an important innovation, with real benefits for application developers.

> We believe that IoC—and, specifically, Dependency Injection—will revolutionize the development of J2EE applications. While the first wave of IoC containers—most notably, Apache Avalon—had a substantial footprint and hefty learning curve, the current crop, such as Spring and PicoContainer, are a different breed. They succeed in avoiding application code depending on the container; they make TDD a delight to practice; and they're not difficult to understand or use.

AOP

AOP has been discussed as the Next Big Thing in middleware for almost two years. (Not merely Java middleware, although there's been perhaps greater interest from the J2EE community than from other communities.) We believe that AOP has arrived, and is ready for you to use to simplify your applications.

AOP is sometimes cynically dismissed as a fad: "another over-hyped paradigm," to quote one such assessment. We believe that this is far from the truth.

AOP provides a powerful means of modularization of concerns that cannot easily be modularized in OOP. While correct use of OOP is crucial for success in J2EE applications, OOP doesn't solve all problems. It fails to modularize **crosscutting** code: for example, code that should run before or after every invocation of a particular method. Such crosscutting concerns often arise in J2EE applications, and EJB owes much of its success to providing one way of addressing them.

We believe that AOP provides a more general, elegant, and powerful solution than EJB for delivering crosscutting enterprise services—most important, declarative services such as transaction management. Of course, AOP is much more than the basis for a replacement for EJB; we're focusing on a subset of AOP's potential, which we believe will have a dramatic impact on J2EE architecture.

- ❑ **AOP is an excellent solution for system-level concerns such as transaction management. AOP allows us to provide declarative services to POJOs, not special objects such as EJB.** As we've seen, Spring's AOP-based declarative transaction management is significantly more capable than EJB CMT, although it can be provided to any POJO.

- ❑ **If you find yourself writing boiler-plate code to address cross-cutting concerns unique to your application or organization, consider using AOP to modularize the duplicated code.** Whether or not you choose to view AOP as a black box behind a framework such as Spring that enables you to benefit from familiar concepts such as CMT or choose to use the framework's infrastructure yourself to implement some of your application code will depend on factors such as your confidence with AOP concepts, performance implications, and the extent of the benefit over a pure OO approach. There are no universal answers.

We advocate fairly cautious use of AOP in this book. We call this "incremental AOP." We don't ask you to take a bold step into the unknown—merely to look at a new application of familiar, proven, concepts.

AOP will have a growing influence on how we design applications in the future. Within a decade, it may well be common to think of application design in terms of aspects, as well as objects. At that point, tools such as AspectJ—that elevate AOP concepts to language level—may become popular.

In the meantime, the first "killer application" for AOP will be a superior replacement for familiar declarative EJB services. Declarative transaction management—once the biggest selling point of stateless session beans—is the best example of how an AOP approach to enterprise services can deliver more power than EJB, yet offer a much simpler programming model. This exemplifies incremental AOP. It doesn't require a new language; it can run without affecting the class loader, using dynamic proxies or runtime byte code generation; its performance is excellent compared to that of EJB; and the implementations are robust. This is not experimentation; it's reality and already in production in many applications.

Testing

We believe that TDD helps to improve code quality and to structure the development process.

Not only does TDD virtually ensure a thorough regression test suite—a tremendous boon in the later stages of development, and during maintenance—it helps to focus development activity, by making it iterative, and dictated by the addition of testable features.

Because TDD has so many advantages, it's important to *design for testability*. This has implications for the design of your own code. It also has implications for the frameworks you use.

We recommend the following guidelines:

- ❑ Remember that unit testing is about testing classes in isolation. Avoid writing tests that indirectly test collaborators of the class being tested.
- ❑ It's essential to be able to run unit tests outside a J2EE application server.
- ❑ *Mock objects* offer a valuable way of achieving these first two goals.
- ❑ It should be possible to run all an application's unit tests within five minutes—preferably, much quicker.
- ❑ The quality of the test suite is as important as the quality of application code.
- ❑ Use a code coverage-analysis tool to help improve the quality of your test suite.
- ❑ If possible, avoid using frameworks or APIs that make testing difficult.

Experience in many projects has shown that the architecture we advocate in this book makes unit testing application code as easy as possible.

Last Words

We believe not only that J2EE development should be much simpler than the mixture of drudgery and complexity it's often made out to be, but that developing J2EE applications should be *fun*.

We hope you've enjoyed reading this book as much as we enjoyed writing it. We hope that after reading it you'll be familiar with the architectural alternatives to the traditional approach to J2EE architecture. We encourage you to base your architectural choices on evidence. While we hope we've been persuasive, don't take our word without proof. Before committing to an application architecture, verify that whatever approach you choose delivers on the goals for your project. And have fun!

Index

W

WAR (Web Application Archive), 325, 404
WAS (Web Application Stress) tool, 479
weaving, AOP, 192
web
applications, Spring Framework, 147–149
interfaces, 38–39
web layers, DAO, 285
web tier design
  application architecture, 368–372
  architectural issues, 364–365
  binary formats, 402
  business objects, 369
  clustering challenges, 457–458
  command-driven controllers, 394–397
  control logic, 366
  controllers, 374
  discussed, 363
  event-driven frameworks, 404–408
  form-driven controllers, 397–399
  interceptors, 374
  IoC-based middle tier, 371–373
  markup generation, 408
  MVC approach, 366
  naive approaches to, 365
  open source frameworks, 368
  portals, 403–404
  portlets, 403–404
  request-driven frameworks, 368, 374–377
  servlets, 366–368
  singletons, 369
  SLBSs (stateless session beans), 369
  static templates, 406
  Struts framework, 375–379
  validation, 374
  view technologies, 401–402
  WebLogSystem class, 386
  WebWork2 framework, 381–385
  wizard-style workflows, 399
web views, lazy loading feature, 292
Web Service Description Language (WSDL), 325–327
web services
accessing, 327–331
ports, 327–328
WSDL-based, 325–327
XML-based, 85
Web sites
Agile Manifesto, 25
Apache, 26

Apache Avalon, 130
AspectWerkz, 201
DynaMock, 429
EasyMock, 428–429
EMCA, 112
FireStorm, 16
FreeMarker, 401
Hibernate, 264
iBatis, 263, 278
JOTM, 63
Maven, 26
MockEJB, 417
Nanning Aspects, 207
NanoContainer, 137
Spring Framework, 10–11
Tapestry, 405
Velocity, 401
WebMacro, 401
WebObjects, 404
WingS, 404
WebApplicationContextUtils **class, 148, 334, 387**
WebLogSystem **class, 386**
WebMacro Web site, 401
WebObjects Web site, 404
WebWork2, web tier design, 381–385
white box testing, 415
wildcard syntax, naming conventions, 225
WingS Web site, 404
wire protocols, remoting services, 317–318
wizard-style workflows, web tier design, 399
WSDL (Web Service Description Language), 325–327

X

XDoclet tool, 98
XML
data binding, 462
performance considerations, 462
populating JavaBeans via, 151–153
web services, 85
XmlBeanFactory **class, 154–155**
XP (Extreme Programming), 86
XWork, WebWork2, 382–383

Z

Zadrozny, Peter (*J2EE Performance Testing with BEA WebLogic Server*), 485